T0211743

Lecture Notes in Computer Science 11786

More information about this series at http://www.springer.com/series/7409

Constantine Stephanidis (Ed.)

HCI International 2019 – Late Breaking Papers

21st HCI International Conference, HCII 2019
Orlando, FL, USA, July 26–31, 2019
Proceedings

Springer

Editor
Constantine Stephanidis
University of Crete and Foundation
for Research and Technology -
Hellas (Forth)
Heraklion, Greece

ISSN 0302-9743   ISSN 1611-3349   (electronic)
Lecture Notes in Computer Science
ISBN 978-3-030-30032-6   ISBN 978-3-030-30033-3   (eBook)
https://doi.org/10.1007/978-3-030-30033-3

LNCS Sublibrary: SL3 – Information Systems and Applications, incl. Internet/Web, and HCI

This Springer imprint is published by the registered company Springer Nature Switzerland AG
The registered company address is: Gewerbestrasse 11, 6330 Cham, Switzerland

Foreword

The 21st International Conference on Human-Computer Interaction, HCI International 2019, was held in Orlando, FL, USA, during July 26–31, 2019. The event incorporated the 18 thematic areas and affiliated conferences listed on the following page.

This year the HCI International (HCII) conference introduced the additional option of "late-breaking work." This applies both for papers and posters with the corresponding volumes of the proceedings published after the conference. A total of 5,029 individuals from academia, research institutes, industry, and governmental agencies from 73 countries submitted contributions, and 1,274 papers and 209 posters were included in the pre-conference proceedings. In addition, 46 papers and 56 posters were included in the post-conference proceedings. These contributions address the latest research and development efforts and highlight the human aspects of design and use of computing systems. The contributions thoroughly cover the entire field of human-computer interaction, addressing major advances in knowledge and effective use of computers in a variety of application areas.

The volumes constituting the full set of the pre-conference and post-conference proceedings are listed in the following pages.

I would like to thank the program board chairs and the members of the program boards of all thematic areas and affiliated conferences for their contribution to the highest scientific quality and the overall success of the HCI International 2019 conference.

This conference would not have been possible without the continuous and unwavering support and advice of the founder, Conference General Chair Emeritus and Conference Scientific Advisor Prof. Gavriel Salvendy. For his outstanding efforts, I would like to express my appreciation to the communications chair and editor of *HCI International News*, Dr. Abbas Moallem.

July 2019   Constantine Stephanidis

HCI International 2019 Thematic Areas
and Affiliated Conferences

Thematic areas:

- HCI 2019: Human-Computer Interaction
- HIMI 2019: Human Interface and the Management of Information

Affiliated conferences:

- EPCE 2019: 16th International Conference on Engineering Psychology and Cognitive Ergonomics
- UAHCI 2019: 13th International Conference on Universal Access in Human-Computer Interaction
- VAMR 2019: 11th International Conference on Virtual, Augmented and Mixed Reality
- CCD 2019: 11th International Conference on Cross-Cultural Design
- SCSM 2019: 11th International Conference on Social Computing and Social Media
- AC 2019: 13th International Conference on Augmented Cognition
- DHM 2019: 10th International Conference on Digital Human Modeling and Applications in Health, Safety, Ergonomics and Risk Management
- DUXU 2019: 8th International Conference on Design, User Experience, and Usability
- DAPI 2019: 7th International Conference on Distributed, Ambient and Pervasive Interactions
- HCIBGO 2019: 6th International Conference on HCI in Business, Government and Organizations
- LCT 2019: 6th International Conference on Learning and Collaboration Technologies
- ITAP 2019: 5th International Conference on Human Aspects of IT for the Aged Population
- HCI-CPT 2019: First International Conference on HCI for Cybersecurity, Privacy and Trust
- HCI-Games 2019: First International Conference on HCI in Games
- MobiTAS 2019: First International Conference on HCI in Mobility, Transport, and Automotive Systems
- AIS 2019: First International Conference on Adaptive Instructional Systems

Conference Proceedings Volumes Full List

Pre-conference Proceedings Volumes

1. LNCS 11566, Human-Computer Interaction: Perspectives on Design (Part I), edited by Masaaki Kurosu
2. LNCS 11567, Human-Computer Interaction: Recognition and Interaction Technologies (Part II), edited by Masaaki Kurosu
3. LNCS 11568, Human-Computer Interaction: Design Practice in Contemporary Societies (Part III), edited by Masaaki Kurosu
4. LNCS 11569, Human Interface and the Management of Information: Visual Information and Knowledge Management (Part I), edited by Sakae Yamamoto and Hirohiko Mori
5. LNCS 11570, Human Interface and the Management of Information: Information in Intelligent Systems (Part II), edited by Sakae Yamamoto and Hirohiko Mori
6. LNAI 11571, Engineering Psychology and Cognitive Ergonomics, edited by Don Harris
7. LNCS 11572, Universal Access in Human-Computer Interaction: Theory, Methods and Tools (Part I), edited by Margherita Antona and Constantine Stephanidis
8. LNCS 11573, Universal Access in Human-Computer Interaction: Multimodality and Assistive Environments (Part II), edited by Margherita Antona and Constantine Stephanidis
9. LNCS 11574, Virtual, Augmented and Mixed Reality: Multimodal Interaction (Part I), edited by Jessie Y. C. Chen and Gino Fragomeni
10. LNCS 11575, Virtual, Augmented and Mixed Reality: Applications and Case Studies (Part II), edited by Jessie Y. C. Chen and Gino Fragomeni
11. LNCS 11576, Cross-Cultural Design: Methods, Tools and User Experience (Part I), edited by P. L. Patrick Rau
12. LNCS 11577, Cross-Cultural Design: Culture and Society (Part II), edited by P. L. Patrick Rau
13. LNCS 11578, Social Computing and Social Media: Design, Human Behavior and Analytics (Part I), edited by Gabriele Meiselwitz
14. LNCS 11579, Social Computing and Social Media: Communication and Social Communities (Part II), edited by Gabriele Meiselwitz
15. LNAI 11580, Augmented Cognition, edited by Dylan D. Schmorrow and Cali M. Fidopiastis
16. LNCS 11581, Digital Human Modeling and Applications in Health, Safety, Ergonomics and Risk Management: Human Body and Motion (Part I), edited by Vincent G. Duffy

Post-conference Proceedings

http://2019.hci.international/proceedings

HCI International 2019 (HCII 2019)

The full list with the Program Board Chairs and the members of the Program Boards of all thematic areas and affiliated conferences is available online at:

http://www.hci.international/board-members-2019.php

HCI International 2020

The 22nd International Conference on Human-Computer Interaction, HCI International 2020, will be held jointly with the affiliated conferences in Copenhagen, Denmark, at the Bella Center Copenhagen, July 19–24, 2020. It will cover a broad spectrum of themes related to HCI, including theoretical issues, methods, tools, processes, and case studies in HCI design, as well as novel interaction techniques, interfaces, and applications. The proceedings will be published by Springer. More information will be available on the conference website: http://2020.hci.international/.

General Chair
Prof. Constantine Stephanidis
University of Crete and ICS-FORTH
Heraklion, Crete, Greece
E-mail: general_chair@hcii2020.org

http://2020.hci.international/

Contents

Learning and Games

Human and Task Models in HCI

HCI, Innovation and Society

User Experience Design and Evaluation

Design Approach for Investigating Multimodal Communication in Dismounted Soldier-Robot Interaction

Daniel Barber[✉] and Rhyse Bendell

University of Central Florida, Institute for Simulation and Training,
Orlando, FL 32826, USA
{dbarber, rbendell}@ist.ucf.edu

Abstract. For several decades there has been continuous growth in the field of robotics, with recent trends driving towards a vision of humans collaborating in a cohesive unit with automated counterparts. Enabling true mixed-initiative teaming between a human and robot will require communication capabilities and cognition comparable to human teammates. Multimodal communication is a framework in which interfaces can be created supporting the flexible selection of different modalities (e.g. speech, gestures) for these transactions. A major challenge for human factors researchers investigating human robot collaboration with multimodal interfaces is the current limitations of robots. Therefore, simulations and wizard-of-oz type experiments are heavily employed to measure performance, workload, and other factors in future mixed-initiative scenarios. Although these techniques facilitate experimentation, it can be difficult to transition findings to working prototypes of today's robots. For example, a researcher finds an effective way to convey a robots decision making rationale in a simulation-based study, but has no working robot that can drive the content in reality. Furthermore, the literature regarding multimodal communication with robots applied to the military domain is limited. For example, evaluation of different modalities as part of an interrupting task has been explored in driving scenarios, but not between robot(s) and soldiers. In many cases there is conflict in findings across domains. To address this challenge, this paper describes how a multimodal interface for a real robotic platform developed under the U.S. Army Research Labs Robotics Collaborative Technology Alliance (RCTA) was extended to support standalone simulation of interactions and integration with simulated virtual environments. This functionality enables researchers to assess new interaction techniques using the same software that will interact with a real platform to facilitate transition of their research. Furthermore, experiment design approaches including theory-based tasks in a military relevant mission (Cordon and Search) are discussed.

Keywords: Multimodal interfaces · Human-robot interaction · Simulation · Tactile display · Communication modalities

C. Stephanidis (Ed.): HCII 2019, LNCS 11786, pp. 3–14, 2019.
https://doi.org/10.1007/978-3-030-30033-3_1

1 Introduction

Robotic technologies have recently made significant advances towards the goal of autonomy. Though some fields may not require or even benefit from autonomous robotic systems (e.g., perhaps we will never be comfortable with fully autonomous surgeons), there are significant improvements that can be made in areas such as search and rescue, emergency response, military operations, etc. which involve high workload, hazardous scenarios. Putting aside fears of potentially malicious AI (a la Isaac Asimov, Stanley Kubrick, or William Gibson), it may be possible to employ such systems to replace humans in life-risking operations to not only protect but to save lives [1–3].

As improvements are made to robotic technologies, it is important for researchers to stay ahead of the curve and attend to the potential directions in which autonomous robots may develop. Anticipating near-future advances improves our ability to curb dangerous approaches as well as optimize the way that technologies are leveraged. A promising direction that is currently the focus of a great deal of research is the transition of near-autonomous robots from tools that may be used to accomplish an operator's goals into teammates that may assist with a human's goal while also attending to separate objectives [4, 5]. The dream of single operator, multi-robot teams may still be a ways off [6, 7]; however, multi-human teams which incorporate intelligent robotic teammates are very nearly a reality. That said, there are a number of challenges beyond the technological (e.g., computer vision, object recognition, artificial intelligence networks, etc.) that will need to be tackled before humans can effectively partner with robots [8].

Our understanding of human-human teaming has been systematically improved for centuries, yet gaps still exist in our knowledge of how best to optimize team performance; the introduction of non-human intelligences into the mix will necessarily complicate matters further [9–11]. Fortunately, we have some understanding of how humans partner with non-humans as a result of human-animal teams which have proven to be extremely effective in a host of scenarios from law enforcement to search and rescue [12]. Human-dog teams, for instance, have functioned effectively both with and without the assistance of technology (see Bozkurt et al. [13] for an interesting use of technology in this field). A fundamental difference between current human-non-human teams and the vision for the future is that autonomous robots may be designed to communicate with a human far more naturally than animals (e.g., speech, graphical depictions, intuitive data arrays) [14]. Though current methods of human-robot communication are primarily limited to video feeds and environmental data transmission [15–17] the future of human-robot teams (HRT) will depend on the expansion of communication modalities to support more natural interactions [10, 18–21] (see Fig. 1).

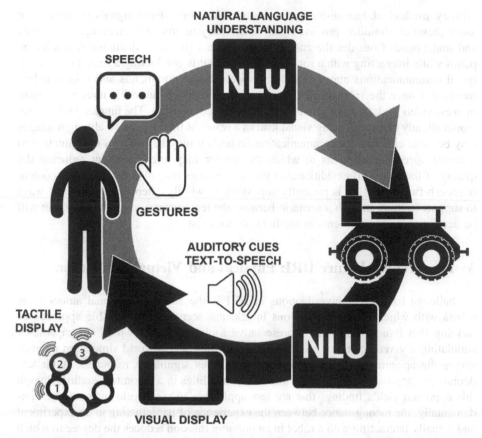

Fig. 1. A diagrammatic representation of the type of multi-modal communication that will be needed to facilitate future HRT communications: bi-directional auditory communication, visual and touch/button interaction facilitated by an interface, and tactile communication which would likely only need to be one way and is represented here as a tactile belt.

2 Multimodal Communication and Teaming

Currently, the needs of human members of HRTs are not clearly understood [22], but it is known that in the context of high-workload situations human performance benefits from reducing cognitive load as much as possible [23–25]. Multi-modal communication (MMC) presents a solution to the danger of overloading human operators by leveraging the fact that the brain is more capable of attending to more information if it is split across modalities [26, 27]. By flexibly utilizing both explicit (e.g., speech, visuals, tactile displays) and implicit communication modes, MMC techniques offload information processing demands to facilitate interactions and improve performance [21].

To emphasis this point, further, one should consider the operational environment in which human-robot teaming will take place. For a soldier, the mission space has potential for noise, low visibility, and many dynamic events. Speech may be the primary method of human-human communication, but visual signals (gestures), or touch (hand on shoulder) provide signal redundancy to ensure the message is received and understood. Consider the case of a HRT consisting of a dismounted soldier on patrol while interacting with a robotic teammate that is conducting a search of an area: initial communications may primarily be speech based commands and acknowledgements, but once the robot begins to encounter objects of interest it must either send images, video feed, or descriptions to their human counterpart. The human, in this case, would already be experiencing visual load as a result of their patrol, so although images may be most effective for communicating findings it may be better in that situation to generate speech descriptions to which the soldier may attend without reducing the quality of the patrol. The additional of tactile messages may also emphasis the content in speech further, [28]. It is presently impossible to wholly determine the optimal ways to support teaming in such a scenario because the teammates and MMC tools that will be needed to run assessments in the field do not exist.

3   Researching Future HRI: Physical and Virtual Simulation

A challenge for current investigations of HRI is the lack of functional autonomous robots with which to test interactions in relevant scenarios. A possible approach to tackling that issue is to create representative tools/teammates which are capable of simulating a given scenario; however, implementing a real-world simulation of even giving the appearance of needed capability requires significant resources. A far less demanding approach is to virtually simulate capabilities in a laboratory setting, though this approach yields findings that are less applicable to real world interactions. Fundamentally, the incongruence between the experience of participating in an experiment and actually interacting with a robot in an ongoing mission reduces the degree to which such investigations can accurately predict interaction outcomes and thereby deduce methods for supporting effective teaming. Though it is important to note those drawbacks, simulating near-future HRI is currently the most viable approach to preparing for the arrival of usable technologies, and therefore it is more relevant to consider the type and design of simulations that can most accurately approximate reality.

Physical simulations are a common tool for evaluating human performance, and can be used for nearly any scenario that does not incorporate undue risk (e.g., firefighters may run drills in burning buildings, but running search and rescue drills in the presence of real radioactive fallout is likely not advisable or necessary) [29]. Jentsch et al. 2010 describe the pros and cons of a scaled Model Operations in Urban Terrain (MOUT) physical simulation that makes heavy use of the "wizard-of-oz" technique to simulate interactions between human operators and remote robotic teammates in a military context. Here, the wizard-of-oz technique essentially describes the use of predetermined events, confederates, and faked information/communications to create the illusion of conducting a real mission in a relevant "environment" without requiring functional autonomous systems or a real world environment in which to test them. Real world technologies and spaces are not required by this approach, however, a great deal of effort, preparation, and maintenance is still necessary to employ a physical simulation such as the MOUT as the faked technologies and environments must still be implemented (see Fig. 2) [30].

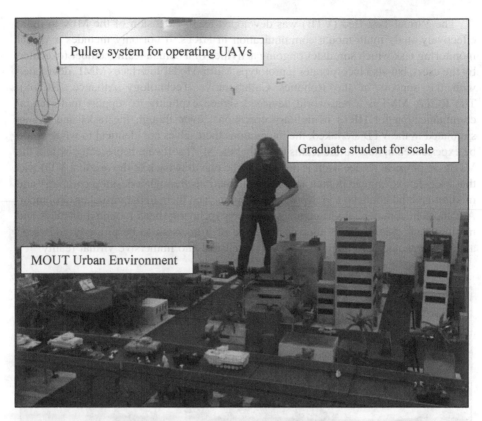

Fig. 2. The scaled MOUT environment including a model urban environment, remote control "autonomous" ground vehicles, and a pulley system for controlling "autonomous" aerial vehicles.

Another approach to simulating near-future HRI is to employ virtual reality simulations. Several such simulations have been developed in the last decade, particularly for the investigation of military focused HRI. The Mixed-Initiative Experimental (MIX) Testbed is one such simulation which provides simulated ground and air robotic systems in a 3D environment as well as an operator control unit (OCU) which allows users to interact with the virtual systems [32]. A benefit of the MIX simulator over physical simulations such as the MOUT is that it does not require a large room to run nor confederates to operate the simulated autonomous teammates. On the other hand, the use of confederates does allow for a larger degree of flexibility than preprogrammed interactions or capabilities which constrain interaction possibilities From an experimental perspective, however, the repeatability of predetermined actions is often better than allowing too much freedom (e.g., two participants who engaged in different interactions may not be directly compared). The MIX testbed has supported several investigations focused on HRT, but did not address the need for MMC which supports verbal communication and virtual multi-tasking (though participants could, of course, be tasked with real-world tasks while interacting with the MIX).

The Virtual Test Bed (VTB) was developed as an extension of the MIX to more effectively study multi-modal communication in HRTs. It not only includes a virtual monitoring task which simulates ongoing activities of a human team member (executed by the user), but also incorporates a prototype Multi-Modal Interface (MMI) developed with the support of the Robotics Collaborative Technology Alliance (RCTA). The RCTA MMI is a real-world device designed explicitly to support multi-modal communication for HRTs in military operations; even though the tasks and events simulated in the VTB are faked, the interactions themselves are identical to what would be experienced in near-future teams (note that the MMI software is presented within the VTB, the physical device itself is not used). The one drawback of the original VTB was that users had to engage in their tasks and interactions through a desktop computer and monitor and did not have a viewpoint which immersed them in the virtual environment. Advances in commercial virtual reality displays (primarily head mounted displays and motion tracked controllers) allowed the issue of immersion to be properly addressed and led to another overhaul of the VTB: extension into immersive virtual reality.

Fig. 3. Participant view of a perimeter monitoring task taking place in a simulated urban environment in the VRMIX.

The immersive version of the MIX/VTB style HRI testing environment, the VRMIX, relies on an HTC Vive and paired handheld controller to put participants right into a virtually simulated mission environment (see Fig. 3).

Much like the VTB, the VRMIX has the capacity to simulate autonomus teammates in addition to a variety of tasks and operations for human-in-the-loop experimentation [31]; however, it also has the vital capability of allowing users to interact with a simulated MMI that they can "hold" (insofar as they hold and interact with a controller which is represented in VR) and use to communicate with a remote autonomous teammate. As indicated in Fig. 1, several wearable devices may be required to support MMC with the RCTA MMI, potentially including wireless headset, a tablet of visual display, and a tactile display such as a tactor belt or vest depending on need. The VRMIX simulation testbed has the capacity to simulate interaction through each of those required modalities by generating simulated events which trasmit real data to most any device in order to elicit natural communication experiences. As such, the VRMIX provides a unique method for evaluating HRT effectiveness in relevant scenarios while supporting environments, tasks, and interactions. Moreover, VRMIX support dismounted HRT while environments like the scaled MOUT and MIX testbed do not.

4 HRI Research Example: Dismounted Solider-Robot Teams

Although it is known that cognitive overload may be ameliorated by distributing loading between processing modes, the optimal method for balancing loading and especially for implementing a system to execute that balancing is far from being well understood. Accordingly, it is important at this stage in MMC research to address the issues of when, why, and how to make use of each available modality. Here, we describe a possible research approach for investigating the specific performance benefits introduced by the tactile modality as a supplementary avenue of communication for human-robot teams.

Tactile communication is a potential untapped resource for use in augmenting robot-to-human communication. The use of haptic cues and feedback is a well known method for notifications in commercial products like cell phone and gaming consoles. Moreover, efforts are ongoing to deliver hands-free navigation using tactile belts for the U.S. Army, enabling a Soldier to maintain light discipline and keep their "heads-up" while traveling in a pre-defined point, [31]. Research to extend a tactile displays ability to convey content similar or complementary to speech are still early, but show promise. Barber, et al., conducted a series of studies to determine the feasibility of delivering two-word phrases within a HRT task, [28]. Results of this effort showed the ability of participants to receive simple reports such as "danger to the north" with high reliability and low response times. Although promising, it is still unclear if one may benefit from having this additional delivery modality paired with speech or other forms of communication from a robot.

The virtual simulation approach that we propose here for investigating tactile communications within MMC makes use of both the VRMIX environment, and the Cordon and Search (C&S) operational context briefly described in the introduction. Though the focus of such an experiment would be centered on the potential performance augmenting effects of tactile communication, it is important to keep in mind that auditory and visual communication may also be provided and evaluated as comparative standards. The basic approach that we suggest is a systematic combination/evaluation of communication modalities in a mission context that allows for empirical performance evaluation (e.g., assessing performance of the Cordon and Search task with the provision of communication via visual, visual + auditory, visual + tactile, auditory + tactile, etc.).

The experimental approach would ideally directly compare each combination of communication modalities with respect to two primary outcomes: performance of the monitoring tasks that are vital to the Cordon aspect of C&S, as well as performance of the Search component of the task. The paradigm that we propose separates the two elements of the task between a human and robotic teammate such that the human (the participant in the context of human subjects research) completes the perimeter monitoring component of the C&S task while also monitoring reports from an autonomous robotic teammate as they ostensibly complete the search component. Using a wizard-of-oz approach, the robot teammate searches the inner cordon area and reports findings using the proposed combinations of modalities. Accordingly, the tasks administered to the human teammate would include the perimeter monitoring task as well as a dedicated robot monitoring or communication task. Evaluation of communication modality effectiveness would therefore be accomplished via investigation of improved or reduced performance of the communication task.

An important a priori decision for such an experiment is the quantification of performance metrics. Performance of a perimeter monitoring task may be quantified well enough through signal detection metrics (see 30, 33), however, the success and effectiveness of communication exchanges as they relate to team performance is not so easily determined by a generalizable paradigm. We suggest that one effective approach to measuring the effectiveness of communications is to measure the development and maintenance of team situational awareness in the context of a given mission context. Situational awareness (SA) generally refers to ones understanding of the current state as well as potential future states of a given situation as it relates to a known (or developing) set of objectives or goals. Given the context of a C&S operation, we propose that evaluation of the quality (and therefore measured effectiveness) of SA should follow from the nature of the search at hand. Consider, for example, a C&S operation that is concerned with the identification of potential bomb-making materials in an urban environment. While the human teammate is busy conducting a monitoring task to ensure the safety of the operation, a robotic teammate may sweep the cordoned area and relay information regarding the presence of potentially dangerous materials. Awareness of the robotic teammate's location, current/past/future actions, findings, and status are all important aspects of communicable information which lends itself to evaluation in that context. Accordingly, if the robotic teammates actions, findings, and communications are predetermined (as they necessarily would be then the following performance data may be assessed during the course of the mission and in the context of communication modalities:

overall team performance in identifying hazardous materials, the human's ability to recall and recognize information regarding reports that occur during the mission, self-reported and objective outcomes with respect to the human teammate's ability to interpret the communications sent by their robotic counterpart, the development and quality of situational awareness as it develops over the course of a mission and in the context of various loading conditions, and the overall performance of the human's primary perimeter monitoring task. Note also that it may be relevant to consider individual differences in the ways that human teammates interact with their virtual counterpart as these variations have been shown to have a significant effect on both individual and team behaviors. Particularly, considering the virtual reality administration method and military focused scenario, some relevant experience should be accounted for to avoid confounding effects. Table 1 below details the possible independent and dependent variables included in the proposed investigative approach.

Table 1. Design approach for investigating MMC

Independent	Dependent
Individual Differences	**Correlated with**
• Biological Sex	• Mental workload (NASA-TLX score)
• Video game experience	• Working memory (recall probe score)
• Virtual reality experience	• Situation awareness (SA probe scores)
• Military experience (e.g. rank, deployment, time in service, etc.)	• Multiple Resource Questionaire (MRQ)
• Education level	
• Robotics Experience	
Multi-modal communication set:	**Effects on:**
• Auditory	–Mental workload (TLX score)
• Visual	–Situation awareness (SA probe scores)
• Auditory + Visual	–Physiological response – Microsoft Band 2
• Auditory + Tactile	(HRV, IBI, HR)
• Visual + Tactile	–Response time (IRT, SDT)
• Visual + Auditory + tactile	–Identification percent accuracy (SDT)
Threat detection task demand levels:	–Identification error rate (SDT)
• Low	–Effects on task performance:
• High	• Percent accuracy
	• Error rate
	• Response time

Additional measures that may be relevant to the evaluation of the effectiveness of MMC pairings/sets include measures of perceived workload which may include self-report measures (such as the NASA-Task Load Index, see [33]) or physiological response measures such as Heart-Rate Variability (HRV), Inter-Beat Interval, or Galvanic Skin Response (GSR) which have been shown to correlate with workload, [18, 34]. Physiological responses may prove especially useful for future implementations of MMC in real world systems as they have the potential to provide real time information that could be used to tailor communication modalities on-the-fly in order to optimize performance.

5 Conclusions

The purpose for this paper is to capture current gaps in the development and assessment of multimodal communication in squad-level human robot teams. Although advances are rapid in the area of machine intelligence, the ability to perform as a cohesive team in environments relevant to the military is not yet achieved. Therefore simulation techniques are necessary to explore how well research findings from human-human communication translate to human-robot teams, as well as how to take advantage of the "super-human" capabilities robots can provide. The VRMIX testbed described provides a platform to emulate future military relevant scenarios with soldier-robot teams to evaluate multimodal communication strategies. Finally, an example experiment focusing on Cordon & Search with a robot team member to investigate tactile communications is proposed with goal of advancing our understanding of how tactile messages may improve communication and situation awareness.

Acknowledgement. This research was sponsored by the Army Research Laboratory and was accomplished under Cooperative Agreement Number W911NF-10-2-0016. The views and conclusions contained in this document are those of the author's and should not be interpreted as representing the official policies, either expressed or implied, of the Army Research Laboratory or the U.S. Government. The U.S. Government is authorized to reproduce and distribute reprints for Government purposes notwithstanding any copyright notation herein.

References

1. Burke, J.L., Murphy, R.R.: Human-robot interaction in USAR technical search: two heads are better than one. In: 13th IEEE International Workshop on Robot and Human Interactive Communication, 2004. ROMAN 2004, pp. 307–312. IEEE, September 2004
2. Casper, J., Murphy, R.R.: Human-robot interactions during the robot-assisted urban search and rescue response at the World Trade Center. IEEE Trans. Syst. Man Cybern. Part B Cybern. **33**(3), 367–385 (2003). https://doi.org/10.1109/TSMCB.2003.811794
3. Micire, M.J.: Evolution and field performance of a rescue robot. J. Field Robot. **25**, 17–30 (2008)
4. Phillips, E.K.: Supporting situation awareness through robot-to-human information exchanges under conditions of visuospatial perspective taking (Doctoral dissertation). University of Central Florida, Orlando (2016). http://stars.library.ucf.edu/etd/4936
5. Phillips, E., Ososky, S., Grove, J., Jentsch, F.: From tools to teammates: toward the development of appropriate mental models for intelligent robots. Proc. Hum. Factors Ergon. Soc. Ann. Meeting **55**(1), 1491–1495 (2011)
6. Chen, J.Y., Barnes, M.J., Qu, Z.: RoboLeader: an agent for supervisory control of multiple robots. In: Proceedings of the 5th ACM/IEEE International Conference on Human-Robot Interaction (HRI 2010), pp. 81–82 (2010)
7. Jentsch, F., Fincannon, T.: Multiple robot-multiple operator control and teamwork: lessons learned and design guidelines. In: Proceedings of Infotech@ Aerospace 2012 (2012)
8. Mouloua, M., Parasuraman, R.: Human Performance in Automated Systems: Current Research and Trends. Lawrence Erlbaum Associates, Publishers, Hillsdale (1994)

9. Jentsch, F., Evans, A., Feldman, M., Hoeft, R., Rehfeld, S., Curtis, M.: A scale MOUT facility for studying human-robot interaction and control. In: Proceedings for the Army Science Conference 2005, (24) (2004)

10. Sawyer, B.: Effects of signal probability on multi-tasking-based distraction in driving, cyberattack, & battlefield simulation. University of Central Florida Electronic Theses and Dissertations, 5169 (2015)

11. Fincannon, T., Jentsch, F., Sellers, B., Talone, A.: Best practices in human operation of robotic/unmanned vehicles: a technical review of recommendations regarding the human-to-robot ratio. Proc. Hum. Factors Ergon. Soc. Ann. Meeting 57(1), 1268–1272 (2013)

12. Phillips, E., Schaefer, K.E., Billings, D.R., Jentsch, F., Hancock, P.A.: Human-animal teams as an analog for future human-robot teams: Influencing design and fostering trust. J. Hum. Robot Interact. 5(1), 100–125 (2016). https://doi.org/10.5898/JHRI.5.1.Phillips

13. Bozkurt, A., et al.: Toward cyber-enhanced working dogs for search and rescue. IEEE Intell. Syst. Cyborg Intell. 29, 32–39 (2014)

14. Phillips, E., Rivera, J., Jentsch, F.: Developing a tactical language for future robotic teammates. Proc. Hum. Factors Ergon. Soc. Ann. Meeting 57(1), 1283–1287 (2013)

15. Yanco, H.A., Drury, J.L.: Rescuing interfaces: a multi-year study of humanrobot interaction at the AAAI Robot Rescue Competition. Auton. Robots 22(4), 333–352 (2007)

16. Chen, J.Y.C., Haas, E.C., Barnes, M.J.: Human performance issues and user interface design for teleoperated robots. IEEE Trans. Syst. Man Cybern. Part C Appl. Rev. 37(6), 1231–1245 (2007)

17. Brown, J., Gray, J.P., Blanco, C., Juneja, A., Alberts, J., Reinerman, L.: Handsfree, heads-up control system for unmanned ground vehicles (No. TARDEC- 22037) (2011). http://www.dtic.mil/dtic/tr/fulltext/u2/a547423.pdf

18. Barber, D., Carter, A., Harris, J., Reinerman-Jones, L.: Feasibility of wearable fitness trackers for adapting multimodal communication. In: Yamamoto, S. (ed.) HIMI 2017. LNCS, vol. 10273, pp. 504–516. Springer, Cham (2017). https://doi.org/10.1007/978-3-319-58521-5_39

19. Barber, D., Lackey, S., Reinerman-Jones, L., Hudson, I.: Visual and Tactile Interfaces for Bi-Directional Human Robot Communication. SPIE Defense, Security, and Sensing - Unmanned Systems Technology. Baltimore, Maryland USA (2013)

20. Bischoff, R., Graefe, V.: Dependable multimodal communication and interaction with robotic assistants. In: 11th IEEE International Workshop on Robot and Human Interactive Communication, pp. 300–305. IEEE (2002)

21. Lackey, S.J., Barber, D.J., Reinerman-Jones, L., Badler, N., Hudson, I.: Defining next-generation multi-modal communication in human-robot interaction. In: Human Factors and Ergonomics Society Conference. HFES, Las Vegas (2011)

22. Sterling, B., Perala, C.: Workload, stress, and situation awareness of soldiers who are controlling unmanned vehicles in future urban operations. Army Research Lab Technical report, ARL-TR-4071 (2007)

23. Lu, S., Wickens, C., Prinet, J., Hutchins, S., Sarter, N., Sebok, A.: Supporting interruption management and multimodal interface design: three meta-analyses of task performance as a function of interrupting task modality. Hum. Factors 55(4), 697–724 (2013)

24. Stader, S.: Impacts of complexity and timing of communication interruptions on visual detection tasks. UCF Stars Library: Electronic Theses and Dissertations (4571) (2014)

25. Wickens, C.D.: Multiple resources and performance prediction. Theor. Issues Ergon. Sci. 3, 159–177 (2002). https://doi.org/10.1080/14639220210123806

26. Duncan, J., Martens, S., Ward, R.: Restricted attentional capacity within but not between sensory modalities. Nature 397, 808–810 (1997)

27. Kahneman, D.: Attention and Effort. Prentice-Hall, Englewood Cliffs (1973)

28. Barber, D., Reinerman-Jones, L., Matthews, G.: Toward a tactile language for human-robot interaction: two studies of tacton learning and performance. Hum. Factors J. Hum. Factors Ergon. Soc. (2014). https://doi.org/10.1177/0018720814548063

29. Jentsch, F., Evans, W., Ososky, S.: Model world: military HRI research conducted using a scale MOUT facility. In: Published in Human-Robot Interactions in Future Military Operations, pp. 419–431 (2010)

30. Bendell, R., Vasquez, G., Jentsch F.: Human performance with autonomous robotic teammates: research methodologies and simulations. In: Human Performance in Automated Systems: Current Research and Trends (2019, in press)

31. Elliott, L.R., Schmeisser, E.T., Redden, E.S.: Development of tactile and haptic systems for U.S. infantry navigation and communication. In: Smith, M.J., Salvendy, G. (eds.) Human Interface 2011. LNCS, vol. 6771, pp. 399–407. Springer, Heidelberg (2011). https://doi.org/10.1007/978-3-642-21793-7_45

32. Barber, D., Nicholson, D., Davis, L., Chen, J.: The mixed-initiative experimental testbed for collaborative human robot interactions. In: International Symposium on Collaborative Technologies and Systems (2008)

33. Vasquez, G., Bendell, R., Talone, A.B., Jentsch, F.: Development of a signal detection-based task for research on distributed human-robot teaming within immersive virtual reality. Proc. Hum. Factors Ergon. Soc. 62(1), 1479–1483 (2018)

34. Matthews, G., Reinerman-Jones, L., Barber, D., Abich IV, J.: The psychometrics of mental workload: multiple measures are sensitive but divergent. J. Hum. Factors Ergon. Soc. (2014). https://doi.org/10.1177/0018720814539505

Accessibility Studies: Abuses, Misuses and the Method of Poietic Design

Gian Maria Greco[1,2(✉)]

[1] Autonomous University of Barcelona, Barcelona, Spain
gianmaria.greco@gmail.com
[2] University of Vigo, Vigo, Spain

Abstract. Over the past several decades, accessibility has been increasingly pervading a vast range of fields, producing a large number of new ideas, theories, and innovations that have already proven to be quite fruitful. A closer look at how accessibility has entered and developed in various research fields shows that said fields have experienced fundamental changes: a shift from particularist accounts to a universalist account of access, a shift from maker-centred to user-centred approaches, and a shift from reactive to proactive approaches. Through these processes, accessibility has birthed new areas within those fields, that have been gradually converging to constitute the wider field of *accessibility studies*. The nature and position of accessibility studies has now become a central topic. This ongoing progression of conceptual clarification may bear some misunderstanding and misinterpretations along the way. In the paper, I first briefly review the principal traits of the process of formation of accessibility studies; then address some possible misconceptions; and finally, introduce a first, very general sketch of poietic design, a method proper to accessibility studies.

Keywords: Accessibility revolution · Accessibility studies · Audiovisual translation · Design · Human rights · Maker-user gap · Maker-expert-user gap · Media accessibility · Poietic design · Universal access in human-computer interaction

1 Introduction

Over the past decades, accessibility has been increasingly pervading a vast range of fields, producing a large number of new topics, theories, and innovations that have already proven to be quite fruitful. Upon closer examination of how accessibility has broken into and developed in these fields shows that the fields themselves have been experiencing a series of shifts. Through these processes, accessibility has given rise to new areas within those fields, that have been gradually converging to constitute the wider field of *accessibility studies* (AS) [1–4]. As in any process of emancipation, where an individual claims her autonomy and individuality once having reached maturity, this ongoing progression of conceptual clarification may bear some misunderstanding and misinterpretations along the way. They are physiological, due precisely to the emancipatory dialectic between an individual (AS) and her peers (other well-established fields). My goal in this paper is threefold: (a) to briefly review the

C. Stephanidis (Ed.): HCII 2019, LNCS 11786, pp. 15–27, 2019.
https://doi.org/10.1007/978-3-030-30033-3_2

principal traits of the process of formation of AS in order to (b) add a few more tiles to the mosaic of AS while (c) addressing some possible misconceptions. Which means that this paper should be read as an additional contribution on the path towards the academic maturity of AS. For this reason, the paper is divided into two parts. In part one, I briefly recall the main characteristics of the process of formation of AS and mention some of its defining features. This part, which corresponds to the next three sections, summarises aspects that I have addressed more extensively in [1]. Therefore, I refer the reader to that paper for a more detailed discussion. In the second part, I begin by addressing some misconceptions that may lead to misuses and abuses of AS and then conclude by introducing a first, very general sketch of a method proper to AS, namely poietic design.

2 The Accessibility Revolution

Access is a central concept in human life. As discussed by Lakoff in his analysis of freedom as a metaphor: "you are not free to go somewhere, get something, or do something if access is blocked, or if there is no path (or road or bridge) to it. Freedom requires not just the absence of impediments to motion but also the presence of access. Inhibiting freedom is, metaphorically, not just throwing up roadblocks, holding one back, taking away power, imposing burdens or threats or harm, but also failing to provide access. [...] The metaphor of freedom as freedom of motion thus has two important parts: freedom from and freedom to. Freedom from concerns those things that can keep you from moving. Freedom to concerns making sure there is access" [5]. The freedom examined by Lakoff is not freedom as a human right but the very general, archetypical concept of freedom.

The importance of access for human life and thought has become even more evident through the debate on human rights. Within this context, accessibility began to make its way to the forefront towards the end of WWI and then subsequently, through the widespread movement that led to the adoption of the *Universal Declaration of Human Rights*. Human rights rest upon two intertwined grounds: human dignity and access. The concept of human dignity usually sets a minimum standard of quality of life an individual is entitled to for the sole reason of being a human being. Such a standard is often defined by a series of material and immaterial goods thought to be essential for every individual. Yet, setting up a public education system does not suffice for a state to claim that it is respecting the right to education for all, if said system does not also provide the means to access for every student. Guaranteeing the conditions for the existence of those fundamental goods is a necessary but not sufficient condition for human dignity. The possibility to have actual access to them also needs to be in place [6]. Thus the reason why human rights, e.g. the human right to education, are expressed in terms of the "human right to access to", e.g. "the human right to access to education" [4]. Having access means, for example, being able to use, interact with, and enjoy those fundamental goods. That is, accessibility entails both quantity and quality of experience. Though human rights consist of a (series of) theory(ies) and there is plenty of scholarship that rejects them, they have indeed shed light on the crucial role of access in many human activities, bringing it to the forefront of theoretical, social and political debate. Thanks to the cultural revolution they have produced, it has become clear that access is a *necessary requirement* in the most varied aspects of our lives. From this point of view, accessibility then acts as a *proactive principle*, which calls for a proactive attitude to comply with the access requirement [4].

In order for the accessibility revolution to fully blossom however, a second condition was needed; this time related to the nature of our world and the ways in which we access it. It needed the information revolution. A 2004 preparatory document for the UNESCO World Summit on the Information Society warns about the "reconfiguration of access" enabled by information and communication technologies (ICTs), which is challenging "fundamental social and political notions of freedom, control, personal responsibility, and shared community values" [7]. By reconfiguring in an unprecedented way how we access the world, ourselves and others, ICTs are creating new social inequalities through the formation of multiple divides, beyond the traditional framing of a digital divide between those who have physical access to ICTs and those who do not. In the information society, accessibility becomes the grounds on which power negotiations and social struggles take place.

Rooted in the human rights revolution and boosted by the information revolution, accessibility has been leading a revolution of its own. The question of access tackles the very foundations of our society. It has become so all-encompassing that some say we are living in "the age of access" [8]. This is highly evident in research. The revolutionary effects of accessibility have been producing a *paradigm shift* in various fields, from transportation studies to human-computer interaction, from geography to engineering, from design to sustainability studies, from translation studies to cultural heritage, from education to tourism studies, just to name a few [9–14]. Briefly mentioning two cases may help highlight this point. Acknowledging that providing access to digital information goes beyond mere technical issues, researchers have started to develop an entirely new approach based on accessibility in order to investigate issues of digital sustainability. It is an approach that has subsequently produced foundational ramifications for the whole field of sustainability studies. Since "access concerns can be considered a prerequisite for sustainability", then accessibility becomes "a necessary step towards conceptualizing the sustainability of human societies and their development" [12]. The transformative effects of accessibility are even more pronounced in the case of transportation studies, where accessibility has played an essential role since at least the 1950s. Over the years, it has grown so as to become one of its main concepts, to the point that many scholars have been rethinking the whole field, because "[accessibility] changes how we think about and measure transport problems and the scope of solutions that are considered for addressing them. As with the Copernican revolution, this shift changes what we consider the system's centre: traffic-based planning places motor vehicles at the centre, while accessibility-based planning places people at the centre of the transport system" [15].

3 The Shifts Produced by Accessibility

A closer look at how accessibility has made its way into and then evolved in various research fields shows that these fields have been experiencing some fundamental changes: a shift from *particularist accounts* to a *universalist account of access*, a shift from *maker-centred* to *user-centred approaches*, and a shift from *reactive* to *proactive approaches*.

Accessibility usually entered these fields through an initial focus on a specific group, often persons with disabilities. Over time, the focus was progressively widened to include other groups, until finally reaching a universal scope. That is, these fields have moved from various particularist accounts, that frame access as *exclusively* or *mainly* concerning specific groups of people, towards a more universalist (or integrated/holistic) account, where access concerns all human beings. The field of human-computer interaction is a clear example. Over the past few decades, the focus on accessibility within this field has given rise to the subdomain called "universal access in human-computer interaction" (UAHCI) [16]. UAHCI was initially grounded on "approaches to accessibility mainly targeted toward providing access to computer-based applications by users with disabilities" [17]. Over time, it gradually expanded its focus to other groups until embracing a universal vision by acknowledging that "accessibility can no longer be considered as a specific problem of people with disabilities [but of] society at large" [14]. The shift is even more evident in the field of audiovisual translation (AVT), the "branch of translation studies concerned with the transfer of multimodal and multimedial texts into another language and/or culture" [18]. When accessibility first came into this field, scholars started to use the term "media accessibility" (MA) to refer to a very specific subdomain of AVT, that concerned with "subtitling for the deaf and the hard of hearing (SDH) and audio description (AD) for the blind and the visually impaired" [19]. Even though it was at times expanded to include other modalities, like audio subtitling and sign language interpreting, this first particularist account framed MA as both specifically related to persons with sensory disabilities and exclusively limited to a precise set of AVT services and modalities. Over time, scholars shifted towards a second particularist account of MA, according to which MA concerned not only sensory but also linguistic barriers [20, 21]. Recently, scholars have started to advocate for the shift to a universalist account, which defines MA as concerning access to media and non-media objects, services and environments through media solutions, for any person who cannot or would not be able to, either partially or completely, access them in their original form [1, 4, 22]. The universalist definition does not limit MA to any specific group but rather, focuses on the functional processes involved in the interaction between users' specificities, the particular contexts within which they act or are placed, and the means to address those specificities in such contexts. According to this account, MA comprises three categories: solutions that allow access to media objects, services, and environments; solutions that allow access to media objects, services, and environments through media tools; and solutions that allow access to non-media objects, services, and environments through media instruments.

While the first particularist account frames MA as a sub-area of AVT and the second particularist account makes it overlap with AVT itself, both frame MA as a sub-area of translation studies. Inversely, by allowing for the inclusion of other groups and access services that would have been otherwise excluded from particularist-based MA, the universalist account favours a convergence of the different conceptions of MA and of MA services developed in other fields. In turn, this positions MA as a broader interdisciplinary area that criss-crosses many fields, including AVT, but that cannot be entirely nor exclusively reduced to any of them because it is a proper subdomain of a new field, which I would refer to as AS. The different positions of MA are exemplified in Fig. 1, which should obviously be considered a mere schematisation of their multi-layered enmeshment.

The Three Accounts of Media Accessibility

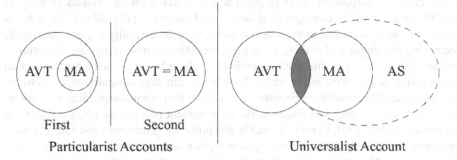

Fig. 1. A simplified schematisation of the three accounts of the area of media accessibility.

The changing tide towards a universalist account of accessibility has been interlaced with a second movement, namely, the increasing attention towards users as bearers of valuable knowledge for the investigation of accessibility processes and phenomena. For years, the dominant attitude was based on the assumption that maker's knowledge is the only one that matters. Whether it be the design of some technology or a theatre performance, artefacts were devised according to the maker's point of view or, in the best case scenario, according to the makers' interpretation of users' needs and capabilities [23]. A major consequence of maker-centred approaches has been a complex series of gaps between the different stakeholders involved. Two of the most prominent are what I have referred to as the *maker-user gap*, a multifaceted gap that can exist between those who make and those who use an artefact, and the *maker-expert-user gap*, which places makers, experts and users at opposite ends of a triangular spectrum of the design process [1, 2, 24, 25]. The need to bridge these gaps has spurred a shift towards inclusive design practices based on user-centred approaches: the knowledge of users, experts and other stakeholders needs to be fully taken into account in the design process because it is as important as maker's knowledge. Evidence of this second shift can be found, for example, in the privileged status that reception studies has achieved in the various fields affected by accessibility.

The recognition that the knowledge of users and experts is as important as the maker's has been posing questions as to how this knowledge should be integrated within the design process, how it should be acquired, and how it should be used. Pursuant to [25–27], the process of artefact design can be broken down into a (series of) *ex-ante*, *in itinere*, and *ex-post* stage(s). For years, access concerns were mainly addressed by adopting reactive approaches. Once produced, artefacts were often modified through ex-post solutions, that is, add-ons in order to render them accessible [28]. In other rare cases, accessibility was addresses at in itinere stages. Ex-post and in itinere solutions bear many limitations, for they may produce a "loss in functionality [or] provide limited and low-quality access" [17]. In some cases, addressing access at the ex-post or in itinere stages is the only possible way. In other cases however, adopting a reactive approach means renouncing accessibility completely, because "it is impossible to 'glue' accessibility onto some of the systems as an afterthought or postmanufacture process" [29]. This has led to a shift towards proactive approaches, which entail "a purposeful effort to build access features into a product as early as possible (e.g., from its conception to design and release)" [17]. Moreover, reactive approaches have often led to the late involvement of accessibility experts, drastically decreasing the chances of making an artefact accessible. These issues are well-known problems in many areas, like web accessibility, where "a main factor for the lack of Accessibility at the Web is the major knowledge gap that normally exists between developers and Accessibility specialists [as well as the] common practice to consider Accessibility at the very last stages of the development process, or when applications are already coded" [30]. In order to tackle this problem, researchers and industry have long been devising specific methodologies that place accessibility concerns – as well as involve users and experts – from the early stages of web application development.

4   The Formation of Accessibility Studies

In order for a new field to be born, one strong, yet not necessarily well-defined, "unique, or at least central, concern" must exist first [31]. This central idea then sets in motion a dialectic between endogenous and exogenous forces that may lead to the formation of the new field [32], if exogenous forces prove to be stronger than the endogenous ones, as will be described below. Some of these forces that scholars widely agree upon are: (a) interdisciplinarity, (b) the formation of a research community, and (c) forms of opposition by well-established fields.

When a new problem emerges on the knowledge horizon, if it cannot be tackled using exclusively the tools of a specific field, a common practice among researchers is to join forces and set up a multidisciplinary programme, each drawing on ideas and methods from her own discipline, to then "split apart unchanged when the work is done" [33]. Yet, some issues are so unique or challenging that the mere juxtaposition of different fields and methods is not sufficient. They demand the "integration and synthesis of ideas and methods", which often leads to the creation of "new hybrid research fields" [33]. Access issues have long proven to demand such an *interdisciplinary* approach, urging researchers from the most diverse fields to not only share their knowledge and tools but to integrate them and devise new ones in order to successfully overcome such challenges.

The uniqueness of accessibility issues has attracted an increasingly broader range of researchers, who have been hybridising their knowledge and methods in order to address said issues. During this journey they have acquired new profiles that neither fully conform to their original fields nor fit within classical boundaries between fields. Regardless of where they started from, they all end up having more in common amongst themselves than with colleagues from their original fields. The area of MA is once more a clear case. Though it was bred within the field of translation studies, MA problems have attracted scholars from the most vastly divergent fields. Researchers from engineering to tourism studies, from filmmaking to computer science, from psychology to the performing arts, have been joining forces, sharing their own methods and creating new ones in order to tackle MA problems. These partnerships have caused them to gravitate beyond the borders of their original fields, detaching themselves from their original colleagues, and forming *a new community of peers*.

While the formation of a new community around accessibility and its interdisciplinary nature have been acting as exogenous forces, they have been opposed by endogenous forces trying to bar that very process. Seeing as "no discipline willingly abdicates its mandated sovereignty" [34], well-established fields tend to resist the formation of a new field, perceived as either a competitor or a threat to their fiefdoms. They tend to shield themselves behind the walls of their orthodoxy, so that their "response is often only to create new subfields – a seemingly endless proliferation that incorporates members of the emerging community of scholars within the larger enterprise without any debate about the significance of their challenge" [35]. In [1] I have discussed several instantiations of these centripetal forces in relation to MA.

5 Some Misuses and Abuses of Accessibility Studies

In the multifaceted process summarised in the previous sections, accessibility has been acting as a magnet. It slowly began applying its attractive force on many fields, leading to the creation of specific subdomains. It simultaneously pulled both these and their researchers out of the spheres of influence of their original fields and has ultimately brought them together on a new, common ground, namely *accessibility studies*. The reader may refer to Fig. 2 which illustrates this, albeit in a very abstract way. Obviously the relationship between AS and other fields is much more complex, seeing as many fields intersect both among themselves and with AS.

AS is the research field concerned with (a) the critical investigation of accessibility processes and phenomena, and (b) the design, implementation and evaluation of accessibility-based and accessibility-oriented methodologies. For a discussion of the definition of AS and its implications, I refer the reader to [1]. As for the goal of this paper, concerning part (a) of the definition, it is sufficient to recall Bradley's words on accessibility in digital sustainability: "[access] is not only about the ability to find and retrieve an item, but also the ability to use, view, listen to, interact with, display, or run the digital item in such a way that users can be assured that what they are viewing satisfies their needs" [36]. Accessibility lies at the heart of a vast gamut of issues, such as acceptability, adaptability, availability, flexibility, personalisation, and usability.

The Formation Process of Accessibility Studies

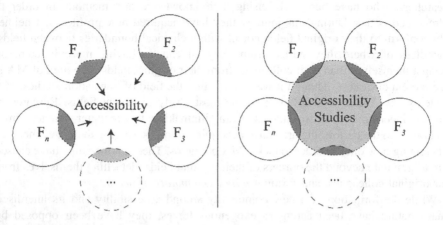

Fig. 2. A simplified schematisation of the formation process of the field of accessibility studies.

Together with many other issues, they are all relevant topics of investigation in AS, as long as some caution is taken, as I will discuss later.

AS has been, de facto, a field for some time, and it is now a central topic in scholarly debate. The journey of a new field towards academic emancipation and recognition is seldom linear and smooth, and may carry some physiological confusion. Therefore, a bit of clarification is called for. In the remaining part of this section, I will address a few of the possible misinterpretations that may lead to misuses and abuses of AS. The list is neither exhaustive nor conclusive. The ultimate goal of the following paragraphs is to contribute to the metatheoretical analysis of the nature of AS while to preventively clear from the path some obstacles that AS may face along the way. Obstacles that, for example, may take the form of argumentations that accept AS but undermine some of its traits, ultimately aiming to keep it under the control of some other field. This even includes fields that may be willing to undergo intense structural renovations to their "castles" so as to make room for AS and exploit its potentials, while keeping it chained to prevent it from walking away from their kingdom. Once more, I will refer mainly to MA to exemplify my point.

A first source of confusion may be related to the distinctiveness of AS. Some may embrace AS, even warmly, while minimising the importance of clarifying the reciprocal positioning and relationship between AS and other fields. Let us consider a possible case in relation to MA, where some may dismiss the value of the distinction between AVT and MA as merely a question of one's point of view. Instead of being a weakness, this is actually a decisive reason for the need to address such a distinction. Having clarity around the perspective from which one conducts her analysis is critical to avoid being stuck in a conceptual, epistemological or methodological muddle. Consider an ancient artefact. A chemist analyses the composition of its materials, a philosopher its aesthetical features. The object being analysed is the same, but the perspectives from which they observe it and the level at which they conduct their analyses differ substantially. In their investigation, the chemist and the philosopher are each guided by a different set of questions, they use different methods, and they elaborate different interpretative models. The chemist may even use the philosopher's results to flesh out some new idea in her own field through metaphorical or analogical thinking. Yet, this does not make the philosopher's statements on the aesthetics of the artefact chemistry statements. Tracing a distinction between MA and AVT does not mean repudiating the role (still being) played by the latter in the development of the former, nor does it mean denying that the two intersect and have much in common. However, they look at the world through different lenses. They are guided by different questions, each of which influence the ways they investigate a problem, the explanations they formulate, and, ultimately, the solutions they devise. As a subfield of translation studies, AVT is concerned with translation, and when it observes the world it frames it in terms of translation problems. As a subdomain of AS, MA is concerned with accessibility, and when it observes the world it frames it in terms of access problems. Obviously, some accessibility problems may be related to translation. Yet, while MA and AVT clearly do intersect: (a) not all translation problems are accessibility problems; and (b) not all accessibility problems are translation problems; therefore (c) not all MA problems are AVT problems and vice versa (see Fig. 1). The fact that MA and AVT intersect and may borrow from each other does not make the need for a distinction a mere fanciful exercise. Mechanical engineering models are used in medicine to gain insight into some mechanisms of the human body and biology. This does not weaken the distinction between medicine and mechanical engineering nor does it make the former a subfield of the latter. As a subdomain of AS, access concerns are ultimately central in MA. Clearly distinguishing between MA (and AS too) and other fields is eventually critical for how one addresses and responds to those concerns. Otherwise, one may run the risk of curing a cold with a hammer. Precisely for these reasons a second possible claim one may advance, i.e. that AVT has become a subdomain of MA, should be discarded as well. Once more, while all problems of MA are accessibility problems, not all problems of AVT are accessibility problems. Which means that, as shown in the third image of Fig. 1, MA is indeed a proper subset of AS (that is, all elements of the MA set are elements of the AS set), while AVT simply intersects with MA (as well as with AS).

The distinctiveness of AS may also give rise to a second form of confusion, that is, the interpretation of AS as either a mere extension or evolution of some other field. This claim usually plays a *hypernym game* with the concepts involved. For example, one can use the concept of translation to talk about design, saying that designing a house is the process of translating the requests of a client into a blueprint and then into a physical building. This formulation plays on the polysemic trait of the words "translation" and "design". While it could be a catchy metaphor or analogy, perhaps useful in inspiring some insights into how the process of design works, accepting it literally would mean classifying design as a hyponym of translation, and thus a *hypernym trap* that leads to conclude that the field of design is a subfield of translation studies. Similarly, claiming that "accessibility is a form of translation and translation is a form of accessibility" [37, see also 38] has a deep heuristic value that, for example, can help us grasp the connection between translation and accessibility at some levels as well as the role they play in addressing and solving social issues. However, it should not be interpreted literally; otherwise it would fall into the hypernym trap. Thus, considering AS as a mere extension or subdomain of some other field, say translation studies, begets the very same controversial conclusion. Ultimately, the hypernym game would engender a field so generic and overpopulated to the point it would become useless.

A third source of confusion may be due to the misinterpretation of AS as a theory instead as a field. AS is not a specific theory of accessibility developed within some fields or subfields, but a field of its own. As such, AS does not aim to provide a unified theory of accessibility but rather, to stimulate the formulation of and, in addition, host many theories of accessibility. Theories that investigate, assess and explain problems, processes and phenomena through the lens of accessibility, while addressing the associated theoretical and the social issues. For example, a theory that rejects the value of users' knowledge in the production of access services has full citizenship in AS. It would probably come into conflict with other theories hosted within AS, but this is part of the healthy internal dialectic of any field.

6   Conclusion: Accessibility and Poietic Design

As mentioned above, AS can be defined as the research field concerned with (a) the critical investigation of accessibility processes and phenomena, and (b) the design, implementation and evaluation of accessibility-based and accessibility-oriented methodologies. In previous works as well as in the pages above, I have focused on (a). In these concluding paragraphs I will briefly examine (b). AS is mature enough to both host a family of theories regarding accessibility-related issues as well as to be organised into subfields, such as *access ethics*, the subfield of AS that investigates the ethical issues raised by accessibility in relation to human life and society. In the course of its emergence, through the enmeshment of the areas that have come together to form it, AS has borrowed specific methodological approaches, and then mixed and restructured them to create its own methods, each concerned with different aspects involved in accessibility. One of these is what I shall refer to as *poietic design* (PD), where "design" should be intended in the most general sense, from policies to software. PD stems from and complies with the inner features of accessibility and applies them to the process of design. The long path that has led to the emergence of AS and the revolution experienced by the different fields have clearly demonstrated the *poietic* trait of accessibility. The focus on users put forward by accessibility, for example, does not imply a secondary role of the makers. On the contrary, it shows that the design process is a co-construction where makers and users, as well as other agents, must work together. Each plays a role that cannot be ignored. Accessibility calls for the responsibility we have both collectively and individually as co-creators and agents. As a method, PD consists of a series of principles:

1. The *Principle of Universality*: accessibility concerns all, not exclusively specific groups or individuals.
2. The *Principle of Personalisation*: one size does not fit all. The design should be able to respond to the specificities of individual users.

3. The *Principle of User-centrality*[1]: design should focus on users and their specificities.
4. The *Principle of Epistemic Inclusivity*: users and other stakeholders, including experts, are bearers of valuable knowledge for the design of artefacts.
5. The *Principle of Participation*: design should be carried out through the active participation of the stakeholders involved.
6. The *Principle of Proactivism*: accessibility should be addressed ex-ante, not ex-post.

The list above should not be considered exhaustive. It merely sketches some of the overarching principles of PD. Others may be added which refer to additional fundamental aspects of accessible design, such as usability and expertise. While I leave a more detailed account of PD, its principles and ethical implications to future work, a few words about the Principle of Personalisation may help to clarify the general point. This principle tells us that universalism should not lead to the annihilation of users' differences and limitation of their freedom. "Design for All" (or Universal Design) identifies the horizon within which the design process should take place: "all" (universalism) means that design has to (potentially) address all users, but not treat them as a homogeneous group of indistinguishable persons. Personalisation means "design for one", that is, we need to design artefacts that can respond to the specificities of each individual. It is design that guarantees individual's choice and makes the adaptation and customisation to her needs, to the environments within which she acts, as well as other factors, possible.

PD is both prescriptive and a descriptive, backward- and forward-looking. It defines the conditions necessary to design an accessible artefact or to make an artefact accessible, in addition to offering an analytic tool for the diagnosis of problems and the devising of strategies of intervention. The poietic trait of accessibility does not simply provide a conceptual tool for the design process, as seized by PD; it also shows the vast potential impact inherent in AS, for example through reframing and successfully tackling old problems. A clear case is the social model of disability. While this model has represented a stepping stone away from the medical model, for years now disability studies scholars have been highlighting its limitations and suggesting the need to move forward, beyond the social model of disability. Yet, this has proven to be very difficult from a disability studies perspective. On the other hand, as I argued in [3, 24, 39], once the problem is framed from its novel perspective, AS allows us to move from a social model of disability to an *atimic model of accessibility* (or *social model of accessibility*), where disability is but an instantiation of a general process of deterioration or negation of the equal status of human beings as imposed by society to anyone who faces barriers to access.

Acknowledgements. I am grateful to Constantine Stephanidis and Margherita Antona for their support as well as to the two anonymous referees and the participants to the 13th conference on Universal Access in Human-Computer Interaction held in Orlando (Florida, US) on 26-31 July 2019. I wish to thank Josh Branson, Kate Dangerfield, Louise Fryer, and Pablo Romero-Fresco

---

[1] I owe the name to Louise Fryer.

for their comments on previous drafts. Teressa Canosa skilfully copyedited the final version of this paper. All remaining mistakes are mine. The research presented in this paper has received funding from the European Union's Horizon 2020 research and innovation programme under the Marie Sklodowska-Curie grant agreement No 752659 (project UMAQ). The author is a member of TransMedia Catalonia (2017SGR113), a research group funded by the Catalan government under the SGR funding scheme, and the GALMA research group, funded by the Galician government under the scheme Proxecto de Excelencia 2017.

References

1. Greco, G.M.: The nature of accessibility studies. J. Audiovis. Transl. **1**, 205–232 (2018)
2. Greco, G.M.: The need for accessibility studies. In: Paper Presented at the Conference the Future of Media Accessibility: Issues and Visions, Lecce, Italy (2017)
3. Greco, G.M.: L'accessibilità culturale come strumento per i diritti umani di tutti. In: Cetorelli, G., Guido, M.R. (eds.) Il patrimonio culturale per tutti. Fruibilità, riconoscibilità, accessibilità, pp. 94–102. Direzione Generale Musei, Ministero dei Beni e delle Attività Culturali e del Turismo, Roma (2017)
4. Greco, G.M.: On accessibility as a human right, with an application to media accessibility. In: Matamala, A., Orero, P. (eds.) Researching Audio Description. New Approaches, pp. 11–33. Palgrave Macmillan, London (2016)
5. Lakoff, G.: Whose Freedom? The Battle Over America's Most Important Idea. Farrar, Straus and Giroux, New York (2006)
6. Francioni, F.: The rights of access to justice under customary international law. In: Francioni, F. (ed.) Access to Justice as a Human Right, pp. 1–55. Oxford University Press, Oxford (2007)
7. Dutton, W.H.: Social Transformation in an Information Society: Rethinking Access to You and the World. UNESCO, Paris (2004)
8. Rifkin, J.: The Age of Access: How the Shift from Ownership to Access is Transforming Modern Life. Penguin, London (2001)
9. Buhalis, D., Darcy, S.: Introduction: from disabled tourists to accessible tourism. In: Buhalis, D., Darcy, S. (eds.) Accessible Tourism: Concepts and Issues, pp. 1–20. Channel View Publications, Bristol (2011)
10. Janelle, D.G., Hodge, D.C. (eds.): Information, Place and Cyberspace: Issues in Accessibility. Springer, New York (2000). https://doi.org/10.1007/978-3-662-04027-0
11. Levine, J., Grengs, J., Merlin, L.: From Mobility to Accessibility: Transforming Urban Transportation and Land-Use Planning. Cornell University Press, Ithaca (2019)
12. Prodan, A.C.: The sustainability of digital documentary heritage. In: Albert, M.-T., Bandarin, F., Pereira Roders, A. (eds.) Going Beyond. HS, pp. 59–69. Springer, Cham (2017). https://doi.org/10.1007/978-3-319-57165-2_5
13. Pullin, G.: Design Meets Disability. The MIT Press, Cambridge (2009)
14. Stephanidis, C., Emiliani, P.L.: Connecting to the information society: a European perspective. Technol. Disabil. **10**, 21–44 (1999)
15. Litman, T.: Evaluating Accessibility for Transportation Planning: Measuring People's Ability to Reach Desired Goods and Activities. Victoria Transport Policy Institute, Victoria (2007)
16. Stephanidis, C. (ed.): The Universal Access Handbook. CRC Press, Boca Raton (2009)

17. Emiliani, P.L.: Perspectives on accessibility: from assistive technologies to universal access and design for all. In: Stephanidis, C. (ed.) The Universal Access Handbook, pp. 2.1–2.18. CRC Press, Boca Raton (2009)
18. Pérez-González, L.: Audiovisual translation. In: Baker, M., Saldanha, G. (eds.) Routledge Encyclopedia of Translation Studies, pp. 13–20. Routledge, London (2008)
19. Orero, P.: Audiovisual translation: a new dynamic umbrella. In: Orero, P. (ed.) Topics in Audiovisual Translation, pp. VII–XIII. Benjamins, Amsterdam (2004)
20. Díaz Cintas, J.: Audiovisual Translation Today. A Question of Accessibility for All. Translating Today, pp. 3–5 (2005)
21. Orero, P., Matamala, A.: Accessible Opera: overcoming linguistic and sensorial barriers. Perspect. Stud. Translatology 15, 262–277 (2007)
22. Greco, G.M.: Towards a Pedagogy of Accessibility. The Need for Critical Learning Spaces in Media Accessibility Education and Training. Linguistica Antverpiensia 19 (forthcoming)
23. Norman, D.A.: The Design of Everyday Things. Basic Books, New York (2013)
24. Greco, G.M.: The normative dimension of cultural accessibility. In: Paper presented at the First Italian Workshop on Cultural Accessibility, Lecce, Italy (2013)
25. Greco, G.M.: Come e perché organizzare un evento culturale accessibile: Dalla teoria alla pratica. In: Paper presented at the Conference ArtLab13, Lecce, Italy (2013)
26. Greco, G.M., Pedone, L.: Accessibilità e sicurezza dei luoghi di spettacolo. Note su criteri impositivi, criteri prescrittivi e buone prassi. AGM, Lecce (2015)
27. Greco, G.M., Pedone, L., Monsellato, E., Rizzo, B., Spinelli, E.: Guida per eventi accessibili ed ecosostenibili. Social Sound-Puglia Sounds, Regione Puglia, Lecce (2012)
28. Adams, R.: User modeling: a universal access perspective. In: Stephanidis, C. (ed.) The Universal Access Handbook, pp. 24.21–24.19. CRC Press, Boca Raton (2009)
29. Vanderheiden, G.C.: Universal design and assistive technology in communication and information technologies: alternatives or complements? Assistive Technol. Official J. RESNA 10, 29–36 (1998)
30. Martín, A., Cechich, A., Rossi, G.: Accessibility at early stages: insights from the designer perspective. In: Paper Presented at the W4A2011–Submission Type Technical (2011)
31. Pietig, J.: Is education a discipline? Educ. Forum 48, 365–372 (1984)
32. Farjoun, M.: The dialectics of institutional development in emerging and turbulent fields. Acad. Manage. J. 45, 848–874 (2002)
33. Committee on Facilitating Interdisciplinary Research, National Academy of Sciences, National Academy of Engineering, Institute of Medicine: Facilitating interdisciplinary research. The National Academies Press, Washington, D.C (2005)
34. Klein, J.T.: The rhetoric of interdisciplinarity: boundary work in the construction of new knowledge. In: Lunsford, A.A., Wilson, K.H., Eberly, R.A. (eds.) The SAGE Handbook of Rhetorical Studies, pp. 265–283. SAGE, Thousand Oaks (2009)
35. Salter, L., Hearn, A.M.V.: Outside the Lines: Issues in Interdisciplinary Research. McGill-Queen's University Press, Montreal (1996)
36. Bradley, K.: Defining digital sustainability. Libr. Trends 56, 148–163 (2007)
37. Díaz Cintas, J., Orero, P., Remael, A.: Media for all: a global challenge. In: Díaz Cintas, J., Orero, P., Aline (eds.) Media for All, pp. 11–20. Rodopi, Amsterdam (2007)
38. Remael, A.: Media accessibility. In: Gambier, Y., van Doorslaer, L. (eds.) Handbook of Translation Studies, vol. 3, pp. 95–101. John Benjamins, Amsterdam/Philadelphia (2012)
39. Greco, G.M.: Accessibility, human rights, and the ghetto effect. In: Paper Presented at the Conference Wounded Places. On the Integrity of the Body, Beirut, Lebanon (2016)

Design Techniques of Ambient Media Advertisements and Message Comprehension

Yen Hsu[1] ⓘ, Chia-Jung Lee[1](✉) ⓘ, and Pei-Ying Yang[2]

[1] The Graduate Institute of Design Science,
Tatung University, Taipei, Taiwan R.O.C.
d10717011@ms.ttu.edu.tw
[2] Ming-Chi University of Technology, Taipei, Taiwan R.O.C.

Abstract. Ambient media advertising is an innovative outdoor advertising format. This type of advertising typically involves placing unexpected advertisements in unusual locations to draw the attention of consumers and leave a memorable impression on consumers. Ambient media advertisements are often integrated into daily surroundings, and these novel advertisements make consumers' daily lives more fun and creative. Unexpected ambient media advertisements draw consumers' attention, provoke their positive attitudes toward the advertisement, and increase purchase intentions and revenues.

Ambient media advertisements that attract people's attention often employ unique media to convey messages, and different presentation designs are applied to incorporate novel and unpredictable factors in the visual display to stimulate the audiences' interests in advertisement messages. For this study, 238 advertisement samples were acquired from the website Bored Panda Ambient Media. After experts eliminated similar samples, a total of 190 ambient media advertisement samples were adopted for this research. By analyzing these samples, five design techniques (i.e., metaphor, similes, allegory, metonymy, and analogy) and three media (i.e., site media, reproducing media, and mechanical media) were identified, and a total of 15 ambient media advertisement sample combinations were obtained. The differences in the message comprehension level were then determined among these samples. The results are as follows:

(1) Among various media with all design techniques, site media resulted in the highest message comprehension.
(2) Among all design techniques under various media, the technique of metaphor resulted in the highest message comprehension.
(3) Regarding the effect of media and design technique interactions, the combination of metaphor and site media resulted in the highest message comprehension.

Keywords: Ambient media · Design technique · Media ·
Message comprehension · Message communication

© Springer Nature Switzerland AG 2019
C. Stephanidis (Ed.): HCII 2019, LNCS 11786, pp. 28–39, 2019.
https://doi.org/10.1007/978-3-030-30033-3_3

1 Introduction

Ambient media advertising first appeared in British media around 1999 before becoming a standard advertising format in the advertising industry [1]. At the time of its inception, this type of advertising attracted great attention among British marketing and advertising media enterprises [2]. Ambient media advertising is an innovative outdoor advertisement format, in which unexpected advertisements are placed in unusual locations to draw consumers' attention [3] and provide unique experiences to the public [4]. Ambient media advertisements have more novelty and are more surprising for recipients than any other advertising media. By placing unexpected advertisements in unusual locations, this type of advertisements successfully encourages their positive attitudes toward the advertisement [5]. Ambient media advertisements provoke new social phenomenon, which increases purchase intentions and sales revenue [6].

In ambient media advertising, a common advertising approach is to integrate advertisements into daily life and use creativity to add some fun to people's lives. By finding a common point between product features and the carrier, advertisers use the happiness and value generated by such novelties to increase ambient media recognition by the public [7]. Ambient media advertisements are usually placed at unexpected locations for targeted audiences. These advertisements are usually well-planned to surprise and excite the audience. Ambient media advertisements often employ unique media to convey messages, and different presentation designs are applied to incorporate novel and unpredictable factors in the visual display to stimulate the audiences' interests in advertisement messages [8].

An increasing number of ambient media advertisements have employed the approach of on-set interactive experiences to achieve promotion purposes [9]. Successful ambient media advertisements effectively communicate advertisement messages through the optimal medium by integrating advertisement contents with designs and media [1]. In response to the increasing popularity of ambient media, the present study analyzed and categorized design techniques and media of ambient media advertisements and then analyzed the differences in the level of message comprehension among different types of advertisements. The objectives of this study are as follows:

(1) Categorize design techniques and medium types of ambient media.
(2) Analyze the effect of design techniques of ambient media advertisements on message comprehension under various media.
(3) Determine the effect of various media of ambient media advertisements on message comprehension under various design techniques.
(4) Determine the effect of media and design technique interactions on message comprehension.

2 Literature Review

The present study focused on determining the process and employment of the rhetoric approach as design techniques for ambient media advertisements. Based on relevant literature review, this study analyzed ambient media advertisements and theories for design techniques to determine the different media characteristics of advertisements and message comprehension. This section is divided into four main topics: ambient media, design techniques, media, and message comprehension.

2.1 Ambient Media

Media are the form of presentation of advertisements, and advertisement messages are information conveyed by companies to the public. Advertisements must provoke the public's interest in the product and promote the brand image. The increasing demand of products and services has led to the generation of various advertisement formats and types. People have learned to apply selection and elimination to process the high amount of advertisement messages. Such behaviors affect the views and purchase intention of consumers [10].

Extraordinary ideas can draw consumers' attention and persuade them to purchase the product. Without extraordinary ideas, advertisements may be overlooked by consumers and hence do not achieve their purpose. Ideas imply creativity [11]. The creativity of ambient media is often based on advertisement messages, and creative ambient media are often realized in locations/spaces that are visually appealing, creating mutual feelings and achieving extensive communication. Advertisement creativity increases the beauty, artistic, and truthful level of the work. Therefore, creativity is the key to the success and quality of an advertisement [12].

2.2 Design Techniques

Languages were created by humans to properly, correctly, and lively convey messages and thoughts. During the process of language use, rhetoric techniques were invented. Rhetoric techniques optimize the effectiveness of language use and emotional expressions [13]. Design techniques refer to the message communication method of an advertisement. Advertisements provide product information that companies want to convey to targeted consumers; advertisements are presented creatively through design techniques and texts to market the product [14].

According to the research results obtained by Trevino (1986), Wimberly et al. (2000), Jeong (2008), Booth (2010), Radden and Kövecses (1999), and Gentner (1983), the present study categorized the design techniques employed by ambient media into five categories.

(1) Metaphor: The carrier can represent the tenor; both objects are considered equal, and their similitudes or differences can only be understood through comprehensive thinking [15]. The public interprets another symbolic element when facing the product. The metaphoric design technique cleverly integrates a cultural element into the product design to create a new creative product. The technique of metaphor

involves pairing two objects and producing new combinations and comprehensions of the relationships and contexts projected by these two objects [16]; for example, bus handles shaped as hands implies contact with unknown individuals.

(2) Similes: Similitudes between the tenor and the carrier are obvious and can be understood without much thinking [17]. For example, containers on a truck represent USB devices with enormous storage capacity. The capacity of storage is the similitude of the two objects.

(3) Allegory: This technique involves counterintuitive thinking by the audience; the product and service portrayed are contradictory to the audience's expectations [18]. For example, the image of a prisoner sitting on the floor of an elevator trying to open the door symbolizes imprisonment in tiny spaces and other possible torture, which contradicts the emphasis of human rights in modern society.

(4) Metonymy: This technique employs partial elements, symbols, or product features to refer to the entire object or concept, and the referral fits the audience's expectation [19]. For example, regarding the image of well-organized clothes stored in each step of a staircase, the visual of well-organized storage represents the products and services of IKEA, and such an interpretation fits the expectation of the public.

(5) Analogy: The tenor and the carrier are absolutely not related, and contexts or written texts are often required to facilitate comprehension [20]. For example, comparing colorful iPods with paint recycling fields implies the effective reuse and recycle of the paint.

2.3 Media

In Understanding Media: The Extensions of Man, Mcluhan proposed that media are messages [21]. People comprehend various messages simultaneously using more than one sense and their comprehension is affected by the conveyance method. Messages and communication media are symbiotic, and such relationships are presented by title font, color, and images of various specifications when people browse through the platform [22].

Ambient media transform messages into symbols through different channels or methods. The nature of these media determines the extent to which the message is conveyed. The media can be divided into three categories and can be applied individually or in combination [23]:

(1) Site media: A communicator is a media. The media communicate through language, facial expression, and hand gestures. Therefore, a communicator must be present. This type of media is confined to the scene and can only occur on site. The communicator conveys the message content through behaviors, actions, or facial expressions such as sitting down or grabbing other people.

(2) Reproducing media: The media were created from the perspective of cultural aesthetics such as images, paintings, and photographs. The media comprise communication works that can exist independently and serve as the basis for site media because they can be reproduced and are creative. Communication is achieved through images, photographs, or nature; for example, images and visual aids such as clouds or the color of the sky.

(3) Mechanical media: This category refers to the use of telephones, televisions, and elevators, which are the transporters of site media and reproducing media. The main differences between reproducing media and mechanical media are that mechanical media operate through mechanics; therefore, technicality must be considered to determine the mechanical output. For mechanical media, the technical aspect is used to communicate messages; for example, the movement of an escalator or the cold air from an air conditioner [23].

2.4 Message Comprehension

Consumers' understanding and comprehension regarding advertisements in surroundings influence their attitude and intention as well as the subsequent purchase behaviors. Therefore, advertisement message comprehension plays a critical role in consumers' purchase decision-making [24]. Through message comprehension, consumers interpret stimulations from the environment and infer knowledge, meanings, and faith. Such inferences then interact with consumers' existing knowledge to produce personal inferences and messages [25].

The following factors influence message comprehension: (1) products, product formats, brands, and marketing methods: Relevant message attributes and benefits obtained by consumers from the product affect consumers' perception of the product [26] and (2) new product benefits, complexity, and perceived risks affect consumers' perception regarding new products [27].

This study aims to determine the differences in the message comprehension level among advertisement samples. On the basis of the research results of Feiereisen, Wong, and Broderick (2008), the present study assessed the level of message comprehension from the perspectives of the advertisement slogan, image descriptions, and main features of a product or service.

3 Experiment

Ambient media communicate a wide variety of concerns including charity, environmental protection, ecosystem, sports, and brand marketing. To understand the design techniques commonly adopted for ambient media advertisements, relevant cases and samples were obtained from the website of Bored Panda Ambient Media. According to the categorization of sites by the website, a total of 238 advertisement samples were obtained in the preliminary stage. Subsequently, further examination was conducted to combine or eliminate similar samples to reduce the possibility of repeated data. Finally, a total of 190 ambient media advertisement samples were obtained. These samples were categorized according to five design techniques (i.e., metaphor, similes, allegory, metonymy, and analogy) and three media (i.e., site media, reproducing media, and mechanical media). The 5×3 experimental design was adopted to generate a total of 15 ambient media advertisement sample combinations. Moreover, 60 participants were recruited for each media. The between-group design was adopted for the experiment. A total of 180 participants were recruited. Before the test, the participants were allowed 5 min to familiarize themselves with the experiment tool and testing samples and to read the operating instructions. The participants were also given time to practice the operation to quickly learn the procedure and content of the experiment and reduce test errors. The operation procedure is as follows: the participants were instructed to look at the center of the screen and click the left button of the mouse for the testing sample to appear on the screen. Each sample was programmed to be displayed for 10 s. Once the sample disappeared from the screen, the participants began to respond to the items. The message comprehension level of these samples was tested.

3.1   Materials

Table 1 presents the 15 ambient media advertisement samples. The samples with images on topics with lesser relevance or with a messy background were eliminated. The image in the sample advertisement and its design concept must be consistent with the advertisement theme; the advertisement text must be readable and be consistent with the original meaning of the situation.

Table 1. Sample numbering according to the media and design techniques

Media	Design technique				
	Metaphor	Similes	Allegory	Metonymy	Analogy
Site media	Sample 1 Metaphor + Site	Sample 4 Similes + Site	Sample 7 Allegory + Site	Sample 10 Metonymy + Site	Sample 13 Analogy + Site
Reproducing media	Sample 2 Metaphor + Reproducing	Sample 5 Similes + Reproducing	Sample 8 Allegory + Reproducing	Sample 11 Metonymy + Reproducing	Sample 14 Analogy + Reproducing
Mechanical media	Sample 3 Metaphor + Mechanical	Sample 6 Similes + Mechanical	Sample 9 Allegory + Mechanical	Sample 12 Metonymy + Mechanical	Sample 15 Analogy + Mechanical

4   Results

4.1   Effect of Design Techniques on Message Comprehension Under Different Media

The experiment with all the ambient media advertisements revealed significant differences in the message comprehension level among advertisements using different media (F value = 8.973, p = .000 < .05).

Table 2. Advertisement comprehension level according to different media

	Media	N	M	Std.	F value	p value	Ranking
Design techniques	Site media	300	5.011	1.4747	8.973	.000***	1
	Reproducing media	300	4.598	1.4754			2
	Mechanical media	300	4.543	1.4906			3

*p < .05 **p < .01 ***p < .001

The mean value of the comprehension level of an advertisement using site media was higher than that of advertisements using the other two media, and the mean values were in the following order: M = 5.011 > M = 4.598 > M = 4.543. This finding implies that the participants had the highest comprehension level for advertisements using site media (Table 2). Slight differences were observed in the mean values of the comprehension level of reproducing and mechanical media.

The simple main effects of these three media variables revealed that for the design techniques of similes, allegory, metonymy, and analogy, the comprehension level of various media differed significantly, whereas for the technique of metaphor, nonsignificant differences were observed (F value = 0.943, p = .391 > .05). The technique of similes showed significant differences in structure (F value = 4.126, p = .018 < .05), and a post hoc test revealed that message comprehension was higher for site media than for mechanical media. The technique of allegory showed significant differences in structure (F value = 33.853, p = .000 < .05), and the post hoc test revealed higher message comprehension for site media than for mechanical media as well as higher message comprehension for reproducing media than for mechanical media. The technique of metonymy showed significant differences in structure (F value = 9.672, p = .000 < .05), and the post hoc test revealed higher message comprehension for site media than for reproducing media. The technique of analogy showed significant differences in structure (F value = 7.578, p = .001 < 0.05), and the post hoc test revealed higher message comprehension for mechanical media than for site media as well as higher message comprehension for mechanical media than for reproducing media (Table 3).

Table 3. Analysis of variance (ANOVA) of main effects of advertisement message comprehension (media)

Source						
Media (A)	SS	Df	MS	F value	p value	Scheffé
Metaphor (b1)	2.594	2	1.297	0.943	.391	–
Similes (b2)	12.337	2	6.169	4.126	.018*	a1 > a3
Allegory (b3)	121.019	2	60.509	33.853	.000***	a1 > a3, a2 > a3
Metonymy (b4)	40.137	2	20.068	9.672	.000***	a1 > a2
Analogy (b5)	32.182	2	16.091	7.578	.001***	a3 > a1, a3 > a2

*p < .05 **p < .01 ***p < .001

4.2 Effect of Media on Message Comprehension Under Different Design Techniques

According to Table 4, different design techniques exerted significant effects on advertisement message comprehension (F value = 28.851, p = .000 < 0.05). Particularly, the mean of the message comprehension level for advertisements employing metaphors was higher than that for advertisements employing similes, allegory, metonymy, and analogy, and the mean values showed the following order: M = 5.488 > M = 4.911 > M = 4.864 > M = 4.187 > M = 4.136. The results revealed that the participants had a uniform perspective of message comprehension for advertisements employing the technique of metaphor (Table 4).

Table 4. Advertisement comprehension level according to different design techniques

	Design Techniques	N	M	Std.	F value	p value	Ranking
Media	Metaphor	180	5.488	1.1724	28.851	.000***	1
	Similes	180	4.911	1.2439			2
	Allegory	180	4.864	1.5632			3
	Metonymy	180	4.187	1.5086			4
	Analogy	180	4.136	1.5098			5

*p < .05 **p < .01 ***p < .001

The main effects test results revealed that under site media, reproducing media, and mechanical media, the design techniques significantly affected the message comprehension level of the participants. Significant differences were observed in site media (F value = 18.144, p = .000 < .05), and the post hoc test revealed higher message comprehension for the technique of metaphor than for the techniques of metonymy and analogy as well as higher message comprehension for the techniques of similes, allegory, and metonymy than for the technique of analogy. Reproducing media showed significant differences (F value = 26.233, p = .000 < .05), and the post hoc test revealed higher message comprehension for the techniques of metaphor, similes, and allegory than for the techniques of metonymy and analogy. Mechanical media showed significant differences (F value = 18.144, p = .000 < .05), and the post hoc test revealed higher message comprehension for the technique of metaphor than for the techniques of allegory and metonymy as well as higher message comprehension for the techniques of similes and metonymy than for the technique of allegory (Table 5).

Table 5. The main effects of advertisement message comprehension (design techniques) according to the ANOVA

Source						
Design Techniques (B)	SS	Df	MS	F value	p value	Scheffé
Site media (a1)	128.393	4	32.098	18.144	.000***	b1 > b4, b1 > b5 b2 > b5, b3 > b5, b4 > b5
Reproducing media (a2)	170.762	4	42.690	26.233	.000***	b1 > b4, b1 > b5, b2 > b4 b2 > b5, b3 > b4, b3 > b5
Mechanical media (a3)	98.771	4	24.693	18.144	.000***	b1 > b3, b1 > b4, b2 > b3, b5 > b3

*p < .05 **p < .01 ***p < .001

4.3   Effect of Media and Design Technique Interactions on Message Comprehension

Two-way ANOVA revealed significant effects of interactions between the three media and the five design techniques (F value = 11.923, p = .000 < .05). The results indicated that the interaction between media and design technique had moderating effects on message comprehension (Table 6).

Table 6. Significance of media and design technique interaction on message comprehension

Independent variables	SS	Df	MS	F value	p value
Media (A)	39.321	2	19.660	11.100	.000***
Design techniques (B)	228.977	4	57.244	32.319	.000***
Media (A)* Design techniques (B)	168.948	8	21.119	11.923	.000***
Error	1567.530	885	1.771		

*p < .05 **p < .01 ***p < .001

Table 7. Effect of design technique and media interactions on advertisement message comprehension

No.	Design techniques	Media	N	M	Std.	F value	p value	Ranking
Sample 1	Metaphor	Site	60	5.657	1.1623	11.923	.000***	1
Sample 2		Reproducing	60	5.388	1.0688			4
Sample 3		Mechanical	60	5.418	1.2778			3
Sample 4	Similes	Site	60	5.275	1.0099			6
Sample 5		Reproducing	60	4.788	1.2061			7
Sample 6		Mechanical	60	4.670	1.4180			10
Sample 7	Allegory	Site	60	5.507	1.3435			2
Sample 8		Reproducing	60	5.378	1.1845			5
Sample 9		Mechanical	60	3.707	1.4677			14
Sample 10	Metonymy	Site	60	4.767	1.6748			9
Sample 11		Reproducing	60	3.610	1.3583			15
Sample 12		Mechanical	60	4.185	1.2548			11
Sample 13	Analogy	Site	60	3.850	1.3655			12
Sample 14		Reproducing	60	3.823	1.5138			13
Sample 15		Mechanical	60	4.733	1.4880			8

*p < .05 **p < .01 ***p < .001

For all ambient media advertisement samples, media and design technique interactions significantly affected the level of message comprehension (F value = 11.923, p = .000 < .05). The mean value of Sample 1 (Metaphor + Site) was higher than that of Sample 7 (Allegory + Site), Sample 3 (Metaphor + Mechanical), Sample 2 (Metaphor + Reproducing), and Sample 8 (Allegory + Reproducing); the mean values presented the following order: M = 5.657 > M = 5.507 > M = 5.418 > M = 5.388 > M = 5.378. The results indicated that the participants' perception of advertisement messages with metaphor, allegory, and site media showed higher uniformity than their perception of advertisement messages with other samples (Table 7).

5 Conclusion

In the present study, the ambient media advertisements collected were analyzed and summarized, and the effects of design techniques and advertising media employed by these ambient media advertisements on the message comprehension level were determined. This study provided the following findings:

(1) Five design techniques: The design techniques identified in this study were metaphor, similes, allegory, metonymy, and analogy. These techniques can provoke the imagination of people. The emotional reaction of people toward the advertisement was achieved by the stimulation of the senses through the media, which draw the public's attention and awaken feelings through the design technique of hidden messages. The interactions of these two factors (media and design technique) can affect the message comprehension level of the advertisement, because people echo with the effects generated in them when they came in contact with the information.

(2) Conveying messages through the three media: Site media communicate the message content through language and eliciting certain behaviors in people at the scene. Reproducing media create new topics by altering images and communicating through the visual sense. Mechanical media create special effects by employing mechanical techniques and technology to overcome time and space limits as well as by stimulating multiple senses.

(3) Among various media, for all the design techniques, site media provided the highest message comprehension. Communication achieved through language and eliciting certain behaviors in people at the scene renders site media the most effective for conveying advertisement messages. Among various design techniques under three media, the metaphor design technique provided the highest message comprehension. In metaphor, the carrier can represent the tenor, and the similitudes and differences in the two objects can only be obtained through comprehensive thinking. The use of metaphor in advertisement design provokes people's comprehensive thinking to understand the meaning of the advertisement and thus comprehend the message.

(4) Regarding media and design technique interactions, the combination of metaphor and site media resulted in optimal message comprehension. Advertisers prefer that advertisements are seen at the adequate time and in the appropriate space for people to interact with the advertisement of their interest. When the advertisement is presented in the image form and the description is consistent or inconsistent with general understanding, the audience will be simulated to seek an answer. Overall, by combining experiences with a series of measures for persuasion, advertising and marketing will improve message comprehension and advertisement values and effectively influence the purchasing intentions of people.

References

1. Barnes, J.: Creating a difference with ambient media. Admap **34**, 46–49 (1999)
2. Shankar, A., Horton, B.: Ambient media: advertising's new media opportunity? Int. J. Advertising **18**(3), 305–321 (2015)
3. Hutter, K., Hoffmann, S.: Guerrilla marketing: the nature of the concept and propositions for further research. Asian J. Mark. **5**(2), 39–54 (2011)
4. Lugmayr, A., et al.: Semantic ambient media—an introduction. Multimedia Tools Appl. **44** (3), 337–359 (2009)
5. Hutter, K.: Unusual location and unexpected execution in advertising: A content analysis and test of effectiveness in ambient advertisements. J. Mark. Commun. **21**(1), 33–47 (2015)
6. Pieters, R., Warlop, L., Wedel, M.: Breaking through the clutter: benefits of advertisement originality and familiarity for brand attention and memory. Manage. Sci. **48**(6), 765–781 (2002)
7. Hutter, K., Hoffmann, S.: Surprise, Surprise. Ambient media as promotion tool for retailers. J. Retail. **90**(1), 93–110 (2014)
8. Hutter, K., Hoffmann, S.: Carrotmob and anti-consumption: same motives but different willingness to make sacrifices? J. Macromark. **33**(3), 217–231 (2013)
9. Gambetti, R.C., Graffigna, G.: The concept of engagement: a systematic analysis of the ongoing marketing debate. Int. J. Mark. Res. **52**(6), 801–826 (2010)
10. Cook, G.: The Discourse of Advertising. Psychology Press, London (2001)
11. Gamson, W.A., et al.: Media images and the social construction of reality. Ann. Rev. Sociol. **18**(1), 373–393 (1992)
12. Ogilvy, D., Horgan, P.: Confessions of an Advertising Man. Atheneum, New York (1963)
13. Lim, C.H., Martin, T.G., Kwak, D.H.: Examining television consumers of mixed martial arts: the relationship among risk taking, emotion, attitude, and actual sport-media-consumption behavior. Int. J. Sport Commun. **3**(1), 49–63 (2010)
14. Ang, S.H., Low, S.Y.: Exploring the dimensions of ad creativity. Psychol. Mark. **17**(10), 835–854 (2000)
15. Trevino, L.K.: Ethical decision making in organizations: a person-situation interactionist model. Acad. Manage. Rev. **11**(3), 601–617 (1986)
16. Wimberly, B.T., et al.: Structure of the 30S ribosomal subunit. Nature **407**(6802), 327 (2000)
17. Jeong, S.H.: Visual metaphor in advertising: is the persuasive effect attributable to visual argumentation or metaphorical rhetoric? J. Mark. Commun. **14**(1), 59–73 (2008)
18. Booth, W.C.: The Rhetoric of Fiction. University of Chicago Press, Chicago (2010)
19. Radden, G., Kövecses, Z.: Towards a theory of metonymy. Metonymy Lang. Thought **4**, 17–60 (1999)
20. Gentner, D.: Structure-mapping: a theoretical framework for analogy. Cogn. Sci. **7**(2), 155–170 (1983)
21. McLuhan, M., et al.: Jak rozumět médiím: extenze člověka. Odeon, Praha (1991)
22. Sherwood, M., Nicholson, M., Marjoribanks, T.: Controlling the message and the medium? The impact of sports organisations' digital and social channels on media access. Digit. Journalism **5**(5), 513–531 (2017)
23. Fiske, S.T., Taylor, S.E.: Social Cognition. Mcgraw-Hill Book Company, New York (1991)
24. Thøgersen, J.: Direct experience and the strength of the personal norm–behavior relationship. Psychol. Mark. **19**(10), 881–893 (2002)

25. Graeff, T.R.: Consumption situations and the effects of brand image on consumers' brand evaluations. Psychol. Mark. **14**(1), 49–70 (1997)
26. Holak, S.L., Lehmann, D.R.: Purchase intentions and the dimensions of innovation: an exploratory model. J. Prod. Innov. Manage **7**(1), 59–73 (1990)
27. Bodnar, A., Corbett, R., Nekrasovski, D.: AROMA: ambient awareness through olfaction in a messaging application. In: Proceedings of the 6th International Conference on Multimodal Interfaces. ACM (2004)
28. Stepanova, E.V., Strube, M.J.: Attractiveness as a function of skin tone and facial features: evidence from categorization studies. J. Gen. Psychol. **145**(1), 1–20 (2018)

How to Define the Passenger's Hazard Perception Level by Combining Subjective and Objective Measures?

Qianjing Hu[1], Gang Guo[1(✉)], Huaji Wang[2], Mingqing Tang[1], Chen Lv[3], and Dongpu Cao[4]

[1] College of Automotive Engineering, Chongqing University, Chongqing, China
Hujingjing_7@163.com, cquguogang@163.com
[2] AVL Powertrain UK Ltd, Coventry, UK
Huaji.Wang@avl.com
[3] School of Mechanical and Aerospace Engineering
and School of Electrical and Electronic Engineering,
Nanyang Technological University, Singapore, Singapore
henrylvchen@gmail.com
[4] Mechanical and Mechatronics Engineering,
University of Waterloo, Waterloo, Canada
Dongp_ca@yahoo.com

Abstract. With the prosperous growing of intelligent technology, the automobile industry is developing towards an unmanned and intelligent generation. However, making a car drive in a human-like way is still a great challenge to engineers, which slows the adoption of such cars in a mass scale. Considering human perception capabilities during the design process might be a solution to this problem, and hazard perception is of great important.

The aim of the study is to propose a theoretical framework for exploring the relationship between driving environment and human perceived hazards to give suggestions on designing human-like vehicle controllers. Correlating objective environmental factors with subjective hazard ratings. Human-in-the-loop experiments were carried out on a high-fidelity driving simulator. 27 driving scenarios were designed and implemented for 14 participants to acquire their subjective hazard ratings, while objective measurements were also recorded.

Specifically, by using the proposed methodology hazard perception level of passenger can be measured by using the subjective parameters adopted during the experiment, which stands for the subjective assessment of passenger's hazard perception. To find what dynamic parameters having a significant correlation with hazard perception level, a seven scale of subjective hazard perception was defined from −3 to 3, namely over dangerous, dangerous, a little dangerous, normal, a little cautious, cautious, overcautious. Objective measures of environment include the velocity and acceleration of the subjective car and the distance between the subjective car and obstacle. A 3*3*3 mixed ANOVA was carried out in our study in order to find out the correlation between the environment and subjective assessment. The finding shows us that the interaction of velocity and acceleration and distance has a strong correlation with the passenger's hazard perception. The others show no correlation be-tween hazard perception assessment.

© Springer Nature Switzerland AG 2019
C. Stephanidis (Ed.): HCII 2019, LNCS 11786, pp. 40–53, 2019.
https://doi.org/10.1007/978-3-030-30033-3_4

This research is with great potential to improve the development of Advanced Driver Assistant System (ADAS) and intelligent automobile from a human perspective. The findings can also be applied to the design of vehicle controllers to improve the passenger's comfort by knowing that on what condition or what kind of control the passenger will feel dangerous and uncomfortable.

Keywords: Passenger · Hazard perception · Subjective · Objective · Driving simulator

1 Introduction

Road safety is achieved when the 'driver-road-vehicle' system works well. Among these three elements, the driver, without any doubt, may best affect the proper functioning of the interaction [1]. However, with the increasing development of internet, the automobile is becoming more and more intelligent and driverless. Every participant in car paly a same important role in the future 'driver-road-vehicle' system.

There are many studies showed that hazard perception is a critical factor to accidents. According to Horswill and McKenna [2], among the different components of driving skill, only hazard perception has been correlated with traffic-accident involvement across a number of studies [3–5]. With the increasing attention on road accident, hazard perception is becoming an increasingly significant research hotpot.

The assessment of hazard perception is often subjective because the perception is highly individual, depending on personal experiences with accidents and potential rewards of risk-taking [6]. Therefore, it is reasonable to measure the passenger's subjective risk perception level. The objective situation can be defined as the subject car's kinematic parameters (acceleration, speed and distance between the subjective car and obstacle on the road.). Moreover, the methods only consider subjective judgments with experiences, but no specific trip. Thus there almost no such study combining the subjective rating, objective dynamic parameter together. The aim of the study is to find out the correlation between passenger's hazard perception and objective environment. Based on study, we can learn about under what kind of condition, the passenger will feel dangerous and uncomfortable. We can adjust the parameters of a car to control the driving behavior in cased of that the passenger is involved in a situation where he or she think is dangerous. It will make a big difference if we adopted this to the Advanced Driver Assistant Systems (ADAS). The aim of the experiment is to find out what is the significant objective environment factor that effect the passenger's hazard perception level based on both objective and subjective parameters. Compared with other literature studies, we retain that the proposed methodology has some advantages, the primarily advantage is that we transfer our focus on passenger's hazard perception not the driver, which could be very different from the other existed study. In addition, our proposed methodology combined both objective parameters and subjective judgment of the hazard perception level.

Numerous studies have focused on the driver's hazard perception. Few of the researches focused on the passengers and their hazard perception, even though passengers are also the car user and should be considered as the same importance as driver.

A brief review about hazard perception would be reported in the next section. After the short introduction, we proposed a literature review in the following section about the hazard perception. Then, we depict our method combing both the subjective and objective measures of hazard perception. A brief description including participants, 27 scenarios, instruments used for collecting data about the objective and subjective judgments of hazard perception will be introduced in detail. Data analysis is described later. Finally, a conclusive section is reported.

2 Literature Review

The literature search was conducted using Google Scholar, because this search engine adopts full-text search and has broad coverage [7–9]. Searches were using the following key words: hazard perception", "situation awareness", "hazard aware-ness", "risk perception".

Hazard perception (HP) has been defined differently by many researchers [10]. Wilde [11] and Mackenna [12] firstly defined hazard perception as the ability to anticipate dangerous situations on the road ahead. While Mills et al. [13] described hazard perception as the ability to read the road. Later on Horswill and McKenna [2] added that hazard perception may be regarded as situation awareness for hazardous, dangerous situations and McKenna, Horswill, and Alexander [12] appended the ability anticipating forthcoming events to the definition. David Crundall [14] said hazard perception (HP) is the process of detecting, evaluating and responding to dangerous events on the road, which have a high likelihood of leading to a collision. One increasingly common description is 'the ability to predict dangerous situations on the road [2, 15].

The literature about the hazard perception almost studied on the driver's hazard perception. Even though there are little few research studied on the passenger's hazard perception, we can still learn something useful to the hazard perception study. Research on driver's hazard perception can be divided into 3 types: (1). the relation between hazard perception and driving experience; (2). the relation between age, gender, nationality and hazard perception; (3). Hazard perception test.

The first type of research focus on whether the driver's driving experience has influence on the hazard perception or not and how the experience affects hazard perception according to references [14, 16–21] relevant to some research about experience and hazard perception. They try to figure out whether or not the driving experiences have influence on the hazard perception and how can we discriminate the driving strategy depend on the driver's experience. The other type about hazard perception is about gender, age or nationality. References [16, 20, 22, 23] study on the relationships between the age and hazard perception to find how the age plays an effects in terms of the ability of hazard perception and what's the differences between different kind of people at different age. References [24, 25] pay their attention on the nationality. That is whether the culture or environment will affect their hazard perception ability or not and how it plays. Meanwhile, there are also some researchers [19, 21, 26–28] who focused on the hazard perception test (HPT), trying to find out the importance of HPT on driver at different period of age or experiences.

Part 1 is mainly talking about what and how the researchers do with the experiment environment where can be broadly divided into four categories: (1). Using a static pictures; (2). Using a traffic clips; (3). PC-based prototype driving-simulator; (4). Real road driving.

There are three categories strategies of evaluating hazard perception ability in the study: (1). Questionnaire; (2). Using a button, which will be pressed when, the participant percept the hazard; (3). Thinking aloud (or Verbal Protocol Analysis);

Using the static pictures and traffic clips can be considered the traditional ways used in hazard perception study. There are a lot of studies based on the traditional ways [14, 16–21, 24, 26]. Recently, the simulator becomes more and more popular in the hazard perception research like reference [23] using it to fulfill the study. With the advantage of allowing researchers to evaluate a driver's ability by parameters such as angles of steering wheel, accelerator, and brake force, driving simulation tests are often used to ascertain driving skills [29–33]. Therefore, it is not only more approaching to reality than desktop neuropsychological tests, but also they are cheaper and more efficient than evaluations of on-road driving test [30]. However, there are some researchers [22, 34] trying to move their experiments to real road, which would be more dangerous and difficult. Considering the convenience, high efficiency and safety of the participant during the experiment, we decided to use a driving simulator to achieve our goal.

A questionnaire is often used to measure the driving experience and the self-assessment of hazard-perception skills [23, 24, 27, 35–38] of the participants. The questionnaire can involve some demographic question and some other question like the frequency they drive, the score to measure how dangerous some traffic scene or something else. Specially, the questionnaire is to find out where, which, what is the hazard [24]. Another way used in hazard perception study is using a press button [16, 17, 20] or using the touch screen [21, 26] or computer mouse [19, 39–41]. The participant can press button or touch the screen or click the mouse when perceive the hazard, which can be collected as response data for researchers. It is a novelty approach called 'Think aloud' (or Verbal Protocol Analysis) used in reference [22]. Participants give continual commentary when they are driving in the real road. In addition, reference [1] combined the objective (like self-assessment) and subjective (speed and acceleration) measure to define the accident risk level. These novelty approaches are very important to improve our study of hazard perception.

In the study about hazard perception, variables about response are widely used, like response time, average response time, response latency, response sensitivity, miss, false, false alarm. In addition, eye tracking is the most used assistant way in the experiment. Also, some studies use some biological indicator to describe the participants' performance, such as palmar sweating response (PSR), electrodermal activity (EDA) in Reference [23]. There are a several of methods used to analysis the experiment data. ANOVA is obvious one of the most popular method used to find out the correlation between factors and hazard perception, which can be proved in References [16, 17, 21] et al. Meanwhile, chi-square analysis is widely used, in particular, to process data in categorization task [17]. Some studies [17, 21] applied logistic regression to fulfill predictive purpose. In their study, the participants watching the clips involve different kind of hazard would have different performance. Then, logistic regression was applied to divide drivers into two groups: novice or experienced, depending on the variables the researchers defined. Moreover, there are some other methods are used, like Poisson regression [26], Paired t-tests [17], Leximancer software [22], Fisher's exact test [17], Cronbach's alpha [25, 26] and Pearson product–moment correlation coefficient [23].

Generally, in the literature, there are many subjects on hazard perception, which were divided into three types before. However, few of them combining the subjective parameters and objective parameters together, neither the study focus on passengers' hazard perception level. However, Eboli [1] defined the accident risk level by introducing a novel methodology, which combines the objective and subjective measures of driving style.

The aim of the study is to find out what parameter standing for the objective environment has a strong correlation with the passenger's hazard perception rating through the methodology, which combines both subjective and objective parameters.

By the use of the proposed methodology, the hazard perception level of the passenger can be tested by using the subjective parameters collected during the experiment. Our study defined a seven scale of passenger's subjective hazard perception (over dangerous, dangerous, a little dangerous, normal, a little cautious, cautious, overcautious), and try to find the dynamic parameters which have significant correlation with hazard perception level.

It is believed that the research can give a great contribution to improving the Advanced Driver Assistant System (ADAS) and the development of the intelligent automobile. What's more, the study can make a big difference in ADAS to improve the passenger's comfort when they are in a road trip if knowing that on what condition or what kind of control the passenger will feel dangerous and uncomfortable.

3 Method

We design a $3 \times 3 \times 3$ mixed experiment depending on three factors, velocity, acceleration and distance. The simulator will be drove in a controlled condition, where the velocity, acceleration and distance is pre-designed. The experimenter will drive at a specific speed Vs (30 km/h, 70 km/h, 110 km/h) and complete a braking task when there is an obstacle appearing in front of the road. By giving a sign to tell the driver where to start braking at the scenario, the acceleration will be controlled at a constant $(-1 \text{ m/s}^2, -3 \text{ m/s}^2, -6 \text{ m/s}^2)$. The distance between the subjective car and the obstacle is settled at $d = (1 + d') \times d0$, $d0 = v2/2a$ and $d' = (5\%, 10\%, 15\%)$. Three velocities represent different speed level (low, normal, high) of the car. As the same, three accelerations standing for three kind of driving style (aggressive, normal, cautious) to stop the car. It also goes for three distance. Participants are required to give a hazard perception rating to describe the own feeling and judgement about the braking task. Each participant is required to complete a questionnaire including a rating scale, which is a subjective self-assessment questionnaire of perceived hazard. Participants express a level from -3 (extremely dangerous) to $+3$ (extremely cautious).

Before the experiment, a hypothesis was proposed that the interaction of velocity, acceleration and distance has a strong relation with the passenger's hazard perception.

3.1 Participants

The participant sample is made up of 14 licensed student drivers and they all are between 23 and 26 years old. Even though they are qualified to be a driver, but during the experiment they are just told to act like a passenger siting on copilot seat and no need to drive.

All of the participants were recruited among university students to be told to know very well the objectives of our research and the proposed methodologies.

To make sure the participants to be representative the age, gender and driving experience of participants should be random.

3.2 Simulator and Questionnaire

To create the virtual driving environment and conduct the experiment, a fixed-base fidelity-driving simulator is used (Fig. 1). The driving simulator is made up of a cockpit, which is equipped with all necessary control systems similar to a real car. The graphics system includes three 42″projectors displays with a front screen resolution of 1920 × 1080 dpi and the two side screens resolution of 1360 × 768 dpi. The displays are situated around the cockpit and provide a 150° horizontal and 40° vertical perspective. The scenarios are presented at a rate of 60 frames per second. Speedometer, rear- and side-view mirror information is visible on the center and side LCD screens. In addition, the driving simulator is equipped a 3D sound system, which can provide a rich audio environment with the sound of the engine, wind and tires. Vehicle vibrations are also simulated via a bass speaker under the driver seat. Steering wheel, gas pedal, brake pedal and car seats are all taken from the vehicle of Ford.

Fig. 1. Fixed-base driving simulator used in the experiment

In order to find the correlation combining the objective and subjective measures. Objective data was pre-designed and controlled by experimenter. For the objective data, we can get it through a questionnaire (Table 1). Each participant in our study is required to finish a questionnaire that includes a rating scale, which is a subjective self-assessment about perceived hazard during the experiment. Specifically, participants is asked to make a self-evaluation of the hazard perception level by expressing a level according to a numerical rating scale about a pair of adjectives representing from over-dangerous to overcautious. We decided to use a Semantic Difference Scale (SDS) to quantify the location which associated with the distance from the center to the corresponding "0" value. The extreme position (near to the adjectives) has the highest value, while the position near to the center have the lowest value. The sign (positive or negative) is associated with the values that identifying the distance from the center for indicating the direction of the distance: it is a convention that the positive sign is on the right, and the negative sign is on the left. Nevertheless, both the extreme position stands for a bad performance: the left means too dangerous under that condition; the right means too cautious which is also considered as a bad performance. There is no doubt that over-aggressive or aggressive behavior will make us feel dangerous. However, it is acknowledged now that driving too cautious also have a terrible influence on the traffic environment and make the passenger feel nervous. Participants express a level from –3 (over dangerous) to +3 (overcautious).

Table 1. Subjective hazard perception rating scale

	Hazard perception rating
Over dangerous and uncomfortable	–3
Dangerous and uncomfortable	–2
Just feel a little dangerous and uncomfortable	–1
Normal and comfortable	0
A little cautious and uncomfortable	1
Cautious and uncomfortable	2
Overcautious and uncomfortable	3

By combining the two kind of data: the objective data controlled by simulator the subjective judgment from participants.

3.3   Driving Scenarios

The survey pre-designed the experiment scenarios (Table 2).

The main task is a braking task, which there is the situation where the experimenter found out the object car and began to brake in one way until the subjective car stopped. Depending on velocity, acceleration, and distance, we created four scenarios including one training scenario and three main task scenarios to stand for different kind of situation. Each main task scenario is made up of nine trips, and in each end of a trip, there will be a van stopped still in front of the lane as an obstacle. When the subjective car driving at a giving condition, the hazard in our study was pre-created.

To make sure the car was drove at one of 27 given scenarios. At first, there will be a speed signal to mind the driver who drive the simulate car to keep the speed as the study asked (30 km/h, 70 km/h, 110 km/h). Then after driving about 200 m later, there will be a sign for driver to start braking. By means of the simulator, when the car was braking, the acceleration of the subject was pre-set at a constant value (–1 m/s², –3 m/s², –6 m/s²). Therefore, it was actually a uniform deceleration. The braking signal was placed in front of the van at a calculated distance, which is 5%, 10% and 15%

Table 2. Pre-designed 27 experiment scenarios

	Vs	a	d'
Scenario 1	30	−1	5%
Scenario 2	30	−1	5%
Scenario 3	30	−1	5%
Scenario 4	70	−1	10%
Scenario 5	70	−1	10%
Scenario 6	70	−1	10%
Scenario 7	100	−1	15%
Scenario 8	100	−1	15%
Scenario 9	100	−1	15%
Scenario 10	30	−3	5%
Scenario 11	30	−3	5%
Scenario 12	30	−3	5%
Scenario 13	70	−3	10%
Scenario 14	70	−3	10%
Scenario 15	70	−3	10%
Scenario 16	100	−3	15%
Scenario 17	100	−3	15%
Scenario 18	100	−3	15%
Scenario 19	30	−6	5%
Scenario 20	30	−6	5%
Scenario 21	30	−6	5%
Scenario 22	70	−6	10%
Scenario 23	70	−6	10%
Scenario 24	70	−6	10%
Scenario 25	100	−6	15%
Scenario 26	100	−6	15%
Scenario 27	100	−6	15%

longer than the uniform deceleration distance of the subject car. The training scenario was built to get the participants warmed up before the main test began, which was almost like the main task scenario, with the number of obstacle and the acceleration different from main scenario. In the training scenario, the number of van is 5, and acceleration was not pre-designed and controlled exactly. However, the subject car will be brake in three way (overaggressive, normal, and overcautious) randomly to simulate our main task.

What's more, the journey on the two lane suburban way is about 15 km.

3.4 Procedure

Fifteen participants (12 men and 3 women) were tested in 27 scenarios lasting approximately 1.5 h. A consent was obtained from each participant after the study being described in detail. Our experimental procedure included a training session and main task session. Participant would be asked to finish the main task after being trained.

Before the training session participant was asked to read the instruction. Then the experimenter would guide the participant to fulfill the training session. Each time the experimenter finished one training task, the participants were required to give a score to describe the own feeling and judgement about the braking task.

Next, the participants would be asked to fulfill the 27 main tasks as a passenger. In each scenario, subject car would be drove by the same driver on the road in a given order. Once driver finished a driving scenario, the participant should give the score of the hazard perception each time. Between each session, participants can had a rest about one minute. The procedure would repeat for 27 times until the main tasks are finished (Fig. 2).

Fig. 2. Experiment scene

3.5   Data Collection

3.5.1   Variables

In our study, we aim to find the correlation between the passenger's hazard perception and objective parameters (velocity, acceleration and distance). Hazard perception rating of each session has been treated as an exogenous variable, and three factors are treated as endogenous variable. The independent variables in the experiment is velocity, acceleration, and distance, which respectively has three levels.

3.6   Design

With the specific aim of finding the correlation between hazard perception rate and objective environment factors the experiment is conducted.

A $3 \times 3 \times 3$ mixed design is used. The between groups factors are the velocity, acceleration and distance between objective car and obstacle when the braking task is finished. The groups factor are different level, such as velocity (low: 30 km/h, normal: 70 km/h, high: 110 km/h), acceleration (overcautious: -1 m/s^2, normal: -3 m/s^2, overaggressive: -6 m/s^2).

To determine whether there is any relationship between the participant's hazard perception rating and the objective environment factors (velocity, acceleration, distance), we carry out a $3 \times 3 \times 3$ ANOVA with velocity (30 km/h, 70 km/h, 110 km/h) and acceleration (low, normal, high) and distance (5%, 10%, 15%) as independent variables, hazard perception rating as the dependent variable.

4 Data Analyze

As is shown in Table 3, we found out that the interaction of velocity, acceleration and distance shows significant influence on hazard perception score, $F(8,351) = 2.324$, $P = 0.019 < 0.05$, that is, the interaction of two independent variables has different influence on the dependent variable at different levels of the third dependent variable. Therefore, it's necessary for us to have a simple two-way interaction test to find out whether the two-factor interactions have significant effect on HP score or not.

Table 3. Test of between subjects effects

Source	df	Mean square	F	p
Velocity	2	120.495	40.703	<0.001
Acceleration	2	144.844	173.052	<0.001
Distance	2	26.963	32.214	<0.001
Velocity*Acceleration	4	68.979	82.412	<0.001
Velocity*Distance	4	1.574	1.881	.113
Acceleration*Distance	4	.852	1.018	.398
Velocity*Acceleration*Distance	8	1.945	2.324	.019

[a]R Squared = .751(Adjusted R Squared = .732)

In our study, we analyzed the impact of acceleration and distance interaction on HP score when velocity at different level. As highlighted in Table 4, when the velocity was 100 km/h, $F(4,351) = 2.755$, $p = 0.028 < 0.05$, it mean that the interaction of acceleration and distance is statistically significant, that is, the acceleration and distance interaction has impact on HP rating when velocity is 100 km/h. However, when velocity was 30 km/h, $F(4,351) = 2.371$, $p = 0.052 > 0.05$, it shows no statistically significance, which means the interaction of acceleration and distance had no influence on HP score (v = 30 km/h). In addition, the results of statistical analyses indicated that the interaction of acceleration and distance has no significant effect on dependent variable when velocity is 70 km/h, $F(4,351) = 0.540$, $p = 0.706 > 0.05$.

According to Table 4, we just need to analyze the influence when velocity is 100 km/h ($p = 0.028 < 0.05$). Pairwise comparisons is shown in Table 5. As is shown in Table 5, there is no statistically significance when velocity is 100 km/h and acceleration is -1 m/s^2 ($p = 1.000 > 0.05$). Table 66 also highlights the comparison between different level of distance, 5% and 10%, 5% and 15%, 10% and -15%, respectively. The correlation between 15% group and HP rating is significantly higher than that in 5% group, $p < 0.001$, and the correlation between 10% group and HP

Table 4. Simple two factor interaction test result

Velocity	source	Sum of Squares	df	Mean Square	F	p
100 km/h	Contrast	9.222	4	2.306	2.755	.028
	Error	293.786[a]	351[a]	.837		
30 km/h	Contrast	7.937	4	1.984	2.371	.052
	Error	293.786[a]	351[a]	.837		
70 km/h	Contrast	1.810	4	.452	.540	.706
	Error	293.786[a]	351[a]	.837		

rating is significantly higher than that in 5% group, p = 0.006 < 0.05. However, there is no significant difference between 15% group and 10% group, p = 1.00 > 0.05. In addition, when velocity is 100 km/h and acceleration is -2 m/s^2, the result of pairwise comparisons shows that The correlation between 15% group and HP rating is significantly higher than that in 5% group, p < 0.001. It also shows that there has significant difference between 10% group and 5% group, p = 0.012 < 0.05. However, there is no sig-indicant difference between 15% group and 10% group, p = 0.119 > 0.05.

Table 5. Result of Pairwise Comparisons

v	a	(I)d	(J)d	Mean difference (I–J)	Std. error	Sig[b]	95% Confidence internal for difference	
							Lower bound	Upper bound
High	High	Max	Mid	.286	.346	1.000	−.546	1.118
			Min	1.357*	.346	<0.001	.525	.546
		Mid	Max	−.286	.346	1.000	−1.118	1.290
			Min	1.071*	.346	0.006	.240	1.903
		Min	Max	−1.357*	.346	<0.001	−2.189	−.525
			Mid	−1.071	.346	.0.006	−1.903	−.240
	Mid	Max	Mid	.714	.346	.119	−.118	1.546
			Min	1.714*	.346	<0.001	.882	2.546
		Mid	Max	−.714	.346	.119	−1.546	.118
			Min	1.000*	.346	.012	.168	1.932
		Min	Max	−1.714*	.346	<0.001	−2.546	−.882
			Mid	−1.000*	.346	.012	−1.832	−.168
	Small	Max	Mid	.071	.346	1.000	−.760	.903
			Min	.214	.346	1.000	−.618	1.046
		Mid	Max	−.071	.346	1.000	−.903	.760
			Min	.143	.346	1.000	−.689	.975
		Min	Max	−.214	.346	1.000	−1.046	.618
			Mid	−.143	.346	1.000	−.975	.689

5 Conclusion and Future Work

In our simulator study, effects of the velocity, acceleration, and distance, which stand for the objective environment on the passengers' hazard perception rating, were examined.

Similar to what we expected, we initially hypothesized that the interaction of velocity, acceleration and distance has a strong correlation with participants' hazard perception rating. As is shown in the result, the interaction of the three subjective parameter shows strong correlation between hazard perception level. However, the simple two factor result demonstrate that only when the velocity is high (v = 100 km/h), the interaction of acceleration and distance has influence on passenger's HP assessment. However, the result shows us that the interaction of acceleration and distance is not statistically significant when acceleration is -1 m/s^2. The pairwise comparisons result also shows us that level of objective parameter (distance) has significant impact on the hazard perception assessment.

In summary, this study, which focused on passenger's hazard perception not the driver's providing a novel experiment that combines both objective measurement and subjective measure together to investigate the relation of hazard perception rating and the objective environment parameters. This study was also the first research to focus the passenger's hazard perception, proving that velocity, acceleration and distance are significantly associated with the passenger's hazard perception.

With the internet industry growing prosperous, the automobile industry is gradually developing towards the unmanned and intelligent way. The most participants when during an automobile will be the passenger not the driver. It is more and more important for us to focus on the passenger. In addition, with the rapidly developing of ADAS, it should not just focus on the driver but also the passenger.

Our study focusing on the passenger would have some disadvantages. Firstly, the simulator will lose some feeling that will be important for passenger to feel the situation. Secondly, it will be more convincible for the study if there will be more participants involved in the study. What's more, the study did not consider about the difference of participant's gender, age, weather a driver and so on.

In our future, we can move the experiment to the real road, which would be less efficient and less convenient but more real. It is possible for us to increase the number of participant, too. In addition, we can take the participants' age, gender, driver or not, novice or experienced into consideration. Furthermore, we can build up a model depending on such researcher to anticipate the passenger's hazard perception. So that the ADAS can be more humanized.

References

1. Eboli, L., Mazzulla, G., Pungillo, G.: How to define the accident risk level of car drivers by combining objective and subjective measures of driving style. Transp. Res. Part F Emerg. Technol. **49**, 29–38 (2017)
2. Horswill, M.S., McKenna, F.P.: A cognitive approach to situation awareness: theory and application. In: Banbury, S., Tremblay, S. (eds.) Aldershot, pp. 155–175. Ashgate Publishing (2004)
3. Peltz, D.C., Krupat, E.: Caution profile and driving record of undergrad males'. Accid. Anal. Prev. **6**, 45–58 (1974)

4. McKenna, F.P., Crick, J.L.: Hazard perception in drivers: a methodology for testing and training. Final Report. Behavioural Studies Unit, Transport and Road Research Laboratory, Crowthorne, UK (1991)
5. Elander, J., West, R., French, D.: Behavioural correlates of individual differences in road-traffic crash risk: an examination of methods and findings. Psychol. Bull. **113**, 279–294 (1993)
6. Nevelsteen, K., Steenberghen, T., Van Rompaey, A., Uyttersprot, L.: Controlling factors of the parental safety perception on children's travel mode choice. Accid. Anal. Prev. **45**, 39–49 (2012)
7. De Winter, J.C.F., Zadpoor, A.A., Dodou, D.: The expansion of Google Scholar versus web of science: a longitudinal study. Scientometrics **98**, 1547–1565 (2014). https://doi.org/10.1007/s11192-013-1089-2
8. Gehanno, J.-F., Rolin, L., Darmoni, S.: Is the coverage of Google Scholar enough to be used alone for systematic reviews. BMC Med. Inf. Decis. Mak. **13**, 7 (2013). https://doi.org/10.1186/1472-6947-13-7
9. Shariff, S.Z., Bejaimal, S.A., Sontrop, J.M., Iansavichus, A.V., Haynes, R.B., Weir, M.A., et al.: Retrieving clinical evidence: a comparison of PubMed and Google Scholar for quick clinical searches. J. Med. Internet Res. 15 (2013). https://doi.org/10.2196/jmir.2624
10. Jackson, A.L., Chapman, P., Crundall, D.: What happens next? Predicting other road users' behaviour as a function of driving experience and processing time. Ergonomics **52**(2), 154–164 (2009)
11. Wilde, G.J.S.: The theory of risk homeostasis: implications for safety and health. Risk Anal. **2**, 209–225 (1982)
12. McKenna, F.P., Horswill, M.S., Alexander, J.: Does anticipation training affect drivers' risk taking? J. Exp. Psychol. Appl. **12**(1), 1–10 (2006)
13. Mills, K.L., Hall, R.D., McDonald, M., Rolls, G.W.P.: The effects of hazard perception training on the development of novice drivers' skills. Report to Department Environment, Transport and Regions (1998). http://www.roads.detr.gov.uk/roadsafety/hazard
14. Crundall, D., Chapman, P.: Some hazards are more attractive than others: drivers of varying experience respond differently to different types of hazard. Accid. Anal. Prev. **45**, 600–609 (2011)
15. Wetton, M.A., Hill, A., Horswill, M.S.: Are what happens next exercises and self-generated commentaries useful additions to hazard perception training for novice drivers? Accid. Anal. Prev. **54**, 57–66 (2013)
16. Borowsky, A., Shinar, D., Oron-Gilad, T.: Age, skill, and hazard perception in driving. Accid. Anal. Prev. **42**(4), 1240–1249 (2010)
17. Borowsky, A., Oron-Gilad, T.: Exploring the effects of driving experience on hazard awareness and risk perception via real-time hazard identification, hazard classification, and rating tasks. Accid. Anal. Prev. **59**, 548–565 (2013)
18. Crundal, D.: Hazard prediction discriminates between novice and experienced drivers. Accid. Anal. Prev. **86**(2016), 47–58 (2015)
19. Horswilla, M.S., Taylora, K.: Even highly experienced drivers benefit from a brief hazard perception training intervention. Accid. Anal. Prev. **52**(2013), 100–110 (2012)
20. Borowsky, A., Oron-Gilad, T., Parmet, Y.: Age and skill differences in classifying hazardous traffic scenes. Transp. Res. Part F: Psychol. Behav. **12**(2009), 277–287 (2009)
21. Scialfa, C.T., Deschênes, M.C.: A hazard perception test for novice drivers. Accid. Anal. Prev. **43**(1), 204–208 (2010)
22. Key, C.E.J., Morris, A.P., Mansfield, N.J.: A study investigating the comparative situation awareness of older and younger drivers when driving a route with extended periods of cognitive taxation. Transp. Res. Part F Traffic Psychol. Behav. **2017**, 145–158 (2017)

23. Takahashi, R., Kobayashi, M.: Driving simulation test for evaluating hazard perception: Elderly driver response characteristics. Transp. Res. Part F Traffic Psychol. Behav. **49**(2017), 257–270 (2017)
24. Lim, P.C., Sheppard, E., Crundall, D.: A predictive hazard perception paradigm differentiates driving experience cross-culturally. Transp. Res. Part F Traffic Psychol. Behav. **26**(2014), 210–217 (2014)
25. Oviedo-Trespalacios, O., Scott-Parker, B.: Transcultural validation and reliability of the Spanish version of the behaviour of young novice drivers scale (BYNDS) in a Colombian young driver population. Transp. Res. Part F Traffic Psychol. Behav. **49**(2017), 188–204 (2017)
26. Scialfa, C.T., Rosemary, S.: Short-term reliability of a brief hazard perception test. Accid. Anal. Prev. **73**(2014), 41–46 (2014)
27. Rosenbloom, T., Shahar, A.: Risk perception of driving as a function of advanced training aimed at recognizing and handling risks in demanding driving situations. Accid. Anal. Prev. **40**(2008), 697–703 (2007)
28. Scialfa, C.T., Borkenhagen, D.: A comparison of static and dynamic hazard perception tests. Accid. Anal. Prev. **51**(2013), 268–273 (2012)
29. Freund, B., Colgrove, L.A., Burke, B.L., McLeod, R.: Self-rated driving performance among elderly drivers referred for driving evaluation. Accid. Anal. Prev. **37**(4), 613–618 (2005)
30. Lee, H.C., Cameron, D., Lee, A.H.: Assessing the driving performance of older adult drivers: On-road versus simulated driving. Accid. Anal. Prev. **35**(5), 797–803 (2003)
31. Andrews, E.C., Westerman, S.J.: Age differences in simulated driving performance: compensatory processes. Accid. Anal. Prev. **45**, 660–668 (2012)
32. Fildes, B., Charlton, J., Muir, C., Koppel, S.: Driving responses of older and younger drivers in a driving simulator. Ann. Proc. Assoc. Adv. Automot. Med. **51**, 559–572 (2007)
33. Stein, A.C., Dubinsky, R.M.: Driving simulator performance in patients with possible and probable Alzheimer's disease. Ann. Adv. Automot. Med. Ann. Sci. Conf. **55**, 325–334 (2011)
34. Eboli, L., Mazzulla, G., Pungillo, G.: The influence of physical and emotional factors on driving style of car drivers: a survey design. Travel Behav. Soc. **7**, 43–51 (2017). https://doi.org/10.1016/j.tbs.2017.02.001
35. Gwyther, H., Holland, C.: The effect of age, gender, and attitudes on self-regulation in driving. Accid. Anal. Prev. **45**, 19–28 (2012)
36. Horswill, M.S., Anstey, K.J., Hatherly, C., Wood, J.M., Pachana, N.A.: Older drivers' insight into their hazard perception ability. Accid. Anal. Prev. **43**, 2121–2127 (2011)
37. Meng, A., Siren, A.: Cognitive problems, self-rated changes in driving skills, driving-related discomfort and self-regulation of driving in old drivers. Accid. Anal. Prev. **49**, 322–329 (2012)
38. Ram, T., Chand, K.: Effect of drivers' risk perception and perception of driving tasks on road safety attitude. Transp. Res. Part F: Psychol. Behav. **42**, 162–176 (2016)
39. Smith, S.S., Horswill, M.S., Chambers, B., Wetton, M.: Hazard perception in novice and experienced drivers: the effects of sleepiness. Accid. Anal. Prev. **41**(4), 729–733 (2009)
40. Poulsen, A.A., Horswill, M.S., Wetton, M.A., Hill, A., Lim, S.M.: A brief office-based hazard perception intervention for drivers with ADHD symptoms. Aust. N. Z. J. Psychiatry **44**(6), 528–534 (2010)
41. Preece, M.H., Horswill, M.S., Geffen, G.M.: Driving after concussion: the acute effect of mild traumatic brain injury on drivers' hazard perception. Neuropsychology **24**(4), 493–503 (2010)

Applying Co-creation Principles
to Requirement Elicitation in Manufacturing

Manuel Oliveira[1(✉)], Andrea Bettoni[2], Eva Coscia[3],
and Hans Torvatn[1]

[1] Department of Industrial Management, SINTEF, Trondheim, Norway
{manuel.oliveira, hans.torvatn}@sintef.no
[2] SUPSI, Manno, Switzerland
andrea.bettoni@supsi.ch
[3] Holonix, Meda, Italy
eva.coscia@holonix.it

Abstract. This paper presents an industrial case of applying co-creation principles for the design of smart industry 4.0 solution within the context of three distinct end-user organizations ranging from aeronautics, robot and furniture manufacturing. The purpose was to develop a digital solution that monitors the operators and their environment to recognise the context and determine whether an operator requires support, subsequently triggering the most appropriate interventions for the operator to excel at their work whilst maintaining their well-being. The paper documents the process followed, results and lessons learnt in applying co-creation principles in the elicitation of requirements in human centered manufacturing work environments.

Keywords: Manufacturing requirement elicitation · Co-creation ·
Digital enhanced operator

1 Introduction

The digitalized factory is a foundational pillar of the European "Factories of the Future" strategy [1] to compete globally. The increasing adoption of automation solutions is essential to stay competitive by facilitating the manufacturing capability to provide advanced products at lower costs. These advances are changing the manufacturing workplace [2], often requiring higher and more specific skills and knowledge levels for workers to succeed. Enterprises' ability to utilize new technologies is a most important competitive advantage, and the specific skills, experiences, competences, and flexibility of workers are pivotal to and at the core of this ability. Consequently, to succeed in the next generation manufacturing requires moving from a production centric perspective, to a human-centric business with greater emphasis on the human capital [3]. To increase the competitiveness of European manufacturing companies while at the same time creating attractive workplaces, it is necessary to create an optimal environment for human automation integration and cooperation that harnesses and leverages the workers' capabilities to increase efficiency whilst improving employee's well-being. However, the ever-increasing introduction of automation and consequent growing

© Springer Nature Switzerland AG 2019
C. Stephanidis (Ed.): HCII 2019, LNCS 11786, pp. 54–61, 2019.
https://doi.org/10.1007/978-3-030-30033-3_5

complexity of tasks are not accompanied by the necessary support for the operator, resulting in inefficiency and misuse (non-optimal use) of workers' capabilities and potential. A key challenge in creating innovative solutions that supplement the human potential within the manufacturing workplace [4], is understanding the requirements of the worker taking into account the rich multi-dimensional context. It is not uncommon that the resulting solution does not address the needs of the worker or there is insufficient acceptance of the solution by workers. This paper describes the co-design process and worker engagement activities in the HUMAN project [5], focusing on the co-design workshops that yielded insights that contradicted the initial perspectives of the project. In addition to describing the tailored co-design methodology, and the key findings from the workshops, the paper also reflects on the lessons learnt on the realization of such activities within manufacturing companies.

2   The HUMAN Project

The HUMAN project [5] is a European research project that aims to digitally enhance the human operator on the shop floor thus assisting them in performing their tasks with the desired quality, whilst ensuring their well-being.

An overview of the conceptual framework of HUMAN, illustrated in Fig. 1 is composed of two distinct cycles:

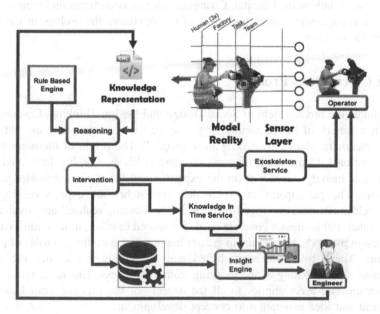

Fig. 1. The HUMAN conceptual framework with short-term reasoning (red track) and long-term reasoning (blue). (Color figure online)

- **Short-term.** The operator is sensorized by the use of wearable devices (e.g.: smart watches, depth cameras, HMD, thermo-graphic cameras, etc.) capturing a wide range of signals that are complemented with sensors in the work environment to generate a digital representation of the workplace environment by the existence of multiple models. Based on the contextual understanding of reality, the system reasons about any anomalies and discrepancies that represent a fallacy in the situation awareness of the operator. As a result, the system determines whether assistance is required and consequently an intervention is triggered that is tailored to the particular needs of the operator;
- **Long-term.** All the data from sensors and events generated from the system are captured for secondary usage through the use of data analytics and process mining by means of the insight engine. Unlike with short-term where the system reasons and determines the best course of action to support the operator, in the case of long-term, an engineer needs to be involved and makes decisions based on the generated insights.

The adoption of advanced manufacturing technologies demands new procedures and working practices as well as modified safety requirements and conditions that workers have to assimilate quickly. Cooperation and easy access to shared knowledge can reduce the reluctance of workers in embracing the change. The challenge is therefore upon modern organisations to come up with solutions for improving the current situation in order to achieve greater agility and reap the benefits of making improved use of their human capital. Changing work environments and their practices requires the engagement and commitment of the operators themselves in the development of the solution.

3   The Co-creation Process

Fostered under the broader field of Social Design and Design Thinking, Co-creation is applied in a variety of fields. Sanders [6] described it very generally as *"an act of collective creativity, shared by two or more people"*. The origin of these approaches can be traced back to the marketing and business fields as a highly facilitated team-based process, heavily dependent on the expertise and the domain knowledge of its practitioners. The participants in Co-creation approaches are experts coming from different fields, all working together in order to design, realize, and evaluate an innovation that will address a concrete need. Compared to other, more traditional user-centred design methods, this results in greater impact on the traditional roles of process participants. These roles are now shifted and the end-user becomes the expert, simultaneously participating in and profiting from the process. This new, active role of the participants/end-users applies to all the aspects of the process from knowledge development and idea generation to concept development.

A major decision of the project was to adopt design-thinking principles to support a co-design approach towards the identification of user needs and capture of user requirements. As such, the emphasis was on the involvement of the relevant stakeholders from each end-user organization, including the key beneficiary of the HUMAN solution – the operator. The flow diagram of Fig. 2 depicts the overview of the co-creation process, with the rectangles representing activities and the circles representing outputs of those activities.

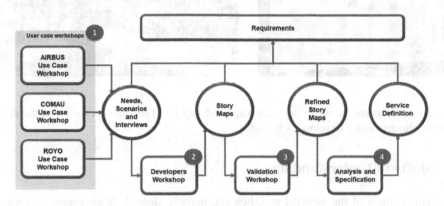

Fig. 2. Co-creation process adopted in HUMAN project

There are four steps in the co-creation process:

- Step 1 – Use Case Workshops: The kick-start to the process was the realisation of 1.5 day workshops at each of the end-user organizations. The process engaged different stakeholders of the end-users, involving operators and management. The output was the prioritisation of operator needs on the shop floor, which then were analysed to create initial scenarios to provide direction for what the HUMAN solution should be. In parallel with the workshops, individual interviews were conducted with operators.
  - Methods and Tools: Brainstorm, Scenarios, Interviews
- Step 2 – Developers Workshop: The analysis of the use case workshops was complemented with thematic analysis of the interviews to define the HUMAN services of interest to the end-user organizations. A workshop involving both researchers and developers used story maps to define each service identified.
  - Methods and Tools: Story Maps, Thematic Analysis of Interviews
- Step 3 – Validation Workshop: A workshop involving the end-user organization representatives, researchers and developers to refine the story maps and contextualise the services.
  - Methods and Tools: Story Maps
- Step 4 – Analysis and Specification: All the outputs from each previous step was analysed to specify the HUMAN solution in terms of the platform that makes sense of the environment and operator's task execution. A set of five distinct services were defined.
  - Methods and Tools: Use case diagrams, activity diagrams, Story Maps

The analysis of the collated data results in a set of requirements for human-centered manufacturing environments (Fig. 3).

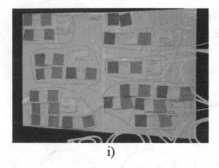

i)   ii)

Fig. 3. (i) illustration of one of the many outputs of step 1; (ii) illustrative example of the story map resulting from the developer's workshop

4   Shifts in Understanding

The engagement of the targeted stakeholders, namely shop floor operators, yielded a deeper understanding of the worker needs and the associated contexts, which led to important insights that have actually challenged the initial assumptions made concerning the interests and focus of the end-user organizations. At the onset of the project, the preliminary analysis of the needs yielded into four distinct use cases of interest to the end-user organizations:

- **Physical Adaptation.** The HUMAN solution intervenes with a physical adaptation to support the operator when they experienced physical stress or tiredness. Without the intervention, the operator slows their productivity and may in some cases result in physical injuries as a result. The technology used would be the exoskeleton, mainly aimed at the upper limb;
- **Cognitive Adaption.** The HUMAN solution intervenes with a cognitive adaptation that supports the worker in performing their task. This intervention is triggered when the operator manifests cognitive stress, tiredness, distraction or cognitive overload. Without the intervention, the operator not only reduces their performance, but may commit errors that impact negatively the production. The key adopted technology would be augmented reality;
- **Knowledge Sharing.** All three end-user organizations rely on highly skilled operators, which have acquired their knowledge through experience over time. The HUMAN solution augments the operator with additional knowledge and provides the means for workers to share their tacit knowledge. The key adopted technology would be social networks supported by gamification for ensuring engagement of the operators;
- **Workplace Redesign.** The analysis of KPIs resulting from the HUMAN monitoring and assessment, complemented by reporting from the operators, triggers cases where there is a need to redesign the workplace to optimise the production. The key technologies to use are augmented reality and virtual reality.

In all cases, both the environment and the operators would need to sensorized for the HUMAN solution to have the necessary situation awareness to intervene when the operator requires support. After the initial co-design activities, the interest of the end-users in the four user cases changed as captured in the Table 1.

Table1 .

Use case	Robot manufacturing	Furniture manufacturing	Aeronautics
Physical Adaptation	High → Low	High	Low → High
Cognitive Adaptation	Medium	High	High
Knowledge Sharing	Medium	Medium → High	High
Workplace redesign	High	High → Medium	Medium → Low

5 Lessons Learnt

Upon reflection of the process, one can distil the following guidelines and recommendations:

- A key ingredient to a successful co-creation workshop is the involvement of end-users and the relevant stakeholders that have an impact in the adoption and usage of the resulting platform. The purpose is to facilitate the process such that end-users move from passive sources of information to active forces that shape the solution. Consequently, the workshop success depends on the involvement of the relevant participants' from the end-user organization, thus it is necessary to have adequate advance preparation to identify and recruit the stakeholders. This type of activity requires the support of management.
  - **Recommendation 1:** Early in the preparation identify and recruit a champion within the end-user organization. This person will represent the team facilitating the workshop, garner support within the organization, negotiate the constrains of the organization, and recruit the participants of the workshop. Consequently, it is necessary to ensure that the champion has the access and reach to support the process.
- In addition to leveraging the expertise and experience of the end-users, one fosters the ownership of the solution by the participants. However, this implies expectations are created that need to be carefully managed to avoid discouragement and disenchantment.
  - **Recommendation 2:** Establish and maintain an open dialogue with the end-users, keeping clear the differences between the phases of discovery and definition of the solution. Do not refrain from frequent and necessary reality checks, to ensure the expectations are managed correctly.
- The very nature of a multidisciplinary team entails the involvement of stakeholders from different disciplines with different expertise and experience, working towards creating new enriched solutions through the intersection of the different perspectives. To engage a multidisciplinary team over a period of time requires frequent and continuous communication amongst the key participants to refine the understanding of the user needs and common shaping of the foundational concepts.

- **Recommendation 3:** Ensure that the multidisciplinary team, in particular when geographically distributed, is aware in advance of the necessary commitment for high level of communication on a continuous basis with frequent interactions. It is not possible to work in isolation as common understanding comes through dialogue.
- In the Co-creation process, namely for the discovery phase, various methods and tools are used with strong visual emphasis (e.g. scenarios, timeline, and storyboards) that are beneficial for facilitating the discussion amongst the different stakeholders. Although the visual artefacts are relevant for exploration, one needs to gauge carefully how to transition to the definition phase and towards ultimately proceeding with development. Otherwise, there is a risk in increasing the specification gap between initial design and implementation, blocking progress.
  - **Recommendation 4:** Attribute a short expiration date to the visual artefacts and adopt the driving principle of discarding the stories and storyboards soon after validation with the end-users.
- The Co-creation process results in visual artefacts supported by some documentation, but a significant amount of tacit knowledge is generated that is not externalised as the effort required makes it impractical considering the fast pace of change. Concepts are shaped by the interplay amongst all the stakeholders; consequently, it is not possible for the co-creation process to be facilitated just with the artefacts created, irrespective of the experience of the facilitator.
  - **Recommendation 5:** Ensure that the co-creation process is facilitated by a team of individuals that remain consistent throughout the process to ensure continuity of the tacit knowledge generated throughout all co-creation activities.

6 Conclusions

The strong emphasis on the operator in the digitized manufacturing workplace puts in question traditional approaches to requirements gathering, thus the adoption of co-creation methods and tools resulted in a four-step process driven by engagement with the end-users complemented by experimentation.

- **Use Case Workshops.** These consisted of co-creation workshops aimed to identification and understanding of the needs of each of the end-user organization. The workshops were organized with multiple stakeholders of each organization, with different roles and responsibilities, but with strong involvement of the operators themselves, whom are the primary end-user of the HUMAN solution. The co-creation approach empowered the stakeholders as experts and active contributors in the process, increasing their engagement and contributing to their ownership as they actively shape the solution from inception to development. The result was a set of relevant needs to be addressed by HUMAN, along with a set of "discovered" scenarios that defined the landscape of the HUMAN solution. Complementing the co-creation workshops were the use of exploratory in-depth interviews that would contribute as rich sources of information in shaping the potential solution.

- **Developer Workshop.** The concept of the HUMAN platform that could perceive the work context and determine what intervention to trigger was crystalized with the analysis of the outputs from the first step. The analysis of the different scenarios, contributed to the identification of services, thus the aim of the developer workshop was to further explore the services and create relevant storymaps that captured the user experience along with the key supporting platform features. In the process of the workshop, where a multidisciplinary team of developers were involved in the elaboration of the storymaps, some of the identified services were discarded as beyond scope of the project, thus contributing to the definition of the HUMAN solution.
- **Validation Workshop.** This workshop involved the multidisciplinary team along with user surrogates and stakeholders representatives of the end-user organizations. The purpose was to further refine and validate the storymaps with the end-users.
- **Analysis and Specification.** The final step consisted on the analysis and specification of the requirements of the HUMAN solution. Unlike the previous steps, this step did not involve a physical meeting with all the discussions leading to maturation of the requirements done by means of virtual meetings and collaboration.

References

1. EFFRA European Factories of the Future Research Association: Factories 4.0 and Beyond: recommendations for the work programme 18-19-20 of the FoF PPP under Horizon 2020 (2016)
2. Thoben, K.D., Weisner, S.A., Wuest, T.: "Industrie 4.0" and smart manufacturing – a review of research issues and application examples. Int. J. Autom. Technol. **11**(1), 4–19 (2017)
3. Emmanouilidis, C., et al.: Enabling the human in the loop: linked data and knowledge in industrial cyber-physical systems. Annu. Rev. Control (2019, to appear)
4. Romero, D., et al.: Towards an operator 4.0 typology: a human-centric perspective on the fourth industrial revolution technologies, In: Computers and Industrial Engineering Proceedings CIE46, Tianjin (2016)
5. HUMAN Manufacturing. http://humanmanufacturing.eu/. Accessed 12 Mar 2019
6. Sanders, E., Stappers, P.: Co-creation and the new landscapes of design. CoDesign **4**(1), 5–18 (2018)

Exploring Color-Universal Design Considering *Kansei* Differences: Color-Vision Types and Impressions of Color Images

Takashi Sakamoto[1]([⊠]) and Yasuyo G. Ichihara[2]

[1] National Institute of Advanced Industrial Science and Technology (AIST),
Tsukuba, Ibaraki 305-8568, Japan
takashi-sakamoto@aist.go.jp
[2] Kogakuin University, Hachioji, Tokyo 192-0015, Japan

Abstract. In this study, the relationship between color-vision types and impressions of color images was examined. Protan, deutan, and trichromatic color-vision participants evaluated the impressions of color images by employing the semantic differentials method, which comprised 13 adjective pairs. In the visual experiment, 20 color images were presented to 31 Japanese male participants, more specifically, 10 trichromatic, 10 protan, and 11 deutan color-vision participants. The experiment revealed that differences of color-vision resulted in different impressions for identical color images. Three factors, named activity, harmony, and potency were extracted from factor analysis. The factor scores were scattered in a three dimensional space on activity, harmony, and potency axes. Furthermore, the protan participants' factor scores did not vary widely along the harmony axis; however, the impression differences sensed in the specific color images by protan and deutan participants were hard to distinguish by using protan and deutan color-vision simulating algorithms. The knowledge of the relationship between color-vision types and color impressions may enable us to develop a concept of a universal design that considers *kansei* differences.

Keywords: Visual experiment · Semantic differentials · Factor analysis · Protan · Deutan · Trichromat

1 Introduction

The purpose of this study was to explore the feasibility of a universal design that considers *kansei* differences. *Kansei* is a Japanese word that may be defined as human characteristics or abilities related to feelings, emotions, intuition, impressions, associations, and preferences that are induced by something tangible or intangible. Furthermore, *kansei* engineering deals with research related to these characteristics or abilities [1]. Previous studies have been conducted on several types of color-vision and their characteristics as well as color-discrimination difficulties caused by color-vision deficiency [2–7]. Nevertheless, not many studies have been conducted on how the impressions of color images differ in relation to color-vision types [8–10]. The differences inherent in the types of color-vision may yield different impressions of color

C. Stephanidis (Ed.): HCII 2019, LNCS 11786, pp. 62–72, 2019.
https://doi.org/10.1007/978-3-030-30033-3_6

images. Analyses and investigations of the impression of color images constitute the major research topics in *kansei* engineering [11–15]. In contrast, color-vision differences have rarely been investigated in *kansei* engineering.

Human color-vision is divided into four types: Trichromatic color-vision, which is normally referred to as normal color-vision, protan color-vision, deutan color-vision, and others. Protan and deutan color-vision are the most common color-vision deficiencies and consist of dichromatic and anomalous trichromatic color-visions. Protan and deutan color-vision have almost the same characteristics of color perception; they cannot perceive reddish and greenish shades. For example, people with protan or deutan color-vision cannot discern facial flushing [16]. Because of these characteristics, it is believed that protan and deutan color-vision differs significantly from trichromatic color-vision in relation to the impressions perceived from colors.

People with protan and deutan color-vision encounter several difficulties in distinguishing and identifying colors. These difficulties in color discrimination have led to the concept of a color-universal design [17, 18]. A color-universal design considers differences between color-vision types, and provides better color discrimination and identification for everyone. However, a color-universal design does not consider impressions perceived from colors; therefore, trichromatic and protan/deutan color-vision people may perceive different impressions from an identical color design even though a color-universal design has been employed.

In order to solve this problem, our research group aimed to offer a new concept in relation to color-universal design that considers *kansei* differences depending on color-vision types. Although our endeavor required knowledge of the relationship between color-vision types and color impressions, this has, as yet, not been clarified. Consequently, this study attempted to clarify the relationship between color-vision types and impressions of color images. It is hoped that such an endeavor will result in a universal design that considers *kansei* differences.

2 Related Studies and Remaining Issues

Please Ichihara [9] found that the impressions of specific colors depended on color-vision types. Furthermore, the results of an analysis based on Osgood's semantic differentials method (SDM) revealed that people with protan and deutan color-vision perceived the colors between red and orange, orange and yellow, yellow and green, and blue and violet to be blight, gorgeous, and lively. On the contrary, they perceived colors between green and blue such as bluish-green, and violet and red, for example, purple to be dark, plain, and lonely. Ichihara [9] only examined single colors by employing color tiles of the Farnsworth-Munsell 100 Hue Color-Vision Test [19]; however, the impressions of plural color combinations or images comprises many colors that have not been investigated.

Chen et al. [8] developed a color-enhancement method to assist people with anomalous trichromatic color-vision and optimized the strength of color-enhancement according to their preferences. Chen et al. [8] examined images that comprised many colors; however, they only dealt with preference among various impressions and did not investigate the other impressions that Ichihara [9] explored.

3 Methods

A visual experiment was conducted to evaluate trichromatic, protan, and deutan participants' impressions of color images in accordance with Osgood's SDM [20]. Experimental methods employed by Ichihara [9] were also used in this study.

The participants included 31 Japanese males that were grouped according to three types of color-vision: Trichromatic color-vision (10), protan color-vision (10), and deutan color-vision (11). By employing an anomaloscope, all the protan and deutan participants were found to be dichromats without anomalous trichromacy.

Twenty color images (see Fig. 2) were selected from a copyright-free image database as visual stimuli in the experiment. The selection of these images was based on whether or not monochrome images converted from the original color images evoked specific emotions in the participants' minds. This selection criterion was employed to examine only impressions of colors contained in the image without impressions of other factors such as objects contained in the image.

The protan and deutan dichromatic simulations are illustrated in Figs. 3 and 4, respectively. These simulated images were created from the 20 color images using Adobe® Photoshop® CC [21]. Although the simulated images were not used in this visual experiment, they were useful to estimate and understand protan and deutan participants' visual performance for the 20 color images.

The 20 color images were presented in a random order to the participants by employing a liquid crystal display color monitor installed in an experimental room, which was illuminated with daylight-white (6700 K) fluorescent light.

Every participant utilized SDM to evaluate the 20 color images. The SDM is a type of a rating scale between two polar adjectives. In this experiment, the SDM consisted of 13 adjective pairs: (1) Bright—Dark, (2) Warm—Cold, (3) Hard—Soft, (4) Heavy—Light, (5) Strong—Weak, (6) Lively—Tranquil, (7) Flashy—Modest, (8) Dense—Sparse, (9) Stable—Unstable, (10) Beautiful—Ugly, (11) Elegant—Inelegant, (12) Concordant—Discordant, and (13) Dynamic—Static. The rating scale between these polar adjectives is divided into seven equal-length segments to produce a uniform-interval scale; this is referred to as the seven points scale (see Fig. 1). After the acquisition of the rating-data, factor analysis [22] was performed so as to analyze the rating scale values of the SDM.

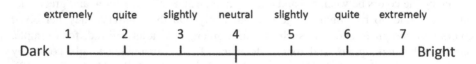

Fig. 1. SDM uses a seven points scale between two polar adjectives.

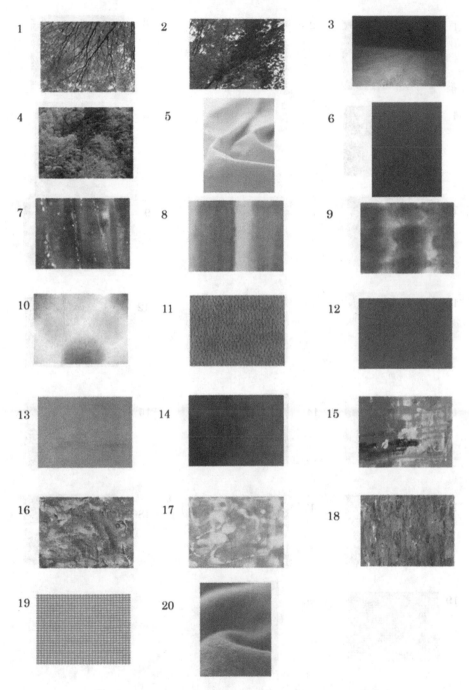

Fig. 2. Twenty color images used in a visual experiment.

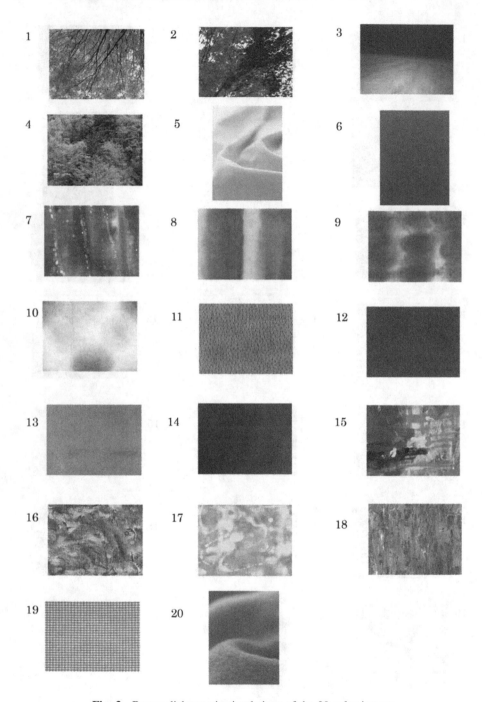

Fig. 3. Protan dichromatic simulations of the 20 color images.

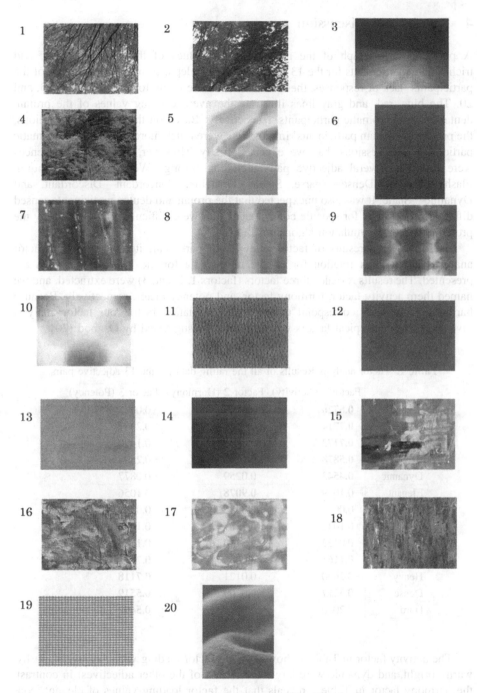

Fig. 4. Deutan dichromatic simulations of the 20 color images.

4   Results and Discussion

A polygonal line graph of the average rating values of the protan, deutan, and trichromatic participants for the 13 adjective pairs is depicted in Fig. 5. Because of the participants' lack of responses, there is no data on the graph for numbers 5, 9, 13, and 20. The blue, red, and gray lines illustrate the average rating values of the protan, deutan, and trichromatic participants, respectively. Based on the overall observations, the protan and deutan participants' impressions were much more similar to trichromatic participants' impressions than we expected firstly. However, significant differences were found in several adjective pairs including Strong—Weak, Lively—Tranquil, Flashy—Modest, Dense—Sparse, Stable—Unstable, Concordant—Discordant, and Dynamic—Static. It was also unexpected that the protan and deutan participants sensed different impressions for specific color images that were difficult to distinguish by the protan and deutan simulation algorithms.

In Table 1, the results of factor analysis, in particular, iterated principal factor analysis and promax rotation for all the rating data for the 13 adjective pairs are presented. The results revealed three factors (factors 1, 2, and 3) were extracted, and we named them activity factor, harmony factor, and potency factor, respectively. Because harmony factor may correspond to Osgood's evaluation factor, our factor analysis revealed that three typical factors were extracted as suggested by Osgood [20].

Table 1. Factor analysis Results of all the rating data for the 13 adjective pairs.

	Factor 1 (Activity)	Factor 2 (Harmony)	Factor 3 (Potency)
Lively	**0.8726**	−0.0293	0.0475
Flashy	**0.7714**	−0.0240	0.2357
Warm	**0.7172**	−0.0150	−0.1490
Bright	**0.5878**	0.1523	−0.2597
Dynamic	**0.4543**	0.0259	−0.0877
Elegant	−0.1049	**0.9078**	−0.1056
Concordant	0.0043	**0.8486**	−0.0399
Beautiful	0.1042	**0.7587**	0.1005
Stable	0.0132	**0.5710**	0.1631
Strong	0.1165	0.0658	**0.7691**
Heavy	−0.2690	0.0121	**0.7118**
Dense	0.3217	−0.0109	**0.5519**
Hard	−0.2030	−0.0917	**0.5492**

The activity factor in Table 1 shows that the factor loading values of lively, flashy, warm, bright, and dynamic were larger than those of the other adjectives. In contrast, the harmony factor in Table 1 reveals that the factor loading values of elegant, concordant, beautiful, and stable were larger than those of the other adjectives, and the potency factor in Table 1 indicates the factor loading values of strong, heavy, dense, and hard were larger than those of the other adjectives.

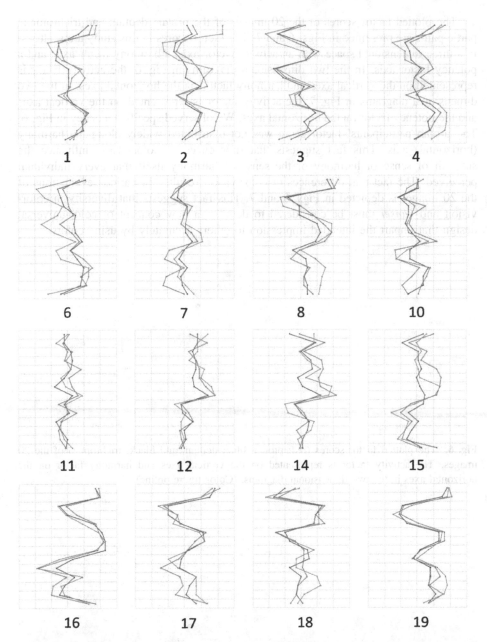

Fig. 5. Polygonal line graphs of the average rating values by the protan (blue lines), deutan (red lines), and trichromatic (gray lines) participants for the 13 adjective pairs. (Color figure online)

The plotted factor scores of the 20 images of the protan, deutan, and trichromatic participants are presented in Figs. 6 and 7. The factor scores in this study are scattered in a three dimensional space with an activity factor axis, a harmony factor axis, and a potency factor axis. In the two dimensional diagrams in Fig. 6, the activity factor is represented on the vertical axes and harmony factor on the horizontal axes. In the two dimensional diagrams in Fig. 7, the activity factor is represented on the vertical axes and the potency factor on the horizontal axes. We observed specific tendency in Fig. 6: The protan participants' factor score was not distributed widely along the harmony (horizontal) axis. This fact suggests that differences of color-vision influence the strength of sense of harmony or the sense of harmony itself that every individual perceived. The fact that differences of color-vision resulted in various evaluations of the 20 images is depicted in Figs. 6 and 7. This fact suggests that diversity in color-vision and *kansei* must be considered to develop a new concept of color-universal design that impart the intended impression to others accurately by using colors.

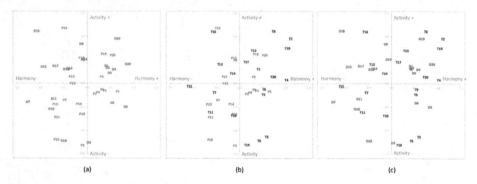

(a)   (b)   (c)

Fig. 6. The plotted factor scores (red: protan, blue: deutan, and black: trichromat) of the 20 images. The activity factor is represented on the vertical axes and harmony factor on the horizontal axes in the two dimensional diagrams. (Color figure online)

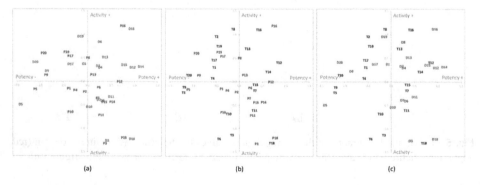

(a)   (b)   (c)

Fig. 7. The plotted factor scores (red: protan, blue: deutan, and black: trichromat) of the 20 images. The activity factor is represented on the vertical axes and potency factor on the horizontal axes in the two dimensional diagrams. (Color figure online)

5   Conclusions

The relationship between color-vision types and color impressions were examined in this study. The results revealed that differences in color-vision resulted in different impressions for identical color images.

In this study, we extracted activity, harmony, and potency factor; these factors corresponded to Osgood's three factors, activity, evaluation, and potency. They were also observed in Ichihara [9] when 100 single colors were used. This fact suggests that the relationship between color-vision types and color impressions does not depend on the number of colors so much. Furthermore, Ichihara [9] found that the values of activity axis were clearly associated with color hue (kinds of colors). In contrast, the present study did not find a significant relationship between color-vision types and color impressions with the exception of the specific tendency that the harmony scores of the protan participants did not vary widely.

Our experimental results suggest that protan and deutan simulation algorithms [21] are not always sufficient when one wants to investigate and classify their impressions for color images (see Figs. 2 and 3). The reason for this insufficiency is that protan and deutan simulation algorithms reduce the color-gamut of original images. Such simulation images cannot reproduce true dynamic ranges that protan and deutan participants see. Based on these experimental results, we could not identify colors that can give common impressions to any type of color-vision. It is recommended that the relationship between color-vision types and impressions of colors be investigated further. Furthermore, in the near future, it is hoped a universal design considering *Kansei* differences will be established if this type of research is continued.

References

1. Nagamachi, M., Lokman, A.M.: Innovations of *Kansei* Engineering, 1st edn. CRC Press, Boca Raton (2010)
2. Mollon, J.D., Pokorny, J., Knoblauch, K.: Normal and Defective Colour Vision, 1st edn. Oxford University Press, Oxford (2003)
3. Kernell, D.: Colours and Colour Vision: An Introductory Survey, 1st edn. Cambridge University Press, Cambridge (2016)
4. Simunovic, M.P.: Colour vision deficiency. Eye **24**(5), 747–755 (2010)
5. Atchison, D.A., Pedersen, C.A., Dain, S.J., Wood, J.M.: Traffic signal color recognition is a problem for both protan and deutan color-vision deficients. Hum. Factors **45**(3), 495–503 (2003)
6. Ichikawa, M., et al.: Preliminary study on color modification for still images to realize barrier-free color vision. In: 2004 IEEE International Conference on Systems, Man and Cybernetics, Netherlands, pp. 36–41. IEEE (2004)
7. Machado, G.M., Oliveira, M.M., Fernandes, L.A.: A physiologically-based model for simulation of color vision deficiency. IEEE Trans. Visual Comput. Graphics **15**(6), 1291–1298 (2009)
8. Chen, Y.C., et al.: Preference for color-enhanced images assessed by color deficiencies. Color Res. Appl. **39**(3), 234–251 (2014)

9. Ichihara, Y.G.: Impression evaluation between color vision types. In: The 4th International Symposium on Affective Science and Engineering, B4-4, pp. 1-4. Japan Society of *Kansei* Engineering, Tokyo (2018)
10. Sejima, Y., Takimoto, H., Sato, Y., Matsuda, K.: Effect of changes in face color on emotion perception in color vision deficiency. J. Jpn. Soc. Kansei Eng. **15**(1), 7–14 (2016)
11. Manami Tamai, M., Hochin, T., Nomiya, H.: Effects of seasons on impressions of pictures. Int. J. Affect. Eng. **17**(2), 109–118 (2018)
12. Thu An, N.T., Hagiwara, M.: An image impression estimation system using adjectives. Int. J. Affect. Eng. **15**(3), 295–303 (2016)
13. Park, H.J., Koyama, E., Furukawa, T., Takatera, M., Shimizu, Y., Kim, H.: An impression evaluation model for apparel product retrieval based on image analysis. Kansei Eng. Int. **3** (1), 11–18 (2001)
14. Du, Y., Gutu, D., Shibata, K., Inazumi, Y., Horita, Y.: National comparison of influence on subjective impression by images in different resolutions. J. Jpn. Soc. Kansei Eng. **16**(1), 147–154 (2017)
15. Eda, T., Koike, Y., Matsushima, S., Ishikawa, T., Ozaki, K., Ayama, M.: Influence of blackness on visual impression of color images. Kansei Eng. Int. J. **10**(1), 49–58 (2010)
16. Nakajima, K., Minami, T., Nakauchi, S.: Interaction between facial expression and color. Sci. Rep. **7**, 41019 (2017)
17. Ichihara, Y.G., Okabe, M., Iga, K., Tanaka, Y., Musha, K., Ito, K.: Color universal design: the selection of four easily distinguishable colors for all color vision types. In: Proceedings of SPIE 6807, Color Imaging XIII: I: Processing, Hardcopy, and Applications. International Society for Optics and Photonics. 68070O (2008)
18. Okabe, M., Ito, K.: Color Universal Design (CUD) -how to make figures and presentations that are friendly to colorblind people-. J* Fly: Data Depository for Drosophila Researchers. http://jfly.uni-koeln.de/color/index.html. Accessed 13 May 2019
19. Farnsworth, D.: The Farnsworth-Munsell 100-hue and dichotomous tests for color vision. J. Opt. Soc. Am. **33**(10), 568–578 (1943)
20. Osgood, C.E., Suci, G., Tannenbaum, P.: The Measurement of Meaning. University of Illinois Press, Urbana (1957)
21. Adobe Photoshop accessibility. https://www.adobe.com/accessibility/products/photoshop.html. Accessed 13 May 2019
22. Child, D.: The Essentials of Factor Analysis, 3rd edn. Bloomsbury Academic Press, London (2006)

Systematic Mapping Study: Use of Design Science in Creation and Evaluation of UX Artifacts

Zlatko Stapić[(⊠)] and Dijana Plantak Vukovac

Faculty of Organization and Informatics, University of Zagreb,
Pavlinska 2, 42000 Varaždin, Croatia
{zlatko.stapic,dijana.plantak}@foi.hr

Abstract. In the recent years, design science has gained significant interest in the information systems development field. In the HCI research community it also proved to be an applicable and often used research framework for design and evaluation of user experience constructs. In this paper we presented the results of a systematic mapping study performed on more than 250 literature sources in order to obtain the information on which UX evaluation techniques are used by researches when performing design science research methodology in creation of UX related artifacts. The analysis resulted in 43 included papers which were classified in five relevant groups. Most of the included studies (21) reported the use different questionnaires in order to evaluate created UX artifacts. The keyword analysis showed that 32 different keywords were used when reporting the UX design and evaluation techniques.

Keywords: Design science · User experience · UX ·
Systematic mapping study

1 Introduction

Design Science (DS) is a research paradigm which aims at creating and evaluating innovative artifacts that address important and relevant organizational problems. Hevner et al. strongly promoted the design science approach in the field of information systems in their book from 2004 [17]. They pointed out that *design science* along with *behavioral science* were two key paradigms used in information systems research. According to their words, design science aims "to extend the boundaries of human and organizational capabilities by creating new and innovative artifacts." A framework of seven guidelines was created by the same authors [17], focusing a design as an artifact, problem relevance, design evaluation, research contributions, research rigor, design as a search process and communication of research.

This framework was adopted and adapted by different authors but Peffers et al. [35] from 2007 made the biggest impact with their definition of Design Science Research Methodology (DSRM) which incorporates principles, practices and procedures required to perform DS research. This methodology included six steps (see Fig. 1)

© Springer Nature Switzerland AG 2019
C. Stephanidis (Ed.): HCII 2019, LNCS 11786, pp. 73–84, 2019.
https://doi.org/10.1007/978-3-030-30033-3_7

including problem identification and motivation, definition of objectives for a solution, design and development of an artifact, demonstration, evaluation and communication.

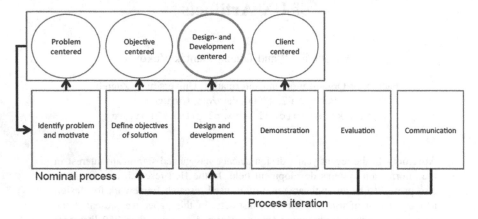

Fig. 1. Design science process model adopted from Peffers [35] and adapted by Dalen and Kraemer [9]

Although the process is structured in a nominally sequential order – in a problem-centered approach, researchers could take different entry points and move outwards, depending on their approach: an objective-centered approach, a design- and development-centered approach or context-initiated approach [35]. For this research we are focusing mainly on a design- and development-centered approach which starts from an artifact which is later proved to be solution for the domain where it will be used. This approach puts special focus on demonstration and evaluation activities which become of special interest for our research as well.

On the other hand, in recent years, design science has gained interest in HCI research community as well, as an applicable research framework for design and evaluation of user experience constructs. User experience (UX), the term coined by Don Norman, is a broad concept explained by Norman itself, as a way a person experiences reality around him/her, e.g. the way he/she experiences the world, a life, a service, an application or a product [28]. More precisely, but still on the high level of abstraction, it refers to every aspects of the user's interaction with the company, its services, and its products [29, 56]. Formalization of the UX term is given by the ISO standard 9241-110:2010 as "a person's perceptions and responses resulting from the use and/or anticipated use of an interactive system, and from the user's interaction with the organization that supplies or delivers the interactive system; from discovering the system, adopting and using it, through to final use" [19], which emphasizes experiences created before, during or after interaction with the system, service or a product and also user's relationship to organization which provide the product.

While there is no consensus on the definition of user experience [16], researchers agree that UX encompasses aspects that go beyond usability and user interface design. Usability is related to the user's accomplishment of the task while interacting with the products, systems or services, while user experience is related to hedonic aspects of that interaction and possession, such as beauty, challenge, stimulation, or self-expression [13]. User experience is subjective category that can change over time and according to the user' internal state. User's state is also underpinned by the definition of Hassenzahl and Tractinsky [14] who define UX as "a consequence of a user's internal state (predispositions, expectations, needs, motivation, mood, etc.), the characteristics of the designed system (e.g. complexity, purpose, usability, functionality, etc.) and the context (or the environment) within which the interaction occurs (e.g. organizational/social setting, meaningfulness of the activity, voluntariness of use, etc.)." Those dimensions, a user, the system and the context, are considered the building blocks of UX.

Djamasbi et al. argue that the user experience and design science research paradigms have much in common; they both contribute to information systems research by providing guidelines for designing successful information technology (IT) systems [10]. The same authors also state that each has weaknesses that could benefit from the strengths of the other, arguing that UX research could benefit from the formal structure of DSR (e.g., the mentioned framework) to better communicate its findings and contribution to theory and practice, while DS could benefit from UX principles that provide specific guidelines, practices, and metrics for measuring the development progress of IT systems designed for a variety of users [10].

To further define our research playground, we must define the key aspect of design science paradigm – an artifact. An artifact may be defined as "*an object that has been intentionally made or produced for a certain purpose*" [18] or it may refer to "*one of many kinds of tangible byproduct produced during the development of software*" [34]. Also, in the context of software development artifact could be defined as "*any piece of software (i.e. models/descriptions) developed and used during software development and maintenance*" [8]. Finally, in the context of design science and human computer interaction, we could adopt and adapt the definition from [55] which points out that *the term artifact denotes any outcome of the activities in a design or an UX design process.*

Thus, taking all into consideration, two important questions within the UX field arise: how to design the system that would evoke positive experience in the user within the given context and how to evaluate the created artifacts to make sure that user's positive experience is achieved. In the context of UX design, various UX design processes could be used, and in the context of UX evaluation, there are many evaluation techniques that could be used.

The goal of our research is to investigate and systematically map available evidence on the use of design science in creation and evaluation of UX artifacts and to determine what type of UX artifact evaluation techniques are used by researchers and practitioners.

The rest of this paper is structured as follows: in the second chapter we describe the research approach and methodology of systematic mapping study that we performed in our research. In the third section we present the results of the study along with the systematic map of found scientific evidence. In the last chapter we bring the most important conclusions and wrap the results presented in this paper.

2 Research Approach

2.1 Systematic Mapping Study

A scientific method of analysing, identifying and structuring all available research evidence and results on a topic of research interest or on a whole research area is called a systematic mapping study (SMS) [3, 37]. As well as a systematic literature review (SLR) [48], SMS also requires the activities of research planning and questions definition, objective setting, rigour search strategies definition etc., but SMS in general has a goal of providing a more coarse-grained overview of the topic, and thus requires less effort to be performed [37]. Petersen et al. [36] state that SMS provides a valuable baseline for subsequent research of a topic. Additionally, mentioned authors state that SMS could save time in subsequent studies, if performed well it presents a solid overview of the researched area, gives very good visualization of research trends, gaps and related work trends etc.

In the context of user experience, a lot of reviews and several SMS's have been performed mostly with the focus on UX evaluation methods. Systematic mapping study performed by Rivero and Conte [39] aimed to identify *technologies (methods/techniques/tools/others) that have been proposed for the evaluation of user experience in the development of applications and how have these methods been used* during period of 2010–2015. Their study revealed the need for new UX evaluation methods, e.g. the one that takes into account both qualitative and quantitative data, the one that suggest improvements of the software once a problem is found etc. Nakamura et al. performed SMS to found out *which usability and UX evaluation techniques were applied on Learning Management Systems and how have they been used?* [25]. Their study showed that inquiry type of evaluation techniques (questionnaires, focus groups and interviews) were the most common ones, while indicating several gaps, e.g. the need for techniques that cover both usability and UX aspects, the need for techniques that suggest improvements of the LMS etc. Subsequently, they have proposed new technique to evaluate UX in e-learning by applying Design Science Research methodology [24].

Typically, SMS is performed through three main phases: planning, conducting and reporting on the mapping.

2.2 Planning the Study

Planning of the study puts the basis for the rest of the scientific activities. During this phase, the objectives and the research questions are defined. Our main research question was: "How is design science (DS) being used in creating and evaluating UX artefacts?". Although the research questions in a systematic mapping could be less specific than in a systematic literature review [36], the search strategy and inclusion and exclusion criteria should be well defined. *Choosing a search strategy* is required in order to determine the way to find information and studies of an area. In our case, a search string was composed of three groups joined by Boolean AND: keywords related to design science, keywords related to UX and usability as UX subset, and keywords related to evaluation and design including alternative spellings and synonyms of those terms. Manual search was planned to be performed on major databases by executing the previously defined and tested search string. *Inclusion and exclusion criteria* must be defined in order to simplify the process of filtering the search results. Final step in this phase was to define extracting data strategy and to establish a classification scheme. *Extracting data strategy* defines what data is needed in a study to enable researchers to classify it. Depending on the field being observed, one can use an existing *classification* found in field literature or apply a new one derived from the search. We planned to use the existing well-known classification scheme of UX evaluation techniques enhanced by our own keyword extraction. The results of each of these steps are as presented in the Table 1.

Table 1. Blueprint for the systematic mapping study

Goal	Identify existing research evidence on the use of Design Science to create and evaluate UX artifacts
Research question	How is design science (DS) being used in creating and evaluating UX artifacts?
Search string	("design science" OR "DSRM") AND ("usability" OR "UX" OR "user experience") AND ("evaluation" OR "assessment" OR "inspection" OR "test*" OR "technique" OR "method*" OR "design")
Inclusion criteria	– Paper or book chapter published in a journal or a conference – Topic of the paper is related to the use of design science in design or evaluation of UX artifacts
Exclusion criteria	– Content in a form of a book, workshop or Master/PhD thesis – Papers describing only the use of design science without UX artifacts present in the paper topic – Papers describing only design or evaluation of UX artifacts without the use of design science research approach – Papers without clear distinction of design science process in design or evaluation of UX artifacts – Papers not written in English – Full papers not available for download after contacting the authors

Classification scheme	– Use existing classification scheme to map the available evidence in one of the following groups:
	• inquiry methods,
	  o interviews including feedbacks;
	  o observations – field or lab; and
	  o questionnaires – SUS, USE, surveys, TAM, UTAUT...,
	• inspection methods (HE, design reviews, analyses...) and
	• usability testing (think aloud, eyetracking, walkthrough...)
	– Extract and map the most important keywords found in the included studies

2.3   Conducting Systematic Mapping Study

By following the previously defined plan, we implemented mentioned strategies and criteria to find, select, classify and map the findings. Petersen et al. [36] note that this process can be iterative and require revisions, and also encourage researchers to document every step in the process since it could be very helpful in subsequent iterations. Thus, as presented in Fig. 2, our process contained several iterations that are presented below.

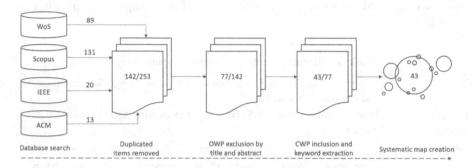

Fig. 2. Systematic mapping process

A search criterion identified a total of 253 sources from the above-mentioned databases. The metadata of obtained papers was exported from the original databases and imported to reference management software which was used by the researchers to maintain the papers during the whole systematic mapping process.

The first iteration was to apply inclusion and exclusion criteria just by reading a title and the abstract of the studies. The reference management tool helped researchers to identify duplicated entries and those entries that were not referring to research results (e.g. the names of events) which were excluded in this phase leaving 142 papers to be included in the analysis. In this process we applied and open-world-principle (OWP), meaning that all papers were included and only those sources that were undoubtedly not passing inclusion criteria where eliminated. This iteration ended up with a total of 77 candidate papers.

The most important phase of the systematic mapping research was to apply inclusion criteria on 77 candidate papers and to identify those that are related to our research questions. In this process we used closed-world-principle approach, meaning that none of the papers were included by default, but only after they passed inclusion and exclusion criteria, and at this point, the content of the paper was taken into consideration as well. Additionally, during this process, keywords relevant to the research question were identified and extracted.

Finally, a total of 43 papers was included and used for systematization and map creation in the last phase of the process.

2.4   Reporting

Mapping report summarizes what was done in previous steps by visualizing the mapping results and using all information collected in the mapping conduction to highlight the findings. The 43 papers are classified into 5 categories related to method and techniques of evaluation of UX artefacts during the design science process. The classification is presented in results section.

3   Results of the Study

A total of 43 papers passed our inclusion and exclusion criteria. These papers are identified as related to our research question and are describing the use of design science research to develop and evaluate UX related artefacts. Due to inconsistent structure of the papers, along with the use of different naming approaches, it turn out that classification and keyword extraction were not a trivial tasks. The analysis of keywords and focused topics in the papers also proved that the research covered rather different and disjunct topics. The studies were classified into five categories related to UX evaluation techniques, and 32 different keywords related to the topic were identified (see Fig. 3).

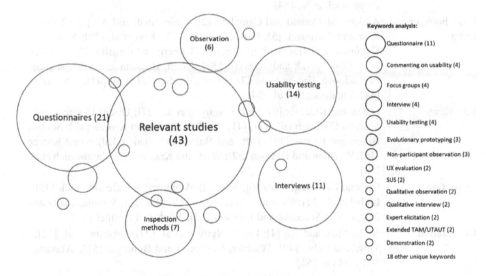

Fig. 3. Studies classification map

Most of the papers (21) reported the use of different types of questionnaires to evaluate created artefacts. These approaches included the use of SUS, USE, TAM, UTAUT and different surveys. The keyword analysis showed that the keyword questionnaire was not in the focus of all of these papers as they used different specific titles as presented above.

The second most covered topic (14 papers) was related to performance of usability/user testing including other related techniques to evaluate the artefacts. This group included the techniques such as thinking aloud, eyetracking and walkthrough.

The use of interviews and related techniques was reported in 11 studies. This group also included the papers mentioning the use of feedbacks, focus groups feedback, commenting, description etc. Finally, different inspection methods were reported in 7 studies: heuristic evaluation, design review and checklist analysis. Last, but not least, field or laboratory observation were reported in the 6 studies.

Some studies reported the use of more than one technique. The detailed list of analysed papers and their relations to the identified topics are presented in the Table 2.

Table 2. Systematization of available research

Questionnaires	Adikari, McDonald and Lynch [1]; Adikari, McDonald and Campbell [2]; Chu, Matthews and Love [7]; Djamasbi et al. [10]; Fink and Nyaga [11]; Haugstvedt and Krogstie [15]; Liebel et al. [21]; Nguyen et al. [26]; Novak and Schwabe [30]; O'Flaherty et al. [31]; Oliveira et al. [32]; Rother, Karl and Nestler [40]; Silva, Berkenbrock and Berkenbrock [43]; Silva et al. [44]; Staden, Biljon and Kroeze [45]; Staden, Biljon and Kroeze [47]; Tufte and Babic [49]; Usener, Majchrzak and Kuchen [50]; Wächter, Hoffmann and Bullinger [51]; Wich and Kramer [53]; Zarabzadeh et al. [54]
Usability/user testing	Adikari, McDonald and Campbell [2]; Ataie, Shah and Ali [4]; Blake, Kerr and Gammack [5]; Firouzian et al. [12]; Kao et al. [20]; Miah, Gammack and Hasan [22]; Mozelius, Torberg and Castillo [23]; Nguyen et al. [26]; Novak and Schwabe [30]; Olsen, Hedman and Vatrapu [33]; Plachkinova, Faddoul and Chatterjee [38]; Schnall et al. [41]; Silva et al. [44]; Zarabzadeh et al. [54]
Interviews	Dalen and Kraemer [9]; Lemai Nguyen et al. [27]; Olsen, Hedman and Vatrapu [33]; Schnall et al. [41]; Staden, Biljon and Kroeze [47]; Staden, Biljon and Kroeze [45]; Tufte and Babic [49]; Staden, Biljon and Kroeze [46]; Weeding and Dawson [52]; Wich and Kramer [53]; Zarabzadeh et al. [54]
Inspection	Choma, Zaina and Silva [6]; Silva, Berkenbrock and Berkenbrock [43]; Liebel et al. [21]; Mozelius, Torberg and Castillo [23]; Scholtz, Calitz and Haupt [42]; Weeding and Dawson [52]; Wich and Kramer [53]
Observation	Ataie, Shah and Ali [4]; Lemai Nguyen et al. [27]; Oliveira et al. [32]; Tufte and Babic [49]; Wächter, Hoffmann and Bullinger [51]; Weeding and Dawson [52]

The keyword analysis performed during the last phase of systematic mapping process resulted in more than 40 different keywords. The list of most common used keywords to explain the UX evaluation techniques and approaches is presented in Fig. 3. Majority of the keyword were used very rarely while just a few keywords were mentioned more than three times: *usability testing*, *interview*, *focus group*, *usability commenting* and *questionnaire*.

4 Conclusions

In this paper we reported the results of the systematic mapping study performed on research evidence related to the use of design science research methodology in creation and evaluation of artifacts related to user experience design. The study analyses more than 250 papers and upon applying inclusion and exclusion criteria 43 papers were included in the results. Those papers were classified into five main classes related to the use of UX evaluation techniques and it turned out that most of the researchers (21 papers) are using different types of questionnaires to evaluate created artefacts. These approaches included the use of SUS, USE, TAM, UTAUT and different surveys. The second most covered topic (14 papers) was related to performance of usability/user testing including other related techniques to evaluate the artefacts. This group included the techniques such as thinking aloud, eyetracking and walkthrough. Other UX techniques were also included but in much lower intensity.

Apart from performing predefined classification, we also performed a keyword analysis and found out that researchers are using more than 30 different keywords which are related to UX design and evaluation techniques.

This research represents a solid ground for additional exploration of the field in terms of fine-grained analysis of the performed processes of DS in general and of the UX evaluation activities.

References

1. Adikari, S., et al.: Design science-oriented usability modelling for software requirements (2007)
2. Adikari, S., McDonald, C., Campbell, J.: Little design up-front: a design science approach to integrating usability into agile requirements engineering. In: Jacko, J.A. (ed.) HCI 2009. LNCS, vol. 5610, pp. 549–558. Springer, Heidelberg (2009). https://doi.org/10.1007/978-3-642-02574-7_62
3. Antonio, E.A., et al.: A systematic mapping of architectures for embedded software. In: 2012 Second Brazilian Conference on Critical Embedded Systems, Sao Paulo, Campinas, Brazil, pp. 18–23. IEEE (2012). https://doi.org/10.1109/CBSEC.2012.22
4. Ataie, F., et al.: Integration social media technology and ethical collaborative learning. Int. J. Eng. Technol. 7(2), 12–15 (2018). https://doi.org/10.14419/ijet.v7i2.34.13898
5. Blake, J., et al.: Development of a DSS and online tools to support sleep disorder consultations using design science. Australas. J. Inf. Syst. 20, 1–12 (2016). https://journal.acs.org.au/index.php/ajis/rt/captureCite/1303/736
6. Choma, J., et al.: Towards an approach matching CMD and DSR to improve the academia-industry software development partnership: a case of agile and UX integration. In: 2015 29th Brazilian Symposium on Software Engineering, pp. 51–60 (2015). https://doi.org/10.1109/SBES.2015.18
7. Chu, M., et al.: Integrating mobile building information modelling and augmented reality systems: an experimental study. Autom. Constr. 85, 305–316 (2018). https://doi.org/10.1016/j.autcon.2017.10.032
8. Conradi, R.: Software engineering mini glossary. http://www.idi.ntnu.no/grupper/su/publ/ese/se-defs.html

9. Dalen, A., Kraemer, J.: Towards a user-centered feedback design for smart meter interfaces to support efficient energy-use choices: a design science approach. Bus. Inf. Syst. Eng. **59**(5), 361–373 (2017). https://doi.org/10.1007/s12599-017-0489-x
10. Djamasbi, S., et al.: Designing and testing user-centric systems with both user experience and design science research principles. Presented at the AMCIS 2016: Surfing the IT Innovation Wave - 22nd Americas Conference on Information Systems (2016)
11. Fink, D., Nyaga, C.: Evaluating web site quality: the value of a multi paradigm approach. Benchmarking Int. J. **16**(2), 259–273 (2009). https://doi.org/10.1108/14635770910948259
12. Firouzian, A., et al.: Conceptual design and implementation of indicator-based smart glasses: a navigational device for remote assistance of senior citizens suffering from memory loss. In: 2015 9th International Symposium on Medical Information and Communication Technology (ISMICT), pp. 153–156 (2015). https://doi.org/10.1109/ISMICT.2015.7107518
13. Hassenzahl, M., et al.: User experience – towards a unified view. In: User Experience – Towards a Unified View: Second International COST294-MAUSE Open Workshop – NordICHI 2006, pp. 1–3 (2006)
14. Hassenzahl, M., Tractinsky, N.: User experience - a research agenda. Behav. Inf. Technol. **25**(2), 91–97 (2006). https://doi.org/10.1080/01449290500330331
15. Haugstvedt, A., Krogstie, J.: Mobile augmented reality for cultural heritage: a technology acceptance study. In: 2012 IEEE International Symposium on Mixed and Augmented Reality (ISMAR), pp. 247–255 (2012). https://doi.org/10.1109/ISMAR.2012.6402563
16. Hellweger, S., Wang, X.: What is user experience really: towards a UX conceptual framework (2015). http://figshare.com/articles/What_is_User_Experience_Really_towards_a_UX_Conceptual_Framework/1319576. https://doi.org/10.6084/m9.figshare.1319576
17. Hevner, A.R., et al.: Design science in information systems research. MIS Q. **28**(1), 75–105 (2004)
18. Hilpinen, R.: Artifact. http://plato.stanford.edu/entries/artifact/
19. International Standardization Organization (ISO): ISO DIS 9241-210:2010. Ergonomics of human system interaction - Part 210: Human-centred design for interactive systems (2010). http://www.iso.org/cms/render/live/en/sites/isoorg/contents/data/standard/05/20/52075.html
20. Kao, H.-Y., et al.: Integrating a mobile health applications for self-management to enhance Telecare system. Telemat. Inform. **35**(4), 815–825 (2018). https://doi.org/10.1016/j.tele.2017.12.011
21. Liebel, G., et al.: Addressing model complexity in automotive system development: selection of system model elements for allocation of requirements. In: 2016 4th International Conference on Model-Driven Engineering and Software Development (MODELSWARD), pp. 168–175 (2016)
22. Miah, S.J., et al.: Extending the framework for mobile health information systems research: a content analysis. Inf. Syst. **69**, 1–24 (2017). https://doi.org/10.1016/j.is.2017.04.001
23. Mozelius, P., et al.: An educational game for mobile learning - some essential design factors. In: Watson, C. (ed.) Proceedings of the 10th International Conference on E-Learning (ICEL 2015), pp. 242–249 (2015)
24. Nakamura, W., et al.: Applying design science research to develop a technique to evaluate the usability and user eXperience of learning management systems. Presented at the XXIX Simpósio Brasileiro de Informática na Educação (Brazilian Symposium on Computers in Education), Fortaleza, Ceará, Brasil, 28 October 2018. https://doi.org/10.5753/cbie.sbie.2018.953
25. Nakamura, W.T., et al.: Usability and user experience evaluation of learning management systems: a systematic mapping study. In: Proceedings of the 19th International Conference on Enterprise Information Systems (ICEIS), pp. 97–108 (2017)

26. Nguyen, L., et al.: Developing an information system for nursing in acute care contexts. Presented at the Pacific Asia Conference on Information Systems, PACIS 2015 - Proceedings (2015)
27. Nguyen, L., et al.: Exploring nurses' reactions to electronic nursing documentation at the point of care. Inf. Technol. People **30**(4), 809–831 (2017). https://doi.org/10.1108/ITP-10-2015-0269
28. NNgroup: Don Norman: The term "UX,". https://www.youtube.com/watch?v=9BdtGj-oIN4E&feature=youtu.be
29. Norman, D., Nielsen, J.: The Definition of User Experience (UX). https://www.nngroup.com/articles/definition-user-experience/
30. Novak, J., Schwabe, G.: Designing for reintermediation in the brick-and-mortar world: towards the travel agency of the future. Electron. Mark. **19**(1), 15–29 (2009). https://doi.org/10.1007/s12525-009-0003-5
31. O'Flaherty, B., et al.: Capturing multi-stakeholder needs in customer-centric cloud service design. Presented at the International Conference on Information Systems (ICIS 2013): Reshaping Society Through Information Systems Design (2013)
32. de Oliveira, F.K., et al.: RECREIO: floss as SAAS for sharing of educational resources. In: 2017 12th Iberian Conference on Information Systems and Technologies (CISTI), pp. 1–6 (2017). https://doi.org/10.23919/CISTI.2017.7975929
33. Olsen, M., et al.: Designing digital payment artifacts. In: Proceedings of the 14th Annual International Conference on Electronic Commerce, pp. 161–168. ACM, New York (2012). https://doi.org/10.1145/2346536.2346568
34. Parker, P.M.: Definition of artifact. http://www.websters-online-dictionary.org/definitions/artifact
35. Peffers, K., et al.: A design science research methodology for information systems research. J. Manag. Inf. Syst. **24**(3), 45–77 (2007)
36. Petersen, K., et al.: Guidelines for conducting systematic mapping studies in software engineering: an update. Inf. Softw. Technol. **64**, 1–18 (2015). https://doi.org/10.1016/j.infsof.2015.03.007
37. Petersen, K., et al.: Systematic mapping studies in software engineering. In: Proceedings of the 12th International Conference on Evaluation and Assessment in Software Engineering, pp. 68–77. BCS Learning & Development Ltd., Swindon (2008)
38. Plachkinova, M., Faddoul, G., Chatterjee, S.: Designing a mobile application for complementary and alternative medicine: a usability approach. In: Stephanidis, C. (ed.) HCI 2015. CCIS, vol. 529, pp. 345–349. Springer, Cham (2015). https://doi.org/10.1007/978-3-319-21383-5_58
39. Rivero, L., Conte, T.: A systematic mapping study on research contributions on UX evaluation technologies. In: Proceedings of the XVI Brazilian Symposium on Human Factors in Computing Systems, pp. 5:1–5:10. ACM, New York (2017). https://doi.org/10.1145/3160504.3160512
40. Rother, K., et al.: Towards virtual reality crisis simulation as a tool for usability testing of crisis related interactive systems. In: Virtual and Augmented Reality: Concepts, Methodologies, Tools, and Applications, pp. 164–179 (2018). https://doi.org/10.4018/978-1-5225-5469-1.ch008
41. Schnall, R., et al.: A user-centered model for designing consumer mobile health (mHealth) applications (apps). J. Biomed. Inform. **60**, 243–251 (2016). https://doi.org/10.1016/j.jbi.2016.02.002
42. Scholtz, B., et al.: A business intelligence framework for sustainability information management in higher education. Int. J. Sustain. High. Educ. **19**(2), 266–290 (2018). https://doi.org/10.1108/IJSHE-06-2016-0118

43. da Silva, D.M.A., Berkenbrock, G.R., Berkenbrock, C.D.M.: An approach using the design science research for the development of a collaborative assistive system. In: Gutwin, C., Ochoa, S.F., Vassileva, J., Inoue, T. (eds.) CRIWG 2017. LNCS, vol. 10391, pp. 180–195. Springer, Cham (2017). https://doi.org/10.1007/978-3-319-63874-4_14
44. Silva, L.D., et al.: Design science research based blended approach for usability driven requirements gathering and application development. In: 2014 IEEE 2nd International Workshop on Usability and Accessibility Focused Requirements Engineering (UsARE), pp. 17–24 (2014). https://doi.org/10.1109/UsARE.2014.6890996
45. Staden, C.J., et al.: eModeration: towards a user experience evaluation framework. In: Proceedings of the 2015 Annual Research Conference on South African Institute of Computer Scientists and Information Technologists, pp. 39:1–39:11. ACM, New York (2015). https://doi.org/10.1145/2815782.2815821
46. van Staden, C.J., et al.: Adopting eModeration: understanding the user experience in this organizational change. In: Devos, J., DeHaes, S. (eds.) Proceedings of the 8th European Conference on Is Management and Evaluation (ECIME 2014), pp. 356–364 (2014)
47. van Staden, C.J., et al.: Using a user experience evaluation framework for eModeration. In: 2017 Conference on Information Communication Technology and Society (ICTAS), pp. 1–6 (2017). https://doi.org/10.1109/ICTAS.2017.7920523
48. Stapic, Z., et al.: Scrutinizing systematic literature review process in software engineering. TEM J.-Technol. Educ. Manag. Inform. 5(1), 104–116 (2016). https://doi.org/10.18421/TEM51-16
49. Tufte, T., Babic, A.: A healthy lifestyle intervention application. In: Gundlapalli, A.V., et al. (eds.) Medinfo 2017: Precision Healthcare Through Informatics, pp. 240–243 (2017)
50. Usener, C.A., et al.: E-assessment and software testing. Interact. Technol. Smart Educ. 9(1), 46– + (2012). https://doi.org/10.1108/17415651211228095
51. Wächter, M., Hoffmann, H., Bullinger, A.C.: Towards an engineering process to design usable tangible human-machine interfaces. In: Bagnara, S., Tartaglia, R., Albolino, S., Alexander, T., Fujita, Y. (eds.) IEA 2018. AISC, vol. 825, pp. 136–147. Springer, Cham (2019). https://doi.org/10.1007/978-3-319-96068-5_15
52. Weeding, S., Dawson, L.: Laptops on trolleys: lessons from a mobile-wireless hospital ward. J. Med. Syst. 36(6), 3933–3943 (2012). https://doi.org/10.1007/s10916-012-9865-8
53. Wich, M., Kramer, T.: Enhanced human-computer interaction for business applications on mobile devices: a design-oriented development of a usability evaluation questionnaire. In: 2015 48th Hawaii International Conference on System Sciences, pp. 472–481 (2015). https://doi.org/10.1109/HICSS.2015.63
54. Zarabzadeh, A., et al.: Utility of electronic international register of clinical prediction rules relevant to primary care. In: 2016 IEEE 29th International Symposium on Computer-Based Medical Systems (CBMS), pp. 146–151 (2016). https://doi.org/10.1109/CBMS.2016.26
55. Artifact. https://www.interaction-design.org/literature/book/the-glossary-of-human-computer-interaction/artifact
56. Usability glossary | Usability Body of Knowledge. http://www.usabilitybok.org/glossary

Development of a Generator System of Parameterized Questionnaires to Evaluate the Usability of Web Pages

William J. Yamada[1]([⊠]), Marcelo Morandini[1], Thiago A. Coleti[2][iD],
and Cinthyan Renata S. C. Barbosa[3][iD]

[1] Princeton University, Princeton, NJ 08544, USA
[2] Informatics Department, State University from North of Parana State,
Bandeirantes, Parana, Brazil
[3] Computer Department, State University of Londrina, Londrina, Parana, Brazil

Abstract. The effectiveness of using websites have a strong dependence on their ergonomic qualities, which affect directly the business. This is more significant when related to the e-commerce, especially considering the little known companies. To verify ergonomic features in a website, the evaluator may conduct inspections based on questionnaires that are answered by him/her or by final users to provide information about the interface.

In this paper, our goal was the development of an application that automatically generates ergonomic questionnaires to evaluate the usability of web sites. The main idea is to select specific questionnaires and specific questions that must be parameterized according to the users choice. Among these parameters, are the interaction elements present in the pages that compose the website, such as scroll bars, buttons, hyperlinks, windows, text fields and others.

The analysis of the questionnaire responses, provides data to build better usability interfaces, resulting in less time and effort to achieve their goals, and thus, delivering positive results. These questionnaires and their responses can be stored in a database for future reference and may support new usability assessments.

The tool was used by 22 evaluators. These users are aged between 19 and 30 years, and have some connection with the University of Sao Paulo. Correlations were also made between some questions to see if there was any relationship between them.

Keywords: Usability · Evaluation · Survey

1 Introduction

Usability is defined as the measure that can be used to achieve specific objectives with effectiveness, efficiency and satisfaction in a given context of use (ISO) and is an important factor in human-computer interaction [4]. With the development

© Springer Nature Switzerland AG 2019
C. Stephanidis (Ed.): HCII 2019, LNCS 11786, pp. 85–100, 2019.
https://doi.org/10.1007/978-3-030-30033-3_8

of the internet and technology, the society has more access to information and as a result, more websites are created and used.

On the web, usability is fundamental. If a site is difficult to use, the users may give up using it, after all, there are several website options that can be used for the same purpose. If the information on a website is difficult to find, or does not answer the key questions of users, or if they get lost on a website, they will give up accessing it.

There is no tutorial for a website. If a user does not feel comfortable, his first line of defense is to leave, and will not access it again, negatively recommending the site to friends and acquaintances [2].

In the current web scenario, more and more, we find applications that seek to exploit to the maximum the interactivity with their users. However, this interaction does not always occur natural or intuitively, what can generate dissatisfaction, either by not finding the desired information, by the difficulty of navigation or by other usability problems. These problems can cause the user to avoid or even quitting the use of the website [2].

A common way to evaluate the usability of a web interface is through the use of usability questionnaires [19], since can be used to collect information at the initial stage of the project and also, to evaluate an existing site. One advantage of using questionnaires is due to their low cost and time saving. However, these questionnaires can be very comprehensive, containing several questions that do not apply to the page or interface in which it is being evaluated.

In this scenario, aiming to optimize these evaluations, we decided to develop a tool that will receive as input, one or more elements of interaction and generate a specific ergonomic questionnaire, which will be based on some questions related to the chosen elements.

Selecting only the most relevant questions for the required interaction elements and based on the application domain provided by the user, we could generate more specific questionnaires that optimize the usability evaluation of the web pages.

2   Related Work

Questionnaires are easy to use and allow the data collection even by professional or traditional users, and could be applied to identify subject aspects of user, interfaces and systems such as usability, acceptance and users engagement. For supporting ergonomic inspections, questionnaires are used as checklists and checkpoints, that guide the evaluator in how he/she must analyze and which are the interface's parameters that must be considered.

However, some kind of questionnaires used for ergonomic inspection have great amount of questions that can be not used for that evaluation context. It happens because the questionnaires are based on guidelines that provide prepared questions, answers and parameters to be followed in the inspection. As an example, the website ErgoList (www.labiutil.inf.ufsc.br/ergolist/) is a widely used ergonomic inspection survey, but it presents about 180 questions based on eighteen ergonomic criteria with the followed answers options: Yes, No, Not Applied and Answer Later.

Due to the amount of questions, conducting an inspection can be an unproductive activity since evaluators must read, analyzed and maybe answer questions not applied for the inspection because the questionnaire is related to a guideline. Also, using practices proposed by several different guidelines can provide more inputs to support inspection and analysis of interface's quality. In this sense, the evaluator should complete two or more questionnaires making the inspection complex even as difficult to analyze data.

Besides ErgoList, other questionnaires can be found such as ISONORM 9241/10 and WCAG 2.0 all of them used to evaluated user interface ergonomic.

The ISONORM 9241/10 is based on norm 9241 and aims to evaluate the compliance of the software products with the recommendations contained in the part of the standard. The questionnaire is applied in two extremely opposing phases of the software project: the first is more traditional, for the evaluation of products already completed and in the commercialization phase, and the second, which is much rarer when it comes to the application of satisfaction assessment questionnaires, for the measurement between the team of designers and the future users of a new module of a software product [23].

The Web Content Accessibility Guidelines (WCAG) are part of a series of web accessibility guidelines published by the Web Accessibility Initiative (WAI) of the World Wide Web Consortium (W3C), the main international standards organization for the Internet. WCAG 2.0 was published as a W3C Recommendation on 11 December 2008 [11,12]. It consists of twelve guidelines (untestable) organized under four principles (websites must be perceivable, operable, understandable, and robust). Each guideline has testable success criteria (61 in all) [13]. The W3C's Techniques for WCAG 2.0 [14] is a list of techniques that help authors meet the guidelines and success criteria. The techniques are periodically updated whereas the principles, guidelines and success criteria are stable and do not change [15].

2.1 Related Questions

As mentioned earlier, questions regarding the feedback and readability questionnaires were analyzed. All questions of each questionnaire can be found in Annex A, which were based on the ErgoList website questionnaires.

3 Materials and Methods

A tool to support the development of personalized questionnaires that could be automatically deployed for user, can improve the process of create ergonomic inspections to ensure a more targeted evaluation according to interface features. So our goal was to develop an application that automatically generates ergonomic questionnaires to evaluate the usability of web sites.

The idea is to select specific questionnaires that generate specific and predetermined questions based on parameters, that must be parameterized according to the user's choice. This parameters are the entry of the respective application domain, for example, if the application domain is social media, then the evaluator could choose as input parameters: user experience, readability, promptness and conciseness, and the corresponding questionnaires to the input parameters will be generated. In this way, it is possible to generate parameterized and customized questionnaires according to the application domain, showing just relevant questions that can be totally useful for the evaluation context.

It is expected that future website developers can use this tool to assist in the implementation of practical environments to be used and that are efficient enough to use, always aiming at the ergonomics and usability of the website.

3.1 Evaluation of the Usability of the Tidia-Ae Portal

The usability assessment can be understood as a set of methods and techniques that must be applied in order to inspect the design quality of an interface. When performing an activity of evaluating the usability of a site, problems can be verified and with this, strategies can be developed so that new projects do not present these problems observed [6].

Tidia-Ae. Ae is an e-learning environment that allows you to manage courses, projects, and collaborative and group learning activities. The environment offers a set of resources or tools to support communication, content distribution, knowledge building, and participant management.

The Ae environment can be used both as a support for face-to-face courses and for courses or projects entirely online. For each virtual space created, called a worksite or site, it is possible to:

- Provide and solve exercises and problems in a collaborative or individual way;
- Set up, make available and take courses of any level of education: primary, secondary, secondary, higher, specialization, training, plan, develop and report on group projects;
- Conduct online meetings and store minutes and documents;
- Perform activities of collaboration and interaction of the participants;
- Support the teaching-learning process in person;
- Carry out teaching and learning activities completely online;

The Ae environment is the result of the efforts of the Tidia-Ae project funded by FAPESP (Foundation for Research Support of the State of Sao Paulo) and associated with the IMS - Global Learning Consortium and the Sakai Foundation, both international institutions that discuss in a collaborative way the use of technology and its results in educational activities [8].

3.2 Development of the Tool

To build the application, was used Java 1.8.0_181 based on Oracle to create the questionnaire interface and MySQL server 14.14 Distribution 5.7.23, as the database manager system, to store the information in the database.

First the tool was developed and hosted on a local computer for some functionality tests and then, was created an online version of it, using google forms, following the same logic of the application (selecting only relevant questionnaires that generates specific and predetermined questions for the user according to the input parameters) with the benefit of sending a link, so that people can access and respond remotely wherever they are, like in a web application. The input parameters are the type of questionnaire available, according to the application domain, so for example, if the input parameter is user experience, the tool will generate the predetermined questions related to the user experience questionnaire.

To each questionnaire (total of 7), which can be: promptness, feedback, readability, user experience, conciseness, error message or location grouping (one questionnaire for each application domain), that necessarily have one to two interaction elements associated with each question. And as a basis for each question, the tool have some types of possible answers, such as: text field, 0 to 10, likert (terrible, bad, reasonable, good and great), not apply and, yes or no. https://www.overleaf.com/project/5bb51feb56227625b1ebb18b It is an initial version of the prototype, that still needs improvements, so that it can be better used by professionals and researchers in the field.

3.3 Data Collection Procedure and Validation

For tool validation, was counted on the participation of 22 volunteers from 19 to 30 years, which have some connection with the University of Sao Paulo and with this, there was no need to explain the site to be evaluated (Tidia-Ae), since it belongs to the university and all students have access to the platform.

The contact with the volunteers and the research guidelines were given in person and via e-mail. The volunteers had to answer all the questionnaires, simulating an application domain that involved all available parameters, with the purpose of qualify the various elements of interaction and usability of the site to be evalued (Tidia-Ae) and validating the tool, whose respective questions, are listed in Annex A. The questionnaires were answered independently (each volunteer on their respective computers and without a defined location), with an average duration of 15 to 20 min.

3.4 Transformation of Variables

In our research, was analyzed the questions belonging to the feedback and readability questionnaires.

For the calculation of the correlations and a better analysis, the variables were standardized and categorized according to the following descriptions:

1. Variables that presented their items arranged in likert scale (terrible, bad, not apply, reasonable, good and great), were transformed as follows in Table 1.

Table 1. Likert factors

Answer	Value
Good/Great	2
Reasonable	1
Not Apply	0
Bad	−1
Terrible	−2

2. Variables with items in 3-point scale such as 'yes', 'no' and 'not apply' were transformed as follows in Table 2.

Table 2. 3-point scale factors

Answer	Value
Yes	1
No	−1
Not Apply	0

We did not analyze text type responses because they were not easily standardized, as there is a wide possibility of possible answers (each user can give different answers).

3.5   Data Analysis

To analysis the data, were calculated correlation between the obtained results, using Spearman's Correlation [3]. The correlation result R is computed from the formula 1, that measures the strength and direction of the relationship between two variables. In terms of the strength of relationship, the value of the correlation coefficient varies between +1 and −1, where the value $R = 1$ means a perfect positive correlation and the value $R = -1$ means a perfect negative correlation.

For a sample of 'n', the 'n' raw score 'Xa', 'Ya' - a raw score is an original datum that has not been transformed - are converted to ranks 'XRa' and 'YRa'. A ranking is a relationship between a set of items such that, for any two items, the first is either ranked 'higher than', ranked 'lower than' or ranked 'equal to' the second [9]. By reducing detailed measures to a sequence of ordinal numbers, rankings make it possible to evaluate complex information according to certain criteria [5].

$$R = \rho_{X Ra, Y Ra} = \frac{Covariance(X Ra, Y Ra)}{\sigma_{X Ra} * \sigma_{Y Ra}} \tag{1}$$

where:

- ρ denote the usual Pearson correlation coefficient [7] but applied to rank variables
- $X Ra$ denote the ranks of X values
- $Y Ra$ denote the ranks of Y values
- σ denote the standard deviation

The calculated correlation is important to understand which usability factors were connected and if together, they have any influence on the usability of the website, whether positive or negative, thus providing important points to be considered by the website developer.

4   Results

From the answers obtained from the feedback and readability questionnaires that were applied to the volunteers, were made correlations between some questions, in order to identify important association.

First, from the answers obtained, a brief discussion will be presented, and then, all the results of Spearman's correlation will be presented in Table 3, for further analysis.

4.1   Feedback Questionnaire

In this questionnaire, was tested the correlations between question 1 and all other questions, except questions 6 and 12, because the answers were in text form, then not standardized. For each correlation, will be presented the respective results.

Question 1 × Question 2. The percentage of response obtained is shown in Fig. 1.

The R value in correlation between question 1 and question 2 is 0.167. By normal standards, the association between the two variables would not be considered statistically significant.

Was not found a correlation, because the question 2 shows that the system provide a feedback to the user, due to some long processing, but the result of question 1 is that the system doesn't provide feedback for all users actions. Then the result obtained is as expected.

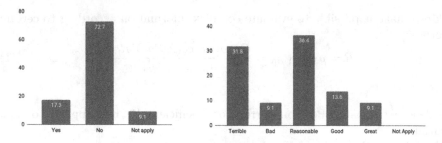

Fig. 1. Percentages - Question 1 and 2 respectively

Question 1 × Question 3. The percentage of response obtained is shown in Fig. 2.

The value of R in correlation between question 1 and question 3 is 0.30941. By normal standards, the association between the two variables would not be considered statistically significant.

Was not found a correlation between question 1 and question 3. Although 31.8% of the answers obtained in question 3 were negative, the majority was positive (in the sense that it provides feedback), which contradicts the answer obtained in question 1.

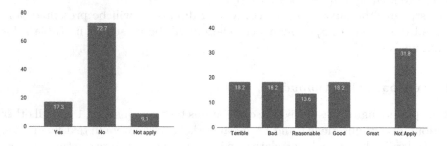

Fig. 2. Percentages - Question 1 and 3 respectively

Question 1 × Question 4. The percentage of response obtained is shown in Fig. 3.

The value of R is 0.12314. By normal standards, the association between the two variables would not be considered statistically significant.

Was not found a correlation between question 1 and question 4. Although 31.8% of the answers obtained in question 3 were negative, the majority was positive (the system highlight the items selected - provide a feedback), which contradicts the answer obtained in question 1, that the system doesn't provide feedback for all users actions.

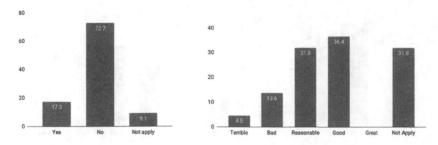

Fig. 3. Percentages - Question 1 and 4 respectively

Question 1 × Question 5. The percentage of response obtained is shown in Fig. 4.

The value of R in correlation between question 1 and question 5 is 0.36478. By normal standards, the association between the two variables would not be considered statistically significant.

Was not found a correlation, because the question 5 shows that the system provide dynamic and contextual feedback on direct manipulation (provide a feedback), but the result of question 1 is that the system doesn't provide feedback for all users actions.

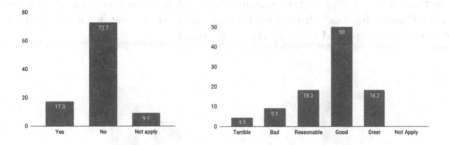

Fig. 4. Percentages - Question 1 and 5 respectively

Question 1 × Question 7. The percentage of response obtained is shown in Fig. 5.

The value of R in correlation between question 1 and question 7 is 0.25645. By normal standards, the association between the two variables would not be considered statistically significant.

Was not found a correlation, because the question 7 shows that the system display a message stating the success or failure of time-consuming processing (provide a feedback), but the result of question 1 is that the system doesn't provide feedback for all users actions.

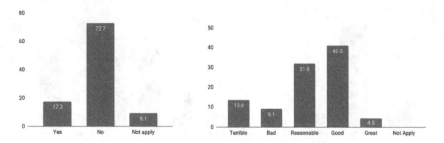

Fig. 5. Percentages - Question 1 and 7 respectively

Question 1 × Question 8. The percentage of response obtained is shown in Fig. 6.

The value of R in correlation between question 1 and question 8 is 0.27015. By normal standards, the association between the two variables would not be considered statistically significant.

This means that there is no important relationship between the system providing feedback with the system provide immediate and continuous feedback from direct manipulations. What is strange, since most of the answers in question 1 (72,7%), was that the system does not provide feedback for all the user's actions and that it corresponds with the answer obtained in question 8, in which more than half (51.8%) of the responses were that do not provide immediate and continuous feedback from direct manipulations. Therefore, some positive correlation was expected between these questions.

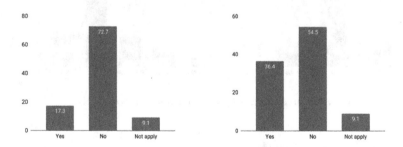

Fig. 6. Percentages - Question 1 and 8 respectively

Question 1 × Question 9. The percentage of response obtained is shown in Fig. 7.

The value of R in correlation between question 1 and question 9 is 0.22679. By normal standards, the association between the two variables would not be considered statistically significant.

Was not found a correlation, between question 1 and question 9. Although 13.6% of the answers obtained in question 9 were negative, the majority was positive (the system set a focus of actions for newly created or newly opened objects - provide a feedback), which contradicts the answer obtained in question 1, that the system doesn't provide feedback for all users actions.

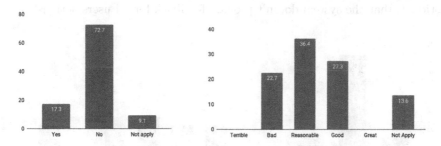

Fig. 7. Percentages - Question 1 and 9 respectively

Question 1 × Question 10. The percentage of response obtained is shown in Fig. 8.

The value of R in correlation between question 1 and question 10 is −0.02164. By normal standards, the association between the two variables would not be considered statistically significant.

Was not found a correlation, between question 1 and question 10. Although 13.6% of the answers obtained in question 10 were negative, the majority was positive (the system provides feedback on object attribute changes - provide a feedback), which contradicts the answer obtained in question 1, that the system doesn't provide feedback for all users actions.

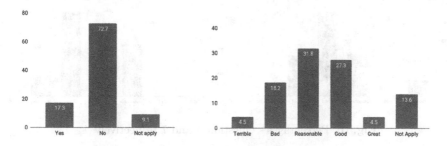

Fig. 8. Percentages - Question 1 and 10 respectively

Question 1 × Question 11. The percentage of response obtained is shown in Fig. 9.

The value of R in correlation between question 1 and question 11 is 0.3942. By normal standards, the association between the two variables would not be considered statistically significant.

Was not found a correlation, between question 1 and question 11. Although 13.6% of the answers obtained in question 11 were negative, the majority was positive (the system notify the user to any change in the current situation of control objects - provide a feedback), which contradicts the answer obtained in question 1, that the system doesn't provide feedback for all users actions.

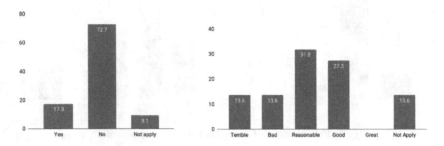

Fig. 9. Percentages - Question 1 and 11 respectively

4.2   Readability Questionnaire

In this questionnaire, was tested the combination of correlation between question 6, 7, 8 and 9. However, a brief analysis will be performed only between the correlations of questions 8 and 9, since no significant correlation was found between the others questions.

The value of R in correlation between question 8 and question 9 is 0.61237. By normal standards, the association between the two variables would be considered statistically significant. This means that there is an important correlation

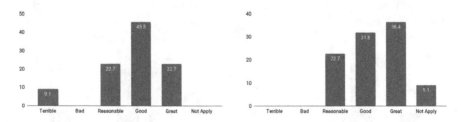

Fig. 10. Percentages - Question 6 and 7 respectively

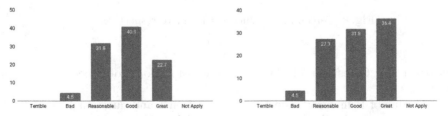

Fig. 11. Percentages - Question 8 and 9 respectively

between the use of bold and the use of underlining in the texts. It is therefore suggested that you use both bold and underline in moderation to have a better quality and usability of the website.

4.3   Discussion

All the results of the Spearman's correlations are presented in the Table 3. In the first line, the results of the correlations between the feedback questionnaire (question 1 and all others, except for questions 6 and 12, as explained above). The other values correspond to the correlations of the readability questionnaire (questions 6, 7, 8 and 9).

Regarding the Feedback questionnaire, no correlation was found between the compared questions, which is a bit strange, as we can see in question 1, more than 70% of the responses were "No", "the system doesn't provide feedback for all user actions", and one of the questions proves this correlation, the question 8, where 54.5% of the responses were that the "system doesn't provide immediate and continuous feedback from direct manipulations". For the other's comparison, it was to be expected that no correlation would be found, since the answer obtained in question 1 contradicted the answers obtained in the other questions, except question 8, as stated above.

So for the feedback correlation, it was expected to find only a correlation between question 1 and question 8, since question 8 proves the answer to question 1 - the system doesn't provide feedback for all user actions - but it was not what happened. This can be a problem related to a small amount of data (answers), since our database contains only 22 answers for each question.

Also, we can conclude that this inconsistency is maybe due to the question 1 have 3 point scale response (yes, no and not apply) and most of the other questions have likert responses, what is a 5 scale point response (terrible, bad, reasonable, good, great and not apply), so the values of the categorical variables compared were often different, that is, not standardized between them. Besides that, how the value of the factor "not apply" used in the Spearman's Correlation was "0", maybe, for the correlation, the "not apply" was may be considered closer to "yes" where the factor is "1", since 0 and 1 is a positive number and the "no" factor is "−1", that is, a negative number. So perhaps if we change the type of answer from question 1 to likert, that inconsistency does not recur, or associating negative responses with negative values, or even, comparing only questions that have the same range of possible answers.

On the other hand, analyzing the Readability questionnaire, it was found a correlation between the use of bold and the use of underlining in the texts, then it is suggested that who is developing a website, to use bold and underline in text with moderation to have a better readability of it and consequently a more ergonomic website. This correlation can be explained by the response graphs, where the question 8 and question 9 has a very similar answer, remembering that the answers "good" and "great" use the same categorical value "2" in the Spearman's Correlation. But we could not find a correlation between the others

Table 3. Spearman's correlation on readability questionnaire

	Question 1	Question 2	Question 3	Question 4	Question 5	Question 6	Question 7	Question 8	Question 9	Question 10	Question 11
Quest. 1	0.167	0.309	0.123	0.365		0.256	0.27	0.227	0.227	−0.022	0.394
Quest. 2											
Quest. 3											
Quest. 4											
Quest. 5											
Quest. 6						0.094	0.159	−0.161			
Quest. 7							0.159	0.216			
Quest. 8								0.612			
Quest. 9											
Quest. 10											
Quest. 11											

questions, which is a bit strange, since all the questions had very similar answers, most of them belonging to "good" and "great".

This inconsistency can be explained by the fact that only questions 8 and 9 had the answers belonging to the same categorical variables "bad", "reasonable", "good", and "great", while questions 6 and 7 had answers belonging to the categorical variables "horrible" and "not apply" respectively.

So, this paper shows us that there are still many things to improve, such as perhaps standardizing the types of responses for a better comparison, as well as make comparisons with the other questionnaires, among them: user experience, concision, error message and location grouping and, of course, expand the number of responses obtained to reduce some user inconsistency, and the main one, make the tool available in a web environment, so that responses are stored directly in the application database, instead of hosted on google forms.

5 Conclusions

The present study analyzed the correlation between the responses of the questionnaires, obtained from the evaluation of the website Tidia-Ae, using the tool developed (still in its initial version), which generates specific questionnaires for the individual application domain. The questions analyzed involved aspects related to the usability features and issues of web sites, mainly referring to feedback and readability.

From the data of the 22 responses, which were correlated from questions 8 and 9 referring to the readability questionnaire, it was verified that the result of Spearman's correlation was equal to 0.61237, that is, a significantly positive correlation. Then, from this correlation, the following inference has been established: the use of bold, along with the use of underlining, brings benefits to the legibility of the website, as long as they are used in moderation. We consider this result is very important for designers, developers and usability evaluation team as this can prove that there is a correlation between these two usability features.

It is hoped that this research can be used as a basis for future researches, and when the tool is completely developed, we plan to allow it to be downloaded free to professionals and researchers, to be used as a tool to help achieve better ergonomics and usability environments.

References

1. Figueredo, A.J., Wolf, P.S.A.: Assortative pairing and life history strategy - a cross-cultural study. J. Hum. Nat. **20**, 317–330 (2009). https://doi.org/10.1007/s12110-009-9068-2
2. Nielsen, J., Loranger, H.: Usabilidade na Web - Projetando Websites com Qualidade (2007)
3. Myers, L., Sirois, M.J.: Spearman correlation coefficients, differences between. In: Encyclopedia of Statistical Sciences (2006). https://doi.org/10.1002/0471667196.ess5050.pub2

4. Liu, F.: Usability evaluation on websites. School Art Des. (2015). https://doi.org/10.1002/0471667196.ess5050.pub2. Wuhan University of Technology
5. Malara, Z., Misko, R., et al.: Wroclaw University of Technology graduates career paths. Econ. Sociol. Biol. (2016). University of Grodno
6. Cybis, W., Betiol, A.W., et al.: Ergonomia e Usabilidade, 3 edn. Novatex Publisher (2015)
7. SPSS Tutorials: Pearson Correlation. https://libguides.library.kent.edu/SPSS/PearsonCorr. Accessed 07 Dec 2018
8. Tidia-Ae, Sobre o Ae. https://ae4.tidia-ae.usp.br/portal. Accessed 9 Nov 2018
9. Merriam Webster - Ranking. https://www.merriam-webster.com/dictionary/ranking. Accessed 9 Dec 2018
10. Web Content Acessibility Guidelines (WCAG) 2.1. http://www.w3.org/TR/WCAG21/. Accessed 15 Nov 2018
11. Web Content Acessibility Guidelines (WCAG) 2.0 - W3C Recomendations, 11 December 2008. http://www.w3.org/TR/2008/REC-WCAG20-20081211/. Accessed 15 Nov 2018
12. W3C Web Standard Defines Acessibility for Next Generation Web. http://www.w3.org/2008/12/wcag20-pressrelease.html. Accessed 15 Nov 2018
13. Web Content Acessibility Guidelines (WCAG) 2.0. http://www.w3.org/TR/WCAG20/. Accessed 15 Nov 2018
14. Techniques for (WCAG) 2.0. http://www.w3.org/TR/WCAG20-TECHS/. Accessed 15 Nov 2018
15. Understanding Techniques for WCAG Sucess Criteria. http://www.w3.org/TR/UNDERSTANDING-WCAG20/understanding-techniques.html. Accessed 15 Nov 2018
16. Stair, R., Reynolds, W.: Princípios de Sistemas de Informação. Centage Learning Publisher, São Paulo (2015)
17. Pressman R.: Engenharia de Software, Uma Abordagem Profissional, 7th edn. AMGII Publisher, Porto Alegre (2011)
18. Colouris, G., Dollimore, J., et al.: Sistemas Distribuídos. Conceitos e Projeto, 4th edn. Bookman Publisher, Porto Alegre (2007)
19. Barros, V.T.: Avaliação da interface de um aplicativo computacional através de teste de usabilidade, questionário ergonómico e análise gráfica do design. In: Dissertação (Pós-Graduação Engenharia de Produção) - Faculdade da Universidade Federal de Santa Catarina (2013)
20. Vanderdonckt, J., Bodart, F.: Encapsulating knowledge for intelligence automatic interaction objects selection. In: Proceedings of the ACM Conference on Human Factors in Computing Systems, INTERCHI 1993. ACM Press, New York (1993)
21. Smith, L.S., Mosier, J.N.: Guidelines for designing user interface software. In: MITRE Corporation and Funded by the U.S Air Force's Eletronic Systems Division (1986)
22. ISO. ISO/DIS9241-16.: Ergonomic requirements for office work with visual display terminals (VDT's) - direct manipulation dialogues. Genebra
23. Prumper, J.: Software-evaluation based upon ISO 9241 part 10. In: Vienna Conference, VCHCI 1993 (1993)

Vehicle Human-Machine Interaction Interface Evaluation Method Based on Eye Movement and Finger Tracking Technology

Mengjin Zeng$^{(\boxtimes)}$, Gang Guo$^{(\boxtimes)}$, and Qiuyang Tang$^{(\boxtimes)}$

Department of Vehicle Engineering, Chongqing University, Chongqing, China
937767411@qq.com, cquguogang@163.com,
qiuyang.tang@foxmail.com

Abstract. The vehicle has been gradually evolving from a traditional delivery vehicle into a complex human-computer interaction system. In view of the increasingly diverse human-computer interaction systems in today's automobiles, the design of HMI (human-machine interact) is very important to driver's safety.

This paper presents a new human-machine interaction evaluation method from both objective and subjective perspective that combined with eye movement tracking, finger tracking, questionnaire and interview which can be used in vehicle design of HMI. It can provide theoretical basis for vehicle design of HMI. Different from other research, one hallmark of it is that this method could directly reflect the problems in HMI design by finger behavior data. Because fingers are the only part of the body that directly touch to the interface during manipulation. In this study, we tested a music selection function of vehicle HMI in domestic with a simple task and find some problems of interaction design.

It is found that the number of steps to complete the task and the total distance of finger movement data can reflect the usability of the logical framework design of music function. The number of tentative steps and the manipulation time can reflect the steps in question and combined with eye movement data and video data can reflect the details of the problem.

From the experimental results, it is seen that some problems in HMI design can be accurately identified by using new evaluation method. It also provides a theoretical basis for the improvement and design of HMI.

Keywords: Finger tracking · Eye movement track · Music player · Evaluation method · In-vehicle information systems · Interaction design

1 Introduction

Recently, the development trend of HMI in vehicles is complex information system that includes car to car, and Car to X [1]. Apart from driving styles, drivers using in-vehicle information systems (IVIS) can also cause distraction [2]. 60% to 70% of the visual attention resources are accounted on the driver's main driving task in their driving.

© Springer Nature Switzerland AG 2019
C. Stephanidis (Ed.): HCII 2019, LNCS 11786, pp. 101–115, 2019.
https://doi.org/10.1007/978-3-030-30033-3_9

With the increase of driver's workload, the degree of distraction increases, which is one of the causes of accidents. And the drivers' workload was revealed to increase with task difficulty and it have relation with the development of smart driving interface designs in the future [3].

The layout of the in-vehicle system must be identified and operated quickly to improve user's efficiency, avoiding serious consequences due to involvement. Many studies had demonstrated that driver's attention will be distracted while operating the IVIS, which will result in a deteriorated driving performance [4].

The design of vehicle information system is an important factor to evaluate the safety impact of interaction between primary driving tasks and secondary tasks while driving [5]. And the development of IVIS is diversity, the manipulation on the system is becoming more and more complex. Therefore, it is meaningful to establish an effective evaluation method for the design of HMI.

In some previous studies, subjective evaluation, questionnaires and interviews were commonly used for evaluation of HMI. In addition, facial expressions, eye tracking system and skin resistance were recently involved in HMI evaluation [6]. In the automobile field, task response time, lane deviation and other indicators based on the state of vehicle were measured for HMI evaluation [7].

Driving simulator, including NASA-RTLX combined with lane deviation and steering wheel angle were used in evaluation of effect on driving performance in the context of music selection [8].

In a driving simulator study of Jeong et al. [9], the position of in-vehicle display was evaluated by physiological and eye movement data. The results showed that the drivers focus of visual field varies with the position of the in-vehicle display, and the conventional location of a display (center console) gave the lowest level of GSR, which means lower mental stress.

Jin et al. [10] established an evaluation method based on driving simulator and eye tracker, which could be used for the evaluation of driving performance when drivers performed in secondary tasks.

Harsham [11] extracted meaningful indicators from vehicle CAN and history data, to evaluate the complexity of the HMI. And came out prediction methods for user behaviors and intentions to improve in-vehicle task manipulation performance.

In the study of Pankok [12], display clutter may have its greatest effect on performance or attention allocation in driving. The more display clutter, the more effect on driver's distraction when operating secondary tasks. And drivers more focus on display clutter than display clear.

Ooi [6] used electrodermal activity (EDA) to investigate stress and anger as primary emotion leading to accidents. They established highly reliability frame of driving emotion recognition by comparative experiments.

Nowadays, there are many devices in the vehicle. These devices are used by drivers to perform secondary tasks related to visual, auditory, vocal, manual or cognitive, and they also were normally associated with more than one type of distribution [13–16]. Especially in the vehicles, driver's hands are mostly engaged in primary driving task, but secondary tasks involved finger movement such as playing music, Bluetooth connection and navigation are increasing rapidly. Thus manipulation an IVIS while driving can distract drivers' attention and further reducing the drivers' performance, drivers' ability to manipulate the IVIS [17, 18] and leading accidents [19].

Fingers are the one of the most important part on the body while operating HMI system. Due to drivers directly manipulate in-vehicle information system by fingers, which behavior can directly reflect driver's experience of it. Finger movement indicators are also significant for evaluation of HMI. Therefore, it is meaningful to measure the movement of fingers.

This paper presents a new human-machine interaction evaluation method from both objective and subjective perspective that combined with eye movement tracking, finger tracking, questionnaire and interview which cloud be used in design of HMI, especially in the field of automobile. In this study, we conducted a music selection task to evaluate a domestic popular IVIS based on the evaluation method mention above.

2 Method

2.1 Apparatus

This experiment adopted a CHANGAN EV200 as the test car. An onboard IVIS system including music was equipped in the middle of the control panel of the car as shown in Fig. 1. The screen was a capacitive screen, and the size was 17.7 (w) × 10.0 (h). Music software was installed on the system, and the icon was on the home page of the IVIS system.

Fig. 1. The middle of the control panel of the car.

Figure 2 was a screen shot of the screen display. It was located on the right side of the steering wheel so that it can be easily viewed and manipulated.

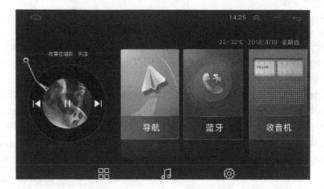

Fig. 2. Home page of IVIS.

As shown in Figs. 3 and 4, the two main interfaces of music function are music playing interface and music list interface, which are also the main interfaces tested in music selection function.

Fig. 3. The music playing interface.

Fig. 4. The music list interface.

EthoVision XT 11.5 software was commonly used to study motion of small animals in two-dimension. We found that the EthoVision XT 11.5 can properly measure the two dimensional motion of thumb on screen. The participant' forefinger movement images were recorded by a camera (Logitech C920) from the vertical direction of the screen. The camera's pixel count of 5 million, and the maximum FPS was 30 frames per second. The camera quality met the experimental requirements. The video files created by the Logitech C920 will be imported into the EthoVision XT 11.5 software, and thumb movement speed was acquired based on image recognition technology. A marker which color was distinguish from the environment will be attached on the nail of thumb, then movement of the marker was considered to be the movement of thumb. The indicators of finger movement total distance, finger movement average angular velocity, finger movement average liner velocity, finger movement total angular, number of clicks and total time of finished task.

A Dikablis Professional eye tracker (Ergnoeers, Germany) was adopted in this experiment to record the image of eye movement at 60 Hz. Two infrared cameras were used record the images of left eye and right eye respectively. Fixation frequency, heat map and visual search pattern were calculated by eye movement analysis software D-Lab (Ergnoeers, Germany).

2.2 Participants

Ten participants (6 males and 4 females ranging in age from 21 to 25 years) were recruited using the following criteria: (1) resident in the Chongqing area; (2) in possession of a valid driver license for at least two years. All the recruited participants didn't use this IVIS before. All participants were in good health and free from eye diseases. Participants were instructed to avoid tea, coffee and cigarette on the day of the experiment.

2.3 Procedure

Before the formal experiment, participants were informed the objective of the study and their task. Each of participant was requested to music selection task. Simultaneously, eye movement and finger movement data were recorded.

We divided the music selection task into seven small manipulation tasks. Thus, to complete the music selection task, participants have to carry out the steps that included (1) clicking music icon (2) clicking music list icon (3) clicking icon of "song" (4) click the "search" (5) click input box (6) input name of song (7) click playing music (8) click icon of collecting. Each task instruction was pre-recorded the sound file and played to participants through audio. After listing to a given item instruction, participants performed the tasks through manual manipulation of center control. Once the last target had been chosen, the experimenter signalled to participants that the task had been completed. Having a five-minute break. After the experiment, the participants were requested to fulfill a questionnaire (PANAS), which was used to reveal relations between positive and negative affect with personality stats and traits.

2.4   Date Analysis

Data analysis had two parts: objective data and subjective data. Objective data include finger behavior data and eye movement data. Subjective data include questionnaires and interview.

The analysis of finger behavior data was recorded the whole process of participants completing interactive tasks with Logitech camera, and then import the video into the EthoVision TX. The finger movement data obtained in this study included two parts, video observation and software processing.

Video data included task completion time, completion task number of steps, each step completion time and number of steps. More specifically, (1) Task completion time referred to the time between the participants' issuance of orders and the completion of tasks. (2) The number of steps referred to all the steps in which participants completed the task. (3) Each step completion task time referred to the time spent between two adjacent correct steps. (4) The exploratory number of steps referred to the keys are pressed the number of errors between two keys being pressed [20].

According to ISO15007-1, a saccade was defined as brief, fast movement of the eyes that changes the point of fixation and a glance was defined as the maintaining of visual gaze within an area of interest [21]. In this study, the details of scanning were extracted by MATLAB encoding, including total fixation time, number of fixation and gaze-on time. To solve the above questions, after testing the participant's manipulation behavior, we found the expert who was very familiar with the manipulation of this car screen to test him in the same way as the participants.

According to the experience, with error rates generally within 30% of observed values, in line with expectations for expert's predictions. Statistical significance was accepted at $p < 0.05$ and conducted using SPSS for Mac 24.

3   Result

Ten participants took part in the experiment. However, three participants' data were excluded from analysis, because of breaking down eye tracker.

As the Figs. 5 and 6 showed, participants required more mean completion the music task time (113 s) than expert (18 s). There was a significant difference between participants and expert on task completion time($p < 0.05$). This result indicated that the task completion time of participants were significant longer than expert.

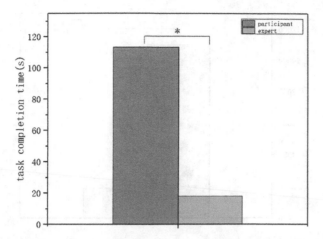

Fig. 5. Task completion time of the music selection task

As can been seen in Fig. 6, the number of step data were analyzed and revealed that participants took significantly more steps to finish task than expert ($p < 0.05$).

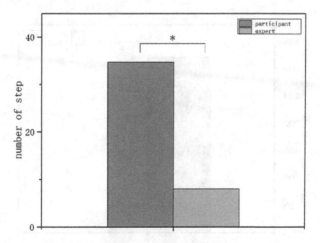

Fig. 6. Number of step of music selection task.

As the Figs. 7 and 8 showed, finger manipulation data of participants were analyzed using One-Samples t-test and showed a significant different in total finger movement distance between participants and expert ($p < 0.05$).

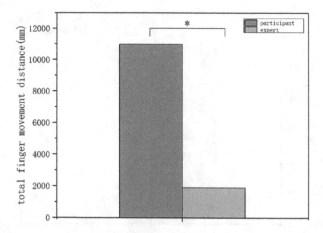

Fig. 7. Total finger movement distance of the completion music selection task (mm).

Compared with the expert, a significant different in participants on total finger movement angle (p < 0.05). Therefore, it can be inferred that participants' fingers take much more workload than experts.

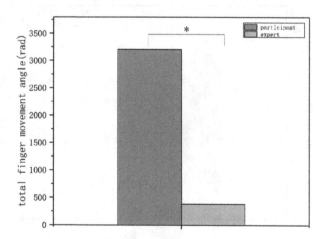

Fig. 8. Total finger movement angle of the completion music selection task (rad).

However, analysis of the accuracy data using a single sample t-test showed no significant difference in average finger movement speed and average finger movement angular speed between the participants and expert (Figs. 9 and 10).

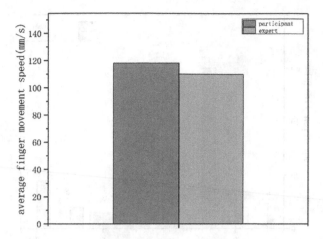

Fig. 9. Average finger movement speed of completion the music selection task (mm/s)

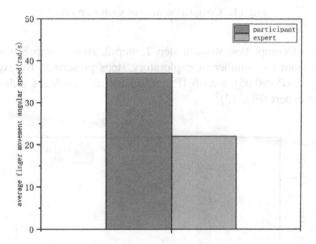

Fig. 10. Average finger movement angular speed of completion the music selection task (rad/s).

Based on the above data, it can be inferred that there are problems in the interactive design of music selection task in this IVIS. Therefore, we analyzed completion time and number of steps for each step to find problems in road of music selection. Each step data including completion time and number of tentative steps of participants were also analyzed by One-Sample t-test.

There were significant differences among the result of five steps in the process of accomplishing the task. Some steps including, step 2, step 4, step 5 and step 6 had no significant different in the completion time of each step with expert. It showed that the interactions involved in these steps are reasonable. However, some steps including step 1 (p < 0.05), step 3 (p < 0.05), step 7 (p < 0.05) and step 8 (p < 0.05) had a significant different in the completion time of each step with expert (Fig. 11).

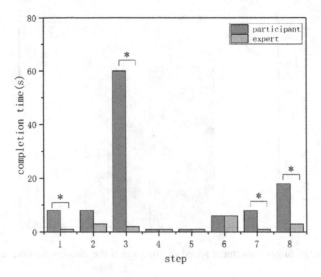

Fig. 11. Completion time of each step (s).

The number of completion steps in step 1, step 2, step 7, step 8 was not significantly different from the number of exploratory steps prescribed by experts. Step 3 ($p < 0.05$), step 5 ($P < 0.05$), step 6 ($P < 0.05$) had a significant different between participants and expert (Fig. 12).

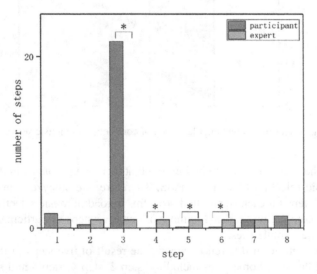

Fig. 12. Each step number of steps.

However, eye movement indicators such as (fixation time, number of fixation, gaze-on time) that were commonly used cannot reflect these problems accurately.

Specifically, there was no significant difference in fixation time, number of fixation and gaze-on time between participants and expert.

To finish music selection task, participants covered two interface. Fixation frequency was used to whether participants cognitive load exceeded normal when their manipulated the music interface. It was found that fixation frequency (number of fixation divided by fixation time) were no significant difference in music playing interface and the music list interface between participants and normal value (4).

Generally, information presentation format or layout has a long history of research in safety-critical domains other than road safety [22]. According to attention track of participants, we found the participants' common operating characteristics.

The PANAS questionnaires was a self-report questionnaire including two scales which were measured both positive and negative affect. Each cell task was scored on a scale of 1 (not at all) to 5 (very much) [23]. Clinical and non-clinical studies have found that PANAS was a reliable and effective tool for evaluation both positive and negative effects [24]. Participants filled out this form after finishing music selection task. The figures showed that Positive emotions accounted for only 42%, while negative emotions accounted for 58%. It can be seen that the experiential feeling of the music selection task on IVIS.

Next, participants filled in some satisfaction questionnaires. These problems could reflect participants' satisfaction with the music selection after completing manipulation. Questions, number of participants and average scores are shown in the Table 1 (1 (not at all) 5 (very much)).

Table 1. The satisfaction scale of music selection function.

Questions	Participant	Score
I don't think it's necessary for this function to be so complicated	10	3.32
I think this function is very simple to use	10	3.16
I think this function is very simple to use	10	3.12

If the mean score reached 80%, it was indicated that most participants were satisfied with the interactive design of music selection. But only 64% of participants were satisfied with the music selection function.

In the interview, participants also asked some questions about manipulation of music task. These problems were summarized and classified.

4 Discussion

As the complexity of the HMI increased, drivers' distraction can contribute to accidents [11]. In previous studies, many scholars have evaluated IVIS by driving performance, emotion, eye tracking or subjective scale. Their concluded that only the usability of IVIS or analysis of driving distraction caused by manipulation IVIS. Now, there is no suggestion on the design of IVIS.

Unlike the previous studies, this paper added finger indicators combined with eye movement indicators and subjective questionnaires to test the music function of IVIS. It was found that, participants' finger behavior data, video data and eye movement data reflected interaction design problems of IVIS and we could accurately find the root where caused of the problem.

The experimental results showed that the new evaluation method was feasible and effective to evaluate In-vehicle information system. Based on the above experimental results, we found three problems in the function of music selection.

First, the task completion time and the task number of step were more than baseline. It suggested that participants had many irrelevant steps when they completed the music task. Experience showed that it was very complicated to complete a task in more than five steps, even expert spent eight steps on completion task. And there is a "15-Second Rule", in a stationary vehicle, if the drivers can complete the task within 15 s, the task may be safe and this task also didn't increase risk of vehicle accidents while driving [25]. It shows that the design of interaction in this task may be reasonable. In this experiment, participants spent 113 s on music tasks and expert also spent 18 s on it. And, in the interview, five participants mentioned that completed task was a lack of consistency. It indicated that the logical framework of music selection task was too complex.

Total finger movement distance and total finger movement angle also had a significant difference with participants and expert. It guessed that participants spent more attention to search the targets and participants' finger had a large number of horizontal movements during music selection tasks, which resulted in a significant increasing in the finger movement angle speed. And this guess was confirmed by video data.

Particularly, according to the data of each step completion time, there were issues with step 1, step 3, step 7, step 8. But the number of steps showed that there were problems with the manipulation of steps 3, step 4, step 5, step 6. Participants had no more steps in step 4 and the number of steps in step 5 and step 6 were less than expert.

Step 1, step 7 and step 8 have significant differences in completion time of each step but no significant difference in number of steps.

It was found that, by watching the participants' manipulation video, all participants could find the music icon in the first time and clicked it. But participants took a lot of time to complete step 1 because the screen wasn't sensitive. So the second problem is that the center console display isn't sensitive.

Step 7, clicking playing music, video data indicated that most participants were considering which song to play when they completed step 7. It looked like a very simple step, participants spent more time on manipulation but it was close to the baseline for participants to complete step 7. Thus it was irrelevant to interaction design.

Step 8, clicking the collection icon, had a significant different with participants and expert. Video data showed that most of participants didn't see quickly the collection icon in music list interface. In interview, I asked participants why they did not quickly find the collection icon. The unanimous answer of the participants was not to see it. Because of the icon color was similar to background color.

Thus there were problems with the interaction design in step 3.

Step 3, clicking icon of "song", from eye movement data, we found that there was no significant difference in fixation time, number of fixation and gaze-on time between participants and expert. It indicated that participants saw the "song" icon, but they did not click on it. So, participants' perception of the "song" icon was low. It also reflected that finger movement data could find problems which eye movement data couldn't find.

As the Fig. 13 showed, we inferred that participants had two common habits in searching for the target in the process of completing the task. First, we found most of participants' eyes swept from left to right and from top to bottom. Secondly, what's more interesting is movement of the fixation point changes with the movement of the finger when participants searched the target and participants searched for target by the way of finger-centered to surroundings. If the guesses are confirmed, it can provide a theoretical basis for the layout of interface information to improve manipulation efficiency.

Fig. 13. One participant's attention track in music selection task.

For example, distribution from left to right according to functional importance and distribution from top to bottom according to using frequency as so on.

5 Conclusion

Different from other research, one hallmark of it is that this method could find the problems in HMI design. The experiment was mainly analyzed finger behavior data and compared finger data between participants and expert. We analyzed problems in the HMI from finger movement data and eye movement data combining with questionnaires and interview. These were results that were not possible from eye movement data.

Further, we resolved the task into simple steps and analyzed those steps by multiply indicators. This evaluation method of HMI can help with design IVIS for manufacturers. And it is also good for reducing driving distraction and decreasing accident risk. Further, the evaluation model built in this study could estimate IVIS effectively under different vehicle.

Analysis of each step should add more finger movement indicators and eye movement indicators to improve the reliability of the analysis results and find more problems in IVIS. There is no improving design and no experiment data of improving design to compare with origin designing data. If the improved data were better than the improved data, the evaluation method would be proved useful. The experiment was carried out in static condition. However, the participants were told to simulate the driving situation in the real vehicle, which was different from the operation of the vehicle information system in driving situation. Therefore, it is suggested that the driver's manipulation data of IVIS should be tested accurately in driving.

References

1. Schmidt, A., Spiessl, W., Kern, D.: Driving automotive user interface research. IEEE Pervasive Comput. **9**(1), 85–88 (2010)
2. Li, X., et al.: Effects of an in-vehicle eco-safe driving system on drivers' glance behaviour. Accid. Anal. Prev. **122**, 143–152 (2019)
3. Birrell, S.A., Young, M.S.: The impact of smart driving aids on driving performance and driver distraction. Transp. Res. Part F Traffic Psychol. Behav. **14**(6), 484–493 (2011)
4. Hao, T., Jianghong, Z., Wei, W.: Vehicle human machine interface design research. Chin. J. Autom. Eng. **2**(5), 7 (2012)
5. Kim, H., Song, H.: Evaluation of the safety and usability of touch gestures in operating in-vehicle information systems with visual occlusion. Appl. Ergon. **45**(3), 789–798 (2014)
6. Ooi, J.S.K., et al.: Driver emotion recognition framework based on electrodermal activity measurements during simulated driving conditions. In: 2016 IEEE EMBS Conference on Biomedical Engineering and Sciences (IECBES), pp. 365–369 (2016)
7. Craig, A., et al.: A controlled investigation into the psychological determinants of fatigue. Biol. Psychol. **72**(1), 78–87 (2006)
8. Mitsopoulos-Rubens, E., Trotter, M.J., Lenné, M.G.: Effects on driving performance of interacting with an in-vehicle music player: a comparison of three interface layout concepts for information presentation. Appl. Ergon. **42**(4), 583–591 (2011)
9. Jeong, C., et al.: In-vehicle display HMI safety evaluation using a driving simulator. Int. J. Autom. Technol. **14**(6), 987–992 (2013)
10. Jin, L., et al.: Research on safety evaluation model for in-vehicle secondary task driving. Accid. Anal. Prev. **81**, 243–250 (2015)
11. Harsham, B.A., et al.: Driver prediction to improve interaction with in-vehicle HMI (2015)
12. Pankok, C., Kaber, D.: The effect of navigation display clutter on performance and attention allocation in presentation- and simulator-based driving experiments. Appl. Ergon. **69**, 136–145 (2018)
13. Oviedo-Trespalacios, O., et al.: Driving behaviour while self-regulating mobile phone interactions: a human-machine system approach. Accid. Anal. Prev. **118**, 253–262 (2018)
14. Oviedo-Trespalacios, O.: Getting away with texting: behavioural adaptation of drivers engaging in visual-manual tasks while driving. Transp. Res. Part A Policy Pract. **116**, 112–121 (2018)
15. Oviedo-Trespalacios, O., et al.: Self-regulation of driving speed among distracted drivers: an application of driver behavioral adaptation theory. Traffic Inj. Prev. **18**(6), 599–605 (2017)
16. Oviedo-Trespalacios, O., et al.: Effects of road infrastructure and traffic complexity in speed adaptation behaviour of distracted drivers. Accid. Anal. Prev. **101**, 67–77 (2017)

17. Horrey, W.J., Wickens, C.D., Consalus, K.P.: Modeling drivers' visual attention allocation while interacting with in-vehicle technologies. J. Exp. Psychol. Appl. **12**(2), 67–78 (2006)
18. Alm, H., Nilsson, L.: The effects of a mobile telephone task on driver behavior in a car following situation. Accid. Anal. Prev. **27**(5), 707–715 (1995)
19. Stutts, J.C., Reinfurt, D.W., Rodgman, E.A.: The role of driver distraction in crashes: an analysis of 1995–1999 Crashworthiness Data System Data. In: Annual Proceedings. Association for the Advancement of Automotive Medicine. AAA Foundation for Traffic Safety (2001)
20. Kolski, C.: Human-Computer Interactions in Transport, p. 375. ISTE Ltd. and Wiley, London and Hoboken (2011)
21. ISO15007-1: Road Vehicles - Measurement of Driver Visual Behaviour with Respect to Transport Information and Control Systems - Part 1: Definitions and Parameters. International Organization for Standardization, Geneva, Switzerland (2014)
22. Singleton, W.T.: The ergonomics of information presentation. Appl. Ergon. 8 (1971)
23. Watson, D., Clark, L.A.: Development and validation of brief measures of positive and negative affect: the PANAS scales. J. Personally Soc. Psychol. **54**(6), 1063–1070 (1988)
24. Crawford, J.R., Henry, J.D.: The positive and negative affect schedule (PANAS): construct validity, measurement properties and normative data in a large non-clinical sample. Br. J. Clin. Psychol. **43**(Pt 3), 245–265 (2004)
25. Green, P.: Visual and task demands of driver information systems. UMTRI, p. 98-16 (1999)

Information, Visualization and Decision Making

Optimizing Exploratory Workflows for Embedded Platform Trace Analysis and Its Application to Mobile Devices

Jonathan Ah Sue[1](✉), Peter Brand[2](✉), Joachim Falk[2](✉),
Ralph Hasholzner[1](✉), and Jürgen Teich[2](✉)

[1] Intel Deutschland GmbH, Munich, Germany
{jonathan.ah.sue, ralph.hasholzner}@intel.com
[2] Friedrich-Alexander-Universität Erlangen-Nürnberg, Erlangen, Germany
{peter.brand, joachim.falk, juergen.teich}@fau.de

Abstract. As 5G wireless communication technology is currently deployed, an increasing amount of data is available from mobile devices out in the field. Exploiting this data, also called system traces, recent investigations show the potential to improve the wireless modem design and performance using data-centric approaches. Such data-centric workflows are exploratory and iterative by nature. For instance, time pattern identification is performed by domain experts to derive assumptions on potential optimizations and these assumptions are continuously refined during multiple iterations of data collection, visualization and exploration. In this context, we propose three optimizations to increase the exploration speed in iterative data-centric workflows. First, we present a methodology based on persistent memoization in order to minimize the data processing duration when additional event sequences need to be extracted from a trace. We show that up to 84.5% of the event extraction time can be spared for a typical modem trace data set. Secondly, we present a novel entropy-based data interaction technique for visual exploration of event sequences and finally, a similarity measure to perform subsequence matching in order to assist the user when identifying frequent time patterns in a trace.

Keywords: Exploratory workflow · Iterative feature extraction ·
Workflow optimization · Time-oriented data visualization · Visual interaction ·
Zoom+Slant · Event sequence similarity measure · Categorical event sequence

1 Introduction

The increasing number of mobile devices out in the field generates a colossal amount of data that can be used to optimize the design and behavior of existing and future devices. As opposed to simulation-centric approaches, such data-centric approaches allow to improve key performance indicators (KPIs) with respect to the user context or behavior. For instance, a low priority data transfer to the network might be delayed if the congestion of the network is expected to be high at a specific time of the day or in a specific location. However, collecting data from mobile devices, also called traces, often requires many efforts, e.g., implementing the tracing system or manually

© Springer Nature Switzerland AG 2019
C. Stephanidis (Ed.): HCII 2019, LNCS 11786, pp. 119–139, 2019.
https://doi.org/10.1007/978-3-030-30033-3_10

collecting traces at different locations. Usually, a maximum amount of hardware and software events is recorded to ensure that the required information is present in the trace in case additional analyses are needed. Because of embedded storage requirements, the raw trace is therefore drastically compressed.

Using such raw traces as input, data-centric workflows, e.g., machine learning workflows [1], often include three steps, as depicted in Fig. 1. In the following, we provide a description of these three steps with related examples for modem power optimization:

1. **Trace processing.** In order to extract meaningful event sequences from a raw trace, computer processing time is required. This extraction usually consists in data decompression, aggregation and sampling.
   Example: In the context of modem power optimization, power-related event sequences are extracted as well as event sequences representing the size of the data packets that are exchanged with the network at different timestamps.
2. **Visual exploration.** The analysis typically starts with a visual exploration of the event sequences. The goal is to identify potential optimizations and discuss them with domain experts.
   Example: Periods of high power consumption for specific components are identified.
3. **Relevance estimation.** Once a time pattern of interest is identified, the relevance of the proposed optimization is assessed, typically by finding a representative amount of similar patterns in the trace.
   Example: A time correlation between high power consumption periods and a specific data packet time pattern is identified.

Finally, such workflows are iterative and exploratory by nature, as relevant optimization proposals often raise questions that can be answered by a new iteration of event sequence extraction and exploration.

Example: An additional event sequence representing the status of the data buffer is extracted. From a domain expert point of view, a high data buffer usage due to specific data packet patterns can lead to a high power consumption. In this case, optimizing the power consumption consists in a modification of the buffer size.

In essence, we argue that optimizing the human-computer interactivity in such iterative data-centric workflows relies on data processing time reduction, human exploration time reduction and analysis time reduction. Therefore, in this paper, we propose three optimizations to increase the exploration speed and improve the interactivity in such workflows. First, in Sect. 2, we present a methodology to minimize the data pre-processing duration in each iteration. Secondly, in Sect. 3, we propose a novel entropy-based data interaction technique for event sequence visual exploration. Finally, in Sect. 4, we evaluate a similarity measure to perform subsequence matching in order to identify frequent modem behaviors.

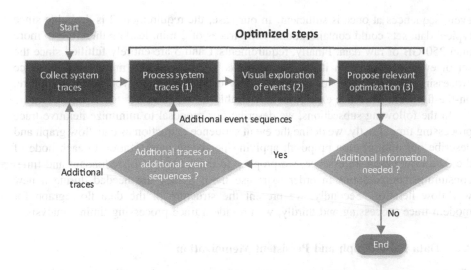

Fig. 1. Exploratory and iterative workflow for modem trace data analysis.

2   Iterative Trace Processing

A modem trace of a LTE/5G device typically contains information reaching 250 MB of hardware and software events logged during 2 min. Due to embedded storage requirements, this information needs to be drastically compressed and a significant amount of pre-processing time is needed to extract and combine the raw data into meaningful *event sequences* (around 10 min for 100 event sequences).

Basically, these event sequences are used as input data for many tasks such as verification, system level optimization or machine learning. In most of the cases, these tasks require multiple iterations of trace preprocessing. For instance, a verification engineer would inspect a set of event sequences to derive some assumptions on the root cause of an anomaly. To refine these assumptions, additional sets of event sequences need to be extracted in order to finally identify the root cause. Similarly, in a machine learning workflow, the initial set of event sequences might be iteratively expanded to add new features that might improve the model performance. Even at early visualization stages, the observation of an event sequence leads to questions that can be answered by observing other event sequences, e.g., identifying causality between event occurrences.

In essence, we argue that such *iterative workflows* often require multiple iterations of trace processing. However, there are some cases where extracting all event sequences at once is more efficient than iteratively extracting them only when needed, i.e., *on-the-fly* extraction. Concretely, on-the-fly event sequence extraction is desirable if one of the following conditions is fulfilled: (1) the set of required event sequences can grow and is not fixed at the beginning of the workflow, (2) extracting every possible event sequence leads to high disk space usage, or (3) trace processing duration needs to be minimized. If none of these requirements is necessary, then extracting all event sequences at once is sufficient. In our case, the requirement 2 is desirable since typical data sets could contain around 1000 traces of 2 min, leading therefore to more than 250 GB of raw data. Finally, requirements 1 and 3 are entirely fulfilled since the set of event sequences in iterative workflows is not fixed and minimizing the trace processing time is crucial for the interactivity of such iterative workflows. Therefore, on-the-fly event sequence extraction is desirable in our case.

In the following subsections, we describe our proposal to minimize iterative trace processing time. Firstly, we define the event sequence extraction as data flow graph and describe our optimization proposal: applying persistent memoization to each node of the data flow graph. In essence, we propose to persist results of redundant and time-consuming computations in order to re-use them if they are needed during a new workflow iteration. Secondly, we present the structure of the data flow graph for modem trace processing and thirdly, we provide a trace processing timing analysis.

2.1 Data Flow Graph and Persistent Memoization

The trace processing steps can be represented by a directed acyclic graph called data flow graph (DFG) where nodes are data transformations, i.e., *functions*, and directed edges represent intermediate data produced and consumed by the nodes, i.e., *variables* [2]. In Fig. 2, we present an exemplary DFG with its associated nomenclature.

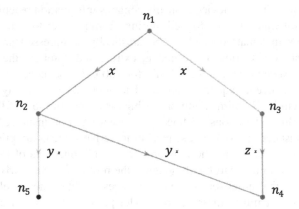

Fig. 2. Exemplary data flow graph. A node represents a function that produces only one output variable and consumes variables produced by one or multiple nodes. Therefore, edges starting from the same node represent the same data, but edges ending at the same node represent different data. For instance, the node n_1 produces the variable x which is consumed by the nodes n_2 and n_3. The node n_4 consumes both variables y and z. The blue subgraph denotes processing steps already executed during the previous iteration whereas the red subgraph denotes additional processing steps executed during the current iteration. Black nodes are not executed yet. (Color figure online)

In Fig. 2, if the variables x and z, produced during the previous iteration (blue subgraph), are persisted, i.e., saved to the disk, they can be retrieved and used during the current iteration (red subgraph). For time-consuming node executions, retrieving intermediate variable is often profitable. However, for fast node executions, the time required to save and load variables might be longer and therefore, intermediate result persistency is not optimal.

Variable persistency could be easily achieved by assigning unique names to files containing persisted variables. If the file exists, the variable could be directly retrieved. However, when designing a DFG for data processing, adjustments of the code often need to be done across multiple iterations, e.g., bug fixing, code cleaning, etc. Therefore, some nodes of the DFG are often modified between two iterations. This leads to modifications of some output variables and possibly all output variables of the child nodes. In this case, saving the node output in a file and checking the file existence is not sufficient to decide whether a result should be retrieved or not. Essentially, avoiding node re-computation only if the node and its input variables remain unchanged can be achieved by memoization [3]. Memoization is often implemented by caching the intermediate variables to the system memory. However, as described in [3], these variables could be persisted, i.e., stored to the disk, in order to be retrieved even across multiple program launches. Therefore, we propose to apply persistent memoization to each node of a data processing DFG in order to avoid unnecessary re-computations.

In order to check whether a variable changed, every time an output variable is produced by a node, it is persisted together with its hash, typically a 128-bit or 160-bit hash value. The more the hashing function is complex, the lower the chances of hash collisions are. However, complex hashing function also take more time. Therefore, we chose simple hashing functions like MD5 or SHA-1. The probability of hash collision of two variables is still less than 1 over 10^{18}. To decide whether a node needs to be re-computed or not, the hashes of the input variables and the hash of the node code is compared with the corresponding hash values stored during the previous execution. If they differ, then we can conclude that either the input variables or the node code have changed. In this case, the node is re-computed. Otherwise, nothing is done and we can ensure that the output variable is up-to-date. Checking the mentioned hashes and eventually re-computing a node is defined as node *evaluation*.

Depending on the results requested, some nodes of the DFG do not need to be evaluated, e.g., in Fig. 2, the node n_5 is not evaluated because the result of n_4 only is requested and does not depend on n_5. Given the entire DFG, defined as G, we also define as *evaluated subgraph* $G_{\{x,z\}}$, the subgraph composed by the nodes and all parent nodes producing the output variables x and z. To obtain these variables, we evaluate each node in $G_{\{x,z\}}$ following their topological order.

2.2 Modem Trace Processing

In the context of modem trace processing, defining the computations as a DFG with persistent memoization is well suited because of the architecture of the tracing system. Usually, the formats of the trace messages logged from two sub-components belonging to the same sub-system have some common semantics. For instance, the sub-component timings will rely on the clock of the sub-system and, therefore, their timeframe will have the same semantics. In Fig. 3, we present the DFG structure for modem trace processing. In the depicted FDG, a node from layer B is typically responsible to extract and retrieve the clock information for a specific sub-system.

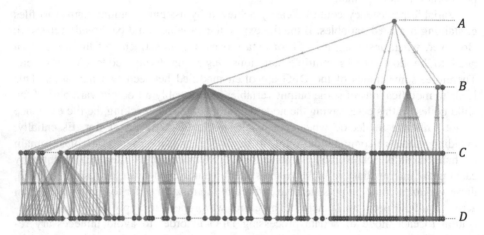

Fig. 3. Data flow graph for modem trace processing. Following the notation of Fig. 2, the blue subgraph denotes node evaluations performed during the previous iteration and the red subgraph denotes additional node evaluations performed during the current iteration. The nodes in the lower layer, i.e., layer D, produce the meaningful event sequences. They are fed by standardized HW/SW modem events produced by layer C nodes. Layer B nodes produce sub-system-specific data and the node in layer A is responsible to import the compressed raw data into the language-specific data structure. (Color figure online)

2.3   Results

In the following, we provide specific trace processing timings recorded for a data set of 20 traces of around 100 MB.

First, the size of the variables produced by the nodes typically does not exceed 10 MB. Therefore, the time required to save a variable and compute its hash, evaluated on a standard computer, typically does not exceed 250 ms. In comparison, the averaged node processing time is 82 s for the layer A node, 11 s for layer B nodes, 3.4 s for layer C nodes and 1.2 s for layer D nodes.

Secondly, we evaluate the iteration processing time by extracting 5 additional event sequences for each trace processing iteration. We perform 19 iterations which finally result in a total of 95 event sequences. In Fig. 4, we compare the processing time between the standard sequence extraction without persistent memoization and our proposed memoized sequence extraction.

We can observe that the first iteration takes a few more seconds for the memoized trace processing compared to the standard one. This is additional overhead is due to data saving and hashing. However, for the next iterations, we notice that up to 84.5% of the processing time duration can be saved. This processing time optimization is crucial when interacting with a trace data set, e.g., in order to iteratively observe additional event sequences or to obtain fast results for a small set of event sequences.

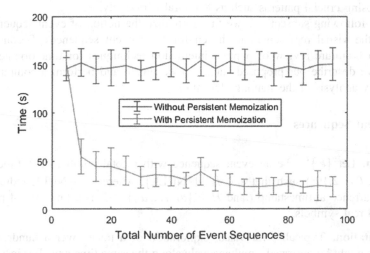

Fig. 4. Time required to iteratively extract 95 event sequences. In each iteration, 5 additional random event sequences are extracted. The timing of each trace processing iteration is evaluated on a data set containing 20 raw traces (100 MB) for both standard processing (without persistent memoization) and optimized processing (with persistent memoization).

3   Entropy-Based Visual Data Interaction

Visual exploration of a trace is a key step for many workflows. When dealing with a modem trace, an efficient visual representation and data interaction mechanism allow to rapidly navigate between key events in order to better understand what is happening in the trace. For instance, a verification engineer needs to check that the connection between the mobile device and the network is well set up, maintained and closed properly. These mechanisms are constantly signaled in the modem trace by events occurring throughout the data exchange. If some anomalies are detected, additional event occurrences from other sub-components need to be visualized, in order to locate the root cause of the anomaly. In general, trace visual exploration helps to understand the behavior of a system in order to detect anomalies, identify possible optimizations or even to ensure that tracing or trace processing is performed correctly. In machine workflows, a predictive model might achieve bad accuracy on one trace compared to the accuracy achieved on the entire data set. In such cases, visually exploring the trace with domain experts is a crucial step to improve the accuracy of such outliers. In these workflows, the interactivity highly depends on the ease of visual exploration of event sequences. Therefore, we propose a data interaction mechanism, which we also called *slanting*, that allows to vary the amount of information presented to the domain expert without losing crucial patterns such as temporal periodicity.

In the following subsections, we first formalize the notion of event sequence and describe the visual representation chosen for trace event sequences. Secondly, we perform a literature review of popular interaction techniques for time-oriented data. Finally, we describe our proposed slanting mechanism and perform a computational complexity analysis of the slanting algorithm.

3.1   Event Sequences

Definition. Let $\{e_t\}_{t=1}^{T}$ be an event sequence with a total number of T timestamps (typically $T \approx 2.10^5$) such that $e_t \in \mathcal{H} \cup \{\text{NULL}\}$, where $e_t \leftarrow \text{NULL}$ indicates no event occurrence at timestamp t and $\mathcal{H} = \{a_1, \ldots, a_H\} \subset \mathbb{R}$ is a finite set of possibly unordered real symbols.

Representation. Typically, for visual exploration of a trace, over a hundred event sequences might be observed simultaneously along the same time axis. For instance, in the DFG of Fig. 3, more than 50 different event sequences might be extracted to be observed together. We propose to use the *lasagna* representation [4]. It is well suited to explore juxtaposition of dozens of event sequences (at most hundreds) as it encodes

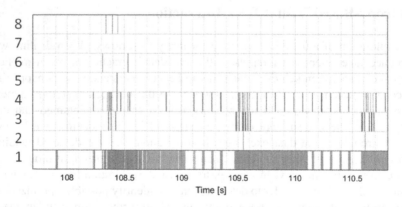

Fig. 5. Modem trace chunk of length 2600 ms containing 8 event sequences. The white color always denotes no event occurrences, i.e., NULL values. Some event occurrences are not displayed due to image downsampling.

values in colors using a small and constant amount of vertical space. Essentially, each event sequence is represented as a layer through time and can have its independent color coding. In Fig. 5, we depict a lasagna representation of event sequences from an exemplary modem trace.

3.2   Time-Oriented Data Interaction

Considering 50 event sequences sampled at millisecond scale and captured during 200 s, we obtain a visualization matrix of size 50×200000. From the higher level perspective, i.e., when visualizing the entire time range, downsampling allows simple overview of the data distribution with a loss of detailed information, e.g., isolated events, and zoom-in enables quick inspection with a better precision at the cost of context information loss.

In the literature [5], 2 popular interaction techniques for time-oriented data are commonly used to present different levels of detail while preserving some context information:

- **Overview+Detail:** This method simultaneously presents an overview and detailed view of the information. The overview plot can be used to rapidly navigate to interesting regions while the detailed plot provides precise insights. However, as explained in [6], the mental effort required to integrate the distinct views as well as the loss of screen space is a notable disadvantage of such approach.
- **Focus+Context:** This method smoothly integrates a distortion centered on the area of interest, also called the focal region. The resulting visualization is a lens effect that allows fast detail exploration when implemented dynamically. However, the distortion effect might prevent the user to make relative spatial judgments [6]. Moreover, the longer the event sequence lasts and the higher the focal length is, the more sensitive the focal region is, i.e., small shifts of a high zoom lens on a long event sequence imply rapid moves of the focal region, which might not be suitable for fine view adjustments.

In some cases, the row height can also be used as supplementary dimension to encode high firing rates and therefore avoiding information loss when zooming out. In CloudLines [7], each row is a white canvas where small colored shapes, usually dots, represent events. When zooming out, nearby overlapping shapes are merged into an equivalent shape of greater height. However, this visualization technique assumes by default that higher firing rates should imply greater attention. In our case, an isolated event might also be crucial for sequence inspection.

3.3 Zoom+Slant

To overcome the limitations highlighted in the previous subsection, we propose a *Zoom +Slant* approach which combines the classical zoom interaction together with a slant interaction, also called *slanting*, described in Fig. 6. Given an event sequence $\{e_t\}_{t=1}^T$, slanting applies such that $e_{t+1} \leftarrow e_t$ only if $e_{t+1} = \text{NULL}$ and if $e_t \neq \text{NULL}$. For each event sequence, this procedure is executed s times, with $s \in \mathbb{N}^*$ defined as the *slant index*. The resulting slanted event sequence will be written as $\{e\langle s\rangle_t\}_{t=1}^T$ in the rest of the paper.

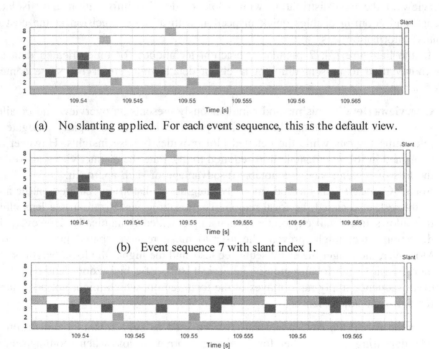

(a)   No slanting applied. For each event sequence, this is the default view.

(b)   Event sequence 7 with slant index 1.

(c)   Event sequence 4 with slant index 2 and event sequence 7 with slant index 19.

Fig. 6. Slanting applied on the same set of event sequences at different slant indexes.

3.4 Algorithm and Computational Complexity

We formally describe the slanting procedure in Algorithm 1.

Algorithm 1. Slanting Procedure

Require: $s > 0$, $\{e_t\}_{t=1}^T$

```
 1:  i ← 0
 2:  E ← {t|eₜ ≠ NULL}
 3:  while E ≠ ∅ and i < s do
 4:     i ← i + 1
 5:     F ← ∅
 6:     for all t ∈ E do
 7:        if eₜ₊₁ = NULL and t + i ≤ T then
 8:           eₜ₊₁ ← eₜ
 9:        else
10:           F ← F + {t}
11:        end if
12:     end for
13:     E ← E − F
14:  end while
```

In practice, slanting can be applied to each event sequence separately and is controlled by a slider. This allows the user to find the optimal slant index for each event sequence. Since the entire line is modified at once, the computation duration can be significantly long. Therefore, we perform a complexity analysis of the proposed algorithm.

Let N_{seq} be the number of slanted event sequences, the algorithm time complexity is $O(sTN_{seq})$. However, it is possible to vectorize the code to handle efficiently multiple event sequence at the same time. Moreover, in Algorithm 1, it is also possible to vectorize the loop from line 6 to 12. These optimizations can significantly optimize the rendering time by reducing the complexity to $O(s)$. In Fig. 7, we summarize the execution time of the vectorized algorithm, implemented with MATLAB® on a 2.80 GHz Intel® Core™ i5-7440HQ with 32 GB of RAM, each value being encoded on 16 bits. A simple linear regression gives an accurate model ($R^2 \geq 0.997$) of the execution time as a function of the slant index. We perform the analysis for different number of event occurrences N_{occ}, different number of event sequences as well as different trace lengths T. In general, we only observe significant variations of the execution time when the slant index changes, which confirms the estimated complexity result of $O(s)$. Typical slant indexes are not greater than 500, and therefore, the rendering time rarely exceeds 3 s which does not harm the interactivity of the visual exploration.

Time (s)

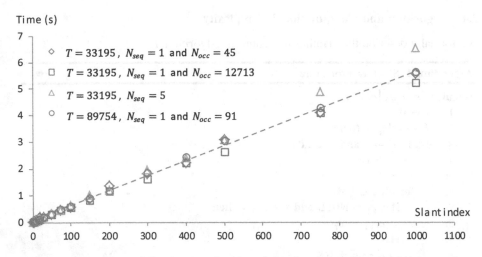

Fig. 7. Rendering time of slanting as a function of the slant index. The simulations are done with event sequences of different lengths T, containing different numbers of event occurrences N_{seq} and on different numbers of event sequences in parallel N_{occ}.

3.5   Slanting Usage

In this subsection, we present three different ways to use slanting as analytical tool:

- **Event sequence magnification.** In Fig. 8, we compare the default view with the slanted view of the same set of event sequences. We can observe that the time patterns are much more visible in the slanted view. Moreover, other meaningful conclusions like anomaly detection can be rapidly drawn in the slanted view. For instance, in Fig. 8b, a regular synchrony pattern can be observed between event sequences 4 and 5. But at timestamp 111.2, we can observe that this synchrony is broken. From a system engineering or verification point of view, such information is crucial to identify potential optimizations or bugs.
- **Periodicity anomaly detection.** Increasing progressively the slant index allows to detect fine periodicity inconsistencies as depicted in Fig. 9. In this case, it is possible to visually identify an atypical event interval of 13 ms when the standard event periodicity is 12 ms.
- **Contextual enhancement.** When observing a small event sequence chunk, e.g., with a width of 100 ms, other events can occur before in the past, outside of the observation window. Thus, they are not visible although they might indicate important contextual information. For instance, in a modem trace, a buffer status message containing information about the number of bits to be transmitted might occur before the observed window containing the actual data transmission events. When the buffer status event sequence is slanted, the buffer status message can be visible in the observation window.

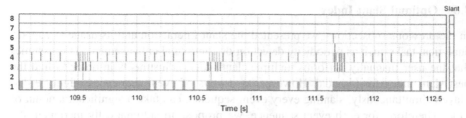

(a)   No slanting applied. Some event sequences seem to be empty because of image downsampling.

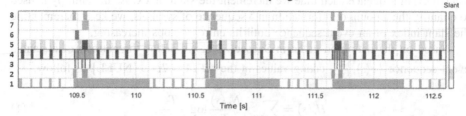

(b)   Slanted view of event sequences with different slant indexes. Event occurrences are visible even in long time chunks.

Fig. 8. Comparison of the default view and the slanted view of the same set of event sequences in an observation window of 3621 ms.

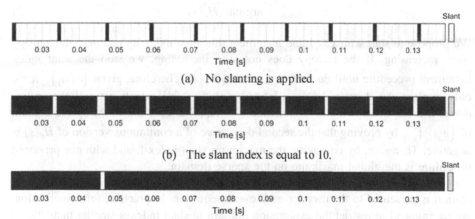

(a)   No slanting is applied.

(b)   The slant index is equal to 10.

(c)   The slant index is equal to 11. One event interval (13 ms) is greater than the others which are all equal to 12 ms.

Fig. 9. Visual detection of fine periodicity anomalies using slanting.

3.6   Optimal Slant Index

In the previous subsections, we presented the slant interaction and its usage to support analytical tasks such as periodicity detection or contextual enhancement. This assumes that the user manually performs multiple slant index adjustments in order to find the best slant index for his goal. However, as dozens of event sequences might be displayed simultaneously, slanting every event sequence can take a significant amount of time. Therefore, for each event sequence, we propose to automatically increment the slant index until a stop criteria is satisfied. In essence, we compute the entropy of the slanted event sequence each time we increment the slant index. As the entropy is used to quantify the amount of information in a sequence of symbols, we keep incrementing the slant index of an event sequence until its entropy stops increasing.

Based on the definition given in Subsect. 3.1, we define the entropy of a slanted event sequence $\left\{e\langle s\rangle_t\right\}_{t=1}^T$ taking values in the set $\mathcal{A} = \mathcal{H} \cup \{\text{NULL}\}$ as follow,

$$H_e(s) = \sum_{a \in \mathcal{A}} \frac{N_a(s)}{T} \log \frac{T}{N_a(s)}, \tag{1}$$

with s being the slant index, $N_a(s)$ being the number of occurrences of event $a \in \mathcal{H}$ in the event sequence $\left\{e\langle s\rangle_t\right\}_{t=1}^T$. Basically, the optimal slant index s_{max} is obtained by solving

$$s_{max} = \text{argmax}_s H_e(s). \tag{2}$$

We propose to start with $s = 1$ and increment this slant index by one until the entropy stops increasing. If the entropy does not stop increasing, we stop the slant index increment procedure until $\exists a \in \mathcal{H} \mid N_{\text{NULL}}(s) \leq N_a(s)$. Therefore, given $\left\{e\langle s\rangle_t\right\}_{t=1}^T$, we only explore the domain $\{s|N_{\text{NULL}}(s) > N_a(s), \forall a \in \mathcal{H}\}$ which we call the *sparse domain*. It can be shown that the function $s \to H_e(s)$ is concave on the sparse domain of $\left\{e\langle s\rangle_t\right\}_{t=1}^T$ by proving that the second derivative of a continuous version of $H_e(s)$ is negative. Therefore, by concavity, the maximum slant index found with our proposed procedure is the global maximum on the sparse domain.

Using this entropy-based slant criteria ensures that a maximum amount of information is presented to the user for each event sequence. In practice, for visualization, we recommend to restrict the exploration domain to slant indexes smaller than s_{max}^{viz}, a maximal visualization slant index such that an isolated event occurrence slanted at this index is represented by only one or two pixels after image downsampling. Essentially, as soon as isolated event occurrences are visible, there is no need to further increase the slant index. Indeed, the more we increase the slant index, the higher the risk is that two isolated event occurrences become visually contiguous, thus losing the information on the absence of event occurrence in between. In Fig. 10, we compare the default view of a trace together with its entropy-based slanted view.

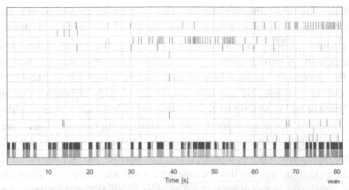

(a)   Default view. Some event occurrences are not visible.

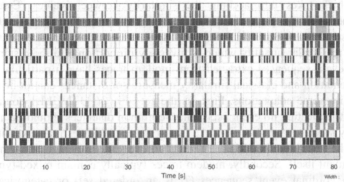

(b)   Entropy-based slanted view. The event occurrences are directly visible. The user can identify the interesting chunks, zoom in and adapt the slant index once zoomed in the chunk. In this case, the slant index is bound to $s_{max}^{viz} = 400$ for every event sequence.

Fig. 10. Two different views of a typical modem trace of length 81479 ms containing 21 event sequences. In one click, it is possible to apply the entropy-based slant modification on every event sequence independently in order to magnify the time patterns as depicted in (b) whereas they are less visible without slanting as depicted in (a).

4 Similarity Measure for Subsequence Matching

When exploring an event sequence $\{e_t\}_{t=1}^{T}$, *subsequence matching* consists in finding subsequences similar to a reference pattern $\{x_n\}_{n=1}^{N}$. This reference pattern can be a subsequence extracted from $\{e_t\}_{t=1}^{T}$ directly or from another event sequence. Subsequence matching is a common task in time-oriented data mining. In particular, for modem traces that typically contain around $T = 10^5$ timestamps, usual data mining tasks often involve subsequence matching with reference patterns containing $N = 100$ timestamps. For instance, in order to optimize timers of specific sub-components, e.g., defining the optimal timer duration before entering low power mode, a system engineer would identify a reference pattern $\{x_n\}_{n=1}^{N}$ where the timer duration is too long. Based on this observation, the timer duration can be reduced in order to save power. However, this optimization would only have a significant impact if the scenario represented by the reference pattern $\{x_n\}_{n=1}^{N}$ is frequent enough along the entire trace. Therefore, quantifying the density of similar patterns in the trace is a crucial step of such analyses.

Although the protocols in mobile communications are well defined, two time patterns representing one specific scenario might be slightly different. For instance, sending one IP packet and receiving its acknowledgment from the server might result in slightly different event sequences for some modem components. Therefore, when evaluating the similarity between time patterns, the similarity metrics usually take into account possible jitters of event occurrences, i.e., the smaller the deviations in time are, the more the time patterns are similar. In essence, a subsequence matching algorithm has a *temporal similarity* component that takes into account the deviations along the temporal dimension. Additionally, such an algorithm also has a *spatial similarity* component which takes into account the similarity between values. Essentially, quantifying the spatio-temporal similarity between two sequences can be done by defining a distance between their mathematical representation. In such cases, the similarity is a real scalar quantity which is inversely proportional to the distance.

However, event sequences extracted from modem traces have a particular mathematical representation and classical similarity measures or distances cannot be directly used and require some adaptations. First, as the set $\mathcal{A} = \mathcal{H} \cup \{\text{NULL}\}$ contains the NULL element, indicating no event occurrence, common distances should be modified as they usually work on sets like $\mathbb{R}$ or $\mathbb{C}$. In our case, the lowest value of similarity should be reached between the NULL element and every other element in $\mathcal{A}$ including the NULL element itself. Secondly, modem traces typically contain mixed-type event sequences, e.g., ordinal event sequences ($\mathcal{H}$ is an ordered set) or categorical event sequences ($\mathcal{H}$ is an unordered set). Therefore, in this section, we propose and define a similarity measure that can be applied on two sequences $\{x_n\}_{n=1}^{N}$ and $\{y_n\}_{n=1}^{N}$ both taking values in $\mathcal{A} = \mathcal{H} \cup \{\text{NULL}\}$ with the set $\mathcal{H} = \{a_1, \ldots, a_H\} \subset \mathbb{R}$ possibly ordered or not.

4.1   Definition

Given two sequences $\{x_n\}_{n=1}^{N}$ and $\{y_n\}_{n=1}^{N}$ taking values in $\mathcal{A} = \mathcal{H} \cup \{\text{NULL}\}$ with $\mathcal{H} = \{a_1, \ldots, a_H\} \subset \mathbb{R}$, we define the discrete signal $X_h[n]$ such that $\forall n \in [\![1, N]\!]$ and $\forall h \in [\![1, H]\!]$,

$$\begin{cases} X_h[n] = e^{-\frac{(x_n - a_h)^2}{\sigma^2}} & \text{if } x_n \in \mathcal{H}, \\ X_h[n] = 0 & \text{if } x_n = \text{NULL}, \end{cases} \tag{3}$$

with σ the *kernel width*. Similarly, we obtain the discrete signal $Y_h[n]$. As second step, we perform the convolution of these two discrete signals with a Gaussian of width τ and obtain the convolved time series $\hat{X}_h[n]$ and $\hat{Y}_h[n]$. Finally, we define the similarity measure between the two sequences $\{x_n\}_{n=1}^N$ and $\{y_n\}_{n=1}^N$ as follow,

$$S(x,y) = \frac{1}{H}\sum_{h=1}^{H}\left(\frac{\sum_{n=1}^N \hat{X}_h[n]\hat{Y}_h[n]}{\sqrt{\sum_{n=1}^N \hat{X}_h^2[n]}\sqrt{\sum_{n=1}^N \hat{Y}_h^2[n]}}\right) \tag{4}$$

4.2 Procedure

In this subsection, we discuss the three key steps involved in the computation of the similarity measure. Essentially, we combine kernel methods and techniques from spike train analysis [8]. First, we propose to map the values to a high-dimensional space to handle non-linear relationships in the data using the kernel trick [9]. Then, as in [10], we compute the correlation of the two high-dimensional signals convolved with a Gaussian filter.

1. **Kernel trick**. Basically, in Eq. 3, using the radial basis function (RBF) kernel, i.e., $k(x,y) = \exp\left[-(x-y)^2/\sigma^2\right]$ with $(x,y) \in \mathcal{H}^2$, is equivalent to compute the cosine similarity between $\varphi(x)$ and $\varphi(y)$ where $\varphi: x \to \varphi(x)$ is a mapping function into an infinite-dimensional space [9]. It is possible to compute the scalar product $\langle \varphi(x), \varphi(y) \rangle$ needed for the cosine similarity without computing explicitly $\varphi(x)$ and $\varphi(y)$. This is called the kernel trick. As the kernel width σ sets the level of inter-action between the symbols, it is tuned according to the statistical data type. For ordinal values, we set σ in the order of the standard deviation of the symbols in $\mathcal{H}$. However, for categorical values, there is no interaction between symbols as they cannot be ordered and σ is kept very low, typically 1% of the minimum symbol distance. Essentially, in this first step, we quantify the spatial similarity between values in $\mathcal{H}$ and obtain a H-dimensional real-valued discrete signal without NULL element.
2. **Convolution with Gaussian**. In this second step, we set the time scale of inter-action for the temporal similarity between two event sequences as described in [10]. Basically, the greater the Gaussian width τ is, the lower is the influence of the event occurrence time jitter. In essence, we transform the multi-dimensional discrete signal in order to enable the application of distances typically used on classical real-valued time series.
3. **Correlation measure**. This last step is described in Eq. 4. For each symbol a_h, we compute the correlation between the two convolved signals, $\hat{X}_h[n]$ and $\hat{Y}_h[n]$, and average on the set $\mathcal{H}$. It can be shown that $0 \le S(x,y) \le 1$ and that $S(x,x) = 1$. In particular, we have $S(x,y) \approx 1$ for similar event sequences, and $S(x,y) \approx 0$ for dissimilar event sequences.

In particular, given the two sequences $\{x_n\}_{n=1}^N$ and $\{y_n\}_{n=1}^N$, if one of these two sequences is empty, e.g., $x_n = \text{NULL}$ for all n in $[\![1, N]\!]$, we have the lowest similarity value $S(x, y) = 0$. Therefore, our proposed similarity measure implicitly assumes that an event occurrence, i.e., $x_n \neq \text{NULL}$, is always more similar to another event occurrence than to an absence of event occurrence, i.e., $x_n = \text{NULL}$.

4.3   Experimental Setup

We propose to compare our approach with two other methods based on classical distance measures, dynamic time warping (DTW) and short time series (STS) distances [11]. Basically, for these two methods, we apply the following procedure. We identically reproduce step 2 and 3 in order to obtain the real-valued time series without NULL element and then, instead of using the correlation measure (COR) described in step 3, we evaluate the DTW or the STS distance averaged over the h dimensions.

In order to compare the COR, DTW and STS-based measure, we propose to apply them for a binary classification task. Given a reference pattern $\{x_n\}_{n=1}^N$, we construct a labelled data set containing both random sequences and sequences similar to $\{x_n\}_{n=1}^N$, in total M sequences $\{y_n^m\}_{n=1}^N$ with $m \in [\![1, M]\!]$. Then, we compute the similarity or distance of each sequence with the reference pattern. Because the DTW and STS-based measures represents positive distances, we apply a strictly decreasing mapping function to obtain the equivalent similarity measure such that the biggest distance corresponds to a similarity of 0 and the smallest distance to a similarity of 1. Then, for the three similarity measures, as evaluation metric, we compute the area under the receiver operating characteristics (ROC) curve, or AUC [12]. The AUC has the desirable property to be independent of the mentioned mapping function chosen for the DTW and STS-based similarities.

Given a threshold $0 \leq \alpha \leq 1$, the sequence $\{y_n^m\}_{n=1}^N$ is considered as similar to the reference pattern $\{x_n\}_{n=1}^N$ if $S(x, y^m) \geq \alpha$ and dissimilar otherwise. Given α, the true positive rate (TPR) and false positive rate (FPR) are defined as follow,

$$\text{TPR}_\alpha = \frac{\text{Number of \textbf{similar} sequences \textbf{correctly} classified}}{\text{Number of \textbf{similar} sequences}}, \tag{5}$$

$$\text{FPR}_\alpha = \frac{\text{Number of \textbf{dissimilar} sequences \textbf{wrongly} classified}}{\text{Number of \textbf{dissimilar} sequences}}. \tag{6}$$

The ROC curve is defined by the points $(\text{FPR}_\alpha, \text{TPR}_\alpha)$ when sweeping α from 0 to 1. The AUC, i.e., the area under this curve, is equal to 1 for a perfect classifier, 0.5 for a random classifier and 0 in the worst case.

4.4   Event Sequence Data Set

In this subsection, we describe the surrogate data sets used for the AUC comparison that we proposed in the previous subsection. First, we generate reference patterns of length $N = 440$ with two parameters:

- **Set cardinality, or $|\mathcal{H}|$.** Based on typical modem event sequences, we randomly pick the symbols from sets of different cardinality, $|\mathcal{H}| \in \{2, 5, 10\}$.
- **Occurrence ratio, or ρ_{occ}.** We vary the number of event occurrences as a ratio of the pattern length, $\rho_{occ} \in \{1/3, 1/5, 1/10\}$.

For each possible combination of $|\mathcal{H}|$ and ρ_{occ}, we randomly generate 5 reference patterns. Therefore, in total, we have 90 reference patterns with varying set cardinality and occurrence ratio. From each reference pattern, we generate similar event sequences by, first, adding Gaussian distributed jitters with standard deviation $\sigma_j \in \{2, 4, 8, 16\}$, secondly, removing randomly $n_- \in \{0, 2, 4, 8, 16\}$ event occurrences and thirdly, adding randomly $n_+ \in \{0, 2, 4, 8, 16\}$ event occurrences. In total, with every possible combination of σ_j, n_- and n_+, we generate 500 similar sequences for each reference pattern. We extend the data set with 500 dissimilar sequences randomly generated with the parameters $|\mathcal{H}|$ and ρ_{occ} as defined previously.

4.5   Results and Discussion

In total, we generate 90 data sets containing 1000 sequences and compute the AUC on each data set using the COR, DTW and STS-based similarity measures as defined in Subsect. 4.3. The Gaussian filter width is chosen in the order of the standard deviation of the jitter, i.e., $\tau = 6$.

We compute the AUC averaged on the 90 data sets and obtain $\text{AUC}_{\text{COR}} = 98.6\% \,(\pm 1.4\%)$ for the COR-based similarity, $\text{AUC}_{\text{DTW}} = 94.7\% \,(\pm 4.5\%)$ for the DTW-based similarity and $\text{AUC}_{\text{STS}} = 92.2\% \,(\pm 4\%)$ for the STS-based similarity. From these results, we can observe that the classifier using our proposed COR-based similarity outperforms the other ones on average. Also, we notice that the COR-based classifier has a lower standard deviation and thus, is more reliable than the other ones. In Fig. 11, we depict the ROC curves obtained for one of the data sets.

The step 3 of the procedure described in Subsect. 4.2 has a time complexity of $O(HN)$ for the COR-based similarity, $O(HN^2)$ for the DTW-based similarity and $O(HN)$ for the STS-based similarity. Therefore, from a computational complexity point of view, the COR-based approach is also better than the DTW-based approach and equivalent to the STS-based one.

From a human-computer interaction point of view, it is crucial to reduce the similarity computation time while preserving the relevance of the results presented to the user. With a time complexity of $O(HN)$ and a AUC of 98.6%, our proposed COR-based similarity measure achieves the best complexity-accuracy trade-off.

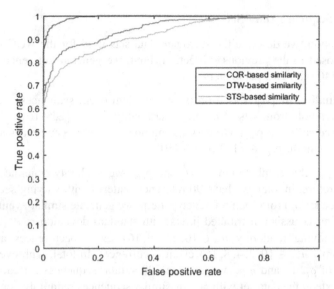

Fig. 11. ROC curves for the COR, DTW and STS-based similarities for one data set generated from one randomly generated reference pattern. The higher the area under the ROC curve is, the better the classifier is. For this data set, the classifier using the COR-based similarity clearly outperforms the classifiers using the DTW-based or the STS-based similarities.

5   Conclusion

In this paper, we propose three possible optimizations to improve the interactivity of data-centric iterative workflows with an application to modem trace analysis. First, we present a methodology based on persistent memoization of intermediate results in order to reduce the trace processing time during a workflow iteration. We show that up to 84.5% of the event extraction time can be spared for a typical modem trace data set. We make available the source code used to implement persistent memoization in data flow graphs[1]. Secondly, we present the Zoom+Slant visual interaction for exploratory analysis of time-oriented data as an alternative to the classical Overview+Detail and Focus+Context interactions. To increase the amount of information shown to the user, we propose an entropy-based algorithm to automatically adjust the slant index. Finally, we present our proposed correlation-based similarity measure for mixed-type event sequences. For a binary classification task, we obtain an averaged AUC of 98.6% with our proposed measure compared to the 94.7% of the DTW-based similarity and the 92.2% of the STS-based similarity.

We believe that our proposed optimizations can efficiently reduce data processing time, data exploration time and analysis time in order to improve the interactivity of iterative workflows. Finally, we think that further real-life experiments shall be

---

[1] Explore: automatic persistent memoization for compute-intensive experiments, Github repository, https://github.com/jahsue78/explore, last accessed 2019/06/24.

conducted with a representative set of users in order to quantify the overall time reduction. In particular, the mental effort to integrate the Zoom+Slant mechanism shall be evaluated in future studies.

References

1. Ah Sue, J., Brand, P., Brendel, J., Hasholzner, R., Falk, J., Teich, J.: A predictive dynamic power management for LTE-Advanced mobile devices. In: 2018 IEEE Wireless Communications and Networking Conference (WCNC), pp. 1–6. IEEE (2018)
2. Dennis, J.: Data flow graphs. In: Padua, D. (ed.) Encyclopedia of Parallel Computing, pp. 512–518. Springer, Boston (2011). https://doi.org/10.1007/978-0-387-09766-4
3. Guo, P.J., Engler, D.: Using automatic persistent memoization to facilitate data analysis scripting. In: Proceedings of the 2011 International Symposium on Software Testing and Analysis, pp. 287–297. ACM (2011)
4. Swihart, B.J., Caffo, B., James, B.D., Strand, M., Schwartz, B.S., Punjabi, N.M.: Lasagna plots: a saucy alternative to spaghetti plots. Epidemiology (Cambridge, Mass.) 21(5), 621 (2010)
5. Aigner, W., Miksch, S., Schumann, H., Tominski, C.: Visualization of Time-Oriented Data. Springer, London (2011). https://doi.org/10.1007/978-0-85729-079-3
6. Cockburn, A., Karlson, A., Bederson, B.B.: A review of overview+detail, zooming, and focus+context interfaces. ACM Comput. Surv. (CSUR) 41(1), 2 (2009)
7. Krstajic, M., Bertini, E., Keim, D.: CloudLines: compact display of event episodes in multiple time-series. IEEE Trans. Visual Comput. Graphics 17(12), 2432–2439 (2011)
8. Brown, E.N., Kass, R.E., Mitra, P.P.: Multiple neural spike train data analysis: state-of-the-art and future challenges. Nat. Neurosci. 7(5), 456 (2004)
9. Schölkopf, B.: The kernel trick for distances. In: Leen, T.K., Dietterich, T.G., Tresp, V. (eds.) Advances in Neural Information Processing Systems, pp. 301–307. MIT Press, Cambridge (2001)
10. Schreiber, S., Fellous, J.M., Whitmer, D., Tiesinga, P., Sejnowski, T.J.: A new correlation-based measure of spike timing reliability. Neurocomputing 52, 925–931 (2003)
11. Zolhavarieh, S., Aghabozorgi, S., Teh, Y.W.: A review of subsequence time series clustering. Sci. World J. (2014)
12. Bradley, A.P.: The use of the area under the ROC curve in the evaluation of machine learning algorithms. Pattern Recogn. 30(7), 1145–1159 (1997)

Evaluating System Sufficiency in a Multimodal, Multiuser Sensemaking Environment Designed for Intelligence Analysis

Shannon Briggs[(✉)]

Rensselaer Polytechnic Institute, Troy, NY 12180, USA
briggs3@rpi.edu

Abstract. This paper discusses a prototype brainstorming tool designed for sensemaking in intelligence analysis and integrates multimodal input in an immersive environment that supports multiple users. This digital tool has been designed using structured analytic techniques already in use through analog methods in the intelligence analysis domain. We discuss an ongoing user study that presents preliminary findings for tool, and suggestions for future development.

Keywords: HCI methods and theories · Multimodal interface ·
Evaluation methods and techniques ·
Qualitative and quantitative measurement and evaluation · User experience

1 Introduction

There have been many digital tools developed for defense and national security venues as a way to enable intelligence analysts and other defense workers to forage for and make sense of information. However, of the software that has been developed, comparatively few overall have been reliably adopted by the intended end users. We propose that developing software that is developed through scenario-based design and sensemaking processes informed by intelligence analysts will create a final product that will be cognitively more approachable and therefore more useful and usable. Currently, the digital brainstorming tool developed and implemented in the Cognitive Immersive Systems Lab (CISL), has been informed by the sensemaking process as described by Pirolli and Card's model [1]. The digital brainstorming tool described in this paper has been designed to support the information-foraging process. We are attempting to transform the analog structured analytic brainstorming technique into an immersive multimodal. We have implemented verbal and gestural technology into the digital, and we have enabled a personal view and a group, or global, view. In this paper, we present preliminary findings of a user study that is currently in progress of the prototype brainstorming digital tool.

© Springer Nature Switzerland AG 2019
C. Stephanidis (Ed.): HCII 2019, LNCS 11786, pp. 140–152, 2019.
https://doi.org/10.1007/978-3-030-30033-3_11

1.1 Previous Work

The following section discusses software that has been developed for the intelligence analysis domain, as well as specific features that have been implemented in these tools to enable sensemaking. These works establish a history of development for the range of functions enabled in software for the intelligence domain.

Taxonomy for Tools Developed for Intelligence Analysis. Prior tools developed for intelligence analysis has approached two of the major problems that analysts face in completing their work: sifting through and filtering large amounts of text data for relevance and representing and manipulating data for improved sensemaking. The former group of tools focus on information management tools, that allows analysts to conduct quantitative measures on text corpora, and provide analysts a space to formalize insight generated by their own expertise and aided by the information provided by the software. The latter group of tools focuses improved sensemaking allowing analysts to represent the data in ways that more easily allow them to draw insights, such as generating timelines, representing data as concept bubbles, and so forth. In both groups the effort is aimed at improving sensemaking for intelligence analysts, while also reducing the cognitive burden of searching for, filtering, and classifying information.

Information Management Tools. Information management is of the major portions of the information-foraging process, and includes searching, filtering, sorting, and marshalling evidence, as described by Pirolli and Card [1]. This stage is important for analysts as they begin to find information that is important to the issues they are concerned with. The cognitive challenge inherent in this stage is information overload, and digital tools, such as those described below, are aimed at assisting analysts in managing information volume, and using algorithms to assist in searching.

Jigsaw is software designed for intelligence analysis especially through text analysis. Gorg et al. [2] discuss the capabilities of the software in their article. Jigsaw is designed to support the sensemaking activities surrounding collecting and organizing textual information by intelligence analysts. The Jigsaw system is designed to provide visualization for different perspectives on information in documents and it supports evidence marshalling through a Shoe Box view. The earliest version of the software focused heavily on visual representation of relationships between entities but did not provide any kind of text analysis. One of the major findings of creating this software was that software functions cannot replace the reading of reports. Repeated careful reading of selected texts tended to be the preferred method to understand the information in texts. As a result, the Jigsaw system incorporated the ability to summarize and cluster similar important text information. From there, the software used packages such as GATE, LingPipe, the OpenCalais system, and the Illinois Named Entity Trigger, to import data from documents.

DIGEST is another tool designed for intelligence analysis, described by Benjamin et al. [3]. Its main capabilities are extracting data from text, such as sentiments, social influence, and information flow structures; the tool also has exploratory data analytics, and finally it uses the stored results to create various knowledge products. After the data collection and processing stage, where analysts can configure the tool to collect data on specific topics, the tool develops a template for information reporting. Finally, the analyst can populate the template with the information the tool has collected. The analyst can choose what information they want included, as well as add any of their own insights to the product.

E-Wall is a visual analytic environment design to support remote sensemaking through the development of what the authors call a virtual transactive memory [4]. The software focuses on object focused thinking, where information is represented as an object, and users construct semantic relations between them. Ewall uses computational agents to infer relationships among data and offer customized insights to users. The E-wall layout is designed to allow users to collaborate while working on information and to allow users to manipulate data in object-like chunks. The E-Wall uses two computational agents to manage information flow, and infers relationships among data types, and another that evaluates databases and suggests data to the user. The E-Wall allows users to navigate large amounts of data independently and minimizes the need for verbal interaction.

Sensemaking Management Tools. Sensemaking is in the second part of the sense-making loop described by Pirolli and Card [1], and includes integrating new information into established schema, generating hypotheses, and presenting analysts' judgements and interpretations. This second group of software can be considered sensemaking management tools, as their scope is to better incorporate information into different types of cognitive frameworks, such as new visualizations, concept maps, and timelines.

The Polestar intelligence analysis toolkit is one of the earliest software suites designed for intelligence analysis [5]. Polestar includes a snippet view of texts, where users could highlight and drag text to the portfolio view for later analysis, and records metadata about the text. Polestar also included a way to start knowledge structuring, such as a wall of facts similar to the sticky-note exercise taught in intelligence analysis classes. This software included a timeline feature, to allow analysts a way to visualize relationships in data. Polestar included an argument tree editor, allowing analysts to structure and formulate hypotheses in a visual fashion. The dependency viewer allowed users to trace back where a document or object was found in the dependency network.

VisPorter, is a collaborative text analytics tool aimed toward allowing sensemaking in a collaborative environment [6]. The software is meant for multi-user engagement and the designers focused on different elements such as haptic touch, lighting, and to explore how people forage for information to share hypotheses. The VisPorter software includes the Foraging tool, which contains the document viewer and the concept map viewer, and the Synthesis tool, which allow users to share information found individually with the foraging tools. Some of the features included in this software was gesture-based interaction, with an example of someone with a small display flipping a document off the left side of their device, and having it be shared and dropped on the right side of a synced large display.

Wright et al. [7] introduce Sandbox, which explains human information interaction capabilities, such as 'put this there' cognition, automatic process model templates, gestures for fluid expression of thought, assertions with evidence, and scalability metrics. The authors take note of the use of Post-its by to organize and sort ideas, and is then translated into a feature called MindManager, which employed concept map strategies to allow diagrammatic visual representations. The software is designed to adapt to different types of analysts and analytical styles. The software also incorporates a source attribution and context function.

GeoTime is a software system designed for analysts to map geo-temporal events. Geo-Time explores part of intelligence analyst's process of using narration to make sense of events of interest [8]. The software employs a space-time pattern finding system, which relieves the analyst from effort of searching for common patterns and events. The second part of the system relies on visual annotations, which takes the visual information and attaches relevant information. The final part of the software is a text editor that allows analysts to make relevant comments on the found information. GeoTime uses a collaborative environment but also emphasizes a data-aware object, where annotations are embedded in time and space, so these become a new piece of information connected to the found information. GeoTime is also interested in allowing analysts to work on a meso-level, such as behavioral trends, events, and plots, rather than an individual unit.

1.2   Digital Brainstorming Tool

The digital brainstorming tool developed by CISL allows a digital space for human analysts to put into practice cognitive techniques already familiar to them. The digital brainstorming tool can be considered as an information visualization tool as well as a schema representation tool. The tool was designed to enable human collaboration and sensemaking during intelligence analysis, and we hope to achieve create a cognitively more accessible product by applying the intended users' domain knowledge to our software development.

Our approach to designing a tool that will assist in sensemaking for the domain was to consult and integrate techniques described in educational materials into the software design of the brainstorming tool. The specific process for the digital tool is a structured analytic technique called brainstorming, and analysts write salient pieces of data on sticky notes and creates topic groups from these notes. This structured analytic technique incorporates timed periods of reading, analysis, and collaboration, to gain a diverse perspective about the information. Our research anticipates that communication between users is an important part of the collaborative process and therefore our tool integrates deliberate periods of interaction among users to collaborate on theories.

One of the major insights from discussion with analysts is that digital tools that are too cumbersome to use, or tools that require analysts to step outside of their workflow to interact with tend to be left behind.

The digital brainstorming tool is a digital tool that is based on the pen and paper version of the structured analytic technique used by intelligence analysts, as described by Beebe and Pherson [9]. The digital tool is displayed via five projectors onto a 360-degree panoramic screen. The digital brainstorming tool allows viewers to generate digital sticky notes, and users can interact with the system through gesture technology using Kinect cameras to capture body frame and gestures [10], and through verbal commands to the Watson system using lapel mics. This system allows user to interact with the digital tool in a manner that mimics the analog interactions that are found in the structured analytic tool, and provides a more immersive experience. The digital brainstorming tool has two major components, the global view and the personal view. The global view can be seen in Fig. 1, and the personal view can be seen in Fig. 2. The global view is projected onto the panoramic screens in the immersive environment, allowing users to discuss with each other and interact with the system; the personal view is accessed through any personal device that is equipped with a web browser.

Fig. 1. Global view of the digital brainstorming tool.

The system is accessible separately and simultaneously through the global and personal views, allowing a myriad of interaction types for users. Users are able to interact remotely with the personal view, viewing others' notes on the global view, and adding and categorizing their own and others' through the touch and type interface of technology such as tablets and laptops. The global view allows users to move sticky

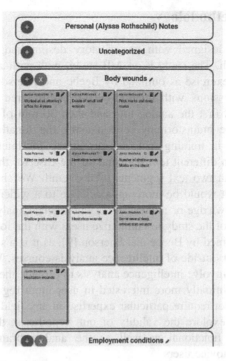

Fig. 2. Personal view of the digital brainstorming tool.

notes on the shared 360-degree screen, and issue verbal commands to interact with the system (Table 1). The breakdown of the current capabilities of the system are as follows:

Table 1. Capabilities of the digital brainstorming tool

Functions	Global view	Personal view
Create note	Voice	All functions are enabled on the personal view's UI
Delete note	Voice	
Move note	Gesture/voice	
Edit note	Voice	
Move note	Gesture/voice	
Categorize note	Gesture/voice	
Create category	Voice	
Delete category	Voice	
Rename category	Voice	

2 User Study Methodology

The user study was designed with participatory design and sensemaking design informing our approach. The study is an A/B study, with participants engaging in an analog brainstorming exercise as outlined by Beebe and Pherson [9]. The study was conducted in 1-hour sessions, with small groups of two to three participants engaging in 30 min segments of first the analog tool and then 30 min of the digital tool. Participants completed the brainstorming session using the Jonathan Luna case study, which is in wide use in training materials developed for intelligence analysts [9]. Participants were given different text segments of the case for the analog portion and the digital portion, with two text segments used overall. We chose the Luna murder case study as we felt it would be more approachable to a wider participant base and required less prior knowledge or interest in the intelligence analysis domain. We also use the analog session of the study to familiarize users with the format of the structured analytic technique outlined by Beebe and Pherson [9], as it is a specific technique that is unlikely to be taught outside of intelligence analysis courses. While later-stage user testing of the tool will involve intelligence analysts to provide their feedback and input for the tool, we were initially more interested in user input regarding basic usability functions that would not require particular expertise in any field or discipline. Particularly, we wanted to explore the validity of our hypothesis: that the digital brainstorming tool would functional as well as the analog brainstorming tool as a sensemaking tool for novice users

We used user surveys for both analog and digital phases. Participants completed separate user surveys after each 30-minute session and were invited to participate in a brief question and answer session at the end of each 30-minute segment. Our surveys asked questions about previous experience with experience in intelligence analysis, experience with brainstorming exercises and software. Participants were recruited from the student body at the university, and overall were novel to this structured brainstorming techniques. All participants were first time or novice users of the interaction technology with the digital tool. We felt this was important to determine the tool's usability to users who are at baseline unfamiliar with the underlying technology, as we posit that most potential users are not going to be familiar with gesture recognition or voice recognition technology in context of an intelligence analysis sensemaking tool. We used think-aloud protocol for our digital tool segment, inviting participants to voice their thoughts as they interacted with the tool, so that we could capture their unfiltered impression of the digital tool as they worked. A more thorough explanation of the digital and analog portions of the experiment is described below

We captured video data and audio data for the experiment, and logged user's actions with the system to determine which users made which notes and categories. Video data is used to record the analog sensemaking process, as well as to give a complete picture of the digital sensemaking process. We are also able to understand users' observations and utterances as pertaining to the system and their interactions.

Analog Testing Procedure. Participants were given a text copy of a text segment of the Jonathan Luna murder case, and each participant was given a pack of differently colored sticky notes. Participants were given a 5-minute period to read the provided text segment, then were given another 5 min to write pieces of evidence from the case study on separate sticky notes. Participants then spent 5 min putting their sticky notes on a shared wall, with each participant laying out their own sticky notes in separate small groups according to topic. Participants then spent 5-10 min discussing and rearranging the notes into shared groups, sorted by common ideas into categories. A brainstorming facilitator was used to time each of the five-minute segments and move participants into the next stage of brainstorming.

Digital Testing Procedure. Participants were given a brief tutorial describing the functions of the digital brainstorming tool, and tablets were distributed to each participant to allow them to access the personal view. Participants were then given a text copy of the second segment of the Jonathan Luna case study, which was also available on the global view of the system and was viewable by all participants. Participants were given 5 min to read the text segment, after which they were given a further 5 min to write pieces of evidence using the personal view on the tablets. Participants were then given 5 min to then use the tablets to send their notes to the global view and sort their notes into separate groups using the gesture technology. Participants were finally given a final 5 min to discuss their notes with each other and rearrange notes and create categories using the personal view and the global view. As with the analog exercise, a brainstorming facilitator timed the five-minute segments and moved participants along the brainstorming session.

Hypotheses. As our user study is an AB comparison study, we are interested in how the digital brainstorming tool performs compared against the traditional brainstorming pen and paper brainstorming tool. We are interested to see if the digital brainstorming tool is as sufficient as the pen and paper process in allowing users to make sense of information as they are working through the case study. We decided to focus on two major aspects of the brainstorming tool that are reflective of the brainstorming process regardless of format: the overall number of sticky notes created per session, and how many notes were put into categories. These two features emphasize participants' interaction with the brainstorming tool and interaction with other participants, as number of sticky notes is the result of participants examining the sample case study, extracting of information from the case study, recording data, and then finally discussing information that was found individually as a group, and notes grouped per category allows us to see how participants' used the system to agree on how the information can be categorized by consensus,

H1: The digital brainstorming tool is as sufficient as the traditional analog brainstorming tool in enabling sensemaking if users are able to create as many notes within the digital system as they can with the analog tool.

H2: The digital tool is sufficient as a sensemaking tool compared to the analog tool if users are able to categorize notes as efficiently as they do with the analog tool.

3 Results

3.1 Digital Sticky Notes

As this digital tool is based on an existing analog cognitive exercise, our current interest is to discover if the digital tool is as sufficient as the analog tool; that is, if the digital tool as a medium for participants to conduct a brainstorming session is as easy to use as the established analog tool. Our way of measuring this is number of sticky notes generated per group per session, as we assume that if the digital tool were much harder to use than the analog tool, then participants wouldn't be able to create as many sticky notes as they had in the analog portion. Therefore, for H1 we examined are number of notes users were able to generate per session. Our hypothesis is that the digital tool can be considered as useful as the previously developed analog tool if users were able to develop as many notes or more on the digital tool as they were able to create using analog sticky notes. The table below shows a breakdown of number of notes users generated across 5 sessions between the analog and digital sessions (Table 2).

Table 2. Number of sticky notes across analog and digital sessions

Session number	Analog session	Digital session
Session 1	16	15
Session 2	25	19
Session 3	20	6
Session 4	16	13
Session 5	46	31

Overall, we had largely positive results in comparing the number of notes users were able to create in the digital tool versus the analog tool. We found that users created nearly as many notes with the digital tool as with the analog tool, save for session 3, which was terminated due to technical problems. We do note that while there are fewer notes overall for the digital session which we further examine in the discussion section.

3.2 Digital Categories

The second point we examine is comparing number of categories and number of notes per category between the analog brainstorming tool and the digital brainstorming tool. Creating categories is a major discussion point between participants, so the number of categories can help us understand if participants are able to use the digital tool to make sense of the information they have collected. The number of notes per category helps us understand if participants can interact with the functions of the system to arrange their notes in a way that makes sense to them. The Table below is a breakdown of categories and notes per session (Tables 3 and 4).

Table 3. Analog categories and number of notes in categories per session.

Session number	# Categories	Category 1	Category 2	Category 3	Category 4
Session 1	3	5	10	1	X
Session 2	4	4	7	5	X
Session 3	3	5	3	5	X
Session 4	4	2	4	3	7
Session 5	3	17	15	15	x

Table 4. Digital categories and number of notes per category per session.

Session number	# Categories	Category 1	Category 2	Category 3	Category 4	Uncategorized
Session 1	2	2	3	2	1	1
Session 2	3	3	2	8	X	X
Session 3	3	7	4	2	X	2
Session 4	3	6	5	2	X	X
Session 5	4	10	7	9	5	X

For H2, we found that users generally created one fewer category using the digital tool than the analog tool and had more uncategorized notes than with the analog tool. We posit that this may be due to the somewhat more difficult process of creating categories through the digital tool function. An alternative interpretation is that using the digital tool allows for more discussion time, as we observed it takes less time to share notes and create categories, which we confirmed in session five that that users of the digital tool create more categories when greater time is allowed during the discussion phase. We feel that further modifying the ability to create categories in a more natural fashion may improve users' ability to create categories and properly categorize notes.

3.3   Discussion

While our current participant pool response is limited in size, we are continuing to run user studies to gain further understanding of the ability of the digital brainstorming tool as a sensemaking aid. We found that users' responses to the tool became more favorable as we implemented usability improvements to the software between user testing sessions. Participants gave valuable feedback in both functionality interactions and interfaces features, which we are continuing to implement for further user studies. Overall, the user experience with the digital tool was mixed, but improved with features that focused on ease of use. Based on user responses, we implemented the ability to edit category names, a clearer way of editing notes via the personal view, and a way to view voice commands on the global view. Similarly, most users responded positively to basic aspects of the digitization of the tool, such as freedom offered by the digital format of the sticky notes, being able to read others' notes clearly, being able to read transcripts of the conversation, and voice interactions. In general, participants felt that the gestures system was intuitive.

Sticky Notes. The content for the sticky notes in the digital session are largely similar across sessions, indicating that the tool is sufficient in allowing users to extract a baseline level of information from the sample case study. Based on the results of the user study so far, we find that the digital tool can aid users in creating nearly as many sticky notes and categories as with the pen and paper tools. The reduced number of notes in the digital sessions may be the result of the changed case study text between the analog and digital session rather than an insufficiency in the tool, which we will examine during future user studies. Finally, while the gestures system is able to support multiple users, users often take turns in using the system regardless, as though it were a single user system. We anticipate that with further modifications to the software to ensure stability and robustness that users should be able to surpass number of notes and categories generated, especially considering that the digital system is able to support an unlimited number of notes or categories generated. This feature was particularly important, as it reflects the success of the digital tool in allowing users to create as many notes as necessary to reflect the personal understanding of the sample case study used as needed by each individual user. Given the prototypical nature of our tool, we are encouraged that with modifications for usability and stability, that the digital brainstorming tool shows potential in enabling sensemaking for our use case.

Categories. One of the major differences in the analog and digital tool is the way categories are created and named. As per the pen and paper method, the creation of categories is delineated by notes grouped in proximity, and a label to describe the content of the category is agreed upon by consensus; the recording of that label can take several forms, either above the categories themselves or on a separate paper, and so on. In our study, participants verbally relay category names to the discussion facilitator to discuss their choices for the analog session. However, the digital tool changes that process by manner of the technology; users switch from the personal view, which can be accessed on any web browser, to the gesture and voice technology of the global view. Multiple participants commented on the ability to clearly read both category names and note content, which we believe is an important improvement from the pen and paper tool. We believe that the affordance of clearly written note content helps facilitate discussion of the case study and creation of category labels, as users are not forced to parse others' handwriting, and can more effectively engage in the presented material.

In early iterations of the prototype tool, deletion of a category resulted in deletion of the notes in that category, which also dissuaded users from creating more categories; however, with user feedback, we implemented the ability to transfer notes within a deleted category to the shared view to preserve their content. We feel that further modifying the ability to create categories in a more natural fashion may improve users' ability to create categories and properly categorize notes.

One of our earliest observations in users engaging structured analytic brainstorming with the digital tool was the collapsed time requirement in sending notes up to the shared view. In the analog sessions, the element of bringing physical sticky notes up to a shared wall space is timed, and usually takes up the allotted time for the activity. We have found, however, that in allowing users to instantly send notes to the shared view reduces that time drastically. This allows for a longer discussion period between participants during the final phase where participants discuss note content and how to categorize their notes.

4 Conclusions, Limitations, and Future Work

We have developed a digital sensemaking tool for intelligence analysis based on analog structured analytic techniques, which were created by intelligence analysts. This software differs from previous work in the field, as discussed above, as we implement our software in an immersive environment to mimic analog interactions, and we have designed the tool to be informed by the cognitive techniques developed by intelligence analysts, which we believe will be more useful and usable to the intended user. Our user study was developed using open source information, available through text books and other educational materials. We plan on refining the functions of our system through direct feedback from intelligence analysts who have worked in the domain.

Our digital brainstorming tool is a prototype, and as can be seen through the progress of the user study is being modified to ensure stability, responsiveness, and robustness in order to support the sensemaking process in intelligence analysis. Future modifications of the tool will be focused on implementing more gestures, overall smoothness of interaction with the different multimodal inputs, and ways in which to link the brainstorming tool with other digital sensemaking tools. We will also be introducing the digital tool to participants in a more formalized demo before testing in order to allow future users to acclimate interacting with the tool.

For future work, we will continue to run our user study to add to the body of data we have collected, and we will supplement our analyses of the data gathered with statistical insight. We are particularly interested in understanding how the medium of the tool affects issues such as how many sticky notes are generated and how many categories are created. We are soliciting feedback and advice from former intelligence analysts, and will run a user study to gain their reactions to the system. We also plan to investigate the issue of cognitive load and how our digital tool can reduce elements of cognitive load during the intelligence analysis process.

Acknowledgements. I would like to acknowledge Matthew Peveler, Jaimie Drozdal, Lilit Balagyozan, and Hui Su, who have all contributed to the material presented in this paper.

References

1. Pirolli, P., Card, S.: Sensemaking processes of intelligence analysts and possible leverage points as identified through cognitive task analysis. In: Proceedings of the 2005 International Conference on Intelligence Analysis, McLean, Virginia (2005)
2. Görg, C., Liu, Z., Parekh, N., Singhal, K., Stasko, J.: Jigsaw meets Blue Iguanodon - The VAST 2007 Contest. In: In IEEE Symposium on Visual Analytics Science and Technology (2007)
3. Benjamin, P., Madanagopal, K., Erraguntla, M., Corlette, D.: Distributed Information Gathering, Exploration and Sensemaking Toolkit (DIGEST). In: Proceedings on the International Conference on Artificial Intelligence (ICAI); Athens. pp. 449–455. The Steering Committee of The World Congress in Computer Science, Computer Engineering and Applied Computing (WorldComp), Athens, United States, Athens (2016)

4. Keel, P.E.: EWall: a visual analytics environment for collaborative sense-making. Inf. Visualization **6**, 48–63 (2007). https://doi.org/10.1057/palgrave.ivs.9500142
5. Pioch, N.J., Everett, J.O.: POLESTAR: collaborative knowledge management and sensemaking tools for intelligence analysts. In: Proceedings of the 15th ACM International Conference on Information and Knowledge Management, pp. 513–521. ACM (2006)
6. Chung, H., North, C., Self, J.Z., Chu, S., Quek, F.: VisPorter: facilitating information sharing for collaborative sensemaking on multiple displays. Pers. Ubiquit. Comput. **18**, 1169–1186 (2014)
7. Wright, W., Schroh, D., Proulx, P., Skaburskis, A., Cort, B.: The sandbox for analysis: concepts and methods. In: Proceedings of the SIGCHI Conference on Human Factors in Computing Systems, pp. 801–810. ACM, New York (2006). https://doi.org/10.1145/1124772.1124890
8. Eccles, R., Kapler, T., Harper, R., Wright, W.: Stories in GeoTime. Inf. Visualization **7**, 3–17 (2008). http://dx.doi.org.libproxy.rpi.edu/10.1057/palgrave.ivs.9500173
9. Beebe, S.M., Pherson, R.H.: Cases in Intelligence Analysis: Structured Analytic Techniques in Action. CQ Press, Washington, DC (2014)
10. Divekar, R.R., et al.: CIRA—An Architecture for Building Configurable Immersive Smart-rooms. 10

CiSA: An Inclusive Chatbot Service for International Students and Academics

Jeongyun Heo[✉] and Jiyoon Lee

Kookmin University, 77 JeongNeong-Ro, SeongBuk-Gu, Seoul 02707, Korea
yuniheo@kookmin.ac.kr, ljiny92@gmail.com

Abstract. In the present study, we developed a chatbot service termed 'CiSA' (Chatbot for International Students and Academics) to enable international students and academics to effectively acquire essential information regarding their academic and campus life. To investigate the pain points and needs of our target user group, user research consisting of interviews and surveys was conducted. Based on the key findings from qualitative analysis, the concept was further refined. A flowchart was constructed to illustrate the designed conversations, while the user interface components were determined to express the responses of the chatbot. The design was further prototyped using Google's DialogFlow, and implemented in Facebook Messenger. Finally, the interviews with the target users were conducted to verify the effectiveness, satisfaction, and extensibility of the service. The outcome of this study provides a powerful way to support the facilitation of communication and social inclusion by using this conversational agent. Furthermore, by focusing on enhancing the accessibility, the research contributes towards the practical understanding of the investigation of its service design for chatbot aimed at inclusivity.

Keywords: Conversational agent · Inclusive design · Chatbot

1 Introduction

1.1 Needs for an Inclusive Design in Academic Field

Expanding international trade volume and globalization has increased, the exchange of personnel globally, and is expected to accelerate further. These changes facilitate the improvement of infrastructure and public services. Such attempts can serve as the basis for instilling a sense of respect for cultural diversity and promoting a positive image worldwide [1]. Accordingly, human exchanges are also becoming more vitalized in universities.

Universities are essential educational institutions where students from various social and cultural backgrounds gather for overall self-development. However, academic experiences at a university vary considerably between domestic and international students [2]. In particular, the local optimized systems may present many issues, including accessibility of sufficient resources in different languages, thus inevitably excluding the international students. This being the case, international students face discomfort while navigating and obtaining suitable information [3].

© Springer Nature Switzerland AG 2019
C. Stephanidis (Ed.): HCII 2019, LNCS 11786, pp. 153–167, 2019.
https://doi.org/10.1007/978-3-030-30033-3_12

Regardless of the issues that international students deal with, they must adapt and successfully carry out their studies in different cultural and social backgrounds. Campus life is a big part of the lives of students who go to another country to fulfil their academic needs [4]. Therefore, it is crucial to provide them with effective informative system to make information gathering feasible.

1.2   Adopting Conversational Agent for Inclusive Design

As internationalized education continuously insists upon novel methods to support the system, solution pertaining to artificial intelligence (AI) have been incorporated to improve existing practices in various contexts. Chatbots are one such solution that improve the way of communication between people, enabling them to find information immediately and conveniently. It leverages intelligent technologies to communicate with people using natural language; its conversational interface has been drawing increasing attention, with major applicabilities for the future.

The chatbots have become a central connector of services in the field of education, E-commerce, customer support, and entertainment [5]. They successfully enhance systems in educational institutions and provide immense support to the faculties and students. Several research practices exist regarding the use of chatbots in an academic environment; however, the designing of a chatbot that could provide inclusive solutions to international students in a university campus environment has not, to the best of our knowledge, been systemically undertaken.

This study focused on applying a chatbot to enhance the quality of campus life for international students by improving the accessibility of information for managing school life. To make this possible, an inclusive chatbot service 'CiSA' was designed and implemented at Kookmin University. The chatbot was aimed at accessing the needs of the students and to proactively solve their queries without time-place and language constrains. It facilitates communication and social inclusion among international students by allowing them to experience a welcoming and satisfactory campus life.

The solution gives the students the ability to immediately retrieve information to achieve various goals. 'CiSA' integrates fragmented information present on the online and offline databases without considerable modification. It is utilized as a gate for information acquisition on the messenger platforms that we are already familiar with. The service can act interact with the international students on a one-to-one basis, preventing them from feeling isolated.

1.3   Methodology Overview

First, we examined previous studies related to the application and effects of chatbots in the area of education. We also reviewed the works of inclusive design to refine our concept. In chapter 3, we describe the analysis of the user research with international students and staff at Kookmin University. The next chapter presents the design process of the CiSA, carried out by combining different design processes for the conversational model. In the last chapter, with high-fidelity prototype of the service, we validated its usability using heuristics. By applying this approach, we considered the usage of the chatbot service in the specific segmentation of user for educational purpose and presented a direction for the development of this chatbot for the future.

2 Related Works

2.1 Chatbot and Conversational Agent

A chatbot is a computer program that automates the work process by communicating directly with users and processes user requirements [6]. It integrates multiple services leveraging AI and interacts through conversational interface using natural language.

The interface of conversational AI takes a form of a dialog, which is the most natural mode of interaction [7]. It is intuitive, instinctive, and has high accessibility without any prior learning requirement. The interface is expressed through either voice, text, graphics, or multimodal. The 'Conversation Design Guide' from Google [8] defines the characteristics of the conversational user interface as 'turn-taking', 'threading', and 'verbal shortcut' which are removed from the nature of the conversation. The interface should be designed to take consider the particular object of the conversation, and sufficient research should be done on the users as the interaction is achieved through dialogs.

The chatbot was first introduced in the ELIZA system [9]. After AI and related technologies become popular, intelligent agent(IA) or virtual assistant were actively applied in various services and products. The IA is based on the interaction of the interface: voice and text. The dominant IA actively applied in the industries include Watson (IBM), Google now (Google), Siri (Apple), Cortana (Microsoft), Alexa (Amazon), and Bot (Facebook Messenger).

The main technologies applied to operate a text-based chatbot are pattern recognition, natural language processing (NLP), semantic web, text mining, and text aware computing [10]. The models of a chatbot are divided into two types: retrieval-based models that respond with pre-made answers to the topics, and deep learning based generative models that automatically generate responses [11]. The more open the topics are, the more complicated the system is.

Til date, an effective usage of service-oriented chatbots in industries include E-commerce, FinTech, personal assistant service, public service, education, and entertainment [6, 12–14]. Particularly, the service has been applied for marketing processes such as customer services and reserving, searching, and buying products online [13]. Chatbots strongly influence the states of informing, connecting and communicating between the products and people. It can instantly solve the requests and efficiently navigate users through the database of the company and the user. It also provides two-way interaction which can increase rapport between the company and its customers. Intelligent assistants and the conversational user interface largely supplant the existing interfaces and interactions, performing tasks for us in our everyday life [14].

2.2   Intelligent Technologies in Education Services

Intelligent technologies have been widely adapted in academic environment. AI-driven solutions create innovative processes for tutoring and communicating such as teaching robots and intelligent tutoring systems. The technologies also enabled the provision of AI-driven distant education programs, via conducting classes using virtual reality [15, 16].

Assistants and bots have been actively studied to improve the convenience process of student services and teaching; popular applications include course program advisor and frequently asked question systems to replace physical information desk. A virtual assistant LiSA [17] was developed to help students in university; the study investigated the kinds of services and information that could be effectively provided through chatbot. It has also been designed to act as a communication hub between the students and the faculties. Lim and Goh [18] developed an intelligent conversational bot for massive open online courses (MOOCs) to enhance the interactivity between the instructor and students using text or speech input via connecting through multiple sites. Krassmann et al. [19] improved the utility and satisfaction by perceiving and relating the moods of the students to enhance the experience of distance education program. Kerlyl, A. et al. investigated the chatbot for the teaching process [20], broadening its utilization. Additionally, studies focusing on technological development of a chatbot were conducted; these comprised of implementation of ALICE Chatbot system, application of generative mode, and development of a system based on text similarity [21, 22].

It is evident that, from a technical perspective, the investigations regarding interactive solutions between the users and the chatbot system in the educational institutions are dominant. However, considerable work still needs to be systematically undertaken, utilizing a user-centered approach, to improve the experience of not just the general users but including people of all other sectors as well.

2.3   Inclusive Design

Designing inclusive services requires the consideration that users differ in identity, age, gender, language fluency, impairment, cultural background, nationality, and socioeconomic status. Inclusive design involves making the services usable and satisfactory for the users [23]. It has been promoted as a way of including the needs of excluded user groups and creating services that work for everyone, particularly for older and disabled people [24]. Inclusive designs share similar approaches with Universal Design [25] and Design for All [26]. The essences of inclusive designs are user-centered, population aware, and business focused [27].

The design strategies of inclusive design include the following three stages should be [26]:

- Stage 1 - the problem definition should explicitly include reference to the intended target users;
- Stage 2 - an appropriate design approach for the target users should be adopted; and
- Stage 3 - the target users should be included in the evaluation process.

Inclusive design method aims to embrace everyone in the community [27]. By defining specific users as "lead users" throughout the product development process, the resulting design output can reflect the users' individual needs. Unlike the overused slogan "for anyone to use", which is often confusing, inclusive design can clearly defines target users that have not been considered so far, provides solution to meet their needs, and include a variety of other users [28].

3 User Research

For the development of the chatbot service in campus environment, international students, and staff supporting the students, at the Kookmin University were chosen as the target users. Combined methodologies of semi-structured interviews, photographs, and surveys were carried out for user research.

3.1 In-Depth Interviews

The target users were divided into two groups for the conduction of in-depth interview: the staff at the Kookmin University in the Department for International Student Services and the international students using the provided information.

Service Provider. We proceeded with the interviews using open questions with the staff in three departments in International Affairs Division at the Kookmin University. The purpose of the interview was to figure out the typology of the information international students need and the methods implemented by the school to support those needs. Thereafter, the collective data from the interviews (n = 3), offline materials such as guide books and brochures, and online resources on the university websites were analyzed. The information sources provided by the school were divided into three categories: academic, administrative, and living aspects (Table 1).

Table 1. Providing information for international students

Divisions of the department	Information provided
Academic	Academic calendar, course registration, programs, courses, transcripts, partner schools and programs
Administrative	Admission, Visa and legal issues, career/job opportunities, guidelines for working, guidelines for pets, counselling
Living	Campus facilities, campus map, dormitory, clubs, activities and events, cultural experience

Service User. In-depth interviews of five international students from different backgrounds (Brazil, China, France, Italy, and Taiwan) were taken. The interviews consisted of questions related to type of information, the contexts for its need, and ways of obtaining it. Questions also addressed the pain points and user needs in relation to accessing and gathering information required for maintaining life on campus, such as that regarding-facilities on and off campus, educational programs and resources, and additional student activities. The usual means of information acquisition is asking other familiar students and faculty. The major issues international students face included low amounts quality of such necessary information in English, and inconvenient processes for searching this information on existing online and offline systems. The students wanted to have the ability to independently access and search for information in various context (Table 2).

Table 2. Summarized results of the in-depth interview

Category of needs	Details of needed information
Information	Facility – Location, operating hours, ways of using Resources for research Administrative documents Stores outside campus School events Clubs Korean language class
Methods	Students – Korean and international Professors School office Guide maps Signs University websites and mobile applications
Limitations	Information in English is simplified and insufficient compared to the Korean version Most of the materials and devices are in Korean Translation is not accurate Sometimes there will be no one to ask in English Have to rely on assistants, friends, and professors Finding information is too long Sometimes one has to give up finding information
Needs	Fast access to information Being able to find information independently University websites and mobile applications should be friendly to international students Do not want to carry around guide books and maps

3.2 Survey

An offline survey was conducted, the objective of which was to study the typology and contexts of required information and the tools used to acquire resources while spending time on campus. The survey questionnaire was developed based on the key findings regarding touch points and pain points from the interviews. The survey was taken by 40 international students from Asia, Europe, North and South America.

The types of information were largely four: Food and drink, location of facilities, using the library and its database, school activities and events. The most valued information is that regarding 'food and drink' for 55.6% of the international students, 22.2% say information related to 'using the library and its database' is the most valuable, and 11.1% voted for the remaining types. For all types of information, more than 75% of the students obtained information through their friends since doing so is easy and convenient. Additional guiding information was about language classes and local events. 83.3% of the students claimed that they plan to use the chatbot, which provides a variety of information in English about campus life, and 83.4% of the students said the service will be useful for the purpose.

3.3 User Experience Analysis

In-depth interviews were carried out concerning both the information provided and that received. We found that the information provided by departments of international student support pertained to all aspects of studies, life, and administration. However, it was somewhat lacking in accuracy and depth.

From the perspective of the interviewed students, the biggest problem was the language barrier. In addition, not knowing where and how to find required information on time made their lives difficult. Even when information could be found, the translation was not accurate enough for students to comprehend or the content was simplified from that in Korean. The alternative process like asking by representative phone number is difficult as well due to the language barrier.

Through the surveys, we discovered that international students want information primarily on food and academics. The situations that information was needed were varied by the type of the information. We also learned that the majority of students had a strong intention to use a chatbot service to which they can ask questions and talk about campus life whenever they choose.

Through analysis of user research, we were able to validate that international students found accessing and exploring information challenging even though they were aware of the current informative systems provided in various languages. Based on the data gathered from the user research, the expected features of chatbot service were defined as follows: (1) Reliable and sufficient in formation in English (2) Fast and easy access to the information.

3.4 Persona

By combining the results of the data analysis, a persona for the target user was created. A user persona is used to present standards that help to incorporate a user's purposes and goals throughout the development [29]. It is also applied to solve issues faced during the process of designing the service [30] (Fig. 1).

The first persona is of Anna, a 26-year old graduate student from France. After a month of beginning studies at Kookmin University, she is still in the process of adapting to the new environment. Her Korean skills are in beginner's level but she is good at English and native in French. For her, it has been difficult to determine how to explore campus and make use of it. The second persona is of Jang, a 32-year old

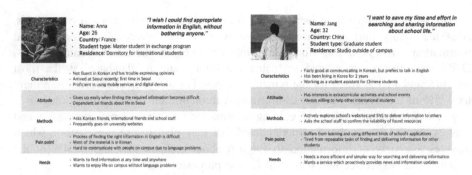

Fig. 1. Examples of persona developed in concept ideation

graduate student from China. After a year study at Kookmin University, he can speak Korean but he prefers to communicate in English. For him, finding information on campus life, such as the time and special venue of special events, continues to be difficult.

Further, the persona of an intelligent agent is vital as it directly engages and interacts with a prospective user. The persona has to be anthropomorphized for it to be able to successfully converse with the user [31]. A human-like chatbot will induce empathy and form a stronger relationship with the user. The persona created for the service is CiSA. CiSA is a Korean undergraduate student attending Kookmin University. CiSA has advanced English communication skills and native Korean language skills, enabling him to gather information from a Korean database and convert it into English and deliver. CiSA is proficient in using a smartphone and converses in non-formal English using emoticons and delivering a familiar tone. The key characteristics of CiSA's persona are smart, multilingual, helpful, and friendly.

4 Design and Implementation

4.1 Design Purpose and Design Process

For the development of an intelligent agent, key stages have to be carefully considered. The steps involved in the design of the CiSA were: (1) Defining the concept, (2) Defining the bot persona, (3) Analyzing features, (4) Designing conversation, (5) Building content strategy, and (6) Prototyping and testing. To refine the details corresponding to interaction with the user, steps 4, 5, and 6 were iterated in the process.

The purposes of CiSA are the following:

- Provides fast access to the source for maintaining campus life
- Conveniently links users with information without a time-space constraint
- Provides fast access to instructions on how to use facilities at the university

The chatbot service will offer international students detailed information in English, based on the user's questions. It quickly responds to the demands of the students with excellent accessibility, reducing the workload for the international student services.

4.2   Designing the Conversational Agent

We proposed features that will help users extract information directly from the chatbot service. Upon analysis of the collective data from user research, the features were prioritized based on most needed information and context beneath. CiSA intends to solve questions on (1) information about dining on campus, (2) guide on how to use the library and its online database (Table 3).

Table 3. Proposed solutions

Category	Solution
Campus Dining	Stores and cafeterias, location, opening hours, daily menu, recommendation, options for a specific dietary preferences
School Facilities	Location, directions, opening hours, information in details
Library Use	Location, opening hours, instructions, floor map
Student Activities and Events	Available activities and events, schedule, recommendations, location, availability of participation

Scenario-Based Dialogues. The prompts of a chatbot must be written within the conversational context for the entirety of a conversation, not just for one turn [32]. To keep track of the context, each prompt has to inform the user what actions they can make. Additionally, figuring out when to switch the dialog with visual clues is also vital because providing text-only answers is not always efficient. When operating on the input query by the user, the chatbot may have to link the user or provide the user with additional visual components [33].

We crafted sample dialogues considering each prompt in the context including error flows. By scripting sample dialogs, we could explore how the actual user experience will be and what changes we have to make to provide a more natural and effective experience. By integrating the persona of a chatbot with the concept of a service, the sample dialogues were created in the context of each feature. The context of a feature was based on the results of the survey, where the environmental situations for requiring information were collated (Fig. 2).

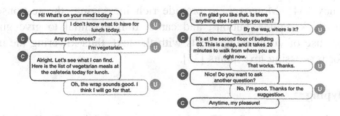

Fig. 2. Sample dialogue for choosing a lunch menu

Task Flow Chart. The task flow chart was designed according to the flow of the dialogue cases, and the fragmentation and error case were also indicated (Fig. 3).

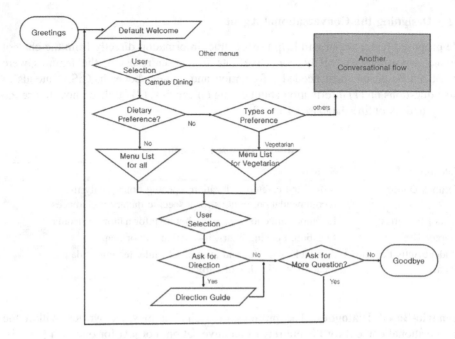

Fig. 3. Example logical task flow of the campus-bot: CiSA

There are two types of dialogues that a chatbot can present: (1) open domain and, (2) closed domain.

- Open domain: The user can input anything and the directions of dialog are unlimited. The inputs will be integrated using NLP.
- Closed domain: The flow restricts users to enter open responses. Instead, the pre-made options are provided for the user to select from. This enables the user to remain in context and reach their goal faster.

In this study, CiSA was created with a combined open and closed conversation domain to help users reach a goal without falling out of context or feeling overly controlled. By adopting predictive recommendation, we tried to improve communication efficiency [34]. Moreover, to provide rich messaging, the responses will be assisted with quick replies, buttons, and cards. It is essential to give guidance by making proper use of visual components with the text, thus lowering the user's cognitive load for processing text inputs [35].

4.3 Prototyping

CiSA was built using Dialogflow(Google) and integrated into Facebook Messenger. Dialogflow acts as an engine for the chatbot [36]. The components of conversation are divided into three groups: (1) intents, (2) entities, and (3) contexts. Intents are the purpose of the user's utterance. Leveraging a machine learning model, intents can be matched to give appropriate multi-turn responses to the user. Entities are the extracts of specific data from user's dialogs. Contexts are the current state of a user's inquiry. Combining contexts allows the agent to carry the pieces of information through the flow of a conversation [37] (Fig. 4).

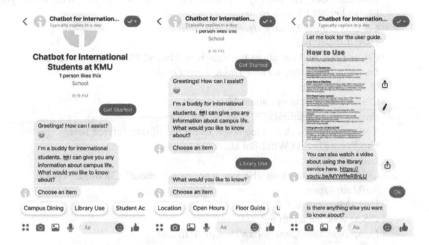

Fig. 4. CiSA running on Facebook Messenger

Facebook Messenger was used to deliver the chatbot providing a more familiar and convenient conversing experience for international students. To test the prototype in the real-world, the chatbot was integrated into a 'Chatbot for International Students at KMU' (Table 4).

4.4 Evaluation with Real Users

Five in-depth interviews with international students were conducted to verify the effectiveness and usability of the chatbot. The evaluation focused on how the chatbot interacts to offer context-sensitive information and how it engages in natural communication. Questions were created to determine the effectiveness, sustainability, satisfaction, and expected extension of the service.

All the participants stated that the service useful, helpful and satisfies the existing needs of information acquisition. They all found the service satisfactory as it provides essential information for everyday life on campus, thus fulfilling fundamental needs. Every participant showed high intent for using the service continuously. In particular, it is very useful for individuals who cannot speak other languages proficiently yet. Participants rated the quick reply buttons, which allowed them to view the features and contents the chatbot at a glance, highly. By using those buttons, they do not have to think about how to ask or what to type when they interacting with the chatbot. This enables the users to converse with chatbots without fail and obtain information efficiently (Fig. 5).

Table 4. Sample dialogue

Feature	Dialogue
Library Use	CiSA: Good day! What can I do for you today? I'm a buddy for international students. I can give you any information about the campus life. What would you like to know? Choose an item. *Campus Dining/Library Use/Student Activities* User: Library use CiSA: Let's find out about the SungKok library! Please choose an item. *Location/Open Hours/Floor Guide/User Guide* User: User guide CiSA: Let me find out about User Guide. (Image of Instructions) You can also watch a video about using the library service here. http://youtu.be/MYWffeR8nLU User: Thanks! CiSA: Is there anything else you want to ask about? Choose an option. *No/Main Menu* User: Main menu CiSA: Ask me anything! *Campus Dining/Library Use/Student Activities*

Fig. 5. Sketch of user interview for prototype validation

5 Conclusion and Future Work

In this study, we devised a new way of effectively delivering accurate information to students regarding campus life using intelligent technology. The chatbot service 'CiSA' was designed and implemented for the inclusion of distantly treated international students in the university environment. This accessible service aims to increase efficiency of information acquisition and accessibility of information by leveraging the current information systems. The effectiveness of a chatbot service was validated with the user research analysis, the result of which indicated that it greatly increases the accessibility of information required for life at a university. Upon analyzing the evaluation, the purpose and features of the service that support the everyday life of the international students were also proven to be satisfactory and efficient. The inclusive agent 'CiSA' will be a powerful way to support communication for marginalized groups of people in various environments.

In future work, the service needs to be equipped with more features that cover areas other than campus life. It also needs to assist in languages other than English. Also, further investigation on the behavior of the system can be conducted including a wider range of international students to see if it can achieve the same purposes. The conclusive findings from this research can also be expanded and can contribute to the development of guide robots at universities to enhance the campus experience for individuals. Moreover, the language barrier free service can be applied to attempt different approaches on a wider scale and provide solutions to universities all over the world.

Acknowledgement. This study has been conducted with support from the "Design Engineering Postgraduate Schools" program, an R&D project initiated by the Ministry of Trade, Industry and Energy of the Republic of Korea. (N0001436).

References

1. Urban, E.L., Palmer, L.B.: International students as a resource for internationalization of higher education. J. Stud. Int. Educ. **18**(4), 305–324 (2014)
2. Sherry, C., Bhat, R., Beaver, B., Ling, A.: Students as customers: the expectations and perceptions of local and international students. In: Higher Education Research and Development Society of Australasia (2004)
3. Gilton, D.L.: Culture shock in the library: implications for information literacy instruction. Res. Strat. **20**(4), 424–432 (2005)
4. Hellsten, M., Prescott, A.: Learning at university: the international student experience. Int. Educ. J. **5**(3), 344–351 (2004)
5. Griol, D., Molina, J.M., Miguel, A.S.D.: Developing multimodal conversational agents for an enhanced e-learning experience. ADCAIJ: Adv. Distrib. Comput. Artif. Intell. J. **3**(1), 13–26 (2014)
6. Følstad, A., Brandtzaeg, P.B.: Chatbots and the new world of HCI. Interactions **24**(4), 38–42 (2017)
7. Why Google A.I. is the last user interface—Computerworld. https://www.computerworld.com/article/3129098/why-google-a-i-is-the-last-user-interface.html
8. Conversation design—Actions on Google—Google Developers. https://developers.google.com/actions/design/
9. Weizenbaum, J.: ELIZA — a Computer program for the study of natural language communication between man and machine. Commun. ACM **26**(1), 23–28 (1983)
10. Zumstein, D., Hundertmark, S.: Chatbots-An interactive technology for personalized communication. IADIS Int. J. WWW/Internet 15(1), pp. 96–109 (2017)
11. Ramesh, K., Ravishankaran, S., Joshi, A., Chandrasekaran, K.: A survey of design techniques for conversational agents. In: Kaushik, S., Gupta, D., Kharb, L., Chahal, D. (eds.) ICICCT 2017. CCIS, vol. 750, pp. 336–350. Springer, Singapore (2017). https://doi.org/10.1007/978-981-10-6544-6_31

12. Alesanco, Á., Sancho, J., Gilaberte, Y., Abarca, E., García, J.: Bots in messaging platforms, a new paradigm in healthcare delivery: application to custom prescription in dermatology. In: Eskola, H., Väisänen, O., Viik, J., Hyttinen, J. (eds.) EMBEC & NBC 2017. IFMBE, vol. 65, pp. 185–188. Springer, Singapore (2018)

13. Piyush, N., Choudhury, T., Kumar, P.: Conversational commerce a new era of e-business. In: 2016 International Conference System Modeling Advancement in Research Trends (SMART), pp. 322–327 (2016)

14. Klopfenstein, L.C., Delpriori, S., Malatini, S., Bogliolo, A.: The rise of bots: a survey of conversational interfaces, patterns, and paradigms. In: Proceedings of the 2017 Conference on Designing Interactive Systems - DIS 2017, pp. 555–565. ACM Press, Edinburgh (2017)

15. McArthur, D., Lewis, M., Bishary, M.: The roles of artificial intelligence in education: current progress and future prospects. J. Educ. Technol. 1, 42–80 (2005)

16. Cumming, G.: Artificial intelligence in education: an exploration. J. Comput. Assist. Learn. 14(4), 251–259 (1998)

17. Dibitonto, M., Leszczynska, K., Tazzi, F., Medaglia, Carlo M.: Chatbot in a campus environment: design of LiSA, a virtual assistant to help students in their university life. In: Kurosu, M. (ed.) HCI 2018. LNCS, vol. 10903, pp. 103–116. Springer, Cham (2018). https://doi.org/10.1007/978-3-319-91250-9_9

18. Lim, S.L., Goh, O.S.: Intelligent conversational bot for massive online open courses (MOOCs). arXiv:1601.07065 [cs]. (2016)

19. Krassmann, A.L., Paz, F.J., Silveira, C., Tarouco, L.M.R., Bercht, M.: Conversational agents in distance education: comparing mood states with students' perception. Creative Educ. 9 (11), 1726–1742 (2018)

20. Kerlyl, A., Hall, P., Bull, S.: Bringing chatbots into education: towards natural language negotiation of open learner models. In: Ellis, R., Allen, T., Tuson, A. (eds.) Applications and Innovations in Intelligent Systems XIV, pp. 179–192. Springer, London (2007)

21. Krisnawati, L.D., Butar-Butar, B.E., Virginia, G.: Prototyping a chatbot for student supervision in a pre-registration process. Commun. Inf. Technol. J. 12(2), 87–96 (2018)

22. Ghose, S., Barua, J.J.: Toward the implementation of a topic specific dialogue based natural language chatbot as an undergraduate advisor. In: 2013 International Conference on Informatics, Electronics and Vision (ICIEV). 1–5 (2013)

23. Stephanidis, C.: User interfaces for all: Concepts, methods, and tools, 1st edn. CRC Press, Boca Raton (2000)

24. Newell, A.F., Gregor, P., Morgan, M., Pullin, G., Macaulay, C.: User-sensitive inclusive design. Univ. Access Inf. Soc. 10(3), 235–243 (2011)

25. Vanderheiden, G.: Fundamental principles and priority setting for universal usability. In: Proceedings on the 2000 Conference on Universal Usability, pp. 32–37. ACM, New York (2000)

26. Keates, S., Clarkson, P.J., Harrison, L.A., Robinson, P.: Towards a practical inclusive design approach. In: Proceedings on the 2000 Conference on Universal Usability, pp. 45–52. ACM, New York (2000)

27. Reed, D., Monk, A.: Inclusive design: beyond capabilities towards context of use. Univ. Access Inf. Soc. 10(3), 295–305 (2011)

28. Clarkson, J., Coleman, R., Keates, S., Lebbon, C.: Inclusive design: design for the whole population, pp. 336–355. Springer, London (2003)

29. Idoughi, D., Seffah, A., Kolski, C.: Adding user experience into the interactive service design loop: a persona-based approach. Behav. Inf. Technol. 31(3), 287–303 (2012)

30. Randolph, G.B.: Use-cases and personas: a case study in light-weight user interaction design for small development projects. Informing Sci. J. 7, 105–116 (2004)

31. Baylor, A., Ryu, J., Shen, E.: The effects of pedagogical agent voice and animation on learning, motivation and perceived persona. Presented at the EdMedia+ Innovate Learning (2003)
32. Cohen, M.H., Giangola, J.P., Balogh, J.: Voice user interface design. Addison Wesley Longman Publishing Co. Inc, Redwood City (2004)
33. Pearl, C.: Designing Voice User Interfaces: Principles of Conversational Experiences. O'Reilly Media Inc, Sebastopol (2016)
34. Yang, L., Dumais, S.T., Bennett, P.N., Awadallah, A.H.: Characterizing and predicting enterprise email reply behavior. In: Proceedings of the 40th International ACM SIGIR Conference on Research and Development in Information Retrieval, pp. 235–244. ACM, New York (2017). https://doi.org/10.1145/3077136.3080782
35. Woods, D.D.: Visual momentum: a concept to improve the cognitive coupling of person and computer. Int. J. Man Mach. Stud. **21**, 229–244 (1984). https://doi.org/10.1016/S0020-7373(84)80043-7
36. Dialogflow. https://dialogflow.com/docs. Accessed 25 May 2019
37. Brabazon, T.: The University of Google: Education in the (post) Information Age. Routledge, London (2016)

Some Mathematical and Practical Aspects of Decision-Making Based on Similarity

Peeter Lorents[1](✉) [iD] and Maryna Averkyna[1,2](✉) [iD]

[1] Estonian Business School, A. Lauteri, 3, Tallinn, Estonia
peeter.lorents@ebs.ee, maryna.averkyna@oa.edu.ua
[2] The National University of Ostroh Academy, Seminarska, 2, Ostroh, Ukraine

Abstract. One type of decision-making processes, which is often applied, based on the similarity of situations and developments. This study examines some approaches to addressing the similarities of situations and developments, including structural similarity and descriptive similarity. Structural similarity and descriptive similarity have been linked in many ways. One of these ways is based on theorems proven in algebraic systems and universal algebra theories. The authors point out that in order to assess two sets of descriptive similarity, it is first necessary to make descriptions of both sets, which must consist of relevant statements. The application of descriptive similarity in the process of managing the development of public transport systems in small towns in Estonia and Ukraine is considered. The authors presented the algorithm of decision-making process' method. The approach how to apply the descriptive similarity between Estonian small towns and their public transport systems, and the small town of Ostroh from Ukraine is proposed. Some concrete examples and derived preliminary conclusions is presented.

Keywords: Situations and developments as systems ·
Types of systems similarity · Structural similarity · Descriptive similarity ·
Numerical evaluation of descriptive similarity ·
Comparison of plausibility based on numerical estimates of similarity ·
Evaluation of the descriptive similarity ·
Public transport systems in the cities surveyed

1   Introduction

The purpose of this work is to clarify certain ways to obtain numerical estimates of the similarities between situations and developments to implement these assessments to manage situations and developments. The reason for this is the fact that people often make decisions based on the degree of to their situation similarity (or development) compared to some other known situation (or development). This can be illustrated by the following scheme:

(I)   The decision-maker examine the current situation (development);
(II) Decision-maker finds sufficiently similar and already known situations (developments);

© Springer Nature Switzerland AG 2019
C. Stephanidis (Ed.): HCII 2019, LNCS 11786, pp. 168–179, 2019.
https://doi.org/10.1007/978-3-030-30033-3_13

(III)   The decision-maker examines what was decided in the case of these situations (developments): In one case, for example, D1, in another case D2;

(IV)   The decision maker will know that the D1 implementation was more positive than the result for D2;

(V)   The decision-maker decides to do what is more like D1 because he believes that in this case, the result is similar (hence positive) to what was achieved with D1 in a known situation (development).

Here, it seems that the more experienced and more successful decision-makers do not rush to recommend D1, which gave positive results if it is not convinced that the situation (development) in which D1 was accepted is sufficiently similar to what the decision-maker is doing in this case. Now we inevitably come to the questions: what is this similarity and is it possible - and if so, how to assess in absolute terms the degree of similarity? There are several ways to study the similarities between situations and developments.

For one approach, it is first necessary to consider situations and developments as so-called structured sets or systems (in algebraic terms, see for example Lorents, Matsak [4]. It is then possible to study the similarity of situations (developments) using homomorphism of algebraic systems. In algebraic system theory and its applications, the observation of systems similarity is usually limited to proving the homomorphism of these systems, in particular the presence of isomorphism (or the lack thereof). At the same time, it has not been discussed what the rate of homomorphism could be and how to calculate it. (Homomorphism or algebraic similarity of finite systems can be numerically estimable by a method developed by P. Lorents only last year – 2018. This research is on publication.)

In the second approach to this work, the description of situations (developments) is based on claims. In this case, descriptions of the situations (developments) are a *set of claims*. In this context, situations (developments) are assumed to be similar if there are similar sets of claims. The numerical estimation of the similarity of the sets is based on a method analogous to that described in the works published in 1901 by Swiss botanist and plant physiologist Paul Jaccard [2, 3]. Very significant and substantive difference here is that the calculation of the Jaccard coefficient is based on the *equal elements* of the two sets. Nevertheless, we rely on *equalized elements* to calculate the similarity coefficient. One relevant approach is presented by Lorents P., Matsak E., Kuuseok A., Harik D. in the work published in 2017 [5].

Of course, the set and set of statements describing this set are not the same. But often we have no other practically usable ways to study the sets, relying on their descriptions. Nevertheless, there is a certain relationship between the set of structures, and the number of statements used to describe them. Indeed – the structural similarity and descriptive similarity are linked in many ways. One of these ways is based on theorems proven in algebraic systems and universal algebra theories (see, for example, Cohn [1], Maltsev [7]), according to which:

– in the case of two isomorphic (or "perfectly similar") systems, all claims that are represented by the corresponding formulas and are correct in one system - are also correct in another system, and all claims that are correct in another system are correct in the first system

– if one system is homomorphic (or "reasonably similar" to another system), all the
claims that can be made with the so-called positive formulas and that "fit" in the
first system - will also "fit" in another system (but not always the other way around -
what is right in another system may not always be right in the first system).

It is useful to use during decision-making process in order to implement Decision
Support Systems in management urban public transportation, and it is important to
develop making-decision approach. Szűts I., András B. emphasized the main approaches in decision-making: the psychological approach, the classical economy, and the
administrative models approach the reality. However, these approaches have limitation.
'The psychological approach application in practice does not serve reliable result. It is
difficult to apply model real situation according to the classical economy approach.
Administrative models allow decision makers to solve the actual issue(s), and they
have not alternative solution' [8]. It is necessary to point out, that descriptive similarity
can be as a basic in the decision-making process management urban public
transportation.

In the present paper, we will first discuss the concept of descriptive similarity and
the calculation of the appropriate numerical estimate. We will then study how to apply
the descriptive similarity between Estonian small towns and their public transport
systems, and the small town of Ostroh from Ukraine. We present some concrete
examples and derived preliminary conclusions. The further aim is to explain how
sensible it is to implement solutions in other cities.

1.1 Descriptive Similarity and Its Numerical Assessment

In order to assess two sets of descriptive similarity, it is first necessary to make
descriptions of both sets, which must consist of relevant statements. Next, it is necessary to clarify what statements from one description and another description can be
considered equivalent. There are now three sets of claims:

– A is a set whose elements are statements from the first description;
– B is a set whose elements are statements from another description;
– C is a set of elements that are ordered pairs, where the first position of the pair has
  the claim A, the second position has the claim B, and these claims have been
  equalized by each other.

Note. Sometimes it is quite useful to find a common, both-for-one formulation for the
claims that are equalized to one another. It is not forbidden, however, that one of these
two formulations be suitable.

We agree that we denote the number of elements of the final set H with the symbol
$E(H)$. In order to calculate the coefficient of descriptive similarity between the sets A
and B, we use the formula, if it is known, which claims are in this case equated with
each other (or set C):

$$\text{Sim}_C(A, B) = E(C) : [E(A) + E(B) - E(C)]. \tag{1}$$

Example. We consider two families F' and F''. Describe the families of the statements S' i and S'' p to these families.

Family F': Living in the countryside. They have their own house. Families have four children. Father is working. Mother is home. There is a big garden around the house. There are two big dogs in the garden. The family has two cars. One usually runs a father, mother with another mother.

Family F'': There are five children in the family. Living in the city. They have a large apartment. Mom goes halfway at work. Grandmother helps deal with children. Father works as a deputy director at a large company. The family has three cars. One uses a grandmother, the mother and the third father travel to the other (Table 1).

Table 1. Families' statements.

The first family describes the claims	Equivalent claims			The other family describes the claims
	Wording from the first	Wording from the second	The wording for both	
Living in the countryside				
	They have their own house	They have a large apartment	They have their own home	
	Families have four children	Peres on viis last	Families have five children	
	Father is working	Father ... as deputy director	Father is working	
Mother is home				
There is a garden around the house				
In the garden ... two big dogs				
	The family has two cars	The family has three cars	Perel has several cars	
	With one ... father, mother with another	One uses grandma, ... and third father	Every adult has a car	
				Mom goes to work ...
				With children ... grandma

We will calculate the similarity rating:

$$5 : [9 + 8 - 5] = 5 : 12 \approx 0.42$$

Perhaps in this case there is an assessment that could be characterized by words: not very high or very low. Or by the words: rather low, than high. Alternatively, just words: not so small.

1.2   Some Explanations of Assessing the Similarity of Sets

We mentioned above that there is an important and substantive difference between the similarity estimation used here and the Jaccard coefficient. Let us explain this in some detail.

Let E(H) be the number of elements of a set H. Let us have two sets A and B.

- Relying on the *same* elements let us calculate the Jaccard's coefficient [2, 3]:

$$Sim_J(A, B) = E(A \cap B) : [E(A) + E(B) - E(A \cap B)] \qquad (2)$$

- Relying on the *equated (matched)* elements let us calculate the Lorents coefficient (Lorents 2017):

$$Sim_{LT}(A, B) = E(equ_T(A, B)) : [E(A) + E(B) - E(equ_T(A, B))] \qquad (3)$$

where **T** this is the way of equalization **equ_T(A,B)** is such a set, where $x \in A$ or $y \in B$ are belonging to *in case, if* x and y **are** *equated*. NB! **We expect**, that
- not any two elements from the set A are equatable with each other
- not any two elements from the set B are equatable with each other
- each element from the set A can be equated with at most one element from the set B and vice versa.

In case we believe that A = B.

Important Note 1. Equating *can* – but does *not necessarily have to* be guided by identity.

Example. Let's observe two sets of shapes:

A = {Δ,□,×,¬,♦,°,+} and B = {+, ×,∇,◊,⌐,•,o,□}. Apparently, in the minds of many, these sets have only two common elements: □ and × . Nevertheless, there are enough people who agree to equate also the following elements

Δ and ∇, + and +, ¬ and ⌐, ° and o. This is a way of equating T (for those people). Let's calculate similarity coefficients:

$Sim_J(A, B) = E(A \cap B) : [E(A) + E(B) - E(A \cap B)] = 2 : [7 + 8 - 2] = \mathbf{2 : 13}$
$Sim_{LT}(A, B) = E(equ_T(A, B)) : [E(A) + E(B) - E(equ_T(A, B))] = 6 : [7 + 8 - 6] = 6 : 9 = \mathbf{2 : 3}!$

Important Note 2. The recent example is one confirmation of the fact that the assessment of similarity depends on how the equalization has taken place! Therefore, it is very important to exhibit in full what elements are equalized to each other. To some extent, a similar phenomenon (depending on how the similarity is determined by the way of identification) can also be observed for structural similarity. For example (by Lorents), if we compare fairly simple systems M 'and M'', where: M' elements are 2, 3, 4, 5, 6 and the relationship between them is "… is non-trivial multiplier for …"; the elements of M'' are shapes O, □, Δ, and the relationship between them "… is more angular than …" – then we can make sure that there are 150 matches between these systems, 18 of which are suitable for homomorphism, and there are several quite similar numerical estimates of similarity (e.g. 0.2 and 0.5!). However, this means that if we limit ourselves to identifying only whether the systems are homomorphic or not homomorphic, we may not notice many aspects. This situation is somewhat reminiscent of what we can notice or not notice in a person's photo, depending on the angle at which it is made.

2   Methodic Approach to Decision-Making Process' in the Public Transportation

It is necessary point out, that descriptive similarity is the basis for developing decision-making process' method in the public transportation (Fig. 1). This method will show relevance of studying and implementing the experience of managing urban public transport.

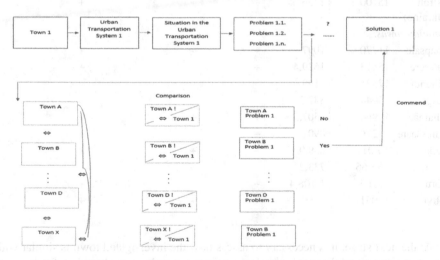

Fig. 1. Algorithm of decision-making process' method

At the first stage of the research, it is necessary to consider the system of the city, to which range it include according to the Working Paper written by Lewis Dijkstra and Hugo Poelman, European Commission Directorate-General for Regional and Urban Policy (DG REGIO) [6]:

1. Densely populated area: (alternative name: cities);
2. Intermediate density area (alternative name: towns and suburbs);
3. Thinly populated area (alternative name: rural area).

It is necessary for research, comparison and situations' analysis of in the same cities in order to implement the experience of managing EU urban transportation systems (Table 2).

It is also necessary to review the urban transport system and the situation in the urban transport system. Then it is important to identify the problems that need to be solved in the urban transport system under the study.

Example. We want to implement in Ostroh the Estonian small towns' experience of managing urban transportation systems (see example Table 2).

Table 2. Data for comparison towns according EU

Towns	Criteria				
	Inhabitants (10000-19999)	Density (at least 300 inhabitants)	A minimum population of 5000	Less than 50% of the population living in rural grid cells	Less than 50% living in a high-density cluster
Ostroh (Ukraine)	15700	1436	+	+	+
Estonian towns:					
Haapsalu	11270	1097	+	+	+
Rakvere	15413	1629,4	+	+	+
Viljandi	17525	1199			
Valga	15044	842,2			
Sillamäe	13964	1307,5	+	+	+
Kuressaare	13276	890	+	+	+
Keila	10 012	889,9	+	+	+
Maardu	16 466	733,2	+	+	+
Võru	12965	1 108,4	+	+	+
Jõhvi	10051	1 319	+	+	+

At the next stage, it is necessary to assess how the investigated town is similar with cities to be compared. For such purpose, we form claims' system based on the study of cities. Listed claims' system is to be filled to the table for both towns. Then we compare the approval of the first list with the second list on this basis. We form a table to assess the general statements of the city as a structure, transport structure and management system (Fig. 2).

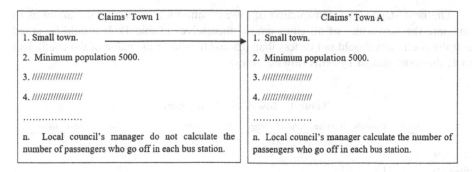

Claims' Town 1	Claims' Town A
1. Small town. ————————————→	1. Small town.
2. Minimum population 5000.	2. Minimum population 5000.
3. /////////////////	3. /////////////////
4. /////////////////	4. /////////////////
....	....
n. Local council's manager do not calculate the number of passengers who go off in each bus station.	n. Local council's manager calculate the number of passengers who go off in each bus station.

Fig. 2. Determination Towns' Equivalent Claims.

Based on comparisons of the list of claims of town, we propose to form a table of similar statements in order to estimate the Lorentz coefficient. Statements that describe town 1 (Ostrog), equal statements between systems, and statements that describe town A (Valga) necessary to write in the table (see Table 3). I case, when all statements are written down, it is necessary to calculate the similarity coefficient. This will allow us to look at how much the systems (towns or cities) are similar, which of the statements should be applied in the decision-making process.

Table 3. Towns' statements.

Town 1 (Ostroh) describes the claims	Equivalent claims			Town A (Valga) describes the claims
	The wording from the first	The wording from the second	The wording for both	
1.	Small town	Small town	Small town	
2.	Minimum population 5000	Minimum population 5000	Population	
3.	Density at least 300 inhabitants	Density at least 300 inhabitants	Density	
4.	Less than 50% lives in high-density clusters	Less than 50% lives in high-density clusters	Concentration	
5.	Intermediate area (towns and suburbs)	Intermediate area (towns and suburbs)	Intermediate area (towns and suburbs)	
n. Local council's manager do not calculate the number of passengers who go off in each bus station				
n + 1				Local council's manager do not calculate the number of passengers who go off in each bus station

The next stage is the construction of towns' similitude matrix, which allow us to compare the similarities of all cities among themselves (Table 4). It should be noted that the coefficient should not be less than 0.5 and the closer the value of the coefficient to 1, the more similar systems (towns, cities).

Table 4. Towns' similitude matrix

	Ostroh	Haapsalu	Rakvere	Viljandi	Valga	Sillamäe	Kuressaare	Keila	Maardu	võru	Jõhvi
Ostroh	1										
Haapsalu	1	1									
Rakvere	1	1	1								
Viljandi	1	1	1	1							
Valga	1	1	1	1	1						
Sillamäe	1	1	1	1	1	1					
Kuressaare	1	1	1	1	1	1	1				
Keila	1	1	1	1	1	1	1	1			
Maardu	1	1	1	1	1	1	1	1	1		
Võru	1	1	1	1	1	1	1	1	1	1	
Jõhvi	1	1	1	1	1	1	1	1	1	1	1

According to the data of towns' similitude matrix, we can see that towns are similar (coefficient similarity equal 1) and we can analyze the urban transport system and the situation in the urban transport system in Estonian towns. If the coefficient similarity lays in the range of 0.5–0.8 during the comparison of systems (cities), it is necessary to make a comparison of the general part of the common parts (Fig. 3). This will allow us to show detailed information about the similarity of cities and common towns' features.

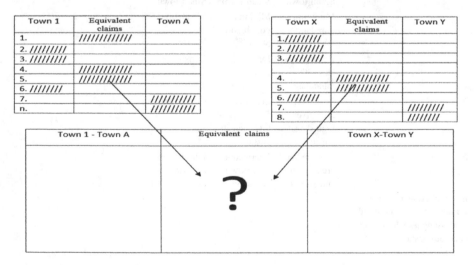

Fig. 3. General part of common parts

The next stage involves an end-to-end comparison of the statements of the city under investigation with another cities simultaneously. This will allow us to show the specific features of the systems under study (Fig. 4). It is also necessary to perform this, since during the comparison of the general part of the common parts of the cities, it may not be possible for the generality to be the same.

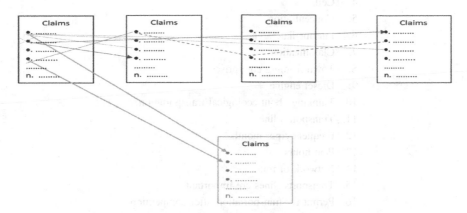

Fig. 4. An end-to-end comparison of the statements of all systems studied.

In order to form the final list of statements after such a comparison (Table 5), we will receive information about differences' features, which are in the urban transport systems and the management of the transport systems. Then it is possible to decide, which a positive experience in the management of public transport systems in Estonian small towns can be implemented for the town (Ostrog, Ukraine).

According to the results of the end-to-end comparison of the statements of all systems studied, we can see 19 similar features. The differences' features between Ostroh and 10 Estonian towns include impossibility to control the buses' time schedule, inconvenient public transportation, deficiency the buses' time schedule at the bus stations. Private carriers dictate their own terms and conditions for the provision of transport services, which leads to non-observance of the schedules on certain routes, deficiency an e-ticket, residents are forced to turn to the services of owners of private vehicles (taxi).

At the next stage of our investigation, we recommend to involve an end-to-end comparison of the statements between Estonian small towns. It is help to find out the similarities and differences' features in order to receive claims for decision-making process for Ostroh local council.

Table 5. Equivalent claims 11 towns (Ostroh-10 Estonian towns)

	Equivalent claims
1.	Small town
2.	Population
3.	Density
4.	Cells
5.	Concentration
6.	Intermediate area
7.	Classification
S.	Town-forming enterprises
9.	Diesel engine
10.	Thinking about ecological transportation
11.	Transport's line
12.	Frequency per month
13.	Peat hours
14.	Network of routs
15.	Transports' lines are important
16.	Permit for transportation after competition
17.	Frequency per route
18.	Calculation emission level is absent
19.	Control

3   Conclusion

Relying on similarity is one of the common ways of shaping decisions. Especially when there are just a few cases to deal with, but decisions have to be made. Whether it is good or bad, is not to be decided by us. However, it is possible to examine what its nature is and how it is implemented. Including if we want to implement or avoid implementing of the public transport arrangement in one small town that has proved useful in another city. So, in this work, we have somewhat explained some of the manifestations of similarity, including the descriptive similarity and the way it is numerally assessed. It was shown the application of the descriptive similarity as basic of the method possibility study and implement the experience of managing urban public transportation. We will present the results of the urban transportation systems similarity and statements to be applied in the decision-making process for Ostroh local council in the next paper.

References

1. Cohn, P.M.: Universal Algebra. Springer, Dordrecht (1981). https://doi.org/10.1007/978-94-009-8399-1
2. Jaccard, P.: Distribution de la flore alpine dans le bassin des Dranses et dans quelques régions voisines. Bull. Société Vaud. Sci. Nat. **37**, 241–272 (1901)
3. Jaccard, P.: Étude comparative de la distribution florale dans une portion des Alpes et des Jura. Bull. Société Vaud. Sci. Nat. **37**, 547–579 (1901)
4. Lorents, P., Matsak, E.: Applying time-dependent algebraic systems for describing situations. In: 2011 IEEE Conference on Cognitive Methods in Situation Awareness and Decision Support (CogSIMA 2011), Miami Beach, FL, pp. 25–31. IEEE Press (2011). (IEEE Catalog Number: CFP11COH-CDR)
5. Lorents, P., Matsak, E., Kuuseok, A., Harik, D.: Assessing the similarity of situations and developments by using metrics. In: Czarnowski, I., Howlett, R.J., Jain, L.C. (eds.) IDT 2017, Part I. SIST, vol. 72, pp. 184–196. Springer, Cham (2018). https://doi.org/10.1007/978-3-319-59421-7_17
6. Dijkstra, L., Poelman, H.: Regional working paper: a harmonized definition of cities and rural areas: the new degree of urbanization, p. 28 (2014)
7. Maltsev, A.I.: Algebraic systems. Science, Moscow (1970)
8. Szűts, I., András, B.: Decision support systems in management. In: 5th International Conference on Management, Enterprise and Benchmarking, 1–2 June 2007

Explorative Visualization of Food Data to Raise Awareness of Nutritional Value

Anna Lunterova(✉), Ondrej Spetko, and George Palamas[ID]

Aalborg University, A. C. Meyers Vaenge 15, 2450 Copenhagen, Denmark
alunte14@student.aau.dk

Abstract. The following research proposes a web based, interactive data visualization of a large food dataset, with an aim to raise awareness of their nutritional value. The system consists of an automatic dimensionality reduction scheme, based on t-SNE algorithm, and an exploratory user interface based on dynamic views of the data. Our approach allows users to effectively compare and relate visual representations of nutritional value in both micro and macro levels. The communicativeness of the application was evaluated regarding user experience and the storytelling functionality. Results show that the participants experienced a shift in perception from one mainly focused on taste to one aware of nutritional aspects. Additionally, the results suggest that a narrative experience can be generated, along with an effective long-term engagement.

Keywords: Big data visualization · Dimensionality reduction · Exploratory data visualization · Interactive data storytelling

1 Introduction

Over the past decades great amounts of data have been accumulated and stored from a variety of sources. These data hold qualities that are not always obvious and comprehensible at first sight. Due to data complexity and high-dimensionality, there is a need to generate a model that can present the data in a simpler and more comprehensible way. Moreover, due to the curse of dimensionality [10], a phenomenon occurring in high dimensional spaces, additional problems such as incoherence in the perception of data might arise. Dimensionality reduction can be performed by selecting the primary components of the dataset and together with using dimensionality reduction algorithm t-SNE, the data can be turned into a 2D visualization. Data visualizations (DV) are commonly used for the representation and presentation of the data. They provide an effective way to transform a data-driven information, such in form of numbers stored in tables, into easily understandable and aesthetically pleasing visuals of various forms [2,6,8,17,19,20]. Additionally, complementing data visualization with storytelling and interactivity elements has been found to enhance and promote user-interaction and further exploration of the presented information [11,18]. From a general audience point of view, this can turn the plain data visualization into a more effective and memorable narrative experience [9,12,26].

© Springer Nature Switzerland AG 2019
C. Stephanidis (Ed.): HCII 2019, LNCS 11786, pp. 180–191, 2019.
https://doi.org/10.1007/978-3-030-30033-3_14

The USDA National Nutrient Dataset of 2017 includes 8400 different foods with each of these holding 41 dimensions. The high density and amount of the information might be one of the reason of generally low nutritional awareness [25]. Combination of above mentioned elements (dimensionality reduction, data visualization, and interactive storytelling) can be used for the design and development of a web-based application, (accessible at https://tinyurl.com/y5lwevp9) offered to the public to explore the food dataset. Furthermore, this combination suggests a way to tackle the problem of effectively communicating complex, high dimensional datasets.

2   Background Research

Even though the roots of DV in forms of maps, charts and graphs go all the way into 17th century, interactive DV are only recently being explored. Moreover, they are mostly used for communicating low dimensional datasets. Visualizing high dimensional datasets in an interactive way is a more advanced topic, with only a few solutions proposed so far [18]. *The infinite drum machine* experiment done by Google Creative Labs [23] is an example of this approach. This experiment use the t-SNE dimensionality reduction algorithm [15] to organize a big dataset of everyday sounds by similar pitch characteristics. The Google interface can be used to create both random and customized beats using the drum sequencer, as well as to explore different sound regions in the interactive DV (Fig. 1).

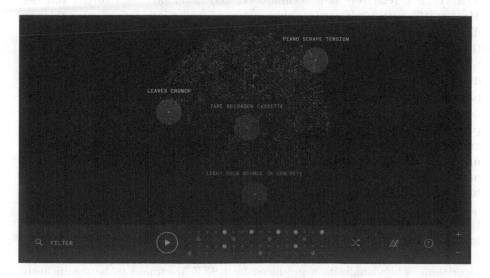

Fig. 1. The infinite drum machine [23]

The exploratory data visualization process consists of the following steps: dimensionality reduction, visualization, user interface and narrative structure. The following sections presents the elements separately.

2.1 Dimensionality Reduction

Dimensionality reduction is a pre-processing stage that is part of the data analysis and data mining phase. By reducing the amount of features in the original dataset, the derived values become more informative, non-redundant, and facilitate comprehension. Two of the most common and most effective dimensionality reduction algorithms are principal component analysis (PCA) and T-distributed Stochastic Neighbor Embedding (t-SNE).

Principal Component Analysis PCA, one of the most common and old (1933) algorithms, uses an orthogonal transformation to manipulate a set of observations of likely similar variables into principal components (a set of values of linearly uncorrelated variables). One downside with linear dimension reduction algorithms is that linear algorithms are not able to describe complex polynomial relations between features. The dissimilar data points are being placed far apart in lower dimensional representations. T-SNE solves these issues by using probability distribution with elements of randomness instead. This allows t-SNE to model distances between points in the low-dimensional map, resulting in an alteration of the Kullback-Leibler divergence curve [7].

T-SNE is a relatively new technique (2008) developed by Laurens van der Maaten [15], with aim to reduce the amount of dimensions by assigning relative distance values. It is based on relative correlations between each datapoint of the raw dataset, resulting in a two or three-dimensional map. The strength of t-SNE lies mainly in its preservation properties of the local distances of the high-dimensional data while mapping them to low-dimensional data. Main tunable parameters of the algorithm are perplexity (sets the number of effective nearest neighbors) and number of iterations. The choice of those parameters has a complex effect on the final picture and depends on the density of the dataset. By exploring its behaviour with different parameters it results in more meaningful information. However, original dimensions are mapped to lower dimensions without preserving any link to their original values, therefore definite assumptions based only on t-SNE output can not be made [20]. Also, the t-SNE algorithm is quite heavy on the system resources as it compares the relations pairwise with the goal of minimizing the sum of the difference of the probabilities in higher and lower dimensions. However, the output of the t-SNE can be used in the process of classification or clustering as an input for further classification or clustering algorithms. The visualization produced by t-SNE are found to be significantly more accurate and informational compared to other dimensionality reduction techniques such as PCA, Sammon Mapping, Isomap, Locally Linear Embedding (LLE) and other.

2.2 Data Visualization

Visualization Tools. The simplest examples of DV includes graphs, maps, 3D models, plots and others [16]. Several online tools and systems are being developed to make the creation of visualizations accessible to non experts and people with low programming skills. (E.g., Many Eyes, Tableau, Power Map, Flourish, iNZight, RAWgraphs, QGIS, Gephi, NodeBox, etc.) However powerful, these solutions are based on predefined templates. The shortcomings are poor customization, visualization of only low dimensional data, mostly static or very little interaction, and exclusively author-driven solutions [11].

Data Visualization Principles. Based on data expert Alberto Cairo's recent book "The Truthful Art" [6], and pioneer in the DV Edward Tufte's "The Visual Display of Quantitative Information" [24], qualities of great visualizations are summarized into five principles. While the name of these principles differ in between these two authors, their characteristics are the same. The order of these design principles are organized by their level of importance, from highest to lowest:

- Truthfulness, or "the lie factor", meaning data are based on thorough and honest research.
- Functionality and low data-ink ratio. Graphic providing accurate and concise depiction of data, that help the viewer to understand and think about the shown information (rather than the design).
- Should be aesthetically pleasing, in the sense of being intriguing and attractive for its audience.
- Insightfulness, revealing otherwise harder to be revealed evidence.
- Enlightening, in a way that if the audience grasps and understand the shown evidence, it changes their understanding or behaviour for the better.

These principles serve as inspiration for evaluation method of an effective data visualization.

2.3 Narratives and Interactive Storytelling

Storified visualizations are DVs that contain story components (structures, elements, and concepts) and are framed within elements that mediate the telling of the story "(people, tools, and channels)" [13,14] . The process of creating data stories in research is mapped out in three phases by author Bongshin Lee and Nathalie Henry Riche in their work entitled "More Than Telling a Story: Transforming Data into Visually Shared Stories" (see the process on Fig. 2).

Firstly the chosen data is explored and analyzed (data analysis). Secondly, after seeing patterns, trends, differences etc., the chosen facts, (story nodes) are connected (story transitions) in meaningful order (plot), to form a story. Lastly, the story is told using a chosen medium and narrative technique. Those "story nodes" are visualized in forms of graphs, charts, maps etc., with the use of clarifying annotations, or narrations [13]. After having created story pieces, that are

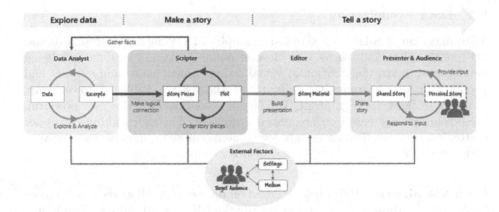

Fig. 2. Storytelling process in DV, taken from *More Than Telling a Story: Transforming Data into Visually Shared Stories* [13]. The process is composed from three main phases: exploration of the data, making of the story, and telling of the story.

the core of the information to be communicated, they need to be transformed into a physical form of a design. The layout of the visual data story, (defined during editor's phase) characterized as "design space dimensions" in research "Narrative visualization: Telling stories with data", where they analyzed 58 visualization, is composed from three characteristics: genre, visual narrative tactics, and narrative structure tactics [22]. Those characteristics are chosen by the author, based on the kind of data (or story nodes) he has, and his rhetorical strategies (story, plot, narration) [1]. This can serve as a foundation for connecting DV within a narrative context.

To further enhance the audience relatedness of the data story, the level of abstractedness or didascalicity, also called author-audience distance, serves as a function of narrative intelligibility and closure that the system achieve or aim to achieve [5].

In relation to the problem of author-audience distance, Hulman & Diakopoulos and Segel & Heer suggest that in data visualizations there needs to be certain balance between author-driven and reader-driven scenarios. This is described as an optimal interplay between an unrestricted exploration from the reader side and a clear story from the author side. A balanced narrative should be a combination of persuasive-rhetorical strategies to transmit an intended information to users, as well as exploratory-dialectic strategies, to give the reader a certain control over the insights. This is specifically called a "Martini glass" structure presenting narrow fully author driven beginnings, and reader driven exploration at the end of the interface [11,22].

Compared to static visualizations, exploratory visualizations give an ability to interact, inviting the reader to be part of the story creation and offers a variety of perspectives on the same information [4,19]. Interactive storytelling is defined as unique user story experiences that go beyond typical clicking, hovering, scrolling and linear structures of the story [3]. Users can choose the new story nodes in an unrestricted way while remaining within the overall story's beginning and ending.

3 Design

The process of design includes the four following topics: dimensionality reduction, visualization, interactivity and narrative structure. The chosen dataset, (USDA National Nutrient Dataset of 2017) reported on 8400 different foods with each of these holding 41 dimensions. These dimensions hold attributes including food category, amount of calories, protein, carbohydrate, fat, fiber values, amount of different minerals and vitamins, and recommended daily amounts of each of the item.

3.1 Dimensionality Reduction

The aim of the reduction of the information is to automatically extract the nutritional composition of each food and organize them in a way that retain nutritional similarities across the data-set. The prioritization of what food attributes should be communicated, was based upon a brief online research of what matters most from a physiological point of view. Moreover, and from the same point of view, a discussion was held regarding the USDA database with two medical students. It was important to be aware of the tuning parameters that are influencing the output of the t-SNE algorithm. The best visual representation was achieved

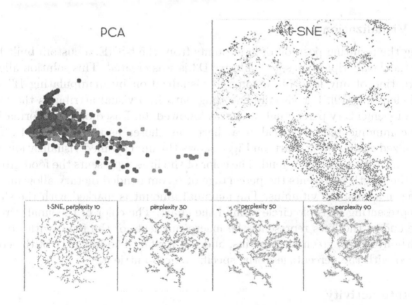

Fig. 3. Dimensionality reduction, visualizations comparison of outputs of PCA and t-SNE algorithm with comparison of t-SNEs maps with perplexity of 10, 30, 50 and 90.

with the number of iterations 4000 and perplexity of 90. The t-SNE performed better than PCA algorithm which resulted in a single cluster formation. Figure 3 shows the comparison of the visualization output of PCA and t-SNE algorithm of perplexity 10, 30 50, 90).

Furthermore, based on the general population selection criteria, a decision was made to color code all 23 food groups. The final t-SNE map (Fig. 4) shows all the points organized in nutritionally similar groups in the 2D space.

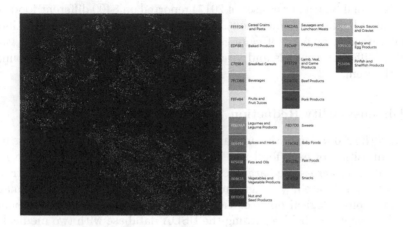

Fig. 4. 2D representation of food data set in nutritionally neighboring positions (Macro level). Color represents food category.

3.2 Visualization

Taking the resulting position of food points from the t-SNE, a custom built DV using the JavaScript open source library D3.js was created. This solution allows the creation of any kind of customized visualization by manipulating HTML DOM elements [19]. For visually encoding data into visual attributes the hierarchy of elementary perceptual tasks was followed [6]. Based on the information being communicated, a cyclical area chart was chosen as a DV type [21]. The customized cyclical area chart, on Fig. 5 shows the final zoomed visualization of a data point with an added legend. The color of the lines represents the food group, while the length represents the percentage of recommended dietary allowance of specific minerals and vitamins. The maximal amount is marked with the short line representing invisible circle around the chart. The color of the small circles at the end of the lines represents the macro-nutrients of the food, with orange for carbohydrates, green for proteins, and red for fat. The intensity of the color is linked with the percentage of the specific macro-nutrient.

3.3 Interactivity

Differences and similarities between food and their associated food groups distribution can be been explored by moving in this 2D space and by zooming in

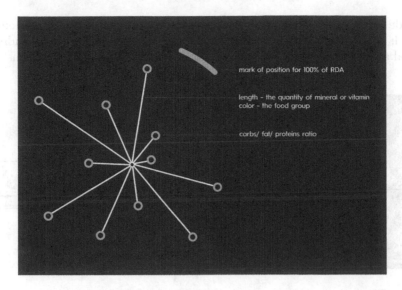

mark of position for 100% of RDA

length - the quantity of mineral or vitamin
color - the food group

carbs/ fat/ proteins ratio

Fig. 5. Graphical representation of the nutritional value of a single food point (Micro level)

and out. Specific foods or food groups can be picked up in the map, customarily searched by name, or selected through the navigation bar. Tool tips and details-on-demand were added to complement the experience and facilitate the understanding of the DV. The aim of this is to strengthen the ability of mental map formation for the audiences, as well as enhance the awareness of how our bodies perceive food.

3.4   Narratives

The goal of the narrative was to acquire narrative closure with the audience, in terms of how they consider the purpose of food and their relationship to it. The chosen plot consisted of three parts: (a) A shortly animated slideshow narrated through gradually appearing text introducing the topic of people's relationship with food. (b) A demo introduction to the food world presented, including a demonstration of the navigation tools. In this phase the user is also invited to choose a character/category to identify with. The choice to be made addresses the user's perspective on food. This was assumed to lead the user to question how and why he chooses his food, and/or to be reminded of what matters particularly to him about a meal. (c) Pure reader-driven exploration of DV, with selective interactions (Fig. 4). This is the conclusion of the story, from a user perspective, as the information presented is large and complex. The points of possible inquiry are in the form of (a) data point stories representing food nutrients, calories, and food groups, (b) comparison of visualizations with other food points, or other food groups, (c) random recommendations of complimentary foods by the system that get highlighted after choosing specific points in the map. The Fig. 6 shows

(a) slide from a short animation introducing the topic of people's relationship to food; (b) A demo introduction to the food Data Visualization, including a tutorial and an invitation to choose a character/category to identify with.

Fig. 6. A user driven narrative (a) with selective interactions (b).

4   Experimental Procedure

The Web-based DV application was tested with 25 participants. Self reported data, regarding the communicativeness and the usability of the solution, were collected from a pre and post-questionnaire. The pre-questionnaire served as an introduction to the exploration and included demographic questions, questions about their interest in the topic of food, and reasons for their interest in participating in the experiment. In the post-questionnaire eight Likert scale questions served for self-evaluating (a) the usability of the interface, (b) the perceived attentiveness, (c) and the degree of relatedness to the information presented. Additional questions for evaluating the insightfulness, the aesthetic level, and the information obtained were given. At the very end of the post-questionnaire, two open questions served for further open reflections on the interest in food and experiment overall. Twenty-five participant's answers were collected, in the span of three days. The experiment took approximately 5 to 10 min, with identical questionnaires and procedures given to all participants.

The results from the questionnaire measuring the effectiveness of the scheme, regarding the communicativeness (attentiveness, relatedness, insightfulness) and the usability of the solution are showed in a radar chart in the Fig. 7(a). The 7(b) shows keywords analysis from two same but differently asked questions regarding what the user cares about the food from before and after-experiment. The questions were: *What do you care about food?* and afterwards *How do you define healthy relationship with food?*

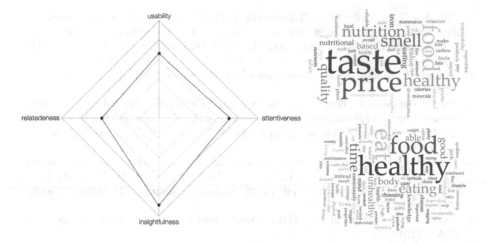

Fig. 7. Usability testing (a) pre and post-questionnaire responses (b).

5   Discussion

From the analysis of over 250 keywords from the pre-questionnaire it appeared that, initially, the prioritization of taste was a common drive for choosing what food to eat (Fig. 7(b)). Post-questionnaire responses, however, show that users were now more concerned about the health side of different foods, even though the definition of "healthy food" here varied for most of the participants and might not be clear as a whole. This suggests that the goal of the narrative was partly fulfilled. For properly evaluating the communicativeness of the visualization and the usability of the interface, more data are needed to confirm the results.

6   Conclusions

The aim of this research was to communicate effectively a large data-set of over 8400 food data points with a trans-disciplinary approach. There were two main focus points of this research, the communicativeness and usability of the visualization. The approach consists of a combination of dimensionality reduction, data visualization and interactive storytelling. Even though further evaluation is needed to confirm the results, the effectiveness of the approach was validated as positive and led us to conclude that there is a big potential that deserves further investigation and study.

References

1. Abbott, H.P.: Story plot, and narration. In: Herman, D. (ed.) The Cambridge Companion to Narrative, pp. 39–51. Cambridge University Press. https://doi.org/10.1017/ccol0521856965.003

2. Billeskov, J.A., Møller, T.N., Triantafyllidis, G., Palamas, G.: Using motion expressiveness and human pose estimation for collaborative surveillance art. In: Brooks, A.L., Brooks, E., Sylla, C. (eds.) ArtsIT/DLI 2018. LNICST, vol. 265, pp. 111–120. Springer, Cham (2019). https://doi.org/10.1007/978-3-030-06134-0_12
3. Bostan, B., Marsh, T.: Fundamentals of interactive storytelling. AJIT-e **3**(8), 19 (2012)
4. Boy, J., Detienne, F., Fekete, J.D.: Storytelling in information visualizations: does it engage users to explore data? In: Proceedings of the 33rd Annual ACM Conference on Human Factors in Computing Systems. ACM Press (2015). https://doi.org/10.1145/2702123.2702452
5. Bruni, L.E., Baceviciute, S.: Narrative intelligibility and closure in interactive systems. In: Koenitz, H., Sezen, T.I., Ferri, G., Haahr, M., Sezen, D., Catak, G. (eds.) ICIDS 2013. LNCS, vol. 8230, pp. 13–24. Springer, Cham (2013). https://doi.org/10.1007/978-3-319-02756-2_2
6. Cairo, A.: The Truthful Art: Data, Charts, and Maps for Communication. New Riders (2016)
7. Canning, J.P., et al.: Network classification and categorization. arXiv preprint http://arxiv.org/abs/1709.04481.pdf
8. Friendly, M., Denis, D.J.: Milestones in the History of Thematic Cartography, Statistical Graphics, and Data Visualization. Springer (2001). http://www.datavis.ca/papers/gfkl.pdf
9. Gershon, N., Page, W.: What storytelling can do for information visualization. Commun. ACM **44**(8), 31–37 (2001). https://doi.org/10.1145/381641.381653. Association for Computing Machinery
10. Houle, M.E., Kriegel, H.-P., Kröger, P., Schubert, E., Zimek, A.: Can shared-neighbor distances defeat the curse of dimensionality? In: Gertz, M., Ludäscher, B. (eds.) SSDBM 2010. LNCS, vol. 6187, pp. 482–500. Springer, Heidelberg (2010). https://doi.org/10.1007/978-3-642-13818-8_34
11. Hullman, J., Diakopoulos, N.: Visualization rhetoric: framing effects in narrative visualization. IEEE Trans. Visual Comput. Graphics **17**(12), 2231–2240 (2011)
12. Kosara, R., Mackinlay, J.: Storytelling: the next step for visualization. Computer **46**(5), 44–50 (2013). https://doi.org/10.1109/mc.2013.36
13. Lee, B., Riche, N.H., Isenberg, P., Carpendale, S.: More than telling a story: transforming data into visually shared stories. IEEE Comput. Graph. Appl. **35**(5), 84–90 (2015). https://doi.org/10.1109/mcg.2015.99
14. Ma, K.L., Liao, I., Frazier, J., Hauser, H., Kostis, H.N.: Scientific storytelling using visualization. IEEE Comput. Graph. Appl. **32**(1), 12–19 (2012). https://doi.org/10.1109/mcg.2012.24
15. van der Maaten, L., Hinton, G.: Visualizing data using t-SNE. J. Mach. Learn. Res. **9**, 2579–2605 (2008). http://www.jmlr.org/papers/volume9/vandermaaten08a/vandermaaten08a.pdf
16. Mallon, M.: Data visualization. Public Serv. Q. **11**(3), 183–192 (2015)
17. Moere, A.V.: Aesthetic data visualization as a resource for educating creative design. In: Dong, A., Moere, A.V., Gero, J.S. (eds.) Computer-Aided Architectural Design Futures (CAADFutures), pp. 71–84. Springer, Netherlands (2007). https://doi.org/10.1007/978-1-4020-6528-6
18. Murray, S.: Engaging Audiences with Data Visualization. O'Reilly Media (2014). https://www.oreilly.com/pub/e/2584
19. Murray, S.: Interactive Data Visualization for the Web: An Introduction to Designing with D3, vol. 2. O'Reilly Media, Inc. (2017). http://opencarts.org/sachlaptrinh/pdf/28380.pdf

20. Nasser, A., Hamad, D., Nasr, C.: Visualization methods for exploratory data analysis. In: 2006 2nd International Conference on Information & Communication Technologies. IEEE (2006). https://doi.org/10.1109/ictta.2006.1684582
21. Raghavan, S.: How to begin your own data science journey (2017). https://towardsdatascience.com/how-to-begin-your-own-data-science-journey-2223caad8cee
22. Segel, E., Heer, J.: Narrative visualization: Telling stories with data. IEEE Trans. Visual Comput. Graphics 16(6), 1139–1148 (2010). https://doi.org/10.1109/tvcg.2010.179
23. Tan, M., McDonald, K.: The Infinite Drum Machine (2017). https://experiments.withgoogle.com/drum-machine
24. Tufte, E.R.: The Visual Display of Quantitative Information, vol. 2. Graphics Press, Cheshire (2001)
25. Wojcicki, J.M., Heyman, M.B.: Adolescent nutritional awareness and use of food labels: results from the national nutrition health and examination survey. BMC Pediatr. 12(1), 55 (2012)
26. Yi, J.S., ah Kang, Y., Stasko, J.: Toward a deeper understanding of the role of interaction in information visualization. IEEE Trans. Visual Comput. Graphics 13(6), 1224–1231 (2007). https://doi.org/10.1109/tvcg.2007.70515

A New Paradigm of Addressing the Complexity of Entrepreneurial Community Design Leveraging Augmented Reality

Ke Ma, Yixiang Zhang, and Jing Cao$^{(\boxtimes)}$

College of Design and Innovation, Tongji University, Shanghai, China
{suta, zyx2929}@tongji.edu.cn,
caojing.tongji@gmail.com

Abstract. Confronting the complex community design challenges, we demonstrated a novel paradigm of addressing the complexity by leveraging Augmented Reality incorporating information visualizations and the CityScope tangible interface. We next deployed CityScope Shenzhen Bay (CSB) as a practical case to quantify the entrepreneurial vitality of the Bay Area community. CSB incorporates information visualization toolkits, tangible interface for the rapid community design together with the simulation matrix of the community performance, which creates a crowd-sourcing platform to engage diverse stakeholders into the design and decision-making process towards the complexity of establishing an entrepreneurial community.

Keywords: Community design · Augmented reality · Tangible user interface · Information visualization · CityScope

1 Introduction

The late two years witnessed the transformative advances of community innovation. Design practices have built up new prototypes of entrepreneurial communities in high-performance and livable cities. Diverse start-ups, labs, services, and talents bring proactive techniques, knowledge, and creativity into communities to create innovative interventions [1]. However, emerging practices have increased the complexity of designing prototypes of networked urban systems and the underlying services. Community curators are seeking for a novel paradigm to address the challenges induced by disruptive entrepreneurial interventions.

We demonstrated a new scheme to empower community stakeholders first to understand the networked situations through quantitative information visualizations and afterward collaboratively sketch the prototype of the target community assisted by the CityScope tangible interface [2]. Meanwhile, real-time simulations can present multi-objective validations, for instances, the diversity and proximity, on the following performances of the community [3]. It is, therefore, feasible to foresee how interventions can improve the situations and optimize the design work before deploying entrepreneurial interventions. We set out to create the impact of reducing the thresholds

© Springer Nature Switzerland AG 2019
C. Stephanidis (Ed.): HCII 2019, LNCS 11786, pp. 192–201, 2019.
https://doi.org/10.1007/978-3-030-30033-3_15

of participating in urban planning activities and engaging diverse stakeholders into the decision-making process of co-creating a consensus of community values.

To exemplify the scheme as an empirical and generalizable solution, we developed "CityScope Bay" (CSB) as a case to represent the systematic framework, scenario-based interaction design, and user practices. See Fig. 1. This research concentrates the gaze on the Bay Area located at the Nanshan District in Shenzhen in China which comes into a characteristic entrepreneurial community gathering numerous enterprises and talents. The purpose of building CSB upon this community is to interpret the entrepreneurial conditions in terms of the networked distribution of diverse categories of enterprises and behavioral patterns of entrepreneurs. Furthermore, CSB gives rise to the rapid prototyping of an initialized entrepreneurial community for multi-users to devise the composition and arrangement of indispensable enterprises.

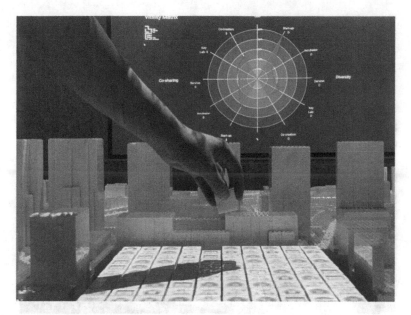

Fig. 1. The tangible user interface and simulation matrix of CSB. A user is manipulating a LEGO module to modify the distribution of entrepreneurial enterprises for community prototyping.

We exhibited CSB at an Open Entrepreneurship Summit in Bay Area, which gathers city managers, community curators, entrepreneurs, and consumers to investigate the future community design and the according lifestyle. In the exhibition, we operated focus group study in which users with specific propositions collaboratively discussed the proposals of designing a novel community aiming at creating either diverse or co-sharing capabilities. Participants manipulated the iterative design decisions on CSB tangible interface which simultaneously represents the distribution and arrangement of enterprises. Figure 2 illustrates the design process of one focus group. Additionally, a validation matrix performed the real-time simulation of the scores on indicators of diversity and co-sharability. Ultimately, each group reached an agreement for the design task and presented the outcome to other audiences. We collected design outcomes as well as simulated scores from three focus groups and yielded out a preliminary analysis. This paper next presents the extensive design work and technical framework of CSB. We also published a website to the public for disseminating recent activities of CSB. An online video of CSB for readers is available via the link[1].

The remainder of this paper is organized as follows: Sect. 2 introduces our method of developing CSB from information visualization, tangible interface, and technical implementation, respectively. In Sect. 3, we demonstrate the community design outcomes from focus groups and evaluate the impact of utilizing CSB as an efficient platform to accomplish complex community design tasks. Finally, Sect. 4 presents conclusions and future work.

Fig. 2. The working process of one focus group at the exhibition. Users are discussing to conclude the design proposition and collaboratively testing design decisions with CSB.

2 Method

CSB incorporates three core modules: (1) information visualization toolkits, (2) CityScope tangible interfaces for prototype design, (3) community performance simulation matrix. Figure 3 demonstrates the scheme and technical framework of CSB. Three modules constitute an iterative architecture for organizing and transferring

---

[1] https://youtu.be/QoVmoLbToVw.

heterogeneous information from internal systems and user actions. Information visualization toolkits provide visual interpretations promptly projected onto CityScope tangible interface. Users' manipulations of interactive LEGO constitutes instantly corresponds with the mathematical simulation matrix to provide users with versatile indicators of community performance at present.

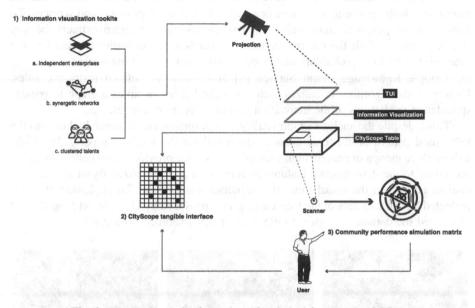

Fig. 3. The conceptual schematic and technical framework of CSB.

2.1   Information Visualization Toolkits

Visualizing heterogeneous data provides the understanding of entrepreneurial conditions to help stakeholders recognize the advantages and issues in the target district. In this case, we identified "Entrepreneurial Vitality" as an indicator for quantifying, analyzing, and visualizing the representations of vitality with regard to three typical scenarios: (1) independent enterprises, (2) synergetic networks, (3) clustered talents showcased in Fig. 4. CSB projects and maps information visualizations onto a LEGO-constructed physical model to achieve the intuitive experience rather than a two-dimensional screen. This paper published the visualizations online as a video[2] capturing the animations for every scenario.

First, we aim to depict the distribution pattern of independent enterprises classified into five primary types: start-up, co-creation space, incubator, service platform, and key lab. With the raw data collected from Open Data Platform certificated by Shenzhen Government [4], we distilled the metadata for each type of enterprises to form a data model. Afterward, with the assistance of the Open API service of Mapbox [5], geographic information is affiliated with each entity such as land, building, and road.

---

[2] https://youtu.be/bJkc1Ucu6mw.

Then, we filtered and marked all the valid location points inside the target region on the map and consequently circumscribed buildings that probably galvanized by innovative enterprises. Color encodings are virtually useful for differentiating the classification of enterprises. To visualize dynamic impacts that independent enterprises are generating to the surroundings, we designed animations for temporary presentations.

Second, our research further investigated network associations among current resources which aggregate to create a new type of innovative products and services. To figure out the potential combinations of enterprises, the algorithm extracts the key competitiveness of all the enterprises into keywords and automatically associate the enterprises with high-probability relevance to drive new kind of innovation assisted by the Google Knowledge Graph Service [6] and manually defined restrictive rules. Moreover, the algorithm visualizes each networked relationship as a graph to present speculative predictions of the innovation and underlying resources.

Third, despite the analysis of the vitality of enterprises, our research looked into the behavioral pattern of clustered talents, which reflects the vitality property. We highlighted three groups of people: high-tech talents, service providers, and college students according to the demographic features in Bay Area and visualized dynamic traces of distinct clusters in the visual form of continuous scatter flow. To implement this, we collected GPS traces data of the target user group provided by Open Street Map [7] and visualized the dataset through the GPX viewer open-sourced library [8].

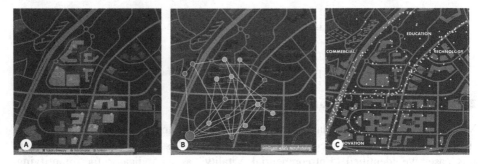

Fig. 4. Visualizations for three identified scenarios. (A) independent enterprises, (B) synergetic networks, (C) clustered talents.

2.2   CityScope Tangible User Interfaces for Prototype Design

CityScope, a tangible visualization and simulation tool, provides the interface to engage community stakeholders in urban intervention design. City Science researchers from MIT Media Lab and global collaborators have been developing CityScopes to simulate the impact of interventions in planned communities and expedite collaborative consensus among stakeholders. As one affiliated member of the City Science Network, City Science Lab @ Shanghai[3] in cooperation with MIT Media Lab harbors the aspiration of transforming insights and techniques into remarkably innovative values in

---

[3] http://www.makeinteractions.com/lab.html.

China. This lab gathers research scientists, urban designers, and entrepreneurs to create sustainable, livable, and entrepreneurial communities by leveraging quantitative simulations and analysis beyond the urban interface. City Science Lab @ Shanghai developed a slew of CityScopes for addressing urban interventions in heterogeneous scales. Figure 5 lists out three additional CityScopes. CSB is the community-scaled CityScope developed by City Science Lab @ Shanghai with the support from open-sourced CityScope repository on GitHub [9]. CSB comprises a 3D model of physical buildings constructed by LEGO bricks, projections for visualizations and simulations onto the model or a vertical screen, a tangible interface for simultaneous interaction with digital information by manipulating semantic LEGO modules, and a CityIO server for processing algorithms and communications.

We selected a district with 1/16 size of the entire 3D model as the tangible interface to simulate the community design process. The interface is divided into a ten by ten grid where each grid can place a four by four LEGO module. Next, we assigned semantic information representing six types of enterprises (start-up, co-creation space, incubator, service platform, key lab, and commercial space) to the LEGO modules. Figure 6A illustrates the grid interface filled with manifold enterprise modules recognized by iconic symbols. Furthermore, CSB cultivates CityScope scanner under CityScope table to capture the grid of recognizable LEGO bricks encoded by six color types (see Fig. 6B) respectively correlating with equivalent enterprise counterparts. Real-time video frames are processed by the Computer Vision algorithm [10] to interpret one hundred color-tagged LEGO modules as semantic enterprises. Figure 6C records the operation of recognizing color types of the LEGO grid system. Therefore, CSB can record the changing distribution of LEGO modules and immediately refresh the interface representing enterprises. This mechanism empowers users to make rapid and iterative design decisions upon the distribution pattern via flexible manipulations of LEGO modules.

Fig. 5. A collection of CityScopes for heterogeneous urban scales developed by City Science Lab @ Shanghai. (A) CityScope Siping Community (http://www.makeinteractions.com/CSSiping.html), (B) CityScope LivingLine (http://www.makeinteractions.com/CSLL.html), (C) CityScope High School (http://www.makeinteractions.com/CSHS.html).

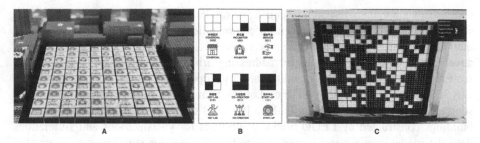

Fig. 6. The tangible interface of CSB. (A) LEGO modules, (B) color types and respective semantic encodings, (C) the LEGO grid system detected by Computer Vision recognition algorithm.

2.3 Community Performance Simulations

CSB provides the scientific simulation of the community performance, which reflects the evaluation of specific indicators towards users' design outcome. In this case, we identified two indicators which are diversity and co-sharing to quantify the entrepreneurial vitality of the focus community. As the tangible interface can calculate the quantities and locations of each type of enterprise via CityScope scanner and LEGO grid system, we defined a mathematical formula to figure out the quantitative scores specific to two indicators. A Radar Map named as "Vitality Matrix" visualizes the measures respectively for six axes (Fig. 7). Each side of the matrix depicts the differences among six types of the enterprise, while comparisons of two symmetric points on the same axis distinguish the performances upon two indicators. Advantageously, users can view the consequences of the recent decision and consider suitable design actions before the next iteration.

$$rmse_{ij} = \sqrt{\frac{1}{5}\sum^{5}\left(\frac{num_{ijk}}{24} - coef_k\right)^2}$$

$$c_k = \left(\sum_i \sum_j rmse_{ijk}\right)^{-1}$$

i: row coefficient

j: column coefficient

k: area type

num_{ijk}: number of k-type area in the 5 * 5 matrix centered on the grid of i rows and j columns lattice

$coef_k$: the ideal ratio coefficient of the k-type area in the 5 * 5 matrix region

$rmse_{ij}$: root-mean-square error of the i-row j-column lattice

c_k: average co-sharing coefficient of k-type area

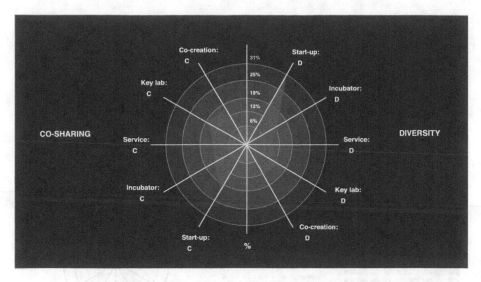

Fig. 7. The Vitality Matrix depicting the community performance of comparative indicators: (1) Co-sharing, (2) Diversity.

3   Evaluation

For evaluating the performance of CSB applied in user scenarios, we picked up three typical design patterns from the focus group study. Final design outcomes from three groups (A, B, C) are yielded out and visualized in Fig. 8. The visualization consists of two sections in which the left grid depicts users' decisions upon the distribution of five types of entrepreneurial entities and the associated commercial amenity while the right Vitality Matrix quantifies scores regarding two indicators: co-sharing and diversity specifically for five counterparts. The intermediate table shows the exact ratios in percentage terms.

We set out to provide preliminary reasonings and interpretations for each group considering the design proposition during the focus group study. Reading the matrix, group A was inclined to create a balanced diversity where five counterparts relatively share equivalent percentage. On the other hand, they tended to increase the co-sharing capability of co-creation spaces and key labs. Nevertheless, group B highly concentrated on the co-sharing performance of three kinds of community-sourced amenities, which are co-creation space, key lab, community service platform. The purpose of the given distribution is to strengthen the openness and accessibility of spaces, technologies, and business. The last group claimed no particular preference for a single indicator. They were aiming to establish a start-up-centered community; consequently, co-creation spaces and key labs are supposed to offer superior incubation service for advanced knowledge and technology.

This paper presents three samples among various possibilities of utilizing CSB for rapid community prototyping with explicit design propositions. Moreover, participators can collaborate to propose promising distribution patterns and finally approach

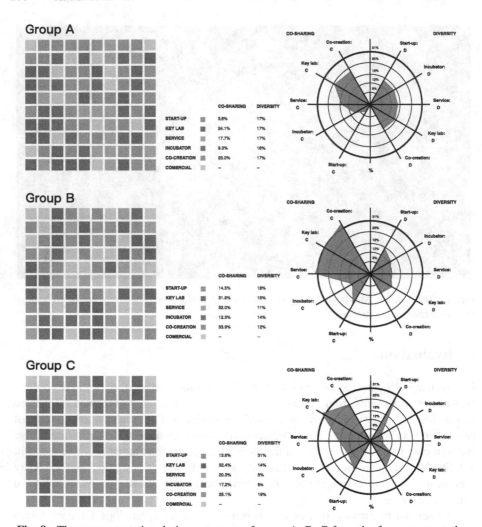

Fig. 8. Three representative design outcomes of group A, B, C from the focus group study.

preferred agreements through precise and quantitative evaluation of proposals calculated by Vitality Matrix. It is advantageous for design spaces that require participatory cooperation to conclude design-makings by multiple stakeholders. Interactive and computational medium effectively galvanize the working process and deliverables. CSB possesses the applicable viability of deploying as a public service in entrepreneurial communities similar to Bay Area community. The community curator can organize workshops and seminars to gather viewpoints from stakeholders, which would serve as a persuasive approach to reach consensus rather than individual disparity.

4   Conclusions

Confronting the complex community design challenges, we demonstrated a novel paradigm of addressing the complexity by leveraging information visualizations and the CityScope tangible interface. To validate the viability of our method, we deployed CSB as a persuasive case to quantify and visualize the entrepreneurial vitality of the Bay Area community. Using multidimensional information visualization toolkits, CityScope tangible interface for and the performance simulation matrix, CSB creates a crowd-sourcing platform to engage diverse stakeholders into the design and decision-making process towards the complexity of establishing an entrepreneurial community from the initial point. This paper distilled three representative design patterns from outcomes of the focus group study to preliminarily evaluate the applicable possibilities towards collaborative design spaces. Our research urges on design practices empowered by the tangible interface and computational evaluation into the innovative community design filed.

Acknowledgments. This work was supported by the Experimental Pedagogy Research Program (Virtual Reality Product Design and Usability Evaluation for Media and Communication Design Discipline, Grant 1400104024). The authors would like to thank Junye Lin, Xinda Guo, Chaoran Chen from College of Design and Innovation, Tongji University for the help of system development as well as doctoral researcher, Ariel Norman, and Ryan Zhang for research instructions.

References

1. Lou, Y., Ma, J.: Growing a community-supported ecosystem of future living: the case of NICE2035 living line. In: Rau, P.-L.P. (ed.) CCD 2018, Part II. LNCS, vol. 10912, pp. 320–333. Springer, Cham (2018). https://doi.org/10.1007/978-3-319-92252-2_26
2. Grignard, A., et al.: Cityscope andorra: a multi-level interactive and tangible agent-based visualization. In: Proceedings of the 17th International Conference on Autonomous Agents and MultiAgent Systems, International Foundation for Autonomous Agents and Multiagent Systems (2018)
3. Alonso, L., Zhang, Y.R., Grignard, A., Noyman, A., Sakai, Y., ElKatsha, M., Doorley, R., Larson, K.: CityScope: a data-driven interactive simulation tool for urban design. Use case volpe. In: Morales, A.J., Gershenson, C., Braha, D., Minai, A.A., Bar-Yam, Y. (eds.) ICCS 2018. SPC, pp. 253–261. Springer, Cham (2018). https://doi.org/10.1007/978-3-319-96661-8_27
4. Shenzhen OpenData Platform. http://opendata.sz.gov.cn. Accessed 18 June 2019
5. Mapbox API Service. https://docs.mapbox.com/api/maps/. Accessed 18 June 2019
6. Google Knowledge Graph Service. https://developers.google.com/knowledge-graph/. Accessed 18 June 2019
7. Open Street Map GPS Traces Service. https://www.openstreetmap.org/traces. Accessed 18 June 2019
8. GPX Viewer Library on GitHub. https://github.com/evrignaud/gpx-viewer. Accessed 18 June 2019
9. CityScope GitHub Repository. https://github.com/CityScope. Accessed 18 June 2019
10. CityScope Javascript Scanning Library. https://github.com/CityScope/CS_cityscopeJS. Accessed 18 June 2019

Sentiment Analysis Through Machine Learning for the Support on Decision-Making in Job Interviews

Julio Martínez Zárate$^{(\boxtimes)}$ and Sandra Mateus Santiago$^{(\boxtimes)}$

Politécnico Colombiano Jaime Isaza Cadavid, Medellín, Colombia
{julio_martinez54172, spmateus}@elpoli.edu.co

Abstract. In this paper, we propose a sentiment analysis model using machine learning for the support on decision-making in the process of job interviews. To do this, a characterization of the analysis of sentiments, job interviews and machine learning algorithms is first performed. Then, supervised machine learning with artificial neural networks is implemented in a prototype, due to the non-linear behavior described in the variables taken in the study and applying the Eye tracking technique. Finally, tests are carried out with people, in which, by asking questions of these, the involuntary movements of the pupil of the eye are analyzed, through the processing of a volume of data and the results of the ocular patterns are interpreted. Correlated with the questions of the test and with it, a final judgment is presented for the support of the decision making.

Keywords: Sentiment analysis · Machine learning · Job interview · Eye tracking · Neural networks

1 Introduction

The sentiment analysis is a process to extract the feelings and emotions of the users [1]. Liu [2] defines it as the field of study that analyzes the opinions, feelings, evaluations, validations, attitudes and emotions of people towards entities such as products, services, organizations, individuals, themes, events and its attributes. Chen [3] speaks about the different forms or computational approaches in which the sentiment analysis can be performed, such as: text-based, voice-based, visual and multimodal. One of the techniques or approaches used for this discipline is machine learning and Mitchel [4] defines it as a sub-area of computer science that studies methods to construct predictive computational models from observational data. The sentiment analysis can be applied to a myriad of disciplines and areas: in economics, in medicine, psychology, state security, politics; for the case of this work, it is applied in psychology and more exactly in the job interviews within organizations. The job interview is the most important process in recruitment and is used for various purposes: measurement of cognitive qualities, personality, motor and physical skills [5].

Job interviews are a popular selection technique from many points of view. In organizations around the world, job interviews are still one of the most widely used methods to evaluate candidates for employment. Among organizational decision

© Springer Nature Switzerland AG 2019
C. Stephanidis (Ed.): HCII 2019, LNCS 11786, pp. 202–213, 2019.
https://doi.org/10.1007/978-3-030-30033-3_16

makers, interviews have been found to be the most preferred assessment method by supervisors and human resources professionals. In addition, applicants perceive that interviews are fair compared to other selection procedures and applicants expect interviews as part of a selection process. In fact, from the perspective of the applicant, obtaining a job interview is essential for success in the search for a job [6].

For the Sentiment Analysis, there are some instruments and techniques that also require a specialist person to interpret that analysis, as well as the costs of some of these devices are relatively high [7–9]. In pre-employment interviews, for example, a person is the one who analyzes behavior, gestures and certain key patterns such as the look, tone of voice and other expressions of the inquired or interviewed. On the other hand, it is worth mentioning one of the most used devices, the polygraph, which measures physiological alterations of people [10]; Furthermore, Chica [11] mentions some disadvantages of this device, where she states that, on the other hand, there are also several "tricks" that can alter the test. Another device is also the Magnetic Resonance Scanner, which uses one of the technologies considered to be the best in the detection of lies, however, it only focuses on this, it is very expensive and requires a rigorous process [12].

Because certain shortcomings and defficiencies in the techniques and devices among others, a low-cost model is proposed that can accurately interpret the feelings of people with eye tracking techniques and provide support to the current decision-making techniques for the personnel in charge of conducting job interviews in organizations, thanks to the information systems, mathematical theories and psychology.

This paper is organized as follows: in Sect. 2, the related works are presented. In Sect. 3, the sentiment analysis model using machine learning. In Sect. 4, the experiments and results. The conclusion is finally presented.

2 Related Works

There are some related works on sentiment analysis using machine learning:

Borth [13] proposed an approach based on understanding of the visual concepts that are strongly related to sentiments. Present a method built upon psychological theories and web mining to automatically construct a large-scale Visual Sentiment Ontology, using a detector library for visual sentiment analysis. Wang [14] proposed a visual sentiment analysis approach with coupled deep adjective and noun neural networks, considers visual sentiment analysis as a binary prediction problem that is to classify an image as positive or negative from its visual content. Baecchi [15] did a study that uses a multimodal feature learning approach, using neural network-based models, to address sentiment analysis of micro-blogging content, such as Twitter short messages, that are composed by a short text and, possibly, an image.

Zadeh [16] presented a model termed "tensor fusion" network (neural network-based) for sentiment analysis, highlighting the growth of research in this area through multiple modes and the use of machine learning. Similarly, Chinsatit [17] used neural networks-based pupil center detection method for a wearable gaze estimation, mentioning the applications that can have this in several disciplines of knowledge, including psychology. For its part, Poria [18] proposed a multimodal affective data analysis framework to extract user opinion and emotions from video content and combines text, audio and video; the paper also proposes an extensive study on decision-level fusion.

On the other hand, Chen [3] uses a convolutional neuronal network for the prediction of sentiments through the joint learning of textual and visual sentiments from training examples. George [19] uses a convolutional neuronal network too, propose a real-time framework for the classification of eye gaze direction and estimation of eye accessing cues.

3   Sentiment Analysis Model Using Machine Learning

In this research, the characterization on sentiment analysis was initially carried out, among which are: textual, voice, visual and multimodal. After this characterization and given the final validation designed to apply it in job interviews, this work focuses on the visual approach. To do this, we use the register of positions through coordinates of the center of the pupil of the eye, following an algorithm called Eye-Tracking [20], which is the process of measuring the movement of an eye in relation to the head or the point where the gaze is fixed (Fig. 1).

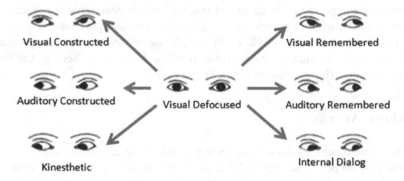

Fig. 1. Eye Accessing cues [21]

The model shown in Fig. 1 establishes that the specific characteristics of the thinking mechanism relate to a non-visual orientation of the gaze [21]. A person is related to the way he moves his eyes [22]. "According to a popular proverb, the eyes are the window of the soul. And, in fact, people have wondered for a long time if there is something in our eyes indicative of character" [23].

For this study, in addition, the exploration of the different automatic learning algorithms used for the sentiment analysis was carried out (Fig. 2).

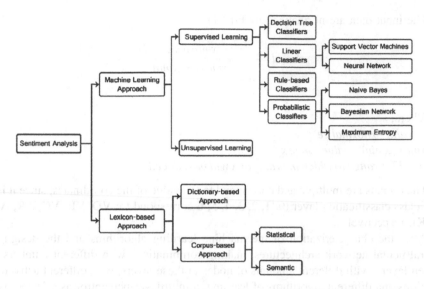

Fig. 2. Approaches and algorithms for sentiment analysis [24].

After making comparisons between the algorithms, the supervised machine learning approach was selected using artificial neural network techniques, using as a criterion that people have different behaviors in their eyes when asked about something and the time of permanence looking towards certain coordinates it is not the same for everyone, nor are the coordinates usually the same, so the relationship between the variables can be considered with a non-linear trend.

3.1 Architecture of the Artificial Neural Network

The prototype used in the sentiment analysis model proposed in the present article has enabled six of the seven patterns (visual defocused, visual created, visual remembered, auditory created, remembered auditory, kinesthetic sensations, internal dialog), excluding the defocused visual pattern.

Next, the architecture of the neural network is proposed to validate the coordinates of the model. The variables of inputs are related to the coordinates of the Cartesian plane (x, y) and the stay time of the gaze. When a question is asked during the job interview at a certain time t, the person fixe his gaze towards certain places, which, when captured, counts the number of times in all the coordinates:

- Number of looks towards visual defocused (#VD)
- Number of looks towards remembered visual (#VR)
- Number of looks towards visual created (#VC)
- Number of looks towards remembered auditory (#AR)
- Number of looks towards auditory created (#AC)
- Number of looks towards internal dialogue (#DI)
- Number of looks towards kinesthetic sensations (#KI)

The input data are normalized by Eq. (1):

$$x' = d1 + \frac{(x - xmin)(d2 - d1)}{xmax - xmin} \tag{1}$$

Where,

x : value to normalize
$[xmax, xmin]$: value range x
$[d1, d2]$: range to which the value of x will be reduced

The outputs are multiple and correspond to the value of the coordinates, since it is a multiclass classification layer (0, 1, 2, 3, 4, 5, 6 correspond to: VD, VR, VC, AR, AC, DI, KI, respectively).

After the characterization of the machine learning algorithms and the design of several neural network architectures, making combinations with different numbers of hidden layers, with different amounts of nodes in these layers, with different activation functions and different algorithms of learning, a multilayer perceptron is selected with two hidden layers of "processing of the sentiments" with 2 inputs (and Bias) and 7 neurons in each hidden layer, and the number of the output is 7 as well, as it was mentioned is multiple (classification). They are activated with the sigmoid activation function, as an error function, categorical cross entropy with Adam optimizer was chosen (Fig. 3).

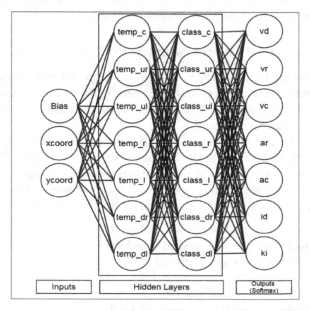

Fig. 3. Architecture of the multilayer perceptron neural network used to validate the patterns [Own development].

The model proposed in this paper can perform the visual sentiment analysis of people with machine learning, performing the interpretation of the eye Accessing cues with the help of the eye tracking technique. It is applied in job interviews now in which an interviewee is asked questions of a personal nature, and this fixes his gaze towards certain coordinates that have a meaning according to the areas of study of psychology. After the results obtained with the variables of the fixations of the gaze, the personnel in charge (usually of human resources), analyze said results and make their own decision about the candidate for the job.

3.2   Interview

The interview is based on the work done in Costa [25] on the five (5) personality dimensions (Big Five): Extraversion, kindness, responsibility, emotional stability, openness to experience. In Rauthmann [23] a study is carried out with the ocular tracking demonstrating with mixed linear models that the personality predicts the number of fixations, the duration of the fixation and the time of permanence in two different abstract animations. Hooft [26] investigate whether ocular tracking technology can improve people's understanding of the response process when it is said. For his part, Broz [27] collects the data from the look of human conversational pairs in order to understand which characteristics of the interlocutors of the conversation influence this behavior. These three (3) works made use of the Costa test [25].

Open questions are carried out based on the Costa test [25] carried out in order to evaluate each of the previous dimensions, so that the person responding projects their gaze towards certain coordinates involuntarily according to their feelings. The human being is capable of manifesting three (3) feelings at the same time with his eye cues.

4   Experimentos y Resultados

Next, the experiments and results made for the sentiment analysis model are presented. For the experiment, it should be suggested to the person not to wear glasses, not to turn the face to the sides, so that the webcam can constantly monitor the movement of the retina.

4.1   Prototype

The prototype consists of a client-server system with graphical user interface (GUI) web client, which captures the coordinates of the gaze and the time spent in these coordinates, using a conventional web camera. The detection of the retina is done with the help of the webcam, this is captured with a javascript library called Webgazer [28], which uses internal machine learning. First the calibration of the "library" is performed, the more it is calibrated, the greater the precision of the detection of the coordinates of the gaze.

In Fig. 4, the user is in front of the computer that has a conventional web camera and captures the movement of the retina, this is reflected in the graphical user interface web on the screen of said computer, capturing the needed information. The collection of the information of the variables is done in real time through the prototype eye-tracking and stored in a database for further processing.

Fig. 4. GUI - prototype for eye tracking [Own development].

In each coordinate where the person interviewed fixes the gaze, the absolute frequency or number of fixations to that coordinate is calculated; then, a point (x, y) closest to the interpolation point described by the data set $(\min(\|X - IP\|))$, if it belongs to the first three (3) major absolute frequencies. It is making a scale of the point (x, y) captured in the width and height (in pixels) of the browser window viewport with respect to the square of the size of the rectangular image of the eye area. A translation of Cartesian coordinates is carried out and then the normalization of the data with respect to the pixel size of the rectangle of the eye region [29].

4.2   Evaluation

For training the neural network, we take the Eye-Chimera data set used in [21], transformed to coordinate matrices of the images. They contain a matrix of (14×2) of each look (described in each image) in which the rows are the coordinates; and the columns, the x and y axes. The five (5) first rows are coordinates of the left eye, as well as the last 2 (two); the rows from 6 to 10 are coordinates of the right eye; the coordinates of the pupil are rows 5 and 10, row 1 is the left end of the left eye, row 6 the left end of the right eye, row 11 is the upper end of the left eye, and row 13 is the upper end of the right eye (which are the variables of interest). Taking these values and performing measurements normalization to a rectangle located in the region of the eye.

The images of the taken dataset have a size of 640 px wide by 480 px high, the region of the eye is reduced to 35 × 18 px.

In Fig. 5, two eyes are shown taking values from a matrix of dotted positions with the pupil in the center.

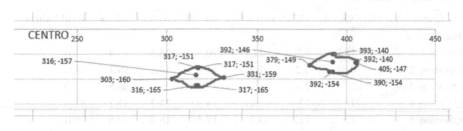

Fig. 5. Coordinates of a matrix of the eye-chimera dataset, person looking at the center [Own development].

The eye coordinates are captured in five (5) volunteers, asking a personality question for each dimension of the Big-Five (5 questions), only explaining to the person who answers the questions that will appear on the computer screen or device, the client was hidden from the interface of capturing the gaze and only the questions that had to be answered appeared and he clicked when he answered it verbally, without explaining what dimension of personality would be measured either. And at the end of the test, present the results of the quantities as shown in Fig. 5, for each question answered.

Fig. 6. End user interview interface. This is a question related to extroversion [Own development].

For each question, the absolute frequencies of fixation in the established coordinates are obtained, and with that the six (6) relative frequencies in each coordinate are calculated and the three (3) first major ones are taken (relative frequencies greater than 10%). The average duration of a fixation ranges between 200 and 350 ms [30].

Table 1 shows the results of the people evaluated and the sentiments corresponding obtained with the eye tracking:

Table 1. Results with absolute frequencies in the coordinates in the determined response time for the five (5) questions.

Sentiment	VD (%)	VR (%)	VC (%)	AR (%)	AC (%)	ID (%)	KI (%)	Total fixings
Volunteer 1								
Question 1	-	**18,7**	6,7	**21,9**	10,9	**25,5**	16,4	1861
Question 2	-	0,8	4,2	1,4	**16,8**	18,6	**58,1**	837
Question 3	-	2,7	2,7	2,7	2,7	2,7	**86,5**	37
Question 4	-	16,2	12,5	**18,1**	14,3	**21,2**	17,7	3011
Question 5	-	1,9	11,1	3,2	**17,5**	16,4	**49,8**	901
Volunteer 2								
Question 1	-	**13,1**	0,2	**20,7**	1,4	**59,0**	5,5	420
Question 2	-	9,0	**19,2**	11,9	**22,4**	12,7	**24,9**	1456
Question 3	-	0,0	**6,8**	0,2	**14,5**	5,0	**73,5**	442
Question 4	-	0,0	4,1	1,0	**7,1**	59,9	**27,9**	197
Question 5	-	11,6	11,9	13,3	**15,0**	16,4	**31,7**	293
Volunteer 3								
Question 1	-	1,0	5,5	8,6	**16,4**	**39,3**	**29,2**	384
Question 2	-	1,6	10,9	7,1	**21,1**	24,1	**35,3**	949
Question 3	-	1,5	10,9	6,8	**21,2**	23,4	**36,1**	980
Question 4	-	1,5	10,9	6,8	**21,0**	22,6	**37,1**	1042
Question 5	-	4,6	13,1	6,8	**17,3**	18,1	**40,1**	237
Volunteer 4								
Question 1	-	5,7	**18,0**	7,4	**21,3**	11,5	**36,1**	122
Question 2	-	9,0	5,4	**22,3**	10,8	**36,7**	15,7	166
Question 3	-	**23,9**	2,0	**24,5**	2,3	**27,0**	20,2	640
Question 4	-	2,5	**25,2**	2,5	**28,6**	9,1	**32,1**	2318
Question 5	-	12,9	11,8	15,1	**15,6**	18,9	**25,7**	1133
Volunteer 5								
Question 1	-	**20,7**	0,4	**20,7**	0,4	21,3	**36,5**	1630
Question 2	-	1,8	**31,0**	2,0	**31,0**	2,8	**31,6**	507
Question 3	-	2,0	**18,1**	2,2	**19,9**	2,4	**22,2**	2137
Question 4	-	**42,3**	12,5	**45,4**	0,0	**58,7**	41,3	489
Question 5	-	**5,6**	0,0	**14,6**	0,0	**77,1**	2,8	144

Each question is about identifying a dimension of the candidate for the job: Question 1, Extraversion; question 2, kindness; question 3, responsibility; question 4, emotional stability, question 5, openness to experience. The response time the person takes is not relevant in the results for the verification, although the absolute frequencies depend on it.

After training of the model with the neural network shown in Fig. 4 with the Eye-Chimera data set (885 samples in total), the results without label are processed, for this the "Tensorflowjs" tool is used.

For each point of the first 3 major ratios of the previous table, take a point closer to the curve described, of each set of points in each of those three (3) coordinates.

Table 2 shows the matrix of validation of the results, showing the percentage of success or certainty with the coordinate. The neural network throws each one of the results of the patterns to be checked with the highest corresponding values with respect to the others.

Table 2. Validation of the results in the corresponding coordinates.

Certainty Sentiment	VR	VC	AR	AC	ID	KI
Volunteer 1						
Question 1	0.9036851	-	0.3852791	-	0.8211777	-
Question 2	-	-	-	0.4530621	0.6093528	0.4601849
Question 3	-	-	-	-	-	0.3797783
Question 4	-	0.4514413	-	-	0.4644437	0.3347794
Question 5	-	-	-	0.3576853	0.4807395	0.3576845
Volunteer 2						
Question 1	0.3706563	-	0.4616654	-	0.6253502	-
Question 2	-	0.538384	-	0.5479685	-	0.5481049
Question 3	-	0.3958438	-	0.3933841	-	0.3079248
Question 4	-	-	-	0.7944366	0.8557455	0.9038013
Question 5	-	-	-	0.4073458	0.9375306	0.3971747
Volunteer 3						
Question 1	-	-	-	0.4683144	0.3150922	0.4673097
Question 2	-	-	-	0.4464874	0.6187378	0.4442834
Question 3	-	-	-	0.4514413	0.4640621	0.5318491
Question 4	-	-	-	0.7093528	0.6101221	0.5213944
Question 5	-	-	-	0.3812893	0.4905789	0.3982546
Volunteer 4						
Question 1	-	0.5383841	-	0.3167358	-	0.3474749
Question 2	-	-	0.4626554	-	0.6586387	0.5432834
Question 3	0.910508	-	0.3852791	-	0.5441523	-
Question 4	-	0.4503414	-	0.4965323	-	0.4184881
Question 5	-	-	-	0.8003421	0.3290811	0.3786671
Volunteer 5						
Question 1	0.912558	-	0.6461454	-	0.5992102	0.2242534
Question 2	-	0.4616415	-	0.2967152	-	0.5425104
Question 3	-	0.3994832	-	0.71549	-	0.5531846
Question 4	0.6712303	-	0.6126548	-	0.2275161	-
Question 5	0.9537871	-	0.5859972	-	0.2372161	-

5 Conclusion

In this paper, we have presented a sentiment analysis model with the use of advanced machine learning techniques, seeing that it is an emergent application area in many fields, for this case, it is applied to decision making in the process of job interviews to assess personality. There are several approaches to analyzing feelings, but in this case algorithms with neural networks were taken because of their advantages analyzed against the subject under treatment.

With the results of the personality test of each question, the person in charge of defining the future of the candidates for a job position (normally a psychologist or human resources professional), relies on the model correlating in the results of the variables to then give their final judgment in this regard.

Acknowledgments. The research work presented in this paper was partially funded by the thesis proposal of Master's Degree in Engineering, from the Politécnico Colombiano Jaime Isaza Cadavid - Colombia; entitled: "Modelo de análisis de sentimientos mediante el aprendizaje de máquina para el apoyo en la toma de decisiones en entrevistas laborales". Thanks to Yamid Asael Arenas Manso, System Engineer.

References

1. Devika, M., Sunitha, C., Ganesh, A.: Sentiment analysis: a comparative study on different approaches. Procedia Comput. Sci. **87**, 44–49 (2016)
2. Liu, B.: Sentiment Analysis and Opinion Mining. Morgan & Claypool Publishers, San Rafael (2012)
3. Chen, X., Wang, Y., Liu, Q.: Visual and textual sentiment analysis using deep fusion convolutional neural networks (2017)
4. Mitchell, T.: Machine Learning. McGraw-Hill, Boston (1997)
5. Dessler, G.: Administración de recursos humanos, enfoque latinoamericano, 5 edn. (2009)
6. Macan, T.: The employment interview: a review of current studies and directions for future research. Hum. Resour. Manag. Rev. **19**, 203–218 (2009)
7. Kron, L.: Polygraph and reliability in psychological assessment: myth or reality? (2016)
8. Pham, T.D., Tran, D.: Emotion recognition using the emotiv EPOC device. In: Huang, T., Zeng, Z., Li, C., Leung, C.S. (eds.) ICONIP 2012, Part V. LNCS, vol. 7667, pp. 394–399. Springer, Heidelberg (2012). https://doi.org/10.1007/978-3-642-34500-5_47
9. Mitsuyoshi, S.: Emotion recognizing method, sensibility creating method, device, and software (2008)
10. Anta, J.: Detección Del Engaño: Polígrafo vs Análisis Verbo-Corporal (2012)
11. Chica, H., Escobar, F., Folino, J.: La Entrevista Psiquiátrica Del Sujeto Simulador (2005)
12. Petisco, J.: Una Mirada A La Detección De Mentiras Empleando fMRI (2015)
13. Borth D., Rongrong, J., Chen, T., Breuel, T., Chang, S.: Large-scale visual sentiment ontology and detectors using adjective noun pairs (2013)
14. Wang, J., Fu, J., Xu, Y., Mei, T.: Beyond object recognition: visual sentiment analysis with deep coupled adjective and noun neural networks (2016)
15. Baecchi, C., Uricchio, T., Bertini, M., Del Bimbo, A.: A multimodal feature learning approach for sentiment analysis of social network multimedia. Multimed. Tools Appl. **75**, 2507–2525 (2015)

16. Zadeh, A., Chen, M.: Tensor fusion network for multimodal sentiment analysis (2017)
17. Chinsatit, W., Saitoh, T.: CNN-based pupil center detection for wearable gaze estimation system (2017)
18. Poria, S., Peng, H., Hussain, A., Howard, N., Cambria, E.: Ensemble application of convolutional neural networks and multiple kernel learning for multimodal sentiment analysis (2017)
19. George, A., Routray, A.: Real-time eye gaze direction classification using convolutional neural network (2016)
20. Llerena, M.: Desarrollo de una metodología basada en la programación neurolingüística utilizando software educativo para mejorar el proceso enseñanza-aprendizaje. Msc tesis. Escuela Superior politécnica de Chimborazo, Ecuador (2016)
21. Florea, L., Florea, C., Vrânceanu, R., Vertan, C.: Can your eyes tell me how you think? A gaze directed estimation of the mental activity (2013)
22. Risko, E., Anderson, N., Lanthier, S., Kingstone, A.: Curious eyes: individual differences in personality predict eye movement behavior in scene-viewing (2012)
23. Rauthmann, F., Seubert, C., Sachse, P., Furtner, M.: Eyes as windows to the soul: gazing behavior is related to personality (2012)
24. Medhat, W., Hassan, A., Korashy, H.: Sentiment analysis algorithms and applications: a survey (2014)
25. Costa Jr., P.T., McCrae, R.R.: Revised NEO Personality Inventory (NEO-PI-R) and NEO Five-Factor Inventory (NEO-FFI) Manual. Psychological Assessment Resources, Odessa (1992)
26. Hooft, V.: Intentional response distortion on personality tests: using eye-tracking to understand response processes when faking (2014)
27. Broz, F., Lehmann, H., Nehaniv, C., Dautenhahn, K.: Mutual gaze, personality, and familiarity: dual eye-tracking during conversation (2012)
28. Papoutsaki, A., Sangkloy, P., Laskey, J.: WebGazer: scalable webcam eye tracking using user interactions (2016)
29. Krishnamurthy, N.: Introduction to Computer Graphics, p. 165 (2002)
30. Tejero, P., Pastor, G., Crespo, A.: Exploración visual y movimientos oculares en conductores con distinta experiencia: una revisión (2004)

Virtual and Augmented Reality

Stereohaptics Toolkit for Dynamic Tactile Experiences

Ali Israr[1(✉)], Siyan Zhao[1,2], Zachary Schwemler[1,2], and Adam Fritz[1]

[1] Disney Research, Pittsburgh, PA 15213, USA
aliisrar@hotmail.com
[2] Carnegie Mellon University, Pittsburgh, PA 15213, USA

Abstract. We introduce a toolkit for creating, editing, storing, sharing and broadcasting dynamic haptic media through current computing devices. Adapted from an audio-based infrastructure, our *Stereohaptics* toolkit uses off-the-shelf hardware components and available software tools to create various haptic interfaces and applications. Core of our toolkit is the *Stereohaptics* engine that processes inputs from embedded sensors and renders high definition haptic feedback on discrete actuator grids. We exploit sensory illusions in touch to generate the perception of objects and their motion on, around and through the user's body and present psychophysical evidence of static and moving tactile illusions between two discretely spaced haptic actuators. The toolkit supports users to craft a variety of haptic effects on and across the body in a variety of grid configurations. We present design of the toolkit and its use in various activities and workshops. Our framework is easy-to-use and simple-to-adopt and can be applied to everyday handheld, wearable, augmented reality, virtual reality and extended reality applications.

Keywords: Haptic toolkit · Haptic illusions · Haptic experience design · Virtual and augmented reality

1 Introduction

Technology devices nowadays trend towards multisensory engagement, including visual, auditory, and haptic modalities. To design for an integrated experience, current computing platforms are equipped with audio-visual displays, frameworks for seamless flow of analog-digital data, and plugins for authoring, recording and playback the sensory media. In order to further enhance the sensory experience, user interactions are monitored via embedded sensors and trigger event handlers in application programs. There is currently an abundance of available application programming interfaces (APIs) and editing software for designing and working with the audio-visual content. Such richness in hardware technologies and software tools is, however, missing in designing coherent haptic feedback, and therefore integrating them with multisensory media is challenging and non-trivial. In this paper, we repurpose the audio-based framework for haptic experience design and utilize audio-based tools to add, save, personalize, and broadcast dynamic haptic media. These tools are well established, mainstream and familiar to a large population in entertainment, design, academic, and the DIY communities, and therefore the toolkit introduce in this paper is easy to use and simple to adopt.

We introduce the *Stereohaptics* toolkit that allows designers, engineers and researchers to use existing hardware and software tools for creating haptics experiences. The toolkit is composed of three main components; One is the database of actuation and sensing technologies easily accessible to consumers and operates with an alternating driving signal; compatible with audio frameworks in our computers, mobile devices, toys, furniture, etc. Second is the suite of software used for authoring and routing audio signals. These software suites are modified to work and design in haptics. Third, in the core of the toolkit resides the *Stereohaptics* engine that renders dynamic haptic feedback based on the user input. The engine utilizes psychophysical models of tactile illusions for creating a phantom tactile sensation and modulating its motion between two or more actuators arranged as a grid on and around the user and couples user inputs to parametric values of the haptic output.

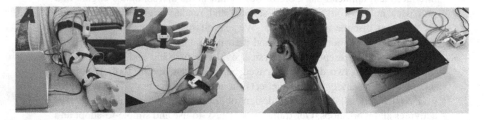

Fig. 1. The Stereohaptics Toolkit is used in a variety of applications including wearable, handhelds and structures.

Organization of the paper is as follow: we first present related background on haptic hardware technologies, common tactile illusions, and available audio and haptic toolkits. We then present the framework of Stereohaptics and design of a sample toolkit that uses off the shelf components and software and demonstrate the work flow with the toolkit on a user's computer. Then we present psychophysical evidence of static and moving tactile illusions on, around and across the user's body using two vibrating actuators (therefore stereo) and approximate the control space of moving tactile illusions in four configurations shown in Fig. 1. Then we report experience with the sample toolkit in a series of workshops and show that the toolkit is useful to familiarize and educate new users with haptic feedback, and provide necessary tools for haptic experience, interaction and product design. Finally, we highlight the scalability and use cases of the toolkit in a variety of applications.

2   Related Background

2.1   Haptic Hardware Technologies

A widely available haptic hardware technology in consumer use, often seen in cellphones and game controllers, is the unbalanced rotating mass dc-motors that produce vibrations as a function of applied dc-voltage. Voice coils and linear resonance actu-ators (LRA) are also popular due to small packaging, reasonable cost and simple drive circuitry. Piezoactuators and electroactive polymers (EAP) have been used in wearable, toys, and handheld devices because of small and flexible design [3, 7, 27, 34]. Piezoactuators, as well as motors, are also used in skin stretch devices to produce shear on the skin [10, 22], and electrostatic devices are designed to vary the friction between the skin and interaction surface or between two surfaces to augment user interactions [4, 11]. These actuators, similar to the speaker technology, give control over both output frequency and amplitude and operate on an alternating driving signal. This time alternating haptic actuation is termed as *tactile* or *vibrotactile*.

Vibrotactile devices are either installed in a single actuator configuration (as in mobile phones) or in a "grid" configuration for varying and moving sensations on and across the body [13, 18, 20]. Surface mounted transducers such as shakers [1, 23], vibrators [29], ultrasonic transducers [32] and electrostatic layers [4, 12] create haptic simulations by propagating acoustic waves in and away from a surface. These haptic technologies operate in bandwidths similar to that of audio channels, and therefore can be applicable to a typical audio framework. Other actuators, such as motors, pneumatic, and Peltier devices, may require special driving circuitry and control framework as in [31].

2.2 Haptic Illusions

A typical vibrotactile stimulus of duration d is defined by a frequency f and amplitude A. Other parameters to characterize the stimulus are temporal onset interval (*SOA* short for stimulus onset asynchrony) and attack and decay fading functions, as shown in Fig. 2. Sequential stimulations at two locations on the skin create a perception of illusory moving sensation between the two points [13, 14, 19, 30]. This moving illusion is known as *Apparent Tactile Motion* shown in Fig. 2A. Simultaneous stimulations at two locations create a "phantom" percept, whose intensity and location are determined by the intensity of two real actuators. This static illusion is known as *Tactile Phantom Sensations* [2, 13] shown in Fig. 2B.

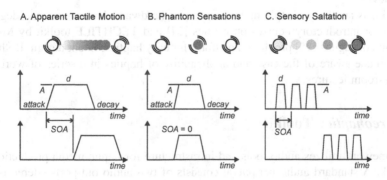

Fig. 2. A set of sensory illusions in tactile perception.

Another illusion is *Sensory Saltation* or the "cutaneous rabbit" illusion [9] shown in Fig. 2C. In this case, three brief stimuli are delivered to the first actuator followed by three stimuli at the second actuator. The user feels a jumping sensation gradually moving from one actuator to the other. These illusions are popular in HCI field and applied towards developing new haptic technologies and interfaces (such as [15, 16, 17, 26, 29 33]. Moreover, these illusions are evoked in contiguous body sites, such as the back, torso, forearm, palm, etc. In this paper, we show that these illusions persist on, across and all around the user's body even when the actuators are not directly in contact with the skin. It has been shown that the frequency and amplitude of the stimulation do not affect illusory percepts [6, 14, 35], and we explore the other two control parameters, d and *SOA*, to evoke moving illusions in our experiments.

2.3   Audio and Haptic Software and Toolkits

A typical audio-based peripheral is shown in Fig. 3A. A personal laptop is equipped with audio input-output ports for microphone input and headphone output. This peripheral is standard in mobile devices (such as phones, wearable, hand controllers), furniture, vehicles, toys and so on. In terms of audio tools, options abound for a user to design and experience various audio content. Mainstream tools, such as Maya, Pro tools, Ableton, Unreal Engine etc. are only a small sample of tools available to edit, route, store and playback audio media. With abundance of audio-based tools, users can easily work with their audio media to create diversified content.

Compared to the variety and flexibility in audio interfaces and tools, haptic media tools are in dearth. The few existing tools with custom APIs are mostly developed for commercial use and only support a specific kind of actuation technology. For example, Immersion Corp. has published developer tools that are compatible with haptic technologies by Immersion Corp. (www.immersion.com). Similarly, D-BOX tools and custom Maya plugins are optimized for motion platforms in theater experiences (www.d-box.com). Research has also proposed tools like Tactons [5], Haptic Phonemes [8], FeelCraft [36], and Tactile Animations [28] to combine rich haptic experience with events, activities and media context. But they are demonstrated to support a specific haptic device.

Hapkit is another example of low-cost open hardware device with one degree of freedom for introductory courses on haptics [24] and TECHTILE toolkit by Minamizawa and colleagues [25] provides a platform for easy haptic content design. Both these toolkits made aware of the ease and applicability of haptics in a series of workshops and classroom lectures.

3   *Stereohaptics* Toolkit

Our framework utilizes audio tools and infrastructure for haptic media production and playback. A standard audio peripheral consists of two audio out-ports (stereo output) and one audio in-port (microphone input) (Fig. 3A). Parallel to the setup, our framework has outputs, inputs and an interface (Fig. 3B). A laptop computer running an audio synthesizer tool (*interface*) generates an *output* of an analog waveform from the audio out-port. The *input* encodes analog measurements through the audio in-port. These input-output analog signals are conditioned through our toolkit's hardware board that comprises of common audio conditioning and amplifier circuitries (Fig. 3B). The output from the board is connected to off-the-shelf haptic actuator in contact with a user's body and the input to the board is connected to an analog sensor that measures a user activity.

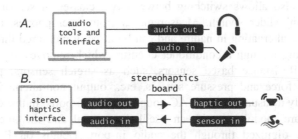

Fig. 3. (A) Typical audio interfaces in a computer. (B) Framework of the Stereohaptics toolkit.

The *interface* is a critical component for accessible and flexible designs, and routing and parsing of input-output signals. The interface also enables parametric models of haptic effects, particularly models of static and moving tactile illusions (Fig. 2). As many computing devices are already equipped with two (stereo) audio outports, we present a toolkit with two haptic points to demonstrate the framework and user experiences.

Figure 4A shows an exemplary toolkit. The toolkit is light, inexpensive, and composed of common electronic components. It consists of a custom hardware board, two voice coil tactors, a pair of stereo audio cables, an USB audio interface, a power adapter and a MEMS accelerometer. The audio cables are plugged to the audio port of a personal computer and the computer interface was developed in a popular visual programing language MAX (cycling74.com). Figure 4B shows the input-output flow of the toolkit and an exemplary use case. The accelerometer is placed under one cup and the tactor is placed under another cup. The toolkit and a software interface are used to couple the activity in the sensed cup to vibrations on the actuated cup [25].

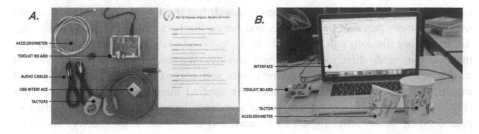

Fig. 4. (A) Exemplary toolkit using off the shelf parts. (B) a typical user case with the toolkit.

The tactors are enclosed in 3D printed housings and operate ~40–300 Hz at ~20–40 dB SL (sensation level) on the body. The board is also housed in a 3D casing, and Velcro straps are used to attach 3D parts to the body and environment. Figure 5 shows details of the hardware board. The board takes 12 V input and drives the circuitry with regulated ±5 V. The stereo audio output passes through a pair of 1 W LM4889 audio amplifiers (Texas Instruments, USA) and outputs the waveform to a pair of Tectonics Element's exciters (model: TEAX13C02-8/RH, USA).

The toolkit also allows switching between two classes of sensor inputs with a 'sensor selection' slider switch. Measurements from microphones, accelerometers, pulse-sensors are alternating in nature and can be directly measured through audio in-ports after passing through a conditioner circuitry which removes any dc bias in the sensor signal. Resistance based sensors, such as stretch sensors, potentiometers, switches, dials, force and pressure sensors, etc., output non-alternating signal that cannot be directly measured through AC-coupled audio in-ports. In this case, the sensor measurements are modulated with an oscillating signal and the alternating sensor voltage is then digitized through the audio in-port. Details on Bill of Material (BOM) and board layout files are accessible at: https://www.researchgate.net/publication/330672632_supplementaryzip.

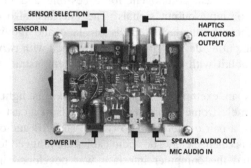

Fig. 5. A Hardware board of the toolkit.

4   Psychophysics of Stereohaptics Illusions

In this section, we demonstrate that a variety of haptic effects can be generated between two or more vibrating elements. Recent research has used vibrotactile grids to create moving illusory percepts on the palm, and across the back and torso [13, 16–18, 26]. These sensory illusions can be parametrically modeled to create a variety of sensations that vary in size, direction, speed and quality. We investigate psychophysics of mechanical stimulations at two active points and approximate the control space of moving illusory percepts between them. We applied three popular sensory illusions (Fig. 2) to evoke static and moving tactile sensations between two voice-coil actuators placed on (i) the forearm, (ii) on each hand, (iii) across the head, and (iv) across an object in contact with the hand.

4.1   Methods

The toolkit described in the previous section is used in the experiments. The purpose of experiments is to determine if moving tactile illusions (Fig. 2) are possible in four actuator configurations shown in Fig. 1. A participant completes a session of eight blocks and each block examines one of the two moving illusions (apparent motion or sensory saltation) at one of the four configurations. The illusion and configuration combinations are presented in random order.

A stimulus set is composed of three repetitions of 2 durations (70 ms and 200 ms) and four SOAs. In the *apparent tactile motion condition*, one actuator sets off, followed by the other separated by an SOA (Fig. 2A). The SOA values are 0 ms (simultaneous), 50 ms, 100 ms and 1000 ms (completely discrete). Attack and decay fading functions are set to 10% of the stimulus duration. In the *saltation conditions*, one actuator is triggered for three times followed by three stimulations of the other actuator (Fig. 2C). Each series of stimulations is separated by an SOA of $d + 10$ ms, $d + 50$ ms, $d + 100$ ms and $d + 500$ ms. Attack and decay fading functions are set to 10 ms. These durations and SOAs are derived from previous research to elicit illusory, non illusory and no motion sensations [6, 13, 35]. Frequency (70 Hz sinusoid) and amplitude (~ 25 dB SL) of stimuli were kept the same throughout the experiment.

In each trial participants report if they feel one point, two, three or more distinct points, or a "continuous motion" sensation from one point to the other point. Participants respond verbally and the experimenter records the response. Participants wear headphone that plays masking noise. Each block (24 trials) takes roughly 5 min to complete and the experiment takes less than 45 min to complete.

4.2   Results and Discussion

Ten participants (5 males, average age: 23 years) took part in the study after they signed a consent form approved by an IRB (Institutional Review Board). Participants' responses were quantified by assigning a number corresponding to the number of distinct spatial points they felt. The response of "more distinct points" was assigned a number 4 and "continuous motion" was assigned a number 5. The results are shown in Fig. 6. Each data point represents the average among participants and the error bars show standard deviation. The results are further analyzed using a repeated measure ANOVA.

Apparent tactile motion is evoked in all four actuator configurations. When SOA was large (1000 ms), the two stimuli were perceived as two discrete vibration points. When the two stimuli were simultaneous (SOA = 0), participants reported a single vibration point in all configurations except for the hands. In the two intermediate SOAs (i.e. 50 ms and 100 ms) participants consistently felt "motion" between the two points. An ANOVA reveals no significant effects of configurations [$F(2.03,18.3) = 1.2$, $p = 0.33$] and duration [$F(1,9) = 4.7$, $p = 0.06$] and a significant effect of SOA [$F(1.5,13.8) = 214$, $p < 0.001$]. All interaction terms failed to show significance ($p > 0.05$). The result suggests that apparent tactile motion robustly persists on the body (arms), along a surface, and across the hands and the head.

Sensory saltation, on the other hand, was not perceived consistently across all four configurations. A 3-way repeated measure ANOVA shows significant effects of configuration [$F(1.4, 12.2) = 4.9$, $p = 0.04$] and SOA [$F(1.4, 12.6) = 5.1$, $p = 0.032$] and no significant effect of duration [$F(1,9) = 3.3$, $p = 0.103$]. All interactions involving the configuration factor were also significant ($p < 0.05$). Therefore, we analyzed each configuration separately using 2-way repeated ANOVAs. On the hands and on the head, the saltation failed to evoke illusory motion. On the arm, both duration [$F(1,9) = 8.6$, $p = 0.017$] and SOA [$F(1.96, 17.6) = 6.4$, $p = 0.009$] showed significant effects. A close examination of the factors indicated that saltation was the strongest at small SOA and short durations (70 ms). On the surface, only SOA had a significant effect [$F(2.3, 20.3) = 8.1$, $p = 0.002$], indicating that sensory saltation was evoked with both long and short durations at low SOAs.

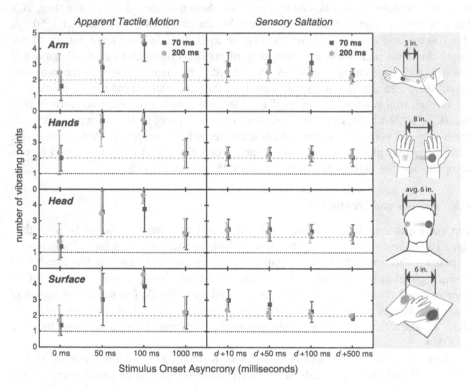

Fig. 6. Approximate control parameter space of apparent tactile motion (left) and sensory saltation (right) in four test configurations.

In summary, the experiments show that apparent tactile motion is robust and persists in the two test durations and four test configurations. Sensory saltation only persists on the arm and surfaces, mostly at low durations and low SOAs, and phantom tactile illusions (merging of two simultaneous vibrations into one virtual actuator [1, 13]) are evoked on the arm, the head and the surface using quick (short duration) stimulations.

5   Workshops and Activities

We have utilized the toolkit in a series of training and activity sessions, ranged from 6-h studio-workshops to 2-h short interactive courses. The sessions are geared towards giving familiarity to designers, artists, engineers, and computer scientists with state-of-the-art in haptic feedback. The goal of the workshop is to utilize the toolkit in hand-on design activities and explore its applicability and accessibility. It is assumed that the attendees of the session are novice in haptic feedback, with varying degree of familiarity with audio tools and framework. A sample instructional material and activities are submitted as supplementary material.

In a typical workshop, the session starts with a brief introduction of haptic perception and technologies, followed by demonstrations of the toolkit and activities (see the supplementary material). The activity sessions introduce attendees with the computer interface, hardware and software tools, and prepare them for working independently or in a small group of 2–3 participants. The activities are: (i) create and modulate a haptic effect – including assembly of the toolkit, familiarity with the interface, set parameters such as frequency, amplitude, waveform, and location; (ii) create and modulate a moving illusion – including experimenting with control spaces of illusions in Fig. 6, experimenting with body locations and familiarity with the quality of sensory effects; (iii) familiarity and playing with a library of tactile effects prepared for the attendees; and (iv) familiarity and playing with the activity sensor.

All activities are prepared in Max (cycling74.com) interface. Figure 7 shows screenshots of Activity 1 and Activity 3, where tactile illusions were parameterized and incorporated in the flow. Users set waveform parameters and tune the quality of both apparent tactile motion and saltation at different speeds. Finally, an interactive ideation, design and demo session concludes the training.

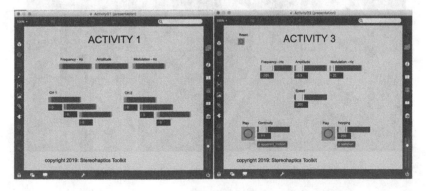

Fig. 7. Screenshots of the interface during user activities.

Our workshops have been highly interactive, and participants prepared numerous everyday scenarios with haptic feedback. These ranged from guiding visual impaired shoppers with directional haptic feedback in a marketplace experience to broadcasting gating actions of a lead-rower to other teammates in order to optimize synchronize rowing. Some ideas were later pursued by participants for their academic advancements. Figure 8 shows some experiences from the workshop. All attendees are asked to fill an online survey, however it is not mandatory. (A survey printout is shown in the supplementary materials.) Out of 54 participants, we received surveys from 22 attendees. These surveys were anonymous and asked for user's background, familiarity with haptics, DIY tasks, open-source software, design, audio production tools and hardware (1: beginners, 2: intermediate, 3: expert), and their ratings (scale 1–5, 1:low and 5:high) to learning experience, topics, activities, applicability and usefulness. Finally, participants were asked for comments and feedback.

On average, attendees rated themselves as beginners in haptics and audio production tools (median = 1) and intermediate in DIY, open source, design and hardware (median = 2). Attendees' ratings to learning (mean = 4.1: mode = 4), topics (4.2:5), activities (4.2:5), applicability (4.5:5) and usefulness (4.5:5) were generous. A few comments highlighting possible improvements were: "nice to have access to the hardware devices after the workshop, replicable either through low-cost or open hardware solutions", "the pacing feels a little uneven: lot's of time in the morning, rushed at the end", "I expect more than vibration", etc.

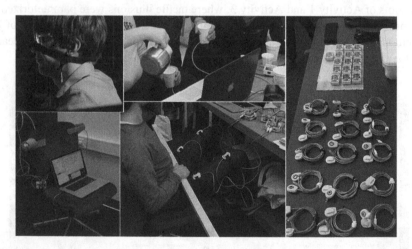

Fig. 8. Some pictures from the workshop-studios.

6 Applications and Use Cases

A key feature of our framework is that it is derived from audio-based tools available in abundance and familiar to creative, professional and academic workforce. We exploit this feature so current workforce can easily apply their skills to construct new haptic technologies and applications using off-the-shelf components.

Perhaps the most common application is in *entertainment* settings, where coherent haptic feedback complements activities and events in video games, movies, sporting events, rides, and in virtual and extended reality. Figure 9 shows a *Haptic Cart* that uses multiple actuators mounted on different elements of the cart and a potentiometer to measure the steering angle. The cart is integrated with a driving game and reacts to collisions, road pavements, and vehicle states. Similar frameworks are also embedded in benches, couches, beds and other furniture to create experience of living environments, where accessories can react to user actions as well as possess unique haptic characteristics [23].

The toolkit can be employed in the *educational* domain in two ways. One, it is used to construct academic material to enhance user's ability in listening, reading and comprehending stories, like in [33, 37], and two, the toolkit can be accessible to students enrolled in the media design, engineering, psychology and HCI course to explore new applications, products and experiences in haptics domain.

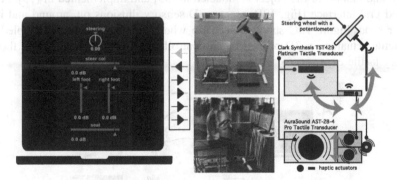

Fig. 9. A Haptic Cart.

The toolkit can also be used for *therapeutic* and *assistive* services. The feedback complements relaxation and meditation, monitor and guide breathing patterns, and provide massage services and applied in smart-vests, smart-belts and headgears to provide directional and awareness cues to motorcycle riders, professional athletes, and construction workers. In *social domains*, personal messages through the Internet and data networks can be shared on personal computers and mobile devices. We demonstrated an application with two remote users interacting via Skype and communicate personal and emotional haptic messages sensed with an accelerometer and rendered on tactors connected with our toolkit (Fig. 10).

Fig. 10. Sharing haptic experiences via internet.

One advantage of the Stereohaptics framework is that it applies to a variety of actuation technologies. We made modifications in hardware electronics to accommodate high-voltage low-power electric pulses and created electrovibration [4] and electro-tactile [21] feedback using audio-based software (see Fig. 11). Similarly, the framework can explore the full capacity of haptic technologies and trigger different sensory modes in touch, such as vibrations and electric stimulations combined together, and with visuals and sound. Figure 12 shows a few extensions of the framework. Figure 12A coupled hand motion to trigger a phantom object in between hands. The location and motion of the object is modeled in [35] and implemented in [15]. A head mounted grid interface (Fig. 12B) creates 3D sensory illusions on, around and inside the user head. Figure 12C shows a scenario where Peltier devices are coupled with vibrotactile actuators in 3D printed touch controllers to render an integrated thermal-vibratory tactile experience.

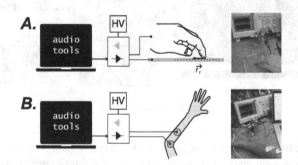

Fig. 11. Adaptation of the framework to electrical systems.

Fig. 12. Scalability of the framework. (A) Wearable, (B) Head mounted gears, (C) 3D printed toys.

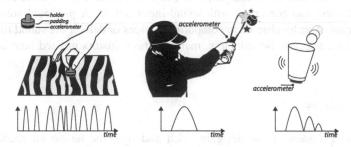

Fig. 13. Applications of haptic recorder.

A key feature of the toolkit is that it senses user activities through high-speed high-bandwidth audio in-ports. Our framework utilizes closed-loop mechanism, where the user activities are monitored in real time and instantaneous feedback is triggered. One application of the closed-loop architecture is a *haptic recorder* that senses haptic features, record them as audio data, broadcast them via audio stream and playback them on demand, all using audio tools. Such a recorder is useful for recording the user's activity during sports, haptic features on surfaces, impacts and other dynamic behaviors as shown in Fig. 13.

6.1   Limitations

Although there are many advantages of our toolkit, currently there are limitations. First, the framework utilizes audio-based tools and input-output. These tools are optimized for audio bandwidth, which is roughly from 20 Hz to 20 kHz. Haptic effects span between ~dc to 400 Hz. Therefore, the low frequency haptic effects are usually attenuated and filtered out. Second, the audio signal is generally sampled at 44.1 kHz which is an over kill for haptic signals. Haptics systems construct clean feedback using 4 kHz sampling rate, which is 10 times slower than audio rates. Therefore, a large bandwidth resource is not utilized and wasted. Our future work includes development of a protocol to utilize the broad bandwidth of an audio channel to drive multiple haptic actuators using simple multiplexing circuitry.

Third, a large variety of haptic actuators are not applicable in the exemplary framework, and custom plugins are utilized in conjunction with our framework. For example, a separate interface was design and used for Peltier devices and dc motors. Fourth, the current toolkit utilizes only two haptic outputs and one sensor input. This limits production of rich haptic interactions needing multiple actuators and sensor. We have extended the toolkit to include mechanical as well as electrical actuators. Another extension includes modular haptic units, where the user adds desired numbers of actuator and sensor channels to a central motherboard unit. These scenarios are briefly discussed in the application section; however, the possibilities are limitless.

Finally, almost all computing devices are equipped with a single audio input-output pair, which is basically for sound purpose. Our framework restricts these channels for haptic production and comprises with sound input-output. A proposed solution is to add another set of audio channel in computing devices or deliver the sound through the same haptic transducers. Nevertheless, many of the actuators utilized here are merely speakers.

7   Conclusions

We propose a framework for designing rich and dynamic haptic interactions using audio tools. The audio infrastructure is already established and available in consumer electronics and everyday objects. This framework allows designers, artists, engineers and everyday users to integrate and design haptic content in their projects. The framework is simple-to-adopt and easy-to-use, and accommodates a wide variety of actuation technologies.

Utilizing the audio infrastructure for haptic experience design is not novel, and it has been used in research and products to enhance users experience (see e.g. [25]). However, haptic experiences are usually limited to homogenous synthetic vibrations presented at one location. We present a framework that utilized psychophysics of moving tactile illusions between two (or more) vibrating points and extend the use to vibrotactile grid arrays for moving tactile sensations on, across and around the body. We show evidence that sensory illusions of objects and motion exist between two actuators placed on the proximal skin locations, across the head, at two hands and on surfaces external to human body.

Acknowledgements. This work is supported by Disney Research, USA.

References

1. Albasini, A., Krause, M., Rembitzki, I.: Using Whole Body Vibration in Physical Therapy and Sport: Clinical Practice and Treatment Exercises. Churchill Livingstone, London (2010)
2. Alles, D.S.: Information transmission by phantom sensations. IEEE Trans. Man-Mach. Syst. 1(11), 85–91 (1970)

3. Bartow, A., Kapadia, A., Walker, I. D.: A novel continuum trunk robot based on contractor muscles. In: Proceedings of the 12th WSEAS International Conference on Signal Processing, Robotics, and Automation (2013)
4. Bau, O., Poupyrev, I., Israr, A., Harrison, C.: TeslaTouch: electrovibration for touch surfaces. In: Proceedings of the 23nd Annual Symposium on User Interface Software and Technology, pp. 283–292. ACM, New York (2010)
5. Brewster, S., Brown, L.M.: Tactons: structured tactile messages for non-visual information display. In: Proceedings of the Fifth Conference on Australasian User Interface, pp. 15–23. Australian Computer Society, Inc. Darlinghurst (2004)
6. Cholewiak, R.W., Collins, A.A.: Vibrotactile localization on the arm: effects of place, space, and age. Percept. Psychophys. **65**(7), 1058–1077 (2003)
7. Cohen, Y.B.: Electroactive Polymer (EAP) Actuators as Artificial Muscles - Reality, Potential and Challenges. PM136, SPIE Press, Bellingham (2004)
8. Enriquez, M., MacLean, K., Chita, C.: Haptic phonemes: basic building blocks of haptic communication. In: Proceedings of the 8th International Conference on Multimodal Interfaces, pp. 302–309. ACM, New York (2006)
9. Geldard, F.A., Sherrick, C.E.: The cutaneous "Rabbit": a perceptual illusion. Science **178** (4057), 178–179 (1972)
10. Gleeson, B.T., Horschel, S.K., Provancher, W.R.: Communication of direction through lateral skin stretch at the fingertip. In: Proceedings of the World Haptics, pp. 172–177. IEEE Computer Society, Washington DC (2009)
11. Hinchet, R., Vechev, V., Shea, H., Hilliges, O.: DextrES: wearable haptic feedback for grasping in VR via a thin form-factor electrostatic brake. In: Proceedings of the 31st Annual Symposium on User Interface Software and Technology, pp. 901–912. ACM, New York (2018)
12. Ishiguro, Y., Israr, A., Rothera, A., Brockmeyer, E.: Uminari: freeform interactive loudspeakers. In: Proceedings of the 9th International Conference on Interactive Tabletops and Surfaces, pp. 55–64. ACM, New York (2014)
13. Israr, A., Poupyrev, I.: Tactile brush: drawing on skin with a tactile grid display. In: Proceedings of the SIGCHI Conference on Human Factors in Computing Systems, pp. 2019–2028. ACM, New York (2011)
14. Israr, A., Poupyrev, I.: Control space of apparent haptic motion. In: Proceedings of the World Haptics Conference, pp. 457–462. IEEE (2011)
15. Israr, A., Zhao, S., McIntosh, K., et al.: Po2: augmented haptics for interactive gameplay. In: ACM SIGGRAPH 2015 Emerging Technologies, p. 21. ACM, New York (2015)
16. Israr, A., Poupyrev, I., Ioffreda, C., et al.: Surround Haptics: sending shivers down your spine. In: ACM SIGGRAPH 2011 Emerging Technologies, Article 14, 1 p (2011)
17. Israr, A., Zhao, S., Schwalje, K., Klatzky, R., Lehman, J.: Feel effects: enriching storytelling with haptic feedback. ACM Transactions on Applied Perception, 11(3), Article 11, 17 p (2014)
18. Kim, Y., Lee, J., Kim, G.J.: Extending "out of the body" tactile phantom sensations to 2D and applying it to mobile interaction. Pers. Ubiquit. Comput. 19(8), 1295–1311 (2015)
19. Kirman, J.H.: Tactile apparent movement: The effects of interstimulus onset interval and stimulus duration. Percept. Psychophys. **15**(1), 1–6 (1974)
20. Konishi, Y., Hanamitsu, N., Minamizawa, K., Sato, A., Mizuguchi, T.: Synesthesia suit: the full body immersive experience. In: ACM SIGGRAPH 2016 VR Village, Article 20, 1 p (2016)
21. Lopes, P., Ion, A., Baudisch, P.: Impacto: simulating physical impact by combining tactile stimulation with electrical muscle stimulation. In: Proceedings of the 28th Annual ACM Symposium on User Interface Software & Technology, pp. 11–19. ACM, New York (2015)

22. Luk, J., Pasquero, J., Little, S., et al.: A role for haptics in mobile interaction: initial design using a handheld tactile display prototype. In: Proceedings of the SIGCHI Conference on Human Factors in Computing Systems, pp. 171–180. ACM, New York (2006)
23. McIntosh, K., Mars, J., Krahe, J., et al.: Magic bench: a multi-user & multi-sensory AR/MR platform. In: ACM SIGGRAPH 2017 VR Village, p. 11. ACM, New York (2017)
24. Martinez, M.O., Morimoto, T.K., Taylor, A.T., et al.: 3-D printed haptic devices for educational applications. In: Proceedings of the IEEE Haptics Symposium, pp. 126–133. IEEE (2016)
25. Minamizawa, K., Kakehi, Y., Nakatani, M., et al.: TECHTILE toolkit: a prototyping tool for designing haptic media. In: ACM SIGGRAPH 2012 Emerging Technologies, Article 22, 1 p. ACM, New York, USA (2012)
26. Pittera, D., Obrist, M., Israr, A.: Hand-to-hand: an intermanual illusion of movement. In: Proceedings of the 19th International Conference on Multimodal Interaction, pp. 73–81. ACM (2017)
27. Poupyrev, I., Maruyama, S., Rekimoto, J.: Ambient touch: designing tactile interfaces for handheld devices. In: Proceedings of the 15th Annual Symposium on User Interface Software and Technology, pp. 51–60. ACM, New York (2002)
28. Schneider, O.S., Israr, A., MacLean, K.E.: Tactile animation by direct manipulation of grid displays. In: Proceedings of the 28th Annual Symposium on User Interface Software & Technology, pp. 21–30. ACM, New York (2015)
29. Seo, J., Choi, S.: Initial study for creating linearly moving vibrotactile sensation on mobile device. In: Proceedings of the 2010 IEEE Haptics Symposium, pp. 67–70. IEEE (2010)
30. Sherrick, C.E., Rogers, R.: Apparent Haptic Movement. Percept. Psychophys. 1, 175–180 (1966)
31. Wilson, G., Halvey, M., Brewster, S.A., Hughes, S.A.: Some like it hot: thermal feedback for mobile devices. In: Proceedings of the SIGCHI Conference on Human Factors in Computing Systems, pp. 2555–2564. ACM, New York (2011)
32. Winfield, L., Glassmire, J., Colgate, J.E., Peshkin, M.: T-PaD: tactile pattern display through variable friction reduction. In: Proceedings of the World Haptics Conference, pp. 421–426. IEEE Computer Society, Washington DC (2007)
33. Yannier, N., Israr, A., Lehman, J. F., Klatzky, R. L.: FeelSleeve: haptic feedback to enhance early reading. In: Proceedings of the 33rd Annual Conference on Human Factors in Computing Systems, pp. 1015–1024. ACM, New York (2015)
34. Zhao, H., Hussain, A.M., Duduta, M., et al.: Compact dielectric elastomer linear actuators. Adv. Funct. Mater. 28(42), 1804328 (2018)
35. Zhao, S., Israr, A.; Klatzky, R.: Intermanual apparent tactile motion on handheld tablets. In: Proceedings of the World Haptics Conference, pp. 241–247. IEEE (2015)
36. Zhao, S., Schneider, O., Klatzky, R., Lehman, J., Israr, A.: FeelCraft: crafting tactile experiences for media using a feel effect library. In: Proceedings of the Adjunct Publication of the 27th Annual Symposium on User Interface Software and Technology, pp. 51–52. ACM, New York (2014)
37. Zhao, S., Lehman, J., Israr, A., Klatzky, R.: Using haptic inputs to enrich story listening for young children. In: Proceedings of the 14th International Conference on Interaction Design and Children, pp. 239–242. ACM, New York (2015)

A Review of Augmented Reality-Based Human-Computer Interaction Applications of Gesture-Based Interaction

Chutisant Kerdvibulvech[✉]

Graduate School of Communication Arts and Management Innovation,
National Institute of Development Administration,
118 SeriThai Rd., Klong-chan, Bangkapi, Bangkok 10240, Thailand
chutisant.ker@nida.ac.th

Abstract. In recent years, augmented reality (AR) is an extremely growing field in information technology, computer science, and computer engineering. Although there are many recent works that use augmented reality for different purposes, most of the existing works do not focus on reviewing recent augmented reality-based human-computer interaction applications regarding gesture-based interaction. Therefore, we focus on a different goal from them. In this paper, we study robust methodologies that researchers have recently achieved gesture-based interaction for using in augmented reality-based human-computer interaction (HCI) applications. To begin with, we explore the recognitions of hand gestures using augmented reality. Next, we explore the possibilities of utilizing augmented reality for gesture-based interaction. We also give a suggestion and present a future scenario for gesture-based interaction and augmented reality. We believe that this would help the interactions that humans would have with modern innovations in an integrated cross-disciplinary area in the near future of human-computer interaction.

Keywords: Augmented reality · Human-Computer interaction ·
Gesture-based interaction · Hand gestures · Distance transform ·
Multimodal augmented reality · Mixed-scale gesture design

1 Background

With the fast development of the machine technology, augmented reality (AR) is a rapidly evolving field in human-computer interaction (HCI), since it helps humans to communicate interactively and also allows humans to visually interact with computing devices in various ways, particularly using gesture-based interaction. Recently, there are some surveys of gesture interaction and gesture recognition. For instance, in 2017, Asadi-Aghbolaghi et al. [1] reviewed systematically methods for gesture recognition and action in various image sequences using deep learning approaches. The fusion strategies, architectures, main datasets, and competition for gesture recognition and action were explained. For the architectures, as displayed in Fig. 1, they categorize the methods of convolutional neural network (CNN) based on how each method handles the temporal dimension of videos into three different groups: 3D convolutions, motion-based

© Springer Nature Switzerland AG 2019
C. Stephanidis (Ed.): HCII 2019, LNCS 11786, pp. 233–242, 2019.
https://doi.org/10.1007/978-3-030-30033-3_18

approaches, and sequential models. For fusion strategies, they categorize each strategy based on timing into three major groups: slow fusion, early fusion, and late fusion. Also in 2016, Kerdvibulvech [2] surveyed some important methods for gesture interaction for helping people with disability. A pose tracker and a combination of superpixels and support vector machine used in gesture interaction applications for supporting disabled people, such as hearing impairment, were explained. In this case, a pose tracker used six-degrees-of-freedom. More recently in 2018, Al-Shamayleh et al. [3] gave a good literature review on computer vision-based recognition techniques, specifically focusing on hand gesture recognition for sign language. Nevertheless, to the best of our knowledge, most of recent literature reviews have not focused on gesture-based interaction for using augmented reality in human-computer interaction applications. For this reason, we have a different goal from the aforementioned review works.

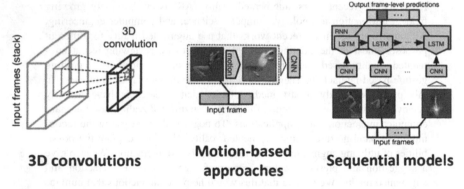

Fig. 1. Three different groups of the methods using deep learning based on how each method handles and deals with the temporal dimension of videos are categorized by Asadi-Aghbolaghi et al. [1].

This paper discusses and studies various state-of-the-art methodologies that researchers, including the author, have recently attempted to achieve gesture-based interaction for using in augmented reality-based human-computer interaction applications. This paper is divided into two main parts: recognitions of hand gestures using augmented reality and utilizing augmented reality for gesture-based interaction. The first main part is, because hand gesture is usually very important and essential for an interaction medium in augmented reality-based human-computer interaction applications, that we explore the recognitions of hand gestures using augmented reality technology. More generally, the second main part is that we explore the possibilities of utilizing augmented reality for human-computer interaction applications of gesture-based interaction. The remainder of this paper is organized for easy to read and understand as follows. Section 2 presents and discusses the recognitions of hand gestures using augmented reality technology in this field of gesture-based interaction research. Next, Sect. 3 reviews the literature on utilizing augmented reality technology for human-computer interaction applications of gesture-based interaction. Finally, Sect. 4 summarizes and concludes the state-of-the-art methods on augmented reality-based human-computer interaction applications of gesture-based interaction.

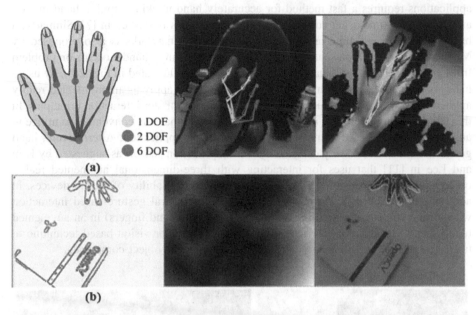

Fig. 2. (a) Kinematic skeleton using convolutional neural networks for localizing the hand and regressing 3D joint locations is developed in [7]. (b) A model-based hand tracking approach for recovering of three-dimensional hand gesture using extended distance transform is implemented in [8].

2 Recognitions of Hand Gestures Using Augmented Reality

Gestures basically convey information through physical movements of some human body parts, such as face, body, hands, legs, and feet. Generally, the hand is utilized for recognitions of gestures compared with other body parts, so that hand gesture is usually very important for an interaction medium in augmented reality-based human-computer interaction applications. The first main part is that we explore the recognitions of hand gestures using augmented reality. For example, because hand gestures can be applied for navigating and manipulating big data, the interactivity of touching the cube with the markerless hand poses utilizing an augmented reality interface [4] is introduced. Their augmented reality cube-like framework is called Augmented Reality for Public Engagement (PEAR).

Furthermore, due to the rapid development of gesture-based interaction using hand gestures, a user-study of hand gestures to design an intelligent in-vehicle interface [5] is researched. Also, Hürst and Wezel [6] built augmented reality-based interaction metaphors on smartphones using finger recognition in front of a smartphone's camera. In their system, people can see the live image of the smartphone's camera, and then computer generated-contents are augmented in the scene that they look at. However, their limitation is about the markerless finger tracking and the user's confusion when using the system. In other words, some users feel confused and face a cognitive overload. In addition, since human-computer interaction in many augmented reality applications requires a fast method for accurately hand tracking rapid, a hand motion analysis in real-time using adaptive probabilistic models is studied in [7]. Similarly, a hand tracking in real-time using convolutional neural networks is also proposed by Mueller et al. [8], as represented in Fig. 2(a), but they aim to handle occlusion problem from a sensor. Moreover, a hand tracking approach, as illustrated in Fig. 2(b), by using hand model and distance transform [9] in real-time for applying in augmented reality application in arts [10] is achieved in term of human-computer interaction principles. In this hand tracking approach, it can run in real-time, so that it is convenient to utilize in augmented reality-based human-computer interaction application. Alternatively, hand gestures can be interactively detected by the Leap Motion sensor, as suggested by Kim and Lee in [11] that uses for interacting with three-dimensional augmented reality objects for three-dimensional transformation to support usability of related-devices. In addition, Frikha et al. [12] presented a method for natural gesture-based interaction with virtual content and gestures from users (i.e., hands and fingers) in an augmented reality heart visualization interface. They used a computer vision-based technique to track gestures and then change the shapes of gestures on object commands.

Fig. 3. A gesture-based interaction study augmented onto the sessions and the table for designing mass volumes of buildings is developed by Gül [13].

3   Utilizing Augmented Reality for Gesture-Based Interaction

The second main part is that we explore the possibilities of utilizing augmented reality for human-computer interaction applications of gesture-based interaction. As gesture-based interaction can be utilized in designing mass volumes of buildings, we explore a gesture-based interaction study on an enhanced mobile augmented reality environment. In 2018, Gül [13] presents a gesture-based interaction work for understanding the concept of the co-design cognition and interaction behavior of the building designers using augmented reality, as shown in Fig. 3. This gesture-based interaction study is expected to further help the development of the augmented reality-based human-computer interaction works for supporting the design activity using multi-touch user interfaces. In fact, the pilot work of Gül et al. for understanding the effect of the employment through smartphone-based augmented reality is introduced in [14] based on a co-design situation and co-modelling situation.

In addition, due to a rapidly aging population's possibility, we explore the augmented reality work for interacting gesture-based interaction. In [15], Sorgalla et al. builds gesture-based interaction using augmented reality for interacting with virtual world to manipulate a variable smart environment using Eclipse SmartHome for supporting senior citizens. Besides, due to the popularity of an untethered mixed reality headset called Hololens from Microsoft, a mixed-scale gesture design using a Hololens augmented reality display with wearable sensors is discussed in [16] by Ens et al. Their aim is to develop a system that can interleave interactively microgestures with larger gestures for human-computer interaction. Figure 4 depicts the demonstration of Ens et al.'s work using wrist-worn sensor mounted under the wrist. For example, a finger's motion can manipulate the speed of a running/walking animation in the virtual world. In their similar study, led by Simmons et al. [17], they explore a comparative evaluation of two hand gesture recognition sensors for micro-gestures. In other words, they evaluate the capabilities of the devices to detect small movement using three distinct gestures.

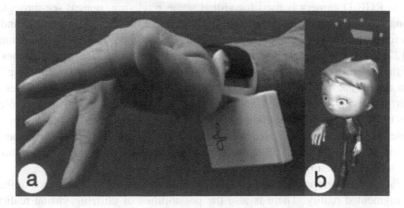

Fig. 4. A wrist-worn sensor, built and designed by Ens et al. [16], is used for controlling animations in the virtual world and designing mixed-scale gesture using a Hololens augmented reality display.

Furthermore, the multimodal augmented reality work is studied in [18] by Lugtenberg et al. for estimating the thickness of the objects, so it is able to allow people to adjust the perception of thickness (hollow or solid) of its material by changing some stimuli factors, including augmenting auditory, in the environment. In other words, their research goal is to find a different perception of thickness of any random material by just changing auditory feedback. However, their limitation is that audio alone is not always successful in every case. In some specific circumstances, it gives an incorrect answer by changing perception from solid to hollow. Therefore, by relying solely on audio alone, haptics and other modalities are believed to possibly help to address this problem. Figure 4 depicts the demonstration of this multimodal augmented reality work. In fact, the initial work of Lugtenberg et al. using multimodal augmented reality is also introduced in [19] for modulating the sound emitted by a material (either a hollow or solid cube) when touched based on the multimodal feedback psychophysically. From their experimental results, the Leap sensor can give more accurate results and lower difficulty than the Soli sensor with their test gesture set using three distinct gestures: a movement of the thumb and forefinger depicting a slider, a movement of moving a finger up and down, and a gesture of moving the hand up and down.

Moreover in 2018, Xue et al. [20] built an interactive hand rehabilitation supplementary system using augmented reality and gesture recognition. Their research purpose is to focus on helping the treatment activity of hand rehabilitation in any circumstance. In this way, their input device is Leap Motion device. Unity3D in this system is used as the development engine in three different parts: conventional training, augmented reality game training, and auxiliary functions. Therefore, because of different levels of challenges in each part using augmented reality, it can increase the attraction and difficulty of the rehabilitation process for users. Next, an optical see-through augmented reality system was explained in [21] by Zhen et al. for gesture-based interaction. In their system, Single-Point Active Alignment Method (SPAAM) based on RGB-D camera is used for virtual scene rendering, optical see-through calibration, and object tracking. Hence, they can achieve the mixture of virtual and real scenes for gesture-based interaction in real-time. Furthermore in early 2019, Aliprantis et al. [22] created a prototype system using gesture-based interaction approaches naturally for several interaction categories (rotation, scaling, and translation) in a Leap Motion device-augmented reality context. Figure 5 shows two different gestures used in their prototype system (high and low level of naturalism each). Their research focuses on gesture-based interaction methods and naturalism levels on the design of 3D user interfaces, called natural user interfaces (NUIs), in augmented reality framework. The Leap Motion device is integrated in a head-mounted display for building an augmented reality natural interface (Fig. 6).

In fact, the developments of gesture-based interaction methods are not limited in using augmented reality. There is also the possibilities of utilizing virtual reality for human-computer interaction applications of gesture-based interaction. Li et al. [23] gave a good overview of gesture interaction in virtual reality. Generally, virtual reality gesture interaction devices are classified into three main types: touch screen-based interaction devices, wearable interaction devices, and computer-vision-based interaction devices. In recent years, a non-contact and non-expensive device, called Leap Motion, is usually used for building gesture-based interaction applications for virtual reality. For instance, Khan et al. [24] discussed and evaluated the effects of adding hand and finger gesture interaction in a virtual world for 360° panoramic movie watching experience. They used Leap Motion, and a SoftKinetic RGB-D camera for tracking the

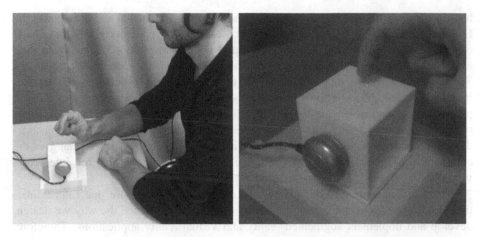

Fig. 5. Augmented sound experiment is designed by Lugtenberg et al. [18] for receiving a perception of thickness of an object differently when tapping it using two cubes (solid and hollow).

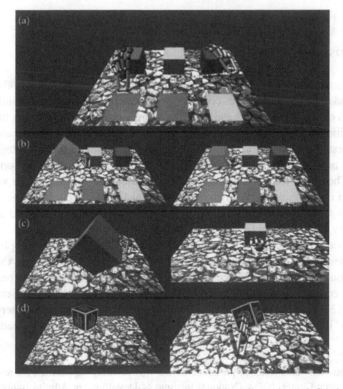

Fig. 6. Two different gestures used in [22] and presented by Aliprantis et al. for the three basic interaction categories.

hand and finger movements and capturing the texture of the hands and arms virtually. In their evaluation, they tested four different cases: showing either a rigged virtual hand or a point-cloud of the physical hand, with and without interaction. Hence from their experimental results, when people can have interact with virtual embedded content in a 360○ panoramic movie, they can feel strong embodiment and ownership from gesture-based interaction. More recently in December 2018, Céspedes-Hernández et al. [25] presented a system of gesture-based interaction for allowing people to navigate environments in a virtual world naturally. They focused on body gestures through user-defined commands within virtual reality environments. Therefore, people can give the commands using navigation tasks and the Wizard of Oz method for interaction virtually.

Therefore, according to our review and discussion, we propose that future directions for gesture-based interaction would be practically reinforced the way we design, develop and implement augmented reality and virtual reality applications. Therefore, we recommend the gesture-based interaction researchers to focus on recent methods of reality-based technologies, especially computer vision-based methodologies. General speaking, the possible methods of augmented reality and virtual reality we mentioned include accurate object tracking, automatic occlusion handling, and robust camera calibration.

4   Conclusions

In summary, we bring a discussion about gesture-based interaction methods for using in augmented reality-based human-computer interaction applications. We introduce the recent works of recognitions of hand gestures using augmented reality. We then outline the possibilities of utilizing augmented reality for human-computer interaction applications of gesture-based interaction. Although discussing about the advantages of each method, we note some limitations involved with using their systems in some specific situations. Therefore, we can understand how the interactions that humans would have with modern innovations do. We firmly believe that future directions for gesture-based interaction would be practically linked to the way we design augmented reality and virtual reality applications. Future work will continue the developments of gesture-based interaction methods for using in human-computer interaction applications of other extended reality (XR) technologies, including augmented virtuality (AV), in more hybrid approaches, such as the hybrid concept of model of human hand motion [26], the hybrid concept of model-based reactive control for robotic system in high dimensions [27], and the hybrid concept of virtual reality and spatial augmented reality [28], in an integrated cross-disciplinary area for the future of human-computer interaction.

Acknowledgments. This research presented herein was partially supported by a research grant from the Research Center, NIDA (National Institute of Development Administration).

References

1. Asadi-Aghbolaghi, M., et al.: A survey on deep learning based approaches for action and gesture recognition in image sequences. In: 12th IEEE International Conference on Automatic Face & Gesture Recognition (FG), pp. 476–483 (2017)
2. Kerdvibulvech, C.: A review of computer-based gesture interaction methods for supporting disabled people with special needs. In: Miesenberger, K., Bühler, C., Penaz, P. (eds.) ICCHP 2016. LNCS, vol. 9759, pp. 503–506. Springer, Cham (2016). https://doi.org/10.1007/978-3-319-41267-2_70
3. Al-Shamayleh, A.S., Ahmad, R.B., Abushariah, M.A., Alam, K.A., Jomhari, N.: A systematic literature review on vision based gesture recognition techniques. Multimedia Tools Appl. 77(21), 28121–28184 (2018)
4. Reski, N., Alissandrakis, A.: Using an augmented reality cube-like interface and 3D gesture-based interaction to navigate and manipulate data. In: 11th International Symposium on Visual Information Communication and Interaction (VINCI), pp. 92–96 (2018)
5. Jahani, H., Alyamani, H.J., Kavakli, M., Dey, A., Billinghurst, M.: User evaluation of hand gestures for designing an intelligent in-vehicle interface. In: Maedche, A., vom Brocke, J., Hevner, A. (eds.) DESRIST 2017. LNCS, vol. 10243, pp. 104–121. Springer, Cham (2017). https://doi.org/10.1007/978-3-319-59144-5_7
6. Hürst, W., van Wezel, C.: Gesture-based interaction via finger tracking for mobile augmented reality. Multimedia Tools Appl. 62(1), 233–258 (2013)
7. Chutisant, K.: A methodology for hand and finger motion analysis using adaptive probabilistic models. EURASIP J. Embed. Syst. Number 18 2014
8. Mueller, F., Mehta, D., Sotnychenko, O., Sridhar, S., Casas, D., Theobalt, C.: Real-time hand tracking under occlusion from an egocentric RGB-D sensor. In: International Conference on Computer Vision (ICCV), pp. 1163–1172 (2017)
9. Kerdvibulvech, C.: Hand tracking by extending distance transform and hand model in real-time. Pattern Recogn. Image Anal. 25(3), 437–441 (2015)
10. Kerdvibulvech, C.: An innovative real-time mobile augmented reality application in arts. In: De Paolis, L.T., Bourdot, P., Mongelli, A. (eds.) AVR 2017. LNCS, vol. 10325, pp. 251–260. Springer, Cham (2017). https://doi.org/10.1007/978-3-319-60928-7_22
11. Kim, M., Lee, J.Y.: Touch and hand gesture-based interactions for directly manipulating 3D virtual objects in mobile augmented reality. Multimedia Tools Appl. 75(23), 16529–16550 (2016)
12. Frikha, R., Ejbali, R., Zaied, M., Ben Amar, C.: Natural gesture based interaction with virtual heart in augmented reality. In: Jackowski, K., Burduk, R., Walkowiak, K., Woźniak, M., Yin, H. (eds.) IDEAL 2015. LNCS, vol. 9375, pp. 457–465. Springer, Cham (2015). https://doi.org/10.1007/978-3-319-24834-9_53
13. Gül, L.F.: Studying gesture-based interaction on a mobile augmented reality application for co-design activity. J. Multimodal User Interfaces 12(2), 109–124 (2018)
14. Gül, L.F., Halıcı, M., Uzun, C., Esengün, M.: Understanding the impact of mobile augmented reality on co-design cognition and co-modelling. In: Luo, Y. (ed.) CDVE 2016. LNCS, vol. 9929, pp. 362–370. Springer, Cham (2016). https://doi.org/10.1007/978-3-319-46771-9_47
15. Sorgalla, J., Fleck, J., Sachweh, S.: ARGI: augmented reality for gesture-based interaction in variable smart environments. In: 13th International Joint Conference on Computer Vision, Imaging and Computer Graphics Theory and Applications (VISIGRAPP), HUCAPP, vol. 2, pp. 102–107 (2018)

16. Ens, B., Quigley, A., Yeo, H.-S., Irani, P., Piumsomboon, T., Billinghurst, M.: Counterpoint: exploring mixed-scale gesture interaction for AR applications. In: Extended Abstracts of the 2018 CHI Conference on Human Factors in Computing Systems (CHI), 2018, Paper No. LBW120 (2018)

17. Simmons, H., Devi, R., Ens, B., Billinghurst, M.: Comparative evaluation of sensor devices for micro-gestures. In: International Conference on Artificial Reality and Telexistence & Eurographics Symposium on Virtual Environments (ICAT-EGVE), Posters and Demos, pp. 23–24 (2017)

18. Lugtenberg, G., et al.: Multimodal augmented reality - augmenting auditory-tactile feedback to change the perception of thickness. MultiMedia Model. (MMM) **1**, 369–380 (2018)

19. Lugtenberg, G., Sandor, C., Hürst, W., Plopski, A., Taketomi, T., Kato, H.: Changing perception of physical properties using multimodal augmented reality: position paper. In: Proceedings of the 2016 Workshop on Multimodal Virtual and Augmented Reality (MVAR), in Conjunction with International Conference on Multimodal Interaction (ICMI), pp. 8:1–8:4 (2016)

20. Xue, Y., Zhao, L., Xue, M., Fu, J.: Gesture interaction and augmented reality based hand rehabilitation supplementary system. In: 2018 IEEE 3rd Advanced Information Technology, Electronic and Automation Control Conference (IAEAC), INSPEC Accession Number: 18311447, Chongqing, China, 12–14 October 2018

21. Zhen, L., Jing, C., Zixiang, Z., Qiushuo, T., Ningsheng, H.: An optical see-through augmented reality system with gesture-based interaction. In: International Conference on Virtual Reality and Visualization (ICVRV), INSPEC Accession Number: 16918263, Hangzhou, China, pp. 447–452, 24–26 September 2016

22. Aliprantis, J., Konstantakis, M., Nikopoulou, R., Mylonas, P., Caridakis, G.: Natural interaction in augmented reality context. Visual Pattern Extraction and Recognition for Cultural Heritage Understanding (VIPERC), Piza, Italy, 30 January 2019

23. Li, Y., Huang, J., Tian, F., Wang, H.-A., Dai, G.-Z.: Gesture interaction in virtual reality. Virtual Reality Intell. Hardware **1**(1), 84–112 (2019)

24. Khan, H., Lee, G.A., Hoermann, S., Clifford, R.M.S., Billinghurst, M., Lindeman, R.W.: Evaluating the Effects of Hand-gesture-based Interaction with Virtual Content in a 360° Movie. In: ICAT-EGVE 63–70 (2017)

25. Céspedes-Hernández, D., González-Calleros, J.M., Guerrero-García, J., Rodríguez-Vizzuett, L.: Gesture-based interaction for virtual reality environments through user-defined commands. In: Agredo-Delgado, Vanessa, Ruiz, Pablo H. (eds.) HCI-COLLAB 2018. CCIS, vol. 847, pp. 143–157. Springer, Cham (2019). https://doi.org/10.1007/978-3-030-05270-6_11

26. Kerdvibulvech, C.: Hybrid model of human hand motion for cybernetics application. In: IEEE International Conference on Systems, Man, and Cybernetics (SMC), San Diego, pp. 2367–2372 (2014)

27. Tzorakoleftherakis, E., Ansari, A., Wilson, A.D., Schultz, J.A., Murphey, T.D.: Model-based reactive control for hybrid and high-dimensional robotic systems. IEEE Robot. Autom. Lett. **1**(1), 431–438 (2016)

28. Roo, J.S., Hachet, M.: Towards a hybrid space combining spatial augmented reality and virtual reality. In: IEEE Symposium on 3D User Interfaces (3DUI), Los Angeles, CA, pp. 195–198 (2017)

The OTC (Object to Camera) Approach to Visualize Behind Stories of Museum Exhibits

Si Jung SJ Kim$^{(\boxtimes)}$, Alexis Sanchez, John Farhad Hanifzai,
Francis Palispis, and Keitaro Nishimura

University of Nevada Las Vegas (UNLV), Las Vegas, NV 89052, USA
sj.kim@unlv.edu

Abstract. Augmented Reality (AR) is a growing field, with great potential purposes in many different environments including public museums and galleries. This paper introduces the use of AR in a public museum that is designed to bridge museum visitors, especially preschoolers to art pieces installed in a public museum. In collaboration with the UNLV Marjorie Barrick Museum, we created an Augmented Reality experience called the OTC (Object To Camera) to showcase one's artwork through an augmented medium that shows the behind scenes of the art pieces. The experience was intended to have a more physical approach, to distinguish itself from other augmented reality experiences the user may have come into contact with. An observation was conducted as a field study with preschoolers at a community event held at the UNLV Marjorie Barrick Museum and showed that interactive AR has potential applications in the museum to enhance the learning process.

Keywords: Augmented reality · AR · Vuforia · Cube · Art · Digital experience · Museum · STEM · STEAM

1   Introduction

The museum is generally a non-profit institution in the service of a community that exhibits the tangible and intangible heritage of humanity environment which include art pieces for which the public use for the purposes of education and enjoyment. The atmosphere in a museum is wide and of an open space. Visitors freely walk around and see different collections of exhibit items, while keeping themselves quiet to not bother other guests. Museum visitors often question themselves about the origin of pieces on display and the stories behind them. Some questions can be about the inspiration, tools used, and or goal of the piece. All the answers to these questions are assumed by the visitors'; unless there is supplementary information available or an attendant to the piece. The attendant could be the artist themselves.

This paper shows an exploratory work of visualizing the story behind museum exhibits by using augmented reality (AR). We proposed another way of gaining insight behind the pieces, by the way of augmenting the "behind the scenes" of museum exhibits. Instead of asking visitors to download a specific application to their smartphones,

© Springer Nature Switzerland AG 2019
C. Stephanidis (Ed.): HCII 2019, LNCS 11786, pp. 243–252, 2019.
https://doi.org/10.1007/978-3-030-30033-3_19

the implementation had a more physical component. The visitor had to use a cube box and position it in front a camera installed on a mobile cart with a television. Once the box was positioned correctly in front of the camera, a side specific augmentation was displayed on the television. The experience was in an open but dedicated space, so that both the user of the AR experience and fellow museum goers were able to see all the different augmentations on the television. We worked with the University of Nevada Las Vegas (UNLV) Marjorie Barrick Museum to create an augmented reality experience that showcased how AR bridges museum visitors to the exhibits. The museum had recently installed a new exhibition which was done by the artist Andrew Schoultz and behind the stories of the artist's exhibits were visualized by AR.

2 Background

Augmented Reality in short AR, is an immerging technology that superimposes computer-generated images on a user's view of the real world generally using a mobile device that is equipped with a camera on it [1]. AR provides the user with a composite view of real world and computer-generated virtual world which is called augmentation [2–4].

There have been several different approaches in AR for museums, art galleries and historical sites [5, 6]. The paradigm of AR is that it is getting more end users based on the dramatic technological advance in AR [7]. One of the most recent examples of using AR in the museum is the Smithsonian Museum's Skin and Bones exhibit that adopted AR for providing visitors with the supplemental information of the skeletons and bones being displayed [8]. The concept behind the project was to augment the bones displayed with the physical body of the animal when it was alive. For example, the users hold their tablet up to the bones and fish are augmented on to the bones.

There are other museums that adopted AR to provide visitors with a unique augmented experience for museum visitors to get a better visualization of the exhibits [9]. The National Museum of Singapore used AR in augmenting various plants and animals as graphics called, Story of the Forest [10]. In the experience, museum visitors use a mobile app equipped with a camera on their phones to view virtual plants and animals in real environment as well as to get supplemental information of them within the drawings. Museum visitors can take photos of or with the augmented scene and then the app provides more information about the plant or animal captured. The Kennedy Space Center in Florida applied AR to provide an immersive experience to visitors called, Heroes and Legends where AR brings holograms of astronaut royalty to life and tells their stories in front of visitors interactively [11]. Jinsha Site Museum in Chengdu, China created 3D models of relics [12, 13]. Visitors to the museum can use an AR app to explore the relics and see them in 3D. It allows visitors to learn more about how the relics look like and what they were used for. Google launched a new feature called Pocket Gallery as art of the Google Arts and Culture app [14]. It uses AR to allow people step inside of an art gallery through their mobile phone. This helps people see every art piece around world without the need to travel, just needed a mobile phone.

All the previous cases are based on an individual's smartphone camera as an AR museum that each user uses his or her own phone to get the augmentation of an object shown in Fig. 1(a). This approach would effective for a large-scale environment where many people visit the site, but it may not be effective in a small-scale environment where the walk flow of the exhibit is less dynamic with the small number of people. What if we trigger the augmentation by a tangible object, that is recognized by a camera from a remote distance? The concept of camera to target is still intact, but the mediums to do so are different, such as displayed in Fig. 1(b). The paper goes over the implementations and concept of object to camera augmented reality; which includes triggering the target and augmented the specific visuals.

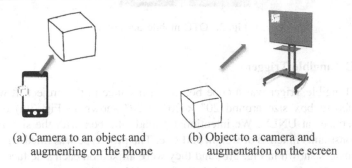

(a) Camera to an object and augmenting on the phone

(b) Object to a camera and augmentation on the screen

Fig. 1. Two different ways of augmenting objects

3   The OTC Design and Prototype

The OTC (Object To Camera) AR system was implemented with three separate components – an OTC (Object To Camera) Mobile Display, an OTC Tangible Trigger and an OTC application. More descriptions of the three components are described below.

3.1   OTC Mobile Display

A structural embodiment of the OTC was based on constructing a portable mobile cart consisting of a 32-in. LED display, an Android phone equipped with a camera, a mobile cart and a battery. These items were chosen so the OTC mobile display can be easily transported and put together for use. The highest of the display was critical, the display should be based on the height on the museum goers. But, also be not too tall to prevent discomfort when trying to position the target object in front of the camera. A battery was used to make the OTC Mobile Display as a standalone mobile AR display and not to rely on positioning near power outlets. Figure 2 shows an overall appearance of the mobile display.

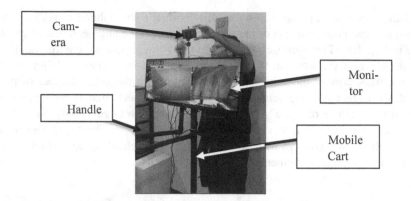

Fig. 2. OTC mobile display

3.2 OTC Tangible Trigger

The OTC Tangible Triger was a cube box as an instance in the project. It was a cube shape cardboard box size around $20'' \times 20'' \times 20''$ shown in Fig. 3(a) donated by shipping services at UNLV. We intentionally made the box with the size in order to give two constraints in terms of weight and size. The prototype was fitted with a total of six target images shown in Fig. 3(b) and they were affixed on each side face of the box shown in Fig. 3(c). Testing occurred thereafter and the testing system was an Android phone with the software downloaded and the cube with the images.

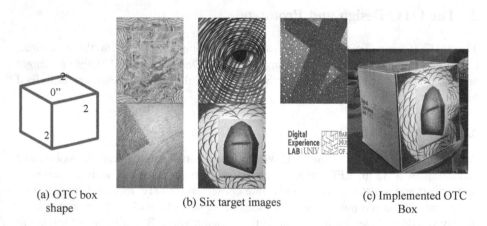

(a) OTC box
shape

(b) Six target images

(c) Implemented OTC
Box

Fig. 3. OTC Tangible Trigger

3.3 OTC App

The OTC application app was developed in Unity and Vuforia [15, 16]. Each side of the cube features an image that triggered an augmentation associated with the picture of the side. Six images corresponding to each surface of the OTC Tangible Trigger were uploaded onto a Vuforia database which Unity uses for image recognition [17]. The overall algorithm implemented in the app is shown in Fig. 4. As shown in the figure, OTC App first detects and recognizes a target image then locate and bring up its corresponding augmentation on the 3D cube model while aligning its size and position. Once triggered correctly, the augmentations would stay with its corresponding side. If the object was rotated with the same side and augmentation being shown, it would follow the objects juxtaposition.

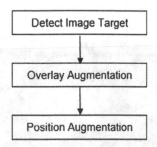

Fig. 4. An overall three steps of augmenting in the OTC app

Augmentation
Each side of the cube has one of Andrew's art pieces on it. We wanted to share some more insight behind his pieces, so we augmented features such as images and video to the art. Some of the augmentations included a time-lapse of Andrew painting one of the murals at the museum and another including a video of his completed artwork done at a local skate park in Las Vegas. Other sides of the cube were augmented with images that had a connection with the artwork. For example, one of Andrew's pieces was a painting of a knight's helmet, so the team augmented an image of the Vegas Golden Knights' logo onto it to connect the piece to the city. The team also included a credits section on the cube in which the DEX and museum team members were augmented.

Distance to recognize
We measured the minimum and maximum distance to recognize an object with the camera. The minimum distance was 5 feet and the maximum distance was 20 feet. However, the 20 feet distance was measured once the image target had already been detected at a closer distance. The initial distance needed for the target to be detected varied but seemed to be more consistent at a distance of less than 10 feet.

3.4   Integration and Testing

Once all the AR effects were being triggered correctly, we started using our event day equipment; which was the OTC object, OTC mobile display and OTC application all used together. The OTC application used the androids phone camera; which was the engine behind rendering the augmentations and displaying them. The android phone running the OTC application then was mounted on the television, with the camera facing objects in front of the television screen, as displayed in Fig. 2. The phone was connected to the television via HDMI port, so the interactions being shown on the cell phone could be displayed on the television. Figure 5 shows the two snapshots of the OTC App showing augmenting a story associated with one side of the OTC Tangible Trigger box displaying on the side of the box. All of the augmentations were positioned to the side of the box, not on top of the target. This was chosen so the connection between the target artwork and the "behind the scenes" augmentation. Figure 5(a) shows when the OTC App does not detect the target and Fig. 5(b) shows when the OTC App does detect the target and align the augmentation on the surface of the physical box.

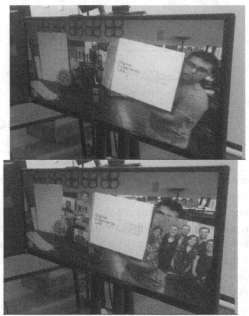

(a) Before recognizing a target   (b) When recognizing the target

Fig. 5. Snapshots of the OTC Setup and Testing

4 Museum Installation

We worked with the UNLV Marjorie Barrick Museum to create an augmented reality experience that would showcase the arts and STEM/STEAM to the community. Figure 6 shows an overall view of the UNLV Marjorie Barrick Museum.

The museum had recently installed a new exhibition which was done by the artist Andrew Schoultz. We wanted to use his art pieces in our OTC approach so we could keep our project relevant to the museum. We decided to create an OTC experience in which the community could learn more about Andrew's art through augmented reality as part of the event's sub-program called, STEAM AT THE MUSEUM and installed the OTC system shown in Fig. 7. We were given a large empty space for this AR

(a)Main Enterance   (b) Lobby   (c) Exhibition Hall

Fig. 6. UNLV Marjorie Barrick Museum

attraction. The AR experience required users to hold the OTC Box, trigger an image target detection using the android phone camera running the OTC application, and overlay augmentations which are associated with his art pieces on the monitor of the OTC Display.

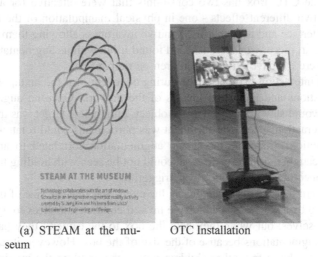

(a) STEAM at the museum   OTC Installation

Fig. 7. Install the OTC system in the museum

5   Results and Discussions

The OTC system was successfully installed in the museum as part of the STEAM at the museum sub program. Figure 8 shows children are experiencing the OTC in the museum.

The OTC experience was a success and received a lot of positive reactions. Most of the visitors were teachers from the community and other were children with their families. Most of the visitors that came to learn more about our project had very little knowledge of AR, but they were excited to learn more about it and where it could go in

Fig. 8. Children visitors experiencing the OTC experience

the future. The OTC Box has two constraints that were effective for adult attendees giving them two different effects - one in physical manipulation of the tangible cube-based user interface and the other in cognitive awareness allowing them to check each surface of the art piece with curiously and found it out with its augmentation. The same constraints were effective with our children participants.

A unique interaction that was made during the event, was the juxtaposition between the augmentations and the target images of the artwork. Once an augmentation was triggered, it would stay juxtaposed to the object; until a new target was triggered. What made this interaction special for the event was participants could rotate both the target and augmentation. Since the target and augmentation correlated to art, participants perspectives caught out information that could not be seen with holding the target in the same place once the augmentation was triggered.

One concern that we observed during the event was that the size of the OTC Box a bit too large to be handled by a child. We invited children attendees to try out the OTC Box for themselves, but when they held the box to the camera; they had a hard time viewing the augmentations because of the size of the box. However, it turned out to be a positive effect that a few other children joined the child on the manipulation of the box and worked together. The box enabled them to collaborate on handling of the box. Another concern that our team captured was that our phone running the AR application was quickly becoming discharged. Thus, it would be better to have the application downloaded on multiple devices to allow other phones to charge while the other is in use and would have demonstrated the portability of the AR application on different devices.

An observation conducted at the community event showed that interactive AR has potential applications in the museum to enhance the learning process of art related STEM/STEAM knowledge. From the media art perspectives, the OTC experience presented in the project was based on displaying art, in which we used both cases listed above. We superimposed digital images/video on a physical object for immersion and to see how much interest would be garnered throughout the event. Some attendees came back for a second trial, after see all of the artist exhibitions in person. During this trial they did not ask questions but made further connections between the augmentations showing the "behind the scenes" information of the pieces displayed at the museum. This was our initial goal, but the uniqueness and separation of our event drew people in before seeing all the exhibitions at the museum. It may have been better to have placed our event at the end of a set path that showcased a majority of the exhibitions, before arriving at ours.

6 Conclusions and Future Works

This paper explored the use of AR in a public museum in collaboration with the UNLV Marjorie Barrick Museum. We introduced the OTC (Object To Camera) allowing users to manipulate a tangible object as a user interface to trigger graphical augmentations. The goal was to make this unique interaction something that a user would not forget; due to its rareness and likeness. Also, to use this experiment as a learning experience for creating new and unconventional ways of using AR as a medium.

As an instance of the OTC experience, we showcased one's artwork through the system that linked the behind scenes of six art pieces. The OTC experience program was a success and we gained more insight on future AR projects. The visitors and collaborators of the project were both satisfied with the new approach showed in the OTC experience and mediums of AR interactions. The OTC experience program was created to cross the boundaries of traditional AR programs that would require just a device to host the AR features. We had a physical object and a larger user interface display, which led to people who have already used AR experience something that felt new. The data we received through feedback and observation will help our team in future experiments and developments. A contribution made in the project was to have a more physical approach in creating AR experiences, to distinguish itself from other augmented reality experiences, in which objects can be more used in the context of AR experience as means of interacting with different augmentations.

As an extension of the work, we planned to extend the installation of the OTC system and invite more people to experience it.

Acknowledgement. We thank Alisha Kerlin, Paige Bockman, Andrew Schoultz, Kris Davidson and UNLV Marjorie Barrick Museum staff members for their help and support on the project. We thank Dean Rama Venkat and Dean Nancy Usher for supporting the budget to implement the OTC system. We also thank all the event attendees who experienced the OTC prototype and provided valuable comments.

References

1. Azuma, R.T.: A survey of augmented reality (1997)
2. Azuma, R., Baillot, Y., Behringer, R., Feiner, S., Julier, S., MacIntyre, B.: Recent advances in augmented reality. IEEE Comput. Graph. Appl. **21**(6), 34–47 (2001)
3. Educause: 7 Things You Should Know About Augmented Reality (2005). http://www.educause.edu/library/resources/7-things-you-should-know-about-augmented-reality

4. Grasset, R., Grascuel, J.D., Schmalstieg, D.: Interactive mediated reality. In: Poster at International Symposium on Mixed and Augmented Reality (2003)
5. Desai, N.: Recreation of history using augmented reality. Accent. Trans. Image Process. Comput. Vis. **4**, 1–5 (2017)
6. Katz, M.: Augmented Reality is Transforming Museums. https://www.wired.com/story/augmented-reality-art-museums/
7. Kim, S.J.J.: A user study trends in augmented reality and virtual reality research: a qualitative study with the past three years of the ISMAR and IEEE VR conference papers. In: Proceedings - 2012 International Symposium on Ubiquitous Virtual Reality, ISUVR 2012 (2012)
8. The Smithsonian Institution: A Hall Through New Eyes. https://naturalhistory.si.edu/exhibits/bone-hall
9. Billock, J.: Five Augmented Reality Experiences That Bring Museum Exhibits to Life. https://www.smithsonianmag.com/travel/expanding-exhibits-augmented-reality-180963810/
10. Ho, V.: Singapore museum adds an interactive virtual forest. https://mashable.com/2016/12/09/virtual-forest-singapore-national-museum-teamlab/#Rlncsq92kOqW
11. Kennedy Space Center: Heros and Legends, https://www.kennedyspacecenter.com/landing-pages/heroes-and-legends
12. Augmented and virtual reality help bring a museum in China to life. https://america.cgtn.com/2017/05/18/augmented-and-virtual-reality-help-bring-a-museum-in-china-to-life
13. Deng, X., et al.: The Future Is Here AUGMENTED REALITY In TOURISM (2017)
14. Schwartz, L.: An art gallery in your pocket: See Vermeer's paintings in augmented reality. https://www.blog.google/outreach-initiatives/arts-culture/art-gallery-your-pocket-see-vermeers-paintings-augmented-reality/
15. Xiao, C., Lifeng, Z.: Implementation of mobile augmented reality based on Vuforia and Rawajali. In: Proceedings of the IEEE International Conference on Software Engineering and Service Sciences, ICSESS (2014)
16. Vuforia: Vuforia
17. Vuforia: Image Targets—Vuforia Library

Through the Realities of Augmented Reality

Thitirat Siriborvornratanakul[(⊠)]

Graduate School of Applied Statistics, National Institute of Development
Administration (NIDA), 118 SeriThai Rd., Bangkapi, Bangkok 10240, Thailand
thitirat@as.nida.ac.th

Abstract. Speaking of Augmented Reality (AR), it is about augmenting an actual world with some virtually generated digital information in order to make the combination of two worlds as seamless as possible. Creating seamless AR effects in real time is non-trivial, requiring interdisciplinary knowledge integration from many fields such as computer vision, signal processing, sensor network, internet of things (IoT), three-dimensional computer graphics, human-computer interaction, and hardware designs. Nevertheless, for the past two decades, it is computer vision that has dominated the field of AR. Hence, common forms of AR that most people are familiar with are about utilizing a hardware device with embedded camera(s) together with a software program powering by computer vision algorithms. Based on our first-hand experiences in AR researches and communities, this paper presents a new summary regarding the world of modern AR from the beginning of the 21st century until now. Our summary divides the modern AR into five major waves based on important trends happening both inside and outside research communities.

Keywords: Augmented Reality · Spatial Augmented Reality ·
Wearable augmented reality · Artificial intelligence · Deep learning

1   The First Wave: Marker-Based AR

We believed that the first wave of modern AR was dated back in 1999 when an open source AR tracking library named ARToolKit [9] was demonstrated at SIGGRAPH 1999. ARToolKit was a C/C++ open source library that only required simple fiducial markers (i.e. black-and-white square markers) and an off-the-shelf camera to work with. Using ARToolKit's built-in functions, it became very easy for researchers and programmers to jump start in AR and obtain real-time camera's 3D pose estimation (with respect to the ARToolKit marker) regardless of indepth 3D computer vision understanding. During the beginning of the 21st century, this library's ease of use triggered rapid development in diverse applications not only in the field of AR itself but also in other 3D-vision applications. Some example usages of ARToolKit included an ARToolKit-based

© Springer Nature Switzerland AG 2019
C. Stephanidis (Ed.): HCII 2019, LNCS 11786, pp. 253–264, 2019.
https://doi.org/10.1007/978-3-030-30033-3_20

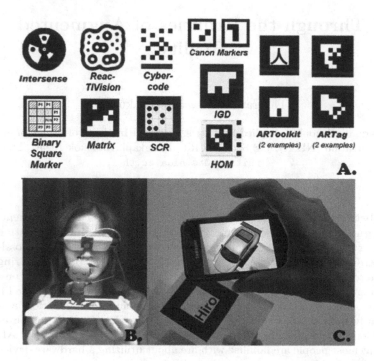

Fig. 1. (A) shows examples of fiducial marker libraries in computer vision; some are specifically designed for AR tasks (e.g., ARToolKit and ARTag) whereas the others are for other tasks in computer vision. (B) and (C) show examples of using ARToolKit markers to generate real-time AR see-through effects. (Image credit: http://campar. in.tum.de/twiki/pub/ISMAR/IarAbstractARTag/IarDetailsFialaSlides.pdf, http:// www.hitl.washington.edu/artoolkit/ and https://alternativeto.net/software/artoolk/)

tangible interface for musician [17], ARToolKit for educational exhibitions [28], and ARToolKit as passive markers for a motion capture system [20].

Inspiring by the success and popularity of ARToolKit, many vision-based fiducial marker libraries were introduced afterwards, mostly for two main reasons—to improve robustness of marker detection and tracking regardless of partial occlusion or difficult lighting situations, and to introduce more visual alternatives of fiducial markers for different tasks. Examples of fiducial marker libraries in computer vision are shown in Fig. 1A. Note that standard barcodes, QR codes and many 2D planar patterns are not suitable as vision-based fiducial markers because they either require some specific camera orientations (relative to the marker) or provide inadequate information for visual computing.

It can be said that in the first wave of modern AR, the key developments heavily relied on computer vision algorithms and applications; the most popular AR features back then were marker-based AR see-through effects using an electronic monitor or a head-mounted device (HMD) as shown in Fig. 1B and C. Nevertheless, during the first wave of modern AR, utilization and popularity of AR outside research laboratories were scarce.

Fig. 2. Examples of Spatial AR for augmenting a physical surface with interactive projected imagery. (Image credit: Office of the future [18] and http://www.pranavmistry. com/projects/sixthsense/)

2   The Second Wave: Spatial AR with Projector

During SIGGRAPH 1998, there was a signal regarding another wave of modern AR. In this conference, Raskar et al. [18] proposed an idea called Office of the Future (Fig. 2 left) where interactive imagery projected from projectors were used to augment arbitrary flat surfaces in a seamless manner; they named this kind of projector-based AR as Spatial Augmented Reality (SAR) [2]. Inspiring by the office-of-the-future proposal as well as the trend of projector miniaturization following afterwards, the first decade of the 21st century was overwhelmed by not only SAR researches using projector-camera devices (a.k.a. pro-cam devices) but also continuous developments for smaller but brighter projection mechanisms. In the following paragraphs, we clarify the rise and fall of SAR in more detail.

Speaking of portable projectors, although they needed not to be firmly fixed on ceiling, their bulky form factors prevented them from being used in truly mobile fashions. After portable projectors became reasonably affordable around the beginning of the 21st century, they were continuously used in diverse researches and applications regarding SAR and computer vision; most of the time, a portable projector was coupled with one or more cameras in order to visually observed the projected results. Some example studies regarding portable projectors included methods to calibrate a pair of projector and camera either geometrically [10] or photometrically [5], methods to calibrate multiple projectors [29], imperceptible [3] or infrared [1] projection techniques, etc.

Another important trigger in the second wave of SAR was probably the Sixth-Sense project (Fig. 2 right) by Mistry et al., published in CHI 2009 [15]. In this project, they built a prototype of wearable pro-cam device where a smartphone-sized laser projector (a.k.a. handheld, mobile or pico projector) and a camera were used to transform any ordinary flat surface into an interactive touch screen.

Their proof-of-concept applications were broadcasted by many news channels, making this project one of the most famous projects in SAR.

When SAR usage scenarios were changed from bulky portable projectors staying (mostly) still on a table to small mobile projectors being moved at all times, problems regarding pro-cam calibration were exaggerated and solutions needed to be provided for dealing with unpredictabilities of projection surfaces. Our previous works started from utilizing a motion sensor for indirect pro-cam geometric calibration [23] and then changed to pro-cam coaxialization using a plate beam splitter in order to completely eliminate the need for geometric calibration [24]; finally, in order to deal with visual crosstalk problems, we decided to maintain projection in the visible light spectrum but change visual analysis tasks into the infrared spectrum [21]. Other popular approaches for dynamic pro-cam geometric calibration included projecting a known pattern on an unknown surface and analyzing the distorted pattern to reconstruct the surface's geometry.

Despite of proof-of-concept demonstrations and few commercial projector-based interactive touchscreen devices, usages of SAR beyond exhibitions and lighting performances were uncommon. Our recent study regarding SAR [22] revealed shared concerns from different experts regarding robustness, price, usability and practicality of SAR in actual usages. Unfortunately, the second wave of modern AR in SAR was not last long. After a decade (approximately) of active development, researchers and manufacturers slowly lost attraction of miniature projector utilization. Our assumption regarding the falling of SAR includes the introduction of Microsoft Kinect Sensor in 2010 and limitations of miniature projectors themselves.

Because of the all-in-one affordable solution provided by Kinect sensor, the needs for developing complicated pro-cam hardwares for geometric calibration or 3D reconstruction were sharply decreased. As for the limitations of miniature projectors, during their golden years, many attempts were pushed towards building brighter, smaller and focus-free projectors. In order to build a focus-free projector (i.e., projected images are always in focus regardless of arbitrary surface depths) with strong brightness, laser projection technologies were once expected as promising solutions. However, because of the international standard of safety for laser devices, the expected solution of laser projection was limited to very small amount of brightness. Even there were other non-laser projection mechanisms that could produce hundreds of lumens in brightness while maintaining their small form factors, without the focus-free ability, our dream of freestyle mobile projection on any desired surface will never come true.

3   The Third Wave: Wearable AR for Corporate

The third wave of modern AR came in the form of professional head-mounted wearable devices as shown in Fig. 3, starting with Google Glass in 2013, Microsoft HoloLens (developer edition) in 2016, MagicLeap One (creator edition) in 2018, and Microsoft HoloLens 2 in 2019; the years specified here are official released years, except for HoloLens 2 that is still in the preorder stage at the moment of writing this paper. Unlike the two previous waves, the third wave of modern

Fig. 3. Leading head-mounted wearable devices for AR from three companies. (A) is Google Glass, (B) is Microsoft HoloLens 1, (C) is MagicLeap One, and (D) is Microsoft HoloLens 2. (Image credit: http://time.com/, https://news.microsoft.com/, https://www.bloomberg.com/ and https://www.microsoft.com/en-us/hololens/buy)

AR has been driven by world famous tech companies whose aims are clearly not just AR prototypes for academic presentations but commercial AR products with (hopefully) mass production. Another uniqueness of this wave is that development of these wearable devices requires high-level interdisciplinary knowledge that goes far beyond computer vision to audio, optics, mechanic, etc. As a result, what most AR researchers do with these wearable AR devices is not to try tweaking their internal mechanisms but to study advantages and disadvantages of using them in each situation. For example, with HoloLens, [12] was able to use the real world geometry as input data and allow a user to define and solve a physical problem by Poisson's equation; [8] conducted experiments using Google Glass for training new scientists in wet laboratory work; [14] created an application on Google Glass that allowed people with Parkinson to monitor their speech volume; [26] discovered that unlike virtual reality headset, users of HoloLens did not suffer from obvious simulation sickness.

In the past, the first Google Glass and HoloLens were promoted with their AR capabilities. However, MagicLeap One and HoloLens 2 are now being advertised as mixed reality (MR). According to the long understanding in reality-virtuality continuum, MR refers to everything where real and virtual worlds are mixed up; this literally means that AR is a subset of MR. Nevertheless, this perspective has slightly been changed since MagicLeap has positioned their wearable device as non-AR but MR where the mixing between two worlds is indistinguishable in a 3D hologram manner. But for the sake of this AR review paper, we will stick with the term AR.

Until now, Google Glass, Microsoft HoloLens and MagicLeap are three big names that have worldly represented the future of wearable AR where the overlaid virtual information is more controllable than the previous wave of SAR as discussed in our previous work [22]. These wearable devices from the three companies share many things in common. They all are packed with sophisticated hardwares and algorithms developed by great engineers. They all are famous not only among AR researchers but also among technologists around the world; this is in particular for Google Glass, the first AR product that successfully popularized AR to end users. Despite of good things in common, they all are struggling the same problem of very high and unaffordable price tags. Their introductory prices are 1,500 USD for Google Glass, 3,000 USD (developer price) or 5,000 USD (commercial price) for HoloLens 1, 2,295 USD for MagicLeap One, and 3,500 USD for commercial HoloLens 2. This problem alone has made utilizations of these wearable AR devices being limited to small groups of researchers or big organizations who can afford (e.g., United State Army, NASA, DHL, General Motors).

For this third ongoing wave of modern AR, there are important lessons learnt from the original Google Glass whose initial aim of being a consumer-grade gadget failed due to privacy laws, driving regulations and social disapproval [7]. This means that the reasons consumers refrain from Google Glasses are not only their unaffordable prices but also their unsuitability regarding consumer life styles. Despite of the previous failure, Google Glass has already come back and this time Google as well as Microsoft have directed their attention to enterprise customers whose personal development and corporate training can take great advantages from these hi-tech and pricey AR headsets.

4   The Fourth Wave: Markerless AR in Smartphone

During the first and second waves of marker-based AR and SAR, one of the most popular techniques is utilizing known visual markers to pinpoint the virtually generated AR contents in world coordinates. Some visual markers are very obvious and not blending to the working environment like those in Fig. 1A. In many researches and AR creator platforms, to avoid using markers with intrusive visibility, natural objects are used as visual markers by help from vision-based feature point matching techniques; this allows us to use something like companies' logos as AR markers.

In our previous work [23], we addressed problems of marker based interactions and proposed a multi-target tracking solution in order to include non-marker objects into AR calculation. Multi-target tracking is a good start to taggle this problem, but in the long run, unless we have a proper map of objects in the environment, augmenting the environment with interactive AR contents remains difficult. To incorporate everything in the environment into AR systems, SLAM (Simultaneous Localization And Mapping) is a promising solution that has become popular recently. Using SLAM techniques, we are able to use camera images in conjunction with other information in order to reconstruct and update a map of an unknown environment in real time. SLAM is especially popular for interactive systems that deal with unknown environments; this includes usage situations of wearable AR devices (Sect. 3) and smartphone AR (Sect. 4).

While the third wave of AR in professional wearable devices is still ongoing, the fourth wave of modern AR in smartphone has already touched the ground with the official releases of Apple's ARKit in 2017 and Android's ARCore in 2018. Like Google's Project Tango proposed back in 2014, ARKit and ARCore utilize SLAM techniques to create markerless AR effects on smartphones. But unlike the discontinued Project Tango relying on specially designed cameras and specific computational modules, ARKit and ARCore use smartphones' built-in motion sensors and cameras to perform SLAM, enabling sustainable smartphone AR in the long run.

Similar to the third wave of wearable AR headsets, the wave of smartphone AR has been driven mainly by big tech companies. However, while wearable AR headsets are very expensive and aim for corporate customers, smartphone AR is mostly free and involves diverse applications for arbitrary smartphone users. Examples regarding smartphone AR include AR DeepCalorieCam [25] that uses ARKit to measure the actual size of the meal (in order to estimate the total calories); interactive AR coding environments where N. Dass et al. [4] show that participant satisfaction is better with smartphone AR (using ARKit) than a traditional tablet or Microsoft HoloLens; a mixed-reality mobile remote collaboration system [6] using ARCore position tracking.

5   The Fifth Wave: AR Underneath Artificial Intelligence

During the years of 2014–2016 (approximately), extended reality technologies (including virtual, augmented and mixed realities) made the headlines that excited many technologists and researchers around the world. But in the past couple of years, majority of the world has turned their interest to Artificial Intelligence (AI) driven by machine learning, particularly the field of computer vision that has been disrupted significantly by deep learning. The popularity in AI (in comparison to AR) during the past decade is illustrated in Figs. 4 and 5. In Fig. 4, it can be seen that the increase in numbers of AI papers is the most obvious in IEEE Xplore Digital Library during 2017 and 2018. As for Google Trends (worldwide) in Fig. 5, popularity in AI keyword has totally beat AR keyword since October 2016.

Because computer vision always plays important roles in AR, disruption in computer vision results in disruption in AR as well. Hence, under the huge umbrella of machine learning and deep learning, there is also AR underneath. For vision-based tasks of recognizing and annotating objects with AR virtual contents, using state-of-the-art pre-trained convolutional neural networks gives researchers and developers a huge jump start with promising image recognition and annotation results. For example, AR DeepCalorieCam [25] uses Inception-v3

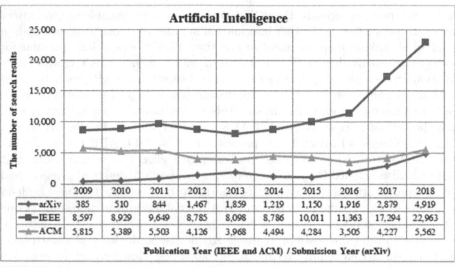

Artificial Intelligence									
	2009	2010	2011	2012	2013	2014	2015	2016	2017	2018
arXiv	385	510	844	1,467	1,859	1,219	1,150	1,916	2,879	4,919
IEEE	8,597	8,929	9,649	8,785	8,098	8,786	10,011	11,363	17,294	22,963
ACM	5,815	5,389	5,503	4,126	3,968	4,494	4,284	3,505	4,227	5,562

Publication Year (IEEE and ACM) / Submission Year (arXiv)

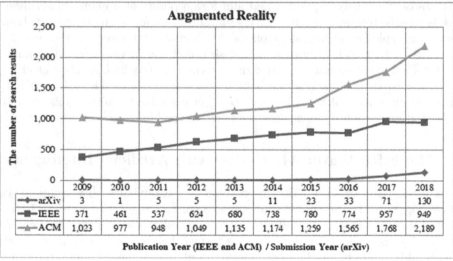

Augmented Reality									
	2009	2010	2011	2012	2013	2014	2015	2016	2017	2018
arXiv	3	1	5	5	5	11	23	33	71	130
IEEE	371	461	537	624	680	738	780	774	957	949
ACM	1,023	977	948	1,049	1,135	1,174	1,259	1,565	1,768	2,189

Publication Year (IEEE and ACM) / Submission Year (arXiv)

Fig. 4. The number of search results during 2009 to 2018 regarding two keywords (i.e., 'artificial intelligence' and 'augmented reality') from three research paper platforms—arXiv.org, IEEE Xplore Digital Library and ACM Digital Library. (Data retrieved on 19 April 2019)

(pre-trained on ImageNet dataset and fined tune on UEC-FOOD100 dataset) to recognize food category from an image before applying ARKit to measure the actual size of each food. Recognizing and annotating humans in images is another task that has received lot of attention recently. The latest proposal from Wang et al. [27] uses a self-supervised deep learning technique to predict human 3D poses from 2D image inputs. This kind of human 3D pose estimation mechanisms

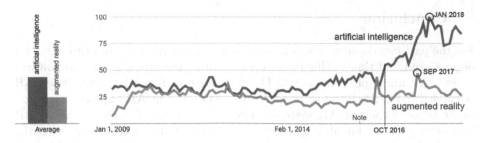

Fig. 5. Google Trends (worldwide) comparing the two keywords of 'artificial intelligence' and 'augmented reality' during 1 January 2009 to 31 December 2018. The vertical axis represents interest over time where 100 is the peak popularity of the corresponding keyword during the specified time interval. (Data retrieved on 19 April 2019)

can help leverage any AR systems that require indepth understanding of human's real-time actions/behaviors.

For interactive virtual makeup applications, it becomes a lot easier to overlay virtual makeups on a moving face as facial landmarks can be precisely located with many free machine learning libraries. An example is in the automatic virtual makeup system of [16] that uses Dlib for extracting 2D facial landmarks from a face image; Dlib is a machine learning library that originally utilizes a combination of Histogram of Oriented Gradients (HoG) and linear Support Vector Machine (SVM). In BeautyGAN [11], more advance technique of deep learning is used to simply transfer a makeup style from a reference makeup face to another non-makeup face. This growth in deep learning techniques helps reform traditional AR virtual makeup systems and strengthen them to become the next generation of artificial intelligence based AR systems.

Superimposing an AR content over a live video of the actual world cannot be more indistinguishable when there is a neural style transfer technique from deep learning to help blend two different image styles together; [13] demonstrates this concept using the neural style transfer and ARKit. Even for AR tasks involving 3D reconstruction for AR headsets (mentioned in Sect. 3), there is a recent proposal from Rematas et al. [19] that uses deep learning to convert a typical youtube video of soccer game into dynamic 3D information; this means that all players in the game are dynamically 3D reconstructed in a way that we can wear a 3D AR headset to see this soccer game in 3D AR style.

It can be said that with recent disruption in artificial intelligence, we can expect AR systems (regarding all four previous waves mentioned earlier) to become more intelligent, more seamless and more interactive in the near future. Once AR can overcome their long-standing technical difficulties, what remain unsolved are the true problems of AR in the long run—problems regarding affordability, user experience and practical usage scenario.

6   Conclusion

For the past two decades, it can be said that modern AR has been through a lot of good and bad times. This paper reviews these two decades and summarizes it into five waves of modern AR. The first wave of fiducial marker based AR is classic and can still be seen until now, especially in AR explorer apps and other proof-of-concept AR systems. The second wave of projector-based AR was once popular; but due to many limitations, it has become slow recently. The third and fourth waves of modern AR have been both driven by big tech companies. The third wave of expensive AR headsets has aimed for corporate training whereas the fourth wave of smartphone AR has directed their attention to mass consumers. Finally, all four waves of modern AR have been elevated by the fifth wave of artificial intelligence disruption where solutions regarding long-standing AR technical difficulties have been proposed one after another.

References

1. Akasaka, K., Sagawa, R., Yagi, Y.: A sensor for simultaneously capturing texture and shape by projecting structured infrared light. In: Proceedings of the 6th International Conference on 3-D Digital Imaging and Modeling, pp. 375–381 (2007)
2. Bimber, O., Raskar, R.: Spatial Augmented Reality: Merging Real and Virtual Worlds. A. K. Peters Ltd., Natick (2005)
3. Cotting, D., Naef, M., Gross, M., Fuchs, H.: Embedding imperceptible patterns into projected images for simultaneous acquisition and display. In: Proceedings of the 3rd IEEE/ACM International Symposium on Mixed and Augmented Reality (ISMAR 2004), pp. 100–109 (2004)
4. Dass, N., Kim, J., Ford, S., Agarwal, S., Chau, D.: Augmenting coding: augmented reality for learning programming. In: Proceedings of the International Symposium of Chinese CHI (ChineseCHI 2018), pp. 156–159 (2018)
5. Fujii, K., Grossberg, M., Nayar, S.: A projector-camera system with real-time photometric adaptation for dynamic environments. In: IEEE Computer Society Conference on Computer Vision and Pattern Recognition (CVPR 2005), vol. 1 (2005)
6. Gao, L., Bai, H., He, W., Billinghurst, M., Lindeman, R.: Real-time visual representations for mobile mixed reality remote collaboration. In: Proceedings of SIGGRAPH Asia 2018 Virtual and Augmented Reality (SA 2018) (2018)
7. Hong, J.: Considering privacy issues in the context of Google Glass. Commun. ACM 56(11), 10–11 (2013)
8. Hu, G., Chen, L., Okerlund, J., Shaer, O.: Exploring the use of Google Glass in wet laboratories. In: Proceedings of the ACM Conference Extended Abstracts on Human Factors in Computing Systems (CHI EA 2015), pp. 2103–2108 (2015)
9. Kato, H., Billinghurst, M.: Marker tracking and HMD calibration for a video-based augmented reality conferencing system. In: Proceedings of the 2nd International Workshop on Augmented Reality (IWAR 1999) (1999)
10. Lee, J., Dietz, P., Maynes-Aminzade, D., Raskar, R., Hudson, S.: Automatic projector calibration with embedded light sensors. In: Proceedings of the ACM Symposium on User Interface Software and Technology (UIST 2004), pp. 123–126 (2004)

11. Li, T., et al.: BeautyGAN: instance-level facial makeup transfer with deep generative adversarial network. In: Proceedings of the ACM International Conference on Multimedia (MM 2018), pp. 645–653 (2018)

12. Logg, A., Lundholm, C., Nordaas, M.: Solving Poisson's equation on the Microsoft HoloLens. In: Proceedings of the ACM Symposium on Virtual Reality Software and Technology (VRST 2017) (2017)

13. MadeWithARKit: Realistic AR brush texture paintings with deep learning style transfer by the ever so creative @Laan Labs. http://www.madewitharkit. com/post/166751998274/realistic-ar-brush-texture-paintings-with-deep. Accessed 28 Feb 2019

14. McNaney, R., Poliakov, I., Vines, J., Balaam, M., Zhang, P., Olivier, P.: LApp: a speech loudness application for people with Parkinson's on Google Glass. In: Proceedings of the ACM Conference on Human Factors in Computing Systems (CHI 2015), pp. 497–500 (2015)

15. Mistry, P., Maes, P., Chang, L.: WUW - wear ur world: a wearable gestural interface. In: Proceedings of the CHI Extended Abstracts on Human Factors in Computing Systems (CHI 2009), pp. 4111–4116 (2009)

16. Park, J., Kim, H., Ji, S., Hwang, E.: An automatic virtual makeup scheme based on personal color analysis. In: Proceedings of the International Conference on Ubiquitous Information Management and Communication (IMCOM 2018) (2018)

17. Poupyrev, I., Berry, R., Kurumisawa, J., Billinghurst, M., Airola, C., Kato, H.: Augmented groove: collaborative jamming in augmented reality. In: SIGGRAPH 2000, Emerging Technologies (2000)

18. Raskar, R., Welch, G., Cutts, M., Lake, A., Stesin, L., Fuchs, H.: The office of the future: a unified approach to image-based modeling and spatially immersive displays. In: Proceedings of the 25th Annual Conference on Computer Graphics and Interactive Techniques (SIGGRAPH 1998), pp. 179–188 (1998)

19. Rematas, K., Kemelmacher-Shlizerman, I., Curless, B., Seitz, S.: Soccer on your tabletop. In: IEEE International Conference on Computer Vision and Pattern Recognition (CVPR) (2018)

20. Sementille, A., Lourenco, L., Brega, J., Rodello, I.: A motion capture system using passive markers. In: Proceedings of the ACM SIGGRAPH International Conference on Virtual Reality Continuum and Its Applications in Industry (VRCAI 2004), pp. 440–447 (2004)

21. Siriborvornratanakul, T.: Vision-based smart mobile projection: a study of infrared projection and sensing in a ubiquitous environment. Int. J. Digit. Content Technol. Appl. (JDCTA) **8**(2), 1–12 (2014)

22. Siriborvornratanakul, T.: Enhancing user experiences of mobile-based augmented reality via spatial augmented reality: designs and architectures of projector-camera devices. Adv. Multimedia **2018** (2018)

23. Siriborvornratanakul, T., Sugimoto, M.: A portable projector extended for object-centered real-time interactions. In: Proceedings of the European Conference for Visual Media Production (CVMP 2009), pp. 118–126 (2009)

24. Siriborvornratanakul, T., Sugimoto, M.: Multiscale visual object detection for unsupervised ubiquitous projection based on a portable projector-camera system. In: Proceedings of the IEEE International Conference on Digital Image Computing: Techniques and Applications (DICTA 2010), pp. 623–628 (2010)

25. Tanno, R., Ege, T., Yanai, K.: AR DeepCalorieCam V2: food calorie estimation with CNN and AR-based actual size estimation. In: Proceedings of the ACM Symposium on Virtual Reality Software and Technology (VRST 2018) (2018)

26. Vovk, A., Wild, F., Guest, W., Kuula, T.: Simulator sickness in augmented reality training using the Microsoft HoloLens. In: Proceedings of the CHI Conference on Human Factors in Computing Systems (CHI 2018) (2018)
27. Wang, K., Lin, L., Jiang, C., Qian, C., Wei, P.: 3D human pose machines with self-supervised learning. IEEE Trans. Pattern Anal. Mach. Intell. (T-PAMI 2019) (2019, to appear). https://arxiv.org/abs/1901.03798
28. Woods, E., et al.: Augmenting the science centre and museum experience. In: Proceedings of the International Conference on Computer Graphics and Interactive Techniques in Australasia and Southeast Asia (GRAPHITE 2004), pp. 230–236 (2004)
29. Zhou, J., Wang, L., Akbarzadeh, A., Yang, R.: Multi-projector display with continuous self-calibration. In: Proceedings of the ACM/IEEE International Workshop on Projector Camera Systems (PROCAM 2008) (2008)

Learning and Games

Development of a Puzzle Game to Learn Coding for Elementary Students

Jaisoon Baek and Gyuhwan Oh$^{(\boxtimes)}$

Ajou University, Suwon, Republic of Korea
{mytaiji, drghoh}@ajou.ac.kr

Abstract. Existing computer games used to teach coding to students have certain shortcomings such as the use of icons that do not convert to actual text-based coding commands, and the fact that teachers cannot follow students' progress in real time. In this study, we have improved upon existing coding games by developing a puzzle game based on coding and a web-based management system to observe the user's learning status in real time and maximize the understanding of how elementary students learn to code. We analyzed the syntax of various coding languages for the school curriculum and provided a menu to convert icons into textual coding language. In addition, the game's management system includes multiple types of tutoring, real-time analysis of user play data, and feedback. Following its application in regular elementary school software classes, we conducted a Likert scale survey. Students reported positive effects on understanding and showed an interest in coding. It is expected that this will contribute to quality improvement in software education by providing content with proven educational value by breaking away from simple learning-oriented coding games.

Keywords: Coding game · Puzzle game · Software education

1 Introduction

As the importance of computational thinking has increased [1], various forms of teaching methods have been proposed to enhance students' thinking skills [2]. Particularly, there are many ways to enable students to acquire computing thinking skills through their own coding experiences [3]. This kind of coding education for computing thinking is being carried out at a very young age [4].

Most coding games for elementary students (7 to 12 years old) are constructed in such a way that the concept of coding is more easily and implicitly understood [5, 6]; they take the form of games so that students will be interested and will naturally acquire basic concepts using icons [7]. Existing coding games using icons [8] are based on once-off experiences and do not contribute to actual textual coding. Additionally, it is difficult for the teacher to understand the students' progress because the game is played on individual devices.

In this study, we attempted to overcome the limitations of existing educational games for elementary students [9–13]. CodePlanet, the puzzle game based on coding that we developed, provides a coding environment similar to textual language coding

© Springer Nature Switzerland AG 2019
C. Stephanidis (Ed.): HCII 2019, LNCS 11786, pp. 267–279, 2019.
https://doi.org/10.1007/978-3-030-30033-3_21

and converts the icons used by the learners into textual coding language. In addition, we have developed a web-based management system that can analyze and provide feedback on the learner's game progress in real-time.

2   Existing Coding Games

With the growing importance of coding learning [14–16], various kinds of content for coding education are emerging in South Korea and elsewhere [17, 18]. This content is in the form of games [19, 20] and often aim to provide learners with interest and motivation in coding rather than teach them specific coding syntaxes [21–23].

2.1   Lightbot

Lightbot [24, 25] is a game that moves characters along a block code the student writes on a three-dimensional isometric map. The goal is to turn all the blue tiles in the map yellow. The coding is performed by a combination of icons having the functions of moving forward, turning left or right, jumping, and lighting up the tile.

It consists of six chapters: Basic, Procedures, Overloading, Loops, Conditionals, and Challenge Level. Although LightBot is structured to teach the concept of sequential progression, function, polymorphism, loop, and condition through six chapters, the loop is processed only in the form of a recursive function that is different from the actual programming language, and executes only the blocks of code that are the same color as the color of the corresponding pixels (Fig. 1).

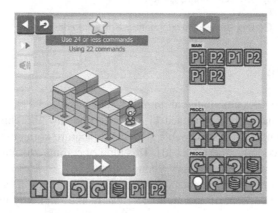

Fig. 1. Lightbot

2.2   Box Island

Box Island [26] is a puzzle game where the user collects stars against the background of a tropical wild environment. It includes the concept of algorithmic thinking, sequencing, and loop.

It consists of a total of 100 levels, and the teacher menu allows parents or educators to adjust the target level to the level of each student. It uses six icons and performs the functions of forward, reverse, left turn, right turn, loop, and condition. It provides solutions and curriculum documents for teachers to use in class (Fig. 2).

Fig. 2. Box Island

2.3 CodeCombat

CodeCombat [27, 28] is a game that students type real code and see their characters react in real time. Before starting the game, you can choose one of the languages Python, JavaScript, CoffeeScript, or Lua, and the syntax of the code used in the game depends on the language you choose. On the left side of the coding layer is a list of currently available cords, and the user must use the code in the list to enable the character to complete all missions. CodeCombat is structured to take advantage of the concepts of sequential progression, loops, conditional statements, functions, and variables. Because it is a Text Programming Language (TPL)-based game and the tutorial is poor, students may have difficulty playing the game if they do not know the basic concepts of programming mentioned earlier (Fig. 3).

2.4 The Foos

The Foos [29] uses a coding language in the form of icons. Each task is represented by an animated icon, which features a story and a screen that looks like a video game. Enter a command in the coding language to solve the mission of each stage according to the story. Students can learn the concepts of sequence, loop, and condition.

It provides various educational resources for parents and teachers, and provides a dashboard for checking and managing students' progress in real time in a separate mode (Fig. 4).

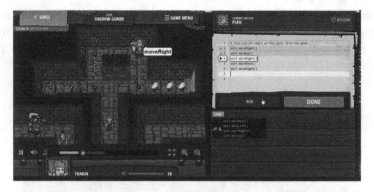

Fig. 3. Code Combat

Fig. 4. The Foos

2.5 Summary

The four coding games discussed above include both game content and coding content, and they all achieve their objective by requiring the player to code certain commands. However, there are some differences in command types, expressions, and coding concepts.

In this study, four aims for the development of our improved coding game CodePlanet were identified, based on our analysis of the existing games. The first is to incorporate the concepts used in programming language as much as possible and design them to relate to game play. Table 1 lists the programming concepts used in a total of six coding games, including the four coding games discussed above. The second is to minimize the confusion of learning the actual coding after the user has played the coding game. Therefore, the User Interface (UI) and User Experience (UX) for screen layout, code input method, and input code representation are configured similar to the actual coding environment. The third is to add appropriate feedback elements to the curriculum so that the coding concepts presented at each stage of the game can be used properly. This is to prevent the user from solving problems in a piecemeal way without using the curriculum required at each stage. Finally, it is possible to learn both the block-based visual-based language and the text-based language used in real coding. Text-based languages are more difficult for younger users to learn. By learning the fundamentals of coding through a block-type language, the text language is experienced naturally and the understanding of the coding language is enhanced.

Table 1. The programming concepts used in coding games

	Lightbot	Box Island	Code Combat	The Foos	Kodable	Code Warrior
Sequence	√	√	√	√	√	√
Loop	√	√	√	√	√	√
Condition	√	√	√	√	√	
Function	√				√	
Variable					√	
Object					√	

3   The Design of CodePlanet

3.1   System Configuration

The mobile game system is structured as shown in Fig. 5. The play information of the mobile game is stored on the server. When the user is offline, the play information of the user is stored on the client terminal and is transmitted to the server when an online connection is established.

3.2   Content Configuration

Each chapter consists of a sequence of progressions, loops, conditions, functions, and concurrent progressions (multi-tasking). This study combines the results of research into and analysis of the precedent cases of the coding games and the common syntax elements of the languages used in actual programming.

Similar to most previous cases, we used icons. However, in order to overcome the difficulty of linking the game to actual text coding, we added a menu that converts the user-input icon into a text language. The game UI for inputting the icon is designed similar to the text language coding environment. Most coding games that use icons can only enter icons in a line. However, Code Planet allows the students to organize complex code through the 'line down' function. This helps students to think analytically in the course of problem solving (Fig. 6).

The mobile game can be set in two modes: a mode in which the individual can play freely and a mode in which learning can be done under the supervision of the teacher or the parent. The game data set in the learning mode is linked with the web-based monitoring site in real time.

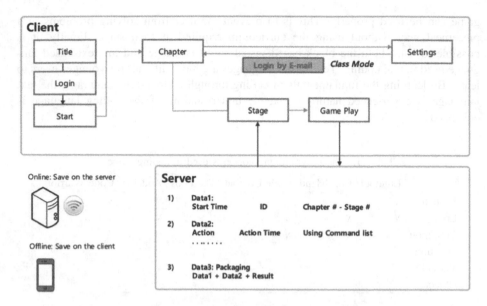

Fig. 5. Game flow

Fig. 6. Screenshot of CodePlanet

3.3   Design of Web-Based Management System for Tutoring

When the student accesses the mobile game with the authentication information (e-mail) registered by the teacher, the teacher can manage the student's progress. The teacher can open the class in this system and manage the data of many students simultaneously. By monitoring the students' real-time play data, it is possible to provide individual feedback and review statistical data on the students' play information (Fig. 7).

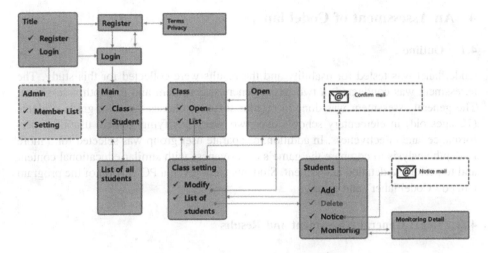

Fig. 7. Flow of the monitoring system

When the teacher registers the students email address with the monitoring system, the student can access the learning mode of the mobile game with the registered e-mail (Fig. 8).

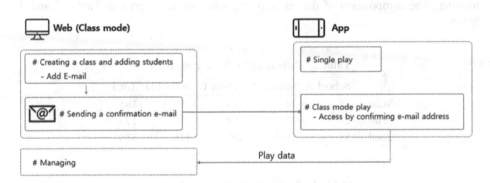

Fig. 8. Flow of the Web-App

Through this system, it is possible to overcome the disadvantage that the teachers cannot understand the learning status of the learners in the game-based class environment, whether using a PC or smart device. Therefore, CodePlanet can be used as an educational tool by allowing the teacher to continuously manage the learner in the educational environment.

4 An Assessment of CodePlanet

4.1 Outline

CodePlanet was tested for usability and the results were collected for this study. The assessment was conducted in two steps: general assessment and in-depth assessment. The general assessment was done in regular software classes for sixth-grade students (12 ages old) in elementary schools over two years, verifying general usability, performance, and effectiveness. In addition, a separate user group was selected for a more in-depth analysis to compare the game's effectiveness with similar educational content and to perform a detailed assessment. Students were given a PC version of the program named "CodePlanet" and tested.

4.2 Step1: General Assessment and Results

Method. Phase 1 of the General Assessment was done in regular software classes of sixth-grade elementary school students (12 ages old) in 4 elementary schools and a total of 358 students participated. Phase 2 was done in 7 regular elementary school students' regular software classes in the following year, and a total of 568 students participated. The schools that participated in the assessment were schools that provided software demonstration training with local government support prior to mandating software training. The composition of the participating students are shown in Tables 2 and 3 below.

Table 2. Participant in Phase 1 of step 1

	School A	School B	School C	School D	Total
Male	28	24	74	59	185
Female	25	27	64	57	173
Total	53	51	138	116	358

Table 3. Participant in Phase 2 of step 1

	School A	School B	School C	School D	School E	School F	School G	Total
Male	54	25	24	55	6	78	38	280
Female	34	26	24	73	16	81	34	288
Total	88	51	48	128	22	159	72	568

During the assessment, we continuously refined CodePlanet based on feedback from students. Students play CodePlanet according to the teacher's instruction for 2 h of class. Immediately after the class ended, we conducted a survey to assess the effectiveness of the education according to the participating students. The questionnaire consists of four quantitative research items that use a five-point Likert scale to score the responses. Three of the four items examined how the software instruction through CodePlanet changed the students' behavior compared to existing school subject lessons. The last one examines general satisfaction with software lessons using CodePlanet.

Results and Discussion. Question A-1 is about how interesting the software lessons through CodePlanet were, compared to existing school classes for students who have not experienced lessons in software. In Phase 1, 99 respondents (28%) answered "Agree" and 135 (38%) answered "Strongly Agree." In Phase 2, 176 respondents (31%) answered "Agree" and 143 respondents (25%) answered "Strongly Agree." Despite the fact that the students had no experience of software lessons, learning through game-based content seems to be more fun than introductory lessons in existing subjects.

Question A-2 asks how the fact that they had to complete a mission in the game affected the attitude of the students. In Phase 1, 119 respondents (33%) answered "Agree" and 96 (27%) answered "Strongly Agree," so more than half of them answered positively. In Phase 2, 161 respondents (28%) answered "Agree" and 145 respondents (26%) answered "Strongly Agree," which means that more than half of them answered positively. It seems that the process of having to solve a problem continuously in the form of a mission encourages students' tenacity and challenges their consciousness more than is the case with lessons where they are simply taught the curriculum.

Question A-3 is a question about how classes through CodePlanet have affected students' perceptions of software. In Phase 1, 121 respondents (34%) answered "Agree" and 115 respondents (32%) answered "Strongly Agree," so more than half of them answered positively. In Phase 2, 166 respondents (29%) answered "Agree" and 147 respondents (26%) answered "Strongly Agree," which means that more than half of them answered positively. The results of the first three questions are shown in Tables 4 and 5 below. The questions are listed below both tables.

Table 4. Assessment of CodePlanet class compared to usual classes (Phase 1 of Step 1; 2017)

	1 (Strongly disagree)	2	3	4	5 (Strongly agree)	Mean
A-1*	9(3%)	23(6%)	92(26%)	99(28%)	135(38%)	3.9
A-2**	7(2%)	32(9%)	104(29%)	119(33%)	96(27%)	3.7
A-3***	12(3%)	24(7%)	85(24%)	121(34%)	115(32%)	3.8

N = 358

Table 5. Assessment of CodePlanet class compared to usual classes (Phase 2 of Step 1; 2018)

	1 (Strongly disagree)	2	3	4	5 (Strongly agree)	Mean
A-1*	20(4%)	52(9%)	177(31%)	176(31%)	143(25%)	3.7
A-2**	21(4%)	51(9%)	189(33%)	161(28%)	145(26%)	3.6
A-3***	28(5%)	63(11%)	167(29%)	166(29%)	147(26%)	3.8

N = 568

A-1*: I was more interested in this class than other subjects such as Korean, math, and science.

A-2**: I have more perseverance and a desire to challenge the problem than ever before.

A-3***: I have a lot more interest and curiosity about software.

Question B, the fourth question (see Tables 6 and 7 below), is about the students' thought and attitudes toward the class. In Phase 1, 103 respondents (29%) answered "Agree" and 146 (41%) answered "Strongly Agree." In Phase 2, 190 respondents (33%) answered "Agree" and 164 respondents (29%) answered "Strongly Agree," which means that more than half of them answered positively.

Table 6. Assessment of the students' thought and attitudes toward the class (Phase 1 of Step 1; 2017)

	1 (Strongly disagree)	2	3	4	5 (Strongly agree)	Mean
B*	5(1%)	6(2%)	93(26%)	103(29%)	146(41%)	4.1

N = 358

Table 7. Assessment of the students' thought and attitudes toward the class (Phase 2 of step 1; 2018)

	1 (Strongly disagree)	2	3	4	5 (Strongly agree)	Mean
B*	11(2%)	14(2%)	187(33%)	190(33%)	164(29%)	3.9

N = 568

B*: I enjoyed this class as it was fun and cooperative with my friends.

4.3   Step2: In-Depth Assessment and Results

Method. An in-depth assessment was conducted on 23 students who participated in the "2017 Junior Game Software Academy," a short-term software training camp for elementary school students. All subjects voluntarily applied to the curriculum and were selected by a lottery held by the organizers of the software academy,. In order to assess the effectiveness of CodePlanet, students played Lightbot and Code Warrior first. Then they played CodePlanet. Afterward, a survey was conducted among the participating students. The questionnaire consisted of four items of quantitative research on Code-Planet that used a five-point Likert scale to score the responses.

Results and Discussion. Twelve (52%) respondents answered "Agree" and six (26%) answered "Strongly Agree" to the first question, on whether it was fun to play CodePlanet, so there was a positive response from more than half of the respondents. Question 2 was to confirm the effectiveness of the education through CodePlanet, and 14 (61%) answered "Agree" and four (17%) answered "Strongly Agree." This shows that game-based software education can be fun for students, which leads to improved interest and comprehension of their software.

Questions 3 and 4 are to test whether the factors that are intended to be educational in CodePlanet have influenced students' learning of the software. In Question 3, 13 respondents (57%) answered "Agree" and one (4%) answered "Strongly Agree," so over half answered positively. In Question 4, 13 respondents (57%) answered "Agree" and two (9%) answered "Strongly Agree," which is a positive response from over half of the respondents. The UI/UX structure of CodePlanet, which is similar to the actual programming environment, seems to have helped students improve their ease of inputting code and understanding text code (Table 8).

Table 8. Assessment of satisfaction and education effect

	1 (Strongly disagree)	2	3	4	5 (Strongly agree)	No answer	Mean
Q1*	0(0%)	0(0%)	5(22%)	12(52%)	6(26%)	0(0%)	4.0
Q2**	0(4%)	0(9%)	4(17%)	14(61%)	4(17%)	4(4%)	3.6
Q3***	1(4%)	3(13%)	5(22%)	13(57%)	1(4%)	0(0%)	3.4
Q4****	0(0%)	2(9%)	6(26%)	13(57%)	2(9%)	0(0%)	3.7

N = 23

Q1*: Was the CodePlanet game fun?
Q2**: Are you interested in programming and improving your understanding with CodePlanet?
Q3***: Did CodePlanet's "Double-Click Code Deletion"/"Line Down" help you enter code?
Q4****: Has the code conversion feature of CodePlanet helped you understand the textual code?

5 Conclusion

Due to the growing interest in software education, coding games have been released on the market and are being used widely in actual education. However, there are many cases where these coding games have not undergone accurate verification, or it is difficult to confirm their actual educational effects. In this study, the curriculum and system for coding game were jointly constructed by analyzing the educational factors of coding learning. We presented a puzzle game based on coding as well as a management system for coding education to overcome the problems and limitations of existing coding learning games. In this way, the learning from the game is valuable for actual coding and effective education is enabled through the learning management system.

More than half of the respondents indicated that software education through CodePlanet produced through this study was effective in terms of interest and participation. Also, it is shown that the software education game of the type proposed in this study has improved learners' understanding of software. This is because learning content with a game format induces the interest of learners, providing a UI/UX similar to an actual coding environment, and showing icon(block language) and text language in parallel can enhance understanding of software of learners.

Based on the results of this study, we can obtain positive results in terms of the interest and satisfaction of learners by adding the programming grammar and coding environment used in actual coding to the contents of a conventional, simple, interest-inducing icon type.

As software education recently has become mandatory in South Korea, this study has highlighted some key elements that can enhance the academic achievement of coding learners more effectively.

It is expected that the assessed content for coding education proposed in this study can lead to the improvement of the quality of overall software education.

5.1   Recommendation for Future Research

This study does not include an analysis of the use of the game play data of students by teachers. We expect students' play level and the pattern of each curriculum to be analyzed through play data collected through the web-based real-time monitoring system. This should lead to a practical evaluation of the effectiveness of the coding learning game and a further improvement in the quality of software education.

References

1. Wing, J.M.: Computational thinking. Commun. ACM 49(3), 33–35 (2006)
2. Barr, V., Stephenson, C.: Bringing computational thinking to K-12: what is involved and what is the role of the computer science education community? Inroads (2011)
3. Rees, A., et al.: An overview of the most relevant literature on coding and computational thinking with emphasis on the relevant issues for teachers, Belgium (2016)
4. Bers, M.U., et al.: Computational thinking and tinkering: exploration of an early childhood robotics curriculum. Comput. Educ. 72, 145–157 (2014)
5. Fyfe, E.R., et al.: Concreteness fading in mathematics and science instruction: a systematic review. Educ. Psychol. Rev. 26(1), 9–25 (2014)
6. Papastergiou, M.: Digital game-based learning in high school computer science education: impact on educational effectiveness and student motivation. Comput. Educ. 52, 1–12 (2009)
7. Strawhacker, A., et al.: ScratchJr Demo.: a coding language for kindergarten. In: Proceedings of the 14th International Conference on Interaction Design and Children, pp. 414–417. ACM (2015)
8. García-Peñalvo, F.J., et al.: A survey of resources for introducing coding into schools. In: García-Peñalvo, F.J. (ed.) Proceedings of the Fourth International Conference on Technological Ecosystems for Enhancing Multiculturality (TEEM 2016), pp. 19–26. ACM, New York (2016)
9. Virvou, M., et al.: Combining software games with education: evaluation of its educational effectiveness. J. Educ. Technol. Soc. 8(2), 54–65 (2005)
10. Jenkins, T.: On the difficulty of learning to program. In: Proceedings of the 3rd Annual Conference of the LTSN Centre for Information and Computer Sciences, vol. 4, pp. 53–58 (2002)
11. Randel, J.M., et al.: The effectiveness of games for educational purposes: a review of recent research. Simul. Gameing 23, 261–276 (1992)
12. Ranum, D., et al.: Successful approaches to teaching introductory computer science courses with Python. In: SIGCSE 2006, Special Session, Houston, Texas, USA, pp. 396–397, 3–5 March 2006

13. Malone, T.W.: What makes things fun to learn? Heuristics for designing instructional computer games. In: SIGSMALL 1980, Proceedings of the 3rd ACM SIGSMALL Symposium and the First SIGPC Symposium on Small Systems, Palo Alto, pp. 162–169. ACM Press (1980)
14. Andreessen, M.: Why software is eating the world. Wall Street J. 20
15. Barr, D., et al.: Computational thinking: a digital age skill for everyone. Learn. Lead. Technol. **38**(6), 20–23 (2011)
16. Yadav, A., et al.: Introducing computational thinking in education courses. In: Proceedings of the 42nd ACM Technical Symposium on Computer Science Education, pp. 465–470. ACM (2011)
17. Moreno-Ger, P.: Educational game design for online education. Comput. Hum. Behav. **24**, 2530–2540 (2008)
18. Kiili, K.: Digital game-based learning: towards an experiential gaming model. Internet High. Educ. **8**, 13–24 (2005)
19. Xie, T.: Where software engineering, education and gaming meet. In: Computer Games and Software Engineering, pp. 114–132 (2015)
20. Swacha, J.: Gamification-based e-learning platform for computer programming education. In: X World Conference on Computers in Education (2013)
21. Park, H.M.: Global SW education trend and tools. Internet & Security Focus, p. 41 (2014)
22. Park, J.H.: Effect of storytelling based software education on computational thinking. J. Korean Assoc. Inf. Educ. **19**(11), 58 (2015)
23. Cho, S.-H., et al.: The effect of CPS-based scratch EPL on problem solving ability and programming attitude. Korea Assoc. Inf. Educ. **12**(1), 77–88 (2008)
24. Lightbot. http://lightbot.com
25. Gouws, L.A., et al.: Computational thinking in educational activities: an evaluation of the educational game light-bot. In: Proceedings of the 18th ACM Conference on Innovation and Technology in Computer Science Education. ACM (2013)
26. Box Island. https://boxisland.io
27. Code Combat. http://lightbot.com
28. Khara, A.: How good is the website CodeCombat.com at teaching JavaScript, Python, and its associated languages? (2015). https://www.quora.com (pristupljeno: 25. Kolovoza 2017)
29. The Foos. https://codespark.com

Which Virtual Piano Keyboard for Children with Autism? A Pilot Study

Maria Claudia Buzzi[1(✉)], Marina Buzzi[1], Marco Maugeri[2,3],
Gabriella Paolini[3], Maria Teresa Paratore[1], Alessandra Sbragia[3,4],
Caterina Senette[1], and Amaury Trujillo[1]

[1] IIT-CNR, via G. Moruzzi, 1, 56124 Pisa, Italy
{claudia.buzzi,marina.buzzi,maria.paratore,
caterina.senette,amaury.trujillo}@iit.cnr.it
[2] Ministry of Education, Rome, Italy
marco.maugeri@istruzione.it
[3] Consortium GARR, Via dei Tizii, 6, 00185 Rome, Italy
gabriella.paolini@garr.it,
alessandra.sbragia@gmail.com
[4] Associazione La Sonda su Marte ONLUS, Rome, Italy

Abstract. Music can be a powerful therapy for many conditions, including autism syndrome. Technology is usually intrinsically attractive for children with autism, who often interact with apps on tablets and smartphones. It can offer structured, repeatable, and coherent training tools, customizable according to the student's need and preferences. Although many apps for rehabilitation of children with autism are available, only a few of them are accessible to students with autism spectrum disorder due to complex interaction environments, the high number of items, and inappropriate stimuli offered. Furthermore, to the best of our knowledge, no apps are available for teaching music to people with autism. The Suoniamo project aims to fill this gap by designing an accessible app for teaching piano playing to students with autism. Customization is a key feature when teaching persons with special needs, even more so if dealing with the complexity of the autism spectrum disorder. This paper describes a pilot test with four adolescents with autism, aimed at evaluating the usability of the Suoniamo app user interfaces for the piano keyboard in three different configurations.

Keywords: Music · Autism · Accessibility: Usability · Web applications

1 Introduction

Literature reports the positive effect of music in treating specific symptoms in autism spectrum disorder, specifically influencing communication, socialization and behavior [7, 8, 13]. Unfortunately, very few studies involve actually teaching music to people with autism. Playing an instrument proficiently requires long training involving many abilities. Individuals with autism may have problems paying attention, decoding notes in the sheet music, interpreting the note values, coordinating hands, and so on. To empower them, it is necessary to exploit their strengths and mitigate their weaknesses.

© Springer Nature Switzerland AG 2019
C. Stephanidis (Ed.): HCII 2019, LNCS 11786, pp. 280–291, 2019.
https://doi.org/10.1007/978-3-030-30033-3_22

Autism spectrum disorder (ASD) is defined by the American Psychiatric Association in the "Diagnostic and Statistical Manual of Mental Disorders" (DSM-5), as delays or anomalies emerging in children before age 3 years in at least one of three areas: social interaction, communicative and social use of language, and symbolic or imaginative play. ASD makes it hard to understand and interpret the world and what is happening around one. Impacting on communication and socialization, it compromises the ability of a person to interact with peers. People with autism often need rigid routines and highly predictable events, move comfortably only in familiar and uncrowded environments and they often display behavior inappropriate to the context, especially in new situations. The spectrum of symptoms varies widely from individual to individual, from mild to severe. For this reason the teaching approach needs to be customized according to the individual's demands and learning pace.

The enormous increase in prevalence of the syndrome, "about 1 in 59, of 8-year-old children," as estimated by the CDC's Autism and Developmental Disabilities Monitoring Network [4], underlines the urgency of applying effective rehabilitation therapy to address all functional areas of the subjects. Early behavioral intervention (possibly before age 3 years) can take advantage of the great plasticity of a child's brain [1].

According to the empathizing-systemizing theory [1], a highly structured intervention can support learning in children with low-functioning ASD. They often need clear and simple interaction patterns, avoiding errors in the initial learning stages to effectively gain skills repeating trials, and facing tasks with a gradual increase in degree of difficulty. A structured learning approach offers a predictable and coherent learning environment. This reduces the subject's frustration or anxious episodes, and thanks to the rewards provided, attention increases while self-stimulation decreases. Evidence in literature suggests the use of technology within a behavioral and holistic intervention, to support the individual in the learning process.

We are carrying out a multidisciplinary study on effective strategies for teaching music to people with autism using the Suoniamo app, a Web tool for teaching music specifically to these users by exploiting mobile devices (tablet or laptop) [3]. The Suoniamo fluid layout enables smooth interface resize to adapt to device screen dimension. All the UI components, basics or augmentatives (described in the following) are the result of literature analysis together with iterative evaluation of mid-term prototypes conducted during co-design sessions involving professionals with different learning experiences with people with autism. We focused on participative design in order to satisfy accessibility/usability aspects that are relevant when designing for special needs people, also taking into account individual needs. Customization is a key feature when teaching people with special needs, even more so if dealing with the complexity of the autism spectrum disorder.

In this paper, we will describe a pilot test with four teenagers with autism, aimed at evaluating the usability of the Suoniamo app user interfaces for the piano keyboard in three different configurations.

2 Related Work

A national project conducted by the National Autism Center in 2009[1] formalized the role of music therapy as an "evidenced-based practice to adopt, exploiting songs and rhythm, when teaching individual skills to subjects with autism" [11]. Several other works in literature report the positive effects of music in treating specific symptoms in autism spectrum disorder. Summarizing a recent review concerning music interventions for children with autism [13], twenty studies focused their attention on music's influence on communication, socialization and behavior.

Concerning communication, music has been used to improve expressive and receptive skills in different ways, such as using text sung or spoken to music or a rhythm [5], or using improvisational music [5, 14]. The use of music for socialization mainly used engagement as a focus of the research, one study using music to decode emotions [9]. All studies showed an improvement in peer-initiated interaction, but generalization and lasting effects were not shown [14, 15]. Finally, most studies cited in this review focused on using music to increase appropriate behavior and reduce vocal stereotypy. Approaches adopted included listening to music and music combined with social stories [2]. General results, reported in the studies examined, were positive, but not all individuals with autism find listening to music a positive experience [6].

Many studies confirmed that music therapy could improve social behavior and joint attention in children with autism; more evidence is needed to determine the impact of group music therapy [12]. The work of La Gasse [10] is an attempt in this direction, providing some evidence that music therapy group sessions targeting social skills may improve joint attention and eye gaze toward other persons.

3 The Suoniamo App

Guidelines for teaching music to children with autism mainly focus on methodology (how to set the didactic environment and to schedule activities), omitting principles for the structured learning environment that guarantees an accessible and effective way to learn. The multidisciplinary Suoniamo project aims to design an accessible highly structured learning environment to teach piano to individuals with low- and medium-functioning autism. The target users are adolescents with autism (age 11–15 years) but the app can be exploited by younger children as well as adults.

The app provides three basic learning units that start the training by following note order (starting from C) and the random modules that verify the concepts previously mastered in a generalized and more challenging way:

(a) Note Discrimination (ND), playing the single notes in sequence (C, C#, D, D#, E, etc.) regardless of duration, in order to identify the position of notes on the piano keyboard. At first, the software proposes notes in ordered sequence to help

---

[1] https://www.umass.edu/doegrants/wp-content/uploads/2014/04/NAC-Standards-Report_2009_2011.pdf.

memorize the scale; afterwards, the student can move to play random notes (program generalization).

(b) Note Value (NV): requires playing the single notes in sequence for the duration (4/4, 2/4, 1/4) indicated by a visual discriminative stimulus. This program also includes training in the pause concept.

The training includes three units: it starts from whole notes (4/4) proposing trials on notes in sequence and then the pause (4/4). Once this concept is mastered, the training moves on to half notes (2/4) and next (after having mastered the previous one) to quarter notes (1/4).

(c) The C Major scale, ascending and descending, to learn the central, left and right scale on the keyboard. This training exercise shows in the pentagram the entire scale to be played, starting from whole notes at the beginning, and once mastered, moves on to half notes and next on to quarter notes

Each learning unit offers a sequence of trials within a predefined workflow. Moreover, colors and visual feedback are used as augmentative stimuli to facilitate task completion without frustration. Errors during task execution are avoided in order to implement the errorless principle of behavioral teaching. After the training, the student should be proficient in decoding pentagram language, playing notes, waiting for pauses and performing simple scores. Another interactive module is provided for supporting the execution of simple pieces of music through graphic cues. Once mastered on the virtual piano keyboard, the program might be generalized on a real piano or via a physical keyboard that can be connected to the app via USB port.

Considering the learning units described above, the student's work environment should guarantee a logical workflow of tasks and fluid design of the graphic components of the user interfaces (UIs). The most relevant insights gained during ongoing tests mainly concern UI design, since potential improvements in the workflow generally require longer evaluation times.

Since people with autism are often visual learners, each UI is a dynamic entity that exploits the user's visual channel to convey information. It includes basic elements such as virtual piano-keyboard, pentagram, notes, etc., and elements defined as 'augmentative' that implement accessible learning strategies. A preliminary pilot study with three students with autism highlighted several limits, especially in the augmentative components; those limits have been overcome through a new version of the app, the target of the current test discussed herein. Of these elements, the most important is note-color mapping to simplify note identification and positioning on the keyboard. We have implemented the association note-color proposing as default combination the rainbow spectrum and providing exercises for note discrimination using a standard piano keyboard (white and black keys). In an earlier version, only the note being tested was colored. As shown in Fig. 1, the discriminative stimulus requires identifying each note on the keyboard and the target note is colored to avoid errors.

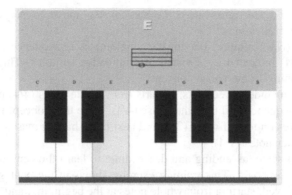

Fig. 1. Note discrimination module - old version

This simplified the task enormously; in fact, results of previous tests showed the complete success of all participants in the discrimination task. Subsequent observations revealed that such a prompt originated only a basic stimulus-response dynamic since the user reacted only to the color and not to the challenging task showed at the top of the UI. Consequently, the new implementation offers the piano keyboard completely colored to make the learner to pay more attention to the task request, thus reducing the stimulus-response effect (Fig. 2).

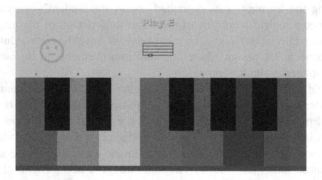

Fig. 2. Note discrimination module (ND) – new version (1-octave)

Another challenge is the concept of note value, in terms of time duration. Learning note value implies the ability to count the flow of time, given a unit of measure, and the ability to inhibit the response to a given stimulus (balance excitation/inhibition). Both have enormous implications in everyday life. In this sense, an active experience of these concepts through music could potentially improve real life behaviors. What could be the best 'augmentative' components to convey this concept? As shown in Fig. 3, the UI proposes two main elements: (i) an emoticon that communicates to the user either positive or neutral feedback related to the completion of the task (the figure shows a neutral case); (ii) A progress bar calibrated on the time signature (the default is 4/4).

As the student presses the key on the virtual keyboard, each quarter progressively fills in. This element helps the user to count the flow of time. Both components have been identified through successive design refinements and are currently once again being tested.

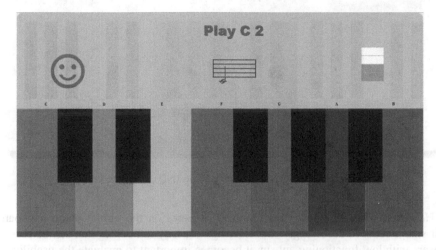

Fig. 3. The Note Value (NV) module (1-octave version)

Finally, since the most common songs (proposed to this specific target of users during music lessons at school) expand at least over 3 octaves and considering that the generalization process will succeed on an electronic piano keyboard composed of three octaves, the size of the virtual piano keyboard has to be carefully analyzed. Specifically, we decided to test three configurations: 1-octave, 1-extended-octave (16 notes centered on the central Do scale), and a 3-octave virtual piano keyboard that generalizes the piano keyboard adopted at school (Fig. 4).

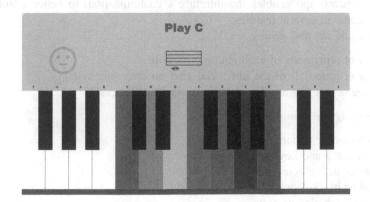

Fig. 4. The Note discrimination module (ND), 1-extended-octave version

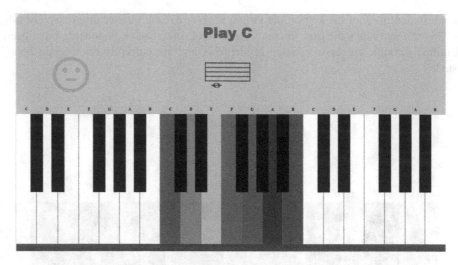

Fig. 5. The Note discrimination module (ND), 3-octave version

However, when expanding the numbers of notes on the virtual piano keyboard, their size is reduced accordingly. Considering motricity difficulties that can be present in users with low-functioning autism, it becomes important to evaluate the usability of the three-octave virtual piano keyboard on the tablet device of about 10.1″ screen size (Fig. 5).

3.1   Customizing the App

Augmentative elements adapt forms and content of the learning program to the individual's characteristics and to the requirements of the music program. The user interface adds these augmentative elements (acting as visual prompts) as default at the beginning but they can be progressively faded (by the music teacher) when the student's learning progress reaches a high percentage of success.

The Suoniamo app enables the interface's customization, to better adapt to the student's needs, in several features:

Customizing the task flow

- Number of repetitions of each learning module
- Number of proposals of the same trial after an error (attempts)
- Including or not any accidental notes in the learning path

Customizing the piano keyboard

- Anglo-Saxon or Italian musical notation
- Sharp or flat piano keyboard notation
- Number of active octaves (1, 2, 3)
- Colored or black & white piano keyboard
- Piano keys labelled or not

4 The Pilot Test

The current form of the Suoniamo prototype is the result of literature analysis together with iterative evaluation of mid-term prototypes conducted during co-design sessions involving professionals experienced in teaching people with autism. Moreover, as previously mentioned, we performed an early pilot study to understand any major usability problems, as well as the app's pleasantness and the degree of acceptance by the children. Thanks to results of the previous test, the prototypes have been updated to reflect changes suggested by observed difficulties and by participant preferences.

The objective of the current test is twofold:

(i) To evaluate the improvements applied to the augmentative elements of each new user interface: colors, notation
(ii) To evaluate potential usability problems arising from the introduction of a simulated three-octave piano keyboard and its variant (1 octave extended) in order to test the feasibility of the future introduction of the additional module, supporting the execution of simple music scores in driven modality. Here we did not discuss the design and implementation of the execution module, which is currently in progress.

For all these reasons, we defined a protocol for the test of the three different versions of the piano keyboard as described in the following.

Who and Where
The test was performed with four adolescents with diagnosed autism, P1, P2, P3 and P4, described in Table 1.

Table 1. Test participants

Subjects	Age	Functional age	Gender	Severity Level[a]	Music knowledge
P1	13	12–13	F	2	Y
P2	13	10–12	M	3	N
P3	14	13–14	M	2	N
P4	18	10–12	F	3	N

[a]Severity level for Autism spectrum disorder: Level 1: "Requiring support", Level 2: "Requiring substantial support", Level 3: "Requiring very substantial support", Diagnostic and Statistical Manual of Mental Disorders (DSM-5), American Psychiatric Association, 2013.

The test was carried out in a natural setting, reassuring for the children in a comfortable and familiar place. We asked participant caregivers to indicate the most comfortable place. Two students performed the test in a lab where they carry out afternoon study sessions twice a week, while two students carried out the test at home. Before starting the test session, a caregiver introduced the researchers and explained the test to each participant. The caregiver was also present during the test, only as an observer, to make the participant more comfortable. The caregiver as well as the researchers verbally reinforced the student in the case of a task performed successfully (also by clapping hands). The user had previously chosen their preferred reinforcement (a piece of music to listen to, a game to play, a piece of candy). After performing each or all tasks of the test (depending on the user's attention), he/she was reinforced with their chosen reward, and if they needed, they could relax by doing something else for a while.

What

All participants had to interact with two learning modules: Note Discrimination in three different configuration settings (i.e., 1 octave, 1 extended octave and 3 octaves) and the Note Duration (performed on the 1-octave setting). During the test, we only collected observational data without interfering. We proposed the following tasks:

(a) T1, Task_1: Note Discrimination module, 1 octave
(b) T2, Task_2: Note Discrimination module, 1 octave extended
(c) T3, Task_3: Note Discrimination module, 3 octaves
(d) T4, Task_4: Note Duration module, 1 octave only for notes of 2/4 value.

The initial order was shifted by one while progressing with the test (i.e., the first user started performing T1, the second started performing T2, and so on), in order to minimize bias due to the effect of familiarization with the exercise and the interaction required. We wanted to investigate the usability of three different configurations of the Suoniamo app user interfaces for the piano keyboard. To this aim, we have collected both objective and subjective data during each task execution related to:

T1, T2 and T3:

- Number of errors (touching a target different from the required note (E1))
- Number of additional wrong interactions (attempt to touch a non-interactive UI element (E2))
- Preference on the different configuration settings (i.e., 1 octave, 1 extended octave and 3 octaves), collected directly by users through Smiley-meter rating scale (Fig. 6).

T4:

- Number of errors touching a target different from the required note (E1)
- Number of wrong interactions touching a non-interactive UI element (E2)
- Number of errors touching the target note for a duration different from the one requested (E3)
- Pleasantness of the UI (1 octave version) collected directly by users through Smiley-meter rating scale (Fig. 6).

Each task is composed of several sub-tasks, each related to a different note.

How – Materials

- Android Tablet with Wi-Fi connection, screen size 10.1″; all participants carried out the test on the same tablet
- Sheet of paper to collect observational data by the mediator (Errors E1, E2 and E3) and other relevant observations.

– A Smiley-meter rating scale of 5 items (I like it very much (5), I like it (4), neutral (3), I do not like it (2), I do not like it at all (1)) to collect subjective data on preferences from the users. Participants with medium-functioning autism were immediately able to use the scale while the users with autism of severity level 3 were supported by the tutor with additional vocal cues.

| I like it very much | I like it | Neutral | I do not like it | I do not like it at all |

Fig. 6. The Smiley-meter rating scale used for the subjective evaluation

5 Results and Discussion

Results of the test are shown in Tables 2 and 3.

Table 2. Results on success (completion without errors, S) and errors (E1, E2, E3)

Subject/Task	T1	T2	T3	T4
P1	S	S	S	S
P2	S	E1 (1)	S	E1 (1)
P3	S	S	S	E1 (1)
P4	S	E1 (1), E2 (1)	E1 (1), E2 (1)	Not completed

Table 3. Results on users' preferences

Subject/Task	T1 (ND 1 octave)	T2 (ND 1 extended octave)	T3 (ND with 3 octaves)	T4 (NV with 1 octave)
P1	4	4	5	4
P2	5	4	4	4
P3	5	4	4	3
P4	4	4	4	3

Regarding observational data, tasks related to the Note Discrimination tasks (T1, T2 and T3) were performed correctly and easily by two of the four users, those who have a lower degree of autism severity. User P2 was confused by the diesis notes, difficult to detect without visual cues for the discrimination.

User P4, a low-functioning girl, was very excited by the presence of the researcher, preferring to interact with her instead of with the app. When it was possible to make her concentrate on the tasks, she interacted very quickly, anticipating the request of the next subtask (e.g., "play F") as soon as the previous was completed, thus making errors and becoming confused about the lack of the visual positive feedback. For this reason, she touched the emoticon in order to make it smile. We need to implement a new version of the UIs that minimize the loading time of subtasks, making the new one available as soon as the previous one has been completed.

Another problem was again related to the diesis notes. To resolve this issue, we plan to use additional visual cues to help the user, such as writing the note with the two colors of the keys surrounding it, e.g. C# with the C red and the # orange.

Task T4 resulted more complex, as expected, but there were some errors, probably due to a weakness of the UI and not due to a real user fault: users play the note for the required duration and the neutral emoticon changes into a smile, but if the user releases their finger 1/2 s after, the system considers it an error. For users P3 and P4, this feedback was confusing (they said, "The smile says I'm doing well, but the same subtask is proposed instead of the next") so they evaluated the UI in T4 with the neutral rate. We need to design more tolerant interaction mechanisms to avoid frustration and misunderstanding in users.

Regarding subjective evaluation, all the users found the user interfaces quite pleasant. Considering the ND module, the simple and clear UI with the piano keyboard in 1 octave was the most highly rated, followed by the one with 3 octaves that a user (with severity level 2) liked because it was the most challenging.

The NV module suffers from the previously described issues and it was the least liked.

Music is an important therapeutic approach for users with autism. This study evaluates the usability of virtual piano keyboards for adolescents with different degrees of autism. As confirmed by literature, a high personalization of the user interface is crucial to match the needs of different subjects, so we have designed different user interface settings. This pilot test with only four users will allow us to refine the app, further simplifying both the interfaces and interaction mechanisms. The aim is to offer an accessible and effective app customizable with visual prompts that can be faded over time to help people with autism play music.

Acknowledgments. We thank the students who participated in the pilot test: Emma, Tommy, Jacopo and Sofia, and their caregivers Claudia, Simona, Francesca, Luca and Susanna.

References

1. Baron-Cohen, S.: Autism: the empathizing-systemizing (E-S) theory. Ann. N. Y. Acad. Sci. **1156**(1), 68–80 (2009)
2. Brownell, M.D.: Musically adapted social stories to modify behaviors in students with autism: four case studies. J. Music Ther. **39**(2), 117–144 (2002)
3. Buzzi, M.C., Buzzi, M., Paolini, G., Paratore, M.T., Senette, C.: Designing an accessible web app to teach piano to children with autism. In: ACM CHItaly 2019 (2019, in press)

4. CDC 2018: US Centers for Disease Control. Community Report on Autism 2018. https://www.cdc.gov/ncbddd/autism/addm-community-report/documents/addm-community-report-2018-h.pdf. Accessed Jan 2019
5. Corbett, B.A., Shickman, K., Ferrer, E.: Brief report: the effects of Tomatis sound therapy on language in children with autism. J. Autism Dev. Disord. **38**(3), 562–566 (2008)
6. Devlin, S., Healy, O., Leader, G., Reed, P.: The analysis and treatment of problem behavior evoked by auditory stimulation. Res. Autism Spectrum Disord. **2**(4), 671–680 (2008)
7. Hallam, S.: The power of music: a research synthesis of the impact of actively making music on the intellectual, social and personal development of children and young people. International Music Education Research Centre (iMerc) (2015)
8. Hetland, L.: Learning to make music enhances spatial reasoning. J. Aesthetic Educ. **34**(3/4), 179–238 (2000)
9. Katagiri, J.: The effect of background music and song texts on the emotional understanding of children with autism. J. Music Ther. **46**(1), 15–31 (2009)
10. LaGasse, A.B.: Effects of a music therapy group intervention on enhancing social skills in children with autism. J. Music Ther. **51**(3), 250–275 (2014)
11. National Autism Center: National standards project: Addressing the need for evidence-based practice guidelines for autism spectrum disorder. Findings and conclusions (2009). http://www.nationalautismcenter.org/pdf/NAC%20Findings%20&%2
12. Rabinowitch, T.C., Cross, I., Burnard, P.: Long-term musical group interaction has a positive influence on empathy in children. Psychol. Music **41**(4), 484–498 (2013)
13. Simpson, K., Keen, D.: Music interventions for children with autism: narrative review of the literature. J. Autism Dev. Disord. **41**(11), 1507–1514 (2011)
14. Simpson, K., Keen, D.: Teaching young children with autism graphic symbols embedded within an interactive song. J. Dev. Phys. Disabil. **20**, 165–177 (2010)
15. Stephens, C.E.: Spontaneous imitation by children with autism during a repetitive musical play routine. Autism **12**(6), 645–671 (2008)

ShadowHunter: Facilitating Children's Outdoor Exploration with Shadows

Yang Chen[1], Yuyu Lin[1], Lijuan Liu[1], Ziyu Liu[2], Cheng Yao[1(✉)],
and Fangtian Ying[3]

[1] College of Computer Science and Technology,
Zhejiang University, Hangzhou, China
{sonnechen,linyuyu,liulijuan,yaoch}@zju.edu.cn
[2] College of Computer Software Technology,
Zhejiang University, Hangzhou, China
miclzy@126.com
[3] China Academy of Art, Hangzhou, China
yingft@gmail.com

Abstract. Currently, HCI researchers focus on novel solutions that combine technology into children's outdoor activities to address the modest decline in such experience. This research presents a novel AR game in which shadows from the outdoor environment are used as AR markers, to facilitate children' motivation and engagement in outdoor exploration experience. Our prototype uses physical shadows as clues with a treasure hunting game mechanism to make a connection with children and their familiar outdoor environment. To evaluate our approach, we designed and implemented the game and then conducted a qualitative user study with children (n = 10) with our initial prototype in a kindergarten. Our striking findings suggest that the use of shadows from the outdoor environment as an AR maker has the potential to expand the approach to facilitate children' engagement and motivation through their outdoor interaction experience.

Keywords: Edutainment/Education games, Shadow · Outdoor exploration · Augmented reality · Children · Head-up game

1 Introduction

Outdoor play has been proven to benefit children's development [1]. The specific features in an outdoor environment which not only be naturalized with plants, trees, flowers, water, sand, animals, and insects but also be rich with a wide range of physical objects and play equipment such as building, cars, statues, swings, slides. When outdoors, children can construct on an expanded scale, explore the world at first hand through a great deal of running and chasing experience, as well as experience natural phenomena such as the changing seasons, the light and shadows [2, 3]. Fjortofit et al. [4] pointed out that children who play in a flexible environment tend to be healthier. By playing outdoors, children engage in social and physical interaction both with competition and coordination, which develop their empathy, increase their social

© Springer Nature Switzerland AG 2019
C. Stephanidis (Ed.): HCII 2019, LNCS 11786, pp. 292–305, 2019.
https://doi.org/10.1007/978-3-030-30033-3_23

competence and strengthen their relationship with the physical world [5–7]. What's more, these benefits are of importance as they play a significant role in children's development of future adult-life [10].

We live in a digital-rich society where digital technology plays a curial role in our lives. These mobile applications in various forms that link the physical world with digital information are changing our practice and the way of perceiving the world. It has been proven that not only adults but also children are exposed to these technologies extensively [9]. Some research evaluated that although these digital contexts provide children various opportunities of an immersive learning experience, it also highlights the massive tension between increased digital learning and decreases physical exploration and interaction with the surrounding world [14, 15].

To solve the tension described above, the HCI community focused on the domain includes Pervasive games, Exertion games, and Heads-Up games to shed light on the decrease in children's outdoor exploration [8]. By embedding novel technology into social and physical interaction experience, more immersive and intriguing outdoor exploration activities have great potential of changing natural outdoor play routine and facilitating children's engagement and motivation in the outdoor experience. Augmented Reality (AR) application, which provides an interactive and digital enhanced view of the physical world, has been reported to success in shifting human mobility patterns. The main feature of AR application is the use of a visual marker, which enables users to link these markers with some specific objects or location and gain different types of information at the same time [11]. This novel technology has the potential to enhance outdoor exploration and learning is already used in the museum, art exhibition, field studies like identification of plants species and educational environment [12, 13]. This entertaining and novel way has the potential to bring real-world into digital-enhanced games that promote the outdoor experience for children.

In this paper, we designed a prototype of an AR application that utilized shadows from physical objects as AR marker and applied it in the context of children's outdoor exploration experience in a treasure hunting mechanism game. We conducted user research to understand how children reacted to this prototype and how technology could be used to motivate children into exploring the open-air environment and strengthen children's relationship with the real world. The main contribution of our research is utilizing more insight on using shadows from physical environment objects in marked-based AR application to enhance the connection between digital knowledge and physical world, which support naturalistic and unobtrusive play experience considering children's perspective. This study provides insights for future research on technological-enhanced outdoor games for children, as well as inspiration and lessons for mobile augmented reality (MAR) development.

2   Related Work

2.1   Head-Up Games

Head-Up Games (HUG) are technology-based outdoor games to promote outdoor interaction with the minimal support of digital devices and screen time [8]. HUGs are a subset of pervasive games that, in contrast to games that mainly use mobile devices as gaming interfaces, does not force players to stick to screen, thus encouraging physical activity and personal engagement. Federica. et al. developed ABBOT [17], which combined a smart tangible object with a mobile application to access new content related to the discovered natural elements.

Another unique feature of HUGs is guiding children with creative thinking. RaPIDO, a sensor-based prototype, as well as an accompanying platform for rule changing [19]. By changing parameters such as buzzing duration and the number of participating teams, children could create various outdoor games from RaPIDO, based on their ideas and concepts. Admittedly, HUGs are practical approaches to enhance children's outdoor play, especially with the feature of no-screen-based interaction and self-exploration settings. In this research, we concentrate on applying novel technology to conventional mobile applications which have the potential of blending the physical and digital world to enhance interactive experience for children, reaching to naturalistic and unobtrusive play experience.

2.2 AR Games

There is a rapidly growing interest in AR application in children's education [18–20]. Research has concluded that AR technology can become innovative tools that combine physical experience, virtual content to develop children's imagination and creativity. Since early research on MAR focusing on interaction design [11]; nowadays, these applications are widely used in various domains. Salmi et al. developed a scientific AR-application [21] which visualizes the invisible physical phenomenon like 'Doppler Effect' and 'Molecule Movement in Gas,' proved to stimulate the interest and situational motivation in the science domains. Amy M. Kamarainen et al. constructed EcoMOBILE project [22], which uses an environmental probe with AR technology in a local pond environment to aid middle schoolers' understanding and interpretation of water quality measurement. There is a wide range of previous research focused on using MAR in nature and environment exploration areas. Oh and Byun [24] have presented an augmented reality learning system called "the interactive flower garden" that makes use of interactive agents in the augmented picture and allows learners to interact with the agents. Current research seems to validate that MAR may provide positive impacts on children's nature subjects education. However, the definition of outdoors can be described as an open and constantly changing environments, where it is possible to experience freedom, gross and boisterous movements, and also physical elements. Given that, we focus on an interactive solution that can use MAR to combine the physical world and digital information in a playful outdoor experience for children.

2.3 Interacting with Shadows

Shadows are ubiquitous around our everyday life, where there is light, there have shadows. Shadows can be seen as a natural information affordance, providing the shape of objects surrounding us [16]. Therefore, we are used to recognizing our surroundings by glancing their projected shadows, which provides a new way of discovering nature and natural environments. What's more, shadows are sensational which are differences from silhouettes, transforming 3D objects into 2D illumination, in consequences make shadows changeable and cunning. Meanwhile, many researchers in HCI have focused mainly on shadow interactive installations [23] such as shadows as input device and shadow transformation through various parameters, without considering about young children's conceptions and creativity of shadows, and particularly the conceptions of very young children (aged below six) in a novel environment exploration approach. In this paper, we seek to utilize shadows as a medium to bridge the physical world and screen time.

2.4   Visual Marker

Visual markers, such as RFID, QR code, barcodes are essential graphic symbols that can be recognized with machine vision through accessing to cameras in mobile devices or tablets. Visual markers may also be utilized without graphical symbols. Ismo et al. [26] designed a mobile augmented reality application in which physical items from nature are used as AR markers to enhance children's nature exploration. Their findings from user interviews suggested that the concept has sound potential in its mixture of physical activity and educational elements in an outdoor context. The main problems of conventional visual markers with mobile devices are their appearance which related to technical looking and has the potential to lead to be obtrusive to children. To solve this problem, design markers which use natural objects may have the chance to use it naturalistic and unobtrusive.

2.5   Main Features of Our Work

Given that our focus on creating an engaging outdoor interaction experience that engages children in observing shadow from physical objects, we concentrate on the aspects that select shadows from the real world and use them as visual markers for MAR. Despite previous research, which focuses on technical issues on image recognition with AR application, our research concentrated on the user perspective and engaging exploration experience for children. We utilize shadows as an unobtrusive and mysterious clue in a treasure hunting game mechanism to create a playful outdoor game for children. Besides, rather than in a fixed nature environment, our work seeks to expand the novel exploration towards the whole physical world, which includes schoolyards, daily routine, botanical gardens, and so on.

3   ShadowHunter

The concept of ShadowHunter is solving the tension between increased addiction to mobile games and decreased outdoor physical exploration in children. Our main goal is to design an unobtrusive and intriguing approach which uses shadows, a natural phenomenon, as physical objects markers to be able to provide contextual information on the real-world objects to children. We also seek to use this MAR way to encourage children to pay attention to their living environment and explore the real world with the mobile AR application.

3.1   Conceptual Design

The paper describes a novel application of AR concept into children's outdoor explo-ration, where children can not merely observe the physical phenomenon and combine these abstract images with real-world objects to form their conceptual explanations, but also be encouraged to explore surroundings which are too familiar to ignore.

The game follows the style of treasure hunting games which players ought to find hidden treasures by following a serious of clues. The concept of ShadowHunter is that children should match given riddles, which are represented as shadows with real physical objects. Thus, they can obtain random shadow monsters as a reward (see Fig. 1).

Fig. 1. The game designed follow the style of treasure hunting game where children should match given riddles (shadows) with real physical objects, thus they can obtain random shadow monsters as a reward

The designed game starts by given shadows of one familiar objects around children everyday life. Because of shadows' unique feature that link 3D and 2D visualizations into one combined visual and information display. The given shadows are different from silhouettes, which to be riddles. Once the mysterious shadow is given on the tablet, each child embarks on treasure hunting through their familiar environment to find appropriate physical objects (facilities, buildings, sculptures, plants, etc.) by pointing the tablet camera at the object. The game identifies the object, gives infor-mation (i.e. videos/text/animation concerning that physical objects) and presents a shadow monster of this object designed by other users as a reward if the shadow matches the object. If the shadow does not match, the children may be given extra information to simplify the exploration. The players can also design their shadow monsters to gain energy for their monsters as well as enrich the game interaction. The monsters can be cultivated by energy children earned by either design popular shadow monsters or exchange shadow monsters with others. After the matching object has been found, children will be able to claim other shadow and embark on the following mission follow the style of treasure hunting game.

3.2 System Design

The prediction-observation-explanation (hereinafter called POE) model proposed by White and Gunstone [25] seeks to promote children's conceptual changes by confronting their prior knowledge through three tasks: prediction, observation, and explanation. This system provides opportunities for children to predict circumstances, clarify discrepancies or congruencies between their prediction and observation.

The applications of the POE model have been widely implemented in a computer-based environment. However, little research has reported the integration of POE model into a game-based context concerning scientific education.

In this paper, we endeavoured to follow POE strategy in AR game design concerning outdoor exploration experience as a game mechanism. As shown in Fig. 2, according to the prediction aspect, the game provided a shadow which functions as clues for children to predict which real physical object it belongs. Considering the deformation of shadows, it can be indeed challenging and confusing. Children proceed to the observation part upon finishing the conceptual speculation.

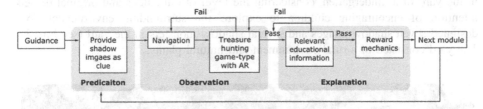

Fig. 2. POE model of ShadowHunter

The observation aspect consisted of seeking with game playing activities. In the seeking activities, the player is assigned a task that explored their outdoor environment to identify objects in a natural world environment. For example, if provided a shadow of a seesaw, the player should speculate and identify it through the tablet camera. As feedback is curial for knowledge improvement and skill acquisition in an educational context. We try to provide an exciting and emotional appealing experience, rewarding (e.g. Collect one random shadow monster/gain energy) and challenge (e.g. impose a time limitation or a competitive system) are embedded into the game.

For the explanation aspect, the players are given an attractive introduction of the physical object educational information, which includes an animation video explaining vividly on how the shadow deforms with sunlight and how this physical object functions in our daily life if they identified the object successfully. If they failed, they could replay the observation aspect with additional information to encourage their exploration.

The game application is implemented in Photoshop, Unity 3D and Qualcomm Vuforia platform. Seven image targets representing AR markers are used in the application. All of the physical objects were photographed straight from a top-down perspective and imported to Unity through Vuforia's Target Manager. All of the markers, physical objects and black-white images were Vuforia image targets in Unity, meaning that each marker is identified only with one 2D image. The majority of the markers gained five stars in Vuforia's target quality rating, means it can be easily recognized.

The videos designed by After Effect and exported in PNG sequential frame were imported, as well as audio resources in this unity projects and coded to follow concept setting.

4   Preliminary User Research

4.1   Research Process

With our preliminary prototype, we tried to confirm on how children reflect, feel and think about ShadowHunter and how this system impact on children outdoor exploration, as well as how can this system motivate children's outdoor activities. Thus, we conducted a game-type experiment in September 2018 in a kindergarten (Singapore). With the cooperation of principal and teachers, the game site was chosen to be located in the yard of a kindergarten, considering the level of difficulties and original design intention of encouraging children to explore the surrounding environment. We designed seven shadow images and several shadow monsters in the yard (see Fig. 3). The yard consisted of a rural environment and natural plants.

Fig. 3. Game map. We chose seven objects and collected their shadows in yard at 12 am.

We collected specified shadow images in advance into Unity database to output designated ShadowHunter application which fit our game-type experiment, regarding variable of shadow formation and practical usability.

The game-type experiment consisted of the following stages and qualitative user study methods:

- Demonstration of ShadowHunter to children
- Presentation of game experience
- Direct observation of children
- Semi-structure discussion with children (prior experience of ShadowHunter with tablets, how they feel about the game etc.)
- Group discussion with teachers (potential use in teaching, identified problems, future work

All users showed great interest in the interaction process, some users said that when they experienced the AquaBot, they were surprised that they could control the underwater robot without touching the water. P3 said the system was very interactive and provides a new water gaming experience. P6 said that this system gave her a new understanding of underwater robots. During the test, we found that the task of controlling the robot's movement was the most popular, and some participants experienced this task many times.

4.2 Methodology

A qualitative approach was chosen as it is a valid approach when trying to achieve a deep understanding of the behavior of individuals and groups. The data collected from semi-structure interview with children and researchers' group discussion, which can yield in-depth information on both learning and playing perspectives.

All the discussions were recorded and transcribed for discussion and future work. Sentences were collected as the unit of analysis and identified into meaningful categories. The records and observations were cross-checked by two researchers and three teachers (Table 1) to ensure validity of the findings.

Table 1. The composition of research team

Code	Gender	Major	Experience (years)
R1	F	Design	6
R2	M	Computer	7
T1	F	Education	14
T2	F	Education	9
T3	M	Design	5

4.3 Participants

In the consideration of the target user of ShadowHunter, six girls and four boys ranging in age from four to six years (mean age = 5.2, sd = 0.92) were selected. We were aware of differences in participant's cognitive abilities due to age and gender. In spite of that, we wanted to gain universal feedback from the assumed potential users that are children.

4.4   Procedure

Before the experiment, a letter was sent to children's parents informing the research study and ask for their consents. The session was started by giving a demonstration and presenting the idea of ShadowHunter to children, which last about 7 min. After that, players were given tablets running ShadowHunter application and instructed to find objects which match given shadow images and collected or designed their shadow monsters in the surrounding area.

The children were divided into four groups of two or three. Each group received a tablet and task sheet of given shadow images which need to be matched with real physical objects. Children were asked to change roles during the game experience.

The main task for children was to predict the provided shadow which functioned as a clue to find one real physical object it belongs to, then examine their prediction with a tablet. The players were a monster as a reward, as well as animation videos and the brief introduction of this object if they identified the right object successfully. If they failed, they could replay the observation aspect with additional information to encourage their exploration. Each group was accompanied by one researcher or teacher, who take charge of observing and notes taking (see Fig. 4).

Fig. 4. Child interact with ShadowHunter

4.5   Semi-structured Interview

After the game-type session, the semi-structured interview was carried out with children, who shared their game experiences and individual development ideas with researchers; the whole process took about 20 min. We utilized Smileyometer published by Read et al. to measure children's fun and satisfaction. We measured enjoyment of POE modal: Prediction (conceptual speculation), Observation (confirm predication) and Explanation (gain multimedia scientific information) with the question of "How much fun was it to do that part?" The answer on the Smileyometer is re-coded to 1 (for awful) until 5 (for brilliant). Almost all the children were satisfied with the game setting and level of difficulties (see Table 2).

Table 2. The result from Smileyometer

	N	Mean	SD
Prediction	10	3.12	1.24
Observation	10	4.23	0.96
Evaluation	10	4.83	0.34

Following are some of the children's comments:

"It's so exciting that I can catch a unique shadow monster" (P3)
"Searching for was fun and so was to design my shadow monster... It was easy; there should have more challenging tasks" (P4)
"It would be great if I can share shadow monsters with my friends" (P6)

The interviews with children indicated that gamified approach motivated them in exploring surrounding areas and engaging outdoor play. They appreciated the game mechanics about feedbacks which encourage them to design and collect shadow monsters in an entertaining way to expand physical activities.

4.6 Group Discussion

Based on the above findings, two researchers and three teachers (Table 1) who observed children and took notes on the both experiment and interview process gathered for a group discussion to form a shared understanding on all the observations and confirm the efficiency and limitation of ShadowHunter.

The discussion themes were as followed:

- First impression and observation
- Pro and cons of using mobile technology in children's outdoor play
- The meaning of physical exploration education
- Feasibility of ShadowHunter in preschool education
- Future exploration and development ideas

The whole discussion process lasted about 45 min and findings were sorted out in order to build practical implications and development directions.

5 Result

The overall responses about ShadowHunter during the semi-structured interview and group discussion were summarized. In general, the use of the surrounding environment with AR technology was considered to be a promising approach for children and especially for their outdoor exploration experience.

Based on the session, we found that it was essential to conduct a brief introduction before the task so that children can grasp the idea and manipulate the application.

Furthermore, our observation broke through the prior studies concerning about children may be too excited to concentrate on external reality. One recognized challenge in the study was the feature of shadow, leading to space and time limitation. An interesting finding was that the children who kept the tablet played a leading role in the group. As was well known that the combination with physical activity and cognitively demanding tasks can support learning achievements. However, it requires further studies with a multidisciplinary approach.

An important observation was that the competition mechanics in gamified approach could empower and motivate those who are not good at this part. As discussed in group discussion, we highly agreed that role-taking, social interaction and coordination needs to be taken account when designing game mechanics and applying novel technology in children outdoor interaction field.

Although teachers have used a large number of educational applications in the classroom, they failed to facilitate a personal engagement in outdoor experience for children, especially the motivation of outdoor exploration. Teachers appreciated the fact that ShadowHunter was intended for children to explore in the real world, outside of the classroom. Some of the teachers were a bit hesitant and sceptical about new technology in education. However, the ShadowHunter application was considered a playful game that could encourage children's outdoor exploration as well as raise their awareness of their surroundings as one teacher noted.

"In general, I am not interested in technology... there is a purpose; ... the opportunity to support independent learning and physical exploration, especially strengthen their emotional connection with the physical world" (T2)

Based on our above result, we draw some practical recommendations regarding edutainment application design for outdoor exploration.

- Use real-life objects as exploring materials
- Stimulate physical activity with scientific phenomenon interaction for a multi-sensory experience
- Considering the gamification mechanics, which includes both competitions and reward to encourage children to explore and learn.
- Design the game process with consideration of the interference of the external environment, including weather, temperature, etc.

6   Limitations and Future Work

The shadow markers worked well technically, albeit with certain limitations. Use of such markers would provide unobtrusive experience in outdoor exploration experience. However, the most serious technical limitation with the technology used in this study lies in the process by which the markers are created.

Every marker has to be created beforehand one by one for the Vuforia Target Manager. Also, due to the unique nature of the markers, transferring between contexts is not straightforward.

A further challenge with our solution is that each shadow is unique, and thus, the same objects in different time are not recognizable due to its slightly changes. This poses an obstacle to more extensive use of physical shadows from real-world objects and calls for other technical approaches, such as computer vision and machine learning.

Also, our work has some methodological limitations. The data were collected from one small group of children and the teachers studied were working in the same school. Thus, we cannot draw any generalizable conclusions on the long-term value of ShadowHunter applications in children's outdoor exploration, expect their initial satisfaction about this game. Also, we fail to conduct a control group to stress on our striking findings. Furthermore, the prototype is rough, and it also contained several technical issues which led to disappointing user experience to some extent.

7 Conclusion

In general, ShadowHunter was seen as a straightforward and intuitive way to interact with real-world objects that could be applied in children's outdoor exploration experience. The advantages of ShadowHunter application from outdoor play are its simplicity and intriguing game which follow treasure hunting game mechanism as well as using natural phenomenon- shadows as a clue in outdoor activity. Using shadows from real-world objects as markers were seen as a good direction for the gaming experience, as it created a naturalistic and unobtrusive play experience to enhance with the open-air environment.

Compared to the previous systems, we focused to utilize shadows from physical objects as a medium to bridge screen game with physical activity in familiar surroundings for children. We followed the POE modal strategy to design the game and conduct a semi-structured interview to confirm children's satisfaction through Smileyometer strategy. We also suggested practical recommendations regarding outdoor interaction for children based on our preliminary study. However, we acknowledge limitations to our approach that our system is limited by time and space, considering the feature of shadows. The future work should address developing the concept further and integrating it with more advanced visual recognition technologies for more extensive trials in varying in-the-wild contexts for outdoor exploration.

Overall we believe this research is a ground-breaking experience towards an unobtrusive and intriguing approach that uses shadows, a natural phenomenon, as physical objects markers to be able to provide contextual information on the real-world objects to children and facilitate their outdoor exploration.

Acknowledgements. The authors thanks all the reviewers for providing valuable insights and suggestions that have helped in substantially improving this paper, as well as all volunteers for general support. This project is supported by the National Natural Science Foundation of China (Grant No. 61332017) and Zhejiang Science and Technology Project (Grant No. 2017C31097).

References

1. Acar, H.: Learning environments for children in outdoor spaces. Procedia Soc. Behav. Sci. **141**, 846–853 (2014)
2. Ouvry, M.: Exercising Muscles and Minds: Outdoor Play and the Early Years Curriculum. National Early Years Network, London (2003)

3. Maynard, T.: Learning in the outdoor environment: a missed opportunity. Early Years **27**, 255–265 (2007)
4. Fjortoft, I., Sageie, J.: The natural environment as a playground for children. Landsc. Urban Plan. **48**, 83–97 (2000)
5. Bento, G., Dias, G.: The importance of outdoor play for young children's healthy development. Porto Biomed. J. **2**, 157–160 (2017)
6. Garvey, C.: Play, vol. 27. Harvard University Press, Cambridge (1990)
7. Loveland, K.K., Gregory Olley, J.: The effect of external reward on interest and quality of task performance in children of high and low intrinsic motivation. Child Dev. **50**, 1207–1210 (1979)
8. Soute, I., Markopoulos, P., Magielse, R.: Head up games: combining the best of both worlds by merging traditional and digital play. Pers. Ubiquitous Comput. **14**(5), 435–444 (2010)
9. Vincent, J.: Mobile Opportunities - Exploring positive mobile media opportunities for European children. http://www.lse.ac.uk/media@lse/documents/Mobile-Opportunities.pdf
10. Moore, R.C., Wong, H.H.: Natural Learning: The Life of an Environmental Schoolyard. Creating Environments for Rediscovering Nature's Way of Teaching. ERIC (1997)
11. Costanza, E., Huang, J.: Designable visual markers. In: Proceedings of the SIGCHI Conference on Human Factors in Computing Systems 82 (CHI 2009), pp. 1879–1888 (2009)
12. Betsworth, L., Bowen, H., Robinson, S., Jones, M.: Performative technologies for heritage site regeneration. Pers. Ubiquitous Comput. **18**(7), 1631–1650 (2014). https://doi.org/10.1007/s00779-014-0766-3
13. Domingo, M.G., Garganté, A.B.: Exploring the use of educational technology in primary education: teachers' perception of mobile technology learning impacts and applications' use in the classroom. Comput. Hum. Behav. **56**, 21–28 (2016)
14. Alakärppä, I., Jaakkola, E., Väyrynen, J., Häkkilä, J.: Using nature elements in mobile AR for education with children. In: MobileHCI 2017. https://doi.org/10.1145/3098279.3098547
15. Manches, A.: Digital manipulatives: tools to transform early learning experiences. Int. J. Tech. Enhanc. Learn. **3**(6), 608–626 (2011)
16. Shadows: Meaning and interpretation. http://astro1.panet.utoledo.edu/~lsa/_color/28_shadowsII.htm
17. Delprino, F., Piva, C., Tommasi, G., Gelsomini, M., Izzo, N., Matera, M.: ABBOT.2018. In: AVI 2018, Castiglione della Pescaia, Italy, 29 May–1 June 2018. https://doi.org/10.1145/3206505.3206512
18. Dunleavy, M., Dede, C.: Augmented reality teaching and learning. In: Michael, S.J., David Merrill, M., Elen, J., Bishop, M.J. (eds.) The Handbook of Research for Educational Communications and Technology, 4th edn, pp. 735–745. Springer, New York (2014)
19. Markopoulos, P.: Design and evaluation of rapido, a platform for rapid prototyping of interactive outdoor games. ACM Trans. Comput. Hum. Interact. **24**(4), 1–30 (2017)
20. Pucihar, K.C., Coulton, P.: Exploring the evolution of mobile augmented reality for future entertainment systems. Comput. Entertain. **11**(2), 1–16 (2013). https://doi.org/10.1145/2582179.2633427
21. Salmi, H., Kaasinen, A., Kallunki, V.: Towards an open learning environment via Augmented Reality (AR): visualising the invisible in science centres and schools for teacher education. Procedia Soc. Behav. Sci. **45**, 284–295 (2012)
22. Kamarainen, A.M., et al.: EcoMOBILE: integrating augmented reality and probeware with environmental education field trips. Comput. Educ. **68**, 545–556 (2016)
23. Zhao, Y., Poupyrev, I., Shiratori, T.: MotionBeam: PicoPet: "Real World" Digital Pet on a Handheld Projector. In: UIST (2011). https://doi.org/10.1145/2046396.2046398

24. Leigh, S.-W., Roseway, A., Paradiso, A., Maes, P.: Remnance of form: interactive narratives through unexpected behaviors of a shadow. In: CHI 2015 Extended Abstracts, Seoul, 18–23 April 2015. https://doi.org/10.1145/2702613.2725434
25. Oh, S., Byun, Y.-C.: The design and implementation of augmented reality learning systems. In: Proceedings of the 11th International Conference on Computer and Information Science (2012). https://doi.org/10.1109/ICIS.2012.106
26. White, R.T., Gunstone, R.F.: Probing Understanding. Falmer Press, London (1992)

An Innovative Employment of Virtual Humans to Explore the Chess Personalities of Garry Kasparov and Other Class-A Players

Khaldoon Dhou[✉]

Drury University, Springfield, MO, USA
kdhou@drury.edu

Abstract. Exploring chess players of different personalities, including the strengths and weaknesses of each remains an essential component in designing new chess applications. Research shows that virtual players play an essential role in helping researchers to explore chess personalities of different classes and playing styles. A virtual chess player is defined as a software simulation that mimics the playing style of a real chess player. The current study employs these players in investigating the personalities of three class-A players while competing against Garry Kasparov. Additionally, it examines the personality of Kasparov and how he performs while competing against the other class-A players. To this end, the study utilizes an experimental design to collect data from simulations of games between three class-A players against Kasparov. The class-A players range in their personalities: a player who prefers chess material, drawish, and a balanced player. The four players in the simulation are virtual humans that are programmed to represent real chess players. The findings reveal that the class-A chess players did not have the same performance. Likewise, the performance of Kasparov varied according to the opponent, although his opponents were from the same category.

Keywords: Games · Chess · Personality · Virtual humans · Chess software · Grandmasters · Kasparov

1 Introduction

Computer chess has attracted much attention over the years and it has been subjected to an extensive investigation by researchers from various disciplines. Recent years witnessed significant developments including computers and chess programs that are able to compete at a very high level and defeat top grandmasters. Nowadays, chess technology is very affordable and is widely used in training. Additionally, it offers many services, including the employment of virtual humans to enable chess players to train and compete against players of different skills and playing styles. For the purpose of this research, virtual chess humans are defined as software simulations that mimic real players including

© Springer Nature Switzerland AG 2019
C. Stephanidis (Ed.): HCII 2019, LNCS 11786, pp. 306–319, 2019.
https://doi.org/10.1007/978-3-030-30033-3_24

many world champions such as Kasparov and Polgar. These virtual humans make it flexible for a chess player to explore the playing styles of many other real players, ranging from beginners to top-rank grandmasters.

Each chess player, including virtual players, is described by two attributes: chess rating and chess personality. Chess rating is a numerical value assigned to each player depending on how he performs versus other opponents in the chess community—the higher the rating, the stronger the player [27, 30]. On the other hand, chess personality is a term utilized in previous HCI research, and it is defined as the perspective of a player during his chess games against other players of different styles [22]. For example, Kasparov's personality is characterized by his ability to make rapid calculations and explore innovative opening styles, which are the result of his extensive development [52]. He often offers piece sacrifices in order to allow his pieces to have extra flexibility to move over the chessboard. Kasparov was the world champion for more than twenty years, and he is considered the greatest player in history. This study investigates the personality of Kasparov by analyzing the games between Kasparov and three class-A players: Rand, Dobie, and Sunny. The three players vary in their chess personalities: Dobie is a player who prefers chess material, Sunny is a player who considers drawing games at an early stage, and Rand is a balanced player. The description of all the players employed in this research, including Kasparov, is offered by Ubisoft [52]. Additionally, the study examines the influences of Kasparov's personality on different class-A players. This study uses three measurements for chess personalities: number of moves in a game, error of a chess player, and the Chessmaster agreement percentage. All these measurements are obtained from analyzing the games in the study using the Ubisoft Chessmaster software.

The reason of choosing Kasparov in this study is that there is a growing body of literature that recognizes the importance of exploring his personality in chess [26, 28, 33, 37, 54]. His personality can play a significant role in addressing many issues in designing chess programs and understanding chess psychology. That is to say, analyzing the games between Kasparov and Deep Blue is still a primary concern for many researchers [11, 16, 38, 40, 51]. To the best of the researcher's knowledge, this is the first article exploring the personality of Kasparov while competing against other class-A players by the utilization of virtual humans. Additionally, the extensive literature review reveals only one study that explores chess personalities via the involvement of virtual humans [22]. Using virtual players to help in understanding chess personalities is crucial because of many reasons: It makes it easier for psychologists to use virtual humans as a tool to understand many aspects of games and their outcomes. Additionally, it can be used as a tool for helping medical students identify particular training techniques as research indicates the employment of tools with chess personalities in surgical training [47]. This research investigates the following questions:

- How does Kasparov perform against different class-A players who vary in their chess personalities?
- Is Kasparov making less or more errors when the personality of his opponent changes?

- How do the personalities of class-A opponents playing against Kasparov affect the length of the game?
- Do class-A players of various personalities perform differently while competing against Kasparov?

The remaining part of the paper proceeds as follows: Sect. 2 provides an overview of the related research in virtual humans, chess psychology, and personalities in HCI research; Sect. 3 describes the approach employed in this study; Sect. 4 outlines the results obtained from analyzing the games between the four virtual players; the findings are discussed in Sect. 5; Sect. 6 concludes the paper.

2   Related Work

Virtual humans are increasingly playing vital roles in our daily lives. They are the outcome of the union of various disciplines such as psychology, human-computer interaction, gaming, and artificial intelligence. Researchers design them to serve in different domains such as medicine, tourism, instruction, and entertainment. Personality is an essential aspect of virtual humans. It has been a subject of many research studies exploring virtual humans in psychology and computer science. For example, Zibrek et al. [57] administered a research study to collect information on how virtual figures are perceived in virtual reality applications and whether their personality makes a difference or not. Their major finding was that the closeness towards virtual figures is described as a composite interplay between the appearance and personality. Similarly, Zhou et al. [56] presented virtual interviewers that communicate with users and judge their personality characteristics. Their study reported that the personality traits and interview context influence people to place trust in virtual humans.

Evidence from the literature suggests that chess is an attractive field to explore many questions about personalities, people, and societies [22,34,47]. A recent study by Dhou [22] explored different aspects of chess personalities from the perspective of virtual humans. In his work, he investigated the personalities of different virtual chess players and linked the findings to existing research in social sciences. Interestingly, the study shows that virtual chess players with identical ratings and different personalities can perform differently depending on their opponent. Additionally, he found that a grandmaster with an attacking style stimulates other less skilled players and causes them to make fewer mistakes as opposed to when they compete against a defensive grandmaster. This finding has roots in psychology, where people attempt to comprehend the difficult events in their lives when they take place [55]. What remains unknown is researching more chess personalities and how they are influenced by each other. Although it is possible to explore chess personalities by investigating real players, virtual chess players give a much greater flexibility in pairing players with different personalities, including world champions against less skilled players. Such flexibility is impractical, if not impossible with real human players.

Several attempts have been made to investigate the personalities of chess players. A classical work was conducted by de Groot [17] who examined players of different levels and attempted to explore the variations between experts and beginners. De Groot observed that chess experts could recall and reestablish meaningful chess patterns over the board as opposed to weaker players. Similarly, Chase and Simon [13] discovered that experts have faster recognition of chess patterns than chess beginners. Later, Vollstädt-Klein et al. [53] examined the personalities of advanced chess players and how they can affect chess performance. They found that female chess players were happier and had higher accomplishments than other females. On the other hand, their study reported that there was not a significant difference between the personality profiles of male players and non-players. Likewise, Stafford [49] employed an extensive database of games and discovered that female chess players exceed the expectations when they play against male chess players. For more studies investigating chess and gender, the reader is referred to [7,9,31,32]. Dhou [19] classified chess applications into different categories and identified the best training approaches in each. Bilalić et al. [6] explored the personalities of children who play chess and their companions who do not. Their study revealed that children who scored higher in particular tests are more likely attracted to chess than their peers. Blanch [8] examined the top one hundred world champions and employed the domain latent curve model to investigate the personal differences. They found a strong association between age and tournament activity. Together these studies provide important insights into the psychology of chess players.

Although all these previous attempts investigated the personalities of chess players and how they perform in different settings, the topic of virtual chess players has still not yet been formally studied. The extensive literature review revealed that there is only one study that explored the personalities of virtual chess players [22]. The main advantage of employing virtual humans over real human players in understanding chess personalities is the flexibility in allowing players from different eras to compete against each other. For example, Dhou [22] investigated the variations between Leko and Anderssen who are grandmasters that exist in different periods. Another advantage of utilizing virtual players lies in the flexibility of designing a controlled experiment between a wide range of players of different skills. Interestingly, research showed that there is a strong correlation between certain moves made by humans and chess computers [36].

It is essential to note that current research recognizes the critical role played by personalities in HCI research. For example, Shohieb [48] developed a game that teaches children how to manage different disaster situations. Additionally, Sarsam and Al-Samarraie [46] introduced a user interface based on personality traits for mobile applications. Other studies investigated the issue of connecting the personality traits to the visual design favorites of users [1,2,45]. Caci et al. [12] explored the motives of Pokémon Game practice, personal variations linked with individual characteristics, and game attitudes. Bacos et al. [5] explored the influence of different personality traits on in-game personality demonstrative of counterfactual thinking. They found that personality relies on players' variations and their experiences of the game itself. In another study, McCreery and Krach [39] investigated the causes of why people appear aggressive in an online setting and explored different types of aggression. They found that proactive aggression was prophesied via agreeableness, extraversion, and emotional stability, while the reactive aggression was prognosticated via agreeableness and emotional stability. More research explored online learning environments and the students' feedback [4, 15]. The investigation of creatures' behavior is not limited to humans. It includes the behaviors of other creatures in different virtual environments such as biological reproduction, ants, and ecological systems [3, 18, 21, 23, 41]. Many of these studies are aimed at reducing the size of binary data that is widely used in text and other formats [20, 24, 25, 44].

To summarize, although psychologists and computer scientists have frequently emphasized virtual humans in different applications, there is only one study investigating their role in understanding chess personalities [22]. This article investigates the personalities of Kasparov and three class-A players to explore how a player from a particular class can be influenced when he competes against a player from another class.

3 Method

3.1 Participants

This study investigates four virtual chess players: three class-A players and Kasparov. The class-A players have different chess personalities, as follows:

- Dobie: He somewhat goes for chess material while competing against other players.
- Rand: He is a balanced chess player and characterized by a profound proficiency in chess openings.
- Sunny: She is not competitive and attempts to draw her games from the beginning. Additionally, she is known for controlling the center, but sometimes ignores the pawn structure.

The three class-A players have almost identical USCF ratings. The USCF ratings of Dobie, Rand, and Sunny are 2118, 2113, and 2115, respectively. In this study, the three class-A players play against Garry Kasparov, who makes rapid calculations and considers creative openings. In addition, Kasparov sometimes chooses neglected opening styles such as Evans Gambit. It is important to emphasize that the four players employed in the current study are virtual humans that mimic real chess players.

3.2 Materials

The present design involves two independent variables:

- IV1: The color of Kasparov's pieces. In this study, each opponent played half of the games with White and the other half with Black.
- IV2: The personality of Kasparov's class-A opponent. This independent variable has three levels: a player who prefers material, a drawish, and a balanced player.

The researcher utilized the Chessmaster developed by Ubisoft to analyze all the chess games in the study [52]. To this end, the researcher considers measurements of five dependent variables generated by the Chessmaster, as follows:

- DV1: The total number of moves
- DV2: The total error of moves played by Kasparov
- DV3: The total error of moves played by a class-A player
- DV4: The Chessmaster's agreement percentage of Kasparov's moves
- DV5: The Chessmaster's agreement percentage of a class-A player's moves

The total error is a metric employed in calculating the errors made by different virtual players. It is calculated as the difference between the actual moves made by players and the optimal moves [14, 22]. The same metric was previously used in exploring virtual humans to understand the differences between chess personalities [22].

3.3 Procedure

In this research study, each class-A player played 98 games against Kasparov, half of them with white, and the other half with black. The researcher collected the data from all the games and analyzed it using the Chessmaster. The Chessmaster generated the five dependent variables for each game. The researcher used these dependent variables in exploring the personalities of the four virtual chess players employed in this study.

4   Results

The researcher analyzed the data in this study using a series of two-way ANOVA tests. Each dependent variable was submitted to a two color of Kasparov (White or Black) by three class-A player personality (drawish, prefers material, and balanced) two-way ANOVA. All the effects were reported as significant at $p < 0.05$.

4.1   Number of Moves

The researcher conducted a series of two-way ANOVA tests to examine the effect of the class-A player's personality and Kasparov's color on each of the five dependent variables. There was a significant main effect of the class-A player, on the number of moves during the games, $F(2, 288) = 6.686$, $p = 0.001$. Paired samples t-tests show that there are statistically significant differences between the number of moves in the games played by different class-A players against Kasparov. There was a significant difference in the number of moves played by Rand ($M = 52.459$, $SD = 10.429$) and the number of moves played by Sunny ($M = 58.888$, $SD = 17.684$); $t(97) = 2.844$, $p = 0.005$. Similarly, there was a significant difference in the number of moves played by Sunny ($M = 58.888$, $SD = 17.684$) and the number of moves played by Dobbie ($M = 51.622$, $SD = 16.358$); $t(97) = 2.968$, $p = 0.004$.

4.2   Kasparov's Total Error

There was a significant main effect of the class-A player, on the total error of Kasparov during his games, $F(2, 288) = 3.108, p = 0.046$. A paired samples t-test reveals a significant difference in the total error of Kasparov when he competes against Sunny ($M = 2.245, SD = 3.197$) and when he competes against Dobbie ($M = 1.290, SD = 2.412$); $t(97) = 2.349, p = 0.021$.

4.3   Class-A Player's Total Error

There are no significant effects.

4.4   Chessmaster's Agreement Percentage on Kasparov's Moves

The interaction between Kasparov's color and the player is significant, $F(2, 288) = 3.262, p = 0.04$ (Fig. 1). To break down this interaction, the researcher conducted a series of paired samples t-tests. Paired samples t-tests show that when Kasparov plays with Black, there are significant differences between the Chessmaster's agreement percentages on his moves when he competes against Dobie ($M = 97.204, SD = 2.041$) and Rand ($M = 96.081, SD = 3.054$); $t(48) = 2.092, p = 0.042$; and when he competes against Sunny ($M = 95.694, SD = 2.823$) and Dobbie ($M = 97.204, SD = 2.041$); $t(48) = 2.931, p = 0.005$.

4.5   Chessmaster's Agreement Percentage on Class-A Players' Moves

There was a significant main effect of the class-A player on the chessmaster's agreement percentage on the moves made by class-A players, $F(2, 288) = 7.791, p = 0.001$. Further paired samples t-tests show that on average, the Chessmaster agrees more on the moves made by Sunny ($M = 88.704, SD = 4.878$) than Rand ($M = 86.418, SD = 4.957$); $t(97) = 3.143, p = 0.002$, and on the moves made by Sunny ($M = 88.704, SD = 4.878$) than Dobie ($M = 85.939, SD = 5.779$); $t(97) = 3.628, p < 0.001$.

5   General Discussion

The purpose of the current research study was to explore the psychology of competition between Kasparov and three class-A players. To this end, the researcher designed a study consisting of four virtual chess players: Kasparov and three other class-A players. In the current experiment, the researcher examined different dependent variables that measure the lengths of the games and the performance of the involved virtual players.

The experimental results showed that Kasparov tends to make more mistakes when he plays against Sunny (drawish) as opposed to playing against Dobie (prefers material). These findings are consistent with the outcomes from the

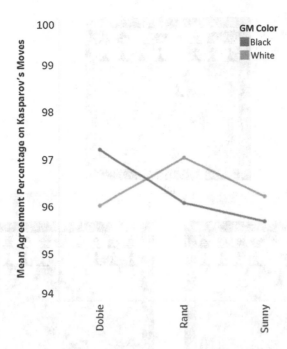

Fig. 1. The mean values of the Chessmaster's agreement percentage on Kasparov's moves. Except for Dobie, the Chessmaster agrees more on Kasparov's moves when he plays with the White color.

previous study [22] investigating the errors made by grandmasters while playing against other class-B players. The study in [22] showed that grandmasters performed differently while playing against different players from the same class. A possible explanation is that Sunny has a good control of the center of the game. That is to say, although she neglects the pawn structure, Kasparov's total error was higher when he competes with her as opposed to competing with Dobie. Her strength is evidenced by the chess literature revealing that controlling the center is more important than having effective pawn combinations [35]. Additionally, one of the standard powerful fundamental postulates in chess is that a strong side attack requires a solid center, which increases the chances of attack [10]. Kasparov did better when Sunny accepted the Queen's Gambit (Fig. 2). The variation of accepting the Queen's Gambit sounds like a favorite direction for Kasparov, and that is probably why he performed better as opposed to the other variation of declining the Gambit. It is essential to mention that Kasparov does well in the opening phase and his game against Deep Blue reveals that the computer could not outplay him during the opening [42].

Controlling the center did not only influence the total error of Kasparov, but it also affected the moves in the games. The paired samples t-tests showed that Sunny was the most resisting player, and the games against her were the most extended in the simulation. Additionally, analyzing two games showed that

(a)

(b)

(c)

Fig. 2. An example showing two variations of the Queen's Gambit. In the two games, Kasparov plays with White and Sunny plays with Black. In (a) Kasparov offers a pawn sacrifice; (b) Sunny decides to choose the accepted Gambit variation that allows Kasparov to control the center; In (b) Sunny decides to decline the Gambit. The results from two games showed that Kasparov made fewer errors and took a greater advantage when Sunny accepted the Queen's Gambit

giving up the center by accepting the Queen's Gambit allowed Kasparov to gain more advantage as opposed to Sunny declining the Gambit. More research is needed to investigate the effects of declining the Gambit. Interestingly, previous research shows a strong relationship between the chess center principle and management. Flamholtz [29] used this principle in his analogy, describing centralized and decentralized management. Another explanation of why Kasparov did better when Sunny accepted the Gambit is probably because of the opening style. In other words, the opening phase determines the direction of the game, and each player has his preferences. For example, when Sunny accepted the Queen's Gambit in one game, the total error of Kasparov was 0, while it was 6.04 when she declined the Gambit. The pawn sacrifice is often offered by Kasparov so that he can get additional mobility to his chess pieces.

The results showing that Kasparov did better when Sunny accepted the Queen's Gambit are consistent with other findings revealing the importance of the opening phase. The opening determines the flow of the game and might even cause a player to lose. For instance, Deep Thought defeated Karpov in the opening and the initial stage of the middle game and had many circumstances to draw the game [43, p. 197]. Different grandamsters and research studies have noted the importance of openings in chess. For example, Michael Adams emphasizes the importance of the opening and believes that working on it is more applicable than working on other phases of the game [50]. Interestingly, in the previous study, the findings showed that a player who is good at the opening did better than a balanced player, although they belong to the same category [22]. Additionally, Levene [36] showed the importance of the opening books as part of chess engines. Chess applications are connected to large databases that contain different openings and their variations.

6   Conclusion

The present study was designed to determine the effect of the personality of chess players on the outcomes of their games against different opponents. To this end, the study involves designing an experiment consisting of four virtual chess players: one grandmaster, and three class-A players. The selected virtual grandmaster was Garry Kasparov, and the three class-A players varied in their personalities. One of the more significant findings to emerge from this study is that Kasparov performed differently while competing with the other class-A players. Additionally, Kasparov did better when the other player followed his line of play (i.e., Accepted Queen's Gambit). Similarly, the three class-A players performed differently although they had the same opponent, Kasparov.

These findings suggest that in general players can behave differently depending on their opponent even if they are within the same class. Additionally, the present findings are consistent with the previous outcomes in [22], showing the differences between players from the same class with different personalities. Furthermore, class-A players performed differently when they were competing with Kasparov, although they have almost identical ratings. The outcomes from this research can help understand the ratings of chess games between players of different personalities and ratings. That is to say, this study paves the way for further research that explores the influence of different chess personalities on each other to investigate new techniques for chess training based on opponents. For example, in the study in [22], the findings showed that less skilled players performed better while competing against an aggressive grandmaster as opposed to a defensive player. Similarly, the current study revealed that the software agrees more on the moves made by a player who controls the center of the game. Such findings reinforce the chess concept that stresses on the importance of controlling the center. Additionally, they can be used as guidelines for chess players to recommend individual personalities for chess training, showing that chess rating is not the only factor to select an opponent for training and personality is also another significant factor.

This research has many practical applications. For example, it helps in designing new chess programs that take the chess personality into consideration and suggest opponents depending on the personality of the player. In other words, some players perform better while competing against certain players, and it would help to suggest different opponents from which they can probably learn the most. Second, further understanding of the chess personalities allows designing new experiments that can probably reveal new findings about social aspects. For example, the study in [22] revealed many interesting findings that are linked to social sciences. In general, therefore, it seems that virtual chess players can contribute to social sciences and prove useful in understanding human behavior.

References

1. Al-Samarraie, H., Sarsam, S.M., Alzahrani, A.I., Alalwan, N.: Personality and individual differences: the potential of using preferences for visual stimuli to predict the big five traits. Cogn. Technol. Work **20**(3), 337–349 (2018). https://doi.org/10.1007/s10111-018-0470-6
2. Al-Samarraie, H., Sarsam, S.M., Alzahrani, A.I., Alalwan, N., Masood, M.: The role of personality characteristics in informing our preference for visual presentation: an eye movement study. J. Ambient Intell. Smart Environ. **8**(6), 709–719 (2016)
3. Alrashydah, E.I., Abo-Qudais, S.A.: Modeling of creep compliance behavior in asphalt mixes using multiple regression and artificial neural networks. Constr. Build. Mater. **159**, 635–641 (2018). http://www.sciencedirect.com/science/article/pii/S0950061817321955
4. Altrabsheh, N., Cocea, M., Fallahkhair, S., Dhou, K.: Evaluation of the SA-E system for analysis of students' real-time feedback. In: 2017 IEEE 17th International Conference on Advanced Learning Technologies (ICALT), pp. 60–61 (2017)
5. Bacos, C.A., McCreery, M.P., Laferriere, J.R.: Interactive narratives, counterfactual thinking and personality in video games. In: Stephanidis, C. (ed.) HCI 2018. CCIS, vol. 850, pp. 340–347. Springer, Cham (2018). https://doi.org/10.1007/978-3-319-92270-6_49
6. Bilalić, M., McLeod, P., Gobet, F.: Personality profiles of young chess players. Personality Individ. Differ. **42**(6), 901–910 (2007). http://www.sciencedirect.com/science/article/pii/S0191886906003515
7. Blanch, A.: Expert performance of men and women: a cross-cultural study in the chess domain. Personality Individ. Differ. **101**, 90–97 (2016). http://www.sciencedirect.com/science/article/pii/S0191886916304111
8. Blanch, A.: Top hundred chess experts: a cross-domain analysis of change over time. Intelligence **71**, 76–84 (2018). http://www.sciencedirect.com/science/article/pii/S0160289618300564
9. Blanch, A., Aluja, A., Cornadó, M.P.: Sex differences in chess performance: analyzing participation rates, age, and practice in chess tournaments. Personality Individ. Differ. **86**, 117–121 (2015). http://www.sciencedirect.com/science/article/pii/S0191886915003852
10. Borik, O.: Kasparov's Chess Openings - A World Champion's Repertoire. Trafalgar Square, North Pomfret (1991)
11. Bory, P.: Deep new: the shifting narratives of artificial intelligence from deep blue to AlphaGo. Convergence, https://doi.org/10.1177/1354856519829679 (2019)

12. Caci, B., Scrima, F., Tabacchi, M.E., Cardaci, M.: The reciprocal influences among motivation, personality traits, and game habits for playing Pokémon GO. Int. J. Hum. Comput. Interact. **35**, 1–9 (2018). https://doi.org/10.1080/10447318.2018. 1519167
13. Chase, W.G., Simon, H.A.: Perception in chess. Cogn. Psychol. **4**(1), 55–81 (1973). http://www.sciencedirect.com/science/article/pii/0010028573900042
14. Chess.com: Chessmaster 9000 questions. Online, June 2019. https://www.chess. com/forum/view/general/chessmaster-9000-questions?page=2
15. Cobos, R., Jurado, F., Villén, Á.: Moods in MOOCs: analyzing emotions in the content of online courses with edX-CAS. In: 2019 IEEE Global Engineering Education Conference (EDUCON), pp. 1467–1474, April 2019
16. Davis, M.: Turing's vision and deep learning. In: Manea, F., Miller, R.G., Nowotka, D. (eds.) CiE 2018. LNCS, vol. 10936, pp. 146–155. Springer, Cham (2018). https:// doi.org/10.1007/978-3-319-94418-0_15
17. De Groot, A.D.: Thought and Choice in Chess, vol. 4. Walter de Gruyter GmbH & Co KG, Berlin (2014)
18. Dhou, K., Cruzen, C.: An innovative chain coding technique for compression based on the concept of biological reproduction: an agent-based modeling approach. IEEE Internet Things J., 1 (2019)
19. Dhou, K.: Chess Software and its Impact on Chess Players. Master's Project at the University of Northern British Columbia (2008). https://doi.org/10.24124/2008/ bpgub1368
20. Dhou, K.: Toward a better understanding of viewers' perceptions of tag clouds: relative size judgment. Ph.D. thesis, Charlotte, NC, USA (2013)
21. Dhou, K.: A novel agent-based modeling approach for image coding and lossless compression based on the wolf-sheep predation model. In: Shi, Y., et al. (eds.) ICCS 2018. LNCS, vol. 10861, pp. 117–128. Springer, Cham (2018). https://doi. org/10.1007/978-3-319-93701-4_9
22. Dhou, K.: Towards a better understanding of chess players' personalities: a study using virtual chess players. In: Kurosu, M. (ed.) HCI 2018. LNCS, vol. 10903, pp. 435–446. Springer, Cham (2018). https://doi.org/10.1007/978-3-319-91250-9_34
23. Dhou, K.: An innovative design of a hybrid chain coding algorithm for bi-level image compression using an agent-based modeling approach. Appl. Soft Comput. **79**, 94–110 (2019). http://www.sciencedirect.com/science/article/pii/ S1568494619301425
24. Dhou, K., Hadzikadic, M., Faust, M.: Typeface size and weight and word location influence on relative size judgments in tag clouds. J. Visual Lang. Comput. **44**, 97–105 (2018). http://www.sciencedirect.com/science/article/pii/ S1045926X16300210
25. Dhou, K.K., Kosara, R., Hadzikadic, M., Faust, M.: Size judgment and comparison in tag clouds. In: IEEE Visualization Poster Proceedings (2013)
26. Drabik, E.: An analysis of the connection between ai development and the creation of games and advanced computer systems. Econ. World **6**(4), 251–262 (2018)
27. Elo, A.E.: The Rating of Chessplayers, Past and Present. Arco Pub, New York (1978). http://www.amazon.com/Rating-Chess-Players-Past-Present/dp/ 0668047216
28. Evans, J.S.B.T.: Human versus machine thinking: the story of chess. Thinking Reason. **24**(4), 498–504 (2018). https://doi.org/10.1080/13546783.2018.1430616
29. Flamholtz, E.: Organizational control systems as a managerial tool. Calif. Manag. Rev. **22**(2), 50–59 (1979). https://doi.org/10.2307/41165320

30. Glickman, M.E.: A comprehensive guide to chess ratings. Am. Chess J. **3**(1), 59–102 (1995)
31. Iqbal, A.: Which gender plays more beautiful chess? In: Social Sciences and Interdisciplinary Behavior: The 4th International Congress on Interdisciplinary Behavior and Social Science (ICIBSoS 2015), Kazan Federal University, Kazan, Russia, 22–23 October 2015, Arya Duta hotel, Jakarta, Indonesia, 07–08 November 2015, p. 375. CRC Press (2016)
32. Iqbal, A., Nagappan, S.: A computational aesthetics assessment of chess playing quality between the genders. In: Proceedings of 2018 the 8th International Workshop on Computer Science and Engineering, WCSE 2018 2018, pp. 313–317 (2018)
33. Kasparov, G.: Chess, a Drosophila of reasoning. Science **362**(6419), 1087–1087 (2018)
34. Ketola, T.: Corporate states or corporate citizens? chess between corporations, states and citizens with sustainable development at stake. Int. J. Sustain. Econ. **3**(1), 107–122 (2010)
35. Kotok, A.: A Chess Playing Program for the IBM 7090 Computer, pp. 48–55. Springer, New York (1988). https://doi.org/10.1007/978-1-4757-1968-0_6
36. Levene, M., Bar-Ilan, J.: Comparing typical opening move choices made by humans and chess engines. Comput. J. **50**(5), 567–573 (2007). https://doi.org/10.1093/comjnl/bxm025
37. Lu, Y.: Artificial intelligence: a survey on evolution, models, applications and future trends. J. Manag. Anal. **6**(1), 1–29 (2019)
38. McBee, M.P., et al.: Deep learning in radiology. Acad. Radiol. **25**(11), 1472–1480 (2018)
39. McCreery, M.P., Krach, S.K.: How the human is the catalyst: personality, aggressive fantasy, and proactive-reactive aggression among users of social media. Personality Individ. Differ. **133**, 91–95 (2018)
40. Min, J.K.: Chess and coronary artery ischemia: clinical implications of machine-learning applications. Circ. Cardiovasc. Imaging **11**(6), e007943 (2018)
41. Mouring, M., Dhou, K., Hadzikadic, M.: A novel algorithm for bi-level image coding and lossless compression based on virtual ant colonies. In: 3rd International Conference on Complexity, Future Information Systems and Risk, Setúbal - Portugal, pp. 72–78 (2018)
42. Newborn, M.: Deep Blue and Garry Kasparov in Philadelphia, pp. 235–278. Springer, New York (1997). https://doi.org/10.1007/978-1-4612-2260-6_9
43. Newborn, M.: Kasparov Versus Deep Blue: Computer Chess Comes of Age. Springer, New York (2012)
44. Pušnik, N., Podlesek, A., Možina, K.: Typeface comparison - does the X-height of lower-case letters increased to the size of upper-case letters speed up recognition? Int. J. Ind. Ergonomics **54**, 164–169 (2016)
45. Sarsam, S.M., Al-Samarraie, H.: A first look at the effectiveness of personality dimensions in promoting users' satisfaction with the system. SAGE Open **8**(2), 2158244018769125 (2018). https://doi.org/10.1177/2158244018769125
46. Sarsam, S.M., Al-Samarraie, H.: Towards incorporating personality into the design of an interface: a method for facilitating users' interaction with the display. User Model. User-Adapt. Interact. **28**(1), 75–96 (2018). https://doi.org/10.1007/s11257-018-9201-1
47. Schlickum, M.K., Hedman, L., Enochsson, L., Kjellin, A., Felländer-Tsai, L.: Systematic video game training in surgical novices improves performance in virtual reality endoscopic surgical simulators: a prospective randomized study. World J. Surg. **33**(11), 2360 (2009). https://doi.org/10.1007/s00268-009-0151-y

48. Shohieb, S.M.: CDMG: crises and disasters management game (video game to teach Arab children how to handle emergencies and crises). In: Proceedings of the 2018 7th International Conference on Software and Computer Applications, ICSCA 2018, pp. 264–268. ACM, New York (2018). https://doi.org/10.1145/3185089. 3185147

49. Stafford, T.: Female chess players outperform expectations when playing men. Psychol. Sci. **29**(3), 429–436 (2018). https://doi.org/10.1177/0956797617736887. pMID: 29364771

50. Summerscale, A.: Interview with a Grandmaster. Everyman Chess, London (2002)

51. Susskind, D., Susskind, R.: The future of the professions 1. Proc. Am. Philos. Soc. **162**(2), 125–138 (2018)

52. Ubisoft: Chessmaster 9000. http://chessmaster.uk.ubi.com/xi/index.php

53. Vollstädt-Klein, S., Grimm, O., Kirsch, P., Bilalić, M.: Personality of elite male and female chess players and its relation to chess skill. Learn. Individ. Differ. **20**(5), 517–521 (2010). http://www.sciencedirect.com/science/article/pii/S1041608010000403

54. Wilkenfeld, Y.: Can chess survive artificial intelligence? New Atlantis **58**, 37–45 (2019). https://www.jstor.org/stable/26609113

55. Wise, D.M., Rosqvist, J.: Explanatory style and well-being. In: Thomas, J.C., Segal, D.L., Hersen, M. (eds.) Comprehensive Handbook of Personality and Psychopathology, p. 285. Wiley, Hoboken (2006)

56. Zhou, M.X., Mark, G., Li, J., Yang, H.: Trusting virtual agents: the effect of personality. ACM Trans. Interact. Intell. Syst. **9**(2–3), 10:1–10:36 (2019). https://doi. org/10.1145/3232077

57. Zibrek, K., Kokkinara, E., Mcdonnell, R.: The effect of realistic appearance of virtual characters in immersive environments - does the character's personality play a role? IEEE Trans. Visual. Comput. Graph. **24**(4), 1681–1690 (2018)

The Relationship Between Game Elements and Player Emotions by Comparing Game Frameworks

Junyao Hu and Tao Xi[(✉)]

Shanghai Jiao Tong University, Minhang District, Shanghai, China
{juliahu, torchx}@sjtu.edu.cn

Abstract. Emotion has become an important part in games. The purpose of this paper is to find whether game elements could influence players emotion? Which elements in a game could evoke player emotions? Previous theories showed game elements could be classified into two layers: the underlying layer and the metaphorical layer. Moreover, aesthetics, narrative, social interaction, and players' ability in games could be emotional triggers. In this paper, we performed a case study to compare the two versions of a game: Game for Peace and PUBG Mobile. By using NLPIR (Natural Language Processing & Information Retrieval) platform, we analyzed 149 reviews of the new version to estimate the influence of specific game elements on player experience and emotion. Our study showed that: (1) even the small change of game elements has potential to influence players experience and emotion. (2) both the metaphorical layer and the underlying layer play a significant role in evoking players' emotion. (3) Without the change of core gameplay, the alteration in theme and a metaphorical layer could alter players experience and emotions.

Keywords: Game frameworks · Game elements · Player emotions

1 Introduction

Due to the practice of many art games and "indie" games, the range of emotional pattern of games is more extensive than before [1]. Many researchers focus on the player experience, and they carried out researches into gamer psychology and behaviour [2–4]. Some researchers tend to show specific strategies for emotion design in games (e.g., character design, narrative design, level design). However, seldom people can clarify the relationship between game elements and player emotions. From theory to practice, there is still a large gap between game design and player experience. Whether game elements could influence players emotion? Which part of the game could evoke player emotions?

First, the paper compared and discussed different game frameworks to find the relationship between game elements and player emotion. Second, in the case study, the authors compared different contents of the same elements in Game for Peace and PUBG Mobile. Third, by using NLPIR platform to analyze 149 reviews the authors provided evidence of emotional impact from particular game elements.

© Springer Nature Switzerland AG 2019
C. Stephanidis (Ed.): HCII 2019, LNCS 11786, pp. 320–329, 2019.
https://doi.org/10.1007/978-3-030-30033-3_25

2   Literature Review

2.1   The Introduction of Game Analysis Frameworks

Table 1. The game analysis frameworks

Author(s)	Years	Sources	Presented elements type
Hunicke et al.	2004	MDA: A Formal Approach to Game Design and Game Research	Mechanics, dynamics, aesthetics
Björk et al.	2005	Patterns in Game Design	Boundary, holistic, temporal, structural
Fullerton	2008	Game Design Workshop	Formal elements, dramatic elements, dynamic elements
Järvinen	2008	Games without Frontiers Theories and Methods for Game Studies and Design	Systemic elements, compound elements, behavioural elements
Schell	2008	The Art of Game Design	Aesthetics, mechanics, story, technology
Bond	2015	Introduction to Game Design, Prototyping, and Development	The inscribed layer, the dynamic layer, the cultural layer

Table 1 shows different frameworks and its elements. Resources, year and authors are also given.

The MDA Framework. The purpose of the MDA framework was to understand games and iterative processes. The fundamental idea of this theory is that games are artefacts, and the result of this artefact is the experience. Moreover, researchers classified the aesthetic goals of games thus encouraging people to analyze games from gamers' perspective, which aimed at the experience-driven design [5].

Patterns in Game Design. These design patterns inspired by the book, A Pattern Language: Towns, Buildings, Construction, which organized design challenges in the architecture field. Similarly, all of them based on design experiences. The patterns in Game Design showed structured knowledge about gameplay, and it was a tool for designers to analyze and design a game. It offered definitions, examples, advice, consequences of the particular pattern, and described relationships between various patterns [6].

Formal, Dramatic, and Dynamic Elements. This framework provided a conceptual tool for designers to analyze games, so they could apply in practice to distinguish which elements in a game caused problems. It also emphasized the "playcentric" approach (design for the player experience) which has a similar core of the experience-driven design in the MDA framework [7].

Games without Frontiers Theories and Methods for Game Studies and Design. This framework was supported by case studies, literature review, and observation. These cases included different kinds of games, such as card and dice games, board games and computer games, which extended a range of game design research. Besides, the author reviewed the psychological theory behind the player experience and built mode to explain the relationship between game elements and player experience [8].

The Elemental Tetrad. Unlike other frameworks, the logic behind the classification was different. It mainly relied on the developers' perspective [9]. These elements were related to different professions in a team. For instance, artists are responsible for the aesthetics of a game; programmers are responsible for technology; designers are responsible for mechanics and writers are responsible for technology [10].

The Layered Tetrad. Based on previous researches, this framework expanded "the elemental tetrad" into three layers and replaced "story" with "narrative" to broaden its content. The inscribed layer described games before playing, while the dynamic layer only appears during playing. The cultural layer is beyond playing, which indicated the impact on society caused by the community of players [9].

2.2 Game Elements and Player Experience

The MDA Framework. The MDA framework chose the word "Aesthetics" to describe player emotional responses evoked by the playing process [5].

This framework linked designers and players through "dynamics". "Dynamics" described behaviours emerging in games and supported by mechanics. This framework showed that designers could influence player emotions by changing the particular mechanics of a game, which could shape the behaviours of players. In this framework, "Dynamics" just like a "black box", we know its inputs and outputs but could not explain its internal working.

Patterns in Game Design. Björk and Holopainen [6] focused on gameplay rather than game elements, which is the interaction structure of players in the game. In their book, Patterns in Game Design, they listed numerous game design patterns and organized them into eleven groups from "game elements" to "meta games, replayability, and learning curves". All these groups have several sub-branches such as "alternative reality", "avatars" and "live". These detailed design patterns generally described particular areas of gameplay and showed the relationship of different patterns in game design. It indicated that "Narrative structures, predictability, and immersion patterns" and "social interaction" play a significant role in the emotional immersion.

Moreover, these patterns such as "game mastery", "empowerment", "transfer of control", "gain ownership", "gain competence" and "player defined goals" were related to players' ability to influence and control a virtual world.

Furthermore, in terms of "exploration", the authors pointed out that aesthetically pleasing rewards could be a "surprise" during exploration. Although authors focus on gameplay and do not demonstrate aesthetics as an independent pattern, in this instance, "aesthetics" linked two patterns that contributed to emotional immersion.

Formal, Dramatic, and Dynamic Elements. FDD framework broke games down into three layers and divided these layers into specific elements. It was transparent for readers to understand their definitions in the game context. "Dramatic layer" in this framework could elicit players powerful emotional reactions, thus contributing to meaningful and engaging experience. This framework listed seven dramatic elements, including challenge, play, premise, character, story, world-building, and the dramatic arc [7].

Without dramatic elements, many games are very abstract. For example, Tetris, there are no characters, no story, even no dramatic arc. It is a bare game mechanic. When players move different blocks to form a horizontal line without any gap, these blocks disappear, and players gain score. This game does not offer compelling context to make all behaviour in game reasonable, so it is difficult for players to be emotionally engaging. Designers could change Tetris into a new one by applying a new background story and changing its appearance. Koster [11] described a mass murder game. Innocent victims are falling to the bottom of the gas chamber. Players should pack victims in tightly enough to ensure the death of them. Nevertheless, when these victims climb on the top of the chamber, players lose and game over. This instance could show how dramatic elements work, and the player experience might be different when neutral blocks turn into innocent victims.

Games without Frontiers Theories and Methods for Game Studies and Design. Järvinen [8] held an opinion that people could analyze player experience by identifying different elements in a game. Besides, the game system is the sum of components, environment, rule set, information, (theme), (interface), players and contexts. It emphasized that theme is the most vital element to form player experience. A theme could provide a game with another layer of meaning beyond minimum information from the rule set. Järvinen pointed out that a theme has a similar function of metaphor (states that one thing is another thing). Therefore, designers could create players experience through theme elements by transforming the information system, such as a rule set, into dramatic, fancy one. In this framework, the theme is the kind of information mapped on a game system, and players could recognize it.

Moreover, theme elements are composed of a setting and psychological elements such as "sacred", which are represented by corresponding game components. However, "Theme" is an abstract idea, and it is not the game components which could represent a theme. It is different from "dramatic elements" described in the FDD framework.

The Elemental Tetrad. Schell [10] chose a static framework to describe games and classified its elements into four parts: aesthetics, mechanics, story, and technology. "Aesthetics" is directly related to player experience, and it describes how players feel about this game through five senses. Although the word "aesthetics" is the same word in the MDA framework, the meanings are different. "aesthetics" in the MDA framework showed player emotions triggered by games. In this framework, "aesthetics" is the most visible elements in a game system such as art resources, sound effects. Unlike other researchers, Schell emphasized that these four elements are equally essential to player experience because they tightly connect and work toward the same goal: player experience.

The author also believed that a unifying theme was essential to a game, although it is excluded in the elemental tetrad. Detailed and practical information was offered about how to choose a better theme and how to use game elements to reinforce it. Additionally, Jarvinen's attitude toward themes was quite similar to Schell's: the theme determines essential feelings that a game delivered to their players.

The Layered Tetrad. Because the concept of the cultural layer was beyond games, the discussion was limited to the dynamic layer and the inscribed layer. Every layer has four parts: aesthetics, mechanics, narrative and technology [9]. The inscribed layer was a static layer which described the condition of a game before playing. Developers entirely control it.

By contrast, the dynamic layer illustrated that all the things appear in a game during playing. Similarly, "dynamics" in the MDA framework, "dynamic elements" in the FDD framework, and "behavioral elements" in Games without Frontiers, all of them relate to "emergence" phenomenon in a game It meant that simple rules could bring unpredictable results in a dynamic system, so it is challenging for developers to clarify the relationship between game elements and player experience.

This framework also pointed out "narrative" and "aesthetics" in these two layers have the goal to evoke players' emotion. "Aesthetics" could set emotional moods in a game.

3 Discussion

All these frameworks and their theory showed that games have the potential power to elicit emotions. To create an emotional experience, every component in a game should work together for a unified theme. Although we could analyze games according to a static framework, it could not deny that a game is a dynamic system. Consequently, researchers need to test these elements in a system.

There was an underlying layer in a game whose elements could be found in every framework. It contained some elements which are essential to a game. In this layer, games are abstract, which only have minimum mechanics. It could be played, but designers and players could not always feel satisfied with it. That is why players need another layer: a metaphorical layer.

As for the metaphorical layer, researchers used these words to describe its elements, such as "dramatic", "narrative", "aesthetics". In these theories, all these elements make games more concrete. They could add more information and emotional triggers in games.

From these frameworks, the function of narrative and aesthetics was emphasized in terms of emotion design in a game. In the game design patterns, which focused on gameplay, social interaction and players' ability in games could promote players emotional immersion.

In conclusion, aesthetics, narrative, social interaction, and players' ability in games could be emotional triggers in a game.

This leads us to hypothesize that:

- The change in the metaphorical layer could influence player experience and emotions.
- The change in underlying layer could influence player experience and emotions.

4   A Case Study

4.1   Introduction of Game for Peace

The authors chose a mobile game called Game for Peace as an object for this case study.

Game for Peace was an alternative to PUBG Mobile in China. PUBG Mobile was the online multiplayer battle royale game, while Game for Peace was developed from it. In "battle royale" game, a large number of players or teams fight in a shrinking zone, and the last survivor will be winners. PUBG Mobile launched in China on February 9, 2018, as a test version and closed on May 8, 2019. On the same day, Game for Peace has been available for players in app store [12, 13]. The game was chosen for several reasons:

Feature of Changes. These two versions come from the same studio in Tencent. Due to new rules of game publication from China's State Administration of Press and Publication (SAPP), PUBG Mobile's developers tried to avoid the "battle royale" context in-game aiming to received monetization approval. At the same time, they maintained core game-play to absorb old players.

Shared Players. Both of these games own a large number of players. Developers remained players' data from PUBG Mobile in Game for Peace. As a result, many players have played both of them.

Players' Reviews. By scanning their reviews in TapTap [14], an online game market in China, we found that most of them pointed out the differences between Game for Peace and PUBG Mobile. Furthermore, they mentioned their experience of these changes, so it could help us to understand players experience toward particular game elements.

4.2   Differences Between the Two Versions

Based on previous analysis of game frameworks, we compared these two versions, as shown in Table 2. The theme of this game has been changed from "military exercises" to "military skills competition". To present the new theme and avoid gory content, developers altered the metaphorical layer and some rules of Game for Peace. There were several dramatic changes in the metaphorical layer of Game for Peace:

New Dying Animation. In this animation, opponents lowered one knee, left loot, waved goodbye before disappearing. It shows that all the participants will not die, and they are just eliminated from competition.

Table 2. The main differences between these two versions

		PUBG Mobile	Game for Peace
The metaphorical layer	**Theme**	Military exercises	Military skills competition
	Dying animation	Died then disappeared	Waved goodbye then disappeared
	Visual feedback on hitting	Green blood and gas	Flash (four color can be selected: green, blue, yellow and pink)
	Shrinking play zone	The electricity field outside of circle	Signal zone inside the circle
The underlying layer	**Equipment for survival**	All kinds of medicine	All kinds of medicine and batteries (to increase signal strength)
	Rule of win	Only one winner	The last five persons will be winners

Visual Feedback on Hitting. When players shoot, the visual feedback is flash to show positions rather than green blood and gas from injured opponents in The PUBG Mobile.

Signal Zone. Developers maintained mechanics of shrinking play zone but changed the safe area into a signal zone. Instead of being injured by the electricity field, players will be eliminated due to a weak signal.

As for the underlying layer of this game, there is a little change in rules:

Signal Zone. Player need batteries to keep them survived on the outside of the signal zone.

Rule of Wins. If there are only five survivors in a competition, players can quit or continue to fight, but an outcome does not change: all of them are winners equally.

4.3   The Analysis of Game Reviews

Review Selection. We crawled 283 reviews in a default sequence in TapTap. The players' name, the number of playing hour and content of reviews are also collected. Next, we filtered-out reviews that the number of playing hours is less than 30 min and removed reviews that were unrelated to this game. In total, the sample contained 149 reviews that showed related information about Game for Peace.

These reviews were posted from May 15 to May 27. All of them spent more than 30 min on this game and over 70% of the players spent over 100 h on this game.

Table 3. The frequencies of game elements

Objects	Frequencies	Objects	Frequencies
Visual feedback on hitting	43	Skin and clothes	25
Signal zone	40	Rule of wins	22
Dying animation	37	Cheater	14
Store	35	Image quality	12
Interaction	30	Anti-addiction system	11

Frequency of Game Elements. We collected 32 objects in total that players talked about in 149 reviews. Table 3 showed the top 10 objects that were mentioned more than ten times. Frequency means the sum of sample which contain this game element, for example, visual feedback on hitting was most frequently mentioned (n = 43), followed by signal zone (n = 40). Most reviews contained more than one game element. To some extent, all of these elements influenced player experience and emotion, so players expressed their sentiment toward them. We classified these game elements into six groups:

(1) *The metaphorical layer.* The superficial part of a game included visual feedback on hitting, signal zone (changed the name of shrinking area), dying animation and image quality.
(2) *The underlying layer.* Rules of game included signal zone (added signal strength) and rule of win.
(3) *Expenditure.* Game elements related to money such as store, skin and clothes. Because of extra attributes such as price, it is different from elements in the metaphorical layer.
(4) *Interaction.* Interaction between players and mobiles, especially for weapon and recoil control in this game which influences players' ability.
(5) *Anti-addiction system.* Limited age and playing hours of underage players (under 18 years old). Players who are younger than 16 years old cannot play this game.
(6) *Cheater.* Cheater could damage the fairness of a game. It also related to players' ability in a game.

Methodology. We used NLPIR platform (Natural language Processing & Information Retrieval) [15] to analyzed reviews. This platform aims to big data research, mining and natural language processing, especially for Chinese. As for polarity analysis of sentiment, this platform employed deep neural networks and a special type of co-occurence to detect emotional words and estimate the emotional weight. It could be applied to different fields and reduce the limitation of emotional dictionaries [16]. As a result, we got the percentage of positive emotion of every review. For example, the figure '40' means that the affective states of this review is composed by 40% positive emotion and 60% negative emotion.

Emotion in Reviews: The percentage of positive emotion in a review ranged from 0 to 100. The frequencies of negative reviews (range = 0–50, n = 96) was higher than positive reviews (range = 50.01–100, n = 53).

Descriptive information about positive emotion (n = 149) showed that players expressed more negative sentiment than positive emotion toward these game elements (mean statistic = 44.9501 < 50, skewness = 0.228 > 0). It indicated that the changes of game elements had more negative effects on players. There was a large difference of players' sentiment (Std. Deviation = 23.27405).

Influence of Game Elements. We analyzed reviews of the specific game elements to estimate the influence of them.

Players had a broadly neutral attitude toward 'store' (mean = 49.0571) and 'skin and clothes' (mean = 48.57). There were more figures that closed to 50 (neutral) than other elements. For example, as for the attitude toward the store, there was a slight difference in the number of positive reviews and negative reviews, at 48.6% and 51.4% respectively. Most players believed that it was reasonable for developers to gain profit, and equipment in store will not damage the fairness of the game. Moreover, skin and clothes shared the similar percentage (positive 48%, negative 52%). Because skin and clothes were sold in store, the attitude toward them was close.

On the other hand, the metaphorical layer (visual feedback on hitting, signal zone, dying animation, image quality), the underlying layer (rule of wins, signal zone), cheater, interaction, anti-addiction system evoked more negative emotion than its positive counterparts. The means of these elements ranged from 40.7484 (dying animation) to 47.6656 (visual feedback of hitting). It showed that these elements have more negative impacts on players experience rather than positive effect.

In terms of the metaphorical layer, 37 players mentioned dying animation. 70% of reviews were negative, while nearly 30% of them were positive. Negative reviews showed that players disliked this animation, furthermore, this visual feedback is noticeable by all the players. Therefore, it could expose players' position to opponents. Similarly, Visual feedback on hitting received more negative reviews (67.4%) than positive reviews (32.6%), some players explained that this feedback disappeared immediately, as a result, it was difficult for players to observe and judge the result of shooting.

As for the underlying layer, changes in rules, such as signal zone (positive 37.5%, negative 62.5%) and rule of wins (positive 31.8%, negative 68.2%), also altered player emotion and experience. For example, due to a new attribute (signal strength) within the signal zone, players had to collect batteries. This new rule set an additional limitation on the players' action which evoked negative emotion.

It proved that changes in the metaphorical layer and the underlying layer have the potential to influence player experience and emotions. Besides, interaction and cheater, which were related to players' ability in a game could affect player experience and emotion.

5   Conclusion and Future Research

The case study proved that a small change of game elements, such as visual feedback, has the potential to influence players experience and emotions. Both the metaphorical layer and the underlying layer play a significant role in evoking players emotions.

Furthermore, without the change of core gameplay (e.g., Game for Peace), the alteration in the theme and the metaphorical layer could alter players experience and emotions. This conclusion means that developers should pay attention to aesthetics, narrative, interaction, and players' ability. It is necessary to adjust these elements to improve the player experience.

The study suffers from some limitation, thus lacking a more comprehensive understanding of the relationship between elements and player experience. Researchers should extend studies into different genres of game and collect a larger sample. Additionally, the labels of emotion are limited. Researchers could consider different types of emotion in the future.

References

1. Isbister, K.: How Games Move Us: Emotion by Design. The MIT Press, London (2016)
2. Ozturkcan, S., Sengun, S.: Pleasure in pain: how accumulation in gaming systems can lead to grief. In: Bostan, B. (ed.) Gamer Psychology and Behavior. ISCEMT, pp. 41–55. Springer, Cham (2016). https://doi.org/10.1007/978-3-319-29904-4_3
3. Bostan, B., Altun, S.: Goal-directed player behavior in computer games. In: Bostan, B. (ed.) Gamer Psychology and Behavior. ISCEMT, pp. 57–71. Springer, Cham (2016). https://doi.org/10.1007/978-3-319-29904-4_4
4. Balkaya, M., Catak, G.: Why games are fun? The reward system in the human brain. In: Bostan, B. (ed.) Gamer Psychology and Behavior. ISCEMT, pp. 21–38. Springer, Cham (2016). https://doi.org/10.1007/978-3-319-29904-4_2
5. Hunicke, R., LeBlanc, M., Zubek, R: MDA: a formal approach to game design and game research. In: Proceedings of the AAAI Workshop on Challenges in Game Artificial Intelligence, vol. WS-04-04, pp. 1-5. American Association for Artificial Intelligence (2004)
6. Björk, S., Holopainen, J.: Patterns in Game Design, 1st edn. Charles River Media, Hingham (2005)
7. Fullerton, T.: Game Design Workshop: A Playcentric Approach to Creating Innovative Games, 2nd edn. CRC Press, London (2012)
8. Järvinen, A.: Games Without Frontiers: Theories and Methods for Game Studies and Design. Tampere University Press, Finland (2008)
9. Bond, J.G.: Introduction to Game Design, Prototyping, and Development: From Concept to Playable Game with Unity and C#, 2nd edn. Addison-Wesley, Boston (2018)
10. Schell, J.: The Art of Game Design: A Book of Lenses. AK Peters/CRC Press, Boca Raton (2014)
11. Koster, R.: Theory of Fun for Game Design, 2nd edn. O'Reilly Media, Sebastopol (2013)
12. Game for Peace Hompage. https://pg.qq.com/main.shtml. Accessed 27 May 2019
13. PUBG Mobile Hompage. https://pg.qq.com/main.shtml. Accessed 27 May 2019
14. TapTap: Game for Peace. https://www.taptap.com/app/83084. Accessed 27 May 2019
15. Natural Language Processing & Information Retrieval Sharing Platform. http://www.nlpir.org/wordpress/. Accessed 5 June 2019
16. Zhang, H., Li, H., Li, Q.: Research on automatic emotional word detection and polarity weighting algorithm. J. Chin. Inf. Process. **31**(3), 48–54 (2017)

Research on Multimedia Teaching in Universities Under Human-Computer Interaction Environment

Xiaoyan Niu[(⊠)]

Shandong University of Finance and Economics,
No. 7366 Er Huan Dong Road, Jinan, Shandong, China
Qiuxiao25@hotmail.com

Abstract. Multimedia teaching has been widely applied in Universities, which has brought good effect and great convenience under human-computer interaction environment in teaching practice. While certain problems arise due to the cognitional misunderstanding and the lack of multimedia technology. This paper discussed the cognitive theory, practical application and effect of multimedia teaching, it also summarized the relevant advantages, disadvantages and required skills to enhance multimedia teaching effect.

Keywords: Multimedia teaching · Cognition theory ·
Human-computer interaction · Multimedia courseware

1 Brief Introduction of the Development of Multimedia Teaching and Human-Computer Interaction

Multimedia teaching refers to the teaching activities that are carried out in accordance with the teaching objectives and learners' characteristics. It combines the traditional classroom teaching means with the modern teaching media, such as text, pictures, sound, video and animation under human-computer interaction environment (Fig. 1). With the rapid development of modern educational technology which relies on computer and network technology, multimedia teaching has become a new popular method with many merits. It has developed into a modern means with the integration of blackboard writing, word processing, image processing, voice acquisition and processing and human-computer interaction.

Human-Computer Interaction (HCI) refers to the technology realizing interrelation and mutual effects between humans and computers via the human-computer interface. After rapid development for nearly thirty years, HCI has been transformed from interrelation with keyboards and mice into human-computer interaction through technology of touch control, multimedia and virtual reality. It seems that the current HCI has been converted from computer-centered interaction into human-centered interaction (Fig. 2).

© Springer Nature Switzerland AG 2019
C. Stephanidis (Ed.): HCII 2019, LNCS 11786, pp. 330–340, 2019.
https://doi.org/10.1007/978-3-030-30033-3_26

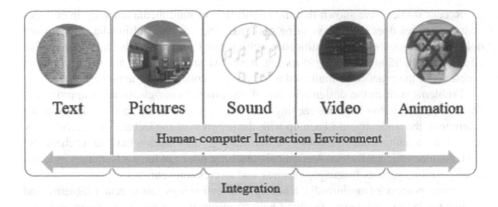

Fig. 1. Multimedia teaching under HCI environment (source: the author)

Fig. 2. Human-computer interaction (source: the author)

Human-Computer interaction focuses on the relationship between human beings and computers; study on the communication between human and computer through mutual understanding and accomplish the functions of information management, service and processing.

Recent studies have shown that the application of multimedia teaching in colleges and universities does not always bring good learning effects. Multimedia teaching not only has the superiority that traditional teaching can't match, but also has the negative effects that traditional teaching does not have. At present, there are some common problems in the practice of multimedia teaching in colleges and universities.

Problems such as the design and use of multimedia courseware are inappropriate; the information is too large in teaching, the display speed is too fast, the focus is not prominent, the students can't keep up with the progress of the lecture; the teachers rely too much on multimedia courseware, which leads to the situation that the teachers and students lose their interaction; Multimedia teaching does not have advantages in terms of expressions such as language, gestures and expressions etc.

In the process of multimedia teaching, the followings are urgent problems and challenges in the multimedia teaching help to eliminate the negative effects and promote the smooth progress of multimedia teaching in colleges and universities: how to determine the specific content of teaching, design multimedia courseware according to the teaching objectives and the characteristics of learners; how to organize or implement teaching by constructing a natural and efficient human-computer interaction environment between teachers and multimedia teaching equipment and how to effective integrate and present teaching information to the learners.

2   Cognitive Theory and Multimedia Teaching

According to the theory and viewpoint of cognitive psychology, students need to cognize multimedia teaching information in the process of multimedia teaching.

2.1   Cognitive Process

The psychological process in the learning process mainly includes cognitive and emotional psychological processes. R.M. Gagne, a famous contemporary educational psychologist in the United States, believes that [1] teaching activities are external stimuli designed to influence the internal psychological processes of learners, so the teaching process design should be consistent with the learners' internal psychological acceptance process in learning activities. Gagne divides the internal psychological process of student learning into nine steps: acceptance, expectation, working memory retrieval, selective perception, semantic coding, response, reinforcement, retrieval and reinforcement, retrieval and induction (Fig. 3).

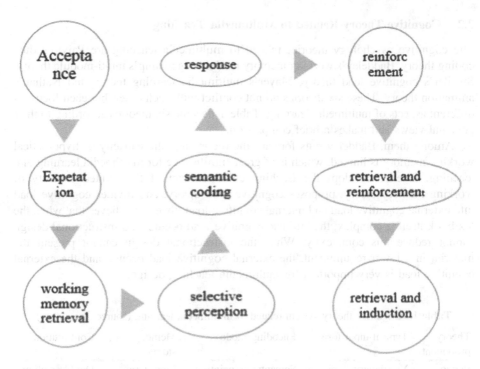

Fig. 3. Nine steps of internal psychological process of student learning (source: the author)

Correspondingly, there are four main psychological activities of learners involved in these nine stages: one is attention, the second is perception, the third is memory, and the fourth is concept formation. These four kinds of psychological activities are closely related to the teaching process, and of course are closely related to the design of teaching activities (Fig. 4).

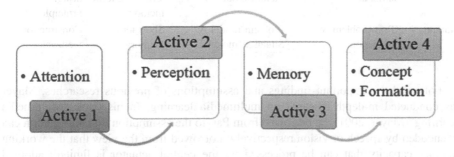

Fig. 4. Four psychological activities of learners (source: the author)

2.2   Cognitive Theory Related to Multimedia Teaching

The cognitive psychology theories related to multimedia teaching are Paivio's dual coding theory, Baddeley's working memory model, Engelkamp's multi-module theory, Sweller's cognitive load theory, Mayer's multimedia learning theory and Nathan's animation theory. These six theories do not conflict with each other, but each focus on different aspects of multimedia learning. Table 1 lists the six theories according to their personal views and makes a brief comparison.

Among them, Baddeley puts forward the theory that the capacity of hypothetical working memory is limited, which is of great significance for multimedia learning and teaching. Sweller develops the teaching enlightenment of the limited capacity of working memory theory, proposes cognitive load theory, and divides cognitive load into external cognitive load and internal cognitive load. Sweller believes that when the textbook itself is complex, the intrinsic cognitive load occurs, and instructional design cannot reduce this complexity. When the instructional design cannot present the material in a lower requirement, the external cognitive load occurs, and the external cognitive load is very important for multimedia teaching design.

Table 1. Cognitive theory system related to multimedia learning (source: the author)

Theory proponent	Typical input form	Encoding mode	Memory storage	Contribution
Paivio	Vocabulary & picture	Semantic association & visual coding	Long-term memory	Double coding theory
Baddeley	Vocabulary & space perception material	Voice & vision/space	Short-term memory	Working memory model
Engelkamp	Action phrase	Motion program & semantic concept	Long-term memory	Multi-module theory
Sweller	Mathematical problems & chart	Schema construction Schema construction	Short-term memory	Cognitive load theory
Mayer	Tech article & animation	Speech model & Picture model	Short-term/long-term memory	Multimedia design principle
Nathan	Text problem & animation	Problem model & Situation model	Short-term memory	Construction feedback

Followed the important findings and assumptions of previous researches, Mayer has conducted in-depth research on multimedia learning. In his book "Multimedia Learning"(Mayer, 2001), he borrowed from Paivio the assumption that information can be encoded by speech or vision respectively; borrowed from the view that the working memory capacity that can be processed by the central actuator is limited; adopted Sweller's idea to divide the cognitive load into external and internal cognitive load; Mayer put forward the idea of setting teaching designed to reduce external cognitive load.

The system proposed by Mayer is shown in Fig. 5. His preferred material presentation is to present in auditory vocabulary so that it is guaranteed that these words do not conflict with the visual coding required for the image. The sound is organized into a speech model, and the visual representation enters in the image model. Working memory is used to integrate verbal models, picture models, and prior knowledge in long-term memory. This integration often begins after receiving a small amount of information rather than completing the instruction.

Mayer's system and his proposed multimedia design principles are based on the numerous experimental results. According to the study, he summarized seven principles of multimedia design as followings:

1. Multimedia Cognitive Principles: students learn words and picture composition better than learning words only.
2. The principle of spatial proximity: The adjacent words and picture display is better than the separate display.
3. The principle of time approach: Students can learn better if the corresponding words and pictures are presented at the same time.
4. Consistency Principle: Students learn better when unrelated materials (words, pictures, and sounds) are excluded rather than included.
5. Formal Principles: Students learn multimedia presentations consisting of animations and commentary better than multimedia presentations that consist of animation and screen text.
6. Redundancy principle: It is better for students to learn the presentation materials that are explained by the animation and explanation than to learn the presentation materials composed of the animation plus the explanation and the screen text.
7. Individual difference principle: The design effect is better for learners with lower knowledge level than for learners with higher knowledge level; the design effect is better for learners with higher spatial ability than for learners with low spatial ability.

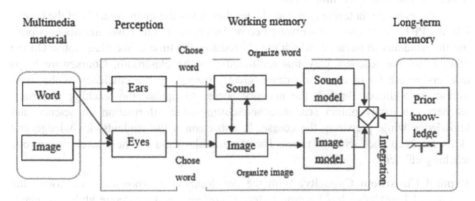

Fig. 5. Mayer's multimedia model (source: the author)

Mayer's model is simple and easy to understand. Many of his principles are consistent with the goal of reducing external cognitive load, such as excluding external and redundant information; presenting text and images in adjacent locations and at similar times also helps to reduce external cognitive load, because it increases the chances of simultaneously activating speech and picture models in working memory, which is easier to accept and understand for learners. And Mayer's model adds a lot of new research findings on multimedia learning, such as the seven multimedia design principles, so this model has strong practicality.

3   Advantages and Disadvantages of Multimedia Teaching

The rapid development of science and technology has also promoted the continuous updating of educational methods and technologies. The teaching method combining traditional teaching with multimedia teaching has been widely applied in the field of teaching, accepted by teachers and students, and has become the focus of teaching reform. Because multimedia is an integrated system of text, sound, video, image and animation, it changes the traditional teaching philosophy and teaching mode, optimizes the teaching process, and promotes the modernization of teaching methods. Therefore, it is of great significance to improve the quality of teaching by correctly understanding the application of multimedia in teaching, and to exert its advantages and avoiding disadvantages.

3.1   Advantages of Multimedia Teaching

Improve Teaching Efficiency. Under the traditional teaching mode, the information imparted through the board, explanation, drawing etc. is very limited; while the students keep taking notes during the lecture, it takes up more classroom time and affects the understanding of the course contents. The classroom efficiency is relatively low under the traditional teaching mode.

In the multimedia teaching mode, the teacher saves the main contents of the course into the PPT, flash and other software before the class. On one hand, the students print out the handouts in advance, which greatly reduces the time of the class notes. On the other hand, the teachers play this multimedia in the classroom. Courseware helps teachers save a lot of time for writing, greatly improving the efficiency of the illustration; in addition, through the network access to update the teaching materials, teachers can easily obtain academic and cutting-edge information on science and knowledge while preparing the course. It also ensures the students' knowledge and skills can keep pace with the times. Therefore, multimedia can help teachers improve teaching efficiency.

Expand Classroom Capacity. With the development of knowledge economy, the renewal of knowledge has become faster. Therefore, the knowledge ability of classroom teaching needs to be improved accordingly, which also brings higher requirements to the teachers responsible for imparting knowledge. Traditional teaching method through books, classroom narration, blackboard writing can't meet the rapidly growing demand for classroom abilities. Computer multimedia technology is a modern technology that combines computer technology with modern communication technology to integrate sound, image, graphics, text and processing the integrated information. Teachers' lectures and burdens can be reduced through the application of multimedia technology in teaching. When the required course contents are presented on a large screen, the classroom information capacity will be greatly expanded. For example, class exercises are showed through large screen layout; or using multimedia technology to show students the reference answers in a short period of time, which helps to solve students' problems in a timely manner (Fig. 6).

Fig. 6. Multimedia teaching helps to expand classroom capacity (source: Baidu)

Make Up the Shortage of Teachers. Teaching activities often require excellent voice and verbal expressions, and sometimes need to be combined with case and graphic explanations. So, it places higher requirements on teachers. Teachers, like ordinary people, cannot be perfect specialists at every aspect. Generalists. So inevitably, they may encounter various problems in their teaching work. For example, when a class needs songs or music performance sometimes, not every teacher has perfect sound and singing skills, at this time, multimedia tools can easily solve this situation; Drawing is usually a weakness of teachers in terms of mathematics or physics teaching. With limited time, multimedia tools can solve such problems well; for example, some teaching contents can only achieve the desired results through specific cases or scenes (such as the founding ceremony), and the application of multimedia teaching can easily achieve the desired effect.

Interactive Multimedia Teaching Methods Create a Good Interactive Environment. In the traditional teaching process, teachers arrange teaching content, teaching procedures etc., students can only passively participate in and accept this process. However, multimedia teaching has the distinctive features of human-computer interaction and timely feedback. Multimedia teaching can make full use of computer interactive man-machine dialogue for two-way teaching. Through timely feedback from the computer, on the one hand, teachers can understand the current situation of each student and coordinate the progress of teaching. On the other hand, students can also change the passive status in traditional teaching to achieve learning autonomy and initiative.

3.2 Disadvantages of Multimedia Teaching

Although multimedia teaching has many advantages, we have found many misunderstandings and improper use through the observation of current multimedia teaching applications.

The Amount and the Content of Courseware is Too "rich" to Distract Student's Attention. The use of multimedia helps to stimulate students' enthusiasm for learning and thus stimulate students' interest in learning. However, some teachers put too much energy into making "gorgeous" multimedia courseware, using limited classroom time to show cute videos or interesting pictures. It diverts the students' attention. The normal teaching is interfered by the useless material. Therefore, the desired teaching effect cannot be achieved.

Teachers Rely Too Much on Multimedia Teaching, Which Affects the Improvement of Teachers' Own Abilities. Advanced multimedia teaching methods bring convenience to teachers, but also bring corresponding negative effects. Some teachers gradually form a reliance on multimedia, and can't even complete a high-quality course without the help of multimedia courseware. Oral illustration and blackboard writing have been replaced by multimedia courseware demonstrations, which results in some teachers' ignorance of oral illustration and blackboard writing and what's more severe even degeneration of teaching ability.

4 Suggestions to Improve Multimedia Teaching in Universities and Colleges

4.1 Increase Investment and Establish a Multimedia Teaching Resource Library

How to make teachers and students easily master the required teaching materials and related background information is a problem that modern teaching must face and also a real way to improve the quality of multimedia teaching. Currently, many colleges and universities establish a variety of subject teaching database (including multimedia courseware database, problem database, etc.), which integrate existing information based on education network and campus network, collect and build teaching resources to achieve resource sharing. The benefits of this approach are: First, teachers can easily obtain high-quality courseware information from the internet and communicate with each other in a timely manner. Second, making full use of the convenience of multimedia teaching resources sharing, students can quickly obtain information from internet learning resources. It helps improve students' ability and efficiency in outside class learning.

4.2 Realize the Organic Combination of Traditional Classroom Teaching and Multimedia Teaching, Accomplish Complementary Advantages

Multimedia teaching is a teaching method, or a form, not a goal. The teaching form needs to serve the teaching content and teaching objectives. Therefore, in multimedia teaching, teachers should correctly understand the relationship between form and content, prioritize the main and minor parts, and rationalize the relationship between people and machines. No matter what kind of media or courseware is used, teachers can't rely too much on machines and give up traditional classroom teaching. Traditional class teaching and multimedia teaching have their own advantages and disadvantages. Teachers should combine the advantages of traditional teaching methods and experience them into multimedia teaching, realize in a way of the multimedia courseware teaching, combined with teachers' body language, emotions, interaction with students and discussion-based teaching mode. Only by realizing the complementary advantages of traditional classroom teaching and multimedia teaching, can we continuously improve the level of multimedia teaching in colleges and universities.

4.3 Improve the Production and Use Level of Multimedia Courseware

Good multimedia teaching needs to be fulfilled based on good multimedia teaching courseware. In order to produce good multimedia courseware and fully display the teaching contents and teaching concepts, teachers need to have strong multimedia design and operation ability. But at present, teachers are not very familiar with computer knowledge and operational skills, and maybe only capable of doing simple text editing and illustration design on PPT. Therefore, it is necessary to strengthen the modern teaching skills training of college and university teachers, such as multimedia teaching design and courseware production skills training. Through these training, teachers will be able to master the latest developments in modern educational technology and the latest information technology applications in teaching, which enables them to produce higher levels of multimedia courseware.

5 Summary

In college and university teaching, multimedia teaching has been one of the most common form of teaching method. After the review of important cognitive theories related to multimedia teach, this paper focuses on the sufficiency and insufficiency of multimedia teaching of Chinese universities under the human-computer interaction environment at the present situation, and put forwards suggestions to overcome the current insufficiencies and to improve multimedia teaching.

How to make better use of the advantages of multimedia technology, overcome the current problems of teaching cognition, methods and technology, establish scientific laws, and create a new talent training method based on multimedia teaching mode? This is a question that teachers and multimedia managers at all levels need to constantly think, study, practice and summarize.

References

1. Gagne, R.M.: Teaching Design Principle. Wang Xiaoming, translated. East China Normal University Press, Shanghai (2006). 5
2. Mayer, R.E., Massa, L.J.: Three facets of visual and verbal learners: cognitive ability, cognitive style, and learning preference. J. Educ. Psychol. **95**, 833–846 (2003)
3. Mayer, R.E., Moreno, R.: Nine ways to reduce cognitive load in multimedia learning. Educ. Psychol. **38**, 43–52 (2003)
4. Li, L.: The pros and cons of multimedia teaching and countermeasures. China Modern Educ. Equipment **2**, 108–110 (2007)
5. Jian, L.: Present situation and the development countermeasures of multimedia teaching in colleges and universities. Educ. Res. Mon. **1**, 110–111 (2011)
6. Zhanxiao, Z.: Problems and countermeasures in multimedia teaching. J. Shanxi Normal Univ. (Philos. Soc. Sci. Ed.) **36**, 180–182 (2007)
7. Gang, W.: Computer multimedia teaching for cultivation of students' innovative ability. Comput. CD Softw. Appl. **7**, 211 (2014)
8. Du, Y.: Thinking on computer multimedia teaching. China CIONews **03**, 160 (2014)
9. Zhang, Y., Ji, Y.: Development and forecast of computer multimedia technology. China Educ. Innov. Herald **01**, 172–173 (2014)
10. Shengbin, T.: Analyses on the influence factors of multimedia teaching. Pioneering Sci. Technol. Mon. **5**, 177–179 (2007)

Employing a Voice-Based Emotion-Recognition Function in a Social Chatbot to Foster Social and Emotional Learning Among Preschoolers

Tsai-Hsuan Tsai[1,3]([✉]), Hsien-Tsung Chang[2,3], Shin-Da Liao[4],
Hui-Fang Chiu[4], Ko-Chun Hung[2], Chun-Yi Kuo[5],
and Chih-Wei Yang[6]

[1] Department of Industrial Design, Chang Gung University, Taoyuan, Taiwan
ttsai.cgu@gmail.com
[2] Department of Computer Science and Information Engineering,
Chang Gung University, Taoyuan, Taiwan
[3] Department of Physical Medicine and Rehabilitation,
Chang Gung Memorial Hospital, Taoyuan, Taiwan
[4] Department of Child Care and Education,
Chang Gung University of Science and Technology, Taoyuan, Taiwan
[5] Metal Industries Research & Development Centre, Kaohsiung, Taiwan
[6] Sampo Corporation, Taoyuan, Taiwan

Abstract. This study will introduce a social chatbot to a child learning site to cultivate children's understanding of emotions and strengthen their emotional expression skills using conversation scenarios between a child and social chatbot under the guidance of a kindergarten teacher to achieve emotional ease and adjustment effectiveness. The use of AI-aided emotional measurement is a completely new direction for academic research regarding the speech emotion and behavioral analysis of preschoolers. The benefits of this study are as follows. (a) The establishment of children's emotional speech database and analysis module. Currently, EMO-DB and Beyond Verbal contain samples of speech emotions, but the analysis of children's emotional speech has not been reported. The speech and conversation data collected from preschoolers in this study might be used to construct speech/emotion characteristic database, an emotional semantic identification database, an image/emotion analysis database, and an interactive script database designed for preschoolers to assist children's emotional development, social learning, and provide references. (b) The development of a voice chatbot with EQ. The setting of this study can be used regarding a voice chatbot with EQ and applied in real-world learning sites, enabling the analysis of real-time emotions based on the emotional speeches and words in dialog with a social chatbot. Moreover, it can pro-vide appropriate conversations based on the different emotional states of the user. The social chatbot developed in this study might help nurture children's EQ and cognitive abilities, as well as improve their emotional adjustment, management, and social support skills.

Keywords: Preschoolers · Emotional intelligence · Social-emotional learning · Voice-based emotion recognition · Socially-assistive robot · Chatbot

© Springer Nature Switzerland AG 2019
C. Stephanidis (Ed.): HCII 2019, LNCS 11786, pp. 341–356, 2019.
https://doi.org/10.1007/978-3-030-30033-3_27

1   Introduction

Artificial intelligence (AI) has made recent outstanding advancements [1, 2]; although AI has improved extraordinarily in terms of outcomes, AI technology remains at the technical level of cognition [3–5], and much room exists for development to reflect the cognition, understanding, emotion, memory, and other functions of the human brain. Currently, two aspects of AI development (i.e., how to make a computer learn to think and natural language processing; NLP) [6] have come into focus. These aspects enable the system to communicate with humans in a natural way. NLP technology has already been applied in numerous ways (e.g., Apple Siri, Google Assistant, Amazon Alexa, Chatbot application of e-commerce, and others), prompting a shift in users' usage behavior from App to Chatbot. Thus, the interactive dialog mode has become increasingly important. Presently, chatbot applications mostly fall under the category of social chatbots, which are instruction- and task-based, can comprehend user speech, and answer using NLP technology. For example, the content of the most commonly used conversational business chatbot is built based on a list of frequently asked questions (FAQs) for customers to provide information to meet users' needs. The social chatbot implements machine learning through constant information input and output during its interactions with users to achieve a better user experience and content services.

AI has also been successfully applied within the medical field; analysis and prediction using AI not only reduce the administrative burden on medical personnel but also achieve better disease prevention, detection, diagnosis, and treatment. The treatment strategies that medical personnel apply to patients can be optimized through smart predictions of patient emotions, which in turn can improve the doctor-patient relationship and patient quality of life [7]. Psychology and neuroscience studies have shown that high-level automatic weighing is involved in many decisions, and emotions are closely related to decision making [8]; therefore, emotions play an important role in rational human behavior. Through the ever-strengthening role that a speech interface plays in human-computer interactions, the importance of automatically recognizing human emotions is increasing [9]. Thus, enabling machines to perceive human emotions might provide a service model that is closer to these emotions.

1.1   Preschoolers' Emotional Development Needs

Early childhood development requires various educational supports from families and caretakers [10], especially with regard to the development of preschoolers' emotional intelligence (EQ) [11, 12]. Children's emotional development becomes more mature and complex with age, especially during the childhood stage when they have the fastest neuronal connection and growth; thus, the development of EQ and cognitive abilities (e.g., emotional understanding, emotional expression, tasks of emotional vocabulary and narrative ability, and others) during this stage is important and helpful for their future emotional management and social-emotional development [13, 14].

Based on Piaget's theory of child cognitive development [15], Dupont, a neo-Piagetian, considered emotions as personal-social constructions that are composed of three components that can develop over the lifespan: cognitive appraisal, an alteration of affect, and a terminal action [16]. Thus, Dupont [16] emphasized that children construct their own emotions. Then, he defined emotional development as mostly associated with children. As Table 1 describes, children's emotions during the egocentric stage are not yet differentiated; rather, they focus on their own bodily feelings and actions, and only have simple positive and negative changes. During the heteronomous stage, children have gradually developed a concept on specific things, are able to produce more lasting feelings for others, begin to have differentiated emotions, and appreciate that they are different from others despite their lack of complete emotion cognition and management capabilities. Thus, preschoolers (i.e., those who are 7 years old on or before September 30th of a school year) gradually come to understand emotions, express emotions, and develop empathy by relying on the help and guidance of a caretaker.

Table 1. The emotional development stages of children

Age period	Stage	Content
From 2–4 years old	Egocentric-Hedonistic	Pleasure, comfort, relief, or freedom from tension are valued during this stage. Feelings relate to pleasure/displeasure, comfort/discomfort, pain/relief, tension/relaxation, global situations (i.e., the weather, the season, or the time of day), or one's mood
From 4–7 years old	Heteronomous I (Getting and Having)	The reasons for feelings relate to a basic dependence on authority figures. Children's feelings are highly dependent on adult approval and authority for getting and having
	Heteronomous II (Going and Doing)	Having permission to go places and to do things is highly valued during this stage. Children's feelings usually relate to going and doing or being restricted in such activities
From 6–10 years old	Interpersonal I (Belonging)	Role-taking skills are poorly developed or nonexistent during this stage. Children's feelings are closely associated with peers, peer interactions, and self-other comparisons
From 10–11 years old	Interpersonal II (Mutuality)	Mutuality is highly valued during this stage. Some older children attribute their feelings to genuine, mutual relationships, where each person is sensitive to one another's feeling; Thus, role-taking skills are well developed
From 10 years old and older	Autonomous	Autonomy is highly valued during this stage. Feelings reflect the need to be self-defining, self-directed, and autonomous. The person can now react upon his or her own actions, thoughts, and feelings
	Integrated	Integrity is valued during this stage. The reason reflects the need to be consistent and honest with oneself and others, adhere to one's principles and convictions, and be whole and integrated

References: Dupont [16, 17].

1.2 EQ Theory

Salovey and Mayer [18] first proposed Emotional intelligence (EQ) as a kind of social intelligence (SQ) that individuals use to differentiate their perceptions from those of others, as well as to think and act; accordingly, EQ consists of three concepts: appraisal and the expression of emotion, the regulation of emotion, and the use of emotion. Later, Salovey and Sluyter [19] considered EQ theory as lacking thinking about feelings and proposed the following four-branch model of the skills involved in EQ.

- "Perceiving and Expressing Emotion" refers when individuals correctly identify emotions and the content of an emotion, perceive their true inner feelings and distinguish them correctly, and empathize with the emotions of others through language, speech, appearance, and behavior.
- "Assimilating Emotion in Thought" refers when emotions promote individuals to think. Through this process, individuals achieve cognitive understanding by thinking of the cause of an event through emotional adjustment. Emotions can also help individuals to diversify their ways of thinking, thereby promoting action and understanding.
- "Understanding Emotions" refers to when, after the above two abilities to identify basic emotions are obtained, individuals connect emotions to life situations and start to learn to understand the meaning of emotions. For example, they differentiate the emotions of anger and upset from emotional situations of sadness and begin to analyze more complex emotional feelings.
- "Reflectively Regulating Emotions" represent the highest level of EQ. This stage refers to individuals who must attend to and care about their own emotions so that they can manage and adjust them. Moreover, they learn to separate emotions from behaviors and think about expressing appropriate emotions and behaviors in appropriate situations. Lastly, they reflect on the cause that triggers the emotion, enabling them to adjust and change their feelings.

Currently, it is well established that children's emotional development and emotional education are important; however, children's speech characteristics, emotional semantics, and emotional cognition and expression abilities have been rarely investigated. Compared with other operation modes of smart devices, speech is the most natural man-machine interface, and it is fairly easy to use for those who are not familiar with the operation of smart devices or language input (e.g., children or the elderly). Thus, the current study aimed to develop a social assistant robot that employed a speech-based emotion recognition function to meet the needs of emotional education of kindergarteners. We also introduced an interactive scripting system in the robot to enable an interactive dialog between the social chatbot and preschoolers to collect data on children's speech and vocabulary. These data were then subjected to the speech and emotion recognition software Beyond Verbal api [20] and the Berlin Database of Emotional Speech (EMO-DB) [21] to identify the emotional characteristics of that speech and classify it and its associated emotion to build children's emotional speech corpus. In this way, a more complete children's dialog experience can be created through the corpus information coupled with machine learning. Importantly, this study was based on Salovey and Mayer's EQ theory [18] and the skills involved in EQ proposed by Salovey and Sluyter [19] to develop the interactive scripts capable of improving children's emotional capacities. In addition, the effects of human-robot dialog on the emotional guidance and adjustment of the child/social chatbot interaction were evaluated by child education experts and kindergarten teachers to indicate the adjustment needed to the scripts regarding child emotional regulation and to verify the applicability of these scripts.

2 Design and Development of a Social Assistant Robot for Kindergarteners

To examine preschoolers' emotional cognitive and expression skills and assist them to develop emotional cognitive and adjustment capabilities and social emotions, we aimed to establish a social assistant robot for kindergarteners to examine emotional judgment. The architecture, robot body, sound recording equipment, dialog script design, and emotional recognition of the system are described below.

2.1 System Architecture of a Social Chatbot for Preschoolers

Figure 1 shows a schematic diagram of the overall system architecture of the social chatbot for preschoolers. This system can be divided into three parts: the robot body, the recording device, and the emotion recognition module. When the robot detects a human face, it starts a conversation with the user, turns on the recording device, and uploads a dialog file between the user and the robot to the database. The server obtains the audio file in the database for emotional recognition analysis. Finally, the emotional recognition result is sent back to the database.

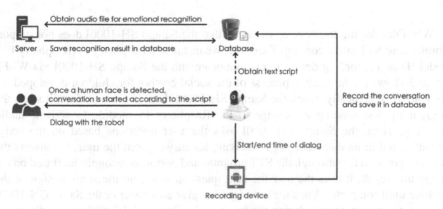

Fig. 1. System architecture of a social chatbot for preschoolers

2.2 Interactive Process of Social Chatbot for Children

We used Sampo wisdom housekeeper (SH-1000I) [22] as the hardware because it supports two-way voice communication, has a built-in text-to-speech (TTS) function, and can connect to the database to obtain a script that is spoken by the robot through TTS. The hardware then converts the speech of the user to text through the robot's speech-to-text (STT) function for analysis. In addition, a camera with a 350° rotating lens on the Sampo SH-1000I provided motion detection and video recording, and the built-in face-tracker/face recognition function is able to recognize a human face and initiate a conversation. Figure 2 show a screenshot of the Sampo SH-1000I face-tracking system.

Fig. 2. Sampo wisdom housekeeper (SH-1000I) (left); Face-tracking function of the Sampo SH-1000I (right)

When developing the system, we found that the Sampo SH-1000I does not support simultaneous STT and recording. Therefore, we installed a Raspberry Pi (Raspberry Pi 3 Model B) as a recording device to communicatewith the Sampo SH-1000I via Wi-Fi. Figure 3 shows the interactive process of the social chatbot for children developed for this system. Specifically, when the Sampo SH-1000I detects a human face, it starts the program by first sending a message to the Raspberry Pi module to activate audio recording. Then, the Sampo SH-1000I asks the user questions based on the script content stored in its database. After receiving an answer from the user, it converts the user's response to text through the STT program and performs recognition. Based on the recognition result, it asks the user the next question based on the script design of the database until complete. When the user does not give an answer or the SampoSH-1000I does not receive an answer during the process, the Sampo SH-1000I repeats the question. The test ends if no response is received. After the test ends, a message is sent to the Raspberry Pi module to stop recording and transmit the audio file to the server to save.

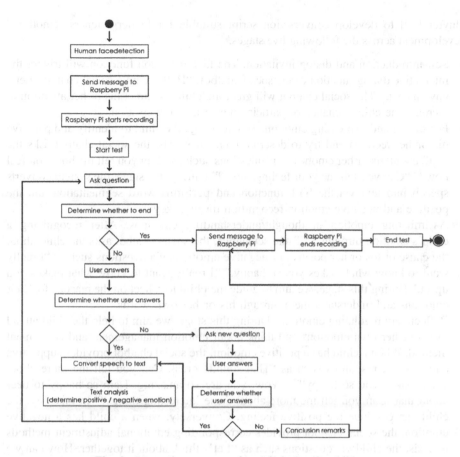

Fig. 3. Interactive process of social chatbot for children

2.3 Dialog Script Planning and Design

The social chatbot developed for this study uses a feedback-type database. The data in this type of database are those collected after accumulation and analyses and used as a control (e.g., various children's voices, conversations, and so on). In this study, we will use the social chatbot to guide children to express their emotions (these data will be collected). According to the previously established positive/negative words table, the branching direction of the dialog script will be determined based on whether the users' answers contain a positive/negative word, and the question related to the branching direction will be played out loud through the TTS engine. The user's speech text information will be obtained through the robot's STT function. After the word segmentation of the speech, the words will then be compared with the positive/negative word table to obtain the branching direction of the script. In other words, when the words are judged as negative, the negative dialog script will be chosen; otherwise, the positive dialog script will be chosen. We will use Salovey and Mayer's EQ theory [18] and the skills of EQ proposed by Salovey and

Sluyter [19] to develop conversation script suitable for kindergarteners' emotional development across the following five stages.

- Self-introduction and dialog invitation. The face-detection function will trigger the interactive dialog function of the social chatbot: "Hello, I am a social chatbot. Let's have a chat." The social chatbot will greet the child to attract his or her attention to increase the child's chance of participating in the conversation.
- Perceiving and expressing emotion. To encourage the child to identify and perceive his or her feelings and try to describe them in words, the social chatbot asks the child about his or her emotions via questions such as "Can you tell me how you feel now?" "Can you tell me your feelings now?" During this stage, the system converts speech into text via the STT function and performs word segmentation and the positive and negative emotion recognition through keywords.
- Assimilating emotion in thought/understanding emotions. After recognizing a child's emotion through STT and semantics, the social chatbot asks the child about the cause of his or her positive or negative emotions via questions such as "I really want to know what makes you so happy." "I really want to know what makes you upset." During this stage, we aim to guide the child to reflect on the reasons for their emotions and understand them through his or her own words.
- Reflectively regulating emotions. During this stage, we aim to help the child attend to his or her own emotions and think about emotion management and adjustment method. When a child has a positive emotion, the social chatbot provides supportive and positive responses such as "That sounds great. Can you tell me more about what makes you so happy?" "Wow, you are so amazing. I am so happy to hear about that. Can you tell me more about these interesting things?" In this way, the child can continue the positive feeling. Conversely, when a child has a negative emotion, the social chatbot provides corresponding emotional adjustment methods to assist the child via questions such as "Let's think about it together. How can we make you feel better?" "Would you like to hold a doll to see if it makes you feel a little better?"
- Concluding remarks: In the end, the social chatbot presents concluding remarks with positive emotion such as "Thank you for telling me so much. It makes me so happy." Thus, the child perceives that positive emotions can be passed on to others. In the case of negative feelings, the concluding remarks are "Thank you for telling me so much. I hope that you are feeling a little better now." Thus, the child feels that the chatbot empathizes with his or her negative feelings.

2.4 Emotional Recognition Techniques and Methods

With regard to speech/emotion recognition, we attempted to determine the audio sample characteristic indicators from the same emotional category by extracting the voice features, adjust them to appropriate categories, and establish the speech feature indicators for each emotion category. The most commonly used voice/emotion recognition resources include Beyond Verbal [20] and EMO-DB [21]. In its speech/emotion recognition service, Beyond Verbal does not analyze the content or the context of the speech. Instead, it identifies the mood of the speaker through a speech-recognition technique. Currently, the Beyond Verbal database has 2.3 million speech samples from 170 countries in 40 languages. The program analyzes the rhythm, time, volume, pause, pitch, and other qualities of speech and compares the voice of the speaker with the voice samples in the company's internal database to find similar emotional characteristics [20]. Unlike Beyond Verbal, EMO-DB is recorded by professional speakers and emphasizes more distinct emotional expressions [21]. As such, we will use the speech/emotion recognition software Beyond Verbal api in combination with the emotion recognition model of EMO-DB api to identify seven emotion categories in the speech for model training: anger, joy, sadness, fear, disgust, boredom, and neutral. However, neither Beyond Verbal nor EMO-DB are emotion-recognition models constructed based on spoken Chinese, and the speeches collected in this study will be taken from the natural conversations of children without distinct characteristics for emotion identification. To more accurately determine the mood of the speech, we will include an emotional semantic judgment when analyzing the emotions of the speech. That is, the audio recordings of the children's speeches will be used to extract speech emotion features and determine the Chinese semantic keywords for emotion recognition. These features will then be used to train the speech emotion recognition model and applied to future intelligent emotion recognition applications (Fig. 4).

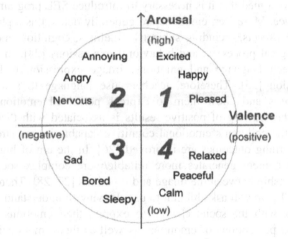

Fig. 4. EMO-DB data can be used to reveal the relative positions of anger, boredom, disgust, fear, joy, neutral, and sadness

3 Experimental Design and Process

With this study, we aim to understand the emotional, cognitive, and expression skills of preschoolers by having conversations with them through a chatbot. Their speeches and conversations will be recorded to construct a speech/emotion database. The speech characteristics, language, and semantic capabilities of preschoolers with regard to emotional expression will be analyzed, and the social chatbot will be optimized to achieve a better conversational and interactive experience for future applications regarding the emotional education and companionship of children.

3.1 Participant Screening and Recruitment

In this study, 30 preschoolers between 3–6 years old will be recruited from middle and senior kindergarten classes of the affiliated Chang Gung University Science and Technology. Three- to 6-year-olds who reach the mid-level standard of the Child Development Assessment Scale administered by the kindergarten teacher will be eligible to participate in this study. The duration of this study will be 20 weeks, and both the participants and their guardians who sign the informed consent agreement have the right to terminate their participation at any time for any reason; the investigators and teachers executing the experiment will also be able to discontinue the test if needed.

3.2 Drawing Emotion Diary

Based on Dupont's emotional development stages [16], preschoolers must rely on the assistance and guidance of a caretaker to gradually understand and express emotions, as well as develop various capabilities such as empathy. Durlak et al. [23] indicated that teaching and learning in schools include strong social, emotional, and academic components and verify the benefits that social and emotional learning (SEL) has on improving social and emotional skills, attitudes, behaviors, and academic performance. These authors also argued that it is necessary to introduce SEL programs into standard educational practice. Moreover, emotions are generally defined as a phenomenon that involves multiple aspects, including subjective feelings, cognition, motivational tendencies, physiological processes, and behavioral expressions [24]. In addition to the association between language and emotions, image expression is likely equal to semantic expression [25]. Therefore, teachers use language to stimulate learners' emotional responses and allow them to express perceived emotional changes by drawing. When the drawing of positive results is associated with that of potentially negative results, the children's emotional cognitive capabilities are strengthened, and their language learning outcomes are improved [26]. In the era of big data, the integration of visual content generates more reliable/more complex social signals and reveals the relationship between the image and emotions [27, 28]. Therefore, based on the concept of SEL, we will ask children to use drawing to understand their emotional states and to talk with the social chatbot to express their emotions to assess their understanding and perceptions of emotions, as well as their emotional word use and emotional expression abilities. Compared with a semantic analysis, however, the emotional analysis of the image is more challenging and involves philosophy, photography, painting, visual arts, and psychology, as well as abstractness and subjectivity [25]. Therefore, we will ask the kindergarten teacher to explain various emotions to the children so that they have a basic understanding of emotional words. The children will be instructed to draw a mood diary while the preschool teachers take notes on the child's mood on site. Subsequently, we will invite child behavioral experts, child emotional experts, and the kindergarten director of the test site to help us understand and analyze the emotions in the children's drawings (Fig. 5).

Fig. 5. Children's mood diary (left: blank; right: a mood diary example); the text below the drawing are the notes taken by a preschool teacher on site

3.3   Emotional Corner Setting

The experiment will be conducted with the middle or senior class in the "emotion corner" of the kindergarten affiliated with Chang Gung University of Science and Technology. This area will be located in one corner of the room, equipped with a few pillows or soft dolls. The social chatbot will play a guiding and listening role, allowing children to have an interactive conversation with the robot in a private space and to express and vent their emotions and thoughts. The emotion corner will be designed based on the following three principles. (a) The space should be appropriately sized. A small and appropriate space should be set aside based on the height of the participants. If the space is too large, then children might feel that the environment is uncontrollable and scary; if the space is too small, then children might feel constricted. The tent used in this study will allow a child 120 cm in height to stand or sit unimpeded. (b) The space should be open while ensuring privacy. The space should have a sense of shelter, although a connection with the outside world can be created, allowing the children to feel at home. (c) The space should be able to encourage the children to express their emotions and help them form a self-concept. The social chatbot in this study will play a guiding role and assist the children to think about and express their emotions via open-ended questions. In addition to space planning, a picture-book manual and expression and emotion textbook will also be designed so that teachers and researchers are able to explain the interactive methods in the emotion corner and have a conversation with the social chatbot through storytelling.

Fig. 6. Emotion corner (Left: senior class; Right: middle class)

3.4 Experimental Protocol

In this study, we aim to examine the emotion cognition and expression skills of preschoolers by having conversations with them through a chatbot and recording their conversations to analyze their speech characteristics and emotional semantics. In addition to the emotion corner (Fig. 6), the kindergarten teacher will introduce the social chatbot to the children using the picture-book manual prior to the test. They will explain the experimental procedure and demonstrate how to talk to the social chatbot. Next, two tasks will be completed. (a) An emotion diary will be distributed to the children and they will draw their feelings. The child will be able to express his or her inner feeling through a pen-and-paper drawing, and it can be used as the basis for speech/emotion recognition. (b) After drawing the emotion diary, the children will enter the emotion corner individually and begin the interactive dialog with the social chatbot; the dialog is triggered by the face-recognition function of the system. When a human face is detected, the social chatbot immediately initiates the dialog function by voicing the self-introduction message ("Hello, I am a social chatbot. Can we have a chat?") to begin a series of questions and answers. After the dialog is complete, the child will be free to leave the emotion corner. Table 2 summarizes the experimental process of this study.

Table 2. Experimental protocol

【Preparation】
Arrange the emotion corner, place the social assistant robot in the tent, and set up the relevant experimental equipment.

↓

【Obtain informed consent from the guardian of the child】
Before the test, obtain consent from the parents or guardian of the child, as well as the child's personal information and permission to visually record. If the child's parents or guardians agree to take the test, then he or she will sign the informed consent document and complete the personal information questionnaire.

↓

【Experimental process explanation and demonstration】
The kindergarten teacher or researcher will introduce the experiment protocol to the participant through the picture-book manual and demonstrate how to interact with the social chatbot.

↓

【Task 1: Drawing the emotion diary】
The participant will attempt to understand his or her own feelings through pen-and-paper drawings in an emotion diary, which (assisted by the kindergarten teacher and investigator) will be used in combination with the speech for emotion recognition.

↓

【Task 2: Talk to social chatbot】
After drawing the emotion diary, the children will enter the emotion corner individually to participate in the test. The dialog process has five stages. Human face recognition triggers the social chatbot conversation that ends after the questioning and answering section is complete; the child is then free to leave the corner.
(The time of the test is not fixed, and the child answers the questions by him or herself. The test sequence is arranged by the teacher and the researcher on site.)

↓

End of test

↓

【System satisfaction evaluation】
Professional preschool teachers complete an assessment to obtain opinions on emotions.

3.5   Data Collection and Measures

The emotional measurements obtained in this system must be reviewed by experts and pretested by kindergarten teachers and children. Furthermore, the drawing of the emotion diary and the setup of the emotion corner suitable for child interactions will be carefully planned. This test will obtain (a) children's emotion diary drawings and the notes on the children's emotions taken by the kindergarten teacher on site; and (b) the speech and dialog data collected through the social chatbot. We will conduct a systematic assessment and emotional behavior analysis on the emotional speech, emotional word, and image data collected in this study. Importantly, to ensure the reliability and validity of the results, we will invite children behavioral experts, children's emotional experts, and the director of the kindergarten of the experimental site to provide revisions and suggestions on the emotion measurement, emotional speech and word analysis; the interactive dialog script based on the systematic analysis results of the image data; emotional words in children's drawings; and their interactive responses to the social chatbot.

4   Conclusions

This study will introduce a social chatbot to a child learning site to cultivate children's understanding of emotions and strengthen their emotional expression skills using conversation scenarios between a child and social chatbot under the guidance of a kindergarten teacher to achieve emotional ease and adjustment effectiveness. The use of AI-aided emotional measurement is a completely new direction for academic research regarding the speech emotion and behavioral analysis of preschoolers. The benefits of this study are as follows. (a) The establishment of children's emotional speech database and analysis module. Currently, EMO-DB and Beyond Verbal contain samples of speech emotions, but the analysis of children's emotional speech has not been reported. The speech and conversation data collected from preschoolers in this study might be used to construct speech/emotion characteristic database, an emotional semantic identification database, an image/emotion analysis database, and an interactive script database designed for preschoolers to assist children's emotional development, social learning, and provide references. (b) The development of a voice chatbot with EQ. The setting of this study can be used regarding a voice chatbot with EQ and applied in real-world learning sites, enabling the analysis of real-time emotions based on the emotional speeches and words in dialog with a social chatbot. Moreover, it can provide appropriate conversations based on the different emotional states of the user. The social chatbot developed in this study might help nurture children's EQ and cognitive abilities, as well as improve their emotional adjustment, management, and social support skills.

Acknowledgments. The authors thank the affiliated kindergarten of Chang Gung University Science and Technology for providing the resources required for this work.

Funding. This research was funded by the Ministry of Science and Technology, Taiwan, R.O.C. under Grant No. MOST 107-2221-E-182-055-, as well as CGMH fund CMRPD2J0021. The funder had no role in study design, data collection and analysis, decision to publish, or preparation of the manuscript.

References

1. Chen, Z., Liu, B.: Lifelong machine learning. Synth. Lect. Artif. Intell. Mach. Learn. **12**, 1–207 (2018)
2. Vorobeychik, Y., Kantarcioglu, M.: Adversarial machine learning. Synth. Lect. Artif. Intell. Mach. Learn. **12**, 1–169 (2018)
3. Cho, J.H., Park, C.G.: Additional feature CNN based automatic target recognition in SAR image. In: 2017 Fourth Asian Conference on Defence Technology-Japan (ACDT), pp. 1–4. IEEE (2017)
4. Wang, X., Gao, L., Song, J., Shen, H.: Beyond frame-level CNN: saliency-aware 3-D CNN with LSTM for video action recognition. IEEE Signal Process. Lett. **24**, 510–514 (2017)
5. Park, S., Jeong, Y., Kim, H.S.: Multiresolution CNN for reverberant speech recognition. In: 2017 20th Conference of the Oriental Chapter of the International Coordinating Committee on Speech Databases and Speech I/O Systems and Assessment (O-COCOSDA), pp. 1–4. IEEE (2017)
6. Mariani, J., et al.: Rediscovering 50 years of discoveries in speech and language processing: a survey. In: 2017 20th Conference of the Oriental Chapter of the International Coordinating Committee on Speech Databases and Speech I/O Systems and Assessment (O-COCOSDA), pp. 1–23. IEEE (2017)
7. Fogel, A.L., Kvedar, J.C.: Artificial intelligence powers digital medicine. NPJ Digit. Med. **1**, 5 (2018)
8. Boureau, Y.-L., Sokol-Hessner, P., Daw, N.D.: Deciding how to decide: self-control and meta-decision making. Trends Cognit. Sci. **19**, 700–710 (2015)
9. Lee, C.M., Narayanan, S.S.: Toward detecting emotions in spoken dialogs. IEEE Trans. Speech Audio Process. **13**, 293–303 (2005)
10. Black, M.M., et al.: Early childhood development coming of age: science through the life course. Lancet **389**, 77–90 (2017)
11. Denham, S.A.: Social cognition, prosocial behavior, and emotion in preschoolers: contextual validation. Child Dev. **57**, 194–201 (1986)
12. Denham, S.A., McKinley, M., Couchoud, E.A., Holt, R.: Emotional and behavioral predictors of preschool peer ratings. Child Dev. **61**, 1145–1152 (1990)
13. Goleman, D.P.: Emotional Intelligence: Why It Can Matter More Than IQ for Character, Health and Lifelong Achievement. Bantam Books, New York (1995)
14. Harris, P.L., Johnson, C.N., Hutton, D., Andrews, G., Cooke, T.: Young children's theory of mind and emotion. Cogn. Emot. **3**, 379–400 (1989)
15. Piaget, J.: Part I: cognitive development in children: piaget development and learning. J. Res. Sci. Teach. **2**, 176–186 (1964)
16. Dupont, H.: Emotional Development, Theory and Applications: A Neo-piagetian Perspective. Praeger Publishers, Westport (1994)
17. Dupont, H.: The emotional development of exceptional students. Focus Except. Child. **21**, 1–10 (1989)
18. Salovey, P., Mayer, J.D.: Emotional intelligence. Imagination Cognit. Pers. **9**, 185–211 (1990)

19. Salevoy, P., Sluyter, D.J.: Emotional Development and Emotional Intelligence. Basicbooks, New York (1997)
20. https://beyondverbal.com
21. http://emodb.bilderbar.info/docu/#home
22. http://www.sampo.com.tw/pdetail.aspx?pd=746
23. Durlak, J.A., Weissberg, R.P., Dymnicki, A.B., Taylor, R.D., Schellinger, K.B.: The impact of enhancing students' social and emotional learning: a meta-analysis of school-based universal interventions. Child Dev. **82**, 405–432 (2011)
24. Scherer, K.R.: The dynamic architecture of emotion: evidence for the component process model. Cogn. Emot. **23**, 1307–1351 (2009)
25. Joshi, D., et al.: Aesthetics and emotions in images. IEEE Signal Process. Mag. **28**, 94–115 (2011)
26. MacIntyre, P., Gregersen, T.: Emotions that facilitate language learning: the positive-broadening power of the imagination (2012)
27. Jin, X., Gallagher, A., Cao, L., Luo, J., Han, J.: The wisdom of social multimedia: using flickr for prediction and forecast. In: Proceedings of the 18th ACM International Conference on Multimedia, pp. 1235–1244. ACM (2010)
28. Yuan, J., Mcdonough, S., You, Q., Luo, J.: Sentribute: image sentiment analysis from a mid-level perspective. In: Proceedings of the Second International Workshop on Issues of Sentiment Discovery and Opinion Mining, p. 10. ACM (2010)

Recommender Systems for an Enhanced Mobile e-Learning

Oswaldo Vélez-Langs[✉] and Isaac Caicedo-Castro

Universidad de Córdoba, Córdoba, Colombia
{oswaldovelez,isacaic}@correo.unicordoba.edu.co

Abstract. In the last years we have been witnesses of the increasing use of on-line educational systems known as e-learning. Every year there are more teaching centers, both public and private ones, which provide their students with web-based access to Learning Management Systems (LMS). Also, it is important to mention platforms for Massive Open On-line Courses (MOOC) which are a type of on-line educational system recently developed according to the design and participation akin to the presential courses at most prestigious universities. These systems provide to all kind of students with didactic resources as well as activities. In another hand the Adaptive and Intelligence Web-based Educational Systems (AIWBES) are made in order to solve the problem of to automate the adaptation of the system to the user features and needs. One more recent alternative is implementing Recommender Systems, which might offer their users customized suggestions to find activities and educational content. Such systems filter user information, for instance, preferences known by a user community for forecasting preferences for the new user, this approach is known as collaborative Filtering. With this proposal we are trying to model and represent the domain knowledge about the learner and learning resources discovering the learners' learning patterns.

Keywords: Recommender Systems · e-Learning · Mobile computing

1 Introduction

One of the problems that exists around the use of Learning Management Systems is that it is necessary to personalize them. This type of problem requires a restructuring of how the teacher has designed the subject, and access to the tools, to support the subject in order of to know which design is better adapted to the characteristics and interests of the learners/students. Then is necessary to ask: How can the use of Learning Management Systems is improved to make them easier to use and learn? How can this interaction is made more effective and satisfactory?

This work has been funded by Universidad de Córdoba (Colombia).

C. Stephanidis (Ed.): HCII 2019, LNCS 11786, pp. 357–365, 2019.
https://doi.org/10.1007/978-3-030-30033-3_28

This paper reflects the ongoing endeavor toward response, in some way, the prior questions. Our approach involves five steps: (1) creating knowledge representation about the learner and learning resources, (2) computing user's similarity based on the frequent pattern mining of learner's actions, (3) generating the recommendation through association rules, and (4) displaying the recommendations into a mobile application taking in account the research challenges (mobile technology).

The remainder article is outlined as follows: in Sect. 2 we discuss the literature review about the application of Recommender Systems in the e-learning context. In Sect. 3 we present the contribution of our work. Finally, Sect. 4 concludes the article and presents our ongoing work.

2   Related Work

In e-learning, Recommender Systems (RS) assist users or learners to discover worthy learning objects which fulfill their needs. To this end, RS aim at providing users with no obvious suggestions about learning objects which, hopefully, might help them to understand the topic of interest. The main recommendation approaches are as follows (Burke 2007; Ricci et al. 2010): (1) content-based RS, (2) collaborative filtering, (3) demographic, (4) knowledge-based RS, (5) community-based RS, and (6) hybrid RS. From previous techniques, the most common adopted in the e-learning domain are content-based RS, collaborative filtering, knowledge-based RS, and hybrid techniques.

In *Content-based RS*, both the history of users taste and content features are used to compute the recommendation to the active user. In the e-learning context, the content is composed of a learning objects collection, each one with its features.

Systems based on *collaborative filtering* suggest to the active user the content which has been preferred to other similar users in the past. In the original approach, the content is not taken into account to compute recommendations (Schafer et al. 2007), whereas matrix factorization has been adopted to infer latent factors which describe the content and the history of users preferences as well (Koren et al. 2009). When the system starts working, most of the users' preferences are unknown, therefore either content-based RS or collaborative filtering based RS tend to fail at suggesting content, this is known as the *cold-start problem*.

On the other hand, *knowledge-based* RS tend to overcome the cold-start problem because recommendations are computed according to specific domain knowledge, and how content features match users' needs and preferences. The knowledge may be represented and encoded either as constraints or cases. The drawback of knowledge-based systems is these RS lack learning components, so knowledge-based systems might be outperformed by other approaches (e.g., collaborative filtering), e.g., where RS use logs of the interaction between users and computers, thus, knowledge-based RS cannot adapt to changes in the domain, such as users who have improved their skills and need new content.

In order to tackle the cold-start and adaptation problem, RS are designed with a combination of several techniques (e.g., collaborative filtering and knowledge based-RS), this kind of systems is named hybrid RS. In the e-learning context, the resulting endeavor has produced hybrid RS. Besides, the e-learning domain poses specific challenges such as learning style (e.g., auditory, kinaesthetic, reader, competency, and visual), both users' preferences and skills are always changing.

In prior research, some hybrid RS for the e-learning domain are based on collaborative approaches besides other ones. Collaborative filtering is combined with other methods such as:

1. Web log mining approach, where the occurrence order between learning objects is used for mining sequential patterns (Li et al. 2011).
2. Modeling attributes of learning objects in a recommendation framework (Salehi and Kmalabadi 2012).
3. Knowledge and content-based approaches, where content features are obtained from the metadata of learning objects, while the knowledge is gathered from users' profile, personal information, interactivity, level, language, preference, learning style, and usage history (Palanca et al. 2018). In another approach, the knowledge is modeled as an ontology, so ratings are predicted for the active user based on the ontology, then collaborative filtering is applied for recommending the top k learning objects, furthermore, the resulting suggestion is computed through a sequential pattern algorithm (Tarus et al. 2017).
4. Collaborative tagging for creating a set of tags, known as folksonomies, which describe learning objects (Klasnja-Milicevic et al. 2018).

Moreover, in the e-learning domain, other research approaches combine content-based with other techniques as follows:

1. Self-organization of the content (i.e., learning objects). Every object is simulated as a smart agent, where these agents interact with one another aiming to improve the adaptability and diversity of the content-based recommendations (Wan and Niu 2018).
2. Personalizing the learning process by matching the compatibility level of the content to the user's learning style as well as the content complexity level and the user's knowledge level. With this approach, researchers aimed at improving the users' performance during evaluations and their satisfaction as well (Christudas et al. 2018).

Besides the above-mentioned kinds of recommendation approaches, data mining algorithms such as K-means and Apriori association rules have also been adopted for designing RS in the e-learning context (Aher and Lobo 2012). Moreover, information retrieval has been combined with knowledge-based systems for suggesting and guiding users in the e-learning environment (Gulzar et al. 2018). Related to user model for recommendations, the research of Chung et al. (2007) has the objective of to propose a framework for recommender systems applications with a focus on supporting personal decision making. The system named VCR - virtual community recommender - Lee et al. (2007) recommends optimal virtual communities for an active user by case-based reasoning (CBR) using behavioral factors suggested in the technology acceptance model (TAM) and its extended models. In addition, it refines its recommendation results by considering the user's needs type at the point of usage. The study of Weng and Chang (2008) utilizes ontology to construct user profiles and makes use of user profile ontology as the basis to reason about the interests of users. Furthermore, this study takes advantage of the spreading activation model to search for other influential users in the community network environment, making a study on their interests in order to provide recommendation on related information The paper of de Gemmis et al. (2010) provides a general (and interesting) overview of the approaches to learning preference models in the context of recommender systems. The work of Polydoropoulou and Lambrou (2012), presents an innovative methodology for the development of a training advisor for e-learning environments. We consider e-learning personalization issues and present an e-learning recommender framework based on discrete choice models and Bayesian theory.

In the context of e-Learning, we can cite some works that adopt recommender systems for personalization of pedagogical content. The work of Baloian et al. (2004) proposes a methodology for characterizing multimedia learning material based on the use of collaborative techniques in order to define a vector of characteristics for a certain document. This vector will reflect the opinion the people who have seen this document before and will evolve as new people express their opinion about the document. Drachsler et al. (2010) is a hybrid recommender system, so-called ReMashe, that takes advantage of the tag and rating data of the combined Web 2.0 sources. The users of ReMashed are able to rate the emerging data of all users in the system. Bobadilla et al. (2009) observed that learners' prior knowledge have a considerable effect on recommendation quality, for this reason he suggested to students a set of tests and introduced the results in recommendation calculation. Durao and Dolog (2010) used similarity between tags defined by learners to provide personalized recommendations. Anjorin et al. (2011) designed a conceptual architecture of a personalized recommender system considering the CROKODIL e-Learning scenario and incorporating collaborative semantic tagging to rank e-Learning resources. A hybrid architecture that combines enhanced case-based recommending with (collaborative) feedback from users to recommend open courseware and educational resources presented in Vladoiu et al. (2013).

Lichtnow et al. (2011) created an approach for collaborative recommendation of learning materials to students in an e-Learning environment considering learning materials properties, students' profile and the context. Addressing more user/learner-centric Technology-Enhanced Learning streams, recommendations seem to be a powerful tool for this solution (Mödritscher 2010). In accordance with Benhamdi et al. (2017): "Personal Learning Environments, information are filtered based on significant context limits thanks to personalized recommendations (Anandakumar et al. 2014; Salehi et al. 2014; Wilson et al. 2007), giving learners the opportunity to take the best of an environment where shared content differed in quality, target audience, subject matter, and is constantly expanded, annotated, and repurposed (Downes 2010)".

Among the above-mentioned approaches, so far there is not enough information to determine which one provides users with the best recommendations. This is because either some of these approaches have been evaluated through user-driven tests with different experimental settings, or no evaluation has been conducted over the other approaches in the state-of-the-art. Besides, in mentioned prior research, authors have not published a public data set to evaluate their contributions in an off-line fashion and reproduce their results. As a consequence, set up an off-line test for comparing all previous approaches is not possible. Furthermore, traditional performance metrics (e.g., precision, recall, F1, etc.) used to evaluate RS do not measure to which extent the RS contribute at improving the users' experience to learn new knowledge or acquire abilities through e-learning environments. For instance, a particular learning object about the multi-layer Perceptron topic might be liked by the user, but it does not mean that the object actually helps the user to understand how the multi-layer Perceptron works.

3 Recommendation Approach

The adopted approach is carried out in two steps as follows:

1. Creating the user neighborhood by mining the use log (see Fig. 1).
2. Computing the recommendation by finding rules which explain how users' actions are associated with one another in the active user neighborhood.

With neighborhood creation we aim at mining use logs to determine aspects such as personalizing the application to a group of users or a single one, regarding

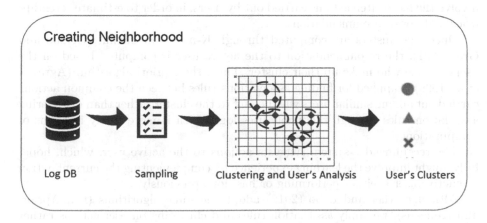

Fig. 1. Steps for computing recommendations

the analysis of advantages and drawbacks, which allows easier and friendlier access to the portal tools.

For use mining and users profile analysis, there are available various candidate techniques, e.g., association rules, sequence patterns and classification, statistics analysis, and clustering. A wider explanation about these techniques is provided as follows:

- Given a database, the association rules technique find causality-based relations between items through conditional probabilities (Agrawal et al. 1996). For instance, an association rule of the form $a \implies b$ means the antecedent a implies the consequent b. In the e-learning context, the item a might be an action such as downloading a content, which implies the item b, that might be the action of solving an exam.
- In sequence patterns, the goal is finding patterns in a set of items, where items are related to each other, according to their chronological order (Han et al. 2007).
- Statistics analysis involve both descriptive techniques (i.e., mean, mode, variance, standard deviation, etc.) and statistical inference (i.e., regression).
- By clustering items, we aim at finding those users who follow similar behavior pattern when they access the system. K-means is a representative clustering technique (Gersho and Gray 1991).

In our context, at Universidad de Córdoba there is a server-based e-learning platform named Campus Virtual, which is a customized version of Moddle. Campus Virtual stores actions carried out by the users in a log. So far, students have no been classified by an expert in the domain, therefore, we adopt clustering of students, with data of access and use frequency (e.g., Quiz view, course view, resource view, etc.). The clustering is performed by taking into account similar actions carried out among students during their learning process.

Currently, the student database and the Campus Virtual data, in particular, the uses logs, are the data sources to model user profiles and features which involve the more often actions carried out by users, in order to estimate serendipitous and novel recommendations.

Once the clusters are computed through K-means algorithm (Gersho and Gray 1991), the recommendation to the active user is computed based on the users' profile who make up their cluster. Thus, the Apriori algorithm (Agrawal et al. 1996) is applied for finding associations rules between the common actions carried out among similar users who belong to the cluster rather than discovering association rules through the whole uses log, which is more costly in terms of computation.

The recommender system suggests actions to the active user, which, hopefully, might improve the learning experience by complementing the current action the active user is either performing or has done previously.

Although Aher and Lobo (2012) adopt the same algorithms (i.e., Apriori and K-means), we apply association rules and clustering on user actions rather than user ratings which represent user tastes. We assume the rating might not represent to what extent the content actually helps the user.

Furthermore, through this approach we avoid dealing with missing values which is a common issue in both collaborative filtering and content-based recommendation, and the one proposed by Aher and Lobo (2012).

4   Conclusions and Ongoing Work

In this work we propose a hybrid recommendation approach based on K-mean and Apriori algorithm to be implemented in the e-learning platform known as Campus Virtual at Universidad de Córdoba. To this end, we have taken into account the problem that e-Learning environments consider that all learners are similar in their preferences and abilities, hence, we have proposed the integration of personalizing tools, focusing on the integration of new recommendation approach in learning scenarios.

By integrating the recommender system into the e-learning platform, our goal is enhancing the personalizing procedure and improving learning quality, while students attain the control of their learning process across different tools and services.

So far we are implementing the recommender systems and setting the evaluation environment to conduct user-driven tests in our approach. Moreover, we will compare its effectiveness to other well-known approaches such as content-based systems and collaborative filtering, the main goal of these experiments is to evaluate the impact of learner's properties on the quality of recommendations and learning processes.

Finally, there are other challenges to be considered for further work, for instance, customizing the content according to the mobile features, and active user skills. The other challenge is providing users with suggestion according to their changing needs and tastes.

References

Agrawal, R., Mannila, H., Srikant, R., Toivonen, H., Verkamo, A.I.: Advances in Knowledge Discovery and Data Mining. In: Fayyad, U.M., Piatetsky-Shapiro, G., Smyth, P., Uthurusamy, R. (eds.) American Association for Artificial Intelligence, Menlo Park, CA, USA, pp. 307–328 (1996)

Aher, S.B., Lobo, L.: Applicability of data mining algorithms for recommendation system in e-learning. In Proceedings of the International Conference on Advances in Computing, Communications and Informatics, pp. 1034–1040. ACM, New York, NY, USA (2012)

Anandakumar, D.K., Rathipriya, K., Bharathi, D.: A survey on methodologies for personalized e-learning recommender systems. Int. J. Innov. Res. Comput. Commun. Eng. 2, 4738–4743 (2014)

Anjorin, M., Rensing, C., Steinmetz, R.: Towards ranking in folksonomies for personalized recommender systems in e-learning. In: Proceedings of the Second International Conference on Semantic Personalized Information Management: Retrieval and Recommendation - volume 781, Aachen, Germany, pp. 22–25. CEUR-WS.org (2011)

Baloian, N., Galdames, P., Collazos, C.A., Guerrero, L.A.: A model for a collaborative recommender system for multimedia learning material. In: de Vreede, G.-J., Guerrero, L.A., Marín Raventós, G. (eds.) CRIWG 2004. LNCS, vol. 3198, pp. 281–288. Springer, Heidelberg (2004). https://doi.org/10.1007/978-3-540-30112-7_24

Benhamdi, S., Babouri, A., Chiky, R.: Personalized recommender system for e-learning environment. Educ. Inf. Technol. **22**(4), 1455–1477 (2017)

Bobadilla, J., Serradilla, F., Hernando, A.: Collaborative filtering adapted to recommender systems of e-learning. Knowl.-Based Syst. **22**(4), 261–265 (2009)

Burke, R., et al.: The Adaptive Web. In: Brusilovsky, P., Kobsa, A., Nejdl, W. (eds.) pp. 377–408. Springer, Heidelberg (2007). https://doi.org/10.1007/978-3-540-72079-9

Christudas, B.C.L., Kirubakaran, E., Thangaiah, P.R.J.: An evolutionary approach for personalization of content delivery in e-learning systems based on learner behavior forcing compatibility of learning materials. Telematics Inform. **35**(3), 520–533 (2018)

Chung, R., Sundaram, D., Srinivasan, A.: Integrated personal recommender systems. In: Proceedings of the Ninth International Conference on Electronic Commerce, pp. 65–74. ACM, New York, NY, USA (2007)

de Gemmis, M., Iaquinta, L., Lops, P., Musto, C., Narducci, F., Semeraro, G.: Learning preference models in recommender systems. In: Fürnkranz, J., Hüllermeier, E. (eds.) Preference Learning, pp. 387–407. Springer, Heidelberg (2010). https://doi.org/10.1007/978-3-642-14125-6_18

Downes, S.: New technology supporting informal learning. J. Emerging Technol. Web Intell. **2**(1), 27–33 (2010)

Drachsler, H., et al.: ReMashed - an usability study of a recommender system for mash-ups for learning. Int. J. Eng. Technol. **5**(S1), 7–11 (2010)

Durao, F., Dolog, P.: Extending a hybrid tag-based recommender system with personalization. In: Proceedings of the 2010 ACM Symposium on Applied Computing, pp. 1723–1727. ACM, New York, NY, USA (2010)

Gersho, A., Gray, R.M.: Vector Quantization and Signal Compression. Kluwer Academic Publishers, Norwell (1991)

Gulzar, Z., Leema, A.A., Deepak, G.: PCRS: personalized course recommender system based on hybrid approach. Procedia Comput. Sci. **125**, 518–524 (2018). (The 6th International Conference on Smart Computing and Communications)

Han, J., Cheng, H., Xin, D., Yan, X.: Frequent pattern mining: current status and future directions. Data Min. Knowl. Disc. **15**(1), 55–86 (2007)

Klasnja-Milicevic, A., Ivanovic, M., Vesin, B., Budimac, Z.: Enhancing e-learning systems with personalized recommendation based on collaborative tagging techniques. Appl. Intell. **48**(6), 1519–1535 (2018)

Koren, Y., Bell, R., Volinsky, C.: Matrix factorization techniques for recommender systems. Computer **42**(8), 30–37 (2009)

Lee, H.-Y., Ahn, H., Han, I.: VCR: virtual community recommender using the technology acceptance model and the user's needs type. Expert Syst. Appl. **33**(4), 984–995 (2007)

Li, Y., Niu, Z., Chen, W., Zhang, W.: Combining collaborative filtering and sequential pattern mining for recommendation in e-learning environment. In: Leung, H., Popescu, E., Cao, Y., Lau, R.W.H., Nejdl, W. (eds.) ICWL 2011. LNCS, vol. 7048, pp. 305–313. Springer, Heidelberg (2011). https://doi.org/10.1007/978-3-642-25813-8_33

Lichtnow, D., Gasparini, I., Bouzeghoub, A., de Oliveira, J.P.M., Pimenta, M.S.: Recommendation of learning material through students' collaboration and user modeling in an adaptive e-learning environment. In: Daradoumis, T., Caballé, S., Juan, A.A., Xhafa, F. (eds.) Technology-Enhanced Systems and Tools for Collaborative Learning Scaffolding. Studies in Computational Intelligence, vol. 350, pp. 257–278. Springer, Heidelberg (2011). https://doi.org/10.1007/978-3-642-19814-4_12

Mödritscher, F.: Towards a recommender strategy for personal learning environments. Procedia Comput. Sci. 1(2), 2775–2782 (2010). (Proceedings of the 1st Workshop on Recommender Systems for Technology Enhanced Learning (RecSysTEL 2010))

Palanca, J., Heras, S., Rodríguez Marín, P., Duque, N., Julián, V.: An argumentation-based conversational recommender system for recommending learning objects. In: Proceedings of the 17th International Conference on Autonomous Agents and MultiAgent Systems, International Foundation for Autonomous Agents and Multiagent Systems, Richland, SC, pp. 2037–2039 (2018)

Polydoropoulou, A., Lambrou, M.A.: Development of an e-learning recommender system using discrete choice models and Bayesian theory: a pilot case in the shipping industry. In: Kalloniatis, C. (ed.) Security Enhanced Applications for Information Systems (chap. 3). IntechOpen, Rijeka (2012)

Ricci, F., Rokach, L., Shapira, B., Kantor, P.B.: Recommender Systems Handbook, 1st edn. Springer, Heidelberg (2010). https://doi.org/10.1007/978-0-387-85820-3

Salehi, M., Kmalabadi, N.: A Hybrid Attribute-based Recommender System for E-learning Material Recommendation. IERI Procedia 2, 565–570 (2012). (International Conference on Future Computer Supported Education, August 22–23, 2012, Fraser Place Central - Seoul)

Salehi, M., Nakhai Kamalabadi, I., Ghaznavi Ghoushchi, M.B.: personalized recommendation of learning material using sequential pattern mining and attribute based collaborative filtering. Educ. Inf. Technol. 19(4), 713–735 (2014)

Schafer, J.B., Frankowski, D., Herlocker, J., Sen, S.: The adaptive web. In: Brusilovsky, P., Kobsa, A., Nejdl, W. (eds.) pp. 291–324. Springer, Heidelberg (2007)

Tarus, J.K., Niu, Z., Yousif, A.: A hybrid knowledge-based recommender system for e-learning based on ontology and sequential pattern mining. Future Gener. Comput. Syst. 72, 37–48 (2017)

Vladoiu, M., Constantinescu, Z., Moise, G.: QORECT – a case-based framework for quality-based recommending open courseware and open educational resources. In: Bădică, C., Nguyen, N.T., Brezovan, M. (eds.) ICCCI 2013. LNCS (LNAI), vol. 8083, pp. 681–690. Springer, Heidelberg (2013). https://doi.org/10.1007/978-3-642-40495-5_68

Wan, S., Niu, Z.: An e-learning recommendation approach based on the self-organization of learning resource. Knowl.-Based Syst. 160, 71–87 (2018)

Weng, S.-S., Chang, H.-L.: Using ontology network analysis for research document recommendation. Expert Syst. Appl. 34(3), 1857–1869 (2008)

Wilson, S., Liber, O., Johnson, M., Beauvoir, P., Sharples, P., Milligan, C.: Personal learning environments: challenging the dominant design of educational systems. J. e-Learn. Knowl. Soc. 3(2), 27–38 (2007)

Human and Task Models in HCI

Using CFD Technology to Simulate a Model of Human Thermoregulation in the Stable Temperature Environment

Sina Dang[1], Hongjun Xue[1(✉)], Xiaoyan Zhang[1,2,3], Jue Qu[1], Chengwen Zhong[1], and Siyu Chen[1]

[1] School of Aeronautics, Northwestern Polytechnical University, Xi'an, China
dsnsw123@126.com, {xuehj,zhongcw}@nwpu.edu.cn,
qujue402@sina.com, zxyliuyan@163.com,
szll0000.csy@163.com
[2] Institute of Human Factors and Ergonomics, Shenzhen University,
Shenzhen, China
[3] Key Laboratory of Optoelectronic Devices and Systems
of Ministry of Education and Guangdong Province,
Shenzhen University, Shenzhen, China

Abstract. A coupling system was developed in the present study to simulate the heat transfer and physiological responses of the unclothed human body in hot and cold environments. This system included a computational thermal manikin controlled by a multi-node thermal model, which could dynamically respond to the environmental conditions. The computational thermal manikin was employed to determine the heat transfer between the human body and ambient environment as well as heat transfer coefficients at each body segment. The CFD simulation was then coupled with a multi-node thermal model to predict the heat transfer and human physiological responses in real time. The performance of coupling system was examined by comparing the simulated skin temperatures with the published measurements from human trials in hot and cold environments. The coupling system reasonably predicted the skin temperatures at local body segments with the maximum discrepancies between the observed values and simulated ones no more than 1.0 °C.

Keywords: Heat transfer · CFD simulation · Environment conditions · Response

1 Introduction

Over the past few decades, many computational thermal manikins ranging from a rectangle to multi-zone have been constructed to resemble the human body. CFD simulation [1] has become a useful tool to calculate heat flux between the human body and ambient environment and heat transfer coefficients using these computational thermal manikins in virtual environments [2]. However, the computational manikin did not contain a thermoregulation system and could not respond to the environment as human beings. Meanwhile, a large number of thermal models [3] have been developed to simulate human thermal responses under transient environments. It is therefore

© Springer Nature Switzerland AG 2019
C. Stephanidis (Ed.): HCII 2019, LNCS 11786, pp. 369–381, 2019.
https://doi.org/10.1007/978-3-030-30033-3_29

necessary to combine the CFD program with the thermal models to better understand the heat transfer and thermal physiological responses [4].

In this study, the three-dimensional model was developed, based on the Fiala's [5] model. It can predict physiological response for stable temperature environments, with taking into consideration of the effects on the pulsatile laminar flow, the peripheral resistance, the thermal effect of food and the composition of viscera [6]. Using the CFD technology to simulate the whole-body 3D human thermoregulation model. This model makes use of the finite volume method to discretize the heat conduction of the differential equation concerning the human body, calculates the distribution of blood flow velocity, pressure and temperature by means of a one-dimensional N-S equation [7], and finally solves numerical values with the CFD method and obtains the change curve of the human body's temperatures with time.

2   CFD Simulation

2.1   Use CFD to Build the Body's Geometric Model and Vascular Geometry Model

A geometric model of human body is established in this paper. This paper select the basic size of human body with height of 174.9 cm, body weight of 66.3 kg and surface area of 1.86 m^2. The i (1–18) shows the human body. The human body is divided into the head, the front 1/2 and the back 1/2 of the head, the neck, the front 2/5 of the trunk, the middle 1/5 and the back 2/5, the upper arm, the lower arm, the hands and thighs, the calves and feet. A total of 18 segments. The k (1–5) is used to represent the layers of human body, which is divided into visceral layer, skeletal layer, muscular layer, fat layer, skin, j (1–7) to represent human visceral organs such as brain, lung, heart, liver, stomach, large intestine, small intestine etc. The specific geometric data of each layer is shown in Table 1 [8]. In order to reduce the difficulty of simulation, the viscera is simplified the regular graphics with CFD. The geometric size of the human body and the geometric size of the blood vessels are modeled through ANSYS 19.0.

Take 1, 2 as a whole, as the heart output. It's length 6 cm, radius 1.285 cm, thickness of blood vessel wall 0.147 cm. Take 3–9 as a whole, as the trunk aorta, length 35.4 cm, radius from 1 cm–0.57 cm uniform change of conical blood vessels, blood vessel wall also changes from 0.12 cm–0.08 cm. Take 10–13 as one, with a length of 32.9 cm, a radius of 0.57–0.24 cm, and a blood vessel wall of 0.08–0.05 cm. Take 14–19 as one, with a length of 65.8 cm, a radius of 0.24–0.13 cm, and a blood vessel wall of 0.05–0.019 cm. Take 20–29 as one, with length 63.5 cm, radius 0.4–0.19 cm, vascular wall 0.062–0.046 cm. 30–35 is the head artery, the length is 39.5 cm, the radius is 0.37–0.06 cm, and the blood vessel wall is 0.063–0.02 cm. The simplified geometric model is shown in the Fig. 1.

Table 1. Human modeling geometric data.

i	Segment	L(cm)	Major semiaxis / Semi-minor axis					Sketch Map
			core	bone	muscle	fat	skin	
1	Head	11.05	17.92/16.59	18.62/17.06	22.62/21.06	23.02/21.46	23.4/21.84	
2	face	11.05	-	18.62/17.06	22.62/21.06	23.02/21.46	23.4/21.84	
3	neck	11.9	-	1.4/1.43	4.01/4.04	4.37/4.39	4.69/4.72	
4	chest	20.87	20.1/13.46	28.17/21.53	29.58/22.95	31.97/25.33	32.46/25.8	
5	Abdomen	10.43	28.17/21.53	10.5/4.035	29.58/22.95	31.97/25.33	32.46/25.8	
6	Waist	20.87	28.17/21.53	10.5/4.035	29.58/22.95	31.97/25.33	32.46/25.8	
7	L- upper arm	30.77	-	5.3/4.9	10.2/9.8	11.1/10.7	11.57/11.2	
8	R- upper arm	30.77	-	5.3/4.9	10.2/9.8	11.1/10.7	11.57/11.2	
9	L- lower arm	22.61	-	5.31/4.18	9.77/8.65	10.59/9.47	11.0/9.9	
10	R- lower arm	22.61	-	5.31/4.18	9.77/8.65	10.59/9.47	11.0/9.9	
11	L-hand	17	-	6.44/1.84	6.98/2.38	7.81/3.22	8.8/4.2	
12	R-hand	17	-	6.44/1.84	6.98/2.38	7.81/3.22	8.8/4.2	
13	L-thigh	42.67	-	6.74/7.14	14.95/15.36	16/16.4	16.63/17	
14	R-thigh	42.67	-	6.74/7.14	14.95/15.36	16/16.4	16.63/17	
15	L-leg	35.57	-	6.75/6.91	12.56/12.72	13.47/13.63	13.96/14.1	
16	R-leg	35.57	-	6.75/6.91	12.56/12.72	13.47/13.63	13.96/14.1	
17	L-foot	23.8	-	1.81/1.2	2.69/2.09	4.14/3.54	5.37/4.77	
18	R-foot	23.8	-	1.81/1.2	2.69/2.09	4.14/3.54	5.37/4.77	

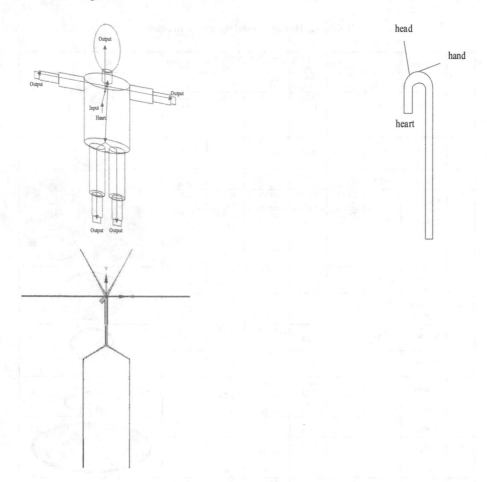

Fig. 1. The geometric size of the blood vessels.

2.2   Computational Grid

Grid division based on the established geometric model of human body and vascular model It was difficult to resolve the complex geometry of the numerical manikin by a structured grid [9]. The unstructured grids were used for the body and the blood models. The human geometric model and the grid division of blood vessels are shown in the figure. The human geometry model contains 2400580 cells and 8569224 nodes, and the vascular models contains 52368 cells and 50175 nodes.

The commercial CFD software ANSYS was used to simulate the heat transfer between the human body and environment. In addition to using ANSYS to solve the equations, the mathematical simulation of the human thermal regulation model also needs to use UDF to compile the equations proposed in this paper.

2.3 Coupling the CFD Simulation with the Thermal Model

Before calculating the change of human temperature over time, the initial human temperature must be given. The core temperature of the human body can be measured by a thermometer, and the skin temperature can also be measured by a skin temperature meter. But the internal initial temperature is uncertain. Therefore, the initial temperature value of each node of the human body in this paper is given as fellows. The body is first considered as a steady state, no internal heat source object, and the internal core layer boundary and skin surface temperature are calculated to obtain a specific initial temperature. The process of calculating the initial temperature using CFD is as Fig. 2.

After calculating the initial temperature, setting the time step, this paper takes the time step length to 0.1 s. The temperature of the outlet section of the heart is used as the output value of the blood vessel temperature. Given the pulsating pressure and velocity curve, the distribution of blood vessel temperature is solved by using the N-S equation. Exporting the vascular boundary temperature at each point of the blood vessels mentioned above, the perfusion temperature is calculated by using the formula, and the perfusion temperature is assigned to the heat source in the heat transfer of human tissues, so that the human heat transfer under unsteady state can be calculated.

The heat source items of human heat transfer include blood perfusion heat production and metabolic heat production. This makes the human body's heat transfer become a heat transfer problem that contains an internal heat source under unsteady state. Heat transfer problems with internal heat sources. On the surface of the human skin, heat exchange with the outside world through respiration, evaporation, radiation, convection, and heat transfer can be regarded as the second and third types of boundary conditions, so the temperature distribution at the next moment can be calculated.

The temperature of the heart output port at the next moment is assigned to the blood vessel input to calculate the perfusion temperature. The skin temperature and hypothalamus temperature at this moment are assigned to the thermal regulation system, and the formula is substituted with the temperature at the previous moment and the set-point temperature to calculate the vasoconstriction and relaxation, as well as the sweating and vibration coefficient. And these coefficients are assigned to the blood perfusion rate of the heat source term in the unsteady heat conduction differential equation and the conditions of the heat production term and the surrounding boundary conditions of the human body, as well as the perspiration term in evaporation heat dissipation. In order to carry out the next calculation. Define $T_{(ijk)n+1} = T_{(ijk)0}$. The flow chart of the human thermal regulation model is shown in Fig. 3.

374   S. Dang et al.

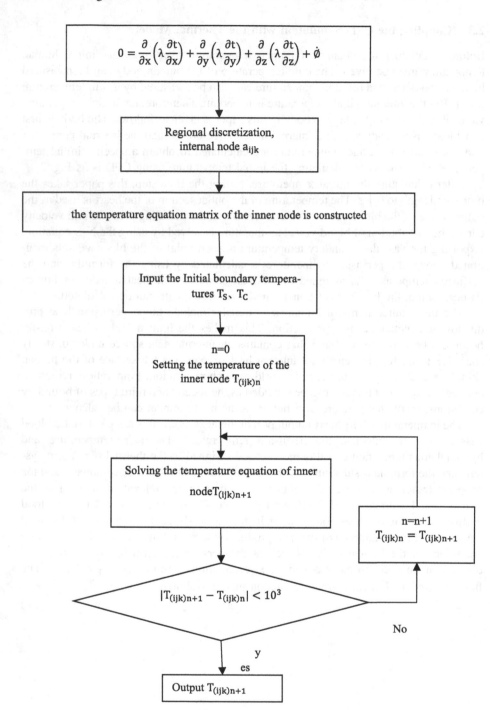

$$0 = \frac{\partial}{\partial x}\left(\lambda \frac{\partial t}{\partial x}\right) + \frac{\partial}{\partial y}\left(\lambda \frac{\partial t}{\partial y}\right) + \frac{\partial}{\partial z}\left(\lambda \frac{\partial t}{\partial z}\right) + \dot{\phi}$$

Regional discretization,
internal node a_{ijk}

the temperature equation matrix of the inner node is constructed

Input the Initial boundary temperatures T_S、T_C

n=0
Setting the temperature of the inner node $T_{(ijk)n}$

Solving the temperature equation of inner node $T_{(ijk)n+1}$

n=n+1
$T_{(ijk)n} = T_{(ijk)n+1}$

$|T_{(ijk)n+1} - T_{(ijk)n}| < 10^3$

No

yes

Output $T_{(ijk)n+1}$

Fig. 2. Initial temperature determination.

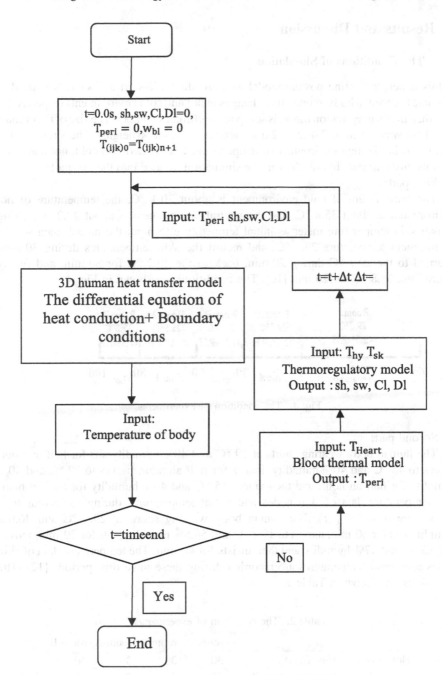

Fig. 3. Flow chart of the coupling thermal model.

3 Results and Discussion

3.1 The Conditions of Simulation

In this paper, the sitting posture model wearing shorts, T-shirt and sandals is used to simulate the human body temperature changes in hot and cold environments respectively. A human thermal regulation model is set up in the climate chamber. The size of the climate chambers was 3.5 m × 3.4 m × 2.0 m (length × width × height). The simulation is conducted in different environmental temperature. It's divided into cold, hot and comfortable environment. In this chapter, the simulation divided into the two parts.

First part:

The temperature of cold environment is about 20.1 °C, the temperature of hot environment is about 35.8 °C, and the neutral environment is about 29.2 °C. Using human skin temperature meter as initial temperature to input the model, then set the environment temperature 29.2 °C, and record the skin temperatures during 30 min, returned to the 20.1 °C during 20 min, back to the 29.2 °C for 30 min, and finally entered the 35.8 °C for 20 min [10]. The conditions are shown in Fig. 4.

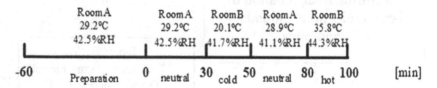

Fig. 4. The condition of experiments.

Second part:

The human body wearing shorts at 29 °C and 40% humidity sits for half an hour, moves to 45 °C and 40% humidity, insists for half an hour, moves to 29 °C and 40% humidity for half an hour, and then enters 45 °C and 40% humidity for half an hour. The temperature data of skin nodes and rectal temperatures during these four time periods are recorded [11]. The human body wearing shorts at 29.4 °C and 46.6% humidity sits for 30 min, moves to 19.1 °C and 54.8% humidity, sits for 20 min, moves to 29.3 °C and 47% humidity and then insists for 40 min. The temperature data of skin nodes and rectal temperatures are recorded during these three time periods [12]. The conditions are shown in Table 2.

Table 2. The condition of experiments.

		room-A	room-B	room-A	room-B
Hot weather	Time (min)	30	30	30	30
	Air temperature °C	29	45	29	45
	Globe temperature °C	29	45	29	45
	Relative humidity (%)	40	40	40	40
	Air velocity (m/s)	0.06	0.06	0.06	0.06
	Time (min)	30	20	40	

(*continued*)

Table 2. (*continued*)

		room-A	room-B	room-A	room-B
Cold weather	Air temperature °C	29.4	19.5	29.3	
	Globe temperature °C	29.5	20.4	29.4	
	Relative humidity (%)	46.8	52.8	47.1	
	Air velocity (m/s)	0.09	0.21	0.09	

These two parts are different. The first part describes a continuous process of entering the cold environment first from neutral environment, into neutral environment and into thermal environment, while the second part describes respectively that neutral environment enters into thermal environment and finally into thermal environment and neutral environment enters into cold environment and enters neutral environment. The process of environment. Regardless of how the experiment is carried out, only different ambient temperature, humidity and wind speed are input into the simulation model. Therefore, the following parameters are input in the simulation, as shown in Table 3. The external temperature envelope of the human body is displayed in CFD as shown in Fig. 5.

Table 3. The simulate temperatures through CFD.

Air temperature °C	19.5	20.1	28.9	29	29.2	29.4	35.8	45
Relative humidity %	52.8	41.7	41.1	40	42.5	46.8	44.3	45
Air velocity m/s	0.21	0.06	0.05	0.06	0.01	0.09	0.07	0.06

The performance of the coupling system was examined by comparing the predicted skin temperatures with the measured ones from experiments. The RMSD values of skin temperatures at the segments of head, trunk, arm, hand, thigh, calf, and foot were 0.452 °C, 0.715 °C, 0.459 °C, 0.635 °C, 0.58 °C, 0.711 °C, and 0.645 °C respectively. The maximum difference between predicted temperatures and measurements at body segments was no more than 1.0 °C. The error analysis diagram of each temperature condition is shown in Fig. 6.

This chapter includes two parts. The first part The author compares the simulation model with the experiment done by the research group. The other part simulation model is compared with the experiment done by others in the references. By comparing the two parts, it can be seen that the experimental error of cold environment is not more than 0.771 °C and the hot environment is not more than 0.851 °C. The simulation system built by this paper can simulate the temperature changes of human body very well.

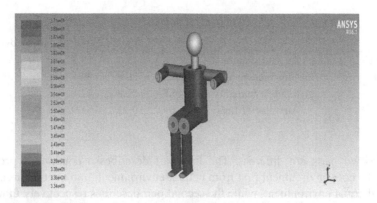

(a) Neutral environment

(b) Cold environment

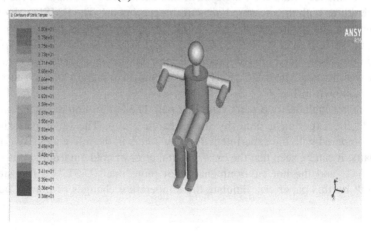

(c) Hot environment

Fig. 5. The conditions of simulation.

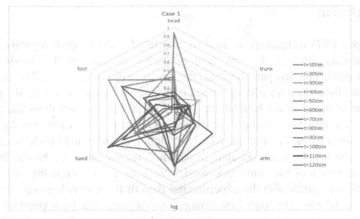

(a) Part 1 hot weather

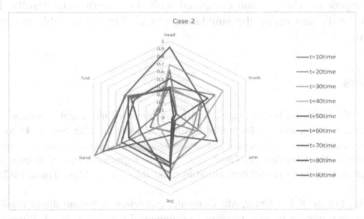

(b) Part 2 cold weather

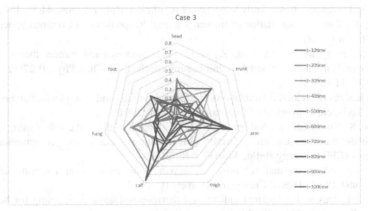

(c) Part 3 cold and hot weather

Fig. 6. Difference between the simulated skin temperatures by coupling system and those from human trials.

4   Conclusion

In this paper, CFD technology is used to simulate human thermal regulation system based on human pulsating flow and heat generation mechanism. The model is simulated in six parts. The first part simulates the structure of human body. The second part simulates the tissue heat transfer of human body. The third part simulates the perfusion temperature of blood in the heat source term. The fourth part simulates the boundary conditions. The fifth part simulates the regulation system. The sixth part is the coupling process between them. Finally, the visual simulation of the human body mathematical model is realized, which can simulate the thermal regulation of the human body very well. The accuracy of the simulation model are proved by comparing the results of other people's research with the experimental data of the research group.

However, whether the model established in this paper can be applied in the environment of instantaneous changes in the external environment is not yet validated. In the next work, the model parameters will be adjusted to adapt to the scene of instantaneous temperature change, and compared with the experimental results. The next work is to verify and revise the simulation model through unstable environmental experiments.

References

1. Jiang, Y.Y., Yanai, E., Nishimura, K., et al.: An integrated numerical simulator for thermal performance assessments of firefighters' protective clothing. Fire Saf. J. **45**(5), 314–326 (2010)
2. Al-Othmani, M., Ghaddar, N., Ghali, K.: A multi-segmented human bioheat model for transient and asymmetric radiative environments. Int. J. Heat Mass Trans. **51**(23), 22–33 (2008)
3. Fiala, D., Lomas, K.J., Stohrer, M.: Computer prediction of human thermoregulatory and temperature responses to wide range of environmental conditions. Int. J. Biometeorol. **45**, 143–159 (2001)
4. Takada, S., Kobayashi, H., Matsushita, T.: Thermal model of human body fitted with individual characteristics of body temperature regulation. Built Environ. **44**(3), 46–70 (2009)
5. Zhang, Y., Yang, T.: Simulation of Human Thermal Responses in a Confined Space. ISIAQ, Copenhagen (2008)
6. Sina, D., Hongjun, X., Xiaoyan, Z., et al.: Three-dimensional human thermoregulation model based on pulsatile blood flow and heating mechanism. Chin. Phys. B **27**(11), 114402-1–114402-11 (2018)
7. Voigt, L.K.: NaviereStokes simulations of airflow in rooms and around a human body. Ph.D. thesis. Technical University of Denmark, Denmark (2001)
8. Tanabe, S., Kobayashi, K., Nakano, J., et al.: Evaluation of thermal comfort using combined multi-node thermoregulation (65MN) and radiation models and computational fluid dynamics (CFD). Energy Build. **34**, 637–646 (2002)
9. Yang, Y.: Indoor thermal response of human body in uniform environment (Warm Conditions). Ph.D. Thesis. Chongqing University (2015)
10. George, H., Dusan, F.: Thermal indices and thermophysiological modeling for heat stress. Compr. Physiol. **6**, 255–320 (2016)

11. Munir, A.: Re-evaluation of Stolwijk's 25-node human thermal model under thermal-transient conditions: prediction of skin temperature in low-activity conditions. Build. Environ. **44**, 1777–1787 (2009)
12. Yang, J., Weng, W., Zhang, B.: Experimental and numerical study of physiological responses in hot environments. J. Thermal Biol. **45**, 54–61 (2014)

Interface Design for Boccia Robot Considering Operation Characteristic

Minzhi Deng[✉], Ruya Chen, Shun Song, Junjie He, Rintaro Onishi,
Rytaro Suzuki, Ryuta Motegi, Naoyuki Takesue, Shin Tsuchiya,
Yoshiki Shimomura, Nami Shida, Osamu Nitta,
and Keiko Kasamatsu

Tokyo Metropolitan University, 6-6 Asahigaoka, Hino, Tokyo, Japan
dengminzhi0717@yahoo.co.jp

Abstract. When designing a product, there are many possibilities of modeling construction. And it is influenced by tacit knowledge such as experiences of the designer and sense of aesthetics. Therefore, sometimes things made with the designer's design model do not conform to the user's mental model, so problems such as unknown usage, unsuited experience to use may occur.

Keywords: User experience · Human-centered · Product design · Design process

1 Introduction

As the process of user experience design becomes more sophisticated, various user survey analyzes to know users, and methods of design assessment have been proposed. However, using the results of user survey analysis, we think that it is necessary to examine the method at the stage of product modeling and construction. If you can use the results of previous user survey analysis successfully and you can think of shaping with consideration of the elements of the next design evaluation in advance, shorten the time required for the project and rely on the tacit knowledge of the designer. We believe that it will be possible to build a more user-friendly product. In this research, We aimed to submit a method of modeling construction that considers general operation usability characteristics without relying on the tacit knowledge of designers.

2 The Concept of Boccia Robot Project

2.1 What Is Boccia?

Boccia is an official event of the Paralympic Games, a sport for severely cerebral paralysis people born in Europe or those with severe extremely severe functional impairment. It is divided into two teams of red and blue, and they compete for how to throw 6 balls of red and blue each, ball, rolling or how to approach the white target ball called jackball.

If you are unable to throw a ball by yourself, use a ramp, a ramp, tell your will to the helper and push the ball with an aid such as a body part or a head pointer.

2.2 Introduction of Boccia Robot Project

Boccia Robot removes both disabled and classified according to the degree of disability in order to promote the health of people with disabilities and to improve the awareness of disabled people in sports. Everyone participates in the same game and together with the competition of Boccia It is a project to develop throwing device "Boccia Robot" (Fig. 1) by application of robot technology for the purpose of enabling enjoyment. In this research, we examine the method of modeling and construction over the design of the interface for operating the throwing device "Boccia Robot".

Fig. 1. Throwing device during trial production

3 Designing Process of Boccia Robot

3.1 Athlete Classification

In the international convention such as the Paralympic Games, depending on the degree of disability, the competitors are divided into 4 of BC 1 to BC 4 (BC is the abbreviation of Brain Cytoplasmic). It is divided into classes:

BC1 Players in this class throw the ball with the hand or foot. They may compete with an assistant who stays outside of the competitor's playing box, to stabilize or adjust their playing chair and give the ball to the player when requested.
BC2 Players in this class throw the ball with the hand. They are not eligible for assistance.
BC3 Players in this class have very severe locomotor dysfunction in all four extremities. Players in this class have no sustained grasp or release action and although they may have arm movement, they have insufficient range of movement

to propel a Boccia ball onto the court. They may use an assistive device such as a ramp to deliver the ball. They may compete with an assistant; assistants must keep their back to the court and their eyes averted from play.

BC4 Players in this class have severe locomotor dysfunction of all four extremities as well as poor trunk control. They can demonstrate sufficient dexterity to throw the ball onto the court. Players are not eligible for assistance.

3.2   Preliminary Survey Analysis

In order to recognize Boccia and gather information on the target person, we participated in the tour of Boccia other than collection of materials on the Internet and other media. The Faculty of Health and Welfare at Tokyo Metropolitan University Tokyo holds the "Boccia Classroom" at the gymnasium of the Arakawa Campus. After grasping basic information such as Boccia rules and flow of competition, behavior observation was carried out, and it summarized in "Thinking to throw" and "Throwing method". Then I set up a persona and analyzed it with an experience map (Fig. 2).

Fig. 2. Introduction of Boccia classroom and appearance of participation

In addition to the stage of the survey and analysis at the previous term, we went to the Boccia classroom as necessary to communicate with participants so that the design can fully consider the situation of people with disabilities in the whole design process.

Experience Map Analysis

The current Boccia Sports experience is good for participants, experiences are not good, especially in order to discover problems for people with disabilities, when observing Boccia classroom Based on six people who participated in the same game persona, And analyzed with an experience map (Fig. 3).

The experience was the most problematic for those who participate in Boccia, as a result of the experience map analysis, for those who throw balls with lamps who can not throw the balls themselves.

One is a matter of communication. For this type of person, ask the assistant to adjust the position and angle of the lamp. As a rule of the game, the assistant only needs to

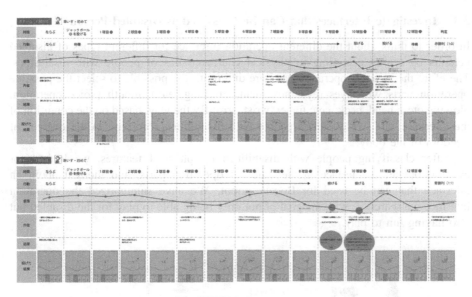

Fig. 3. Experience map

move in response to the instructions of the athlete, and keep turning his eyes off the game with his back on the coat. However, people with disabilities such as cerebral palsy often have difficulties in language function, and therefore often can not convey their intention well. There are two ways to throw (Figs. 4, 5):

Fig. 4. Method A: Rolling from the bottom   **Fig. 5.** Method B: Throw from the top

Method A is used when throwing to a distance or throwing near by force adjustment. Method B tends to stop at the position where it fell. As a result of analyzing the method of throwing, a person who throws the ball using the lamp found a problem that can not be thrown in Method B.

Compared with the case of throwing the ball by himself, the machine makes the weak hand feel the part of operation. However, depend on the experience of the participants, many cases lead to fail, the ability of the person, the condition at the time of the match, so when developing a throwing device, it can't be too accurate. We must think with consciousness that the outcome of practice can be reflected.

3.3   Investigate Interfaces that Can Be Classified as Disabled Persons

In order to think about the different operation interface for different types of disabled persons by typing according to physical characteristics of people with disabilities. Therefore the possible operation parts are different, it is possible to select the possible operation parts with eyes (eye movement, blinking, etc.), mouth (voice operation, blowing etc.); head, neck, jaw; finger, wrist, arm; By the way, based on the condition of the operation site, we classified people with disabilities according to the degrees of freedom of the body.

After classifying people with disabilities by physical features, we looked for existing operation interface in the order of operation parts, and thought about an interface that can be used for Boccia Robot. We have summarized the operation interface we searched, with the goal of not only being able to play for the disabled but also having fun to play.

Fig. 6. Mapping existing operation interface

Therefore, I thought that it is necessary to analyze concrete behavior such as the degree of disability of the operation site and the range of movement. Finally the Japan Para Athletics Federation's Paralympic Sports.

Considering the physical characteristics of people with disabilities, within the range of moderate physical strength without resorting to intense exercise capacity, the elements that can be enjoyed fun are classified into "feeling of exercise moving the body", "feeling of tension thinking strategy in the head", "There is a challenge feeling" "There are three". Then, mapping the existing operation interface on the horizontal axis: brain power → physical strength, vertical axis: operative → intuitive, the core interface zone of the operation interface which is likely to be used for robotics, "tablet type", "remote control type", "sensor" There were three tendencies (Fig. 6).

3.4   Re-type Disabled People for Behavior Analysis

Therefore, I thought that it is necessary to analyze concrete behavior such as the degree of disability of the operation site and the range of movement. Finally I referred to para-sports track and field classification 7 by the Japan Para Athletics Federation.

In the track sports classification of Paralympic Sports, "T" in the previous English letter means running race, jumping competition, "F" means throwing competition. Among the following numbers, the preceding number represents the type of disability and the number behind it represents the degrees of disability.

If designing with consideration of the disability of each class with a high degree of disability, considering applying light persons with a slight degree of disability, basically the type with a high degree of disability in each class is represented as a representative type Extracted (Fig. 7).

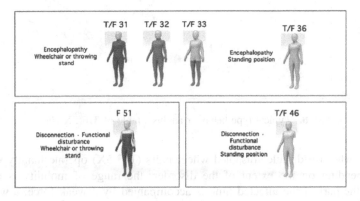

Fig. 7. Representative type of each extracted class

As a method of motion analysis, first of all, in order to share the image within the design team, from the explanation about the representative type by parachuting athletics classification, search for examples of people with disabilities that match the situation, collect Fig. 7, A possible operation part of this type of person and the possible operation are analyzed by a sketch and summarized in a table.

According to Paralympic sport's athletics classification, people with disabilities are divided into two types: disabled and disabled due to cerebral hemiplegia.

Disabled people with TB (T/F 3X) is symptoms such as spastic paralysis, ataxia, athetosis (involuntary movement) who cannot control their own body well. A person with severe cerebral neuropathy disorder (T/F 31) cannot operate with limbs, and as an operation part, it is a part of the head (eye: eye movement, blinking etc.; mouth: voice operation, blowing etc.; jaw: It is possible to do only within the movable range). A person with moderate EEG (T/F 32.33.36) can operate with limbs but cannot control the body well, so when moving the body, the movement is larger than the desired motion and within a small range cannot operate precisely (Fig. 8).

T/F51

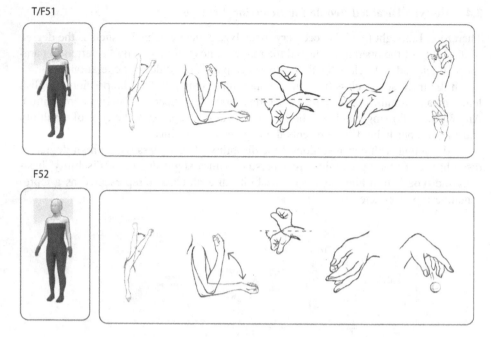

Fig. 8. Typical type behavior analysis table of T/F 5X class

People who use disabled/disabled wheelchairs (T/F 5X) operate mainly with arm parts. Depending on the extent of the disorder, the range of mobility is different, generally the part of the affected limb is accompanied by a weak force, a weak sensation (Fig. 9).

T/F31

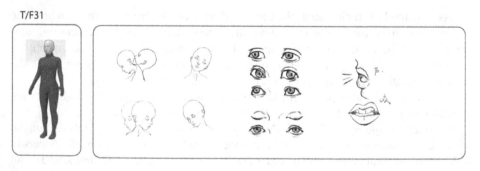

Fig. 9. Typical type behavior analysis table of T/F 3X class

According to the above analysis, the operation part is divided into head parts (eyes, mouth, chin), part of the arm (finger, wrist, elbow), foot part to the eyes. Person's habits, the situation of each type of person above Also, "the feeling of movement to move the body" as the "element that can be enjoyed and played" which the project is aiming, "the feeling of tension thinking strategy in the head", "Taking a comprehensive view of the "challenging feeling of", in this time except for interfaces with less exercise such as brain waves, eye movement and the like, the order of the operating parts considered is: arm part (finger, wrist, elbow) > head part Mouth, jaw) ≥ It was made to part of the foot.

3.5   Prototype Evaluation

Operating Procedure:
See Fig. 10.

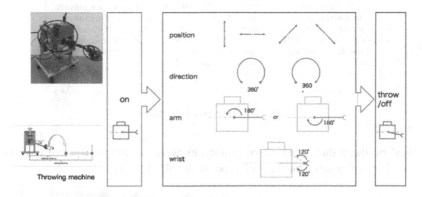

Fig. 10. Operating procedure

3.6   Idea Submission by Type

From the previous disabled type classification behavior analysis, we divide it into types 1 to 3 that can be operated with the arm this time, and severe encephalopathy paralyzed T/F 31 that can only be operated with the head, perform idea sorting by type It was.

There were three kinds of controller proposals as shown in Fig. 11 among idea ideas issued at the stage of the previous idea issue. Since the throwing device has four parameters of machine position, machine orientation, machine arm angle when throwing a ball and machine throwing angle when throwing a ball, if you divide it into four parts, the controller size Is large or the interval between each part is small, there is a risk of erroneous operation, so the idea made out mainly focused on operation simplification.

Controller 1	Controller 2	Controller 3
Switch between position, direction, arm, wrist adjustment function with one button, adjust with the joystick in the middle, throw the ball with one button.	Position, direction, arm, wrist with "BACK" "NEXT" button below Switch between the adjustment functions, adjust with the joystick in the middle, push the top button and throw.	With one joystick, switch it between position, direction, arm, wrist adjustment function, tilt back and forth to adjust the machine, push the joystick and throw.

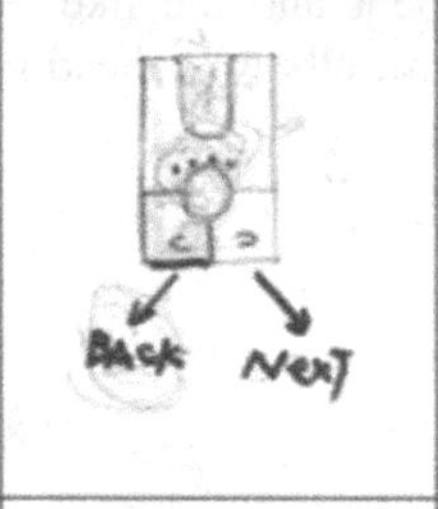

Fig. 11. Three selected plan

Based on these three controllers, prototypes were created to separate easy-to-use size and shape of controllers for each type of people (Fig. 12).

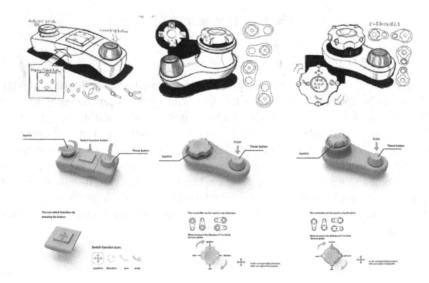

Fig. 12. Prototype

3.7   Prototype Evaluation

Before evaluating the prototype, first of all, type 1 of the type that operates with the part of the arm, before manipulating the prototype, so that it is possible to separate the problem in operation and the controller's easy-to-use shape and size for each type of person, 3 persons of type 2, 1 person of type 3, 1 person of severe encephalopathy paralyzed T/F 31 operated at the head part, features of the body of a total of 6 persons, the operation site and the method of setting the controller I made a persona (Fig. 13).

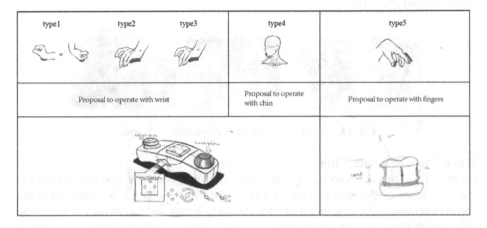

Fig. 13. Proposed controller in the first stage

Type 1: Can not use only fingers
Type 2: Can not use elbows, wrists, fingers. Joint is stiff
Type 3: Weak force Involuntary movement. Joint is stiff
Type 4: Paralysis (non-cerebral) can be operated with chin, gaze, expression
Type 5: Elbow can not be raised from the desk; Wrist, you can use fingers; Grip strength is weak, but toothbrush, spoon etc. are grasped;

Can be used with an auxiliary device According to the result of the evaluation, for each type of person, it is easier to use an interface that operates with a momentary completion operation such as pressing. Therefore, the idea of the type to operate with the next wrist and the type to operate with the jaw will be considered based on the proposal A of the combination button, the throw button and the joystick. For finger operated type you need to think about a new smaller size.

In addition, it is necessary to consider the switching button, the distance between the throwing button and the joystick, and the arrangement of the three parts.

3.8 Examination of Size Based on Operation Characteristics

When Operating with the Wrist

According to the results of the prototype evaluation, people of Persona I, II, V who operate with the wrist have a possibility of misoperation if the distance between the toggle button, throw button and the joystick is not enough, so the minimum between these three parts In order to understand the interval, we measured the size of the back of the hand, the width of the hand, the width of the fist, the height of the fist as the operating part (Fig. 14).

Fig. 14. Measurement part to be operated with wrist

When Operating with Chin

People of Persona VI who manipulates with chin is a type that operates within the movable range of the jaw, so there is a possibility that it can not be delivered if the distance between the toggle button and the throwing button and the joystick is far, so the optimum distance that can be operated with natural posture, We measured the distance when the left and right movement of the jaw naturally acts as the operation site (Fig. 15).

Fig. 15. Measuring part operated with chin

When Operating With Fingers

When operating with fingers, the size is small, so even if there is a difference in spending there is a possibility that operability may be affected. For this time, we conducted an experiment focusing on the difference between the range of movement of fingers naturally and the height.

4   Redesign from the Results of Review

From the results of the examination, since it is understood the basic size such as the switching button, the throwing button and the distance between the joystick, the arrangement position, the height, etc., "a plan to operate with the wrist", "a proposal to operate with the chin", "Draft" to adjust the size of each type, redesign was done (Fig. 16).

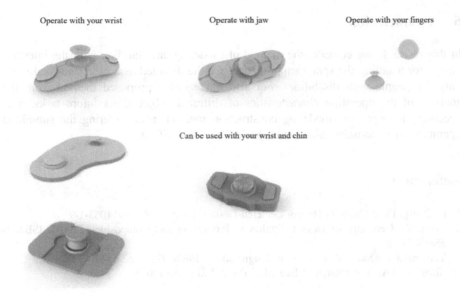

Operate with your wrist   Operate with jaw   Operate with your fingers

Can be used with your wrist and chin

Fig. 16. Consider by prototype

5 Styling

After deciding all the design requirements, the styling part firstly starts from the image collage about "sporty", the styling keyword of Boccia Robot this time "less is more", "Professional: Paralympics, For Olympic athletes", "Easy to use: Processing details focused mainly on easy-to-use". And styling based on these three keywords (Fig. 17).

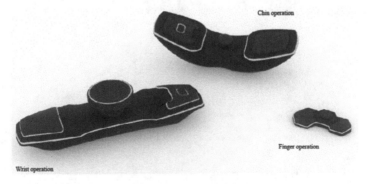

Chin operation

Finger operation

Wrist operation

Fig. 17. Finger operation

6 A Conclusion

In this research, we consider the method of modeling and building with the interface design for handling the sports support robot for the disabled as a case, and finally not only for people with disabilities, but also make out a proposed method from the analysis of the operation characteristics of different subjects. As future tasks, it is necessary to apply the modeling construction method in considering the submitted operation characteristics in an actual project and to verify it.

References

1. IDEOorg: Field Guide to Human-Centered Design. ISBN: 978-0-9914063-1-9
2. Elam, K.: Geometry of Design: Studies in Proportion and Composition (2001). ISBN I-56898-249-6
3. Yamanaka, S.: Skeletal structure of design (2011). ISBN 978-8222-64470-3
4. Norman, D.A.: The Design of Everyday Things? Shunsha (2015)

Development and Evaluation of a Model of Human Comfort and Cognitive Ability for Moderate Differences in Thermal Environment

Shane T. Mueller[(✉)] ⓘ, Yin-Yin (Sarah) Tan, and Isaac Flint

Michigan Technological University, Houghton, MI 49931, USA
shanem@mtu.edu

Abstract. Past research has established systematic effects of thermal stress on human comfort and cognitive performance. However, this research has primarily focused on extremes of temperature, ignoring moderate temperature ranges typically found in work environments and vehicles. Furthermore, models predicting the psychological impact of thermal environment have typically focused solely on perceived comfort, or when accounting for cognitive performance (e.g., Anno et al. 1996; Mueller et al. 2011) focused on in relatively extreme thermal conditions. As a consequence, there is limited empirical data, and no viable predictive models, for understanding the impact of moderate thermal stress on human comfort and performance. We report on an experimental study with 24 college-age participants that assessed cognitive performance (across a number of cognitive dimensions including manual dexterity, speed, dual-task performance, task switching, executive function, and attention), subjective measures of comfort and workload (including the CALM comfort scale, the affect grid, NASA-TLX, perceived effort, and other measures related to the thermal environment), and physiology (including heart rate, skin temperature, and breathing rate). Participants were tested during three 90-min sessions in a controlled thermal chamber in which the temperature was either cool (15 °C/59 °F), room temperature (22.5 °C/72.5 °F), or warm (30 °C/86 °F), during which they completed repeated rounds of comfort ratings, cognitive task performance, and rest. Results showed strong responses in physiological and comfort measures over time to differences in thermal environment. However, the thermal environment had differential effects on cognitive measures, with some producing little impairment, and others showing increases or decreases over time that were moderated by thermal environment. The results were examined within a latent variable model that suggests that comfort alone is not an adequate proxy for performance, even for moderate thermal stressors, and more complex predictive models are needed.

Keywords: Performance prediction · Mental stressors · Environmental conditions

© Springer Nature Switzerland AG 2019
C. Stephanidis (Ed.): HCII 2019, LNCS 11786, pp. 395–411, 2019.
https://doi.org/10.1007/978-3-030-30033-3_31

1 Background

1.1 Purpose

The goal of this paper is to discuss the design, methodology, and results of a study to investigate how variations in the thermal environment impact aspects of physiological state, comfort, subjective assessments of workload, and cognitive measures of performance. The goal of this project was to develop a statistical latent factor model (based on the Task-Taxon-Task model) that could account for the variety of effects that the thermal environment has on human outcomes, and collect data that demonstrated the utility of a latent factor model in accounting for human response to thermal environment. The practical significance of this study is to understand the human response to moderate variations in their environment—those typical of indoor spaces—to help support future intelligent climate control systems.

Traditional physiological models of thermal stressors on human outcome variables have focused on modeling a single outcome variable (e.g., comfort) based on variations in thermal environment. However, the comfort and performance outcomes are known to have differential and complex relationships to thermal environment. Consequently, traditional models are unable to account for these impacts prima facie. However, past data establishing this has focused on extreme thermal environments (e.g., extended physical labor under heat stress conditions in military settings), making the past models ill-suited for the expected smaller ranges of sedentary passengers within the typical thermal environment of vehicle designed space. Consequently, we conducted a new study which used multiple dependent measures under different conditions of thermal stress and time, to develop a latent-variables model to account for the differential effects on various outcome measures.

2 Method

2.1 Participants

Twenty-four participants were recruited voluntarily from the local university and community. The criteria for recruiting participants included adults (1) aged 20–40, (2) at least 4 years of driving experience, (3) normal or corrected-to-normal vision and no color-blindness, (4) no history of heat strain injury, seizure related issues, and (5) no claustrophobia or discomfort in small rooms. Participants fell within a range of gender-dependent height/weight requirements to be included in this project. Participants were required to wear long-sleeve, button-down shirt and long pants, and were instructed to not consume alcohol or drugs 24 h before any study session. Each participant was paid $12 for each hour of participation. All methods were approved by the MTU IRB.

2.2 Experimental Design

This study implemented a within-subject experimental design, with all participants completing the same set of tests in a counterbalanced order under different environmental conditions. The study took four sessions, each lasting about 2 h. The first session was intended as practice and familiarization in order to counteract any learning effects and obtain baseline measures. The remaining three experimental sessions involved manipulated environmental conditions controlled with an environmental chamber: normal condition (22.5 °C/72.5 °F), cool condition (15 °C/59 °F), and warm condition (30 °C/86 °F). The order of these sessions was counterbalanced across participants.

Each session was conducted either on different days or by at least two hours apart if different days could not be scheduled. Within each session, participants were assessed in four study cycles each lasting approximately 25 min. Each study cycle involved a sequence of cognitive behavioral tasks and self-assessments.

2.3 Procedures

Participants took part in a battery of cognitive tests, including the Anti-Saccade Test, Pursuit Rotor Test, Dual-task Test, Hick's Law Task, Switcher Task, and the Minnesota Dexterity Task (see Table 1 and Fig. 1 for detailed descriptions). All computerized tests were implemented using a free, open-source software, Psychology Experiment Building Language (PEBL, [23, 25]). The primary independent variables were environmental state (cycle and ambient temperature). The major dependent variables were performance measures, physiological states (i.e., heart rates, breath rates, and skin temperatures), and subjective user comfort and workload ratings.

Each of the four cycles within each session involved the same sequence of tasks. These started with comfort ratings (which lasted about three minutes), then five cognitive tasks (five computerized tasks, each taking 2–5 min to complete), followed by the NASA-TLX workload and comfort ratings (3 min to complete). The entire sequence took under 25 min, and when complete, the participant rested until the next round started (25 min after the previous). Tasks were selected based on several criteria: (1) they were likely to be sensitive to decrements in attentional and executive control, which have previously been found to be most highly sensitive to the distraction and discomfort caused by thermal stress; (2) they were relevant for in-vehicle environments, with analogs to many of the control processes and decisions drivers must make, as well as those facing non-drivers who may wish to engage in a focused work task while ignoring external stimuli; (3) they could produce reliable measures in a relatively minimal timeframe (permitting 25-min cycles), and they could be repeated without inducing substantial learning effects. We used a set of self-report measures related to the thermal environment, perceived workload, and affective state. Physiological monitors recorded real-time heart rate, breathing rate, skin temperature, and several other non-invasive measures (e.g., posture and movement) throughout the sessions, with the Equivital SEM-02 system.

Table 1. Description and Rationale of the measures used in the present experiment.

Task type	Task	Purpose
Behavioral and performance	Pursuit rotor [1, 3]	Assess continuous motor control. Coupled with Minnesota Dexterity to provide dual-task manipulation
	Minnesota Dexterity [24, 26]	Assess dual-task aimed movement under dual-task conditions. Manual control
	Anti-saccade [2, 12, 14, 19, 21]	Executive control; suppressing attention-capturing visual stimuli. Maintaining focused attention under distraction
	Dual-task [8, 29, 30]	Executive control and task management; responding to multiple simultaneous stimuli
	Hick's Law [16, 28]	Rapid decision making; choose quickly among options with increasing set size
	Switcher [4, 18, 21]	Executive control; switch decision making rapidly between rules. Task-switching for managing attention
Physiological measure	Skin temperature	Contact measure under clothing using Equivital SEM-02
	Breathing rate	Belt-derived breathing rate using Equivital SEM-02
	ECG heart rate	Contact-derived measure using Equivital SEM-02
Subjective self-report	Borg Scale/RSME [7, 31]	Rating of perceived mental effort
	Comfort [9, 13]	Rating of perceived comfort (CALM)
	Hot/Cold [17, 27]	Assess perception of temperature
	Wet/Dry skin [17, 27]	Assess perception of skin moisture (typically related to sweat and humidity)
	Preferred temperature [17, 27]	Assess whether they would prefer a warmer or cooler room temperature
	Affect grid [6]	Two dimensions: Pleasantness and Arousal
	TLX [11, 15]	Rating of six dimensions of workload

Pursuit Rotor Task and Minnesota Dexterity Task. The Pursuit Rotor Task employed a 4 (cycles: time in the environment) $\times$ 3 (temperatures: cold, normal, & warm) $\times$ 2 (level of difficulty: easy & difficult) within-subjects, repeated-measures design. The Minnesota Manual Dexterity Test was used along with Pursuit Rotor Task to examine participants' motor skills regarding the capability for eye-hand-finger movement and to create a scenario of dual task performance. All the participants completed the task with five trials in the same sequence. Each trial was set to be 30 s with either slow (1 rotation/10 s = 0.1 RPS) or fast (1 rotation/5 s = 0.2 RPS) mouse control rate. In the first trial, participants were instructed to just watch the task (slow) while flipping the disks as quickly as possible. Participants completed the pursuit rotor task alone on the 2nd (slow) and 4th (fast) trials; however, in the 3rd (slow) and 5th (fast) trials, they completed both tasks, executing the task and also flipping the checkers simultaneously.

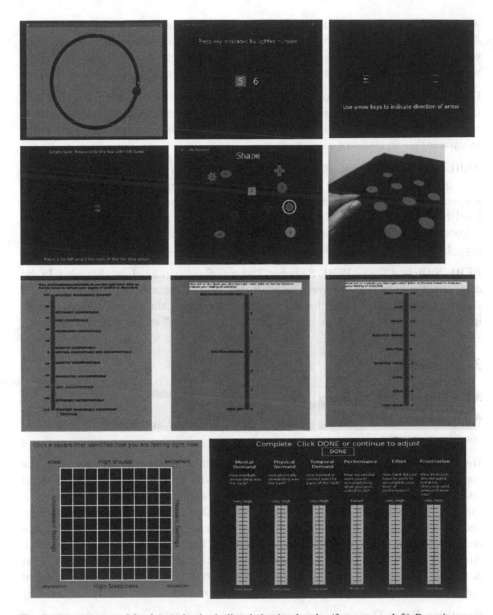

Fig. 1. Measures used in the study, including behavioral tasks (from upper left) Pursuit rotor, Hick's law task, Anti-saccade task, Dual-task test, Switcher task, and Minnesota Dexterity Task. Subjective assessment tasks used in the study, including CALM comfort scale, Wet/Dry, Hot/Cold, Affect grid and NASA-TLX.

Anti-saccade Task. Similar to Pursuit Rotor Task, the Anti-Saccade Task employed a $4 \times 3 \times 2$ factorial within-subject design. The two levels of difficulty include easy level where participants only judged the direction of one single arrow, and difficult level where they had to use both hands to respond to the direction of two arrows.

Dual-Task Test. Identical to previous tasks, the Dual Task employed a $4 \times 3 \times 2$ factorial within-subject design. In the easy condition, participants were required to respond to the direction of one arrow, while in the difficult condition, they were asked to answer the directions of two arrows.

PEBL Hick's Law Task. PEBL Hick's Law Task was used to measure stimulus-response compatibility, motor control, and interference suppression. The task employed a $4 \times 3 \times 2$ factorial design as previous tasks. There are two levels of difficulty. Easy level has one (i.e., 5) or two (i.e., 5 & 6) numbers for participants to press on the keyboard corresponding to two fingers on their two hands, while difficult level had four (i.e., 4, 5, 6, & 7) or eight numbers (i.e., 2, 3, 4, 5, 6, 7, 8, & 9).

PEBL Switcher Task. PEBL Switcher Task involved two levels of difficulty. In the easy condition, participants were asked to follow one "match rule", such as color, shape, or letter, and searched for the symbol that matches the current symbol. Participants were required to follow more than one "match rule" in the difficult condition.

3 Results

3.1 Physiological Measures

We first examined the physiological measures across time in the three environmental conditions (see Fig. 2).

Heart Rate. The warm thermal environment led to a higher overall heart rate. The cool and normal environments began (on average) with a lower heart rate, and the heart rate reduced by about 10 bpm over the 90-min session. In contrast, the warm environment began higher and remained elevated. On average, elevated temperature resulted in elevated heart rate that increased over time in comparison to neutral, while cool temperature produced no differential impact on heart rate in comparison to neutral. An ANOVA showed that there was a significant main effect of environment on heart rate ($F(2,42) = 9.3$, $p < .001$; means for CNH = 96.9, 97.5, 102.7), and a significant temperature by time interaction ($F(6,43) = 5.01$, p = .01).

Breathing Rate. There was a general elevation in breathing rate over the course of each session. There were substantial differences across individuals, some of which likely arose because of sensor and algorithm errors. Overall, there were not large systematic differences in breathing rate across conditions, which is expected in our study that involved low-impact cognitive testing. When cool and warm environment breathing rates were compared to neutral, no differential effects in comparison to neutral were observed. An ANOVA showed no significant main effect of environmental condition ($F(2,42) = .47$, $p = .6$; means for CNH = 12.5, 13.0, 11.5), and also no significant temperature by time interaction ($F(6,43) = .46$, p = .6).

Skin Temperature. Measured skin temperature rose over the session for each of the conditions—even for the cool condition. This is likely a consequence of the skin temperature being measured underneath clothing in a sedentary environment, where the heat of the body generally increased the measure over time. Notably, in the warm condition, skin temperature was substantially higher even during the first cycle. When skin temperature of the two extreme conditions was compared to neutral, we found that the temperature elevation in the warm condition was relatively constant over time, and that the cool temperature condition produced a relatively constant decrease in skin temperature over time. An ANOVA showed a significant main effect of environmental condition (F(2,42) = 13.8, p < .001; means for CNH = 32.8, 33.6, 34.7), and a marginally significant temperature by time interaction (F(6,43) = 2.66, p = .08).

3.2 Subjective Measures

Subjective comfort and workload measures were assessed at the beginning of each session, between each cycle, and after the final cycle. Mean values for each condition are shown in Fig. 3. The results indicate that environmental temperature condition has both immediate and time-varying effects on these ratings. A factorial ANOVA showed ambient temperature has significant main effect on CALM (F(2,44 = 19.9, p < .001), Hot/cold (F(2,44) = 326, p < .001), Skin wetness (F(2,44) = 18.9, p < .001), Preferred temperature (F(2,44) = 129, p < .001), Pleasantness (F(2,44) = 4.0, p = .02), and Arousal (F(2,44) = 5.6, p = .007), but not perceived effort (F(2,46) = 2.28, p = .11). Moreover, most of the interactions were also significant, indicating generally that at least one difference got larger over time, including a significant interaction between cycle and condition for Perceived effort (F(2,43) = 3.4, p = .04), CALM (F(2,46) = 24.3, p < .001), Hot/cold (F(2,46) = 23, p < .001), Preferred temperature (F(2,46) = 24, p < .001), and pleasantness (F(2,46) = 9.3, p < .001). There was no interaction for skin wetness (F(2,46) = .86, p = .43) or arousal (F(2,46) = 1.5, p = .228). There were no significant main effects or interactions with the NASA-TLX scores.

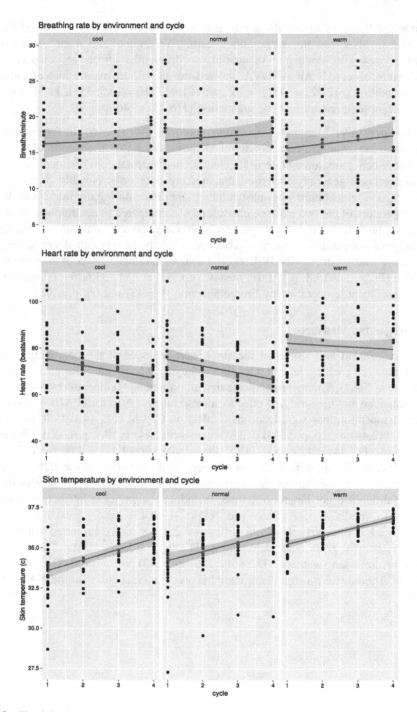

Fig. 2. Physiological responses for each environmental condition, across consecutive 25-min cycles.

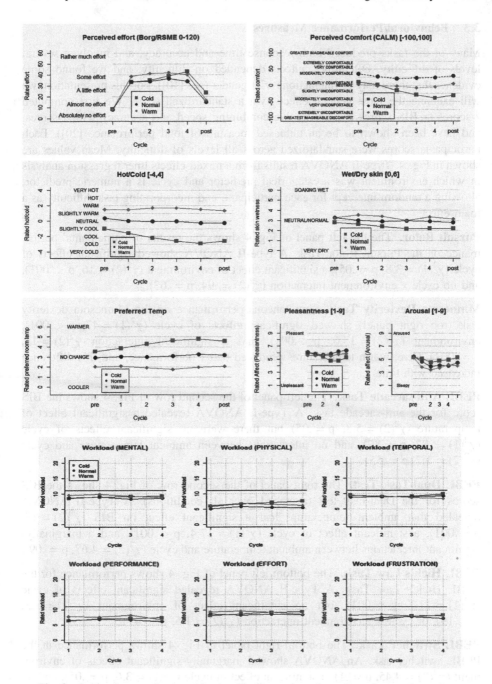

Fig. 3. Subjective comfort, workload, and affect ratings throughout four study cycles.

3.3   Behavioral/Performance Measures

Many of the tasks produced both response time and accuracy, and involved several levels of difficulty. Oftentimes, effects depended on difficulty, and we found some evidence that there may be interactions with gender (see [10]). For this presentation, we will examine the most general effects, via a standardized score. We first computed z-scores or BIS scores (which involve combining speed and accuracy with z-scores, and have been shown to be an unbiased measure of total performance [20]). Each participants scores were standardized across all levels of difficulty. Mean values are shown in Fig. 4. Type-II ANOVA results from a mixed-effects lmer regression analysis in which environment was a categorical predictor and cycle is a numeric predictor, allowing a random intercept for each participant, and incorporating task difficulty as a main effect.

Pursuit Rotor. The top left panel of Fig. 4 shows the results of participants' performance on the Pursuit Rotor Task. A type-II ANOVA showed significant effects of cycle ($\chi^2(1) = 3.8$, p = .05), a significant effect of environment ($\chi^2(2) = 16$, p < .001), and no cycle x environment interaction ($\chi^2(2) = .94$, p = .63).

Minnesota Dexterity Task. Simultaneous performance on the Minnesota dexterity task (top right panel) showed significant effects of cycle ($\chi^2(1) = 47$, p < .001), environment ($\chi^2(2) = 13.6$, p < .001), and a significant interaction $\chi^2(2) = 13$, p = .001). Here, warm temperatures produced better performance, and this difference increased with time.

PEBL Anti-saccade Task. The left panel of the second row of Fig. 4 shows the BIS score for the anti-saccade task. A Type-II ANOVA revealed a significant effect of temperature ($\chi^2(2) = 5.8$, p = .05) but there were no significant effects of cycle ($\chi^2(1) = .02$, p = .87), and no interactions between ambient temperature and cycle ($\chi^2(2) = 1.2$, p = .55).

PEBL Dual-Task Test. The right panel of the second row of Fig. 4 shows the BIS scores for the Dual-task test (averaged over all conditions). A Type-II ANOVA revealed that ambient temperature had a significant effect on BIS ($\chi^2(2) = 15$, p < .001), a significant effect of cycle ($\chi^2(1) = 17.4$, p < .001), and a marginally-significant interactions between ambient temperature and cycle ($\chi^2(2) = 4.67$, p = .09).

PEBL Hick's Law Task. The bottom left panel of Fig. 4 shows performance for the PEBL Hick's Law Task. A Type-II ANOVA revealed significant effects of cycle ($\chi^2(1) = 11.7$, p < .001), but no significant effect of environment ($\chi^2(2) = 3.3$, p = .19), or cycle x environment interaction ($\chi^2(2) = 1.5$, p = .47).

PEBL Switcher Task. The bottom right panel of Fig. 4 shows performance in the PEBL switcher task. An ANOVA showed marginally-significant effects of environment ($\chi^2(2) = 4.45$, p = .1), a significant effect of cycle ($\chi^2(1) = 3.6$, p = .05), and no cycle x environment interaction ($\chi^2(2) = 2.1$, p = .34).

Summary. Overall, each test showed the impact thermal environmental. For most measures, the neutral condition was the best, and cooler and warmer conditions produced relatively worse performance. But these effects were not uniform across tasks, suggesting a complex relationship between thermal environment and performance.

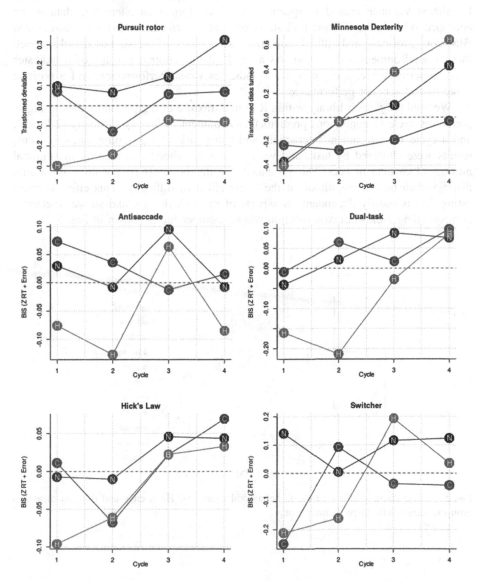

Fig. 4. Participants performance on the behavioral tasks. Performance is displayed as transformed z-scores, or on relevant tests, speed and accuracy were combined into a composite (BIS) measure. In each case, higher values indicate better performance.

3.4   Latent Variable Model (T3)

The Task-Taxon-Task (T3) model [5, 24, 26] was originally developed to model the impact of large environmental and chemical stressors on human performance. Typically, subject-matter experts would provide ratings of the importance of different skill taxa on different tasks, and use this as the basis for fitting performance impact functions for shared variance related to specific taxa. We adopted an alternative data-driven approach to fitting the T3 model. First, we computed performance using the normalized BIS scores, for easy and difficult conditions across each of the six tasks, and for each thermal environment and session. As a result of this coding, a value of 0 indicates average performance, a negative value indicates worse performance, and a positive value indicates better performance.

We used the *flexmix* library within R to fit a mixture of regression models, using as predictors cycle (1 continuous predictor), environment (3 levels), difficulty (2 levels), and a cycle x environment interaction; and using task as a grouping variable. Thus, results were clustered by task, and we used a BIC criterion to identify the optimal number of clusters or taxa. This produced five distinct clusters, but three were only distinguished by the magnitude of the linear effect of difficulty. This effect is interesting, but is mostly dependent on aspects of the task design, and so we selected a corresponding 3-cluster/taxon solution whose membership is shown in Fig. 5.

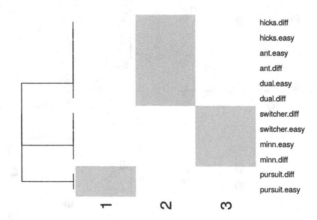

Fig. 5. Three-taxon solution based on behavioral measures. Here, easy and difficult measures group together, with three distinct groups.

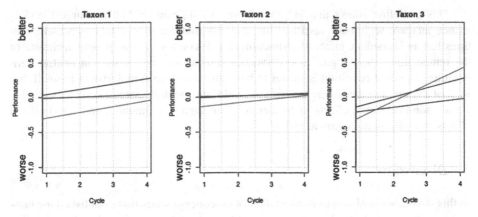

Fig. 6. Results of Taxon 1–3. For each taxa, we see distinct patterns of how performance changes over time, under different temperature conditions.

Each individual taxon is a group of measures that behave similarly in response to time and temperature. The predictions of each of these three models is shown in Fig. 6. The patterns of data captured here suggest that overall, performance tended to increased with time under all temperatures. This means that participants were not getting fatigued, but rather were becoming better at the task. This is not simply a learning process, because this happened despite the fact that participants had an entire practice session prior to the testing in which they needed to meet a performance criterion, and the temperature conditions were counterbalanced.

For the first taxon, which was comprised of the two difficulty levels from the Pursuit Rotor task, normal temperature produced the best performance, which improved over time. Warm temperature produced the worst performance, which improved a similar amount. The cold temperature started at about the same level as neutral, but did not improve. This suggests that warm temperature had an immediate negative impact which lessened over time, and cool temperature had no initial impact but its negative effect (in comparison to neutral) increased over time. For the second taxon (several executive function tasks), there was little impact of cold temperatures, and no real improvement over time for the neutral or cold conditions. However, warm temperature again led to an immediate decrement—but this decrement diminished over time. This is a similar pattern as seen in Taxon 1, except with a lack of improvement for neutral. Finally, for taxon 3 (pursuit rotor and switcher), each condition starts out at about the same level, but warm improves the most, then neutral, and cold the least.

This modeling shows that in general, warm temperatures had the largest performance increase within the session. This suggests that our moderately-warm temperatures has an immediate effect of distraction and discomfort, but as people acclimate to the temperature, their cognitive performance returns to what is seen in neutral temperature. The cool condition is slower to have an impact; its initial impact is small, but in 2 of the taxons, the difference between cold and neutral increases over time. This shows non-symmetric effects of temperature on cognitive function, and non-uniform effects over different cognitive tasks.

4 Discussion

In this study, our goal was to conduct a proof-of-concept study that established the non-unitary effects of thermal environment on human responses, in a highly-controlled laboratory environment. Our results showed impacts on physiology, subjective measures, and cognitive function. We examined several physiological outcomes. We found that heart rate was slightly elevated and did not change substantially in the warm-temperature condition, but neutral and cool temperature lead to lower and decreasing heart rate over time. In contrast, thermal environment had no substantial impact on breathing rate (although breathing rate increased slightly across the session), but thermal environment had a more substantial effect on skin temperature (with cool environment producing lower temperature and warm environment producing a higher temperature than neutral), all of which increased uniformly over time. So, even for relatively direct measures of physiological state, we observed three distinct patterns of results. These patterns (and others) were reproduced in comfort and human performance measures. Notably, self-report workload measures appear to have not been impacted by thermal environment or duration, but different measures of comfort and affect were impacted in different ways—often very strongly. In contrast, behavioral measures are not as strong, but we still found impacts of thermal environment on most of the behavioral measures.

This suggests several lessons:

- The impact of thermal environment on performance cannot be uniformly predicted by physiological measures, because thermal environment has different impacts on different types of performance.
- Although subjective measures of comfort and thermal preference are very reliable, they also cannot account for the varied impacts of thermal environment on different measures of performance
- Behavioral measures are less reliable and subject to more individual variability than the subjective measures. Nevertheless, we were able to measure the negative impact of thermal environment on a number of performance tasks.
- Larger studies with more participants, across a larger variety of tasks, will be necessary to more fully map out the cognitive, performance, and comfort impact of thermal environment.

Although the details of the results are informative from a basic theoretical perspective, the larger implications are that thermal environment has non-unitary effects on human comfort and performance. We anticipate that as additional dependent measures and thermal environment manipulations are explored, this fact will remain true. As control of the thermal environment becomes more intelligent, this fact will impact the basic approach to human-systems integration, control theory, and trust in intelligent automation.

For example, traditional in-vehicle environment control systems required the driver or rider to be instrumental in adapting the environment to their desired state. Until recently, even thermostatic controls (a technology more than a century old) were only available in luxury vehicles. Thermostatic controls work on simple principles that adjust the environment to match a minimum deviation from a set point, which is a well-understood problem, both from an engineering perspective and human factors perspective. Although there are many technical issues in dealing with engineering a proper environment and dealing with variations in anthropometry and individual differences, these problems are addressable because the optimization-control problem is fairly straightforward.

The next generation of systems will aim to work more intelligently. Rather than simply minimizing error to a set-point, they might aim to adapt the environment optimally for many other factors, including driver safety, comfort, work throughput, perceived workload, alertness, stress, and the like. This will require user models that incorporate the differential effects of thermal environment on these different outcomes, including individual differences (possibly stemming from gender, geography, or other factors). Furthermore, this presents several obvious challenges from a human-system integration (HSI) perspective.

For example, an appropriate model may be created that can predict the comfort or work throughput of a typical driver or rider, and these models may even be adaptable to individual differences based on preference or anthropometry. However, the system will likely not be able to infer the goals of the rider directly—for example, whether they want to work, or want to stay awake, or want to take a nap, may by supported by separate environmental-control modes in a vehicle. This means that there are issues in designing a system that a rider can control, give feedback to, change settings, and interrogate the internal state of.

But even getting to that point is a challenge for research and development, and may require substantially different control approaches. Existing naive models based on PID controller schemes may still be running at the core of the system, but these controllers will need to incorporate some specific models of the human within their control scheme. Just as image and audio compression libraries incorporate psychophysical models of human vision and hearing to best optimize the outcome, intelligent control models will need to incorporate models of human response to temperature in order to optimize human comfort and productivity. Furthermore, as we have demonstrated in this study, models of the physiology alone will be insufficient, because there will be no single physiological state that is optimal for all particular goals and outcomes.

Acknowledgements. This research was supported by a gift from the Ford Motor Company to the Michigan Tech Fund. We thank Megan Volaski and Lamia Alam for assisting in data collection, and John Elson for advice and guidance on the conduct of the research, and for comments on this and earlier drafts of this manuscript.

References

1. Adams, J.A.: Warm-up decrement in performance on the pursuit-rotor. Am. J. Psychol. **65** (3), 404–414 (1952)
2. Ainsworth, B., Garner, M.: Attention control in mood and anxiety disorders: evidence from the antisaccade task. Hum. Psychopharmacol. Clin. Exp. **28**(3), 274–280 (2013)
3. Ammons, R.B.: Rotary pursuit apparatus: I. Survey of variables. Psychol. Bull. **52**(1), 69–76 (1955)
4. Anderson, K., Deane, K., Lindley, D., Loucks, B., Veach, E.: The effects of time of day and practice on cognitive abilities: the PEBL Tower of London, Trail-making, and Switcher tasks. PEBL Technical report Series, #2011-01 (2012). https://sites.google.com/site/pebltechnicalreports/
5. Anno, G.H., Dore, M.A., Roth. T.J.: Taxonomic model for performance degradation in combat tasks. Pacific-Sierra Corporation Technical report, Contract #DNA-001-90-C-0139 (1996)
6. Barrett, L.F., Russell, J.A.: The structure of current affect: controversies and emerging consensus. Curr. Dir. Psychol. Sci. **8**(1), 10–14 (1999)
7. Borg, G.A.: Psychophysical bases of perceived exertion. Med. Sci. Sports Exerc. **14**(5), 377–381 (1982)
8. Brown, R.G., Marsden, C.D.: Dual task performance and processing resources in normal subjects and patients with Parkinson's disease. Brain **114**(1), 215–231 (1991)
9. Cardello, A.V., Winterhalter, C., Schutz, H.G.: Predicting the handle and comfort of military clothing fabrics from sensory and instrumental data: development and application of new psychophysical methods. Text. Res. J. **73**(3), 221–237 (2003)
10. Chang, T.Y., Kajackaite, A.: Battle for the thermostat: gender and the effect of temperature on cognitive performance. PLoS ONE **14**(5), e0216362 (2019)
11. Colligan, L., Potts, H.W., Finn, C.T., Sinkin, R.A.: Cognitive workload changes for nurses transitioning from a legacy system with paper documentation to a commercial electronic health record. Int. J. Med. Inform. **84**(7), 469–476 (2015)
12. Deuter, C.E., Schilling, T.M., Kuehl, L.K., Blumenthal, T.D., Schachinger, H.: Startle effects on saccadic responses to emotional target stimuli. Psychophysiology **50**(10), 1056–1063 (2013)
13. Gagge, A.P., Stolwijk, J.A.J., Hardy, J.D.: Comfort and thermal sensations and associated physiological responses at various ambient temperatures. Environ. Res. **1**(1), 1–20 (1967)
14. Hallett, P.E.: Primary and secondary saccades to goals defined by instructions. Vis. Res. **18** (10), 1279–1296 (1978)
15. Hart, S.G., Staveland, L.E.: Development of NASA-TLX (Task Load Index): results of empirical and theoretical research. In: Hancock, P.A., Meshkati, N. (eds.) Advances in Psychology, vol. 52, pp. 139–183. North-Holland, Amsterdam (1988)
16. Hick, W.E.: On the rate of gain of information. Q. J. Exp. Psychol. **4**(1), 11–26 (1952)

17. Hultzapple, K., et al.: Chemical protection garment redesign for military use by the laboratory for engineered human protecton years 2005–2011. In: Performance of Protective Clothing and Equipment: 9th Volume, Emerging Issues and Technologies. ASTM International (2012)
18. Jersild, A.T.: Mental set and shift. Arch. Psychol. **14**(89), 81 (1927)
19. Levy, D.L., Mendell, N.R., Holzman, P.S.: The antisaccade task and neuropsychological tests of prefrontal cortical integrity in schizophrenia: empirical findings and interpretative considerations. World Psychiatry **3**(1), 32–40 (2004)
20. Liesefeld, H.R., Janczyk, M.: Combining speed and accuracy to control for speed-accuracy trade-offs (?). Behav. Res. Methods **51**(1), 40–60 (2019)
21. Miyake, A., Friedman, N.P., Emerson, M.J., Witzki, A.H., Howerter, A., Wager, T.D.: The unity and diversity of executive functions and their contributions to complex "frontal lobe" tasks: a latent variable analysis. Cogn. Psychol. **41**(1), 49–100 (2000)
22. Mueller, S.T.: PEBL: the psychology experiment building language (Version 2.1) [Computer experiment programming language] (2018). http://pebl.sourceforge.net
23. Mueller, S.T.: Adapting the Task-Taxon-Task methodology to model the impacts of chemical protective gear. In: The 19th Annual Conference on Behavior Representation in Modeling and Simulation, Charleston, SC (2010)
24. Mueller, S.T., Piper, B.J.: The psychology experiment building language (PEBL) and PEBL test battery. J. Neurosci. Methods **222**, 250–259 (2014)
25. Mueller, S.T., Simpkins, B., Anno, G., Fallon, C.K., Price, O., McClellan, G.E.: Adapting the task-taxon-task methodology to model the impact of chemical protective gear. Comput. Math. Organ. Theory **17**(3), 251–271 (2011)
26. Pierce, J., Hirsch, S., Kane, S., Venafro, J., Winterhalter, C.: Evaluation of thermal comfort of fabrics using a controlled-environment chamber. In: Performance of Protective Clothing and Equipment: 9th Volume, Emerging Issues and Technologies. ASTM International (2012)
27. Proctor, R.W., Schneider, D.W.: Hick's law for choice reaction time: a review. Q. J. Exp. Psychol. **71**(6), 1281–1299 (2017)
28. Schumacher, E.H., et al.: Virtually perfect time sharing in dual-task performance: uncorking the central cognitive bottleneck. Psychol. Sci. **12**(2), 101–108 (2001)
29. Wickens, C.D.: Processing resources and attention. In: Damos, D.L. (ed) Multiple-Task Performance. Taylor & Francis, London (1991)
30. Zijlstra, F.R.H.: Efficiency in work behaviour: a design approach for modern tools. Doctoral Thesis (1993). https://elibrary.ru/item.asp?id=6863266

Measuring Nursing Workload in an Intensive Care Unit Using NGOMSL Model

Sivamanoj Sreeramakavacham[1], Jung Hyup Kim[1(⊠)],
and Laurel Despins[2]

[1] Industrial and Manufacturing Systems Engineering Department,
University of Missouri, Columbia, MO 65211, USA
ssxx9@mail.missouri.edu, kijung@missouri.edu
[2] Sinclair School of Nursing,
University of Missouri, Columbia, MO 65211, USA
DespinsL@health.missouri.edu

Abstract. The purpose of this study is to understand the impact on nursing workload due to patient severity and nurse experience by using Natural GOMS Language (NGOMSL) model. To develop the model, a time and motion study was conducted using a real-time location system. After that, the nurse's location and time data were used to develop multiple hierarchical task analysis charts. These HTA charts were used to create the NGOMSL model and identified the ICU nurse's workflow patterns. The analysis results from the NGOMSL model showed that the patient severity and the nurse's experience had significant impacts on nurse's workload for in-room patient care activities, out of room activities, peer support, and talking to other healthcare professionals. This research empirically demonstrates that patient severity and nurse's experience significantly influenced the nursing workload in an intensive care unit, and the NGOMSL model could measure the workload.

Keywords: Nursing workload · RTLS · Nursing workflow · Intensive care unit

1 Introduction

Patient care in an intensive care unit (ICU) is characterized by highly demanding tasks to support urgent therapeutic intervention and to provide intensive patient monitoring. The nurses working in ICU perform various clinical procedures, document the patient's clinical status, engage in clinical discussions, and perform other tasks (Carayon and Gürses 2005). Due to the increasing complexity of the work environment in ICU, the amount of time spent on each task increasing resulting in time scarcity (Gigerenzer 2007). Studies had found that time scarcity can create time pressure on nurses when they need to do other assigned tasks (Bowers et al. 2001). Time pressure has always been associated with increasing workload as it would activate the emotional component anxiety which causes allocation of more attention resources to the task (Galy et al. 2012; Monod and Kapitaniak 2003).

© Springer Nature Switzerland AG 2019
C. Stephanidis (Ed.): HCII 2019, LNCS 11786, pp. 412–421, 2019.
https://doi.org/10.1007/978-3-030-30033-3_32

Currently, ICU managers are implementing various strategies (e.g., minimizing the time spent on required clinical tasks, rescheduling tasks, and so on) to deal with time scarcity and workload problem. Although the strategies have improved the time scarcity and the workload problems, ICU nurses' clinical workflows are still unorganized (Bowers et al. 2001). In this study, we focus on identifying the impact on nurse's workload due to the patient's severity of illness and nurse experience in an ICU and suggest a new way to measure nursing workload by using a Natural Goal Operator Methods and Selection Rules Language (NGOMSL) simulation model. As the outcomes of this study, we were able to provide better and more profound insights related to the tasks where the nurses are experiencing high workload.

2 Literature Review

The workload is a multidimensional and complex construct that is used to describe the extent to which an operator has engaged the cognitive and physical resources for task performance (Backs et al. 1994). A more comprehensive definition of nursing workload is defined as the amount of time and care that a nurse has devoted (directly and indirectly) towards patients, workplace, and professional development (Alghamdi 2016). A primary concern identified in an ICU is the high workload of healthcare professionals. Nurses commonly experience a heavy workload. There are five main reasons for this: (1) increased work demand for each nurse, (2) inadequate nurse supply, (3) reduced staffing (De Cordova et al. 2010), (4) reduction in patient length of stay (Carayon and Gurses 2008), and (5) increased information overload caused by networked information technologies in the healthcare system. Many researchers have studied the nurse workload in an ICU. There are several different approaches to measure the nursing workload. In the first approach, called patient-based approach method, Kiekkas applied the newer version of Therapeutic Intervention Scoring System (TISS) to study the association between nursing workload and patient mortality (Kiekkas et al. 2008). Also, Duffield et al. (2011) implemented Project Research in Nursing (PRN) to identify the effects of nurse staffing and the nursing workload based on patient outcomes. In the second approach, called operator based approach, the nurse's interaction with the work environment is used to determine the causes of high workload on the nurses and identify strategies to reduce the workload (Hoonakker et al. 2011). Some of the other techniques of the operator based approach include the Cooper-Harper scale, the Subjective Workload Assessment Technique (SWAT), the Rating Scale Mental Effort (RSME) and the NASA Task Load Index (NASA-TLX). All these rating techniques can be used as direct indicators to measure nurse's workload.

In this current study, to apply both patient-based approach and operator-based approach, Patient Severity Level (PSL) and Nurses Experience (NE) were used as two main factors that could influence nursing workload in an ICU. The Sequential Organ Failure Assessment (SOFA) score was used to measure the PSL. The SOFA is a scoring system primarily designed to determine the extent of a person's organ function or rate of failure (Rosa et al. 2015). It is commonly used to track a patient's status during admission to an ICU. SOFA scores are commonly used in ICUs to predict a patient's mortality rate.

For the NE, Benner (2004) interpreted skill acquisition and clinical judgment between more experienced and less experienced nurses. The study showed that the more experienced nurses were better able to change their perception of the nature of the situation and act accordingly in response to the new situation. A study by Roffman et al. (2016) also showed that the nurse's experience level had a significant influence on the workload experienced.

3 Methodology

3.1 Study Setting and Data Collection

A time and motion study was conducted in the medical ICU at the University Hospital, the University of Missouri, Columbia for four months. The ICU consists of two pods with 18 single patient rooms and a reception area located at the center of the two pods. Each pod is equipped with a nurse station that provides access to computers, monitors, table telephones, and medicine cabinet. The primary tasks in the ICU include assessing and re-assessing the clinical status of the patients, documenting in medical records, providing physical care and emotional support to patients, responding to routine, urgent and emergency situations, identifying and communicating existing patients' problems with the physicians, preparing and administering medications to patients, and providing education to the patients and/or their families. Eleven nurses with a range of working experience from 0.83 to 35 years participated in the study. The volunteer nurses were all registered nurses and were provided with a description of the study in a Waiver of Documentation of Consent form attached to a recruitment email. They were informed that the completion and return of an attached demographics questionnaire signified their consent to participate in the study. The information collected about the nurses and the patients was kept confidential.

The Near-Field Electromagnetic Ranging (NFER) system was used to collect the ICU nurses' real-time location during their nursing tasks (Song et al. 2017). Each observer shadowed two to three nurses on the observation day, and the observers recorded the start time and end time of each task the nurses performed in the observation form. The observation data was collected one day per week for thirteen weeks. Each observer made notes of any special events that occurred during the observation. Also, the nurses documented all information related to the patient's health conditions in the Electronic Medical Record (EMR) system. All nurses' documentation activities in the EMR system was recorded in a database, called Real-Time Measurement System (RTMS). After the data collection, the observation data was combined with the data from the NFER system and RTMS data.

3.2 HTA Chart and NGOMSL Model

By using the data from manual observation, NFER, and RTMS, multiple hierarchical task analysis (HTA) charts were created to understand the workflow of the ICU nurses. The HTA charts showed the working patterns of ICU nurses. Each HTA chart consists of high-level tasks and subtasks, and each level of tasks has its own goals and subgoals.

Once the goals and subgoals were identified, a plan was created for each level of tasks. Based on the HTA charts, all ICU nursing tasks were categorized into eight primary categories: (1) verbal report, (2) primary care (in-room activities), (3) peer support, (4) out-of-room activities, (5) Talking to someone about patient's clinical processes, (6) Take notes about patients, (7) Teaching residents/students, and (8) non-nursing activities, The top-level goal of the HTA chart is to complete all clinical nursing tasks during a day shift. The multiple subgoals must be completed to achieve the goal shown in the top level.

By using the HTA charts, a Natural Goals Operators Methods and Selection Rules Language (NGOMSL) simulation model was developed. The NGOMSL model shows the step by step procedure of how ICU nurses perform health care services to the patients. Figure 1 shows the ICU nurse's NGOMSL model for the different tasks they perform during the day shift.

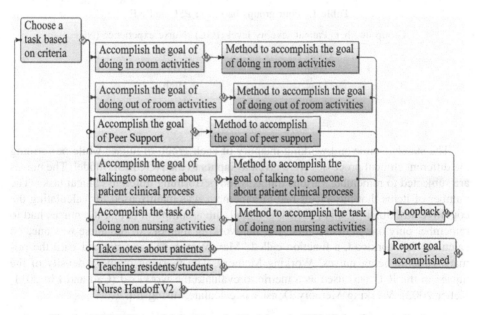

Fig. 1. NGOMSL model for Nurse's Workflow in ICU (Color figure online)

The tasks shown in green indicate that they have certain subgoals that must be accomplished. All activities, within the task network model, were represented as nodes and connected by arrows that denoted the sequence in which the tasks were performed. There are two types of dynamic variables: (1) model variables, used to control how the model itself would run based on the input condition and (2) data collection variables, used for data collection. The process times to perform the different tasks were recorded in the model variables while the cognitive workload to complete each task was recorded in the data collection variables.

3.3 Data Analysis

The time and motion study data was combined with the NFER data. Also, the RTMS data and sequence diagrams were created to understand the nurses' workflow. The sequence diagrams were then analyzed to identify the time taken to perform each task. After that, the nurses were aggregated into four groups based on the severity level of the patients assigned to the nurse and the nurse's experience level. In this study, the SOFA score was considered as patient severity level. A HIGH patient severity level indicates that the patients assigned to the nurse had high SOFA score greater than the threshold value of 8.6. The threshold value is the mean value of the SOFA scores for the collected data set. The nurse experience is HIGH if the nurse had experience working in an ICU for more than 2 years. Based on the threshold values, the four groups are shown in Table 1.

Table 1. Four groups based on PSL and NE

Group number	Patient severity level (PSL)	Nurse experience (NE)
1	High	High
2	High	Low
3	Low	High
4	Low	Low

The standard time and working memory of each group of nurses while performing the different clinical processes were given as inputs to the NGOMSL model. The nurses are subjected to remember various things while performing different clinical tasks. The number of items that the nurses had to remember was mainly used for calculating the cognitive workload. In this NGOMSL model, the assumption is that the nurses had to remember only one item at a time, i.e., the working memory of the nurse was one. To calculate the workload, a function called "Max_Workload" was defined with the primary variable being nurses' Working Memory. The working memory density of the nurses in the ICU was used as a metric to evaluate the workload (Cao and Liu 2011; Keller 2002). Working Memory Density is calculated using Eq. 1.

$$\text{Working Memory Density} = \frac{\text{Items Remembered}}{\text{Total Number of Statements}} \tag{1}$$

In Eq. 1, the items remembered is the summation of all the working memory used by the nurse while performing the subgoals to accomplish the main goal. The total number of statements in the simulation model was used to measure the total number of physical/mental operators. Using Eq. 1, the nursing workload for each clinical process can be calculated.

4 Results

The simulation model was executed for 180 times, i.e., about 6 months data. Along with the nursing workload for each task, the time taken by the nurses for each task was also collected. A one-way ANOVA was conducted to analyze the impact of patient severity level (PSL) and nurse experience (NE) on the nursing workload for all the tasks combined. The results showed that there was a significant difference between the low and high level of PSL and NE at $p < 0.05$ [F = 120.05, P < 0.001]. Another one-way ANOVA was conducted to analyze the impact of the two factors on time taken to do all the tasks. The results showed that there was a significant difference between the low and high level of PSL and NE at $p < 0.05$ [F = 11.25, P < 0.001]. The workload analysis and time analysis results are shown in Fig. 2.

To investigate the impact of PSL and NE on the nursing workload and time taken between the four groups of nurses, two-way ANOVA tests were conducted for each of the eight categories (subgoals) of tasks that the nurses did in ICU. The significant results from the workload analysis are shown in Table 2.

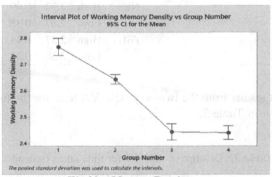

Working Memory Density

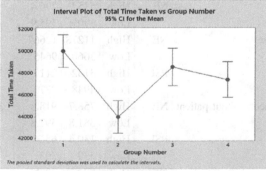

Total Time taken (Secs)

Fig. 2. Interval plots for all the tasks combined

Table 2. Descriptive statistics for Working Memory Density

Sub Goal	Factor	Level	Mean	St. Dev.	F	P
In-room activities	PSL	High	2.77	0.18	538.77	<0.001
		Low	2.51	0.27		
	NE	High	2.83	0.25	301.69	<0.001
		Low	2.65	0.22		
Out room activities	PSL	High	2.74	0.31	137.15	<0.001
		Low	2.50	0.27		
	NE	High	2.60	0.37	7.89	0.005
		Low	2.64	0.29		
Peer support	PSL	High	2.41	0.53	4.17	0.044
		Low	2.31	0.35		
	NE	High	2.44	0.45	4.2	0.043
		Low	2.31	0.44		
Talking to someone about patient's clinical processes	PSL	High	2.51	0.42	12.09	<0.001
		Low	2.31	0.38		
	NE	High	2.32	0.49	6.98	0.008
		Low	2.47	0.38		
NVA activities	PSL	High	2.57	0.48	20.52	<0.001
		Low	2.38	0.35		

The significant results from the two-way ANOVA tests for the total time taken for the tasks are shown in Table 3.

Table 3. Descriptive statistics for time taken (seconds)

Sub goal	Factor	Level	Mean	St. Dev.	F	P
Handoff	NE	High	575.9	296.4	8.3	0.004
		Low	690.4	395.9		
In-room activities	NE	High	11278	12667	78.11	<0.001
		Low	3660	9645		
Peer support	PSL	High	3132	2117	13.63	<0.001
		Low	4948	2870		
Talking to someone about patient	NE	High	758.7	918.6	33.51	<0.001
		Low	381.8	597.8		
Note taking	PSL	High	130.4	65.3	7.7	0.017
		Low	339	303		
	NE	High	82.5	28.2	16.82	<0.001
		Low	247.2	215.1		
NVA activities	PSL	High	2410	3514	14.83	<0.001
		Low	2557	2910		
	NE	High	5067	4376	148.04	<0.001
		Low	1365	1735		

From Tables 2 and 3, PSL and NE had a significant impact on the nursing workload and the time taken to do each task in ICU. These results are further discussed in the next section.

5 Discussions

For the Handoff task, the patient severity level and the nurses' experience level had no significant impact on the nursing workload. This task only involves transferring information about the patient, and the steps involved in this task are very similar regardless of the patient's severity level and the nurse experience. Hence, there was no significant difference in the nursing workload between the groups. However, the time for performing the Handoff task was significantly influenced by the nurses' experience level. The results showed that the less experienced nurses took a longer time compared to the high experienced nurses. It could be caused by a lack of problem-solving skill, clinical judgment, time management, or administrations skills (Khoza 1996; Zhang et al. 2001).

For the In-Room Activities, the nurses who took care of more severe patients experienced higher workload and spent longer process time by doing more clinical tasks associated with providing primary care. According to our data set, the nurses with longer working experience in ICU usually performed more supplementary clinical tasks as a precaution to prevent any deteriorations of patient condition. Based on our definition of workload, those additional in-room tasks led to increasing the nursing workload during the tasks.

For the Out of Room Activities, the results showed that the patient severity level significantly influenced the nursing workload due to the Out Room EMR charting task. More information has to be charted in the EMR system for the patient with a high severity level which implies more sub-sections need to be accessed. In other words, the average number of steps and the items to be remembered to accomplish EMR documentation were significantly increased compared to the patient with a low severity level.

According to our data analysis, ICU nurses usually performed peer support tasks after finished the In-Room activities. For that reason, the nurses who assigned to more severe patients had to remember more information about the previous In-Room tasks compared to the nurses who assigned to less severe patients. Also, the results showed that the nurse's experience level had a significant impact on the nursing workload in ICU due to additional clinical tasks, helping other nurses, or communicating with patient family members. The nurses who had less severe patients spent more time performing peer support tasks compared to the nurses who took care of more severe patients.

In addition, we identified that the less experienced nurses performing In-room or Out-of-Room Activities were more often interrupted than more experienced nurses by family members or physicians to discuss the patient's conditions. It significantly influences the nursing workload. It significantly influences the nursing workload. According to the study done by Parameshwara et al. (2016), interruption is one of the main factors that increase the nursing workload in an emergency department.

For the Note Taking, there was no significant difference in the nursing workload between the patient severity level and the nurses' experience level. However, the time for taking notes was significantly influenced by the patient's severity of illness and nurse experience. It might be caused by the contents that noted down by ICU nurses. We observed that the amount of information written in the Note Taking task related to medication requirements, assessment results, and physician's notes were significantly influenced by the patient severity level and nurse experience.

6 Recommendations

There are several recommendations based on the findings from the current study. For the In-Room Activities, the nurses should not combine two or more tasks due to the heaviness of nursing workload. For the Out of Room Activities, the EMR charting task was the most critical factor to increase the nursing workload. Hence, we recommend to the EMR system to be more user-friendly by simplifying the number of steps of data input with less scrolling and fewer tabs to access multiple pages. For the peer support task, the nurses who took care of more severely ill patients should be cautious for any peer supports in order to focus more on their assigned patients. Also, specific time slots for communication should be negotiated between the patient's family members or other healthcare professionals and the nurse to avoid interrupting the nurses during their clinical activities.

References

Alghamdi, M.G.: Nursing workload: a concept analysis. J. Nurs. Manag. 24(4), 449–457 (2016)

Backs, R.W., Ryan, A.M., Wilson, G.F.: Psychophysiological measures of workload during continuous manual performance. Hum. Factors 36(3), 514–531 (1994)

Benner, P.: Using the Dreyfus model of skill acquisition to describe and interpret skill acquisition and clinical judgment in nursing practice and education. Bull. Sci. Technol. Soc. 24(3), 188–199 (2004)

Bowers, B.J., Lauring, C., Jacobson, N.: How nurses manage time and work in long-term care. J. Adv. Nurs. 33(4), 484–491 (2001)

Cao, S., Liu, Y.: Mental workload modeling in an integrated cognitive architecture. In: Paper presented at the Proceedings of the Human Factors and Ergonomics Society Annual Meeting (2011)

Carayon, P., Gurses, A.P.: Nursing workload and patient safety—a human factors engineering perspective (2008)

Carayon, P., Gürses, A.P.: A human factors engineering conceptual framework of nursing workload and patient safety in intensive care units. Intensive Crit. Care Nurs. 21(5), 284–301 (2005)

De Cordova, P.B., Lucero, R.J., Hyun, S., Quinlan, P., Price, K., Stone, P.W.: Using the nursing interventions classification as a potential measure of nurse workload. J. Nurs. Care Qual. 25 (1), 39 (2010)

Duffield, C., et al.: Nursing staffing, nursing workload, the work environment and patient outcomes. Appl. Nurs. Res. 24(4), 244–255 (2011)

Galy, E., Cariou, M., Mélan, C.: What is the relationship between mental workload factors and cognitive load types? Int. J. Psychophysiol. **83**(3), 269–275 (2012)

Gigerenzer, G.: Gut Feelings: The Intelligence of the Unconscious. Penguin, New York (2007)

Hoonakker, P., et al.: Measuring workload of ICU nurses with a questionnaire survey: the NASA task load index (TLX). IIE Trans. Healthc. Syst. Eng. **1**(2), 131–143 (2011)

Keller, J.: Human performance modeling for discrete-event simulation: workload. In: Paper presented at the Simulation Conference, Proceedings of the Winter (2002)

Khoza, L.B.: The competencies of newly qualified nurses as viewed by senior professional nurses (1996)

Kiekkas, P., et al.: Association between nursing workload and mortality of intensive care unit patients. J. Nurs. Scholarsh. **40**(4), 385–390 (2008)

Monod, H., Kapitaniak, B.: Ergonomie: Elsevier Masson (2003)

Parameshwara, N., Kim, J.H., Guo, W., Pasupathy, K.S.: NGOMSL simulation model in an emergency department. In: Paper presented at the Proceedings of the 2016 Winter Simulation Conference (2016)

Roffman, C.E., Buchanan, J., Allison, G.T.: Charlson comorbidities index. J. Physiotherapy **62** (3), 171 (2016)

Rosa, R.G., et al.: Comparison of unplanned intensive care unit readmission scores: a prospective cohort study. PLoS ONE **10**(11), e0143127 (2015)

Song, X., Kim, J.H., Despins, L.: A time-motion study in an intensive care unit using the near field electromagnetic ranging system. In: Paper presented at the IIE Annual Conference, Proceedings (2017)

Zhang, Z.X., Luk, W., Arthur, D., Wong, T.: Nursing competencies: personal characteristics contributing to effective nursing performance. J. Adv. Nurs. **33**(4), 467–474 (2001)

Modeling Drone Crossing Movement with Fitts' Law

Kaito Yamada(✉), Hiroki Usuba, and Homei Miyashita

Meiji University, Nakano, Tokyo, Japan
`kite171@me.com`

Abstract. Drones have begun to find extensive use in commercial, scientific, recreational, agricultural, and military applications in recent times. Drone maneuvers involve several pointing and crossing operations. In this regard, previous studies have shown that drone pointing operations can be modeled by the two-part model. In this study, we conduct a crossing operation experiment to control a drone to fly through a frame with a target width. Subsequently, we verify the applicability of Fitts' law and the two-part model to drone crossing operations. Fitts' law and the two-part model are both found to be suitably valid for crossing operations ($R^2 > 0.940$). Upon comparing the AIC values of the two models, we find that Fitts' law, which has fewer parameters, is a better model for the crossing operation. Our results indicate that the drone operation time in crossing operations can be suitably predicted. In addition, based on models, we can compare drones and evaluate interfaces in drone crossing operations.

Keywords: Drone · Pointing · Crossing · User performance model · Fitts' law · Human-drone interaction

1 Introduction

Operations in graphical user interfaces (GUIs) are composed of pointing, crossing, and steering operations, and these operations have been suitably modeled. Pointing operations in GUIs involve the selection of a target (Fig. 1 left panel), whereas crossing operations involve the movement of the cursor across a boundary line (Fig. 1 right panel). The factors affecting pointing and crossing operations in GUIs are well known, and the movement time for these operations can be predicted with high accuracy by using Fitts' law. Meanwhile, steering operations in GUIs involve the movement of the cursor along a given path. Here, we note that the steering law is also derived from Fitts' law [1]. In the larger context, it has been reported that via the modeling of these operations, a general evaluation of interfaces and input devices is possible [2–5].

Against this backdrop, drone maneuvers also involve pointing and crossing operations. An example of a drone pointing operation involves directing a drone

© Springer Nature Switzerland AG 2019
C. Stephanidis (Ed.): HCII 2019, LNCS 11786, pp. 422–432, 2019.
https://doi.org/10.1007/978-3-030-30033-3_33

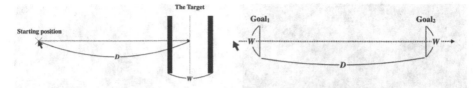

Fig. 1. Pointing task (left panel) and crossing task (right panel) in graphical user interfaces (GUIs)

Fig. 2. Examples of drone pointing operations: landing on desk (left); Self-portrait captured by drone (right)

to land on a desk[1] (Fig. 2 left panel). Further, the use of a drone to capture a self-portrait may also be considered as a pointing operation (Fig. 2 right panel). An example of a crossing operation is a drone race[2] (Fig. 3 left panel). In a drone race, the drones must pass through a frame of a certain width. As an example, the video entitled "Mirai Hikou[3]" shows a video shot by a drone passing through a circle formed by human arms and plastic (Fig. 3 right). Even in this scenario, the drone must pass through a frame of a certain width, i.e., this is a crossing operation. These two crossing operations can be maneuvered in the first-person view (FPV), whereas the operation of passing through a door can be executed in the third-person view (TPV). Thus, drone maneuvering involves many pointing and crossing operations. Here, we note that if these maneuvers are modeled, the operation time of the drone can be predicted. In addition, we can compare devices (such as drones and controllers) in a manner similar to GUI comparisons, and we can, for example, make a statement that "drone A can be controlled faster than drone B in this difficulty level." In addition, new drone control interfaces can be evaluated over a wide range of difficulty levels. In this regard, previous studies have already demonstrated that pointing operations can be modeled by the two-part model [6] (Fitts' law was found unsuitable). Against this backdrop, in this study, we conducted a crossing operation experiment to control a drone to fly through a frame with a target width (Fig. 4) in an attempt to model the crossing operation with both Fitts' law and the two-part model.

---

[1] https://www.tethertools.com/product/aero-launchpad/.

[2] https://youtu.be/4u7C-tx2ho0.

[3] https://youtu.be/2dceR6Ya79w.

Fig. 3. Examples of drone crossing operations: drone race (left); Video production by drone (right)

2 Related Work

2.1 Drone Maneuvering

In the FPV operation of a drone, it is difficult to accurately determine the drone height and position. In certain studies, this problem has been solved using XR [7,8]. Further, Erat et al. proposed a TPV maneuvering system using a HoloLens to address the difficulty of maneuvering a drone from the FPV in narrow paths, as might be required in disaster scenarios [9].

Meanwhile, several other studies have explored many drone maneuvering methods and interfaces. Hall et al. investigated three maneuvering techniques and determined which among them could capture pictures in the fastest possible time (methods included maneuvering from the TPV, the FPV on a tablet, and the FPV with a headset) [10]. Further, Hansen et al. determined the optimal combination by combining eye movements and controller manipulation methods [11]. Cho et al. discussed the difficulty of users in perceiving the actual direction of a drone [12]. Kasahara et al. proposed a method to control a drone by means of a touch screen [13].

2.2 Modeling and Evaluating Devices

Input devices in GUIs have been evaluated in many studies; Card et al. [3] evaluated devices such as the mouse and joystick, while Ramcharitar et al. [14] have compared game controllers. Here, we again note that these devices are modeled by using Fitts' law [3,14].

Other devices have been also modeled, such as sewing machines [15], forklifts [16], the turning of a two-handled crank [17], and driving simulators [18]. Thus, there are precedents for Fitts' law or the steering law also being suitable for operations other than those in GUIs.

3 Experiment

In our study, we conducted a drone crossing operation experiment to control a drone completely and fly it through a frame with a target width.

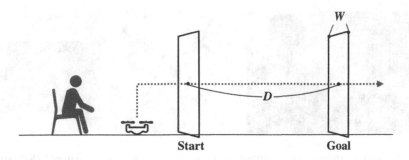

Fig. 4. Crossing experiment outline

3.1 Participants

The participants of our study included 12 undergraduate and graduate students (7 male and 5 female students, average 23.2 years, $SD = 0.80$ years). Two participants had little experience in drone control, while nine had been subjected to previous experiments conducted by us for about two hours, and one had a total of about ten hours of drone operation experience.

3.2 Task

The participants were required to control a drone on a path through two frames (Fig. 4). To reduce the effect of the difference in the height of each participant, they were made to sit on a chair at a distance of 1.0 m from the starting area (Fig. 5, left panel). The participants were requested to perform the task as quickly and accurately as possible. The participants were informed that the flight position of the drone was freely adjustable until drone passage through the start frame. In this experiment, a trial was considered successful if the drone passed from the start frame to the goal frame without colliding with either frame; otherwise, it was considered to be unsuccessful. Participants were notified of their success or failure in each trial.

3.3 Apparatus

The experiment was conducted in a room (6.0 m in length, 2.5 m in width, and 2.5 m in height) containing no obstacles. The air-conditioning in the room was turned off. To prevent collision of the drone with the wall, a mat was positioned behind the goal frame (Fig. 5, left panel). A drone called "Parrot Mambo Fly (180.0 mm in length, 180.0 mm in width, 40.0 mm in height)[4]" was used for the experiment; this drone has a dedicated iPad application called "Free Flight Mini[5]" as the controller (Fig. 5 right). The speed of the drone is controlled by the inclination of the drone; the maximum inclination can be adjusted in the range of 5° to 25° in the application. We chose the default setting (15°) in the experiment.

---

[4] https://www.parrot.com/global/drones/parrot-mambo-fly.
[5] https://www.parrot.com/global/freeflight-mini.

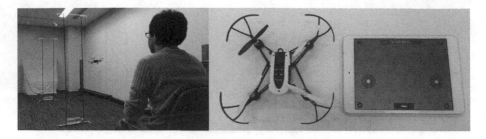

Fig. 5. Crossing experiment environment: photograph of actual experiment (left panel); Drone and controller used for experiment (right panel)

3.4 Design and Procedure

The target width W was 0.3, 0.4, or 0.5 m, while the target distance D was either 2.5 or 3.5 m. The frame used in the experiment was 1.8 m in height, which we believed to be sufficient for controlling and maneuvering the drone. The participants were given a time of approximately 10 min to familiarize themselves with the drone controls; we selected one condition from the six conditions ($2D \times 3W$) and the participants performed the task as practice until they succeeded three times. Subsequently, they performed the task 10 times, from which experimental data was obtained. Participants repeated the above procedure six ($2D \times 3D$) times. The order of selecting the conditions was counterbalanced by the Latin square. In total, 720 trials (i.e., $2D \times 3W \times 10$ sets $\times 12$ participants) were conducted; the time required was approximately 40–80 min per participant.

3.5 Measurement

The movement time MT (the time difference between when the center of the drone passes through the start frame and when it passes through the goal frame) and error rate were recorded for each trial. Parameter MT was measured from the videos obtained during the experiments.

4 Results

The acquired data were analyzed by means of repeated measures ANOVA and the Bonferroni post hoc test. The data of ten trials were deleted by mistake, and hence, the data of only 710 trials were used as experimental data. The number of errors was 124 (17.4%).

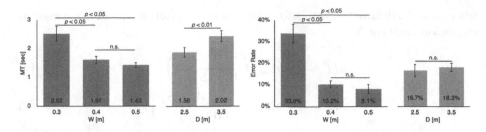

Fig. 6. Effects of distance D and width W on movement time MT (left panel) and error rate (right panel) in crossing experiment

4.1 Effects of D and W on MT

First, we examined the main effects of W ($F_{2,22} = 25.06$, $p < 0.01$) and D ($F_{1,11} = 13.28$, $p < 0.01$) on MT (Fig. 6 left panel). From multiple comparisons, it was observed that an increase in D ($p < 0.01$) and/or decrease in W ($p > 0.10$ for W values between 0.4 m and 0.5 m; otherwise, $p < 0.05$) resulted in an increase in MT (Fig. 6 left). The interaction in $D \times W$ on MT was not observed ($F_{2,22} = 0.50$, $p > 0.10$).

4.2 Effect of D and W on Error Rate

We next observed the main effects of W ($F_{2,22} = 31.95$, $p < 0.01$) on the error rate; however, we could not observe the main effects of D ($F_{1,11} = 0.55$, $p > 0.10$) on the error rate (Fig. 6, right panel). From multiple comparisons, we found that decreasing W ($p > 0.10$ for W between 0.4 m and 0.5 m; otherwise, $p < 0.05$) resulted in an increase in the error rate (Fig. 6 right). The interaction in $D \times W$ on error rate was not observed ($F_{2,22} = 0.70$, $p > 0.10$).

4.3 Model Fitness

The movement time (MT) of crossing operations in GUIs can be modeled by Fitts' law (Eq. 1); thus, Fitts' law can be considered as a candidate model. In the crossing experiment, for example, if the drone collides with the frame, the drone may crash, and therefore, it is necessary to ensure clear passage of the drone completely within the frame. Therefore, taking into account the size of the drone ($S = 0.18$ m), the model in which the target width W for Fitts' law is replaced by $W - S$ becomes a candidate model (Eq. 2, the log term of this equation is represented as ID_{cf}). Meanwhile, a previous study [6] has demonstrated that the two-part model is also a good fit for pointing operations; thus, the two-part model also forms a candidate model (Eq. 3, the log term of this equation is represented as ID_{ct}).

$$MT = a + b \log_2 \left(\frac{D}{W} + 1 \right) \tag{1}$$

where a and b denote the regression constants (hereafter, a, b, and k are used as regression constants).

$$MT = a + b \log_2 \left(\frac{D}{W - S} + 1 \right) \qquad (2)$$

$$MT = a + b \log_2 \left(\frac{D + (W - S)}{(W - S)^k} \right) \qquad (3)$$

Next, we verified whether Fitts' law (Eq. 2) suitably fits our results. The relationship between MT and ID_{cf} is depicted in left panel of Fig. 7. We note from the figure that Fitts' law affords a good fit for the crossing operation ($R^2 = 0.940$). Next, we verified whether the two-part model (Eq. 3) could suitably fit our results. The relationship between MT and ID_{ct} is shown in the right panel of Fig. 7. Again, it can be observed that the two-part model affords a good fit for the crossing operation ($R^2 = 0.948$). In this regard, Shoemaker has demonstrated that when the MT curves for each D and W value do not intersect, the two-part model is more suitable than Fitts' law [19]. However, as shown in Fig. 8, the MT curves for each D and W value do overlap; thus, we can consider both Fitts' law and the two-part model to be good fits. Meanwhile, from Fig. 9, we note that the MT curves for each D and W value do not intersect in the pointing experiment.

Table 1 lists the fitness of each model for the crossing operation. In general, a model with higher R^2 and lower AIC is a better model. From the table,

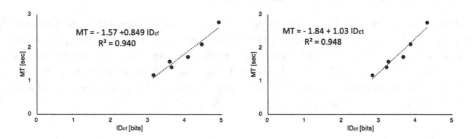

Fig. 7. Model suitability for Fitts' law (left panel) and two-part model (right panel) for crossing operation

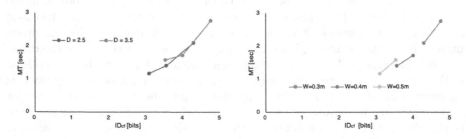

Fig. 8. Relationship between ID_{cf} and MT for each value of D (left panel) and W (right panel)

we note that R^2 is slightly higher for the two-part model, whereas AIC is slightly lower for Fitts' law. Therefore, Fitts' law, which has fewer parameters, is a better model for the crossing operation.

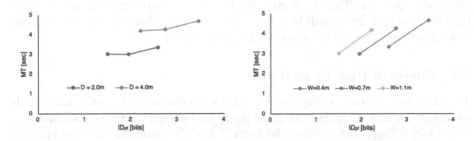

Fig. 9. Relationship between ID_{pf} and MT for each value of D (left panel) and W (right panel) (corresponding to Figures 11 and 12, respectively, in [6])

Table 1. Comparison of models considered for crossing operation

	Eq.	a	b	k	R^2	AIC
Fitts' law	$MT = a + b\log_2\left(\frac{D}{W-S}+1\right)$	-1.57	0.849		0.940	0.153
Two-part model	$MT = a + b\log_2\left(\frac{D+(W-S)}{(W-S)^k}\right)$	-1.84	1.03	0.806	0.948	1.42

5 Discussions

5.1 Effect of Target Width

Participants made comments such as, "I felt that reaching the target was difficult when the width was reduced, but I did not feel it was very difficult even when the target distance was increased," and "It was much more difficult to reach the target for narrower widths." These comments are consistent with experimental results, wherein we observed that the error rate is affected only by the target width W. In this experiment, the target distance D was varied as 2.5 m and 3.5 m, that is, the difference was only 1.0 m; thus, it appears that more participants were affected by the width than the distance.

5.2 Difference in Model Fitness Due to Experimental Environments

Fitts' law was found to be a good fit for the crossing operation ($R^2 = 0.940$); however, it was not suitable for the pointing operation ($R^2 = 0.672$) [6]. The drone used in the pointing experiment was slower than the drone used in the crossing experiment. The slower is the drone speed, the more pronounced is the effect of target distance D. The change in the D value in the crossing experiment was 1.0 m; however, the change in the D value in the pointing experiment was 2.0 m. The larger is the difference between the D values, the more will each D curve in the graph show a separation, as in the results of the pointing experiment (Fig. 9). For these reasons, for the pointing experiment, only the two-part model afforded a good fit. Therefore, even in the crossing experiments, we speculate that the two-part model will be a better fit over Fitts' law when a slower drone is used or when the gap between the D values is increased.

5.3   Causes of High Error Rates

The error rate of the crossing task was 17.4%. In this regard, participants made comments such as, "I thought that the drone had passed the frame (however, the drone had actually not reached the frame)" and "I would like to maneuver the drone from the side of the frame." Based on these comments, we assumed that participants struggled to perceive the distance between the drone and the frame. Therefore, we considered that the error rate of this experiment is higher than the error rate of crossing on the GUI, which does not require depth perception (7.4%) [1].

6   Limitation and Future Work

The drone used for the experiment was prepared by experimenters, not participants. In the experiments, the drone was unlikely to break down. Further, the frame was composed of a soft material, and thus, the drone did not break down even when it collided with the frame. Moreover, we note that although we asked the participants to maneuver the drones "quickly and accurately," when maneuvering under the risk of break down and when using their own drone, users will generally focus more on not making mistakes than reducing the movement time. That is, users will want to maneuver the drones more "accurately" than "quickly." We considered that if the emphasizes would have been on "accuracy", the experiment would have been closer to the actual drone operations.

Further, the user standing position and viewpoint are of importance. In this experiment, the participants stood on the takeoff side of the drone. Although there are many such situations, there are also cases in which the drone is maneuvered to return to the users or in the middle of the takeoff and the target. In the experiment, the participants maneuvered the drone while watching the target and the drone at the same time (i.e., TPV). However, as in the case of drone races, there are situations in which users need to maneuver drones from the FPV; thus, we should also verify how the FPV affects drone maneuvering. Via examining the results for various standing positions and viewpoints, we can demonstrate the effects of the standing position and viewpoints on the movement time; this will form the topic of future studies.

The steering (e.g., flying a drone through a corridor[6], Fig. 10) operation forms a major component of drone operation. In GUIs, the steering law is derived from

---

[6] https://youtu.be/MI2tgUKK3Ds.

the crossing law [1]. Thus, even for drones, because crossing operations can be modeled, we hypothesize that even steering operations can be modeled.

Fig. 10. Example of drone pointing operation: flying drone through corridor

7   Conclusion

In this study, we performed crossing experiments with a drone, and we studied the effects of the target distance and target width on the drone movement time and the error rate. Our results demonstrated that the movement time was affected by the target distance and target width, whereas the error rate was only affected by the target width. Further, an analysis of our results indicated that Fitts' law could be applied to the crossing operation. This indicates that with the use of suitable models, we can predict the drone operation time in crossing operations. In addition, we can compare various drones and controllers and evaluate the drone control interfaces in crossing operations. We believe that our findings will further contribute to advancements in drone operations across a wide range of applications.

References

1. Accot, J., Zhai, S.: Beyond Fitts' law: models for trajectory-based HCI tasks. In: Proceedings of the ACM SIGCHI Conference on Human Factors in Computing Systems, pp. 295–302 (1997)
2. MacKenzie, I.S., Sellen, A., Buxton, W.A.S.: A comparison of input devices in element pointing and dragging tasks. In: Proceedings of the SIGCHI Conference on Human Factors in Computing Systems, pp. 161–166. ACM (1991)
3. Card, S.K., English, W.K., Burr, B.J.: Evaluation of mouse, rate-controlled isometric joystick, step keys, and text keys for text selection on a CRT. Ergonomics **21**(8), 601–613 (1978)
4. Accot, J., Zhai, S.: Performance evaluation of input devices in trajectory-based tasks: an application of the steering law. In: Proceedings of the SIGCHI Conference on Human Factors in Computing Systems, pp. 466–472 (1999)

5. Kobayashi, M., Igarashi, T.: Ninja cursors: using multiple cursors to assist target acquisition on large screens. In: Proceedings of the SIGCHI Conference on Human Factors in Computing Systems, pp. 949–958. ACM (2008)

6. Yamada, K., Usuba, H., Miyashita, H.: Modeling drone pointing movement with Fitts' law. In: Extended Abstracts of the 2019 CHI Conference on Human Factors in Computing Systems, CHI EA 2019, pp. LBW2519:1–LBW2519:6 (2019)

7. Zollmann, S., Hoppe, C., Langlotz, T., Reitmayr, G.: FlyAR: augmented reality supported micro aerial vehicle navigation. IEEE Trans. Vis. Comput. Graph. **20**(4), 560–568 (2014)

8. Hedayati, H., Walker, M., Szafir, D.: Improving collocated robot teleoperation with augmented reality. In: Proceedings of the 2018 ACM/IEEE International Conference on Human-Robot Interaction, pp. 78–86. ACM (2018)

9. Erat, O., Isop, W.A., Kalkofen, D., Schmalstieg, D.: Drone-augmented human vision: exocentric control for drones exploring hidden areas. IEEE Trans. Vis. Comput. Graph. **24**(4), 1437–1446 (2018)

10. Hall, B.D., Anderson, N., Leaf, K.: Improving human interfaces for commercial camera drone systems. In: Proceedings of the 2017 CHI Conference Extended Abstracts on Human Factors in Computing Systems, pp. 112–117. ACM (2017)

11. Hansen, J.P., Alapetite, A., MacKenzie, I.S., Møllenbach, E.: The use of gaze to control drones. In: Proceedings of the Symposium on Eye Tracking Research and Applications, pp. 27–34. ACM (2014)

12. Cho, K., Cho, M., Jeon, J.: Fly a drone safely: evaluation of an embodied egocentric drone controller interface. Interact. Comput. **29**(3), 345–354 (2017)

13. Kasahara, S., Niiyama, R., Heun, V., Ishii, H.: ExTouch: spatially-aware embodied manipulation of actuated objects mediated by augmented reality. In: Proceedings of the 7th International Conference on Tangible, Embedded and Embodied Interaction, pp. 223–228. ACM (2013)

14. Ramcharitar, A., Teather, R.J.: A Fitts' law evaluation of video game controllers: thumbstick, touchpad and gyrosensor. In: Proceedings of the 2017 CHI Conference Extended Abstracts on Human Factors in Computing Systems, pp. 2860–2866. ACM (2017)

15. Montazer, M.A., Vyas, S.K., Wentworth, R.N.: A study of human performance in a sewing task. In: Proceedings of the Human Factors Society Annual Meeting, vol. 31, pp. 590–594. SAGE Publications, Los Angeles (1987)

16. Drury, C.G., Dawson, P.: Human factors limitations in fork-lift truck performance. Ergonomics **17**(4), 447–456 (1974)

17. Reed, K., Peshkin, M., Colgate, J.E., Patton, J.: Initial studies in human-robot-human interaction: Fitts' law for two people. In: 2004 IEEE International Conference on Robotics and Automation, Proceedings, ICRA 2004, vol. 3, pp. 2333–2338. IEEE (2004)

18. Zhai, S., Woltjer, R.: Human movement performance in relation to path constraint-the law of steering in locomotion. In: Virtual Reality, Proceedings, pp. 149–156. IEEE (2003)

19. Shoemaker, G., Tsukitani, T., Kitamura, Y., Booth, K.S.: Two-part models capture the impact of gain on pointing performance. ACM Trans. Comput.-Hum. Interact. (TOCHI) **19**(4), 28 (2012)

Research on the Differences of Risk Perception Ability Between Novice and Experienced Drivers

Jie Zhang$^{(\boxtimes)}$, Gang Guo$^{(\boxtimes)}$, Peizhi Wang, Qiuyang Tang$^{(\boxtimes)}$, and Zijian Zhang

Department of Vehicle Engineering, Chongqing University, Chongqing, China
1090791670@qq.com, cquguogang@163.com,
qiuyang.tang@foxmail.com

Abstract. Driving safety has been an important issue of common concern among countries around the world and novice drivers continue to have the high fatality rate. Researches have shown that driver's risk perception plays a leading role in driving safety. This research establishes a driver's risk perception ability evaluation method including subjective cognition, risk perception and risk response to test and evaluate the differences in risk perception ability between experienced and novice drivers from both subjective and objective perspectives. Forty participants (20 novice drivers and 20 experienced driers) were asked to drive through six dangerous scenarios (both visible and hidden hazards were included) connecting to an eye tracking system and were requested to identify hazardous situations. The results indicated that novice drivers performed worse in subjective cognition, risk perception and risk response. There were significant experience differences in risk perception ability. The results could provide guidance for the further development of driving assistance system.

Keywords: Novice and experienced drivers · Eye movements ·
Risk perception · Subjective scale · Risk response

1 Introduction

The traffic issue has become increasingly severe in the past ten years and traffic accidents have been the most common cause of abnormal deaths [1]. Statistics shows that 90% of traffic accidents are caused by drivers. In China, novice drivers (with driving experience less than 3 years and 10000 km mileages) caused more than 40% of traffic accidents and nearly 50% of deaths in traffic accidents [2]. Novice drivers have become the high-risk population who are easily involved in traffic accidents, posing serious threats to society.

Drivers' ability to acquire and assess information relevant to the recognition of risks in the road has been the focus of more recent studies [3]. The risk perception ability is an important driving ability which is most closely related to traffic accidents [4]. A previous study has shown that risk perception ability is negatively correlated with the rate of traffic accident [5], namely, the higher risk perception ability of drivers, the less likely occurrence of traffic accidents. It can be inferred that an important reason

© Springer Nature Switzerland AG 2019
C. Stephanidis (Ed.): HCII 2019, LNCS 11786, pp. 433–447, 2019.
https://doi.org/10.1007/978-3-030-30033-3_34

for the high accidental rate of novice drivers is their poor risk perception ability. Therefore, studying the differences of risk perception ability between novice and experienced drivers and proposing solutions based on the research results is a good idea to solve the problem of novice drivers.

Hazard perception test (HPT) is used for the detection of risk perception ability. Researchers have done a lot of researches on HPT and some nations have applied HPT into driver's license test [6]. There are three standard methods for HPT at present: driving simulator [7], dynamic videos [8] and static images [9]. In existing studies, most experiments are conducted by playing static pictures or dynamic videos to participants. After experiment, participants are required to describe their feelings about the dangerous situation and score the dangers showed in pictures or videos. These subjective evaluations of dangers may contain problems like evaluation distortion, evaluation ambiguity and largely individual differences. Some researches use tasks like pushing a button [10] or clicking mouse [11] to assess drivers' risk perception, which cannot completely reflect driver's true risk perception ability comparing to driving on the real road.

Previous study has shown that driving in a simulator is comparable to driving on the real road [12] and simulator is an essential tool for driver assessment because it can eliminate the consequences of exposing drivers to actual driving hazards and give the driver dynamic vision of driving on the real road. Eye movement techniques can be used in the field of traffic safety research [13] as eye movement is closely related to cognitive activities and 80% of traffic information is provided by vision. Questionnaire evaluation has the advantages of flexible in design, simple in operation and wide in implementation, and is not limited by time and space so that it is a commonly used tool to study dangerous feelings of drivers. Some scholars [14] believe that using questionnaire to measure driver's risk perception may be more comprehensive than other methods. Therefore, this research seeks to establish an effective method using advanced driving simulator, eye tracking and subjective scales to test and evaluate drivers' risk perception ability from both subjective and objective perspectives which can make up for the inadequacies in existing researches.

1.1 Risk Perception

Cognition includes processes such as perception, recognition, attention, memory, problem solving, language processing and so on. According to information process theory, hazard perception process of drivers can be described as follows: firstly, drivers receive information of surroundings through the sensory channels (vision, hearing, etc.). Then, the information is processed in cerebral cortex according to corresponding priori knowledge, e.g. driving experience and driving technology. The processing result will tell whether hazards are present. If the hazards exist, the muscular system will response to the risk according to the order given by cerebral cortex. Therefore, the risk perception process consists of three phases: sense, perception and response.

Driver's risk perception ability is an ability to judge the existing traffic environment or predict the subsequent events based on emerged information which allows drivers to perceive risks as early as possible and take necessary steps to resolve potential dangers.

Therefore, this paper divides driver's risk perception ability into three parts: subjective cognition, risk perception and risk response.

2 Method

2.1 Participants

40 drivers (20 novice drivers and 20 experienced drivers) who met the following requirements were selected to participate in the experiment: (1) in possession of a valid driver license; (2) not participated in HPT before; (3) with eyesight of 1.0 or above and normal color vision; (4) not professional social vehicle driving member. In order to exclude interference factors like age [15] and gender [16], there were 15 males and 5 females for each group and ranging in age from 20 to 35 years old (Table 1).

Table 1. Basic information of participants

Participants information	MEAN (SD)	
	Experienced drivers	Novice drivers
Age (year)	28.6 (3.86)	21.3 (0.47)
Total driving mileage (km)	6500 (63015.87)	366 (280.54)
Driving experience (year)	5.6 (1.27)	1.05 (0.82)

2.2 Apparatus

Driving Simulator

The Realtime Technologies driving simulator was used. It can accurately and realistically simulate the vehicle's motion from the overall performance of human-vehicle-environment closed-loop system. Participants sit inside the fixed-base car, and maneuver through the virtual environment displayed on the three screens (one in front of the car and two on each side) which can change appropriately just as they would go through in the real environment.

SimVista Modeling Software was used to build virtual world that include various types of static roadway geometries (freeway, intersections, signs, etc.). Buildings, tree lines and forests can be efficiently represented by only those surfaces. Moreover, it is possible to control the traffic flow and program vehicles or pedestrians to move along a fixed path at a normal speed.

Eye tracker

The Dikablis Eye Tracking System is a latest high-precision, low-invasive and high-end eye tracker developed by Ergoneers of Germany to track driver's sight and superimpose the viewpoint data on scenario video to study driver's vision and attention. It is equipped with two cameras, which are responsible for tracking the eyes and recording scenarios respectively. The 1920 × 1080 high-definition camera clearly records the scenario video image with sampling frequency of 50 Hz. The driving simulator and eye tracker are shown as Fig. 1.

Fig. 1. The driving simulator and eye tracker

2.3   Scenarios

Hazardous scenarios are generally divided into two categories: scenarios with obvious source of danger or potential source of danger, namely dominantly risky scenarios and potentially risky scenarios. Dominant hazards are those currently visible to driver and potential hazards are hidden hazards, such as the blind spots in the right turn, requiring drivers to predict possible dangers in the future. The following six dangerous scenarios (both visible and hidden hazards were included) with ten hazardous areas (divided to facilitate the analysis of eye movement data) were built in the driving simulator as shown in Table 2 and Fig. 2.

Table 2. Ten hazardous areas of six scenarios

Scenario	Area	Hazard description	Key point
S1	a1	When driving a car at a straight road without crossing, one pedestrian cross the road ahead. Dominant danger of Human category	We note whether drivers brake in time and pay attention to the rear car to prevent rear-end collision
S2	a2	Trucks parking by the side of the road may suddenly change its driving state. Dominant danger of Other Vehicles category	We note whether drivers fixate near the left front edge of the truck as they pass by the truck
	a3	Trucks obscure driver's sight so it's hard to predict if pedestrians will walk out in front of the truck. Potential danger of Human category	
S3	a4	When turning left at the intersection, there is a vehicle turning left in front. Dominant danger of Other Vehicles category	We note whether drivers brake to follow the traffic lights and the front car and pay attention to the rear car to prevent rear-end collision
	a5	Intersection ahead with traffic lights. Dominant dangerous of Intersection category	

(continued)

Table 2. (*continued*)

Scenario	Area	Hazard description	Key point
S4	a6	There is a road maintenance section ahead, and the driver needs to driver over the centerline. Dominant danger of Road Environment category	We note whether drivers slow down and observe the left edge of the obstacle to see if there are vehicles coming from the opposite direction and be careful to the rear-end collision
	a7	The view is blocked by the obstacle, and it's not obvious for drivers to know if there are vehicles coming from the opposite lane. Potential danger of Other Vehicles category	
S5	a8	On the intersection without traffic lights, the right side is blocked by buildings and there may be vehicles running out laterally. Potential danger of Intersection category	It requires the drivers to slow down when crossing the intersection and consciously look at the rearview mirror to prevent rear-end collision in the case of the possibility of slamming the brakes
	a9	There may be vehicles appear on the left side of the intersection. Potential danger of Intersection category	
S6	a10	A sharp turn suddenly appears without any prompt when the driver's driving speed is easily getting faster on a straight road Potential danger of Road Environment category	We note if the driver can notice the linear structure of the road and improve his vigilance to make a correct judgment

Fig. 2. Six scenarios built on the driving simulator

2.4   Variables

The independent variable in this research is driving experience. Novice driver is lack of driving experience and experienced driver is more skilled with rich driving experience, which results in the differences of their risk perception ability and driving performance.

There are three dependent variables: subjective cognition, risk perception and risk response. Each variable contains several secondary indicators which are measured from different ways. Subjective cognition is measured by the scores of scales, risk perception is analyzed by eye movement data and risk response is obtained from vehicle data during driving process and in-depth interviews.

Subjective Scales
The subjective scales of driving safety was designed to evaluate driver's subjective cognition of driving safety in driving attitude, driving skill and hazard perception.

Driving Attitude Scale was taken from Li's driver attitude questionnaire [17] which was based on the research of Ulleberg [18], including questions about driver's attitude towards traffic fluency and compliance, speed, driving entertainment. The Likert 5-point scoring method was used to arrange the options as: very disagree, disagree, neutral, agree, very agree, and the corresponding score was 5 points, 4 points, 3 points, 2 points, 1 point.

Driving Skill Scale was taken from the Driving Skill Inventory (DSI) of Lajunnen [19]. The options were arranged as: very bad, bad, average, good, very good, and the corresponding score was 1 point, 2 points, 3 points, 4 points and 5 points.

Hazard Perception Scale was taken from the risk perception questionnaire developed by White [20]. The options were arranged as: not dangerous, not too dangerous, no feeling, dangerous, very dangerous, and the corresponding score was 1 point, 2 points, 3 points, 4 points and 5 points.

Besides the subjective scales, we also conduct in-depth interviews to let participants score and describe the dangers in the scenarios, which reflects their feeling and reactions towards dangers and can be combined with objectively measured data from eye tracking and simulated driving to support the analysis of differences in risk perception ability between experienced and novice drivers. The following questions will be mainly asked: (a) Have you recognized the danger during driving? (b) Was it dangerous? How many levels do you want to score it from 1–10? (c) What was your reaction during driving? (d) Which areas did you concern about in this scenario? These questions are designed to know their dangerous feelings about the scenarios.

Risk Perception Sorted by the speed of eye scanning, there are three types of eye movements: glance, fixation and saccade. 8 refined indicators of eye movement related to glance, fixation and saccade are selected.

Risk Sensitivity
Time to first glance (TFG)/Time to first fixation (TFF): Time to first glance/fixation represents the time from the occurrence of hazard to the first time the driver scans/gaze at the risky area. The shorter TFG/TFF is, the more sensitive the driver is to the danger.

Number of rearview mirror glances: This indicator can be counted from the driving video, which shows the driver's sensitivity to the rear-end collision when changing lanes or taking turns.

Hazard Perception

Total glance time/Fixation duration: The sum of all glance/fixation time in risky areas. It indicates the complexity of processing dangerous information in risky areas [21];

Number of fixations/Number of saccades: This indicator reflects the cognitive process of dangerous information. Drivers will be more concerned about the risky area and get more information if the number of fixations and saccades are larger.

Saccade length: It indicates the processing of dangerous information. The greater the saccade distance, the more information is obtained when gazing at one time.

Risk Response

Generally speaking, after perceiving the danger, it takes drivers a period of time t1 to react which affects the braking distance of the vehicle that plays a key role in driving safety. The faster risk response shows the stronger cognitive ability of drivers. Reaction time and intra-group response sensitivity were used to evaluate the difference in risk response ability between experienced and novice drivers.

Reaction time was calculated from the appearance of hazards (in dynamic scenarios) or from the time of test vehicle arriving at a certain position (in static scenarios) to the time that drivers react. In order to obtain the reaction time in a dangerous situation, the driver's first reaction time was found from vehicle data such as brake pedal force, acceleration and so on.   Intra-group response sensitivity shows the sensitivity of the two groups of drivers responding to an event. It's defined as the proportion of drivers who notice the danger when it appears and react to avoid the danger when drive and can accurately describe the danger after drive. The result was obtained from the in-depth interview. In summary, the driver's risk perception ability evaluation model is establish as shown in Table 3.

Table 3. Driver's risk perception ability evaluation model

Variables	Secondary indicator	Measurement
Subjective cognition	Driving attitude	Compliance with regulations
		Over-speed driving situation
	Driving skill	Driving operation technology
		Driving safety motivation
	Hazard perception	Assessment of danger
Risk perception	Risk sensitivity	Rearview observations
		Time to first glance
		Time to first fixation
	Hazard perception	Fixation duration
		Total glance time
		Saccade length
		Number of fixations
		Number of saccades
Risk response	Response time	Reaction time
	Response accuracy	Intragroup response sensitivity

2.5 Procedure

Firstly, asking the participants to fill out an informed consent form and giving them written instructions about the experiment, telling them to follow the voice navigation and obey traffic rules throughout the drive. After the participants read the instructions and know clearly about the experiment, they were asked to fill the subjective scales which lasted about 5 min. Then, they got into driving simulator with the head mounted eye tracker and were given adaptive drive to get comfortable with the simulator and eye tracker. After that, calibrating eye tracker to track their sight and starting the test drive with designed scenarios while eye movement data and vehicle data were recorded from the eye tracker and driving simulator, which lasted about 20 min. Finally, the in-depth interview was carried out and participants' answers about the designed questions were recorded in this phase.

2.6 Data Analysis

We could get rich data from the following three aspects: (i) the scores of subjective scales, which represents driver's subjective cognition of driving safety, (ii) eye movement data, such as time to first fixation, number of fixations and saccade length were obtained, and (iii) vehicle data, including velocities, coordinates, accelerations and other vehicle data were obtained. The independent sample t-test was used for data conforming to normal distribution, otherwise the independent sample u-test was used to analyze whether data between novice and experienced drivers has significant differences. Statistical significance was noted when p-values were less than 0.05.

3 Results

3.1 Subjective Scales

There was no significant difference in driving attitude (P = 0.11) between novice and experienced drivers, and novice drivers' driving attitude score was even higher than experienced drivers. There were significant differences in driving skills (P < 0.01) and hazard cognition (P < 0.05) between novice and experienced drivers. The total score of subjective scales was tested. There was significant difference in subjective cognition (P < 0.05) between experienced and novice drivers, and the subjective cognition of experienced driver was better than novice driver, as shown in Fig. 3.

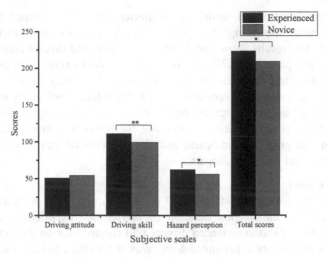

Fig. 3. Scores of subjective scales

3.2 Risk Perception

Risk Sensitivity

The eye movement data of novice and experienced drivers in the 10 hazardous areas were extracted and analyzed. a1, a3, a4 and a9 are dynamic hazardous scenes that only when the test vehicle reaches the set positions will the vehicle and pedestrian be triggered. There were significant differences of TFG in potentially hazardous areas a3 ($P < 0.001$) and a9 ($P < 0.01$) and experienced drivers noticed the risk earlier. There were significant differences of TFF in a3 ($P < 0.05$) and a9 ($P < 0.001$), and novice drivers had a longer TFF. There were no significant differences in a1 and a4 (dominantly risk interest areas) of TFG and TFF between novice and experienced drivers, as shown in Fig. 4.

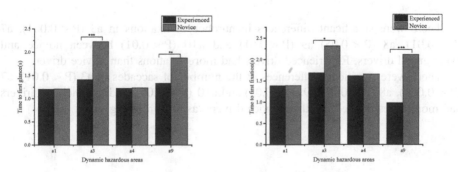

Fig. 4. TFG and TFF in dynamic hazardous areas

We counted the number that novice and experienced drivers scanned the rearview mirror and correctly turned signal to analyze the driver's sensitivity to the potential danger behind. The results show that 83.8% of experienced drivers correctly opened turning signal, compared to 54.7% of novice drivers. And experienced drivers recognized the left and right rearview mirror much more frequently than novice drivers. During the driving process, drivers could check the vehicles behind by observing the rearview mirror, or they could remind rear vehicles by turning signal. The higher the frequency of the experienced drivers observing the rearview mirror and the correctly lighting when changing lanes indicated that the experienced drivers were more sensitive to the rear-end potential dangers.

Hazard Perception

In potentially risky areas a3 (P < 0.001), a7 (P < 0.05), a8 (P < 0.001), a9 (P < 0.01), and a10 (P < 0.05), the fixation duration of novice and experienced drivers were significantly different and experienced drivers had shorter fixation durations.

The total glance time of experienced driver was shorter than novice drivers and there were significant differences in a3 (P < 0.01), a7 (P < 0.001), a8 (P < 0.05), a9 (P < 0.001) and a10 (P < 0.05) between novice and experienced drivers, as shown in Fig. 5.

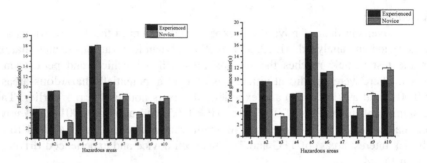

Fig. 5. Fixation duration and total glance time in the 10 hazardous areas

There were significant differences in number of fixations in a3 (P < 0.001), a7 (P < 0.01), a8 (P < 0.05) a9 (P < 0.01) and a10 (P < 0.01) between novice and experienced drivers. Experienced drivers had more fixations than novice drivers.

There were significant differences of the number of saccades in a3 (P < 0.01), a7 (P < 0.001), a8 (P < 0.05) a9 (P < 0.05) and a10 (P < 0.05), and experienced drivers had more times of saccades than novice drivers, as shown in Fig. 6.

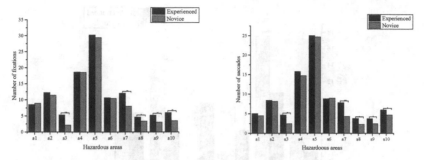

Fig. 6. Number of fixations and saccades in the 10 hazardous areas

There were significant differences in saccade length in a3 (P < 0.01), a7 (P < 0.01), a8 (P < 0.001), a9 (P < 0.01) and a10 (P < 0.05) between novice and experienced drivers. Experienced drivers had longer saccade length, as shown in Fig. 7.

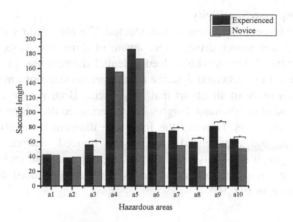

Fig. 7. Saccade length in the 10 hazardous areas

In areas with dominant dangers, there were no significant differences in indicators above. In short, there were significant differences between novice and experienced drivers in the eight indicators of risk perception in potentially risky situations, while no significant difference in dominant dangers.

3.3   Risk Response

Reaction Time
In all risky scenarios, the driver must brake to avoid dangers so we extracted the response time of drivers in six dangerous scenarios, and the reaction time was significantly different in S1(P < 0.05), S2(P < 0.001), S3(P < 0.01), S4(P < 0.05), S5 (P < 0.001) and S6(P < 0.05), which indicated that experienced driver responded faster and took timely measures to avoid risks, as shown in Fig. 8.

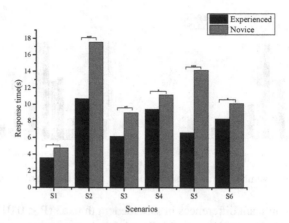

Fig. 8. Reaction time in the six scenarios

Intra-group Response Sensitivity

After driving, the in-depth interview was conducted. The recorded results indicated that both experienced and novice drivers were aware of dominant dangers, but the proportion of experienced drivers who noticed potential dangers was higher than novice drivers. Experienced drivers could describe the dangerous situations in a more accurate way and gave a variety of situations that may occur. Both novice and experienced drivers had responded to dominant dangers, but experienced drivers performed better in potentially risky scenarios. Drawing the following diagram by multiplying the proportion of novice and experienced drivers who noticed, reacted, and accurately described the danger, it's obvious to see that intra-group response sensitivity of novice drivers to judge and response to hazards was poor than experienced drivers in the six scenarios, as shown in Fig. 9.

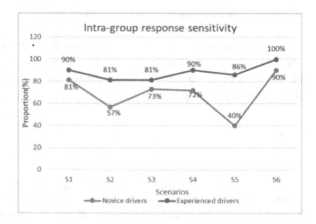

Fig. 9. Intra-group response sensitivity of experienced and novice drivers in the six scenarios

4   Discussion

According to the previous analysis, novice drivers' driving safety awareness was worse than experienced drivers. Although novice drivers' driving attitude was relatively good, which might be attributed to their tendency to be conservative, cautious to strictly abide by traffic rules when driving, they were often at risk due to the limitation of driving skills and deficiency in hazardous cognition. The subjective cognition of hazards includes assessing both the level of risk and their ability to deal with the hazard effectively, which can provide the requisite information for risk perception.

From the in-depth interview we knew that in the same scenario, novice drivers believed it was not that dangerous while experienced drivers thought there was a certain danger and generally scored higher than novice drivers, which in turn indicated that novice drivers had a higher threshold for dangerous reactions. In addition, most experienced drivers said that they would observe the rear vehicles in advance before turning or changing lanes to confirm that there was no danger of collision. Experienced drivers were more concerned and sensitive to the potential danger behind and had a higher sense of driving safety while novice drivers mainly pay attention to the road ahead during the driving process.

The eye movement data indicated that novice drivers performed poorer in risk perception. It was easier for novice driver to ignore the existence of the potential dangers or notice the dangers slower than experienced drivers. The results proved Derry's research [22] that compared to novice drivers, experienced drivers detect hazards more quickly and efficiently and perceived them more holistically.

The significant differences in risk response indicated that novice drivers reacted more slowly in the presence of dangers. Huestegge [23] pointed out that the reaction time of experienced and novice drivers was affected by different processing speeds after a hazard was detected. Sometimes novice drivers noticed the danger but made a slower response to it. The lack of novice drivers' driving skills, which made it unable for them to control vehicles well, affects their reaction time in dangerous scenarios. Another probability was that novice drivers made a lower evaluation of dangers so it was hard to reach the threshold for response until the distance between the ego vehicle and the obstacle shortened to a certain extent.

Due to the space limitation, we didn't analyze the correlation of subjective assessment and objective measurement, but we could recognize that the subjective cognition was consistent with objective measurement. The disadvantages of this research was the limitation of number and backgrounds of participants who were mainly recruited from Chongqing University. Although some participants complained that the eye tracker was too heavy, no one ever discontinued the experiment because of this problem. Despite this, it still provides an effective method to test and evaluate driver's risk perception ability.

5 Conclusion

This paper constructs a complete cognitive test and evaluation method based on advanced driving simulator and eye tracker, exploring risk perception ability of novice and experienced drivers from three dimensions: subjective cognition, risk perception and risk response. The specific experience differences in dangerous scenarios are obtained, including the significance and manifestations of differences, which would facilitate the implement of experiment and design of training programs to compensate the risk perception ability of novice drivers. The method in this research is proved to be feasible and comprehensive in evaluating risk perception ability.

The results are mainly the following three aspects: (i) The subjective cognition of driving safety between novice and experienced drivers was significantly different and experienced drivers had a better sense of driving safety than novice drivers. (ii) The risk perception of novice and experienced drivers in potential dangers were significantly different, while in dominant dangers there was no significant difference. (iii) There were significant differences in risk response capability in both potential dangers and dominant dangers, and experienced drivers are more responsive to dangers.

If the experimental database is large enough, we will be able to provide accurate development and improvements for future ADAS and HMI systems based on the specific differences in drivers' risk perception ability. It is of great significance for promoting safe driving and reducing traffic accidents.

References

1. Zimasa, T., Jamson, S., Henson, B.: Are happy drivers safer drivers? Evidence from hazard response times and eye tracking data. Transp. Res. Part F: Traffic Psychol. Behav. **46**, 14–23 (2017). https://doi.org/10.1016/j.trf.2016.12.005
2. Ma, L., Tang Z., Cheng L.: Analysis of the danger perception ability of new and old drivers. China Science and Technology. Paper Online, (11), 854–857 (2011)
3. Pradhan, A.K., Hammel, K.R., DeRamus, R., Pollatsek, A., Noyce, D.A., Fisher, D.L.: Using eye movements to evaluate effects of driver age on risk perception in a driving simulator **47**(4), 840–852 (2005). https://doi.org/10.1518/001872005775570961
4. Fisher, D.L.: Can novice drivers be trained to scan for information that will reduce their likelihood of a crash? Injury Prev. **12**(suppl_1), i25–i29 (2006). https://doi.org/10.1136/ip.2006.012021
5. Crundall, D.: Hazard prediction discriminates between novice and experienced drivers. Accid. Anal. Prev. **86**, 47–58 (2016). https://doi.org/10.1016/j.aap.2015.10.006
6. Wetton, M.A., Hill, A., Horswill, M.S.: The development and validation of a hazard perception test for use in driver licensing. Accid. Anal. Prev. **43**(5), 1759–1770 (2011). https://doi.org/10.1016/j.aap.2011.04.007
7. Martinussen, L.M., Møller, M., Prato, C.G.: Accuracy of young male drivers' self-assessments of driving skill. Transp. Res. Part F: Traffic Psychol. Behav. **46**, 228–235 (2017). https://doi.org/10.1016/j.trf.2017.03.001
8. Scialfa, C.T., Deschênes, M.C., Ference, J., Boone, J., Horswill, M.S., Wetton, M.: A hazard perception test for novice drivers. Accid. Anal. Prev. **43**(1), 204–208 (2011). https://doi.org/10.1016/j.aap.2010.08.010

9. Finn, P., Bragg, B.W.E.: Perception of the risk of an accident by young and older drivers. Accid. Anal. Prev. **18**(4), 289–298 (1986). https://doi.org/10.1016/0001-4575(86)90043-6
10. Borowsky, A., Shinar, D., Oron-Gilad, T.: Age, skill, and hazard perception in driving. Accid. Anal. Prev. **42**(4), 1240–1249 (2010). https://doi.org/10.1016/j.aap.2010.02.001
11. Smith, S.S., Horswill, M.S., Chambers, B., Wetton, M.: Hazard perception in novice and experienced drivers: the effects of sleepiness. Accid. Anal. Prev. **41**(4), 729–733 (2009). https://doi.org/10.1016/j.aap.2009.03.016
12. Underwood, G., Crundall, D., Chapman, P.: Driving simulator validation with hazard perception. Transp. Res. Part F: Traffic Psychol. Behav. **14**(6), 435–446 (2011). https://doi.org/10.1016/j.trf.2011.04.008
13. Coeckelbergh, T.R.M., Cornelissen, F.W., Brouwer, W.H., Kooijman, A.C.: The effect of visual field defects on eye movements and practical fitness to drive. Vis. Res. **42**(5), 669–677 (2002). https://doi.org/10.1016/s0042-6989(01)00297-8
14. Farrand, P., McKenna, F.P.: Risk perception in novice drivers: the relationship between questionnaire measures and response latency. Transp. Res. Part F: Traffic Psychol. Behav. **4** (3), 201–212 (2001). https://doi.org/10.1016/s1369-8478(01)00024-9
15. Underwood, G., Phelps, N., Wright, C., Van Loon, E., Galpin, A.: Eye fixation scanpaths of younger and older drivers in a hazard perception task. Ophthal. Physl. Opt. **25**(4), 346–356 (2005). https://doi.org/10.1111/j.1475-1313.2005.00290.x
16. DeJoy, D.M.: An examination of gender differences in traffic accident risk perception. Accid. Anal. Prev. **24**(3), 237–246 (1992). https://doi.org/10.1016/0001-4575(92)90003-2
17. Li, T.: Analysis of the characteristics and discriminant indicators of improper driving behavior of motor vehicle drivers. Tsinghua University (2012)
18. Ulleberg, P., Rundmo, T.: Personality, attitudes and risk perception as predictors of risky driving behaviour among young drivers. Saf. Sci. **41**(5), 427–443 (2003). https://doi.org/10.1016/s0925-7535(01)00077-7
19. Lajunen, T., Summala, H.: Driving experience, personality, and skill and safety-motive dimensions in drivers' self-assessments. Pers. Indiv. Differ. **19**(3), 307–318 (1995). https://doi.org/10.1016/0191-8869(95)00068-h
20. White, M.J., Cunningham, L.C., Titchener, K.: Young drivers' optimism bias for accident risk and driving skill: Accountability and insight experience manipulations. Accid. Anal. Prev. **43**(4), 1309–1315 (2011). https://doi.org/10.1016/j.aap.2011.01.013
21. Ābele, L., Haustein, S., Møller, M., Martinussen, L.M.: Consistency between subjectively and objectively measured hazard perception skills among young male drivers. Accid. Anal. Prev. **118**, 214–220 (2018). https://doi.org/10.1016/j.aap.2018.02.022
22. Deery, H.A.: Hazard and risk perception among young novice drivers. J. Saf. Res. **30**(4), 225–236 (1999)
23. Huestegge, L., Skottke, E., Anders, S., Müsseler, J., Debus, G.: The development of hazard perception: dissociation of visual orientation and hazard processing. Transp. Res. Part F Traffic Psychol. Behav. **13**(1), 1–8 (2010). https://doi.org/10.1016/j.trf.2009.09.005

Design and User Experience Case Studies

Feasibility Assessment of Cloud SaaS Enabled Collaboration and Information Confidentiality for the Public Accounting Industry

Lior Baron[1](✉) and Tzipora Halevi[2]

[1] CUNY Graduate Center, New York, NY 10016, USA
lbaron@gradcenter.cuny.edu
[2] Brooklyn College, Brooklyn, NY 11210, USA

Abstract. In recent years, the growing use of Software as a Service (SaaS) presents both new opportunities and challenges for organizations. Specifically, building trust in SaaS as an alternative to traditional methods of conducting business presents unique challenges for the CPA industry, who deals with sensitive financial client information and strict regulations.

This study seeks to understand the attitudes and behavior of CPA industry staff members facing changing technology in the workspace. It investigates the usability of cloud SaaS collaboration platform, utilizing Microsoft Office 365 based solution and Microsoft SharePoint Online technology. It examines whether CPA staff members can overcome preconceptions about trust in SaaS tools. Specifically, can these tools, which store client information in the cloud, be used to safely exchange sensitive information between two parties while allowing CPA firms and clients to effectively collaborate on projects. The study design included a walk-through experiment as well as a semi-structured interview survey consisting of both open and closed-ended questions. The study participants were asked to use a pre-configured SharePoint collaboration portal and execute several predefined financial common tasks, following prescribed testing script, as well as fill an online survey regarding their experience. The study results demonstrate that CPA team members felt the software provides a better platform for communicating with clients than the currently used tools. However, participants' comfort level managing specific sensitive client information on the new online portal was lower, pointing to the potential need for follow-up training and improved education for CPA team members on the SaaS platform capabilities.

Keywords: Secured online collaboration · SaaS · Cloud · Accounting · Usability

1 Introduction

The interaction between public account firm and their clients makes an interesting case for secured human computer interaction investigation. The nature of the services CPA firms offer to their client requires sharing of large amount of sensitive financial and operational information between clients and CPA firms which typically clients will not share with outsiders.

© Springer Nature Switzerland AG 2019
C. Stephanidis (Ed.): HCII 2019, LNCS 11786, pp. 451–467, 2019.
https://doi.org/10.1007/978-3-030-30033-3_35

Public accounting firms in the US and elsewhere offer several services to clients which require collaboration during time bound projects. For example, most tax compliance work, whether personal or corporate tax filings, require the CPA firm to meet deadlines set by the federal or state government and missing deadlines could potentially result in financial penalties to clients. During the preparation of a tax return, the accounting firm will ask the clients to produce sensitive financial information and will use this information to prepare the tax return. The challenge many CPA firms face is how to effectively collaborate with clients while not compromising the client's sensitive financial information and maintaining a high level of trust with the client.

Before the age of electronic records, firms and individuals communicated with accounting firms either in person (e.g. delivering required documents for tax preparation) or via US Postal Mail, in which case both parties trusted the US post office and mail delivery to be secured and had high confidence that the information sent by mail will not be compromised. Since electronic records became the prevailing methods during the 1990s, secured means of electronic communication had to be established directly between the accounting firm and their clients since no third-party standard (like the US postal mail) was acceptable as reliable and secured. Many software companies rose up to the challenge and provided secured email communication and secured file transfers. As a result, CPA firms have many software solutions available for secured collaboration from several vendors which don't integrate well and present challenges for effective collaboration. For example, a CPA company might use a product like ShareFile or sFTP site for secured file transfer and MimeCast for secured email communication. When interacting with a client, the CPA firm will ask the client for sensitive information in an email with instructions on how to set up MimeCast secure email login and send the client a ShareFile password using secure email enabled by MimeCast before collaboration can take place. The client will then use 'the ShareFile password to upload the file. Thus, the client's staff is required to maintain two additional login credentials for collaborating with the CPA firm. If the CPA firm uses other products for collaboration (Chat software or online survey tools) the number of credentials managed by the client will increase. The collaboration process requires the CPA firm's client to manage a set of passwords for several tools and client standards for maintaining password could become an issue, especially in situations where there are several people at the client organization that require login to ShareFile and/or secured email and other tools.

1.1   SaaS Cloud Technologies for Collaboration

There are several SaaS platforms for collaboration that offer secured file transfer, secured communication and secured online collaboration space from which Microsoft's Office 365 and Google's G Suite are probably the most common. These platforms provide an integrated secured environment for individuals and firms to collaborate on files, communications, calendars and tasks. Both platforms [5, 6] use security at rest, secure file transfer S/Mime protocols, secured online access using https and two-step verification along with email spam and phishing filtering to ensure secure communication. Both platforms are certified by ISO, AICPA and HIPPA standards. In addition, the platforms integrate with a company's corporate directory, so there is no need for additional password management or risk that a departed employee will maintain access to the company's sensitive information. The integration with corporate security is an important feature of these enterprise collaboration software since it ensures that only active employees of the firm have access to online corporate resources. Once an employee leaves the corporation, their access to corporate resources including online collaboration software is eliminated.

Microsoft Office 365 software is the more robust option for both small and large corporations. It does not only include email and file sharing capabilities [5], but also a wide range of products which offer enhanced online collaboration experience. These include tools like SharePoint for online capabilities rich collaborative work space, MS Teams for small team collaboration, MS Flow for data integration, OneDrive for cloud file storage, and other management/survey/editing tools that are useful for collaboration between CPA firms and their clients.

1.2 Study Contribution

This is the first usability study in a CPA firm examining online collaboration SaaS software that we know of. Since this software is intended to replace current tools which facilitate information exchange with the client, developing internal methods of assessing the acceptance of such a tool is useful both for understanding the improvements needed for this tool as well as create a method for future tools evaluation. The CPA firm is seeking new and more efficient ways to work with clients and to leverage the available SaaS technology without negatively impacting client experience or information confidentiality. The CPA company is looking to integrate more SaaS software as a strategic direction to both cut costs on IT infrastructure and improve operational efficiency of its staff. Therefore, the contribution of this study is twofold. First, this study introduced an assessment methodology for new products in-house, which can be used for follow-up evaluations as well. Second, the study provided insights that helped the CPA firm to assess adoption challenges in using a new SaaS software with Microsoft's Office 365 platform implementation as a client collaboration platform to deliver work efficiently. The findings from this assessment are discussed in detail in the results section.

2 Theoretical Background

Qualitative methods have been shown to provide deeper insights into the user experience when working with a new product [7] and have been utilized in previous usability studies in the financial industry by Conway et al. [1]. Accounting staff are facing deadline driven work schedule with pressure to execute a large volume of high-quality work while interacting confidentially with their client. The tight deadlines and pressure to maximize productivity may result in behavior that will compromise client information confidentiality. The qualitative part of our assessment seeks to better understand frame of mind and decision around client information confidentiality. The quantitative testing will assess whether the CPA staff members were able to complete common collaboration tasks while avoiding common mistakes that impact client information confidentiality.

Maxion et al. [11] pointed to usability challenges when conducted a study of file permission interface, developing an alternative file access management system. We use similar testing methods to conduct the usability part of our study. This work assesses whether the file permission interface of our chosen SaaS collaboration platform addresses some of the original challenges pointed out in [11]. Our work further explores additional challenges (beyond file sharing) related to online questionnaires, collaborative work planning, online discussion boards and team announcements.

3　HCISEC Considerations

3.1　Client Information

CPA firm's client might be either a corporation or an individual seeking help with tax return, corporate audit, estate planning or other services. Whether the client is an individual entity (e.g. a person or a family) or a corporation, there are norms and guidelines that are generally accepted for interactions between CPA firms and clients as well as regulations set up by AICPA (in the US) and prevailing laws that specify what information the CPA firm needs to collect from clients to perform services. For example, an individual that hires a CPA firm to help with filing an individual federal tax return (form 1040 in the US) will be asked to provide the CPA firm with personal and financial information that will assist in tax preparation. A corporation seeking help with corporate tax might be required to provide information about sources of income (clients), vendors, payroll and products. Although the amount of client information could be large, the client is the source of information and is in full control of what information is shared with the CPA firm. According to those guidelines, the CPA firm must use the information for the sole purpose of providing the tax advice to the client and cannot use it for any other purpose.

3.2　Client Information Security

CPA firms are required to ensure the safety of information provided by clients from the moment the information is shared with the CPA firm. The information might come in several formats, like printed materials, electronic files, emails, and electronic media (DVD or tape). Regardless of the format, the CPA firm must ensure that no outside party can access the data and that only authorized CPA staff members can access it to perform services. In the case of online collaboration portal for corporate clients, the client information security requirement can be satisfied by using a combination of factors:

- Client access – strict external user access provisioning in Office 365 collaboration portal in SharePoint Online using the clients' existing accounts Office 365 can provide the authentication needed for sharing data between clients and the CPA firm. The CPA sends an invitation to collaborate to the user account and the client must accept within a given timeframe. Since the invitation is personalized to a specific corporate named user account, the method will simply piggy-back on existing client authentication capabilities.

- CPA staff access – the Office 365 groups provide an intuitive access provisioning interface for client team with ability to check effective access to verify correct configuration. In addition, by using a SharePoint feature called Site Collection for client collaboration, the chance for unintended staff access is further reduced since each site collection has a dedicated access configuration setup and does not share access credentials with other sites outside the collection. The CPA firm needs to have procedures in place to make sure client team access is properly maintained (by the client team) and change in team membership is reflected in the online collaboration portal.
- Hardware/Server unintended access risk – since the online collaboration portal uses cloud-based SaaS – Office 365, IT staff or non-client team staff member do not need access to the client information at all. The CPA firm does not need to maintain the infrastructure that stores this information, as the software provider (Microsoft) ensures the safe storage of the client information on its cloud servers.

3.3   Encryption Consideration for Online Collaboration

Encryption at rest - File storage for Office 365 collaboration is using Microsoft product called OneDrive for Business. Encryption for the OneDrive for Business product is facilitated by using BitLocker at the disk level and file/transaction level encryption and are compliant by Federal Information Processing Standard (FIPS) 140-2 according to Microsoft [9]. Encryption-in-transit for SharePoint online and OneDrive for Business uses SSL/TLS connections with 2048-bit keys. The SSL/TLS connections are used by both CPA firm staff and clients to upload or access shared information in OneDrive for Business and SharePoint Online.

4   Portal Implementation

To examine how an accounting firm can successfully collaborate with clients using a cloud based online collaboration tool, we used Microsoft Office 365 based solution which used Microsoft SharePoint Online technology for collaboration. The collaboration portal is used for collaboration between the accounting firm and corporate clients seeking to benefit from R&D tax credits at the federal or state level (IRS Form 6765 and various state tax forms). The tax credit work requires an investigation by the accounting firm of activities that will allow the client to maximize R&D tax credits given by the US federal government or states in which R&D activity took place. Typically, the process of collecting evidence for R&D tax credit requires the following collateral to be provided by the client-

1. A qualified R&D activity (a questionnaire is used to identify activities)
2. Identify R&D related investments to support these activities – Those include

    – An assessment of payroll expenses related to R&D (By employee, how much time allocated for R&D support)
    – Supplies cost related to R&D
    – Contracted support (vendor) cost in support of R&D work

3. For each of the three areas of R&D cost identification, the client needs to provide proof in the form of documentation and answering questions in pre-defined criteria. Depending on what the initial set of questions uncovers, more questions might be used to correctly classify R&D related activities that pertain to tax credit by federal or state level tax return.
4. The online collaboration portal support functionality needed for the R&D tax credit work (questionnaire and ability to upload documents as evidence).

The collaboration portal included the following features to enable successful collaboration:

- A dedicated SharePoint site collection using the accounting firm's Office 365 subscription
- Sharing with external users feature enabled

The user interface screens used for setup are shown in Figs. 1, 2, 3 and 4.

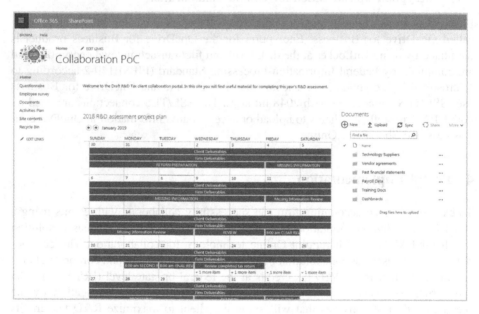

Fig. 1. The Primary landing page of the collaboration portal, displaying a team calendar and a list of online folders

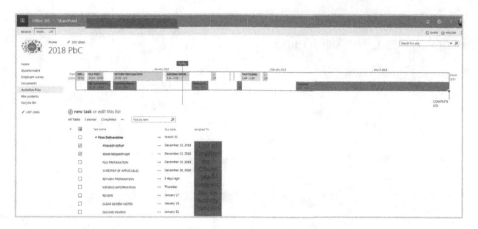

Fig. 2. SharePoint task list for tracking activities, assignments, dependencies and dates

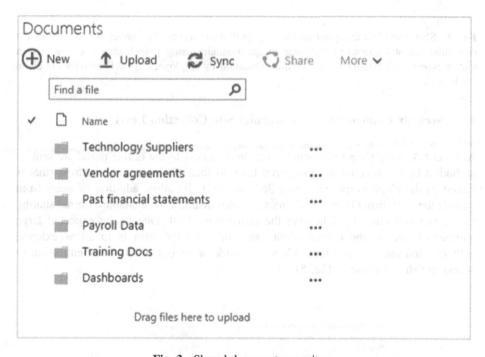

Fig. 3. Shared documents repository

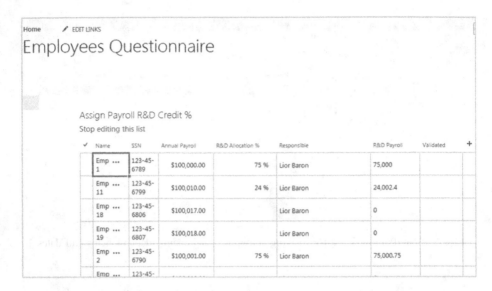

Fig. 4. SharePoint List to capture employee payroll R&D survey. The survey is a SharePoint list containing client's employee classification questionnaire using payroll data – Client subject matter experts will classify portion of time allocation by employees to R&D activities to claim tax benefits

4.1 Security Configuration - SharePoint Site Collection Level

A. Client Access. Client personnel which need access to the online portal are sent an invitation by the accounting firm portal team to their business email address (that is linked to the client corporate Office 365 account). To allow addition of users from outside the CPA firm Office 365 domain, an administrator must enable external sharing to the site collection by following the instructions [10]. Due to the expected large number of clients, the configuration used for the CPA firm is to allow external authenticated users to use their Microsoft work or school account authentication to access the shared content (Fig. 5).

Fig. 5. SharePoint site collection external user access configuration screen

The email request has a link by default to accept the invitation. Only after accepting the invitation will the client staff members get access to the portal. The invitation is linked to the Office 365 account of the client staff user's email. If somehow another person tries to use the link with a different account (other than the named user in the email) it access will not be granted.

Example of a system generated client invitation to the online collaboration portal sent to client (Fig. 6).

Fig. 6. Example of system generated email inviting an external user to log on

B. User Access Right Provisioning. Access rights in R&D credit portal use group membership to allow/restrict access to content in the collaboration portal. Each module in the portal can either inherit access rights from the parent site or specify unique access rights with view/edit/administer privileges. An example of the groups used in the solution is in the image below (Fig. 7):

Assessing effective user or group access (View/Download/Modify) can be viewed by using a built-in feature in SharePoint Online under the security setting for the site/folder/page/item section (Fig. 8).

Fig. 7. List of user security groups in SharePoint used for information access provisioning

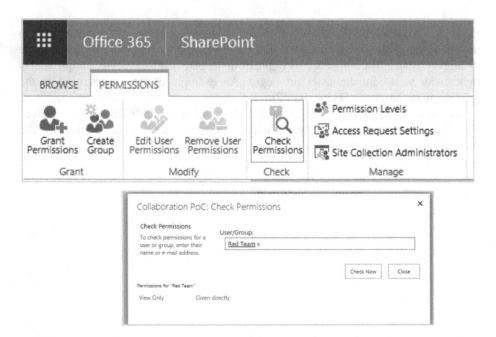

Fig. 8. SharePoint Security Permission Screen Ribbon. By clicking on "Check Permission", the user can enter the name of group or individual user and click on "Check Now" to view effective permissions

5 Study

The participants were divided into two groups, one simulating a CPA staff member and the other simulating a CPA client subject matter expert (CPA). The scenario used for the testing was an employee classification for R&D tax credit in which both CPA staff members and clients collaborate to complete information. This process is typically done in the context of R&D tax work with client by CPA firms in the US. All participants were CPA company employees. Half of the participants played the role of the client and the other half played the role of CPA firm team members. Participants were asked to complete a survey at the end of the study to provide feedback. In addition, to assess understanding of security and access, the study administrator played the role of the CPA firm's client staff trying to access non-authorized information using a non-CPA firm Microsoft Office 365 account with a Client SME role (SharePoint Online security group membership).

Study Tasks. The testing team was divided into two roles

- CPA team – CPA staff that provide a specific R&D Tax Credit Study service to a client
- Client SME team

Below is a description of the test tasks that the team members were asked to perform during the study.

CPA Team

> Step 1 - View the list of qualified projects (do not add new project or change project description - This will be done in future phases)
> Step 2 - Assign SME to help with employee classification - Use the "Responsible" column

Client SME Team

> Step 3 - Select each employee from the list and assign relative time to each on the projects on the right part of the screen

CPA Team

> Step 4 - Ask two questions in the client Questionnaire per instructions below:
> - Click on "Client Questionnaire" link and review the list of existing questions and answers
> - Post a question on the questionnaire list
> - Assign a person to answer from the client
> - Ask a sensitive question to client finance team in questionnaire list
> - You'll need to ensure that the Client SME Team does not have access to view the question

5.1 Survey

Participants in the test were asked to complete a survey – see below and Sect. 6 for questions and results.

In the survey, the participants were asked to fill out the Likert table below. The results of the Likert were statistically analyzed to assess user experience (Fig. 9).

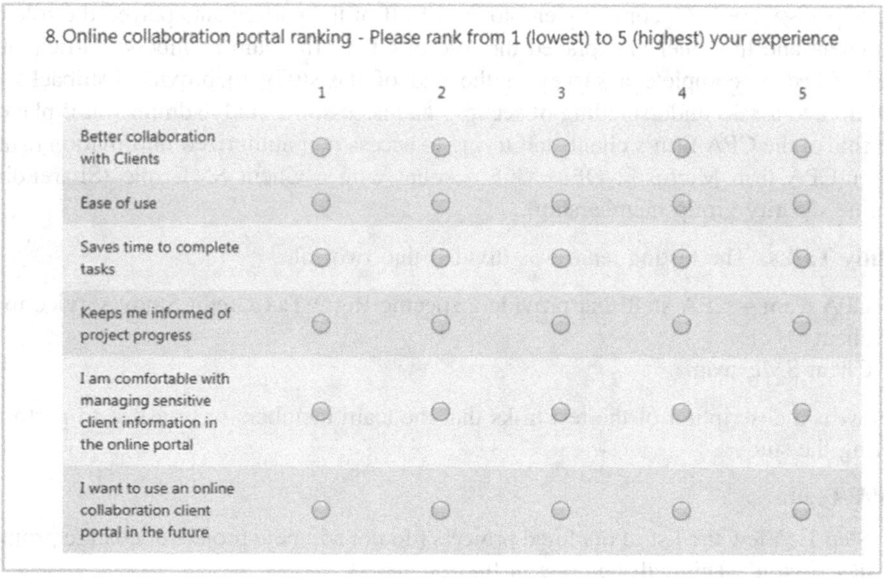

8. Online collaboration portal ranking - Please rank from 1 (lowest) to 5 (highest) your experience
1
2
3
4
5
Better collaboration with Clients
Ease of use
Saves time to complete tasks
Keeps me informed of project progress
I am comfortable with managing sensitive client information in the online portal
I want to use an online collaboration client portal in the future

Fig. 9. Likert part of online survey asking participants to rank from 1 to 5 different categories

Summary of Likert Results
0
1
2
3
4
5
6
1
Better collaboration with Clients
Ease of use
Saves time to complete tasks
Keeps me informed of project progress
I am comfortable with managing sensitive client information in the online portal
I want to use an online collaboration client portal in the future

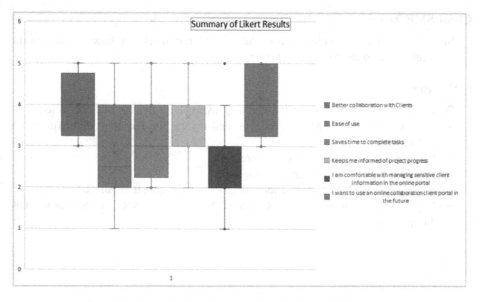

Fig. 10. Likert results summary using box and whiskers chart

The results from the survey to the Likert question appear in the summary table below in a box and whisker chart. Note that x in the indicating the median value of responses (1 being the lowest and 5 being highest). The box boundaries represent the 2nd and 3rd quartiles (Fig. 10).

5.2 External User Access and Information Security Assessment

Members of the CPA team were asked to perform step 4 in the testing script which includes asking a sensitive question to the client finance team in the questionnaire. The expectation from the investigator is that the CPA team member would check access to the sensitive question and its answers and adapt as necessary by changing the permission level to the questions (a SharePoint list item) from the default setting which allows access by all client teams to just the client finance team. There are two aspects to this step in the testing which are of interest from HCI-SEC perspective.

- Would the user be aware that they need to change default permission?
- Would the user be successful in changing the default permission using the software interface?

At the completion of testing, the principal investigator used an external user account simulating client SME role to assess proper access to sensitive questions. There were only two questions posted by the team (out of 12 participants) that simulated sensitive questions. None of the sensitive questions had its default access setting modified.

6 Results Analysis and Discussion

The open-ended questions were designed to capture feedback from the participants regarding tool usability, relevance to current work practices and client experience. A summary of the main point is below:

What is your role in the organization?
To evaluate whether there were differences in experience between a junior vs. a more experienced user, we collected responses from several roles, including R&D Tax Team Associates, Seniors and Managers. Note that in the R&D team, Associates are the more junior team members and will focus on information collection, while Seniors and Managers will focus more on work quality and supervision responsibilities.

In your opinion, what are the benefits of using the online collaboration when compared with how you previously collaborated with clients?
To understand how CPA staff perceived future work using SaaS tools when compared with current tools and methodologies. The responses included a view that efficiency and client experience will improve since all information will be available to both client and CPA team in one location, better use of time by client and CPA staff member and shifting more work to the client which will increase utilization of CPA staff members.

One response summarized few points shared by other participants well

> "Using the online collaboration tool will provide our teams with the ability to seamlessly communicate with our clients on a real-time basis. The tool will enable efficient communication channels, real-time updates on engagement status, and the ability to effectively manage client engagements from an external and internal perspective. The tool will provide greater engagement transparency for our clients and provide us with a multitude of options on improving our internal and external processes."

Where you successful in completing your task in the online portal?
This question was designed to gauge how CPA staff perceived their own success in completing all testing activities. The results indicated some challenges and confusion regarding client role access and the information participants were required to provide. Out of 11 responses, two indicated successful completion, four indicted no success and the rest five responses indicated partial success. Comments included:

> "Validating access wasn't assigned to me. I didn't see sensitive data, such as wages on the SME facing page."

> "No, in the SME role I could still see all of the questions and answers, not just those assigned to me."

Where you able to validate proper access to client files with sensitive information?
This question examines the perception of the CPA staff regarding their own success in setting up proper client information to sensitive question (the last step in the testing script). Two responses out of 11 indicated successful completion (although when we tested the actual configuration we discovered only partial success in securing access to sensitive survey questions). The rest of the responses indicated none or partial success, which corresponds with our findings of only two question responses two step 4 in the test script.

In your opinion, will our clients like to use the new online portal?
As the CPA staff is familiar clients, their estimate of client's impression would provide an indication to their trust in the platform. The CPA staff study participants work closely with clients regularly and are familiar with client's behavior. Responses were mixed and indicated that the tool needs to be properly tested and enhance the user experience with configuration and proper training.
    Example for a response which captures key points:

> "It will depend on the client. Some clients will love this tool while others will not have the time, patience, or capabilities to effectively use it. When evaluating whether we should use this tool for a client or not, we can always provide options and different processes on a case by case basis. Overall, I see a lot of potential with this, especially in R&D where we could even use SharePoint as a more "tech savvy client" option or even "the budget friendly" option where there are clients that prefer to be more hands on with their engagements or prefer to work on engagements on their own time."

> "I think it could be useful, given there aren't too many communication channels in use. If there are too many places to check for information/sending messages, information can be missed. However, it would be nice to have a platform that is less unwieldy than GoFileRoom and more organized than outlook."

The overall impression from the team to using the online collaboration tool was positive given that the overall median score for the Likert data (median above 3) and narrative of feedback was positive [See Appendix A]. The two main areas that scored unfavorably (median below 3) were the "Ease of use" and "I am comfortable with managing sensitive client information in the online portal". The narrative comments in the survey supported this view with several participants indicated that they found the information access management confusing. Apart from the ease of use and information access management, the narrative feedback to tool usability in the survey was mostly positive with main takeaways appear to be around training and configuration.

Efficiency. An interesting takeaway we observed is that the vision of using SaaS for collaboration to increase team efficiency was well received and accepted as a strategic direction for the CPA firm by the more senior participants (Manager and senior) while the junior staff member who participated in the study feedback focused more on time saving for their own work while working with their clients. The senior members were more likely to point out where the software did not meet their expectations and the additional work needed to bring the collaboration portal to broad adoption with clients.

Access Rights to Information. This aspect is a main security concern, as it deals with sensitive client information. The default setting of the software allows access by all the different client teams. Users can change this setting to allow access just to the client finance team. To test participants understanding of this setting, participants were asked to enter sensitive questions that they client than needed to respond to. Users of the software are expected to change this setting if sensitive information is being asked from the clients. users were asked whether they were able to validate proper access to information (Q5) with few respondents indicating that they believed that the access right to the sensitive question's scenario in step 4 of the testing was successful while in fact sensitive questions in the client questionnaire were not properly configured for access as confirmed by the authors. The gap between user perception and actual access management is concerning and demonstrate the need for additional user training and/or simplified UI design for access management in SharePoint.

7 Summary and Future Work

Finally, the significance of this study captures the experience of a mid-size CPA firm (with about 500 employees) trying to challenge the client collaboration status quo software by leveraging emerging SaaS collaboration capabilities in the hope for improving client experience and in parallel improve their own staff team efficiency and experience. The collaboration challenges CPA staff members face are unique to their industry who is very specialized and require a high level of trust to deliver services. Future work will focus on finding the right balance between SaaS configuration, user training and client experience setup to enable the CPA firm to achieve the efficiency and client experience it desires.

Appendices

8.1 Appendix A - Table of Terms

See Table 1.

Table 1. Table of terms

SaaS	Software as a service
ShareFile	Secured File Sharing software by Citrix https://www.sharefile.com/fileshare
MimeCast	Secured email software https://www.mimecast.com/
Office 365	SaaS collaboration platform by Microsoft https://www.office.com
CPA	Chartered Public Accounting
HCI-SEC	Human/Computer Interaction - Security

8.2 Appendix B – Training Materials

Testing Preparation Instructions. Thank you for helping our firm assess the functionality of the new collaboration portal for R&D projects. We would like you to perform a few activities in our portal to help our team deliver better client experience and collaboration for R&D Tax credit work.

Note - As a part of the assessment, you will be asked to provide feedback on both functionality and information access. You can see a step by step instructions at this link. To view access for any item (Task, question or document) select the item by clicking on its row and then click on "Share" and then in the popup window click on the three little dots next to the close screen X button and then on "Manage Access" –> Advanced. In this access management window, click on a button called "Check Access" and then enter the person's name you want to check access for. In this screen you will be able to assign/remove access by first "Stop Inheriting" access and then remove/add access as needed. For questions please contact Lior Baron

And now for the actual testing activities:

You are asked to complete a series of activities that will be like how the R&D team interacts with some clients. You will be asked to play one of these roles:

CPA Firm team member

Client Finance Team

Client SME team.

The testing will be made of steps 1–4.

Training Slide - User access management in SharePoint
See Fig. 11.

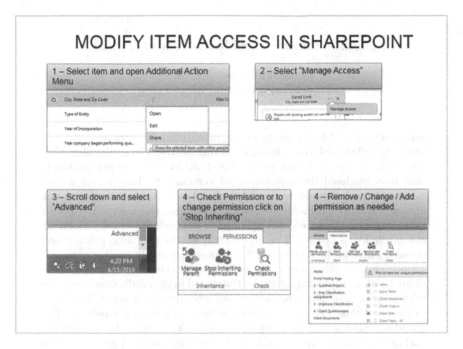

Fig. 11. Training slide provided to study participants

References

1. Conway, D., Taib, R., Harris, M., Yu, K., Berkovsky, S., Chen, F.: A qualitative investigation of bank employee experiences of information security and phishing. In: Thirteenth Symposium on Usable Privacy and Security (SOUPS 2017). USENIX Association, pp. 115–129 (2017)
2. https://customers.microsoft.com/en-us/story/plante-moran-professional-services-office-365
3. https://big4careerlab.com/big-4-accounting-firms/
4. https://www.smartvault.com/resource/setting-up-shop-in-the-cloud/
5. https://products.office.com/en-us/business/office-365-trust-center-security
6. https://gsuite.google.com/security/?secure-by-design_activeEl=data-centers
7. https://www.ftc.gov/tips-advice/business-center/guidance/protecting-personal-information-guide-business
8. https://www.aicpa.org/interestareas/frc/assuranceadvisoryservices/cybersecurity-resources-for-organizations-and-cpa-firms.html
9. https://docs.microsoft.com/en-us/office365/securitycompliance/data-encryption-in-odb-and-spo
10. https://docs.microsoft.com/en-us/sharepoint/external-sharing-overview
11. Maxion, R.A., Reeder, R.W.: Improving user-interface dependability through mitigation of human error. Int. J. Hum.-Comput. Stud. **63**(1–2), 25–50 (2005)
12. Trauth, E.M.: Qualitative Research in IS: Issues and Trends. IGI Global, Hershey (2001)

Frictionless Web Payments with Cryptographic Cardholder Authentication

Francisco Corella$^{(\boxtimes)}$ and Karen Pomian Lewison

Pomcor, Carmichael, USA
{fcorella,kplewison}@pomcor.com

Abstract. The 3-D Secure protocol, introduced 20 years ago, aims at reducing online credit card fraud by authenticating the cardholder. Version 2 of the protocol, not yet deployed, addresses usability problems that have hindered the deployment of version 1 by introducing a frictionless flow for low risk transactions. But the frictionless flow does not authenticate the cardholder. Instead, it requires the merchant to send information to the issuer through a back channel, potentially violating the cardholder's privacy. The paper analyzes the usability, privacy and security provided by 3-D Secure 2 and proposes an alternative protocol, simpler and less expensive to implement, where the cardholder is authenticated with a cryptographic credential stored in the cardholder's browser with zero friction. The scheme can take advantage of a native bank app in the cardholder's device to further authenticate the cardholder by fingerprint scanning or face recognition as made available by the device, and can be used for credit card purchases made on the merchant's web site or on a merchant app.

Keywords: Usability · Privacy · Security ·
Cryptographic authentication · Credit card · Certificate · Private key ·
Biometric authentication · Bank app · Issuing bank

1 Introduction

The addition of EMV chips to credit cards has reduced credit card fraud for in-store transactions, but fraudsters have shifted their efforts to online transactions, and the rate of online credit card fraud has increased.

Providing serious security for online credit card purchases requires authentication of the cardholder. This was recognized by the credit card industry and addressed, first by the specification of the Security Electronic Transactions (SET) protocol [12,17], which was never deployed, then by the introduction in 1999 of version 1 of the *3-D Secure* protocol [19], created by Visa and marketed under different names by different credit card networks (Verified by Visa, MasterCard SecureCode, American Express SafeKey, etc.). In 3-D Secure 1.0 the merchant's web site redirects the cardholder's browser to the web site of the issuing bank, which authenticates the cardholder and redirects the browser back to the merchant's site.

© Springer Nature Switzerland AG 2019
C. Stephanidis (Ed.): HCII 2019, LNCS 11786, pp. 468–483, 2019.
https://doi.org/10.1007/978-3-030-30033-3_36

But two decades after its introduction 3-D Secure 1.0 is still unevenly used in European countries and rarely used in the United States.

One reason for the limited deployment of 3-D Secure 1.0 is the friction that it causes. Traditionally, the bank authenticated the cardholder by asking for a password. The cardholder had to wait for the redirection to the issuing bank, enter the password, and wait for the redirection back to the merchant's site. Today some banks use two-factor authentication, adding to the friction by requiring a one-time password in addition to a static password. Consumers "hate" 3-D Secure [2], and merchants are wary of transaction abandonment.

Another reason for the limited deployment of 3-D Secure is the withering criticism with which it was met for asking for a password after a redirection, a bad practice that makes users more likely to become victims of phishing attacks [10, 11, 16]. Yet another reason may be its cost to merchants and banks. Merchants who want to use 3-D Secure are required by the credit card networks to use a "merchant plug-in (MPI)" provided by a licensed provider, and banks must use an access control server (ACS).

To address the limited deployment of 3-D Secure, the credit card networks have tasked EMVco with the specification of version 2 of the protocol [5]. But the new version has flaws that make it less likely to be successfully deployed than the original version.

3-D Secure version 2 (3DS2) reduces friction for low risk transactions by introducing a *frictionless flow*. But friction is reduced by eliminating cardholder authentication altogether for those transactions. Instead of authenticating the cardholder, the frictionless flow creates a back channel through which the merchant sends transaction, device and cardholder information to the issuing bank without going through the cardholder's browser. The bank uses the information to decide whether to require a subsequent *challenge flow* that does authenticate the cardholder.

The frictionless flow is depicted in a Visa infographic [18], which shows many little icons traveling from the merchant to the issuer and states that "3-D Secure 2.0 delivers 10 times more data, such as device channel and payment history, than a previous version". This should raise a red flag among privacy advocates and government regulators. The issuing bank does not need a history of payments made with cards issued by the same bank, and sharing payments made with cards issued by other banks without cardholder's consent could be deemed a violation of the cardholder's privacy by the merchant in some jurisdictions. As further discussed below in Sect. 2.3, the current version of 3-D Secure (version 2.2.0) does not actually specify any payment history data to be sent in the frictionless flow, but the specification is still incomplete, and it is not clear if such data will be specified in a future version.

An important selling point of 3DS2 has been that it supposedly features biometric authentication of the cardholder by fingerprint scanning or facial recognition. Such authentication would be implemented by a bank app, but how the bank app would be used by 3-D Secure is declared to be outside the scope of the specification. As further discussed below in Sect. 2.1, figures showing user interface templates suggest that, after being taken to the bank's web site, the cardholder would be shown written instructions asking him/her to manually open the bank's native app in order to be authenticated. It is hard to imagine the cardholder reading and following the instructions instead of abandoning the transaction. Such an awkward user experience would create at least as much friction as version 1 of 3-D Secure.

3DS2 is very complex, and requires a lot of infrastucture. While version 1 of 3-D secure required an ACS server, version 2 now requires three servers (an ACS server, a Directory Server (DS), and a 3DS Server). The cost of this infrastructure will have to be borne by merchants and banks.

Thus 3-D Secure 2 raises privacy issues and adds complexity and cost for merchants and banks without achieving the goal of frictionless authentication of the cardholder.

Yet it is possible to provide strong cardholder authentication for all transactions with zero friction and negligible infrastructure cost without raising privacy issues, using a cardholder authentication scheme that uses a cryptographic credential and optional biometric authentication as we propose in this paper.

In brief, the cardholder authenticates with a cryptographic credit card credential stored in the cardholder's browser, where it is protected by the *same-origin policy* of the web and controlled by a *service worker* registered with the browser by the issuing bank. The credential consists of a private key and a credit card certificate that binds the associated public key to a hash of credit card data. A hash of the data is used instead of the data itself to protect the data against an attacker who gains physical possession of the cardholder's device. At checkout, after the cardholder enters the credit card data, the merchant's site redirects the browser to the issuer's site with the data and a description of the transaction. But the redirected request never reaches the issuer's site. It is intercepted by the service worker and handled within the browser. The service worker checks the data against the hash, asks the cardholder to confirm the transaction, signs the transaction with the private key and sends the signature and the certificate to the merchant, which retains the signature on the transaction for non-repudiation purposes.

If the bank has a native app in the cardholder's device, the credit card credential is kept in storage controlled by the app rather than in the browser, and the app authenticates the cardholder using the credential in the same way as the service worker would in the absence of a bank app. Optionally, if the cardholder's device provides a biometric API for native apps, the bank app may further authenticate the cardholder by means of a fingerprint scan or face recognition. The role of the service worker when the bank has a native app is just to further redirect the merchant's authentication request to the bank API, then redirect the authentication result back to the merchant's site.

In the cardholder authentication scheme that we propose in this paper the cardholder is authenticated with a strong cryptographic factor, possession of the private key, in addition to the weak factor used today as the only factor in most online credit card transactions, knowledge of the credit card and cardholder data.

We refer to this combination of a strong factor and a weak factor as $1\frac{1}{2}$-factor authentication ($1\frac{1}{2}$FA). If the issuing bank has a native app in the cardholder's device the cardholder may be further authenticated with an additional biometric factor, in what we call $2\frac{1}{2}$-factor authentication ($2\frac{1}{2}$FA). In either case the cardholder is strongly authenticated without having to enter a static password or a one-time password, and with no password exposure to back-end breaches or reuse at malicious sites.

The rest of the paper is organized as follows. Section 2 provides a brief analysis of the 3DS2 specification, including a description of the frictionless and challenge flows in Subsect. 2.1 and a discussion of usability, privacy, security, and cost in Subsects. 2.2, 2.3, 2.4, and 2.5. Section 3 describes the proposed cardholder authentication scheme. Subsection 3.1 describes the infrastructure required to implement the scheme. Subsections 3.2 and 3.3 describe the credit card credential and how it is stored in the browser. Subsection 3.4 explains how the credential is provisioned to the cardholder by the issuing bank. Subsection 3.5 describes the protocol for cryptographic authentication of the cardholder, Subsect. 3.6 explains how a native app provided by the issuing bank can be used to add biometric authentication, and Subect. 3.7 describes the case where the cardholder uses a merchant app instead of accessing the merchant's site through a web browser. Subsections 3.8, 3.9, 3.10, and 3.11, evaluate the usability, security, privacy and cost of the proposed scheme. Section 4 concludes with a comparison between 3-D Secure 2 and the proposed cardholder authentication scheme.

2   Brief Analysis of 3-D Secure 2

The version of the specification referenced in this section is version 2.2.0, published December 13, 2018 [5]. It consists of two documents, the Protocol and Core Functions specification, more briefly called the *Protocol Specification*, and the *SDK Specification*.

2.1   Frictionless and Challenge Flows

In a traditional web payment by credit card, the cardholder enters credit card and cardholder data and clicks a button to submit the payment. Then the merchant's web site sends a payment authorization request that goes through the merchant's acquirer bank and the card's network to the card's issuing bank. The issuing bank's response to the authorization request takes the same route in reverse to reach the merchant. We shall refer the authorization request/response roundtrip as the *authorization processing*.

When 3-D Secure is used, it takes place between the payment submission by the cardholder and the authorization processing. 3-D Secure causes the authorization processing to be omitted if cardholder authentication fails, but is otherwise entirely separate and independent from the authorization processing.

3-D Secure 1.0 has a simple flow where the cardholder's browser is redirected to the issuer's ACS, which typically prompts the cardholder for a static password, plus possibly a second factor such as a one-time password, and redirects back to the merchant's site with the result of the authentication.

3-D Secure 2 has a *frictionless flow* that may or may not be followed by a *challenge flow*. In the frictionless flow the merchant's site sends transaction, device and cardholder information to the issuer, using a back channel to transmit the information instead of a redirection through the cardholder's browser. The back channel is not a direct connection. The information goes from the merchant's site to the 3DS server, then to the Directory Server, then to the issuer's ACS, before finally reaching the issuer.

Based on the information provided by the frictionless flow the issuer decides whether cardholder authentication is required. If it is not required the merchant initiates authorization processing right away. If it is required, the merchant responds to the payment submission with a redirection to the issuer's ACS, which initiates the challenge flow. As in 3-D Secure 1.0, the issuer's ACS authenticates the cardholder and redirects back to the merchant's site, which initiates the authorization processing if the authentication succeeded, or displays an error message to the cardholder otherwise.

Version 1 of 3-D Secure, released 20 years ago, was only concerned with web apps, but 3DS2 is concerned with native apps as well.

The SDK Specification is concerned with how a native app downloaded from the merchant's site into the cardholder's device can use a *3DS SDK*. The SDK implements functionality that includes gathering device information to be sent to the issuer in the frictionless flow, and interacting with the issuer's ACS in the challenge flow.

After the cardholder submits payment information on the merchant's app, the app sends transaction and device information to the merchant's site, which communicates with the issuer to execute the frictionless flow, implemented as in the case where the cardholder uses a web app.

The SDK implements the challenge flow without using a web browser. It sends a message to the issuer's ACS asking for a "challenge". The ACS responds with a message asking the cardholder to enter authentication data such as a password. After the SDK sends the requested data, the ACS may ask for additional authentication data, such as a one-time password for two-factor authentication. Eventually the issuer's ACS tells the SDK whether the cardholder authentication has succeeded or failed.

3-D Secure 2 is also concerned with the case where the issuing bank has a native app on a device controlled by the cardholder. (The specification does not make it clear whether this must be the same device used for payment submission or may be a different device.) The issuer's app may be used in the challenge flow to authenticate the cardholder, but the issuer's ACS is still involved in the flow. The ACS is asked to authenticate the cardholder as described above, but it delegates authentication to the native app instead of asking the cardholder for authentication data such as a static password or a static password plus a one-time password.

The specification does not specify how the ACS uses the native app, but it makes two suggestions. One suggestion can be found in Sect. 3.2 of the Protocol Specification, which states that the issuer's ACS may send "a push notification to a banking app that completes authentication and then sends the results to the ACS". Another suggestion can be found in user interface templates depicted in Figs. 4.6, 4.12 and 4.17, which contain the following instructions to the cardholder: "For added security you will be authenticated with YourBank application. Step 1 — Open your YourBank application directly from your phone and verify this payment. Step 2 — Tap continue after you have completed authentication with your YourBank application."

2.2   Usability Analysis

The frictionless flow, when not followed by the challenge flow, requires no cardholder interaction. This improves the user experience for low risk transactions when compared to 3-D Secure 1.0, which requires the cardholder to authenticate to the issuer's ACS for all transactions. On the other hand the frictionless flow adds the latency of a roundtrip through three intermediate servers for all transactions, which reduces usability for high risk transactions.

3DS2 allows the cardholder to be authenticated biometrically using a native app provided by the issuing bank. However, the user experience for doing so is extremely awkward. The cardholder has to read instructions and manually locate and open the bank's native app before authenticating. This cannot compete with payment methods such as Paypal or Apple Pay that feature tight integration of biometric authentication with the checkout process.

2.3   Privacy Analysis

In the frictionless flow the merchant shares cardholder information with the issuing bank. This may or may not violate the cardholder's privacy, depending on what information is shared, and whether the cardholder is notified and asked for consent.

A Visa infographic [18] states that the information sent to the issuer includes the cardholder's payment history, which should raise a red flag. Annex A.7 of the Protocol Specification specifies data elements that the merchant sends to the issuer in the frictionless flow. Sections A.7.1–A.7.4 include 32 data elements, none of which are payment history entries. (Sections A.7.5–A.7.10 are unrelated to the frictionless flow and may have been included in Annex A.7 by mistake.) However some of the data elements are not defined in detail yet, suggesting that the specification of the frictionless flow has not been finalized and could include a payment history in the future. One checkout software provider states that its implementation of 3DS2 sends over 100 data elements to the issuing bank, including the payment history [3].

2.4   Security Analysis

The frictionless flow does not authenticate the cardholder. Therefore 3DS2 provides less security for low risk transactions than 3-D Secure 1.0.

In the frictionless flow the merchant sends transaction, device and cardholder information to the issuer, which the issuer uses to assess transaction risk. Today, without 3-D Secure, merchants or merchant processors make their own risk assessment before submitting a transaction for authorization processing, and issuers make their own risk assessment when they receive the payment authorization request. 3DS2 will not increase the sum total of information that is used today for risk assessment, but there may be a security advantage at allowing the issuer to combine its own information with information received from the merchant.

Both in 3-D Secure 1.0 and 3DS2, the issuer is free to use any method it wants to authenticate the cardholder. Password authentication was used traditionally in 3-D Secure 1.0, and two-factor authentication has begun to be used recently. The word "challenge" in "challenge flow" might suggest that 3DS2 has replaced password authentication with a cryptographic challenge-response protocol, but this is not the case. The glossary in the Protocol Specification defines "challenge" as "the process where the ACS is in communication with the 3DS Client to obtain additional information through Cardholder interaction" and "challenge flow" as "a 3-D Secure flow that involves Cardholder interaction as defined in Sect. 2.5.2". There is no reason to believe that passwords will not continue to be used in version 2 of 3-D Secure, with their well-known vulnerabilities to phishing attacks, back-end breaches and password reuse.

EMVCo and the FIDO Alliance announced collaborations in July 2016 [6], June 2018 [7] and April 2019 [8], with the latest collaboration also involving the W3C. The FIDO Alliance has developed standards for web authentication by means of a cryptographic key pair (UAF, U2F and FIDO2) [9]. The 3-D Secure Protocol Specification mentions FIDO authentication, but only in connection with authentication of the cardholder to the merchant prior to the credit card transaction. The Protocol and SDK specifications make no other mention of cryptographic authentication of the cardholder.

Biometric authentication of the cardholder by a native app provided by the issuing bank, as described above, would be more secure than password-based or two-factor authentication methods currently used in 3-D Secure 1.0.

2.5   Cost

3DS2 is very complex, specially for the merchant, which is called the Requestor in the Protocol and SDK specifications. Section 2.1.1 of the Protocol Specification mentions the following components or entities involved in the 3DS Requestor Environment: 3DS Requestor, 3DS Client, 3DS Server, 3DS Requestor App, 3DS Method, 3DS SDK, 3DS Integrator. The app-based authentication flow comprises 25 steps and 90 "requirements". The browser-based authentication flow comprises 22 steps and 71 "requirements". This complexity will result in high development, outsourcing and licensing costs for merchants, merchant processors and issuing banks. 3DS2 also requires 3DS Servers, Directory Servers and Access Control Servers, whose cost will have to be borne by merchants and issuing banks.

3   Frictionless Cardholder Authentication

In this section we describe the proposed scheme for authenticating the cardholder by means of a cryptographic credit card credential, plus optional biometric authentication if the issuing bank has a native app on the cardholder's device.

All communications over the Internet take place over secure TLS connections.

3.1   Infrastructure

The infrastructure required to implement the proposed scheme consists of a public database of issuing banks that support the scheme (the *scheme database*). Each issuer is identified in the database by its issuer identification number (IIN), which consists of the first six digits of the credit card number. (Eight digits will be used in the future.) The database maps the IIN of each issuer to two data items used by the scheme:

1. The URL of a cardholder authentication endpoint, to which the merchant redirects the cardholder's browser to authenticate the cardholder and obtain a signature on the transaction.
2. The public key associated with the private key that the issuer uses to sign credit card certificates.

Merchants can download the scheme database or use an HTTP API to query the database. The database, downloads of the database, and queries to the HTTP API must be integrity-protected but need not be confidentiality-protected.

3.2   Credit Card Credential

The credit card credential consists of a private key and a certificate that binds the associated public key to a cryptographic hash of credit card data. A hash of the data is used instead of the data itself to protect the data against an attacker who gains physical possession of the cardholder's device. The data is entered as usual by the cardholder when submitting a payment with the credit card. A hash of the data is then computed and compared with the hash in the certificate. If credentials for multiple credit cards from the same issuer are stored in the browser, the hash also serves to uniquely identify the one to be used for the current transaction. The data hashed into the certificate is the data printed on the physical credit card, viz. the credit card number, the expiration date, the security code, and the cardholder name. Cardholder data such as address, telephone number, email address, etc., is not included in the hash, but it may be required as usual by the merchant, and if required it may be used by the merchant to accept or reject the transaction before asking for authorization, and by the issuer when processing the authorization.

The credit card certificate is an X.509 certificate as profiled by the IETF [4] with an empty subject field, containing the hash of the credit card data in a subjectAltName extension. It is signed by the issuer and the signature can be verified with the public key associated with issuer's IIN in the scheme database. By issuing the certificate, the issuer plays the role of a certificate authority (CA), but there is no CA hierarchy and no certificate chain to be verified. The certificate becomes useless when the card expires or is invalidated. Hence there is no need to revoke it or assign a meaningful expiration time to it. The expiration time of the certificate must not coincide with the card expiration date, to avoid revealing the latter to an attacker who steals the cardholder's device. A bogus validity period is used instead for the certificate with a "notAfter" field that is far enough in the future and a "notBefore" field that is far enough in the past, so that the same bogus validity period can be used for all certificates from the same issuer.

3.3 Credential Storage

The credit card credential is stored in the browser, where it is protected by the same origin policy of the web [1,14] and used by a service worker [15,21]. The credential can be stored in an "object store" of an IndexedDB database [13,20], as an object having the private key and the certificate as properties. The hash is included in the certificate, but it is also stored as a third property used as a database primary key for fast retrieval of the object. If the Web Cryptography API [22] is used for cryptographic computations, the private key can be wrapped in a CryptoKey object, from which it can be made non-extractable.

3.4 Credential Provisioning

The cardholder may obtain the credit card credential on demand, by asking for it on the issuer's web site, or on the fly, when a merchant asks for cardholder authentication.

In on-demand provisioning, the cardholder logs in to the issuer's site and requests a credential for a particular credit card, possibly among multiple credit cards issued by the same issuer to the same cardholder. The issuer's site computes the hash of the credit card data and responds to the request with a script (i.e. JavaScript code embedded in a web page) that contains the hash. The script displays an error message if it finds a credential with the same hash already stored in the browser. If no credential is found, the script creates a key pair and sends a certificate signing request to the issuer's site, containing the hash, the public key and a proof of possession of the private key. The site verifies that the cardholder is still logged in and may ask for a refresh of the login session or additional authentication. The site verifies that the hash is the same one that was computed earlier and downloads a signed certificate binding the hash to the public key, with the above-mentioned bogus validity period. The script creates a credential comprising the certificate and the private key and stores it in the browser. There may already be a service worker configured to intercept requests that target the issuer's cardholder authentication endpoint; if not, the script registers one.

On-the-fly provisioning takes place when the merchant's site redirects the cardholder's browser to the cardholder authentication endpoint but there is no service worker to intercept the request, or there is a service worker that cannot find a credential with the hash of the credit card data. If there is no service worker, the redirected request reaches the issuer's site. If a credential cannot be found, the service worker does a further redirection to a secondary cardholder authentication endpoint. In either case the issuer's site receives the cardholder authentication request, which contains the credit card data, a description of the transaction and a callback URL that targets the merchant's site.

The issuer's site asks the cardholder to log in if a login session is not already in progress. Then it responds to the request by displaying a transaction confirmation page, augmented with a check box that the user can check to ask for the provisioning of a credit card credential to the browser. Additional authentication may be required if the cardholder checks the box.

If the cardholder confirms the transaction and checks the box, a script in the transaction confirmation page provisions a credit card credential to the cardholder's browser and registers a service worker if there is not one already that is configured to intercept requests to the cardholder authentication endpoint. Then it signs the transaction with the private key and sends the signed transaction and the credit card certificate to the callback URL.

If the cardholder confirms the transaction but does not check the box, the script creates a one-time credit card credential, uses it to sign the transaction, and sends the signed transaction and the credit card certificate to the merchant as if the cardholder had checked the box. But it does not save the credential and it does not register a service worker.

The cardholder may repeatedly confirm transactions without checking the credential-creation box. In that case the cardholder is repeatedly authenticated by logging in or having logged in to the issuer's site. The merchant does not know whether the transaction has been signed by the issuer's site with a one-time credential, or by a service worker with a credential stored in the cardholder's browser, unless explicitly told by the issuer.

3.5 Cryptographic Authentication with a Credit Card Credential

The protocol for cryptographic authentication of the cardholder comprises the following steps, illustrated in Fig. 1.

1. In the checkout page of a purchase transaction, the merchant's site asks the cardholder to enter credit card and cardholder data as usual. Knowledge of this data is the weak authentication factor that is used today for authentication of web transactions. Combined with strong authentication by means of the credit card credential it provides what we call $1\frac{1}{2}$-FA. The cardholder enters the data and clicks "continue" to go a confirmation page.

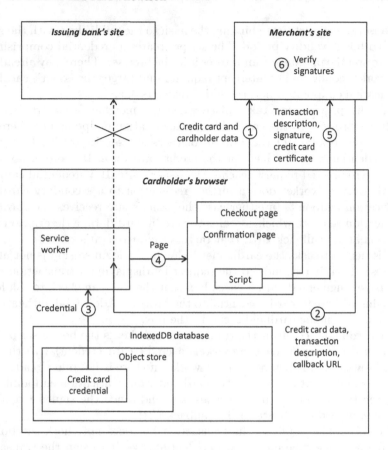

Fig. 1. Cryptographic cardholder authentication

2. The merchant looks up the IIN prefix of the credit card number in the scheme database. If there is no entry for the IIN in the database, the merchant may proceed without cardholder authentication or use a different method of cardholder authentication such as 3-D Secure. If there is an entry for the IIN prefix, the merchant redirects the cardholder's browser to the cardholder authentication endpoint of the issuer, using a script in the checkout page to submit a POST request that conveys the credit card data, a description of the transaction, and a callback URL that targets the merchant's site. If there is no service worker in the cardholder's browser configured to intercept requests to the authentication endpoint, the request reaches the issuer's site, which attempts on-the-fly credential provisioning as described above in Sect. 3.4.
3. If there is a such a service worker, it intercepts the request, hashes the credit card data, and looks for a credential containing the hash in the object storage of the IndexedDB database where the issuer stores credit card credentials. If no credential is found there, the service worker forwards the request received from the merchant to a secondary authentication endpoint of the issuer's site,

and the issuer's site attempts on-the-fly credential provisioning as described above in Sect. 3.4.

4. If the service worker finds a credential, it creates a transaction confirmation page and delivers it to the browser in response to the intercepted request. The browser renders the page as if it came from the issuer's site, showing the URL of the cardholder authentication endpoint in the address bar. The page describes the transaction using the description received from the merchant and has buttons that the cardholder can use to confirm or cancel the transaction. The page contains a script that includes the hash of the credit card data and the description of the transaction as JavaScript literals.

5. If the cardholder cancels the transaction, a script in the confirmation page sends a POST request to the callback URL notifying the merchant that the transaction has been canceled. If the cardholder confirms the transaction, the script uses the hash to retrieve the credential, signs the description of the transaction with the private key component of the credential, and sends a POST request to the callback URL containing the description of the transaction, the signature, and the credit card certificate.

6. When the merchant's site receives the POST request sent upon confirmation, it verifies the signature on the transaction using the public key in the certificate, and the signature in the certificate using the public key of the issuer found in the scheme database.

3.6   Biometric Authentication with a Bank App

If the issuing bank has a native app in the cardholder's device, the app can be used to provide biometric authentication for transactions that are deemed exceptionally risky by the merchant or the bank. Biometric authentication is used in addition to, rather than instead of cryptographic authentication because cryptographic authentication creates zero friction. Cryptographic and biometric authentication in combination with the knowledge of the credit card and cardholder data amounts to what we call $2\frac{1}{2}$-FA.

If there is a bank app in the cardholder's device, the credit card credential is stored by the app, using any secure storage made available by the platform. When the service worker intercepts the POST request that carries credit card data, the transaction description and the callback URL, it relays the request to the bank's app, using a URL with a custom scheme registered by the app. The app asks the cardholder for confirmation and may authenticate the cardholder biometrically by means of a fingerprint scan or face recognition, using an API made available by the platform. If all goes well the app signs the transaction and causes the browser to open a javascript URL (i.e. a URL where the scheme is "javascript" instead of "http" or "https") where the script in the URL (i.e. the JavaScript code that follows "javascript:") sends a POST request to the callback URL with the signed transaction and the credit card certificate.

3.7   Using a Merchant App

The case where the cardholder uses a native app provided by the merchant is handled in essentially the same way as the case where the cardholder uses a web app, using either the default browser or a bank app to store the credit card credential.

After the cardholder enters the credit card and cardholder information, the merchant's app asks the default browser to open a javascript URL where the script in the URL sends a POST request with the credit card data, the transaction description and a callback URL to the cardholder authentication endpoint of the issuing bank. The POST request is intercepted by a service worker as described above, the cardholder is asked to confirm the transaction by the browser or a bank app, the description of the transaction is signed with the private key component of the credit card credential, and a POST request conveying the signed transaction is sent to the callback URL. In this case, however, the callback URL does not target the merchant's site. It is instead a URL with a custom scheme registered by the merchant's app, so that the cardholder is returned to the merchant's app after confirming the transaction in the browser or the bank's app.

3.8   Usability Analysis

The proposed scheme allows the cardholder to be strongly authenticated by possession of a private key with zero friction and zero latency.

The only action that the cardholder has to take to be authenticated cryptographically is to click a button to confirm the transaction. The cardholder's user experience is the same as in an ordinary online credit card transaction with a separate confirmation page, except that the page is a bank page rather than a merchant page. The bank page is generated in the browser itself by a service worker, without a roundtrip to the bank. It may thus be displayed faster than a confirmation page retrieved by the browser from the merchant's site.

If there is a native app supplied by the issuing bank in the cardholder's device, it can be used to further authenticate the cardholder using a biometric facility made available by the device to the app through an API, such as fingerprint scanning or face recognition. The biometric facility that a device makes available to native apps is typically the same one that is used for unlocking the device. It should therefore be highly usable and familiar to the cardholder.

3.9   Privacy Analysis

In the proposed scheme, the merchant does not share any information with the issuing bank beyond what it already shares today through the payment authorization process.

The credit card certificate that the cardholder sends to the merchant together with the signed description of the transaction only contains data printed on the card. Such data is required to be provided by the cardholder in most online credit card transactions.

3.10   Security Analysis

Since cryptographic authentication causes no friction, the cardholder can be strongly authenticated for all transactions, not only for some transactions deemed to be riskier than others.

No passwords are used in the proposed scheme. The well-known vulnerabilities of passwords are therefore avoided.

No shared secrets are used in the proposed scheme. Therefore the scheme is not vulnerable to backend database breaches.

3.11   Cost

The proposed scheme is simple, easy to describe and specify as can be seen by the length of this paper, relatively easy to implement for the issuer, and trivial to implement for the merchant or merchant processor. This simplicity will translate into low implementation costs.

The only infrastructure required by the scheme is the scheme database, which merchants may download or access online. The contents of the database must be integrity-protected but need not be kept secret. There will thus be very low infrastructure costs to be borne by merchants and banks.

4   Conclusion

The addition of EMV chips to credit cards has reduced credit card fraud for in-store transactions. But the rate of online credit card fraud has increased, because cardholders are authenticated online by their knowledge of credit card and cardholder data, which is a weak secret.

Reducing online fraud will require strong authentication of the cardholder. Version 1 of the 3-D Secure protocol, introduced 20 years ago, provides authentication of the cardholder, typically by password or two-factor authentication. But it is rarely used in the US abd unevenly used in other countries because merchants fear transaction abandonment caused by poor usability. It is also expensive to implement for merchants and card issuing banks.

Version 2 of 3-D Secure, not yet deployed, addresses the usability problem of version 1 by introducing a frictionless flow to be used for low risk transactions. But the frictionless flow does not actually authenticate the cardholder, and may violate the cardholder's privacy by requiring the merchant to share cardholder information with the issuer through a back channel. Furthermore, version 2 is very complex and requires a heavy infrastructure whose cost will have to be borne by merchants and banks.

It is possible to do much better. We have proposed a cardholder authentication scheme that provides strong authentication of the cardholder without causing any friction. The cardholder is authenticated with a cryptographic credential consisting of a private key and a certificate that binds a cryptographic hash of credit card data to the associated public key. The credential is stored in the cardholder's browser, or in a bank app if available on the cardholder's device, and used automatically to sign a description of the transaction upon confirmation of the transaction by the cardholder.

Since the scheme introduces no friction it can be used for all transactions, not only some transactions deemed to be riskier than others. Cryptographic authentication can be combined with biometric authentication provided by a bank app and can be used for credit card purchases made on the merchant's web site or using a merchant app.

The proposed scheme is trivial to implement for merchants, and only requires a lightweight infrastructre consisting of a database that maps the IIN of each participating bank to the URL of a cardholder authentication endpoint and to a public key used for verifying the certificates issued by the bank. It can therefore be deployed inexpensively.

References

1. Barth, A.: The Web Origin Concept. IETF RFC 6454. https://tools.ietf.org/html/rfc6454
2. Brignall, M.: MasterCard and Visa to simplify hated verification systems. The Guardian, 13 November (2014) https://www.theguardian.com/money/2014/nov/13/mastercard-visa-kill-off-verification-systems
3. Checkout.com. 3-D Secure payments. https://docs.checkout.com/docs/3d-secure-payments
4. Cooper, D., Santesson, S., Farrell, S., Boeyen, S., Housley, R., Polk, W.: Internet X.509 Public Key Infrastructure Certificate and CRL Profile, May 2008. http://datatracker.ietf.org/doc/rfc5280/
5. EMVCo™. EMV® 3-D Secure. https://www.emvco.com/emv-technologies/3d-secure/
6. FIDO Alliance. EMVCo and the FIDO Alliance Collaborate on Mobile Payment Authentication, July 2016. https://fidoalliance.org/fido-emvco-mou/
7. FIDO Alliance. EMVCo and the FIDO Alliance to Address FIDO Authentication in EMV® 3-D Secure Use Cases, June 2018. https://fidoalliance.org/emvco-and-the-fido-alliance-to-address-fido-authentication-inemv-3-d-secure-use-cases/
8. FIDO Alliance. EMVCo, FIDO Alliance, and W3C Form Interest Group to Enhance Security and Interoperability of Web Payments, April 2019. https://fidoalliance.org/emvco-fido-alliance-and-w3c-form-interest-group-to-enhance-security-and-interoperability-of-web-payments/
9. FIDO Alliance. Specifications Overview. https://fidoalliance.org/specifications/
10. Baker-Bates, J.: Phishing with 3-D Secure. 13 August (2009). https://webtorque.org/phishing-with-3-d-secure/
11. Laurie, B.: More Banking Stupidity: Phished by Visa. March 28 (2009). https://www.links.org/?p=591
12. Mastercard and VISA. SET Secure Electronic Transaction Specification. Version 1.0, May 1997. http://www.maithean.com/docs/set_bk1.pdf, http://www.maithean.com/docs/set_bk2.pdf, http://www.maithean.com/docs/set_bk3.pdf
13. Mozilla. IndexedDB API. https://developer.mozilla.org/en-US/docs/Web/API/IndexedDB_API

14. Mozilla. Origin. https://developer.mozilla.org/en-US/docs/Web/HTTP/Headers/Origin
15. Mozilla. Service Worker API. https://developer.mozilla.org/en-US/docs/Web/API/Service_Worker_API
16. Murdoch, S.J., Anderson, R.: Verified by Visa and MasterCard SecureCode: or, How Not to Design Authentication (2010)
17. Stallings, W.: The SET Standard & E-Commerce. November 1 (2000). http://www.drdobbs.com/the-set-standard-e-commerce/184404309#
18. Visa. New and improved 3-D Secure. Originally retrievable from https://www.visaeurope.com/media/pdf/visa-infographic.pdf. Accessed June 8, 2019. https://usa.visa.com/dam/VCOM/global/visa-everywhere/documents/visa-3d-secure-2-program-infographic.pdf. Archived at https://web.archive.org/web/20190608194449/usa.visa.com/dam/VCOM/global/visa-everywhere/documents/visa-3d-secure-2-program-infographic.pdf
19. Visa. Visa 3-D Secure 1.0. https://technologypartner.visa.com/Library/3DSecure.aspx
20. W3C. Indexed Database API. https://www.w3.org/TR/IndexedDB/
21. W3C. Service Workers. https://www.w3.org/TR/service-workers/
22. W3C. Web Cryptography API. https://www.w3.org/TR/WebCryptoAPI/

A Robust and Real-Time Face Anti-spoofing Method Based on Texture Feature Analysis

Aasim Khurshid[(⊠)], Sergio Cleger Tamayo, Everlandio Fernandes, Mikhail R. Gadelha, and Mauro Teofilo

SIDIA Instituto de Ciência e Tecnologia, Manaus, Brazil
{aasim.khurshid,sergio.tamayo,everlandio.fernandes,
mikhail.gadelha,mauro.teofilo}@sidia.com
https://www.sidia.org.br/en/home/

Abstract. Face spoofing attack is an attempt to obtain unauthorized access by using photos, videos or 3D maps of an user's face. In this work, we propose a software-based anti-spoofing method that extracts multiple texture features based on Local Binary Patterns (LBP) in the grayscale and YCbCr color spaces to train binary Support Vector Machine (SVM) classifier, which is then used to classify faces. The proposed method is compared with state-of-the-art methods using Attack Presentation Classification Error Rate (APCER), Normal Presentation Classification Error Rate (NPCER), Average Classification Error Rate (ACER), True Positive Rate (TPR), True Negative Rate (TNR), False Positive Rate (FPR), and Accuracy. Our method performs better than the other state-of-the-art methods when classifying spoofed and non-spoofed faces of the NUAA dataset. In particular, our method presents the smallest FPR, and thus guarantees robustness against spoofing attacks. Furthermore, our anti-spoofing method can be used in real-time applications with an average of 26 frames per second, providing high accuracy with little overhead to authentication systems.

Keywords: Face anti-spoofing · Spoofing ·
Local Binary Patterns (LBP) · YCbCr image space

1 Introduction

Face-based biometrics is currently the most studied topic in image-based authentication applications [1]. There are older authentication methods available such as passwords and barcode readers; however, once an unauthorized party has access to the key, it is incredibly challenging to prevent unauthorized access of systems using these authentication methods. Recent research on authentication methods is focused on biometrics such as iris, fingerprint, or face recognition to verify the authenticity of the user. Iris and fingerprint authentication systems

© Springer Nature Switzerland AG 2019
C. Stephanidis (Ed.): HCII 2019, LNCS 11786, pp. 484–496, 2019.
https://doi.org/10.1007/978-3-030-30033-3_37

have been actively researched and tend to be more accurate than older techniques [2]; such techniques, however, require intentional and active user contact with the device, which might feel unpleasant to the user. Face-based authentication is the most user-friendly and secure method [3], requiring little to no user contact with the device. Face-based authentication, however, is still vulnerable to spoofing, i.e., using photos, videos, or 3D maps of the user to gain unauthorized access [4]. Some systems try to prevent this by acquiring some live face feature, such as yawning [5], but most face-based authentication methods do not provide a built-in anti-spoofing mechanism. In principle, the problem of anti-spoofing is usually treated as an independent problem from face-based authentication.

Different techniques have been proposed in the literature to classify spoofed images of a person, including hardware-based, challenge-response, and software-based anti-spoofing methods. Hardware-based solutions use specific hardware, making it difficult to implement it in simple cameras or smartphones and, while challenge-response methods ask users to perform specific actions for their authentication. However, performing these challenges might feel unpleasant to the user. Software-based methods can be cheap and user-friendly; in the literature, most software-based anti-spoofing methods use gray-scale images to classify among spoofed and non-spoofed faces, capturing images using conventional cameras, thus reducing costs. We extend these methods by combining luminance and chrominance components of color images, and our experiments show that our novel method not only improves detection accuracy but also minimize detection errors.

YCbCr color space allows differentiating between luminance (Y) and chrominance (Cb and Cr) components. In this paper, we propose to extract texture information using Local Binary Patterns (LBP) from both the luminance and chrominance (provided by the YCbCr color space). Gray-scale LBP features and co-occurrence of the LBPs are also used to avoid false positives. These features are combined in a feature matrix, and a binary Support Vector Machine (SVM) classifier is trained using the training set. In the testing phase, these features are computed for each face and concatenated in a feature vector. This feature vector is classified by the already trained classifier as spoofed or non-spoofed (real-person).

The main goal of our method is to ease user interaction with a system, while also increasing security. Current trends in security include two-factor authentication methods [6], but it burdens the user with extra steps, both for the configuration and the usage. In this regard, our method is transparent to the user and allows pleasant user interaction with the system. Our proposed software-based anti-spoofing solution increases security, and also, it can be deployed in real-time systems without incurring any major processing overhead.

For experimental evaluation, we use the NUAA database [7]. We compare our method against other state-of-the-art methods [7–10] using the following metrics: Attack Presentation Classification Error Rate (APCER), Normal Presentation Classification Error Rate (NPCER), Average Classification Error Rate (ACER), False Positive Rate (FPR), True Positive Rate (TPR), True Negative

Rate (TNR) and accuracy. Results show that our method not only presents better results for each metric (lowest APCER, NPCER, ACER, FPR, and highest TPR, TNR and accuracy) but also runs in real-time with an average of 26 frames per second in our experiments, providing high accuracy with little impact to authentication systems.

The paper is organized as follows: Sect. 2 refers to the recent studies on spoofing detection and compares theoretical aspects that motivated this work, Sect. 3 explains the important concepts used in the development of the proposed method. Next, the proposed method is presented in detail in Sect. 4, followed by the experimental evaluation in Sect. 5. Finally, conclusions are drawn in the Sect. 7.

2   Related Works

Software-based spoofing detection motivated many studies. Pioneer solutions to spoofing detection started with a focus on texture-based methods. Li et al. analyzed frequency distribution to differentiate between live and non-live face images [11]. The authors assumed that the photo image has less high-frequency components because of the flat structure of the photo and that the standard deviation of frequency components in the photo image is small because of invariant expressions. These assumptions, however, do not hold for more sophisticated attacks, which include video attacks or 3D map attacks. Anjos et al. created a database and indicated protocols for the evaluation of the spoofing attack solutions [12]. Sun et al. proposed an eye blinking based face liveness detection [13]. Bao et al. used optical flow to detect face liveness [14]; however, the accuracy of the method drops substantially with people using glasses.

Furthermore, iris-based liveness detection methods are not practical because it is not uncommon to use sunglasses in outdoor scenarios. Chingovska et al. utilized Local Binary Patterns to analyze texture to prove liveness [15]; the authors also include alternative LBPs such as transitional LBP (tLBP), direction-coded LBP (dLBP) and modified LBP (mLBP). These LBPs are used as feature vectors and are compared using X^2 histogram classification.

Research on software-based anti-spoofing was usually based on grayscale image analysis until recently. However, some recent works exploited the color properties as vital visual cues for discriminating spoofed faces from the real ones [3,16]. Boulkenafet et al. proposed a color-based technique that analyses contrast and illumination changes in the captured image or video [3]. LBP is used as a feature vector, and are combined to train a Support Vector Machine (SVM) based classifier. In addition to these features, Co-occurrence of Adjacent Local Binary Patterns (CoALBP), Local Phase Quantization (LPQ), Binarized Statistical Image Features (BSIF) and Scale-Invariant Descriptor (SID) are used as a feature vector for the classifier. This method has high accuracy; however, the feature vector is too big, which makes it slow in training and testing. In our proposed method, we use texture features extracted from multiple color spaces to classify between spoofed and non-spoofed face images. Several methods use luminance information to extract texture features to detect spoofing. However, the chrominance component provides important cues for spoofing detection. Our method extends these methods by combining luminance and chrominance components. It is worth mentioning that LBPs are computed independently in luminance and chrominance component of YCbCr color spaces. Furthermore, gray-scale LBP features and Co-occurrence of the LBPs are also used to avoid false positives. These features are combined as a feature matrix, and SVM based classifier is trained using the training set to classify spoofed face images.

Convolutional Neural Networks (CNN) are also used to face anti-spoofing [17]. Yang et al. trained a CNN with five convolutional (Conv) layers, followed by three fully connected (FC) layers. After learning the CNN, the features from the last connected layer are used to train the SVM classifier. However, in order to use the full potential of neural network based solutions, plenty of pre-processed and labeled training data and hardware capabilities. Furthermore, Kim et al. [8] proposed to use Local Speed Patterns (LSP) based on diffusion speed as a feature vector and to train a linear classifier to detect spoofing. The key idea behind this method is that the difference in the surface properties between live and fake faces can be estimated using the diffusion speed.

In this method, we propose to utilize minimal texture features based on LBPs which are extracted in multiple color spaces. These features tend to be robust and perform real-time. The important building blocks of the proposed method are explained in the next section.

3 Fundamental Concepts

This section elaborates the fundamental concepts used to develop our proposed method. Color spaces are explained in Sect. 3.1, followed by LBP feature extraction in Sect. 3.2, which is used as texture features instead of using all the pixels. Finally, the computation of the Co-occurrence of Adjacent Local binary patterns (CoALBP) is explained in Sect. 3.3.

3.1 Color Spaces - YCbCr and Grayscale

YCbCr is a digital color space that represents the image in three channels, i.e., luminance (Y), chrominance difference blue (Cb) and chrominance difference red (Cr) [18]. The ability of YCbCr to differentiate among luminance and chrominance component makes it easier to handle these components independently. Along with the luminance component, the chrominance components also provide important cues for image analysis. In our proposed method, we use the chrominance and luminance components independently to compute texture features.

Grayscale images also provide important information about the image: it represents the amount of light present in the image, which provides a more meaningful luminance component value than the Y channel of YCbCr color space. For this reason, grayscale images are also used to compute the texture features. In particular, grayscale image is used to compute grayscale LBP and CoALBP features.

3.2 Local Binary Patterns

Local Binary Patterns (LBP) is a local descriptor which generates a binary code for a pixel neighborhood. Figure 1 shows two examples of LBP computation of a center pixel by comparing its intensity with the neighboring pixel intensities. For one pixel, the value of the center pixel is used as a threshold, and the threshold is operated on the eight neighborhood pixels [19]. For LBP, each neighboring pixel value greater than the threshold is assigned 1 and value smaller than the threshold is assigned a value of 0. These values of $0's$ and $1's$ are concatenated in a clockwise manner, and the final vector of binary values is converted to integer form, which is the LBP of the central pixel, as can be seen in Fig. 1. The advantages of LBP include its invariance to illumination changes and low computational complexity. Therefore, LBP can be computed at real-time and is capable of discriminating the local texture.

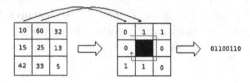

Fig. 1. Example of LBP computation, the binary 01100110 is converted to 24 and neighboring pixels are signed 1 if greater than this value, or 0 otherwise. Image reproduced from [19].

3.3 Co-occurrence of Adjacent Local Binary Patterns

Original LBP features seem to ignore the spatial relationship among the adjacent LBPs, which tends to contain important information about the details of the image [20]. Nosaka et al. [20] computes sparse LBPs and then compute the correlation between the spatially adjacent LBPs in four directions. The directions are defined as: $A = \{(\Delta r, 0), (0, \Delta r), (\Delta r, \Delta r), (-\Delta r, \Delta r)\}$. For each direction $a \in A$ a 16×16 2-D histogram is created. The resulting histogram is then reshaped and concatenated to a feature vector. Figure 2 shows the computation of CoALBP in all four directions: the LBP is computed in a 4-neighbor manner instead of 8-neighbor to reduce the computation costs.

4   Proposed Method

Mostly face spoofing is performed using printed targets faces, displaying videos or masks to the input sensors [8]. The simplest attacks, e.g., using mobile phone

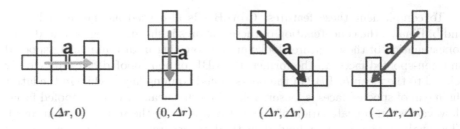

$(\Delta r, 0)$ $(0, \Delta r)$ $(\Delta r, \Delta r)$ $(-\Delta r, \Delta r)$

Fig. 2. Computation of CoALBP - image reproduced from [20]

displays, can be detected easily using texture analysis because of the artifacts in the image. However, higher quality spoofed faces are difficult to detect [3]. Some examples of the real and spoofed images from NUAA database [7] are shown in Fig. 3. Real and spoofed images look very similar, and the task of spoofing detection is not trivial. The distribution of luminance, however, is a bit uniform in spoofed images (as shown in the second row of Fig. 3). This is because human eyes are more sensitive to luminance. Furthermore, chrominance components are important cues for the detection of the recaptured images. For this reason, this work focuses on utilizing both the luminance and chrominance components.

In order to analyze the luminance and chrominance cues for spoofing detection, LBP histograms are computed and tested against the mean of the LBPs from the training data. The training data contains spoofed and non-spoofed face images. Two LBP means are computed: the mean of spoofed images represented by μ_s is computed by taking the average of all the training spoofed images, and the mean (μ_c) of non-spoofed images, where c is a representation of client/non-spoofed image. After computing the means, the difference between the test face image and the means is computed to classify spoofing. Chi-square distance is robust for computing the difference between histograms, and is computed using:

$$d_{x^2}(H_x, \mu_c) = \sum_{i=1}^{n} \frac{(H_x(i) - \mu_c(i))^2}{(H_x(i) + \mu_c(i))}, d_{x^2}(H_x, \mu_s) = \sum_{i=1}^{n} \frac{(H_x(i) - \mu_s(i))^2}{(H_x(i) + \mu_s(i))}, \quad (1)$$

where $H_x(i)$ represents the ith bin of the tested face image.

Figure 4a shows the chi-square distances $d_{x^2}(H_x, \mu_c)$ and $d_{x^2}(H_x, \mu_s)$ of the LBP histograms taken from non-spoofed (client or live) faces in the test set, and Fig. 4b shows the chi-square distances $d_{x^2}(H_x, \mu_c)$ and $d_{x^2}(H_x, \mu_s)$ of LBP histogram in grayscale image space of the spoofed faces in the test set. The smaller distance means that it belongs to that particular class. For example, if the distance $d_{x^2}(H_x, \mu_c) \leq d_{x^2}(H_x, \mu_s)$, the image is non-spoofed, otherwise the image is spoofed.

Similarly, the chi-square distances of the chrominance components are shown in Fig. 4c and d. It can be seen that the chrominance component is more robust in the detection of spoofed images than grayscale, while grayscale has better detection of non-spoofed images.

To complement these features, CoALBP is also used as shown in Fig. 5a and b. Finally, the concatenation of these features is shown in Fig. 5c and d. The concatenation of these features looks more promising in discriminating spoofed and non-spoofed faces. In the former, the LBP of non-spoofed faces are closely related to the mean μ_c LBP of the non-spoofed training faces, while in the latter the mean of spoofed faces is loosely related to the mean μ_s of the spoofed faces. However, when concatenation of the features is used, the results are improved. This analysis allows our extended method to accurately classify spoofed and non-spoofed faces.

Fig. 3. Example images from NUAA database; Original images in the first row and spoofed images in the second row

4.1 Feature Extraction

In our proposed method, multiple features are computed and then concatenated to make it robust against the spoofing attacks. We use five LBP based features which are computed in either gray scale or YCbCr color space. Firstly, an RGB image retrieved from the camera is converted into grayscale image (I_g) and YCbCr image (I_yc). LBP features are extracted from a gray scale face images and the YCbCr images of the training dataset. Furthermore, grayscale images are also used to compute the Co-occurrence of the Adjacent Local Binary Patterns (CoALBPs), as described in Sect. 3.3. After the computation of these features for each image, each of the feature is reshaped into a vector, and then these feature vectors are combined to one big feature vector. After completing this process for each image, the feature vectors from the whole dataset is combined into a feature matrix of size $n \times m$, where m is the size of the feature vector and n is the size of the training data.

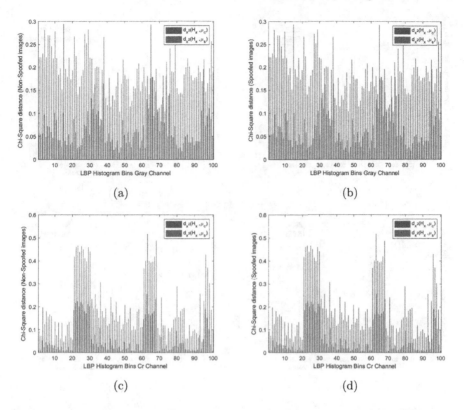

Fig. 4. Chi-square distance of the μ_c and μ_s with (a) non-spoofed and (b) spoofed face images LBPs in Grayscale; (c) non-spoofed and (d) spoofed face images LBPs in Chrominance (Cr) channel of YCbCr color space.

4.2 Training

After the training matrix is computed, a binary SVM classifier is trained with the labels of the training data to classify the spoofed and non-spoofed images. For SVM training and testing LibSVM library is used [21].

4.3 Classification

When a test image is given, all the features are computed the same way as computed for the training set (as described in Sect. 4.1). After the feature vector is computed, the feature vector is given to the already trained SVM classifier for spoofing detection.

5 Experimental Evaluation

Our proposed method was implemented using Matlab on a PC with a core i7-7500U CPU@2.70 GHz processor, 12 GB of RAM and Windows operating system. For the quantitative evaluations, the following metrics are used to compare

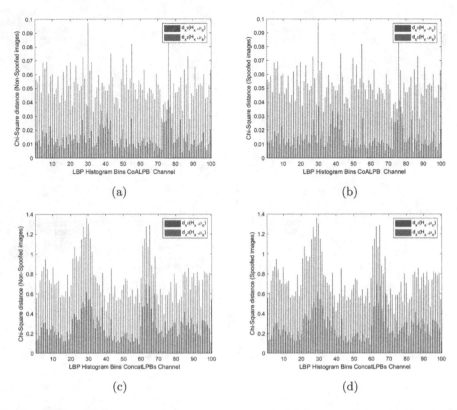

Fig. 5. Chi-square distance of the μ_c and μ_s with (a) non-spoofed and (b) spoofed face images of CoALBPs; (c) non-spoofed and (d) spoofed face images when using concatenated LBPs.

the proposed method with the state-of-the-art methods: Attack Presentation Classification Error Rate (APCER), Normal Presentation Classification Error Rate (NPCER), Average Classification Error Rate (ACER), False Positive Rate (FPR), True Positive Rate (TPR), True Negative Rate (TNR) and accuracy.

Attack Presentation Classification Error Rate (APCER):

$$APCER = \frac{FP}{TN + FP} \tag{2}$$

Normal Presentation Classification Error Rate (NPCER):

$$NPCER = \frac{FN}{FN + TP} \tag{3}$$

Average Classification Error Rate (ACER):

$$ACER = \frac{APCER + NPCER}{2} \tag{4}$$

True Positive Rate (TPR):

$$TPR = \frac{TP}{TP + FN} \tag{5}$$

False Positive Rate (FPR):

$$FPR = \frac{FP}{FP + TN} \tag{6}$$

Accuracy:

$$Accuracy = \frac{TP + TN}{TP + TN + FP + FN} \tag{7}$$

The goal of the anti-spoofing algorithm is to achieve smallest value of APCER, NPCER, ACER, FPR and highest TPR, TNR and accuracy values.

5.1 Dataset

For experimental evaluation, the NUAA database was used. The NUAA database was constructed as part of the method called Face Liveness Detection from A Single Image with Sparse Low Rank Bilinear Discriminative Model [7]. It has 11752 original and spoofed face images from 15 subjects, which are divided into training and test sets. The database is recorded using a webcam at 20 fps in varied illumination conditions in a span of two weeks. Spoofing in the NUAA database is done by printing the photos and taking the photos of these photos to re-capture the image. Some examples from the database are shown in Fig. 3. The first row in Fig. 3 shows the original captured images and the second row shows the spoofed images.

6 Quantitative Evaluation

Table 1 shows the results of our proposed method with different sets of features. Our proposed method is compared against the following methods: Total variation models for variable lighting face recognition [9], Face Liveness Detection from a Single Image with Sparse Low Rank Bilinear Discriminative Model [7], Deep Feature Extraction for Face Liveness Detection [10] and Face Liveness Detection From a Single Image via Diffusion Speed Model [8].

In Table 1, the first four rows report the accuracy of three state-of-the-art methods for the NUAA dataset. Each row indicates the results of its respective feature independently, and the last row shows the results of these combined features. For APCER, NPCER, ACER, and FPR smallest value indicate the best result. On the other hand, higher values are expected for TPR, TNR and accuracy. Table 1 shows that our proposed combined LBP method (last row) performs better on all metrices. In terms of accuracy, Kim et al. [8] performs relatively better than other state-of-the-art methods.

The simplest method such as Grayscale LBP performs better than state-of-the art methods based on accuracy, however, grayscale LBP method has some

APCER, which can allow some frauds. For this reason, robustness against spoofing attacks is achieved by combining LBP histograms of luminance and chrominance components, along with Co-occurrence of LBP. Our proposed combined LBP method has the smallest APCER and FPR, and thus guarantees robustness against spoofing attacks, and it can be used in real-time with an average of 26 frames per second in our experiments, providing high accuracy with little impact of time to authentication systems.

Table 1. Experimental evaluation of the proposed feature set and comparative methods accuracy (best results in **bold**, second best results in *italic*).

Method	APCER	NPCER	ACER	FPR	TPR	TNR	Accuracy
Chen et al. [9]	N/A	N/A	N/A	N/A	N/A	N/A	0.6844
Tan et al. [7]	0.2073	0.2267	0.2170	0.2073	0.7733	0.7927	0.7856
Sengur et al. [10]	N/A	N/A	N/A	N/A	N/A	N/A	0.8809
Kim et al. [8]	N/A	N/A	N/A	N/A	N/A	N/A	0.9845
GrayLBP	*0.0025*	*0.0033*	*0.0029*	*0.0025*	*0.9967*	*0.9971*	*0.9967*
YLBP (Luminance)	0.0035	0.0041	0.0038	0.0035	0.9959	0.9967	0.9964
CbLBP (Chrominance Blue)	0.0661	0.1132	0.0896	0.0661	0.8868	0.9331	0.9146
CrLBP (Chrominance Red)	0.0410	0.0725	0.0567	0.0410	0.9275	0.9587	0.9457
CoALBP	0.0413	0.0879	0.0646	0.0413	0.9121	0.9583	0.9357
Combined LBPs	**0.0002**	**0.0008**	**0.0005**	**0.0003**	**0.9992**	**0.9995**	**0.9994**

7   Conclusions

This work proposes a robust anti-spoofing algorithm that performs in real-time. Our proposed method uses LBP features as texture descriptor in YCbCr color space and grayscale. Furthermore, CoALBP is used to exploit local spatial information. These multiple LBP features are concatenated in one feature vector to represent a face image. The proposed method has two phases: a training phase and a test phase. In the training phase, the concatenated LBPs and CoALBPs of the training images are combined in a feature matrix, that is used to train a binary SVM. In the test phase, the test image's LBPs and CoALBP are computed and concatenated into a feature vector, which is then classified by an already trained SVM. Experimental results show that our proposed method performs better than state-of-the-art methods. In particular, our proposed concatenated LBP method has the smallest APCER and FPR, and thus guarantees robustness against spoofing attacks. Our proposed anti-spoofing method can be used in real-time environments with an average of 26 frames per second in our experiments, providing high accuracy with little impact of time to authentication systems.

Acknowledgment. The authors would like to thank the support provided by SIDIA Instituto de Ciência e Tecnologia and teams.

References

1. Wang, M., Deng, W.: Deep face recognition: a survey. CoRR arXiv:abs/1804.06655 (2018)
2. Galbally, J., Marcel, S., Fierrez, J.: Image quality assessment for fake biometric detection: application to iris, fingerprint, and face recognition. IEEE Trans. Image Process. **23**(2), 710–724 (2014)
3. Boulkenafet, Z., Komulainen, J., Hadid, A.: Face spoofing detection using colour texture analysis. IEEE Trans. Inf. Forensics Secur. **11**(8), 1818–1830 (2016)
4. Khurshid, A., Scharcanski, J.: Incremental multi-model dictionary learning for face tracking. In: 2018 IEEE International Instrumentation and Measurement Technology Conference (I2MTC), pp. 1–6, May 2018
5. Omidyeganeh, M., et al.: Yawning detection using embedded smart cameras. IEEE Trans. Instrum. Measur. **65**(3), 570–582 (2016)
6. Aloul, F., Zahidi, S., El-Hajj, W.: Two factor authentication using mobile phones. In: 2009 IEEE/ACS International Conference on Computer Systems and Applications, pp. 641–644. IEEE (2009)
7. Tan, X., Li, Y., Liu, J., Jiang, L.: Face liveness detection from a single image with sparse low rank bilinear discriminative model. In: Daniilidis, K., Maragos, P., Paragios, N. (eds.) ECCV 2010. LNCS, vol. 6316, pp. 504–517. Springer, Heidelberg (2010). https://doi.org/10.1007/978-3-642-15567-3_37
8. Kim, W., Suh, S., Han, J.: Face liveness detection from a single image via diffusion speed model. IEEE Trans. Image Process. **24**(8), 2456–2465 (2015)
9. Chen, T., Yin, W., Zhou, X.S., Comaniciu, D., Huang, T.S.: Total variation models for variable lighting face recognition. IEEE Trans. Pattern Anal. Mach. Intell. **28**(9), 1519–1524 (2006)
10. Sengur, A., Akhtar, Z., Akbulut, Y., Ekici, S., Budak, U.: Deep feature extraction for face liveness detection. In: 2018 International Conference on Artificial Intelligence and Data Processing (IDAP), pp. 1–4, September 2018
11. Li, J., Wang, Y., Tan, T., Jain, A.K.: Live face detection based on the analysis of fourier spectra. In: Biometric Technology for Human Identification, vol. 5404, pp. 296–304. International Society for Optics and Photonics (2004)
12. Anjos, A., Marcel, S.: Counter-measures to photo attacks in face recognition: a public database and a baseline. In: 2011 International Joint Conference on Biometrics (IJCB), pp. 1–7. IEEE (2011)
13. Sun, L., Pan, G., Wu, Z., Lao, S.: Blinking-based live face detection using conditional random fields. In: Lee, S.-W., Li, S.Z. (eds.) ICB 2007. LNCS, vol. 4642, pp. 252–260. Springer, Heidelberg (2007). https://doi.org/10.1007/978-3-540-74549-5_27
14. Bao, W., Li, H., Li, N., Jiang, W.: A liveness detection method for face recognition based on optical flow field. In: 2009 International Conference on Image Analysis and Signal Processing, pp. 233–236. IEEE (2009)

15. Chingovska, I., Anjos, A., Marcel, S.: On the effectiveness of local binary patterns in face anti-spoofing. In: 2012 BIOSIG-Proceedings of the International Conference of Biometrics Special Interest Group (BIOSIG), pp. 1–7. IEEE (2012)
16. Wen, D., Han, H., Jain, A.K.: Face spoof detection with image distortion analysis. IEEE Trans. Inf. Forensics Secur. **10**(4), 746–761 (2015)
17. Yang, J., Lei, Z., Li, S.Z.: Learn convolutional neural network for face anti-spoofing. CoRR arXiv:abs/1408.5601 (2014)
18. Shaik, K.B., Ganesan, P., Kalist, V., Sathish, B., Jenitha, J.M.M.: Comparative study of skin color detection and segmentation in HSV and YCBCR color space. Procedia Comput. Sci. **57**, 41–48 (2015). 3rd International Conference on Recent Trends in Computing 2015 (ICRTC-2015)
19. Karis, M.S., Razif, N.R.A., Ali, N.M., Rosli, M.A., Aras, M.S.M., Ghazaly, M.M.: Local binary pattern (LBP) with application to variant object detection: a survey and method. In: 2016 IEEE 12th International Colloquium on Signal Processing Its Applications (CSPA), pp. 221–226, March 2016
20. Nosaka, R., Ohkawa, Y., Fukui, K.: Feature extraction based on co-occurrence of adjacent local binary patterns. In: Ho, Y.-S. (ed.) PSIVT 2011. LNCS, vol. 7088, pp. 82–91. Springer, Heidelberg (2011). https://doi.org/10.1007/978-3-642-25346-1_8
21. Chang, C.C., Lin, C.J.: LIBSVM: a library for support vector machines. ACM Trans. Intell. Syst. Technol. **2**, 27:1–27:27 (2011). http://www.csie.ntu.edu.tw/~cjlin/libsvm

Impacts of Emotional Ambient Sounds on Face Detection Sensitivity

Dong Liu and Pei-Luen Patrick Rau[(⊠)]

Department of Industrial Engineering,
Tsinghua University, Beijing 100084, China
rpl@tsinghua.edu.cn

Abstract. Emotion affects human activities in our everyday lives. Therefore, it is quite normal to expect that emotion can act on our common human–computer interaction behaviors. In the present study, ambient sounds or pictures were provided to create emotional contexts and examine their influences on the initial stage of information processing—information detection. Three traditional cognitive experiments were conducted to test whether emotional information can exert influences on detection performances for briefly presented faces. The results showed that fear ambient sounds could enhance detection sensitivity for neutral faces but not fear faces. Moreover, such modulation existed only when human voices were applied. When music or pictures with fear expressions were presented, no enhancement in face detection performances was found. The findings suggest that emotional contexts affecting visual detection largely depend on the valence and presentation forms of emotion information.

Keywords: Emotional context · Ambient sounds · Face detection

1 Introduction

Traditional human–computer interaction (HCI) studies have considered the users as rational individuals who can discard all their emotional selves to interact efficiently and rationally with computers. However, more and more psychology and technology researchers have held a different view that emotion plays a critical role in every human–computer-related activity [1–3]. Nevertheless, not only can HCI itself induce users' different emotional states, but also environmental characteristics can convey emotional information (e.g., pleasant sounds make users feel pleasant). Researchers have found that emotional information from the surrounding environment can affect our basic cognitive activities, such as early visual perception [4], and high-level cognitive processing, such as problem solving [5], sentence understanding [6], purchase decisions [7]. The extensive influences of emotional information on cognitive activities imply that our common HCI behaviors can also be affected by emotion, because HCI activities involve different kinds of simple and complex cognitive processes. Taking web searching as an example, when individuals search for information online, they first have to detect the information, identify it, and then select the related information. Researchers have found that information selection results can be largely affected by the emotional contexts [8]. For example, under negative emotional contexts individuals

© Springer Nature Switzerland AG 2019
C. Stephanidis (Ed.): HCII 2019, LNCS 11786, pp. 497–506, 2019.
https://doi.org/10.1007/978-3-030-30033-3_38

were more likely to perceive the negative information [9]. Nevertheless, it is still unclear whether such modulation effect could occur in the initial stage (e.g. information detection) of the searching process. Hence, in the present study we adopted three cognitive experiments to test how emotional information from the surrounding environment affecting information detection performances.

2 Related Research

2.1 Emotion Classification

Emotions are the response mechanism by which individuals give proper answers to external inputs and internal changes. Some researchers believe there are six basic emotions—fear, anger, sadness, joy, disgust, and surprise—that are shared by all humans [10]. Psychologists and neuroscientists have explored many methods to test whether different types of emotion, such as fear or happiness, are processed identically, but the results are rather inconsistent [11–13]. Some studies found that negative information, e.g., fear or anger, receives better processing than neutral or happy emotions [11, 14], while others supported the superiority of happiness [12].

In contrast to basic-emotion classification, researchers have described emotions with different dimensions or scales, such as valence and arousal [15]. Emotional valence refers to the extent to which the stimuli can be considered as positive or negative, and arousal corresponds to the intensity of the stimuli. Generally, emotional valence decides the direction of human behavior either going forward or withdrawing, and the arousal level may strengthen that behavior. Researchers have proposed that emotional processing is a bimodal process [16], and sounds and pictures can evoke the same emotional responses. Therefore, in the present study, whether emotional contexts created by sounds or pictures can have the same influences on the information-detecting process was tested.

2.2 Emotion Affects Information Processing

Emotion affects information processing in myriad ways. Researchers found that emotion information itself can affect the time we get access to it [17, 18]. For example, researchers found that emotional information with a highly negative valence, e.g., a fear face, can be detected more quickly than information with neutral or positive valence [18]. Similar findings were found when individuals were required to search for a fear face from a number of neutral or happy faces [13]. Researchers have explained the above phenomenon with a threat superiority theory, according to which threat-related information is important for surviving and, thus, has the priority to get processed. Moreover, studies have further indicated that an emotional stimulus can affect the processing of information presented shortly afterward [4]. For example, researchers applied a rapid serial visual presentation (RSVP) paradigm and found that, when an emotional stimulus was presented as a distractor, the target that followed the emotional stimulus could hardly be detected [19]. Such impairments in information processing performance were also found in information identification or recognition tasks [20, 21] and even existed when the emotional stimulus had no relationship to the task goals [19]. The reason researchers gave for such impairments was that not enough attention could be allocated to subsequently presented targets, because attention were first captured by the emotional stimuli presented before. However, how emotional contexts affect information detection when visual information is presented briefly and without much attention required has received little attention.

On the other hand, researchers have also found that emotional contexts modulating subsequent task performance were largely affected by the emotional valence of the contexts. For example, individuals under negative emotional contexts (e.g. under a gossip condition) but not neutral contexts are more easily to detect the negative information [9]. Nevertheless, research about emotional information acting on visual perception produced inconsistent results. Some researchers found that neutral information can facilitate a subsequent visual perception task [22], while others supported the notion that fear or happiness emotions can boost the subsequent visual processing task [4, 23]. These contradictory findings reveal the need to test how different emotional contexts, e.g., neutral or fear, act on visual detection.

2.3 Present Study

Here, the aim was to test how environmental characteristics (i.e., emotional contexts) exert influences on our common HCI behavior, e.g., information detection. In the present study, three psychological experiments were conducted to examine how emotional contexts affect subsequent detection of briefly presented visual information, e.g., face images. For all experiments, after exposure to the emotional contexts created by ambient sounds or pictures, participants were required to detect a face image presented briefly with colorful patterns following as mask stimuli. Two questions were raised.

(1) Can emotional contexts affect our face detection performances when emotional contexts are not related to the task goals?
(2) Can emotional contexts created by ambient sounds or pictures play the same role in detection performances?
(3) Can different emotional contexts e.g. neutral or fear make same influences on detection performances?

3   Method

3.1   Participants

A total of 30 participants (mean age = 24.34 years) took part in the study. 10 participants (7 female, 3 male) were engaged in Experiment 1, 10 (8 female, 2 male) participated in Experiment 2, 10 (6 female, 4 male) participated in Experiment 3. None declared any hearing impairments and all had normal or corrected vision. All participants were naive to the purpose of the experiments and were paid after they finished the experiments.

3.2 Stimuli

All stimuli were presented using MATLAB (The MathWorks, Natick, MA) together with the Psychophysics Toolbox extensions. Face stimuli used in the first three experiments were photographs of 8 actors (4 male and 4 female) with the most recognized expressions selected from the NimStim face-stimulus set. Both neutral and fear expressions were selected in Experiment 1 and only neutral expressions were selected in Experiment 2 and 3. All hair and nonfacial features were removed, and only the central face area (1.53° × 1.86°) was left. The face image was spaced at a random position along an imaginary ring 2° from the fixation. Sound stimuli used in Experiment 1 were 12 human voices speaking the vowel \a\ to express fear or neutral emotions. Sound stimuli used in Experiment 2 were 12 digital music samples from the Chinese sound database with fear or neutral emotions. All the sounds were presented with a sample rate of 44.10 kHz. 8 pictures selected from the International Affective Picture System (IAPS) were used as emotional stimuli in Experiment 3. The visual stimuli used for masking the face images were scrambled colorful patterns with a size of 6° × 6°. All stimuli were presented against a gray background at a viewing distance of 58.5 cm.

3.3 Procedure and Data Analysis

Experiment 1. Each trial began with a human voice lasting 600–800 ms, and participants were just required to listen passively to the sound and view the central fixation mark (0.98° × 0.98°). And 100 s after the sound, a face image was presented for 15 ms, and then a mask stimulus was presented for 150 ms. When the mask disappeared, the central fixation mark was presented on the screen and observers were required to make a response with a left arrow or right arrow key to indicate whether a human face was presented before the mask. Observers had to make the response within 1500 ms. The intertrial interval was 800–1000 ms (see Fig. 1).

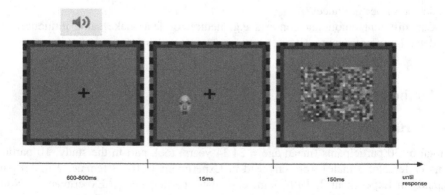

Fig. 1. Illustration of stimuli sequence in Experiment 1

Each participant finished 192 trials, which comprised 48 trials in each of four conditions. These conditions were created by crossing the emotional valence of the human voice (fearful vs. neutral) and the emotional valence of the detected face (fearful vs. neutral). For each condition, 24 trials were used as catch trials and no human face images but scrambled face images were presented for 15 ms. All test trials were presented in a new random order for each participant.

Experiment 2. The procedure in Experiment 2 was the same as that in Experiment 1, except that digital music rather than the human voices were used as the sound stimuli. Moreover, only neutral faces were presented. In Experiment 2, participants had to complete 96 trials. Half of the trials were presented with fear sounds and the other half were presented with neutral sounds.

Experiment 3. The procedure for Experiment 3 was the same as that for Experiment 1, except that not human voices but emotional pictures were provided as the attended stimuli. As in Experiment 2, only neutral faces were presented. Participants also had to finish 96 trials. Half of the trials were presented with fearful pictures and the other half were presented with neutral pictures. In both Experiment 2 and Experiment 3, the number of catch trials for each condition was half as that in Experiment 1.

For all the experiments, observers' response times and sensitivity (A′) were collected for further data analysis. A′ was calculated based on observers' hit rate (H) and false alarm (F) data for each test condition based on the equation as below [24].

$$A' = .5 + (H - F)(1 + H - F)/[4H(1 - F)] \tag{1}$$

After finishing the experiment task, participants had to make a 9-point rating of the emotional sounds (Experiment 1 and 2) or pictures (Experiment 3) to evaluate their emotional valence and arousal levels. In the ratings, 1 represents the most negative emotion, while 9 represents the most positive emotion; 1 represents the least arousal level and 9 represents the highest arousal level.

4 Results

In Experiment 1, A′ were entered into a 2×2 two-way repeated measures analysis of variance with the emotional valence of the face (fearful vs. neutral) and the human voice (fearful vs. neutral) as within-subjects factors. Results revealed a significant interaction effect, $F(1, 9) = 8.30$, $p = .018$, $\eta p2 = .48$. Simple effect further showed that, when neutral faces were masked by colorful patterns, observers' sensitivity was enhanced when fearful voices were presented compared with when neutral voices were presented, $t(9) = 3.46$, $p = .007$, $d' = 1.10$. However, when fear faces were masked by colorful patterns, observers' sensitivities were not different between the condition when fearful sounds were presented and that when neutral sounds were presented, $t(9) = .46$, $p = .653$. Furthermore, we also conducted the Pearson's correlations between the differences in sensitivity of neutral faces (fearful sounds presented condition minus neutral sounds presented condition) and the rating differences of emotional valence (fearful sounds minus neutral sounds). The results revealed a marginal significant correlation, r = −.56, p = .092, suggesting that the larger differences in the emotional valence ratings, observers' sensitivity for neutral faces followed by fear voices were much smaller than those followed by neutral voices. Similar Pearson's correlations were conducted with sensitivity differences for neutral faces and the rating differences of arousal levels, and no significant correlation was found, r = .23, p = .415. When response times were entered into the above analysis, no main effects or interaction effects were found, all ps > .05 (see Table 1). The results found in Experiment 1 implied that only the neutral face detection performances could be modulated by the emotional contexts, e.g., fear human voices. Therefore, in Experiment 2 and 3, whether different emotional contexts (e.g., created by digital music or pictures) can have identical influences on neutral face detection as human voices was examined.

Table 1. Mean RTs and A' results across three experiments

	Measurement	fear-fear	neutral-fear	neutral-neutral	fear-neutral
Experiment 1	RTs (ms)	0.81 (0.19)	0.86 (0.20)	0.89 (0.15)	0.81 (0.19)
	A'	0.71 (0.11)	0.68 (0.15)	0.55 (0.15)	0.71 (0.12)
Experiment 2	RTs (ms)			0.78 (0.16)	0.80 (0.23)
	A'			0.57 (0.16)	0.62 (0.16)
Experiment 3	RTs (ms)			0.86 (0.22)	0.83 (0.26)
	A'			0.58 (0.14)	0.59 (0.11)

In Experiment 2, observers' response times and A' were compared between the fear sounds presented condition and those of the neutral sounds presented condition, and no significant differences were found, $t(9)$ = .42, p = .684 for response times, $t(9)$ = .68, p = .513 for A'. Although observers' subjective rating differences in emotional valence (neutral sounds minus fearful sounds) for digital music were significantly larger than those of human voices, p = .013, it still was not possible to find an emotional modulation effect on response times or sensitivities of neutral faces.

In Experiment 3, detection times for neutral faces followed the fearful pictures were not different from those followed the neutral pictures, $t(9)$ = −.81, p = .439. Similarly, observers' sensitivities for neutral faces were not different, $t(9)$ = .34, p = .741. Again, observers' subjective rating differences in emotional valence (neutral stimuli minus fearful stimuli) for emotional pictures were significantly larger than human voices, p < .001, however, we still failed to find an emotional modulation effect on observers' detection performances of neutral faces.

5 Discussion

Previous studies have suggested that threat information as its significance for survive has privilege to get processing [13, 14, 18]. In this study, we found that emotional contexts created by ambient sounds could affect visual detection of face images presented shortly after the sounds. And this modulation effect was specific to neutral but not to fear face images. Moreover, such modulation effect existed only when human voices but not digital music were provided, suggesting a stimulus specificity of emotional modulation on face detection. Our study extended previous findings about emotional contexts acting on simple feature detection [4] and further indicated that emotional contexts could affect detection performances of complex stimuli (e.g., face images), even when the emotional contexts had no direct relationship with the current goals.

In the present study, we found that emotional contexts, especially the ambient sounds with fear emotions, could enhance but not impair neutral face detection sensitivity. The possible reason for the above findings was that the face presentation time was too short and participants did not have enough time to pay much attention to the masked face. Thus, whether attention was captured by emotional stimuli or not could not affect subsequent visual processing. Furthermore, neuroimaging studies have found that, when one processes emotional information, especially threat-related information, the amygdala (a brain area responsible for emotion processing) could be activated automatically [24]. Studies have further found that the amygdala has bidirectional connections with visual processing areas, such as face processing areas, e.g., fusiform areas [25]. Thus fear ambient sounds activate the amygdala, which sends neurofeedback to the face processing areas, and make the neurological representations of the faces enhanced. However, sensitivity enhancement for fear faces was not found in Experiment 1, which is possibly because individuals typically have better capability in detecting fear information because of the significance of fear information for our survival [13, 14, 18]. Therefore, it is possible that fear face detection performances cannot be further enhanced by emotional contexts, e.g., fear ambient sounds.

Previous studies have suggested that each emotional stimulus can be described in terms of valence and arousal [15]. Therefore, it is also desirable to determine whether emotional influences on face detection are largely affected by valence types or arousal levels. Studies have found that emotional information modulating information processing depended greatly on the arousal levels rather than valence types [26]. For example, individuals' visual search efficiency was better for a happy face with a high arousal level than the counterpart of an angry face [12], or emotional stimuli with different arousal levels can affect individuals' simulated driving performance, e.g., braking times [27]. However, contrary to previous findings, a marginal correlation was found between face detection sensitivity and individuals' subjective evaluation in emotional valence. Additionally, there are still a small number of studies supporting the emotional valence modulation on subsequent visual performances [4, 28]. For example, individuals' hazard perception can be impaired when threat-related stimuli rather than neutral stimuli are presented beforehand [22]. Although the emotional modulating on visual perception found in this study was different from that in the previous studies, it still can be concluded that emotional valence can affect subsequent visual perception. Nevertheless, arousal levels for fear stimuli were generally larger than neutral ones, so one cannot detach the role of arousal engaged in modulating visual perception. More research is needed to test more types of emotional valence (e.g., fear, happiness, and anger) on subsequent visual perception performances.

Emotional meaning can be conveyed by different kinds of stimuli such as speaking voice, affective speech melody, environment sounds, and visual scenes. Even though individuals' emotional states can be induced by different types of emotional stimuli but brain areas responsible for these emotional stimuli are quite different [16]. On the other hand, human voices and faces are important for human emotional understanding and social communications, and were found have overlapped or directly linked brain areas responsible for them [29, 30]. Such close links in brain regions responsible for human voices and faces could result in the human voice's effect on face detection being different from that of digital music. So, in the present study, only human voices, rather than digital music, were found to modulate face detection processing.

Researchers have proposed an implicit HCI concept and suggested that not only the behaviors of users but also the surrounding environment can convey information that is important for HCI activity [31]. For example, when the output displays of a smart phone are designed, designers should consider the current environment in which users are involved. If the user is in a dynamic environment, it is better to present output such as characters with a big font size, while, in a static environment, the font size of characters should be small to present more information. Emotion information is also a kind of environmental information, and one cannot ignore the influences of emotional contexts on HCI behaviors. More importantly, HCI activity sometimes can be significantly impaired under some emotional contexts, such as threat alerting. It is typically considered that threat-related information acts on HCI behavior just like the flight-or-fight response under stress, so that moderate intensity of fear stimuli may not impair but boost human behavior. Thus, an enhancement in face detection performance could be found in a fear-related emotional context.

6   Conclusions

Emotional contexts created by fear ambient sounds could enhance neutral but not fearful face detection performances. Such a modulation effect was found only when human voices were used as ambient sounds. The findings again show that one cannot ignore the influences of environmental characteristics (e.g., emotional contexts) on common HCI behavior, e.g., information detection.

References

1. Franzoni, V., et al.: Emotional machines: the next revolution. Web Intell. 17(1), 1–7 (2019)
2. Hudlicka, E.: To feel or not to feel: the role of affect in human–computer interaction. Int. J. Hum Comput Stud. 59(1), 1–32 (2003)

3. Partala, T., Surakka, V.: The effects of affective interventions in human-computer interaction. Interact. Comput. **16**(2), 295–309 (2004)
4. Nicol, J.R., et al.: Emotion-specific modulation of early visual perception. Cogn. Emot. **27**(8), 1478–1485 (2013)
5. Spering, M., Wagener, D., Funke, J.: The role of emotions in complex problem-solving. Cogn. Emot. **19**(8), 1252–1261 (2005)
6. Ihara, A., et al.: Language comprehension dependent on emotional context: a magnetoencephalography study. Neurosci. Res. **72**(1), 50–58 (2012)
7. Yi, S.W., Baumgartner, H.: Coping with negative emotions in purchase-related situations. J. Consumer Psychol. **14**(3), 303–317 (2004)
8. Nabi, R.L.: Exploring the framing effects of emotion - do discrete emotions differentially influence information accessibility, information seeking, and policy preference? Commun. Res. **30**(2), 224–247 (2003)
9. Anderson, E., et al.: The visual impact of Gossip. Science **332**(6036), 1446–1448 (2011)
10. Ekman, P.: Strong evidence for universals in facial expressions - a reply to Russells mistaken critique. Psychol. Bull. **115**(2), 268–287 (1994)
11. Pinkham, A.E., et al.: The face in the crowd effect: anger superiority when using real faces and multiple identities. Emotion **10**(1), 141–146 (2010)
12. Craig, B.M., Becker, S.I., Lipp, O.V.: Different faces in the crowd: a happiness superiority effect for schematic faces in heterogeneous backgrounds. Emotion **14**(4), 794–803 (2014)
13. Ohman, A., Flykt, A., Esteves, F.: Emotion drives attention: detecting the snake in the grass. J. Exp. Psychol. Gen. **130**(3), 466–478 (2001)
14. Blanchette, I.: Snakes, spiders, guns, and syringes: how specific are evolutionary constraints on the detection of threatening stimuli? Q. J. Exp. Psychol. **59**(8), 1484–1504 (2006)
15. Lang, P.J., et al.: Looking at pictures - affective, facial, visceral, and behavioral reactions. Psychophysiology **30**(3), 261–273 (1993)
16. Fruhholz, S., Trost, W., Kotz, S.A.: The sound of emotions-towards a unifying neural network perspective of affective sound processing. Neurosci. Biobehav. Rev. **68**, 96–110 (2016)
17. Stein, T., et al.: Rapid fear detection relies on high spatial frequencies. Psychol. Sci. **25**(2), 566–574 (2014)
18. Yang, E., Zald, D.H., Blake, R.: Fearful expressions gain preferential access to awareness during continuous flash suppression. Emotion **7**(4), 882–886 (2007)
19. Mathewson, K.J., Arnell, K.M., Mansfield, C.A.: Capturing and holding attention: The impact of emotional words in rapid serial visual presentation. Mem. Cogn. **36**(1), 182–200 (2008)
20. Bocanegra, B.R., Zeelenberg, R.: Dissociating emotion-induced blindness and hypervision. Emotion **9**(6), 865–873 (2009)
21. Zeelenberg, R., Bocanegra, B.R., Pecher, D.: Emotion-induced impairments in speeded word recognition tasks. Exp. Psychol. **58**(5), 400–411 (2011)
22. Jones, M.P., Chapman, P., Bailey, K.: The influence of image valence on visual attention and perception of risk in drivers. Accid. Anal. Prev. **73**, 296–304 (2014)
23. Zeelenberg, R., Bocanegra, B.R.: Auditory emotional cues enhance visual perception. Cognition **115**(1), 202–206 (2010)
24. Haase, S.J., Theios, J., Jenison, R.: A signal detection theory analysis of an unconscious perception effect. Percept. Psychophys. **61**(5), 986–992 (1999)
25. Pessoa, L., Adolphs, R.: Emotion processing and the amygdala: from a 'low road' to 'many roads' of evaluating biological significance. Nat. Rev. Neurosci. **11**(11), 773–782 (2010)
26. Mather, M., Sutherland, M.R.: Arousal-biased competition in perception and memory. Perspect. Psychol. Sci. **6**(2), 114–133 (2011)

27. Trick, L.M., Brandigampola, S., Enns, J.T.: How fleeting emotions affect hazard perception and steering while driving: the impact of image arousal and valence. Accid. Anal. Prev. **45**, 222–229 (2012)
28. Farran, E.K., Branson, A., King, B.J.: Visual search for basic emotional expressions in autism; impaired processing of anger, fear and sadness, but a typical happy face advantage. Res. Autism Spectrum Disord. **5**(1), 455–462 (2011)
29. Schirmer, A., Adolphs, R.: Emotion perception from face, voice, and touch: comparisons and convergence. Trends Cogn. Sci. **21**(3), 216–228 (2017)
30. Blakemore, C.: The range and scope of binocular depth discrimination in man. J. Physiol. **211**(3), 599–622 (1970)
31. Schmidt, A.: Implicit human computer interaction through context. Pers. Technol. **4**(2), 191–199 (2000)

Human-Centered Manufacturing Challenges Affecting European Industry 4.0 Enabling Technologies

Manuel Oliveira[1](✉), Emrah Arica[1], Marta Pinzone[2], Paola Fantini[2],
and Marco Taisch[2]

[1] Sintef, Trondheim, Norway
{manuel.oliveira, emrah.arica}@sintef.no
[2] Politecnico di Milano, Milan, Italy
{marta.pinzone, paola.fantini, marco.taisch}@polimi.it

Abstract. Industry 4.0 implies the digitization of the shopfloor combining technologies such as sensors, augmented reality, and wearable robots that transform the manufacturing environment into a workplace where human-machine interactive symbiosis. As manufacturing companies develop strategies to innovate and engage with the digital transformation, the reality of the enabling technologies demonstrate serious challenges to the wider organizational adoption beyond the pilot phase albeit the promising evaluation results. This paper presents two cases based on two European research projects encompassing representatives of different industrial sectors and distils the challenges encountered that raise barriers to wider adoption.

Keywords: Digital enhanced operator · Enabling technologies ·
Smart manufacturing · Industry 4.0

1 Introduction

The digital transformation of the manufacturing environments is accelerating significantly with the recent introduction and promotion of the Industry 4.0 technologies (e.g. internet of things, data analytics, wearable technologies, artificial intelligence, mixed reality) all around the world. Although automation and digital transformation is touted as the innovation driver for establishing manufacturing competitiveness in the global marketplace, workers will remain as a critical resource for manufacturers [1], especially in complex, high-tech, and customized manufacturing industries. Highly skilled, independent, and flexible workforce is foundational to solve problems, address root causes, drive continuous improvement efforts, and innovate towards short-term and long-term changes [2].

The previous work conducted in the manufacturing planning and control literature [3, 4] have shown the importance of human factors in the performance of manufacturing operations and the interdependent relations between HTO (human, technological, and organizational) factors. It is now well-recognized in literature that successful utilization and implementation of the digitalization and automation technologies largely

© Springer Nature Switzerland AG 2019
C. Stephanidis (Ed.): HCII 2019, LNCS 11786, pp. 507–517, 2019.
https://doi.org/10.1007/978-3-030-30033-3_39

rely on the compatibility of the technological support with human factors. The integrity of the technological support to the tasks of human [3], the interaction of the human with the digitalized support system [5], and cognitive abilities (e.g. attention, perception) of humans [6], make them a critical component of the decision-making process together with the digital systems. It is therefore critical to digitalize the manufacturing environments in synergy with the human factors of workers.

This paper gives an overview of existing Operator 4.0 frameworks and taxonomies (Sect. 2), followed by an analysis of two relevant European research projects pertaining successful digitalization of Industry 4.0 manufacturing environments (Sect. 3), distilling and characterizing the relevant limitations (Sect. 4) that affect human-centered manufacturing work environments, which limit the effective deployment and use of the associated enabling technologies.

2 Operator 4.0 Frameworks and Taxonomies

There is an overall consensus in Europe on naming Fourth Industrial revolution the current process of transformation undergone by the manufacturing sector, following to the first one consisting on mechanization of processes, based on water and steam power; the second one consisting on mass production, based on division of work and electricity; the third one consisting in automation, based on information and communication technologies [7]. The fourth industrial revolution consists in integrating the vertical layers of the traditional automation hierarchy; the horizontal nodes of the supply chain; the phases of the design and engineering process; based on cyber-physical-systems (CPS) [8]. These systems consists of material entities empowered by sensorial, computational, actuating and communication capabilities that collaborate with each other [9] and enable the integration between manufacturing machines and equipment on the shop-floor with the manufacturing execution, enterprise information systems, and with the digital world in general.

The integration of the cyber and physical world is pursued through the implementation of a set of different technological solutions or enabling technologies, such as Additive Manufacturing, Augmented Reality, Big Data and Analytics, Autonomous Robots, Simulation, Industrial Internet [10].

The deployment of the Industry 4.0 solutions has been limited so far to narrow scopes within manufacturing enterprises and a full integration of a manufacturing system has not been achieved, so far. Therefore, there is not a large base of evidence concerning what the implications of the fourth industrial revolution are for the organization of work when considering the augmentation of the operator.

Scholars, while waiting for richer and more mature empirical studies, have developed a conceptual reference, based on two opposite scenarios [11]. The first one assumes that the power and autonomy of artificial systems will be so high to allow for a tight control on the workers exerted through the technologies: technologies master humans. The second scenario speculates that workers will be in control of the processes and technologies will be used for support: technologies as tools for humans. From the human-centric perspective of this last scenario the concept of the Operator 4.0, a "Smart and skilled operator who performs work aided by machines if and as needed"

[1] developed as an emerging paradigm. According to this view, the Operator plays the key role on the shop-floor and various technologies enhance his/her capabilities and support his/her activities. Examples of technologies to augment operators are exo-skeletons to increase strength; augmented reality to transfer knowledge and increase cognitive capabilities; wearable technologies improve health through monitoring of physiological conditions.

Indeed the Operator is a fundamental resource for manufacturing, especially if he/she focuses on activities in which the uniqueness of human contribution is valued [12] and not for mere execution of routine tasks either physical or cognitive. Indeed the human worker represents an extraordinary driver for flexibility in manufacturing environment with high levels of automation, no matter how flexible and advanced these systems are [13]. The Operator 4.0 is mainly a decision maker and a problem-shooter, his/her intervention develops by leveraging and collaborating with the artificial systems along all the phases, from the initial understanding of the situation to the final decision and performance [14]. Most of the effectiveness of human actions depends on situation awareness, that is on the perception and comprehension of the current status of a system, and on the projection of future status [15].

3   Enabling Technologies Case Studies

3.1   Case 1: HUman MANufacturing Project

The HUMAN project [16] is a H2020 research project aiming to digitally enhance the operator on the shop-floor to support them in their work, augmenting their physical and cognitive capabilities, thus avoiding loss of productivity and poor quality due to errors done in their work, whilst contributing to greater well-being.

An overview of the conceptual framework of HUMAN, illustrated in Fig. 1, is composed of two distinct cycles:

- Short-term. The operator is sensorized by the use of wearable devices (e.g.: smart watches, depth cameras, HMD, thermo-graphic cameras, etc.) capturing a wide range of signals that are complemented with sensors in the work environment to generate a the digital representation of the workplace environment by the existence of multiple models. Based on the contextual understanding of reality, the system reasons about any anomalies and discrepancies that represent a fallacy in the sit-uation awareness of the operator. As a result, the system determines whether assistance is required and what would be the appropriate level of assistance. When appropriate an intervention is triggered that is tailored to the particular needs of the operator, who may always decide to over-rule the system;

- Long-term. All the data from sensors and events generated from the system are captured for secondary usage by additional services used for learning, supporting decision making and workplace optimization. Unlike with short-term where the system reasons and determines the best course of action to support the operator, in the case of long-term, an engineer needs to be involved and makes decisions based on the generated insights.

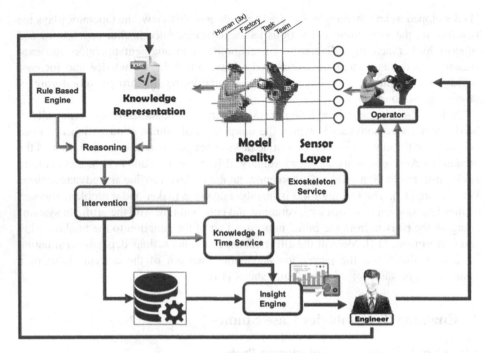

Fig. 1. The HUMAN conceptual framework with short-term reasoning (red track) and long-term reasoning (blue) (Color figure online)

Two of the short-term services are:

- Knowledge In Time (KIT) service [17], which uses augmented reality combined with machine learning to address the detrimental effect of cognitive overburden of the operator that ultimately affects their productivity and quality of the work output. The understanding of the operator's context permits a tailored delivery of support;
- Exoskeleton service, where the operators don a semi-passive exoskeleton along with wearable device to measure real-time physiological data. The service determines the probable level of physical fatigue experienced by the operator and adjusts the level of physical assistance (Fig. 2).

Taking the KIT service in more detail, it has been deployed at all three of the end-users organisations, covering a range of different industries, namely aeronautics, robot manufacturing and furniture manufacturing. Each of the end-users has differing production rates and product/process complexities, which have their own challenges:

- Furniture Manufacturing. The primary use of the KIT service is for training purpose to reduce the time to competence of operators. However, the system is also used by the experienced operator by bringing to their attention intricacies of the assembly

Fig. 2. Use of the HUMAN short-term services at the end-user organizations

operation based on their past performance and evidence of retention concerning process. The secondary use of the system is to verify the quality of the training and decide on potential workplace optimisation.

- Robot Manufacturing. The system provides step-by-step instruction support, whilst monitoring the operator's activities to assess the quality of their work and capturing evidence of the work. The secondary use of the captured data is to support quality auditing of the production process.
- Aeronautics. The system is used to support the operator in their process, indicating the mistakes that were incurred in the recent past. The system in this case monitors the operator's actions, indicating the probability of error in the task, thereby bringing to the attention of the operator. The secondary use of the system is to improve the process optimisation.

The operators have appreciated the use of augmented reality with machine learning to increase their cognitive capabilities tailored to the particular context of work being carried out. However, the secondary use of the system to support long-term cycle provides the means to augment and improve existing company knowledge.

3.2 Case 2: MAN-MADE Worker-Centric Adaptive Workplace

The MAN-MADE (MANufacturing through ergonoMic and safe Anthropocentric aDaptive workplacEs for context aware factories in EUROPE) project aims at defining new socially sustainable workplaces where workers are foreseen at the centre of the factory [18], especially in terms of workplace adaptation. The worker-centric manufacturing model is, then, demonstrated in a pilot implementation at the training assembly line of an Italian producer of white-goods.

According to the MAN-MADE approach, in order to build a personalized workplace that fits each individual worker, specific anthropometric data of each worker are gathered to build a detailed 3D digital mannequin characterized by significant dimensions of the human body (e.g., standing height, elbow height). The anthropometric characterization of the worker is also enriched with information on her capacities, skills and needs [19]. As a result, a comprehensive, consistent and evolving knowledge base is created to enabling the digital design and configuration of the worker-centric workplace and its physical adaptation, so that it can sustain workers' performance and wellbeing at best [21].

From a technological viewpoint, the characterisation of the worker is realised with the support of a non-invasive data capture systems meant to collect relevant anthropometric dimensions of each worker (Fig. 3). Specifically, a stereo camera-based imaging system is used. It consists of two cameras, landmarks to place on the worker's body, a data analysis software, and a screen to visualize the data capture process. The system has low costs due to non-complex hardware; it is accurate with measurements performed in 3D, and easy-to-use, as all measurements are performed automatically from the acquired images, and the measurement procedure requires less than 5 min.

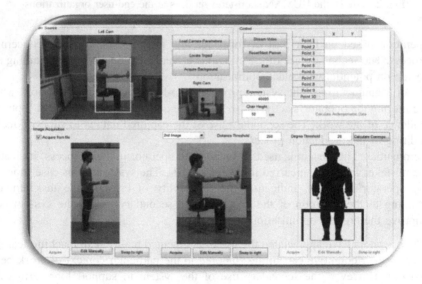

Fig. 3. User interface of the stereo camera-based imaging system

The captured data and information enable the creation of a digital 3D mannequin. Then, an ad-hoc CAD plug-in is used to transfer the data to/from a Computer Aided Design software to define a new adaptable workplace, and to configure its parameters so that it ergonomically fits the worker as well as production objectives.

Finally, from the physical point of view, the workplace adaptability is realized by introducing a collaborative robot instead of complex automation alternatives (Fig. 3). Collaborative robots enable direct interaction between operators and cobots, thus overcoming the classical division of labour, which requires industrial robots to be confined in safety cages [21]. As an example, in one of the MAN-MADE scenarios, the worker approaching the workstation is recognized and the worker's parameters are directly transferred to the motors to automatically adjust the workstation plan. The cobot hands the worker a part in the most ergonomic way or adjust the position of the bins where the worker fetches components, taking into account the specific traits of the individual worker (e.g., if the worker is right- or left-handed). Equipping the workplace with a collaborative robot to implement adaptability leads to a more flexible, scalable, and economic system than other traditional electromechanical approaches, which usually lack in flexibility and cannot efficiently adapt to frequent changes and dynamic working environments (Fig. 4).

Fig. 4. Training assembly line and collaborative robot

4 Challenges

In both projects, different technologies were used in researching solutions to address human-centred manufacturing work environments, whether by changing the workplace (MAN-MADE) or by digitally enhancing the operator on the shopfloor (HUMAN). The results from the research projects were promising, but there remains a significant gap between the research results and the industrial uptake, which are briefly described in the subsequent subsections.

4.1 HUMAN

In the HUMAN project, the focus on digitally enhancing the operator on the shopfloor is faced with several challenges associated to the enabling technologies that are used in the digital transformation of the workplace, namely:

- Production readiness. The devices used for the different services were afflicted with shortcomings that make their adoption harder when considering a factory roll-out. In the case of wearables, the level of accuracy of the readings in terms of time synchronization raises difficulties in construing an accurate context from the different sources; in the case of the exoskeleton, one requires certification for deployment in the factory; in the case of hololens (device used in KIT), the over-heating presented itself as a problem due to passive dissipation of the heat, the battery lifetime was limited, the reduced field of view (FOV) caused concerns with some operators when trying to gauge the big picture and the accuracy of the holograms invalidated some processes due to quality constraints.

- Privacy and Trust. A fundamental premise of the HUMAN project was for the system to build a context of the work environment, the operator and the task being carried out. In addition to the traditional digital information originating from production systems and the environment, the operator themselves was sensorized with wearable devices, depth cameras, video and audio. Whilst this richer data sets provided the means of creating more accurate understanding of the work context at hand, serious concerns regarding privacy were raised [22, 23], which consequently had an impact on the trust operators would have in the service and affecting their acceptance.
- Integration with the Work Practice. The use of new solutions with innovative work practices have an impact on existing processes that need change. The use of process analytics and mining contribute to a measured approach to improving the workplace.
- Training and Reasoning. The advent of machine learning is transforming the opportunities in the workplace, but approaches such as deep learning, require inordinate amounts of data for training purposes. However, within manufacturing environments, access to data is in most cases sparse and difficult to acquire taking into account the practical constraints of production schedules, environment conditions (e.g.: lighting, noise, etc.), intellectual property involved and the requirement of contextual knowledge for labelling. Therefore, one needs to create proprietary data sets that benefit from contextual information that make learning transfer difficult to achieve.

4.2 MAN-MADE

The approach proposed by MAN-MADE for workplace adaptation is considered as promising by the main company stakeholders. However, some challenges must be addressed to guarantee its successful implementation in real factories. The main ones are briefly described:

- Contextual Knowledge. Health professionals of the company medical service are needed to perform the acquisition of the measurements, with standardized protocols to be followed with instructions for preparation (kind of clothing to be worn, calibration method of the system, anatomical land markers), the correct positioning of the worker, and taking the images.
- Privacy and Trust. Data privacy and protection concerns regard how workers' personal data are being stored, protected and re-used. These concerns may be also amplified when a dynamic worker profile is created and updated by monitoring the worker status trough wearable devices to enable the adaptation of the workplace in real-time [24].
- Environmental Constraints. Industrial environments are often complicated and may not have optimal lighting conditions. Therefore, it is crucial to select carefully hardware and software components that are suitable for use in real-life industrial environments.
- Safety. safety and trust in the cobot are essential. Additional certification for the cobot's tools is required to guarantee the physical safety of operators. Similarly,

issues related to mental stress and anxiety induced by close interaction with the cobot must be considered to ensure that the worker feels comfortable and safe when cooperating with the cobot.

- Training and Reasoning. Operators and maintenance technicians must be trained to develop the skills needed not only to perform new tasks together with the cobot but also to re-programming the cobot in case of adjustments, minor product changes, or stoppages [25].

5 Conclusions

The industry 4.0 digital transformation of the manufacturing landscape is promising [26] but unlike many proponents, it will not deliver the vision of a fully automated manufacturing site, as the human operator remains necessary due to the nature of tasks, in particular when creativity and problem solving is required. Therefore, the emphasis has been of exploiting the synergies between the human operator and technology, to cognitively and physically enhance the operator whilst making the work environment adaptive to the needs of the operator.

This paper has presented some of the research results from two European projects, involving end-users organizations from different industrial sectors. The cases demonstrate the potential of adopting enabling technologies to digitally enhance the operator and the work environment, but the paper delved into the challenges that raise barriers concerning the wider deployment of the devised solutions albeit the pilots yielded promising results with attractive performance indicators.

Some of the challenges are related to the maturity and production readiness of the enabling technologies, which gradually will improve over time (e.g.: the hololens 2 provides a wider FoV, more sophisticated sensors and an ergonomically much improved design that offsets the heavy load from the front). However, there are many of the limitations are rooted in non-functional features, namely the concerns over trust and privacy as significant amounts of data from the operators are captured so a digital solution may understand the context and determine the best way to support the operator. It becomes essential to consider privacy by design from the onset and adopting engagement strategies that involve the operator in the designing and deploying the solution in their work environment.

References

1. Romero, D., Bernus, P., Noran, O., Stahre, J., Fast-Berglund, Å.: The Operator 4.0: human cyber-physical systems & adaptive automation towards human-automation symbiosis work systems. In: Nääs, I., et al. (eds.) Advances in Production Management Systems: Initiatives for a Sustainable World, pp. 677–686. Springer International Publishing, Cham (2016). https://doi.org/10.1007/978-3-319-51133-7_80
2. de Snoo, C., van Wezel, W., Wortmann, J.C., Gaalman, G.J.C.: Coordination activities of human planners during rescheduling: case analysis and event handling procedure. Int. J. Prod. Res. 49(7), 2101–2122 (2011)

3. Arica, E., Haskins, C., Strandhagen, J.O.: A framework for production rescheduling in sociotechnical manufacturing environments. Prod. Plan. Control **27**(14), 1191–1205 (2016)
4. Arica, E., Buer, S.V., Strandhagen, J.O.: Organizational capability in production scheduling. In: Umeda, S., Nakano, M., Mizuyama, H., Hibino, H., Kiritsis, D., von Cieminski, G. (eds.) APMS 2015. IAICT, vol. 459, pp. 383–390. Springer, Cham (2015). https://doi.org/10.1007/978-3-319-22756-6_47
5. van Wezel, W., Cegarra, J., Hoc, J.-M.: Allocating functions to human and algorithm in scheduling. In: Fransoo, J.C., Waefler, T., Wilson, J.R. (eds.) Behavioral Operations in Planning and Scheduling, pp. 339–370. Springer, Berlin (2011). https://doi.org/10.1007/978-3-642-13382-4_14
6. Cegarra, J.: A cognitive typology of scheduling situations: a contribution to laboratory and field studies. Theoret. Issues Ergon. Sci. **9**(3), 201–222 (2008)
7. Thoben, K.-D., Wiesner, S.A., Wuest, T.: "Industrie 4.0" and smart manufacturing-a review of research issues and application examples. Int. J. Autom. Technol. **11** (2017). https://doi.org/10.20965/ijat.2017.p0004
8. Kagermann, H., Wahlster, W., Helbig, J.: Recommendations for implementing the strategic initiative INDUSTRIE 4.0 - Final Report of the Industrie 4.0 Working Group (2013)
9. Wang, L., Törngren, M., Onori, M.: Current status and advancement of cyber-physical systems in manufacturing. J. Manuf. Syst. **37**, 517–527 (2015). https://doi.org/10.1016/j.jmsy.2015.04.008
10. Rüßmann, M., et al.: Industry 4.0: the future of productivity and growth in manufacturing industries. Bost. Consult (2015). https://doi.org/10.1007/s12599-014-0334-4
11. Dworschak, B., Zaiser, H.: Competences for cyber-physical systems in manufacturing – first findings and scenarios. Procedia CIRP **25**, 345–350 (2014). https://doi.org/10.1016/j.procir.2014.10.048
12. Fantini, P., Pinzone, M., Taisch, M.: Placing the operator at the centre of Industry 4.0 design: modelling and assessing human activities within cyber-physical systems. Comput. Ind. Eng (2018). https://doi.org/10.1016/j.cie.2018.01.025
13. Fantini, P., et al.: Exploring the integration of the human as a flexibility factor in CPS enabled manufacturing environments: Methodology and results. In: IECON 2016 - 42nd Annual Conference of the IEEE Industrial Electronics Society, pp. 5711–5716. IEEE (2016). https://doi.org/10.1109/IECON.2016.7793579
14. Emmanouilidis, C.: Enabling the human in the loop: linked data and knowledge in industrial cyber-physical systems. Annu. Rev. Control (2019). https://doi.org/10.1016/j.arcontrol.2019.03.004
15. Endsley, M.R.: Measurement of situation awareness in dynamic systems. Hum. Factors **37**, 65–84 (1995). https://doi.org/10.1518/001872095779049499
16. http://humanmanufacturing.eu/
17. http://www.kit-ar.com
18. Bettoni, A., Cinus, M., Sorlini, M., May, G., Taisch, M., Pedrazzoli, P.: Anthropocentric workplaces of the future approached through a new holistic vision. In: Grabot, B., Vallespir, B., Gomes, S., Bouras, A., Kiritsis, D. (eds.) APMS 2014. IAICT, vol. 439, pp. 398–405. Springer, Heidelberg (2014). https://doi.org/10.1007/978-3-662-44736-9_49
19. Pinzone, M., Fantini, P., Fiasché, M., Taisch, M.: A multi-horizon, multi-objective training planner: building the skills for manufacturing. In: Bassis, S., Esposito, A., Morabito, F.C., Pasero, E. (eds.) Advances in Neural Networks. SIST, vol. 54, pp. 517–526. Springer, Cham (2016). https://doi.org/10.1007/978-3-319-33747-0_51
20. May, G., Taisch, M., Bettoni, A., Maghazei, O., Matarazzo, A., Stahl, B.: A new human-centric factory model. Procedia CIRP **26**, 103–108 (2015)

21. Villani, V., Pini, F., Leali, F., Secchi, C.: Survey on human–robot collaboration in industrial settings: safety, intuitive interfaces and applications. Mechatronics **55**, 248–266 (2018)
22. Mannhardt, F., Petersen, S., Oliveira, M.: Privacy challenges for process mining in human-centered industrial environments. In: 15th International Conference on Intelligent Environments, Rome, June 2018
23. Petersen, S.A., Mannhardt, F., Oliveira, M., Torvatn, H.: A framework to navigate the privacy trade-offs for human-centred manufacturing. In: Camarinha-Matos, Luis M., Afsarmanesh, H., Rezgui, Y. (eds.) PRO-VE 2018. IAICT, vol. 534, pp. 85–97. Springer, Cham (2018). https://doi.org/10.1007/978-3-319-99127-6_8
24. Pinzone, M., et al.: A framework for operative and social sustainability functionalities in human-centric cyber-physical production system. Comput. Industr. Eng. (2018)
25. Fantini, P., Pinzone, M., Sella, F., Taisch, M.: Collaborative robots and new product introduction: capturing and transferring human expert knowledge to the operators. In: Trzcielinski, S. (ed.) AHFE 2017, pp. 259–268. Springer, Cham (2018). https://doi.org/10.1007/978-3-319-60474-9_24
26. EFFRA European Factories of the Future Research Association, Factories 4.0 and Beyond: Recommendations for the work programme 18-19-20 of the FoF PPP under Horizon 2020 (2016)

When to Take a Break? Exploring the Role of Peers on Sedentary Office Workers' Resting Behaviors

Ling Qin, Xu Sun[⊠], Bingjian Liu, and Luis Moreno Leyva

The University of Nottingham Ningbo China,
199 Taikang East Road, Ningbo 315100, China
{zyl8427, Xu.Sun, Bingjian.Liu,
Luis-Moreno.Leyva}@nottingham.edu.cn

Abstract. For sedentary office workers, occupational sitting is a health hazard [1]. Excessive sitting, especially prolonged sitting (i.e. sitting more than one hour) without rest is highly likely to increase the risks of metabolic syndrome, obesity, cardiovascular disease and a range of other conditions, all of which cannot even be compensated for by taking exercise [2, 3]. Peer effect is a phenomenon whereby the behavior of an individual is affected by the behavior of their peers. It has been identified in the workplace with regards to wages, absenteeism and investment decision making in recent studies [4–7]. This paper contributes to the stream of research on peer effects on sedentary office workers by proposing a model to quantify the peer effects on office workers' break behaviors, and by exploring how individual break behaviors can be affected by peers in the same workspace. In conclusion, peer effects have been detected in offices and have proved to have a marked influence on sedentary office workers' resting behaviors.

Keywords: Sedentary behaviors · Peer effects · Social norms · Organizational behaviors

1 Introduction

Sedentary Behavior is defined as any waking behavior characterized by an energy expenditure ≤ 1.5 metabolic equivalents (METs), while in a sitting, reclining or lying posture. A metabolic equivalent is deemed to be 3.5 ml O2/kg/min in adults without mobility impairment or chronic disease [8]. The various types of physical activities can be categorized into sedentary behavior (1.0–1.5 METs), light-intensity (1.6–2.9 METs), moderate-intensity (3–5.9 METs), and vigorous-intensity (≥ 6 METs) activities. Table 1 describes the metabolic equivalent of several physical activities in an office [9].

© Springer Nature Switzerland AG 2019
C. Stephanidis (Ed.): HCII 2019, LNCS 11786, pp. 518–527, 2019.
https://doi.org/10.1007/978-3-030-30033-3_40

Table 1. Metabolic equivalents of physical activities in an office.

Physical activities	MET
Sedentary behaviors	**1.0–1.5**
Sitting quietly (watching TV, listening to music)	1.0
Sitting - reading books	1.3
Sitting - typing	1.5
Light-intensity	**1.6–2.9**
Standing-talking/talking on the telephone	1.8
Walking on the job, ≤ 2.0 mph (in the office)	2.0
Moderate-intensity	**3–5.9**
Walking on the job, ≤ 2.5 mph and carrying light objects	3.0
Walking on the job, 3.5 mph and carrying light objects	4.0
Vigorous-intensity	**≥ 6**
Jogging	7.0

Sedentary lifestyle has been reported to have severe negative effects on health, and this is now a global issue. A previous study of 17,013 Canadians suggested that people who spent the majority of their time sitting were 50% more likely to die in early ages than those who sit the least. The results of this study remained similar even after sex, age, smoking status and body mass index were controlled [10]. In Australia, more than half of the adult citizens are reported to be too inactive, and physical inactivity has contributed to the second major cause of cancer, following that of smoking [11].

As a matter of fact, office workers have already paid attention to their sedentary behaviors. A recent survey has indicated that prolonged periods of sitting has raised concerns among office workers, 88% of whom believed that time spent sitting is directly associated with their health status. Musculoskeletal complaints, followed by general health and obesity, were identified in the survey as their most significant considerations [12]. In particular, taking breaks is essential for office workers' well-being. It is clear that break activities during working hours may maintain productivity over the entire working day [13]. Office workers may need to have a break from their work to restore energy and remain focused [14]. It is also probable that they self-interrupt or rest to manage their workload and productivity [15].

Peer effect, in which the behavior of an individual is affected by the behavior of their peers [16], have been evidenced to exist in the workplace in terms of wages, absenteeism, entrepreneurship decisions, and investment decision making in recent studies [4–7]. Nevertheless, little research has addressed whether peer effects have an impact on the sedentary behaviors of office workers. In this paper, peer effects on the resting behaviors of office workers, refer to how their resting behaviors are influenced by their peers, as including when to take a rest and what to do during the break periods are influenced by. This implies that resting decisions do not depend on one's physiological needs in isolation, as individuals may take breaks when they realize that their peers are doing so. The purpose of this paper is to propose a model to quantify the peer effects on office workers' break behaviors, and to explore how individual break behaviors can be affected by peers in the same workspace. Since sedentary behaviors are health hazards and sedentary office workers are keen to make a difference, the potential implications of this model will be discussed in the conclusion.

2 Methodology

We define an individual i's peers as all the individuals excluding i in the same workspace w. We then hypothesize a linear regression model to illustrate the existence of peer effects on individual resting behaviors:

$$R_{i,w} = \beta_0 + \beta_1 P_{i,w} + \beta_2 H_i + \varepsilon_{io}$$

where $R_{i,w}$ refers to the resting behaviors of the individual i in the workspace w. $P_{i,w}$ denotes the corresponding effects of resting behaviors of the peers. H_i is a vector of individual i's physiological characteristics, β_0 represents the constant term, and ε_i is the error term. β_1 stands for the major coefficient of interest between peer effects and resting behaviors. As the duration of hourly rest periods can be estimated by oxygen uptake [23], it can be reasonably expected that physiological condition (such as age, gender, cardiovascular states) is a dependent factor of one's resting behaviors. Therefore, the purpose of the following experiment is predominately to examine the relationship between $R_{i,w}$ and $P_{i,w}$.

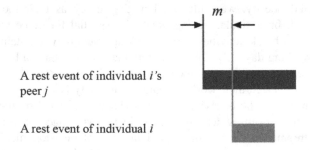

A rest event of individual i's peer j

A rest event of individual i

Fig. 1. An illustration of time interval m (j's rest behavior has an influence on i)

To quantify the above items, we introduced a parameter, time interval m (unit: minutes), to quantify the peer effects among individuals. It designates the time difference between the starting time of the two nearest successive rest events of individual i and i's peer j, assuming that the earlier event has an impact on the later one. Figures 1 and 2 may explain it.

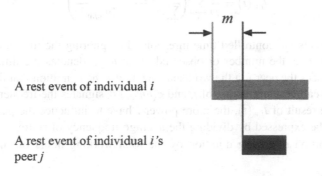

Fig. 2. An illustration of time interval m (i's rest behavior has an influence on j)

By using time interval m and the frequency of each time interval $C(m)$, $P_{i,w}$ can be calculated as the reciprocal of the weighted average of the time intervals (j's rest behavior has an influence on i).

$$P_{i,w}(t) = \frac{1}{D} \sum_{1}^{D} \left(\frac{\sum c(m_{j,i,w})}{\sum (m_{j,i,w} \cdot c(m_{j,i,w}))} \right)$$

where t, represents the controlled time threshold i.e. ignoring the time interval that is longer than t; D refers to the number of observed days; $m_{j,i,w}$ denotes the time interval that j influences i in the workspace w, under the condition that the rest event of j happened earlier than the rest event of i; and $c(m_{j,i,w})$ designates the frequency of $m_{j,i,w}$. The larger the results of $P_{w,i}(t)$ is, the easier it is for i to be influenced by the peers. $R_{i,w}$ can be calculated by dividing the average frequency of resting events by the average proportion of resting duration to the total working hours of individual i:

$$R_{i,w} = \frac{H}{D} \sum_{1}^{D} \left(\frac{f_{i,w}}{t_{i,w}} \right)$$

where H represents the regulated working hours of the workspace w, D refers to the number of observed days; $f_{i,w}$ and $t_{i,w}$ are the total amount of frequency and duration of i to take breaks in the workspace w respectively. The larger the result of $R_{i,w}$, the more likely i is to take breaks.

Similarly, we define Individual Power ($I_{i,w}$) as the ability of individual i to influence the resting behaviors of i's peers in the workspace w and $R_{(i),w}$ as the resting behaviors of individual i's peers in the workspace w. $I_{i,w}$ can be expressed as the reciprocal of the weighted average of the time intervals (i's rest behavior has an influence on j):

$$I_{i,w}(t) = \frac{1}{D} \sum_{1}^{D} \left(\frac{\sum c(m_{i,j,w})}{\sum (m_{i,j,w} \cdot c(m_{i,j,w}))} \right)$$

where t represents the controlled time threshold (i.e. ignoring the time interval that is longer than t); D is the number of observed days; $m_{i,j,w}$ denotes the time interval in which i influences the peer j in the workspace w, under the condition that the rest event of i happened earlier than the that of j; and $c(m_{i,j,w})$ designates the frequency of $m_{i,j,w}$. The larger the result of $I_{i,w}(t)$, the more power i have to influence the peers.

$R_{(i),w}$ can be expressed by dividing the average frequency of resting events by the average proportion of resting duration by the total working hours of all individuals excluding i:

$$R_{(i),w} = \frac{H}{D} \sum_{1}^{D} \left(\frac{f_{(i),w}}{t_{(i),w}} \right)$$

where H represents the regulated working hours of the workspace w, D is the number of observed days; $f_{(i),w}$ and $t_{(i),w}$ are the average frequency and average time for taking breaks in one day of all the individuals in the workspace w, excluding i. The larger the result of $R_{(i),w}$, the more likely i's peers are to take breaks.

By exploring the relationship between $R_{i,w}$ and $P_{i,w}$, we can identify the role of peer influence on individual resting behaviors. By contrast, the role can be double proved by testing the relationship between $R_{(i),w}$ and $I_{i,w}$, as individual i can be also treated as another individual j's peer.

3   Research Experiment

Two-week field observations were conducted with 12 participants (F = 7, M = 5) of at three offices to detect whether individuals may take a break in response to others' similar behavior. Office workers at a university who were healthy and had predominantly desk-based jobs were recruited by email. During the observation, researchers sat in the natural surroundings of the participants' offices for two days, unobtrusively observing and recording their activities when they left their seats to take breaks and what they did during those periods. We also interviewed the participants at the end of each day to further explore their resting behaviors based on the observations. Several rules were set to identify and record resting behaviors.

1. The minimum unit used to record the time is one minute, the same as that of to record time interval. Therefore, the case may appear in which one independent rest event of one individual was recorded as happening at the same time that another rest

event ended for the same individual, but they were recorded as two events rather than one whole event.

2. The recorded resting behaviors have been categorized into the following events, for which we also estimated the energy expenditure of each activity according to Table 1:

(A) Looking for something/reaching for something (4.0 METs)
(B) Talking with colleagues (1.8 METs)
(C) Going to the toilet (3.0 METs)
(D) Filling containers with water (3.0 METs)
(E) Standing for a rest/stretching (1.8 METs)
(F) Answering the telephone (standing/walking around) (1.8 METs)

3. A multitasking rest event was recorded as a single rest event. For example, refilling a teacup while talking with a colleague.

4 Results

Our finding indicates that one office worker's resting behaviors may result in another one or more other office workers to show similar behavior. Such events have been witnessed frequently, confirming the existence of peer effects on the resting behaviors of sedentary office workers.

The statistical data provides strong support for the observational findings. We plotted a diagram of the frequency of each time interval ($C(m)$) against occurred time intervals (m) of all participants during the observations. Figure 3 clearly demonstrates that it was when the time interval approached 0 that the successive events were most likely to take place. The frequency tends to decline dramatically with the growing time interval. A case that was observed on numerous occasions supports the perspective, where one person left the seat to go to talk to another person, causing that person stood up and replied. Another example was when one individual went to refill his/her teacup and invited his/her colleague to do so as well, so both of them were prone to filling their cups with hot water. These two examples demonstrate how an office worker may have an almost immediate influence on the activities of their peers by verbal invitation or enquiry. In addition, a previous paper has suggested that there are probably many circumstances in which office workers invite each other to take breaks [17].

Table 2 demonstrates the linear regression estimates of the impact of peer effects on resting behaviors under certain time interval threshold controls. These controls were based on Fig. 3, where saltation occurs (at a time interval of approximately 5, 10, 15, 20, 25 and 30 min). The results in row (1) show that peer effect ($P_{i,w}$) is a significant indicator for predicting individual resting behaviors ($R_{i,w}$) when the time interval threshold is at approximately 20 min. Row (2) describes how the reasonability of the above conclusion can be confirmed by the relationship between the peers' resting behaviors ($R_{(i),w}$) and individual power ($I_{i,w}$) under the same control. The conclusions are in conformity, since peers' resting behaviors can also be predicted and indicated by the effects of individuals.

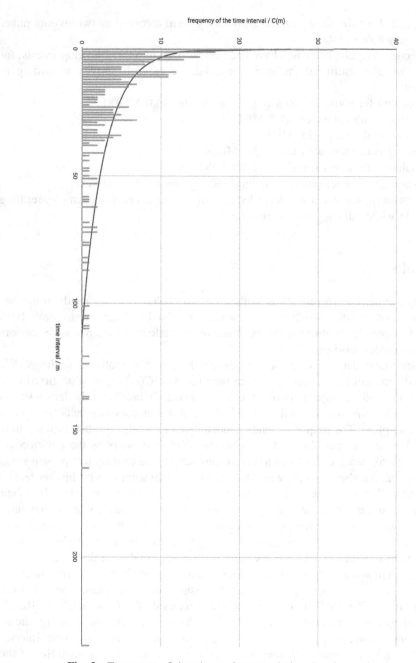

Fig. 3. Frequency of time interval occurs during the observations

Table 2. Linear regression estimates of resting behaviors and peer effects

	Controlled threshold (1)	Without control (2)	30 mins (3)	25 mins (4)	20 mins (5)	15 mins (6)	10 mins (7)	5 mins (8)
(1)	$R_{i,w}/P_{i,w}$	-28.147	10.650***	5.882*	7.492**	7.842**	3.911	-0.213
	$\overline{R_{i,w}}$	1.936						
	95% CI	[1.563, 2.309]						
(2)	$R_{(i),w}/I_{i,w}$	0.460	13.021*	7.283***	7.457***	2.540	3.130	0.410
	$\overline{R_{(i),w}}$	2.107						
	95% CI	[1.503, 2.711]						

The dependent variables are controlled peer effects and controlled individual power respectively. 95% confidence intervals (CI) are shown in brackets. *$p < 0.1$, **$p < 0.05$, and ***$p < 0.01$.

5 Conclusion and Recommendation

In conclusion, it is evident that peers have a noticeable effect on individual break behaviors within a certain range. The effects are mutual and significant, indicating that, in turn, an individual is also able to affect the break behaviors of peers. Thus, certain design implications are derived regarding the application of peer effects on office workers to reduce their sedentary behaviors.

Social interactions are direct influential factors on rest frequency. Taking some offices as an example, it was clear that they had a culture of staff inviting each other to go for a drink break, while others demonstrated the practice in which that one person would bring drinks for the peers who remained sitting for a long time [17]. The promise of peer effects provides policy makers with suggestions that can be employed to increase the overall performance by realizing peer groups [18]. Combined with this research, managers may apply the above model to evaluate the resting behaviors of their employees to test whether they are sufficiently active. The model also makes it possible to recognize employees who positively and actively influence peers' resting behaviors, and those whose behaviors are easily affected by peers, following which managers may attempt to group them together in the same workspace. Consequently, the overall activity of the workforce is expected to be augmented.

Social norms are major barriers to behavior changes among office workers [19]. Team leaders may properly utilize the peer effect on employees to improve their well-being, as senior managers can implement tremendous shifts in the organizational norms [20]. For instance, the leaders themselves could take the initiative to spend less time siting -and thereby encourage their employees to follow suit. This may lead to health improvements for both leaders and employees.

Moreover, social networks, such as online discussion forums and social networking sites, showed a promising consequence regarding a decrease in prolonged sitting [21, 22] and another strong factor is that communication technologies can be employed to encourage peer effects [16]. A previous survey indicated that users are extremely unsatisfied with the current reminders such as pop-up windows on computer screens and wearable devices with vibrating inactivity alerts [17], it is therefore possible for designers to apply social media into the design of systems or products to reduce sedentary behaviors in the workplace by increasing the peer effect. One potential suggestion could be an application that enables a group of office workers to discuss the subject and thereby motivate each other to reduce their levels of physical inactivity.

References

1. Ryan, C.G., Dall, P.M., Granat, M.H., Grant, P.M.: Sitting patterns at work: objective measurement of adherence to current recommendations. Ergonomics **54**(6), 531–538 (2011). https://doi.org/10.1080/00140139.2011.570458
2. Tremblay, M., Colley, R., Saunders, T., Healy, G., Owen, N.: Physiological and health implications of a sedentary lifestyle. Appl. Physiol. Nutr. Metab. **35**(6), 725–740 (2010)
3. Pate, R.R., O'neill, J.R., Lobelo, F.: The evolving definition of "sedentary". Exerc. Sport Sci. Rev. **36**(4), 173–178 (2008)
4. Thomas, C., Dustmann, C., Schönberg, U.: Peer Effects in the Workplace. Am. Econ. Rev. **107**(2), 425–456 (2017)
5. Ichino, A., Maggi, G.: Work environment and individual background: Explaining regional shirking differentials in a large Italian firm. Quart. J. Econ. **115**(3), 1057–1090 (2000)
6. Brown, J., Ivkovic, Z., Smith, P.A., Weisbenner, S.: Neighbors matter: causal community effects and stock market participation. J. Financ. **63**, 1509–1531 (2008)
7. Bursztyn, L., Ederer, F., Ferman, B., Yuchtman, N.: Understanding peer effects in financial decisions: evidence from a field experiment, NBER Working Paper 18241 (2012)
8. Tremblay, M.S., et al.: SBRN terminology consensus project participants. sedentary behavior research network (SBRN) – terminology consensus project process and outcome. Int. J. Behav. Nutr. Phys. Act. **14**(1), 75 (2017)
9. Ainsworth, B., et al.: 2011 compendium of physical activities: a second update of codes and MET values. Med. Sci. Sports Exerc. **43**, 1575–1581 (2011). https://doi.org/10.1249/MSS.0b013e31821ece12
10. Katzmarzyk, P.T., Church, T.S., Craig, C.L., Bouchard, C.: Sitting time and mortality from all causes, cardiovascular disease, and cancer. Med. Sci. Sports Exerc. **41**(5), 998–1005 (2009). https://doi.org/10.1249/MSS.0b013e3181930355
11. Australian Bureau of Statistics (ABS): Australian Health Survey: Physical Activity, 2011–12. ABS Cat. No. 4364.0.55.004. ABS Canberra: (2013)
12. McGuckin, T., Sealey, R., Barnett, F.: Planning for sedentary behaviour interventions: office workers' survey and focus group responses. Perspect. Public Health **137**(6), 316–321 (2017). https://doi.org/10.1177/1757913917698003
13. Mark, G., Iqbal, S., Czerwinski, M., Johns, P.: Capturing the mood: Facebook and face-to-face encounters in the workplace. In: Proceedings of the 17th ACM Conference on Computer Supported Cooperative Work & Social Computing (CSCW 2014), pp. 1082–1094. ACM, New York (2014)
14. Mark, G., Iqbal, S., Czerwinski, M., Johns, P.: Focused, aroused, but so distractible: temporal perspectives on multitasking and communications. In: Proceedings of the 18th ACM Conference on Computer Supported Cooperative Work & Social Computing (CSCW 2015), pp. 903–916. ACM, New York (2015)
15. Skatova, A., et al.: The role of ICT in office work breaks (2016). https://doi.org/10.1145/2858036.2858443
16. Eckles, D., Kizilcec, R., Bakshy, E.: Estimating peer effects in networks with peer encouragement designs. Proc. Natl. Acad. Sci. U.S.A. **113**(27), 7316–7322 (2016)

17. Huang, Y., Benford, S., Hendrickx, H., Treloar, R., Blake, H.: Office workers' perceived barriers and facilitators to taking regular micro-breaks at work: a diary-probed interview study. In: de Vries, P.W., Oinas-Kukkonen, H., Siemons, L., Beerlage-de Jong, N., van Gemert-Pijnen, L. (eds.) PERSUASIVE 2017. LNCS, vol. 10171, pp. 149–161. Springer, Cham (2017). https://doi.org/10.1007/978-3-319-55134-0_12
18. Feld, J., Zölitz, U.: Understanding peer effects: on the nature, estimation, and channels of peer effects. J. Labor Econ. 35(2), 387–428 (2017)
19. Nooijen, C., Kallings, L.V., Blom, V., Ekblom, Ö., Forsell, Y., Ekblom, M.M.: Common perceived barriers and facilitators for reducing sedentary behaviour among office workers. Int. J. Environ. Res. Public Health 15(4), 792 (2018). https://doi.org/10.3390/ijerph15040792
20. Hadgraft, N.T., et al.: Reducing occupational sitting: workers' perspectives on participation in a multi-component intervention. Int. J. Behav. Nutr. Phys. Act. 14(1), 73 (2017). https://doi.org/10.1186/s12966-017-0530-y
21. Ganesan, A.N., et al.: International mobile-health intervention on physical activity, sitting, and weight: the stepathlon cardiovascular health study: the stepathlon cardiovascular health study. J. Am. Coll. Cardiol. 67(21), 2453–2463 (2016)
22. Puig-Ribera, A., et al.: Patterns of impact resulting from a 'sit less, move more' web-based program in sedentary office employees. PLoS ONE 10(4), E0122474 (2015)
23. Murrel, K.F.H.: Ergonomics: Man and His Working Environment. Chapman and Hill, London (1971)

NTSB Investigation of Weather-Related Aviation Incidents and Accidents

Sathya Silva[✉] and Paul Suffern[✉]

National Transportation Safety Board, Washington, DC 20594, USA
{sathya.silva,paul.suffern}@ntsb.gov

Abstract. This paper describes the current investigative process for weather-related events, explores the challenges facing weather investigations, and discusses potential solutions to enable better data capture for time-sensitive events to better understand the human factors associated with why these events occurred. Challenges discussed include (1) investigative data loss due to delayed notification of weather encounters and duration of flight following weather encounters if flight continued to destination, and (2) increasing lack of investigative information regarding pilot use of weather resources due to increasing availability of online sources that do not necessarily archive pilot or flight information. A review of available weather sources is presented with respect to investigative quality and availability of such information. Lastly, several mitigations are discussed for industry consideration to improve these investigative challenges.

Keywords: Safety · Human performance · Weather

Disclaimer: The views expressed in this paper are those of the authors and are not necessarily endorsed by the Safety Board or reflect the position of the Safety Board.

1 Overview of Investigative Process

After the National Transportation Safety Board (NTSB) gets notified of an air safety event (incident or accident), a multi-disciplinary decision process begins to coordinate the response. Investigative teams vary in size, but can consist of expertise in operational factors, human performance, meteorology, and multiple other areas. For weather related events in particular, once an event is reported, the investigators gather pertinent weather information (observations, forecasts, satellite and radar imagery, etc.), and conduct interviews of relevant personnel (which can include pilots, meteorologists, air traffic controllers, observers, and others). Once investigators assess the integrity of gathered weather information, analysis of the actual weather observed, available weather information, and flight path, is conducted to understand the pilot decision making likely involved. This information can directly impact findings, probable cause, and most importantly safety recommendations.

C. Stephanidis (Ed.): HCII 2019, LNCS 11786, pp. 528–537, 2019.
https://doi.org/10.1007/978-3-030-30033-3_41

One example of demonstrated safety impact of a comprehensive weather investigation was the identification that latency in in-cockpit Next Generation Radar (NEXRAD) was involved in several accidents related to encounters with weather. An NTSB safety alert was issued in 2012 warning pilots that the actual age of NEXRAD data could differ significantly from age indicated on their display [1]. This alert was the result of accident investigations where enough data were available on the weather information the pilot had accessed. One of these accidents occurred in 2010 where a helicopter impacted terrain in Tennessee after encountering thunderstorms inflight [2]. Information from the cockpit display memory indicated that it had received one NEXRAD image via XM roughly halfway through the flight. By requesting information from XM archives, investigators were able to obtain the image that was sent and timing of the message which had indicated to the pilot that it was about 1 min old. Upon comparison with NWS radar however, it was found that the weather conditions sent to the aircraft were actually about 5 min old. The image indicated that the severe weather was about 7 miles away from the heliport where the pilot was attempting to land, but the severe weather was actually just crossing over the heliport at about the time the display received the NEXRAD image. Using this information and pilot communications with ATC, the investigation was able to understand how the pilot was using his onboard radar information and how it contributed to the accident.

This example shows how valuable reliable weather data that pilots were using during an event can be when conducting a comprehensive investigation. Unfortunately, data are not always available and the lack thereof can limit the safety impact provided by investigations. Although the NTSB has been successful in identifying causes and contributing factors to many weather-related events, there can be challenges in conducting these investigations. These are further explored below.

2   Challenges in Investigating Weather Related Events

The identification of potential weather hazards that may have impacted an accident flight is straightforward in many cases using readily-available meteorological data sources or other information. However, the answer to understanding "why" the event happened is often tied to human decision making. Assessing the decision-making process is based on understanding what information the human had, and how they interpreted and used this information. Sources for these data come from crew interviews, cockpit voice recorder, images or video, potential uplink sources, and/or recordings of weather display and display settings. Perishability of human memory and limited recording capability of onboard recorders create a time pressure to capture these data. Often times, much of these data are not captured in time for investigative use (or are not available), for example in cases where the pilot perished in the accident or recorders were not installed on the aircraft. In cases like these, investigations rely on evaluating pilot behavior, which may or may not reflect the pilot's full decision making process.

2.1   Delayed Notification of Events

One challenge involves delayed notification of the event to the NTSB. In certain circumstances, this delay results in relevant human performance and operational information being no longer available for the investigation. For example, in weather related cases, notification usually occurs if the aircraft was substantially damaged or serious injury/death occurred. While substantial damage to the aircraft may be immediately noticed, awareness of the severity of injuries to persons can sometimes take time to ascertain.

According to 14 CFR Part 830, "the operator of any civil aircraft, or any public aircraft not operated by the Armed Forces or an intelligence agency of the United States, or any foreign aircraft shall immediately, and by the most expeditious means available, notify the nearest National Transportation Safety Board (NTSB) office, when an aircraft accident … occur[s]" [3] Aircraft accident means an occurrence associated with the operation of an aircraft which takes place between the time any person boards the aircraft with the intention of flight and all such persons have disembarked, and in which any person suffers death or serious injury, or in which the aircraft receives substantial damage. Serious injury means any injury which: (1) Requires hospitalization for more than 48 h, commencing within 7 days from the date of the injury was received; (2) results in a fracture of any bone (except simple fractures of fingers, toes, or nose); (3) causes severe hemorrhages, nerve, muscle, or tendon damage; (4) involves any internal organ; or (5) involves second- or third-degree burns, or any burns affecting more than 5% of the body surface.

Case Study: In 2013, a Boeing 747-400 aircraft encountered moderate turbulence over the Pacific Ocean enroute from Sydney to San Francisco during which a flight attendant was injured [4]. After the aircraft landed in San Francisco, the flight attendant was transported to a hospital where she was diagnosed with a broken wrist. This diagnosis qualified as a serious injury per definition and therefore, the event was then classified as an accident. However, the post-flight diagnosis caused a delay in classifying the encounter with turbulence as an accident therefore resulting in the CVR being overwritten and limiting the information available to investigators once the NTSB was notified.

2.2   Duration of Onboard Recording Devices

A further challenge relates to how the duration of onboard recording devices can affect the quality/quantity of data available. For example, even if an event is reported to the NTSB and power to the cockpit voice recorder was removed after landing, it's still possible that cockpit voice recorder information would not be available due to limitations in recording time. The following table lists several accidents involving encounters with enroute turbulence where CVR data was lost due to limitations in the duration of recording devices [5] (Table 1).

Table 1. Non-exhaustive list of accidents caused by encounters with enroute turbulence where CVR information was unavailable (adapted from [5])

Date	NTSB accident number	Location
03/09/2017	DCA17CA079	Dallas-Fort Worth (DFW), TX
07/29/2011	DCA11FA091	Tangshan, China
12/25/2007	SEA08LA051	Honolulu, HI
02/23/2007	CHI07LA078	Chicago, IL
09/16/2006	NYC06LA223	Hastings, NE
03/15/2006	CHI06LA099	Omaha, NE
10/22/2005	NYC06LA016	Atlantic Ocean
07/25/2004	DCA04MA061	Miami, FL
06/04/2004	CHI04LA148	Liberal, KS
04/21/2003	CHI03LA113	Lithonia, GA
04/22/2002	NYC02LA088	Atlantic Ocean

2.3   Documentation of Pilot Reference of Weather Information

Lastly, Part 121 operations are typically dispatched flights with weather information attached to a flight release, however this structured practice of reviewing weather isn't as common for general aviation flights. Pilots are taking advantage of advances in technology that have enabled the weather data industry to develop and display information in more creative and potentially more "user friendly" ways. In a survey conducted by AOPA, results reported an 13% increase of pilots using an aviation application such as ForeFlight as a primary source of weather prior to a flight in "challenging conditions" compared to a 10% decrease in use of flight service (telephone) between 2017 and 2019 [6–8]. In general aviation or Part 135 accidents however, the increase in availability of online or commercial weather sources has created investigative difficulties in determining whether a pilot referenced any weather information prior to the flight and evaluating the quality and display of this weather information in cases where archived sources of weather were not used.

From an investigative standpoint, investigators can confidently determine preflight weather reference when pilots use a telephone weather briefing, online briefing, or commercial services with user log-in. Indirectly, investigators can ascertain pilot reference to other sources of weather information in cases where pilot cell phone browser or computer history shows visits to weather websites or where witnesses observe pilots checking the weather. The following table displays different sources of weather and investigative quality of each source (Table 2).

Table 2. Investigative value of pilot weather sources

	Can with confidence determine			Investigative quality of source (if obtained)
	If source was used	What info was provided	Presentation of what was provided	
Flight Service	Yes	Yes	Yes	Good
Company – Part 121	Yes	Yes	Yes	Good
Automated recorded broadcasts	Conditionally	Yes	Yes	Good
FAA aviation weather cameras	Conditionally	Conditionally	Yes	Good
Commercial weather and FIS-B (preflight & inflight)	Conditionally	Conditionally	No	Good
Onboard weather sensing	Conditionally	Conditionally	No	Good
Internet weather website	Conditionally	No	No	Good
TV/Radio weather	Conditionally	No	No	Marginal

Flight Service. Pilots can request information regarding weather from flight service, via telephone, radio, or online. Aircraft IDs are logged when using this service and can be traced to an accident aircraft if necessary. Phone calls and radio communications are recorded and investigators can use that information to not only document what information was provided but also to understand pilot intent and understanding of the information received. For example, the following quotes were heard on the recording of the FSS line.

- In a 2013 accident in Florida, the pilot told flight service "I'm looking at the radar trying to figure out how we can 'scud-run' and get home" [9].
- In a 1992 accident in Arizona during a medical evacuation mission, the pilot stated to flight service "...I think I can meander my way through the mountains on that one" regarding weather enroute [10].

When pilots use flight service for weather briefings, the NTSB can typically, with ease, understand and have access to what information was provided and how that information was presented to the pilot.

Company. The dispatch process of part 121 carriers provides pilots with a weather package prior to each flight. These packages are retained and are made available to investigators in the case of an accident or incident. Therefore, it is typically straight-forward for investigators to determine whether information was provided, what information was provided, and what form that information came in.

Part 135 carriers vary in their processes for ensuring pilots obtain weather. While some implement formal dispatch procedures similar to a Part 121 carrier, others rely on their pilots alone to obtain weather information. In the latter cases, unless the pilot contacted flight service, witness testimony is necessary to determine what weather information the pilot had, if any. Oftentimes there are no witnesses that have information on pilot weather review, and if there are, it can be difficult to locate these witnesses. In these cases, many witnesses aren't expert observers and may not be able to recall details on what information was obtained or sites accessed making it difficult for investigators to ascertain what information the pilot had and how it was presented to them.

Case Study: In 2013, an Alaska State Troopers helicopter impacted terrain in Alaska during a search and rescue flight in deteriorating weather conditions [11]. Investigators interviewed family members who stated that after receiving the initial call for the flight the accident pilot went upstairs to his home computer and checked the weather. However, the weather information that was checked on the home computer was not able to be determined or obtained. There was no other record or knowledge of additional weather information received by the accident pilot. This precluded the investigation from determining the efficacy of any weather information the pilot received and how such information impacted his decision making. Correspondingly, without this understanding, no recommendations could be made regarding improvements to decision making using preflight weather.

Case Study: In 2012, a medical transport helicopter impacted the ground in Illinois during inclement weather fatally injuring the three people on board [12]. Interviews revealed that the pilot had WSI and Aviation Sentry Weather available to him as weather resources before the flight, but neither system logged access, so there was no record or knowledge of the weather information obtained by the pilot before the flight. Weather observation stations along the route of flight were reporting VFR conditions about the time the pilot accepted the flight, however an investigative question remained regarding whether the pilot had relied solely on observation stations or had assessed synoptic information that would have indicated risk for inclement weather. Knowing the pilot's awareness of the weather risk or whether he was aware when he accepted the flight would have led the investigation towards different findings and recommendations reflecting his decision making. However, without knowing what information the pilot had when he accepted the flight, conclusions could not be made regarding this factor, possibly precluding an opportunity to issue certain recommendations to improve the system and prevent future accidents of this type.

Automated Recorded Broadcasts (ATIS, ASOS/AWOS, HIWAS, or Similar). Automated recorded broadcasts of weather can be a valuable tool for pilots, particularly inflight. The quality of this information is also good for investigators as there is little ambiguity as to the information provided on the recording and investigators have access to the data feeding these recordings for the investigation. It can be difficult for investigators to determine whether a pilot tuned into the weather frequency and listened for the entire recording, particularly when a CVR isn't available. Investigators are dependent on ATC recordings where they exist where the pilot reported they received the ATIS. In cases where an FDR is available that recorded frequency inputs and comm settings, it is also possible to ascertain whether a recording was accessed.

In cases where the pilots obtained information via an ASOS/AWOS however, it can be difficult to ascertain which ASOS/AWOS report was obtained depending on how often the ASOS/AWOS reports are broadcast and what information is available about when the pilot listened to the recording.

FAA Aviation Weather Cameras. While more often used in areas with rapidly changing weather and less weather reporting infrastructure, such as Alaska, weather cameras are commonly used to witness actual conditions along a route of flight including ceiling, visibility, and precipitation. Determining whether a pilot used cameras during preflight is still limited to witness interviewing or URL trace. However, if statements indicate a pilot did use the weather cameras and approximately what time they accessed them, investigators have the capability of pulling archived camera images. These images, however, are only archived for two weeks, and therefore must be requested within that time period in order to be accessible to investigators. If obtained, these images can be invaluable for investigators to both document actual conditions in addition to conditions apparent during a pilot's preflight decision-making process.

Commercial Weather Products (XMWX, ForeFlight, or Similar) and Flight Information Services- Broadcast (FIS-B). Commercial weather products can be a valuable tool for pilot preflight planning as well as inflight decision making. From an investigative standpoint, investigators can only ascertain whether a pilot accessed this information inflight if they mentioned it to ATC or was logged into their account and uplink information was available. If they were logged into their account, a record of text information viewed may be available, however actual recordings of the dynamical graphics accessed by pilots are generally not available. Therefore, while it's possible to reconstruct the information likely shown on a display, it is impossible for investigators to assess any display settings or page settings inflight without video footage. Archiving graphical products requires extensive memory, however some manufacturers do archive select graphics which can ultimately provide investigators with clear documentation of certain aspects of the preflight briefing that could have been available to the pilot. But the exact settings or screen selected the pilot was using will remain unknown. While rare, this is very useful to investigators.

Flight information system-broadcast (FIS-B) is a component of the Automatic Dependent Surveillance – Broadcast (ADS-B) In service that periodically, automatically uplinks weather and airspace system information to aircraft who are equipped with an ADS-B In receiver[1] [13]. A 2015 survey of 1400 U.S. pilots indicated that pilots who had used the service considered weather information provided by FIS-B to be useful and over 70% reported frequent use of the information [14]. The study also found that over 50% of respondents who did not use ADS-B services were planning on equipping in the future. This suggests that the increased use of FIS-B in general

---

[1] FIS-B information is uplinked on 978 MHz and is available to aircraft capable of receiving ADS-B on that frequency.

aviation combined with the availability of archived uplinked data could provide more information to investigators in the event of an accident.

Onboard Weather Radar. Access to the raw data on onboard weather sensing technologies such as onboard radar is limited to cases where FDR or video is available for the investigation.[2] If FDR information is not available, usage of onboard weather radar systems can be ascertained if the pilot discusses aspects of the radar with air traffic control. In these cases however, it's difficult for investigators to determine what information was being displayed to the pilot due to variation in display range, tilt angle, and other controls. While the information can be useful to assess the pilot decision making process, cases where usable evidence on onboard weather radar data is obtained are rare.

Internet Websites (ADDS, AWC, HEMS Tool, or Similar). Internet website sources of aviation weather are commonly used by pilots. However, because these sites do not archive name or aircraft ID, it is difficult for investigators to trace any accessed website to a certain aircraft or pilot. There are occasions where cell phone records or computers provide a browsing history with weather information, or eyewitnesses were in proximity when the pilot was checking weather. The quality of the data the investigation receives in these cases, is dependent on the eyewitness. In the cases where witnesses are trained observers (other pilots, dispatchers, etc.) they can be a useful source of evidence, however again, these cases are very rare.

TV/Radio Weather. TV and radio can also be a source for weather that pilots may use. Again, the documentation of these weather checks are dependent upon witnesses. The data obtained and how it was presented from the TV or radio however can be difficult to track, even if investigators have knowledge that a pilot used TV or radio sources.[3]

3   Discussion of Solutions for Mitigating Investigative Challenges

3.1   Extended Duration Cockpit Voice Recorders

Current US regulations require a minimum of 2-h recording capability for CVRs But, if an event occurred in an earlier phase of the flight and beyond the recording duration it is possible that it would not be available for investigative use. In October of 2018, the NTSB issued a recommendation to the FAA to issue a requirement for 25 h CVRs. If adopted, this would provide an opportunity for much more robust investigation of weather-related events [5].

---

[2] In limited cases it can also be possible to retrieve investigative data from radar unit's internal, non-volatile memory.

[3] It is possible for NTSB to request archived television footage if investigators have information on which station and what time the pilot referenced the television weather footage.

3.2   Development of Guidance for Pilot Preflight Weather Reference

Increased availability of internet and commercial weather services introduced more variability into the weather content provided to the pilot and how this information is displayed. This greater variance in presentation of information combined with the trend towards increased pilot use of online self-briefings revealed a timely opportunity to develop consistent guidance on what information should be referenced when checking weather, where it can be found, and how it can be used. The increased variability in presentation can be countered by more systematic guidance, such as a FAA advisory circular or checklist, on what information should be referenced prior to flight to more easily enable a pilot's comprehensive review of weather preflight. This guidance would provide additional benefit to investigators by defining a consistent expectation of what weather information should be referenced preflight.

3.3   Industry Programs to Encourage of Pilot Weather Log-in

Considering the preference some pilots have for using aviation applications and potential benefits to timeliness and graphical representation of the information, it's important for solutions to accept the trend toward state-of-the-art technologies and work with them for mutual benefit.

Several weather source applications track what is provided to pilots who have logged into their system. However, if a pilot accesses the system without logging in, no contextual information is recorded on how pilots use the system. Consistent logged in use provides the pilot with opportunities to get relevant information pushed to them. In addition to motivating increased use and better weather understanding by the PIC, logged systems can provide more definitive insight to investigators in the case of an accident on the information the pilot accessed and how the pilot may have used it.

It is possible that industry incentives for pilots to log in to these systems when they check weather could incentivize pilots to provide this information. This could come in the form of FAA programs such as WINGS or potentially insurance incentives for consistent reference to weather briefings. Ultimately, tracking of this information would benefit accident cases by providing an additional path to improve these systems if necessary. Given the increased use of aviation applications over more traditional Flight Service tools this can serve as an important source of information for investigators to verify the quality and display of such information provided.

References

1. National Transportation Safety Board: Safety Alert – In-Cockpit NEXRAD Mosaic Imagery, Washington, DC. Safety Alert Website (2012). https://www.ntsb.gov/safety/safety-alerts/Documents/SA_017.pdf. Accessed 1 June 2018
2. National Transportation Safety Board: Accident Brief ERA10MA188, Washington, DC. Accident Brief Website (2012). https://www.ntsb.gov/about/employment/_layouts/ntsb.aviation/brief.aspx?ev_id=20100325X93604&key=1. Accessed 1 June 2018
3. Immediate Notification, 49 CFR § 830.5 (2015)

4. National Transportation Safety Board: Accident Brief WPR13LA131, Washington, DC. Accident Brief Website (2015). https://www.ntsb.gov/_layouts/ntsb.aviation/brief.aspx?ev_id=20130220X51849. Accessed 1 June 2018
5. National Transportation Safety Board: Safety Recommendation Report – Extended Duration Cockpit Voice Recorders, Washington, DC. Recommendation Letter Website (2018). https://www.ntsb.gov/investigations/AccidentReports/Reports/ASR1804.pdf. Accessed 1 June 2018
6. Aircraft Owners and Pilots Association: 2017 Weather Study. Study Website (2017). https://download.aopa.org/advocacy/2017WxSurvey.pdf. Accessed 1 June 2018
7. Aircraft Owners and Pilots Association: 2018 Weather Study. Study Website (2018). https://download.aopa.org/advocacy/2018/0803-AOPA_2018_Weather_Survey_Report.pdf. Accessed 1 June 2018
8. Aircraft Owners and Pilots Association: 2019 Weather Study (2019)
9. National Transportation Safety Board: Accident Brief ERA13FA133, Washington, DC. Accident Brief Website (2013). https://www.ntsb.gov/_layouts/ntsb.aviation/brief.aspx?ev_id=20130215X10538&key=1. Accessed 1 June 2018
10. National Transportation Safety Board: Accident Brief LAX92FA136, Washington, DC. Accident Brief Website (1993). https://www.ntsb.gov/_layouts/ntsb.aviation/brief.aspx?ev_id=20001211X14306. Accessed 1 June 2018
11. National Transportation Safety Board: Accident Brief ANC13GA036, Washington, DC. Accident Brief Website (2015). https://www.ntsb.gov/about/employment/_layouts/ntsb.aviation/brief.aspx?ev_id=20130331X41252&key=1. Accessed 1 June 2018
12. National Transportation Safety Board: Accident Brief CEN13FA096, Washington, DC. Accident Brief Website (2014). https://www.ntsb.gov/_layouts/ntsb.aviation/brief.aspx?ev_id=20121210X32953&key=11. Accessed 1 June 2018
13. Federal Aviation Administration: ADS-B In Pilot Applications (2018). https://www.faa.gov/nextgen/programs/adsb/pilot/#fisb. Accessed 1 June 2018
14. Silva, S., Jensen, L., Hansman, R.: Safety benefit of automatic dependent surveillance-broadcast traffic and weather uplink services. J. Aerosp. Inf. Syst. **12**(8), 579–586 (2015)

HCI, Innovation and Society

III.1 Innovation and Society

Evaluating Citizen Scientists' User Experience and Engagement Using a Mobile Watershed Data Management App

Ann Fruhling[1]([✉]) [iD], Shannon L. Bartelt-Hunt[2] [iD],
and Alan Kolok[3] [iD]

[1] University of Nebraska at Omaha, Omaha, NE 68182, USA
afruhling@unomaha.edu
[2] University of Nebraska-Lincoln, Lincoln, NE 68588, USA
[3] University of Idaho, Moscow, ID 83844, USA

Abstract. Environmental problems, such as climate change are global in scope and multivariate in complexity. Today, citizen scientists can make important contributions by providing observations to further understand environmental related issues and by playing an important role in data collection. Citizen scientists now have the ability to use EPA certified testing tools that increase their ability to collect accurate and precise environmental data. Smart phones allow citizens to efficiently submit timely data. Given that citizen scientists now have the capacity to be involved in scientifically meaningful data acquisition campaigns, it is important to evaluate the citizen scientists' experience and engagement using technology to fully maximize their potential contribution.

For this study we developed an interactive mobile app, called mWatershed, which enabled citizen scientists to be involved in all aspects of the campaign: environmental monitoring, information gathering, data collection and analysis, and reporting. Specifically, the citizen scientists were given EPA tools to test their drinking water or neighboring surface waters for: toxic metals, certain pesticides, nutrients and certain bacteria. Citizen scientists had the option to use the mWatershed app. At the end of the campaign they were invited to take a survey assessing their experience and engagement.

The survey utilized the MUX instrument, which provides a holistic assessment of mobile software-device use. In addition, we included tailored engagement questions. We report on the results from our study and discuss implications for future citizen scientists' efforts. We also examine the MUX instrument in the context of this research.

Keywords: User engagement · User experience · MUX · Citizen science

1 Introduction

Many environmental challenges, such as climate change, are global in scope and multivariate in complexity. It has been suggested that a citizen observatory, that is a group of citizen scientists who can provide observations and understanding of environmentally related issues, may play an important role in data collection relative to

© Springer Nature Switzerland AG 2019
C. Stephanidis (Ed.): HCII 2019, LNCS 11786, pp. 541–554, 2019.
https://doi.org/10.1007/978-3-030-30033-3_42

large-scale environmental problems. Citizen science, or crowd-sourced data collection is the act of utilizing members of the general public to collect scientific data. In many different fields, the use of citizen scientists has enabled the collection of large amounts of data that would have otherwise been uncollectible. Projects involving citizen scientist are growing exponentially in recent years due to technological advancements [1].

Relative to water quality, advancements in analytic chemistry have put EPA certified testing tools into the hands of citizen scientists, thereby increasing their ability to collect accurate and precise data [2]. Furthermore, the advent of smart phones has created an opportunity for citizens to rapidly and efficiently share the data they collect using an interactive mobile watershed data management app (mWatershed app) on their phone. The mWatershed app allows citizen scientists to upload their data onto maps that are readily available for consumption. The mWatershed app permitted citizen scientists to be involved in all aspects of data collection, including environmental monitoring, information gathering, data management and analysis, as well as data assessment and reporting. While this capacity dramatically increases the breadth and depth of the scientific community to acquire first tier data, such as large data sets collected using relative unsophisticated tools, it also generates a number of compelling questions at the interface between the technological advancements and the engagement of citizen scientists. To further maximize citizen scientists' impact this research evaluated the citizen scientists experience and engagement using the mWatershed app.

2 Background

Modern environmental issues, such as global climate change and the pollution of freshwater resources share a number of similar characteristics. These include: adverse impacts that occur over vast geographies, and contamination from multiple, non-point source inputs. For example, the nutrient (phosphorus and nitrogen) contamination of the Mississippi River is due to the runoff of fertilizers that have been applied to fields scattered across much of the Midwestern United States. A watershed refers to a geographic area where water is ultimately channeled to a single outlet (e.g. lake, stream, or river). When precipitation occurs, the water that does not infiltrate into the soil flows over the land surface and can carry chemicals into surface water bodies. The diffuse nature of the chemical inputs, as well as the continental geography of impact create a context in which systematic data collection, monitoring and remediation is extremely challenging.

2.1 Citizen Scientists

The term "citizen science" can be applied to a wide variety of projects that share the core feature of nonscientists engaging in doing science. Citizen science projects have several characteristics. These characters are: (1) actively engage participants (2) specifically engage participants with data, (3) use systematic approaches to produce reliable knowledge, (4) meet widely recognized standards of scientific integrity, (5) use practices common in science, (6) engage participants who are (primarily) not project-relevant scientists, (7) seek to use the knowledge gained to contribute to science and/or community priorities, (8) generally provide some benefit to the participant for participating, and (9) involve the communication of results [1].

The enlistment of citizen scientists in data acquisition is not new. The Christmas bird count for example, has been using citizen scientists to collect data on the range of North American wild bird populations for the last 117 years. These data have proven to be quite useful, and have provided information leading to a large number of scientific publications [3].

Fortunately, two recent technological innovations have enabled citizen scientists to increase their participation in data collection: the development of smart phone technologies for data acquisition and retrieval, and the development of novel environmental testing tools that can be used by the citizen scientists. Currently, citizen scientists have the tools available to test their drinking water or neighboring surface waters for: toxic metals (lead, copper), certain pesticides (atrazine, organophosphate insecticides), nutrients (phosphates, nitrogen) and certain bacteria (coliforms). Given that citizen scientists now have the capacity to be involved in scientifically meaningful data acquisition campaigns regarding water quality, the next series of questions in the field will focus on whether the citizen scientists can collect data that are scientifically robust, and whether the citizen scientist networks that are developed can be sustained over time periods that are long enough to identify long term changes in environmental quality.

2.2 Water Quality Campaigns

The Nebraska Watershed Network (NWN) is a student-driven organization, founded in 2012, that strives to promote water quality awareness through outreach, education, and research. The NWN is concerned with monitoring water sources to track chemical contaminations and concentrations over time. With their findings, the NWN hopes to build restoration assessment programs to clean up the watersheds in the Midwestern area [4].

The main focus of the NWN's citizen scientist testing campaign is for the chemical atrazine. Atrazine is a common herbicide prevalent in agriculture runoff and has been shown to have detrimental effects on wildlife in concentrations as low as only a few parts per billion [5]. Atrazine is often used by farmers in the Midwest. It is one of the most common pesticide found in surface water. Other chemicals the Nebraska Watershed Network tests for are nitrite, nitrate, and phosphate.

When the Nebraska Watershed Network first started recording the information gathered by citizen scientists, the information was collected by postcards. The citizen scientist would first conduct the tests at the specified location, then fill out the postcard and send in the information through the postal service. This process was slow and made it difficult to analyze data quickly.

Citizen scientists were provided with a water sampling kit to measure the water temperature and dissolved oxygen. These samples were then used to evaluate quantitatively the nitrite, nitrate, phosphate, turbidity and pH levels and then qualitatively investigate whether atrazine is detected or not and if discovered, at what amount.

Recently, a statewide citizen scientist network called NEST was created within Nebraska as a result from funding from the National Science Foundation (CBET-1644595.) NEST citizen scientists' goals are to collect accurate and precise data regarding the state's environmental quality. For NEST to function effectively, it required a series of tasks (e.g. data collection, data management, data interpretation and dissemination of results) to collect robust data regarding environmental issues.

2.3   mWatershed App

The aim of the mWatershed app was to support NEST tasks for NWN citizen scientist watershed testing campaigns. Further, the mWatershed app was designed to enhance the citizen scientist experience, streamline the data collection processes, and increase overall participant engagement. Past studies report increased participation when there were capabilities for citizen scientists to more easily report results, establish dialogue, and exchange data [6].

The software requirements for the mWatershed app included enabling citizen scientists to record their observations conveniently, accurately and in a timely manner. The mWatershed app encompassed a database and web application that allowed citizen scientists to easily use a smartphone or other connected device to add water test results to projects in real time while still in the field. For each data point entered, the citizen scientist needed to be able to enter the latitude and longitude, comments about the test, as well as the result, and have the option to upload a relevant photo. Citizen scientists could immediately view their newly entered data points on a dynamic map and compare them to other citizen scientists' data points for the same campaign.

The mWatershed app used responsive design techniques. Special attention was given to the graphical interface design in order to make it easy to learn, easy to navigate and appealing to the eye. The UI colors and styles aligned with the Nebraska Watershed Network's branding. Every webpage was clearly labeled so that citizen scientists knew where in the application they were and which campaign they were entering data points. Clickable buttons and page redirects were carefully considered so that the user experience was pleasant and site navigation was effortless. Filtering options were added to appropriate pages to assist the user in customizing the pages to their specific requests.

A major feature of the app was the ability to display all data points for a particular campaign on a dynamic map. The map display included scrolling, zooming in or out, and clickable data points for additional detail (e.g. date, GPS coordinates, test results data, and image).

The map display uses tabs to differentiate attributes for each water test type and then display each test type data on separate pages. The map markers for the data points are color coded based on the legend and are filterable both by the items in the legend and by which week of the project the data point was added. For example, on a project that tested for atrazine, nitrate, nitrite, and phosphate, a citizen scientist could use the filtering to display only data points entered in the second week of the project that have a test result indicating high levels of phosphate, or all data points not entered during the last week of the project that have a test result indicating low or medium levels of nitrate. An example of the map display is shown in Fig. 1.

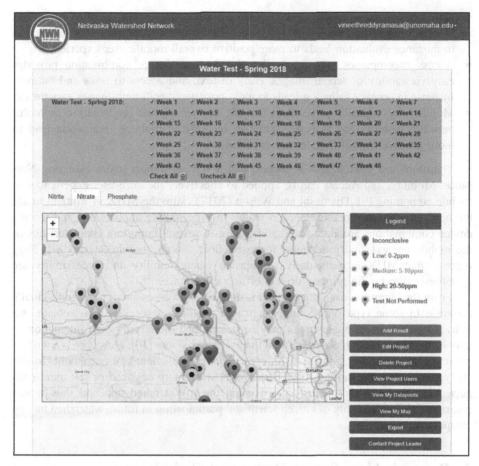

Fig. 1. Example map display

2.4   User Experience and User Engagement

In this study we were particularly interested in the impact the interactive mWatershed app had on the users' experience and engagement. This is especially important for sustainability of future watershed testing campaigns utilizing citizen scientists. User experience (UX) researchers emphasize that UX research needs to focus on representing a holistic vision for interaction between humans and technology [7].

The MUX survey is a new instrument introduced by Djamasbi and Wilson (2017) that supports assessing applications from a holistic perspective in the context of mobile computing which includes mobile devices and the software application. MUX consists of three scales: Nuisance, Access and Mobility [9]. Djamasbi and Wilson (2017) define the scales as follows:

- Nuisance encompasses perceptions that the device/software combination slows use, is inconvenient, and evokes feelings of isolation and disconnectedness. Reduction in nuisance evaluation leads to more positive overall mobile user experience.
- Access encompasses perceptions that the device/software combination provides easy viewability of screen images, entry of text, and access to links and buttons. Increase in access evaluation leads to more positive overall mobile user experience.
- Mobility encompasses perceptions that the device/software combination promotes personal mobility and is easily portable. Increase in mobility evaluation lead to more positive overall mobile user experience.

Djamasbi and Wilson (2017) suggest that MUX self-report scales assessing Nuisance, Mobility, and Access can be applied to effectively measure user experiences in mobile computing [9]. Djamasbi and Wilson (2017) claim the MUX instrument meets the need as a holistic measurement in which specific mobile applications and mobile device combinations are assessed, it is sensitive to several important characteristics of the mobile context, and it accounts for distinctions among mobile devices [9]. They propose that MUX is particularly appropriate when mobility and accessibility are hypothesized to be the primary drivers of user experience.

From the literature, user engagement is defined as an assessment of an individual's response to some type of offering, such as a product, a service or a website. An individual's degree of engagement may be determined directly through interaction or may be assessed through observation of the user's behaviors [10]. However, we wish to point out that user engagement is different than citizen scientist engagement. In our study we wanted to examine if the participants were more engaged or felt more connected to other citizen scientists when using the mWatershed app and thus would contribute to sustainability of citizen scientists' participation in future watershed testing campaigns.

3   Research Aims, Survey Design and Study Design

3.1   Research Aims

Our research study had two aims. The first aim was to assess the mWatershed app and its impact on the users' (citizen scientist) experience and user engagement during the watershed testing campaign. The second aim was to employ the MUX instrument scales Nuisance and Access to assess the users' experience and examine its applicability.

3.2   Survey Design

The assessment survey for the mWatershed app consisted of 14 questions on user experience and engagement and two questions on technical aspects. Some of the questions were adopted from the MUX instrument. User engagement questions were determined by the expertise of the researchers. In our study we focused on the MUX Nuisance and Access scales to assess the users' experience. For our study we included six questions that aligned with the MUX questions as shown in Table 1. We did not ask questions related to Mobility because we could not compare devices, nor would we know the kind of device the participant would use and if s/he would consistently use the same type of device throughout the campaign. We also included two questions that evaluated technical issues and concerns identified from our previous pilot study. We wanted to make sure they had been resolved. Table 2 presents the complete set of questions.

Table 1. Survey questions

MUX	mWatershed App MUX Related Questions
I feel using [device] to access [software] would slow me down. Inverse	Using the mWatershed app helped me work efficiently
I feel using [device] to access [software] would slow me down	Using the mWatershed app slowed me down
Quasi – I had no problem entering text when using a [device] to access [software]	Using the mWatershed app made it convenient to enter data
Using a [device] to [access] software made me feel disconnected. (Reverse)	Using the mWatershed app gave me the feeling that I was a part of a larger community
A [device] provided a good view of information when accessing [software]	When using the mWatershed app, I had difficulty clicking on links or buttons
Clicking on links or buttons was easy to accomplish using a [device] to access [software]	Navigating between screens using the mWatershed app was easy

3.3 Study Design

Citizen scientists received in-depth training from the Nebraska Watershed Network team via instruction packets and electronic resources. Citizen scientists were provided with the appropriate, tested quantitative tools to conduct water quality tests across large spatial and temporal scales. They could contact the environmental scientists by email or phone if needed during the campaign. The mWatershed app assessment survey was administered at the end of the watershed testing campaign. The survey was conducted according to IRB guidelines.

4 Results

4.1 Demographics

The watershed testing campaign for this study was conducted in Illinois. Ninety citizen scientists participated in the Illinois campaign. The Illinois citizen science campaign accumulated 2,105 data points across 35 watersheds each week for five weeks for atrazine, nitrates, and phosphates. Citizen scientists included college students and environmental enthusiasts.

Table 2. Subjects' number of citizen science campaigns participated

Answer	Percentage	Number
None	29.82%	17
1–5	57.89%	33
5–10	7.02%	4
More than 10	5.26%	3
Total	100%	57

Out of the 90 participants in the water quality testing campaign, 60 (67%) participants answered the UX survey. Although, not every questions were answered by all 60 respondents. As shown in Table 2, 70% of the respondents have participated in a citizen scientist water quality testing campaign in the past and almost 30% or 17 of the respondents were new recruits. Figure 2 shows the respondents had a wide age range, e.g. 20 years old to over 70 years old. More women (55%) than men (44%) participated in the survey and most respondents (77%) had some college education as shown in Table 3.

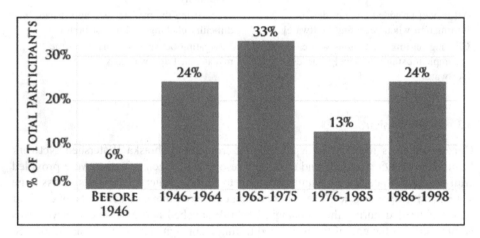

Fig. 2. Subjects' year of birth

4.2 Survey Statistical Analysis

Statistical analysis was conducted on the survey data to determine the scales for the survey. Using the Kaiser Meyer Okin measure our results indicate the overall Measure of Sampling Adequacy is .91 and is acceptable. Next, the Principal Component Analysis was performed on survey data to extract factors followed by the Varimax Orthogonal rotation. The number of scales extracted were based on Kaiser's criterion and have considered factors with an eigenvalue greater than 1. Four factors (scales) emerged from the EFA. They are presented in Table 4. In addition to Nuisance and

Table 3. Subjects' highest level of education

Answer	Percentage	Number
High School Graduate	1.75%	1
Some College	26.32%	15
College Graduate	57.9%	33
Masters	7.02%	4
PhD	5.26%	3
Other	1.75%	1
Total	100%	57

Access, two other scales emerged. We labeled them as Engagement and Technical. One question was dropped from the analysis due to low responses.

Table 4. EFA scales

Question	Scale
Using the MWatershed app helped me work efficiently	Nuisance
Using the MWatershed app slowed me down	Nuisance
The MWatershed app was fully functional with the computer technology I used	Access
It was easy to view the mapped data using the MWatershed app	Access
When using the MWatershed app, I had difficulty clicking on links or buttons	Access
Entering data is difficult when using the NEWatershed Data Management System	Access
Navigating between screens using the MWatershed app was easy	Access
Using the MWatershed app made it convenient to enter data	Engagement
In addition to uploading my data to the NEWatershed website, I used the MWatershed app to follow the project's progress	Engagement
Using the MWatershed app gave me the feeling that I was a part of a larger community	Engagement
Using the MWatershed app increased my interest in participating in this citizen science campaign	Engagement
Instantly viewing my data on a map using the MWatershed app increased my motivation to complete this citizen science campaign	Engagement
Interacting with the NEWatershed Data Management System increased my desire to participate in this citizen science campaign	Engagement
Using the MWatershed app increased my interest to participate in a future citizen science campaign	Engagement
At the start of the project, I had trouble (logging on, uploading data, changing my password) with the MWatershed app	Technical
I did not experience issues when uploading images onto the MWatershed app	Technical

Two questions factored with Nuisance in our study. One of the questions was different than used previously in MUX; however, it aligns closely to the inverse of the question "Using [device] to access [software] would slow me down. The environmental scientist partners on this project were interested in efficiency. Therefore, we asked a question related to efficiency. The question on convenience factored with Engagement rather than Nuisance as reported by Wilson and Djamasbi [8]. This may be because we asked the question from a positive angle rather than negative (inconvenient) and Nuisance is a negative scale. The four MUX questions on Access we included in our survey factored with Access. An additional question asking if the app was fully functional with the computer technology used also factored with Access. All of the questions asked that were proposed for Engagement factored together. The two technical questions factored together.

4.3   User Experience

With regards to the Nuisance scale, approximately, 80% of the respondents reported that using the mWatershed app did not slow them down in their participation. Correspondingly, 89% of the respondents agreed or strongly agreed that the app helped them work efficiently.

Most respondents (85%) agreed or strongly agreed that the app was fully functional with the technology they used. 95% reported the app made it easy to view the mapped data. Only 7% of the respondents had some difficulty clicking on links or buttons. Likewise, only two respondents (3.3%) had difficulty entering data. The majority (93%) of the respondents answered it was not difficult to enter data. 100% of the respondents were positive or neutral when assessing the ease of navigation between screens.

4.4   User Engagement

Regarding assessing the impact the app had on respondents' engagement in the campaign, five respondents reported they did not use the app to follow the campaign's progress. However, 78% of the participants agreed or strongly agreed they used the app to follow the campaign's progress. In addition, 91% of the participants reported that the app gave them the feeling that they were part of a larger community. 95% of the respondents agreed (40%) or strongly agreed (55%) that using the mWatershed app made it convenient to enter data. 80% of the respondents stated using the app increased their interest in participating in the water quality testing campaign. This is further supported by the 86% positive responses to the survey question "instantly viewing my data on a map using the app increased my motivation to complete the water quality campaign."

The campaign lasted over a 5-week period, so there was potential for citizen scientists to drop out. The data showed that on average 66% citizen scientists participated each week during the campaign. Some citizen scientists did not get started until week 2. Further, 83% responded positively that interacting with the app increased their desire to participate in the water quality campaign. And, 88% agreed that using the app increased their interest to participate in a future water quality campaign. A summary to the responses to the mWatershed survey are presented in Table 5.

Table 5. Summary of mWatershed App assessment survey responses

Question	Total	Strongly Agree	Agree	Neutral	Disagree	Strongly Disagree
Using the MWatershed app helped me work efficiently	59	53%	36%	10%	2%	0%
Using the MWatershed app slowed me down	59	0%	0%	20%	46%	34%
Using the MWatershed app made it convenient to enter data	58	55%	40%	5%	0%	0%
Using the MWatershed app gave me the feeling that I was a part of a larger community	60	48%	42%	7%	2%	2%
Using the MWatershed app increased my interest in participating in this citizen science campaign	59	47%	32%	14%	5%	2%
Instantly viewing my data on a map using the MWatershed app increased my motivation to complete this citizen science campaign	59	39%	47%	14%	0%	0%
Interacting with the NEWatershed Data Management System increased my desire to participate in this citizen science campaign	59	39%	44%	14%	3%	0%
Using the MWatershed app increased my interest to participate in a future citizen science campaign	59	47%	41%	8%	3%	0%
I did not experience issues when uploading images onto the MWatershed app	47	26%	4%	45%	19%	6%
The MWatershed app was fully functional	59	53%	34%	7%	5%	2%

(*continued*)

Table 5. (*continued*)

Question	Total	Strongly Agree	Agree	Neutral	Disagree	Strongly Disagree
with the computer technology I used						
It was easy to view the mapped data using the MWatershed app	59	42%	41%	12%	3%	2%
When using the MWatershed app, I had difficulty clicking on links or buttons	59	0%	7%	3%	44%	46%
Entering data is difficult when using the NEWatershed Data Management System	59	0%	3%	3%	41%	53%
Navigating between screens using the MWatershed app was easy	58	41%	53%	5%	0%	0%
At the start of the project, I had trouble (logging on, uploading data, changing my password) with the MWatershed app	60	7%	27%	3%	23%	40%

4.5   Qualitative Data

At the end of the survey, respondents were given the opportunity to provide additional comments. Five respondents wrote very appreciative remarks to be a part of the citizen scientist watershed testing campaign. Some of the remarks were: "Thank you for opportunity to college river data.", "Thoroughly enjoyed being part of this project.", "Great program and my students really learned from it." Other remarks further supported their feeling of being part of a community and user engagement. Three respondents wrote "I really enjoyed being a part of this!" and asked to be notified of other citizen scientist projects slated for the future. There were some suggestions on requesting improvement on the mWatershed app in the areas of map resolution and additional data entry options for latitude and longitude.

5   Discussion

At this time, the MUX instrument has not been utilized enough to have established "benchmarks" as to what values constitute low Nuisance, high Access and high Mobility [8]. However, the responses from the survey assessing the mWatershed app suggest the app minimizes Nuisance issues. Both the quantitative and qualitative results from this study advocate that the mWatershed app enhanced the citizen scientists' user experience and increased their level of engagement. On average, every participant submitted 23 data points and participated four out of the five weeks. The open ended comments were enthusiastic and the majority of the responses to all survey questions were positive.

The MUX instrument helped assess the user experience from the Nuisance and Access standpoint. A limitation of the study is that we could not control for the type of device the citizen scientist used; therefore, we did not compare devices because each citizen scientist had their own device. Thus, we could not fully implement the MUX instrument. Further studies need to be conducted to examine if it would be useful for the MUX instrument to add an additional scale for Engagement.

This study is an important example where an interactive citizen scientist app showed positive impact on the users' experience and engagement while participating in a watershed testing campaign. Our study can be used as a model for other citizen scientist projects to assess the impact of using mobile technology to interact with the user community.

6   Conclusion

The citizen scientists' experience using the mWatershed app was found to be positive. Further, for many of the citizen scientists using the mWatershed app also indicated it increased their engagement in the watershed testing campaign.

We anticipate the mWatershed app will continue to positively impact citizen scientists' interest, commitment, and participation levels in current and future water quality testing campaigns. Future studies could build on assessing our engagement questions and also explore what other factors may contribute to citizen scientists' engagement. We believe providing interactive technology will help increase citizen scientists' engagement and will in turn maximize citizen scientists' contribution overall.

Acknowledgements. This project was supported by the National Science Foundation (CBET-1644595). Krystal Herrmann played a critical role in this project by facilitating recruitment of citizen scientists, scheduling of workshops and logistical support. The authors would like to thank all the citizen scientists who participated in this research.

References

1. National Academies of Sciences Engineering, and Medicine: Learning Through Citizen Science: Enhancing Opportunities by Design. National Academies Press, Washington (2018)
2. Ali, J., Noble, B., Nandi, I., Kolok, A., Bartelt-Hunt, S.L.: Assessing the accuracy of citizen scientist reported measurements for agrichemical contaminants. Environ. Sci. Technol. **53** (10), 5633–5640 (2019)
3. Link, W.A., Sauer, J.R.: Seasonal components of avian population change: joint analysis of two large-scale monitoring programs. Ecology **88**(1), 49–55 (2007)

4. Aquatic Toxicology Laboratory. https://www.unomaha.edu/college-of-arts-and-sciences/aquatic-toxicology-lab/index.php. Accessed 01 June 2019
5. Pesticide Action Network. https://www.panna.org/resources/atrazine. Accessed 01 June 2019
6. Liu, H.Y., Kobernus, M., Broday, D., Bartonova, A.: A conceptual approach to a citizens' observatory–supporting community-based environmental governance. Environ. Health **13** (1), 107 (2014)
7. Hassenzahl, M.: The thing and i: understanding the relationship between user and product. In: Blythe, M.A., Overbeeke, K., Monk, A.F., Wright, P.C. (eds.) Funology, vol. 3, pp. 31–42. Springer, Dordrecht (2003). https://doi.org/10.1007/1-4020-2967-5_4
8. Wilson, E.V., Djamasbi, S.: Measuring mobile user experience instruments for research and practice. Commun. Assoc. Inf. Syst. **44**(1), 8 (2019)
9. Djamasbi, S., Wilson, V.: MUX: development of a holistic mobile user experience instrument. In: Proceedings of the 50th Hawaii International Conference on System Sciences (2017)
10. WhatIs.com. https://whatis.techtarget.com/definition/user-engagement. Accessed 01 June 2019

UX Analysis of the North Korean Information Technology

Xianglian Han[1], Sung Woo Kim[1(✉)], and Chunghak Oh[2]

[1] Kookmin University, Seoul 02707, Republic of Korea (South Korea)
hyangryeonhan@gmail.com, caerang@gmail.com
[2] Sogang University, Seoul 04017, Republic of Korea (South Korea)
ohchunghak@gmail.com

Abstract. In this paper we introduce our latest findings and insights we have acquired from our UX analysis on various North Korean IT products. The objective of this research is to understand the current status and the characteristics of the North Korean UX. Little is known about UX in North Korea. Based on the fact that UX has progressed in parallel with the advancement of information technology, we have obtained a number of North Korean IT products and services to grasp their UX. The products we used in our research include a smartphone, a tablet, a computer operating system and a website all made in North Korea. This paper describes the 1st phase of our research journey on North Korean UX through analysis on these products of 'made in North Korea.'

Keywords: North Korea · Information technology · UX · Design for unity

1 Introduction

1.1 Research Background

Little is known about UX in North Korea. UX has now become a core area of design in parallel with the advancement in information technology. For example, in South Korea a number of universities offer graduate degree programs and produce high-educated specialists every year. North Korea, on the other hand, has little information on how they nurture UX experts, what process they take to create UX, etc.

Considering the trend that UX has traditionally developed along with the information technology industry, there's possibility to look into the North Korean UX indirectly through its IT industry. The level of North Korea's software technology is known to be quite high [1]. On the other hand, the hardware sector is weak because it requires enormous investment in infrastructure. In the daily lives of North Koreans living in major cities like Pyongyang, information technology is somewhat prevalent [2]. In the case of mobile communication [3], North Korea started its 3G service in 2008, and about 4 million people are known to be using smartphones as of 2018. 'Arirang' and 'Pyongyang' are the popular smartphones [4].

Although the Internet access for North Koreans is extremely limited, the North Korean government has set up an internal network called 'Gwangmyeong Network', which provides somewhat similar Internet experience to its people. For example, the Gwangmyeong Network has a portal site called 'Gwangmyeong.' Many government

© Springer Nature Switzerland AG 2019
C. Stephanidis (Ed.): HCII 2019, LNCS 11786, pp. 555–568, 2019.
https://doi.org/10.1007/978-3-030-30033-3_43

and public organizations have set up their websites in this network. In 2015, North Korea's 'People's Services Administration' unit opened an online shopping mall named 'Okyu,' followed by 'Manmulsang' and 'Eunpasan'. In 2018 'Pyongyang No.1 Department Store' has opened its first online shopping mall in Gwangmyeong Network.

Globally, North Korea operates websites for foreigners. Many of them are in fact political propaganda websites. But we can also find a number of websites for practical use. A good example is the Air Koryo - the state-owned national flag carrier airline of North Korea - website for foreigners to fly to North Korea. Popular software applications for personal computers developed in North Korea include a word processor called 'Changdeok' and Korean IME for Microsoft Windows called 'Dangun.' In fact, the latest version of Changdeok is expanded to an office suite including spreadsheet and presentation tools. In addition, a variety of games and e-book apps are available on smartphones and tablets used by North Korean residents. North Korea produces Android-based tablets such as 'Ryongheung' and 'Myohyang.' Also, North Korea has developed an operating system called "The Red Star," a modified version of Linux, and has announced it as a national standard operating system [5].

A brief look into the current status of the North Korea's IT industry as described above tells us that North Korea indeed designs UX on their products. Various computer software, apps and web sites developed are equipped with UX made in North Korea. By analyzing North Korea's IT products, we will be able to grasp the current status and characteristics of North Korean UX.

1.2   Research Objectives

The objective of this research is to identify the current status and the characteristics of North Korean UX through analysis of UX in IT products made by North Korea. We are particularly interested in investigating the similarities and differences of UX between South and North Korea that share the same Korean language system. We aim to achieve this goal through comparative analysis of similar products from the two nations.

2   UX Analysis Process and Methods

2.1   Research Steps

This study was conducted through the following procedure. First, we defined 4 representative IT product groups, and for each group we chose products of South and North Korea. Second, for each product we listed ten to twenty five elements and ten use scenarios, conducted in-house comparative UX analysis on each element and scenario. Third, we conducted a user research with 8 South Korean participants on North Korean products. Fourth, we hosted a workshop with 15 to 25 attendees in an UX related academic conference. Finally, we consolidated all the collected, summarized them, and drew key insights on the current status and the characteristics of the North Korean UX.

2.2   Selection of the Products

We selected the four representative IT product groups. They are smartphone, tablet, computer operating system and website. For each product group we obtained North Korean products first, and then looked for matching South Korean products.

Selected North Korean products are as follows: 'Pyongyang 2423' is the North Korea's latest Android based smartphone released in the October of 2018 (Fig. 1). 'Ryonghung' is one of the most popular tablets used in North Korea. It's a 7 inch Android based tablet with 8 GB memory and 30 mega-pixel built-in camera (Fig. 2). The Red Star is the national standard computer operating system in North Korea (Fig. 3). The one we used in our study is version 3.0 released in 2014. North Korea runs political propaganda websites such as 'Uriminzokkiri (Among Korean People)' and 'Today in North Korea.' Access to these political websites are restricted in South Korea. In this study, we chose Air Koryo's website (Fig. 4) as we wanted a website with little political propaganda and instead focuses on practical purpose.

Fig. 1. Pyongyang 2423

Fig. 2. Ryonghung

Fig. 3. The Red Star 3.0

Fig. 4. Air Koryo's Website (www.airkoryo.com.kp)

South Korean products have been selected in consideration of technical specification and use context of North Korean products (Table 1). Also, we chose products made in South Korea except for Microsoft Windows 10 Korean version. South Korea does not have a national standard OS made in South Korea.

Table 1. Selected products from both Koreas

Product Group	North Korea	South Korea
Smartphone	Pyongyang 2423	Samsung Galaxy J3 2017
Tablet	Ryonghung	LG G Pad II
Operating System	The Red Star ver 3.0	Korean MS Windows 10
Website	Air Koryo	Korean Airline

2.3 Selection of Elements and Use Scenarios

For each product group, 10 to 25 elements were selected for UX analysis. Elements include product features such as functions, UI components, etc. For each product group, 10 use scenarios were created. Table 2 shows the selected elements. Below are the lists of 10 use-scenarios for each product group.

Smartphone

1. Enter and save the following contact in the address book (Name: Hong Kildong/Cell phone number: 010-9876-2345/Address: 101, Birthday: 2019.2.13/Record: University student)
2. Take a picture and view the picture just taken
3. Open the web browser and connect to Naver (a South Korean portal)
4. Make a call to Hong Gil Dong in the address book
5. Change the date to January 1st, 2019
6. Turn on your phone's flashlight
7. Enter and save the following schedule (Classification: Conference/Time 2019.2.13 12: 00-15: 00/Repetition: Weekly/Notification: 30 min before)
8. Choose "Hong Kildong" from the address book and send the following text to him; make sure to add smiley emoticon from your mobile phone emoticon list at the end: "Are you coming? (smiley emoticon)"
9. Change the background image of the phone's lock screen and top-menu screen by choosing an image from the built-in image list in the phone.
10. Launch an app corresponding to Korean dictionary and browse 'Daehanminguk (South Korea in Korean language)' in that dictionary app

Tablet

1. Move the file tool window to another position
2. Adjust the volume
3. Switch between the front and rear camera
4. Change the wallpaper
5. Record your voice, save it and play it back
6. Make a quick note and add a gallery photo into it
7. Calculate a mathematical expression using a calculator
8. Take a photo, and immediately jump right into the gallery to crop it (edit photo)
9. Adjust the screen brightness directly from the current screen without entering the setting menu
10. Change the date and time

OS

1. Change wallpaper
2. Capture current screen to make a screenshot
3. Change the date and time
4. Write and post a sticky note on a screen
5. Recover it back after deleting a file
6. Create a simple document; use copy, cut and paste function

7. Add a new event to a calendar
8. Write an email
9. Calculate a mathematical expression using a calculator
10. Create a simple presentation document (1 slide)

Website

1. Sign up
2. Change your password from My Page
3. View the following international flight schedules: Beijing - Pyongyang/New York - Seoul
4. Book a round-trip ticket: Beijing - Pyongyang/New York-Seoul
5. Check my reservation
6. Make a payment (reach to the last step of the transaction page)
7. Change your reservation: To the closest date after the scheduled date
8. Add passengers
9. Checking for information on: in-flight baggage/in-flight meal services
10. Cancel your reservation

Table 2. List of elements for analysis

Smartphone	Tablet	OS	Website
Korean keyboard layout	Korean keyboard layout	Korean keyboard layout	terminology
terminology	terminology	terminology	features only in this website
icon (visual design)	icon (visual design)	icon (visual design)	font
font	font	built-in application	site map
built-in app	built-in app	features only in this OS	ads & banner
features only in this phone	features only in this tablet	Korean dictionary	contents in the first page
app store	app store	video player	membership
web browsing	web browsing	system on/off	login/logout
technical spec	technical spec	warning message	account management
Call	video player	file window	transaction
text (SMS)	file transfer to computer	task bar	flight reservation
taking a photo	screen rotation	tree menu style	flight schedule
emergency call	drop-down menu	dialogue box	'My...' menu
background image	global navigation bar	tooltip	
map, car navigation	screen brightness control	START menu	
touch interaction set	sound control	control window	
	camera	slider	
	photo gallery	screen saver	
	touch interaction set	calculator	

2.4   In-House Analysis

Feature inspection and comparative analysis were used as analysis methods. Each element was reviewed, and each use scenario was run on both South and North Korean products. The objectives of this in-house analysis were (1) for researchers to get familiar with North Korean products (2) to prepare user research.

2.5   User Research

Once internal analysis mentioned above was completed, we conducted user research with 8 participants composed of 5 master and 3 doctoral students majoring in UX. For each product two participants were assigned. Of the ten use scenarios 3 were selected as task scenarios based on the findings from the in-house analysis. Participants were asked to execute the three task scenarios in turn, and give any thoughts and opinions of their experience.

2.6   Workshop

In order to collect various thoughts and opinions, we hosted a 'North Korean UX Research' workshop at the Korean HCI Conference 2019. About 15 conference attendees joined our workshop. We made four breakout groups and assigned North Korean product to each group. Based on cognitive walkthrough we ran the same three task scenarios used in the user research for each product.

3   Analysis Summary

As mentioned earlier, the goal of this study is to understand the current status and the characteristics of each North Korean product. We have collected a vast amount of factual data through three UX analysis activities and consolidated them. Below are the summaries of our insight of each product from our data.

3.1   Smartphone: Pyongyang 2423

Thanks to its a high level of design and performance most participants didn't see it as a smartphone from North Korea at first (Fig. 5). The visual style is somewhat a mixture of material design and squeegee morphism. It comes from the mix of newly created apps and the old apps from the previous smartphones.

There were opinions from participants that its design is not filled up with explicit political ideas as they had imagined. For example, all of the built-in wallpapers were either about nature or abstract concept but no image of their supreme leader portraits. The wallpaper containing the text image of 'Pyongyang' is the only one that reveals this product is from North Korea (Fig. 6). Of course, the phone is equipped with several built-in apps with a plain political propaganda (Fig. 7) so it is not fully free from politics.

Fig. 5. Pyongyang 2423

Fig. 6. Built-in Wallpapers. The image on the middle-left has 'Pyongyang' text in Korean

Fig. 7. Built-in political propaganda app

As it follows the basis of Google Android on the whole, participants using the Android phones were able to carry out task scenarios without much difficulties. The most unfamiliar UX factor for South Korean users was terminology. Many participants gave comments that those foreign terminologies overly translated into the North Korean style expression seemed very strange and unfamiliar, but also interesting on the other hand.

3.2   Tablet: Ryonghung

Being an Android-based tablet, participants who have experience with Android tablets produced in South Korea found themselves easy to adapt to Ryonghung. The basic UI skeleton such as the button positions or input windows are similar. Touch interaction and gesture sets conform to the original Android standard.

The visual style basically followes skeumorphism. Material Design, the standard GUI for Google Android, was hard to find in Ronchung. One reason is the one we used in our research is manufactured before the birth of Material Design. However, the latest North Korean Android Tablet called 'Dayang 8321' released in 2018 seemed not to have adopted the Material Design either (Figs. 8 and 9).

Fig. 8. Ryonghung's Visual UI style

Fig. 9. Daeyang 8231 (screen capture from North Korea's Central Television News)

A number of participants expressed their thoughts that Ryonghung was better than they expected. For example, its PDF reader showed smooth transition between pages, and its UX was similar to a popular e-book reader in South Korea. Of course, there were a several comments on inconveniences due to usability deficiencies too.

The slight difference in terminology was the most unfamiliar for South Korean users. In addition, the North Korean keyboard layout was also slightly different from the standard South Korean keyboard layout. Thus a number of participants showed common usage pattern of making a typo during the task of entering text.

It was interesting to see that built-in apps of Ryonghung were focused on the two conflicting areas of education and entertainment. Among the education apps, some showed explicit political propaganda. On the other hand, game apps showed a tendency to pursue entertainment itself than political intention. Ryonghung has game apps like 'Motorcycle Race' or 'Joy of Billiard.'

3.3   OS: The Red Star Version 3.0

The first characteristics pointed out by our participants was that the overall design of the Red Star 3.0 was very similar to Mac OS. Many of our participants were industrial designers and they generally use Apple product either at work or at home. Those familiar with Mac OS also had little trouble carrying out the task scenarios.

The basic UI elements - controls or widgets - were also familiar to our participants (Fig. 10). The most disturbing element was terminology and expression. Like other products, North Korea overly translated globally well known English words into North Korean words, which were unfamiliar to even South Korean users who use same Korean language.

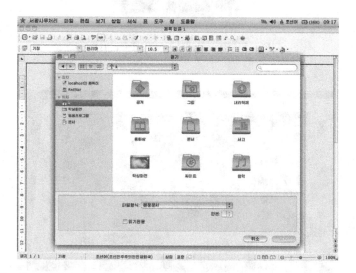

Fig. 10. 'Open File' Dialogue Box in the Red Star version 3.0 (Color figure online)

3.4   Website: Air Koryo

Many participants expressed their surprise with comments such as "I thought North Korea' s website would be very outdated," "I imagined everything would be in red because it is a communist nation," "It is not too distanced from my own web experience." In overall, 'better than imagined,' 'clean,' 'wonderful' and 'simple' were common expressions from our participants. Of course, some expressed unfamiliarity and uncomfortability.

Material The basic layout of the website is not much different from the Korean Air's website in South Korea. The main menu is located on the top right, and the very center of the screen has a large banner. A notable difference is that Air Koryo website has no advertising. It is also a very simple and clear website that is faithful to its functional purposes (Fig. 11). It is in contrast to the fact that Korean Airline's site is full of capitalistic elements such as promotions and special offers (Fig. 12).

Fig. 11. Air Koryo Website (2019.2)

Fig. 12. South Korea's Korean Airline website (2019.2)

Figure 13 shows flight schedule for Beijing-Pyongyang. Scheduled days were marked with the 'flying bird' logo, which is the trademark of Air Koryo. However, some commented that it was not easy to recognize what it meant to have those marks on the days.

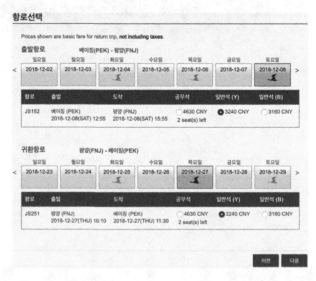

Fig. 13. Flight schedule between Beijing and Pyongyang

Air Koryo's website is not equipped with online payment methods. Instead, customer is asked to make deposit to Air Koryo's bank accounts of the banks in China or Russia. This contrasts with Korean Airline's various online payment methods. In addition, participants pointed out that UX was not well structured to cover various use patterns of flight users such as 'changing reservations' or 'selecting seats.' On the other hand, in some parts the website showed very detailed customer service message. Examples are "There is a vegetarian diet" or "You can take a monkey with you as a pet." Unfamiliarity with terminologies and heavily translated expressions were major confusions to the participants as in other products too.

4 Round-Up

4.1 Conclusion

In overall, South Korean participants' impressions on the North Korean IT products were "better than I thought." For most of the South Koreans the first impression on North Korea is one of the poorest nation in the world where thousands starve to death. For them, it was amazing to find out that North Korea has such good IT capability, and many North Korean residents do enjoy information technology in their everyday lives.

On the UX side, there was no huge difference between South Korean and North Korean products. Most of the smart devices tend to conform to the DNA of their platform owners (e.x.: Google Android), so basic UX structure tend to be similar. This is evident from the comparison of websites. Web does not have such market-dominant platform owner - only open standard - thus showed relatively more differences between the two Korean websites than that of smart devices.

To summarize our participant's opinions into one sentence: "very similar to South Korean products with some obvious differences." One participant expressed his experience using the metaphor "time difference of 3 h." Big countries like the US has domestic time difference among their cities. When we travel to another city in different time zone - for instance, you live in San Francisco and you travel to NYC - we feel there is no big difference in general. However time to time you confront unfamiliar cases that are different from your routine experience. Shops close earlier than you thought for instance. Physically there is no time difference between South Korea and North Korea. For UX, there's is 3 h time difference, metaphorically speaking.

4.2 Future Research

Although the Red Star is officially North Korea's national standard operating system, it is not widely in use. Computer is not yet an everyday home electronics in North Korea and penetration rate is still low. Universities and research institutes with relatively higher computer usage are known to use illegal copies of MS Windows. Thus the Red Star is being developed as a server OS in order to lower the dependence of using OS made in USA - particularly OS for servers with sensitive national security issues. This is somewhat similar situation in South Korea. We also have 'made in Korea' operating system such as 'Harmonica' and 'Gurum' specialized for server systems. The initiative for developing these products was a concern on using foreign-made OS for servers related to national security. We plan to compare these 'made in Koreas' server OSs in the future.

This study focused on identifying current status and the characteristics of the North Korean UX. In order to keep this goal, we intentionally ruled out evaluating the quality of North Korean UX. The two Koreas are in military and political confrontation, and each individual's political judgment on North Korea varies. Individuals less fond of North Korea have high chance to point out only the negative aspects of North Korean products. We didn't want participants' personal political opinions to cloud factual characteristics. In other words, by not judging the quality we strove to keep objective view on North Korean UX and focused on 'fact-finding.' In our second phase of the study we plan to conduct in-depth assessment on the quality. Maintaining objectivity will continue to be a key concern in the second study.

References

1. Kim, J.S., Lee, C.G.: History of North Korean IT industry development. Issues Policy **25**(8), 24–33 (2015). STEPI
2. Jang, Y.H.: Spread of IT device among North Korean the young generations, Midus, pp. 26–27 (2016)
3. Kim, B.S.: Current status of North Korean wired and wireless communication service. Inf. Commun. Broadcast. Policy **29**(10) (2017). KISDI
4. Kang, D.W.: A study on the introduction of foreign culture into North Korea and changes to the North Korean society: with an interview survey with North Koreans in a third country. Humanit. Unification **60**, 167–202 (2014)
5. Kim, J.S., Lee, C.G.: Analysis on North Korean OS "The Red Star." Issues Policy 1–16 (2010). STEPI

Integration and Development of Science, Technology and Innovation in Developed Countries: Perspective from Ocean Policy

Yuta Komori[1]([✉]), Yasuyuki Matsuura[2], and Riho Gojo[3]

[1] The Ocean Policy Research Institute,
The Sasakawa Peace Foundation, Tokyo, Japan
y-komori@meiji.ac.jp
[2] Department of Cross-Cultural Studies,
Gifu City Women's College, Gifu, Japan
[3] Meiji University, Tokyo, Japan

Abstract. This presentation aims to consider the process of inclusion and development of science and technology in developed and industrialized countries based on the experience of Japan's efforts as well as to present some observations on its prospects.

After the Meiji Restoration, Japan aimed at catching up with the Western Great Powers and pushed for the rapid modernization with "Wealth and military strength". At that time, Japan was not only changing political systems drastically but also integrating the Western Great Powers' advanced science and technology positively. As a result, in the days of World War I, Japan achieved entering permanent member of the League of Nations and came to occupy a big position globally. Although Japan was put under the control of allied powers, after the World War II, Japan planed integrating the overseas advanced technology again and will have current prosperity in one's hand afterwards.

On the other hand, when we pay more attention abroad, the utilization of science and technology is essential to the right profit in the achievement of "Sustainable Development Goals" that is an action plan shown in "Transforming our world: the 2030 Agenda for Sustainable Development" adopted in the United Nations General Assembly of September 2015.

In Japan, 3rd Basic Plan on Ocean Policy approved by the Cabinet in May 2018 prescribes about promoting measures such as "Improve scientific knowledge", "Promote Arctic policy" and others based on science and technology. Therefore, we must consider modality of science and technology for save the ocean as Japan's lifeline.

In this presentation, we will focus on inclusion and development of science and technology in Japan's ocean policy and present modality of science and technology in developed and industrialized countries.

Keywords: Science and technology policy · Ocean policy · Blue economy ·
Capacity building

© Springer Nature Switzerland AG 2019
C. Stephanidis (Ed.): HCII 2019, LNCS 11786, pp. 569–579, 2019.
https://doi.org/10.1007/978-3-030-30033-3_44

1   Introduction

This presentation aims to consider the process of inclusion and development of science and technology in developed and industrialized countries based on the experience of Japan's efforts as well as to present some observations on its prospects.

After the Meiji Restoration, Japan aimed at catching up with the Western Great Powers and pushed for the rapid modernization under the slogan of "Enrich the state, strengthen the military". At that time, Japan was not only changing in its political systems drastically but also integrating the Western Great Powers' advanced science and technology positively. As a result, after the World War I, Japan became one of the permanent members of the League of Nations and occupied an important position at the international scene. Although Japan was put under the control of the allied powers after the World War II, Japan integrated the overseas advanced technology again, which has led to its current prosperity [1–3]. This process could be equated with the social development process starting from "Hunting society" (Society 1.0), "Farming society" (Society 2.0), "Industrial society" (Society 3.0) to "Information society" (Society 4.0), and is an important step forward for "Society 5.0" advocated by the Japanese Government (Fig. 1).

Fig. 1. Sustainable development goals (SDGs) (Source: United Nations Information Centre)

On the other hand, utilization of science and technology is essential for the achievement of "Sustainable Development Goals (SDGs)" that is an action plan contained in "Transforming our world: the 2030 Agenda for Sustainable Development" adopted in the United Nations General Assembly in September 2015. In Japan, the 3rd Basic Plan on Ocean Policy approved by the Cabinet in May 2018 sets forth promoting measures such as "Improve scientific knowledge", "Promote Arctic policy" and others based on science and technology. Japan must consider seriously how to apply science and technology to save the ocean for its prosperity (Fig. 2).

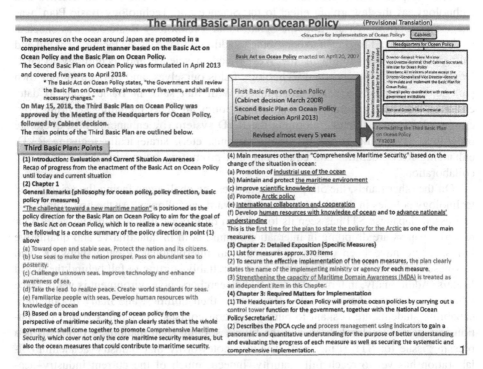

The Third Basic Plan on Ocean Policy (Provisional Translation)

The measures on the ocean around Japan are promoted in a comprehensive and prudent manner based on the Basic Act on Ocean Policy and the Basic Plan on Ocean Policy.
The Second Basic Plan on Ocean Policy was formulated in April 2013 and covered five years to April 2018.
* The Basic Act on Ocean Policy states, "the Government shall review the Basic Plan on Ocean Policy almost every five years, and shall make necessary changes."
On May 15, 2018, the Third Basic Plan on Ocean Policy was approved by the Meeting of the Headquarters for Ocean Policy, followed by Cabinet decision.
The main points of the Third Basic Plan are outlined below.

Third Basic Plan: Points

(1) Introduction: Evaluation and Current Situation Awareness
Recap of progress from the enactment of the Basic Act on Ocean Policy until today and current situation
(2) Chapter 1
General Remarks (philosophy for ocean policy, policy direction, basic policy for measures)
"The challenge toward a new maritime nation" is positioned as the policy direction for the Basic Plan on Ocean Policy to aim for the goal of the Basic Act on Ocean Policy, which is to realize a new oceanic state. The following is a concise summary of the policy direction in point (1) above
(a) Toward open and stable seas. Protect the nation and its citizens.
(b) Use seas to make the nation prosper. Pass on abundant sea to posterity.
(c) Challenge unknown seas. Improve technology and enhance awareness of sea.
(d) Take the lead to realize peace. Create world standards for seas.
(e) Familiarize people with seas. Develop human resources with knowledge of ocean
(3) Based on a broad understanding of ocean policy from the perspective of maritime security, the plan clearly states that the whole government shall come together to promote Comprehensive Maritime Security, which cover not only the core maritime security measures, but also the ocean measures that could contribute to maritime security.

(4) Main measures other than "Comprehensive Maritime Security," based on the change of the situation in ocean:
(a) Promotion of industrial use of the ocean
(b) Maintain and protect the maritime environment
(c) improve scientific knowledge
(d) Promote Arctic policy
(e) International collaboration and cooperation
(f) Develop human resources with knowledge of ocean and to advance nationals' understanding
This is the first time for the plan to state the policy for the Arctic as one of the main measures.
(3) Chapter 2: Detailed Exposition (Specific Measures)
(1) List for measures approx. 370 items
(2) To secure the effective implementation of the ocean measures, the plan clearly states the name of the implementing ministry or agency for each measure.
(3) Strengthening the capacity of Maritime Domain Awareness (MDA) is treated as an independent item in this Chapter.
(4) Chapter 3: Required Matters for Implementation
(1) The Headquarters for Ocean Policy will promote ocean policies by carrying out a control tower function for the government, together with the National Ocean Policy Secretariat.
(2) Describes the PDCA cycle and process management using indicators to gain a panoramic and quantitative understanding for the purpose of better understanding and evaluating the progress of each measure as well as securing the systematic and comprehensive implementation.

<Structure for implementation of Ocean Policy>   Cabinet
Headquarters for Ocean Policy
Basic Act on Ocean Policy enacted on April 20, 2007
First Basic Plan on Ocean Policy
(Cabinet decision March 2008)
Second Basic Plan on Ocean Policy
(Cabinet decision April 2013)
Revised almost every 5 years
Formulating the Third Basic Plan on Ocean Policy *FY2018

Fig. 2. Abstract of the 3rd basic plan on ocean policy (Source: National Ocean Policy Secretariat, Cabinet Office, Government of JAPAN)

2 Method

For the above-mentioned purpose, we will survey official documents (laws, government ordinances, Imperial ordinances, publicized documents), international treaties (bilateral and multilateral treaties) and preceding researches in the relevant areas, consider inclusion and development of science and technology in Japan, present the prospects concerning science and technology in developed and industrialized countries.

3 Research

3.1 Japan's Science and Technology Policy Since 2001

The science and technology policy in Japan is promoted in an integrated and consistent manner based on the Science and Technology Basic Plan made according to the Basic Act on Science and Technology (Act No. 130 of November 15, 1995). So far, the 1st plan (1996–2000), the 2nd plan (2001–2005), the 3rd plan (2006–2010) and the 4th plan (2011–2015) have been established, the 5th plan having been in effect since January 2016.

The 5th plan summarizes the situations in which the Basic Act on Science and technology, as the law giving effect to the Science and Technology Basic Plan, was enacted as follows: "At the time the Science and Technology Basic Act was enacted, there was a demand for Japan to contribute to addressing the issues facing mankind and shift our policy from following the West's lead in science and technology to challenging unexplored science and technology fields ourselves, and to opening our own path to the future as a world frontrunner. With that said, in Basic Plans to date, emphasis has been placed on strengthening policy in areas including securing government R&D investments, reforming the R&D system (by enhancing post-doctorate programs, developing competitive environments, etc.), strategically focusing R&D, enhancing R&D facilities and equipment, and promoting international exchange and collaboration."

On the other hands, the 5th plan summarizes the challenges facing the science and technology policies in the 21 century and afterwards as follows: "As the first point to be addressed, Japanese STI has seen its foundation rapidly weakened in recent years. Our research papers are dropping in international rank, both in quantitative and qualitative terms. There have been delays in building an international research network, and Japanese science and technology activity is regrettably starting to fall behind the world leaders. Additionally, in terms of active STI researchers, no environment is yet in place where young researchers can fully demonstrate their abilities, and many of our high-capability students are hesitant to pursue doctoral courses. As Japan's young population is expected to shrink further in the future, solving such manpower problems is a pressing issue for STI. (Line feed) It is also noteworthy that industry–academia collaboration has yet to reach full maturity. Indeed, much of the current industry–academia collaboration is on a small scale, and there is still little mobility for researchers across organizations and sectors. Venture companies and the like have yet to reach the point of structurally transforming Japanese industry. Therefore, we need to clearly recognize that the mechanism for filling the gap between company needs and the knowledge and technology produced by universities has not fully performed its function to date. This is leading to deficiencies in Japan's ability to innovate through science and technology. In addition, due to the Great East Japan Earthquake and the followed nuclear power incident, as well as the recent case of research fraud and other incidents, confidence in Japanese science and technology, as well as our researchers and technical experts, is falling. Thus, the importance of rethinking the relationship between science, technology, and society, as well as promoting STI together with the various stakeholders of society, is increasing." And the 5th plan points out that "As has been described to this point, Japan's world standing in science and technology is falling as a whole, just as other countries are further strengthening their STI policies. In addition, the shift from science and technology policy to STI policy as given in the Fourth Basic Plan may not be progressing sufficiently. These issues must be addressed with bold reforms driven by a strong sense of crisis and speed. In the interest of extracting the most out of the results of the R&D investments of the past 20 years, it is particularly important to reform the systems for addressing the various issues faced by STI researchers, and to reorganize and enhance the function of universities and national R&D corporations."

Based on these recognitions, the 5th plan includes as "Target National Image", "Sustainable growth and self-sustaining regional development", "Ensure safety and security for our nation and its citizens and a high-quality, prosperous way of life", "Address global challenges and contribute to global development" and "Sustainable creation of intellectual property". And it also includes as "fundamentals for STI (science, technology, and innovation)", It thus states that Japan should promote efforts for "Acting to create new value for the development of future industry and social transformation", "Addressing economic and social challenges", "Reinforcing the "fundamentals" for STI (science, technology, and innovation)" and "Building a systemic virtuous cycle of human resource, knowledge, and funding for innovation", while "bolster(ing) global brain circulation and position(ing) a framework capable of disseminating Japan's science and technology to the world, within its science and technology diplomatic strategy, as part of the visible face of the nation."

3.2   Trend and Application Possibility of Japan's Science and Technology Policy

Japan's science and technology policy has been formed on the principle of "not to perform the scientific research for military affairs". In this respect, Science Council of Japan (SCJ), the representative organization of Japanese scientist community covering all fields of sciences including humanities, social sciences, life sciences, natural sciences, and engineering, clearly describes this tendency in its "Statement on Research for Military Security" publicized in March 2017.

According to the Statement, "Science Council of Japan (SCJ) was established in 1949, and the following year, SCJ adopted a statement on its commitment not to be engaged in scientific research that would help conduct war, and in 1967, issued again a statement on its commitment not to be engaged in scientific research for military purposes. Behind these statements, there existed remorse for the scientist community's past cooperation with war efforts and a deep concern for a possible resurgence of similar situations. In recent years, the distance between scientific research and military endeavors has been narrowing again. Therefore, by recognizing the tension between two sides, namely, academic freedom and a sound development of the sciences on one side, and research for national security employing military measures, in other words, research for military security conducted at universities and research institutions, on the other, we affirm the previous two statements." SCJ further emphasizes "what the scientist community should pursue, above all, is a sound development of the sciences through which it can respond to the responsibilities entrusted to it by society. Past experience demonstrates that scientific research is often restricted or mobilized especially by political powers. Therefore, autonomy of research, especially the unrestricted publication of research results, must be guaranteed. However, for military security research, there exist concerns that government intervention in the activities of researchers might become stronger in regards to the direction of the research and the preservation of confidentiality during project periods and thereafter." In this respect,

"The Acquisition, Technology and Logistics Agency (ATLA) of the Ministry of Defense started a research funding program called National Security Technology Research Promotion (Anzenhoshougijutsu-kenkyuu-suisin-seido) in the fiscal year 2015. In this funding program, research proposals are invited and reviewed with a clear objective of awarding prospective projects which are likely to produce results useful to the future development of defense equipment. In addition, officials of the ATLA, not outside experts, administrate on-going research and their progress during funding periods. It should be pointed out that this funding program has many problems due to these governmental interventions into research. From the standpoint of a sound development of the sciences, funding should be increased further for research in civilian areas where autonomous research by scientists and unrestricted publication of research results are assured.". SCJ suggests that "Contrary to the original intentions of scientists, research results may sometimes be diverted to military applications and for aggressive goals. Therefore, prudent judgment is required on sources of research funding and other conditions before actual research activities begin. Universities and research institutions are responsible for the management of their facilities, information, intellectual properties, and other resources, and for the preservation of unrestricted research and educational environments open to domestic and foreign nationals. Accordingly, each university or research institution should create a system to review research proposals that might be used for military security research for their appropriateness, both technologically and ethically, based on the validity of their research objectives, methods, and potential applications. Academic societies and other communities are required to develop guidelines depending upon the characteristics of their respective disciplines and fields." and concludes that "As to appropriateness of the research, a shared understanding should be formed within the scientist community based on cumulative academic deliberations and judgments. Sincere discussions should be ongoing among not only respective scientists, but also universities, research institutions, academic societies, and the scientist community as a whole, and should be open to the rest of society. SCJ, an organization that represents the scientist community in Japan, will continue to lead deliberations on relevant issues to provide viewpoints and findings that contribute to this discussion."

4 Discussion

4.1 Japan's Ocean Policy Since 2001

Though there seem various opinions on the origin of the concrete ocean policy in Japan, no doubt the adoption of "United Nations Convention on the Law of the Sea: UNCLOS" in 1982, "Rio Declaration on Environment and Development" in 1992 and "Agenda 21" in 1992 have been significant watersheds in its history. These events gave rise to increasing interests in ocean policy in Japan, and various institutional frameworks including the setting of the exclusive economic zone as a result as well as led to the enactment of "Basic Act on Ocean Policy" in 2007 and "Basic Plan on Ocean Policy" (established in 2008, revised in 2013 and in 2018). "Johannesburg Declaration on Sustainable Development" (adopted in 2002) and "The Future We Want" (adopted in 2012) were also developed on the basis of these instruments [4, 5].

On the other hand, while it is true that the formation of the ocean policy in Japan has been driven by global factors including UNCLOS or Rio declaration, there is no reference about the relationship with domestic factors such as asset price bubble in 1980s, political reform in 1990s and Central Government Reform in 2001. In practice, the so-called cabinet-led policy making process has been developed as a result of the changes in domestic factors, which has had significant impacts on the formation of Japan's ocean policy.

With regard to contribution of science and technology to promoting ocean policy, the 2nd Basic Plan on Ocean Policy includes "Promotion of marine surveys and integration and disclosure of marine-related information" and "Developing human resources and improving technological ability" in the "Measures to be Intensively Promoted Under the Plan".

However, the survey by Ocean Policy Research Institute, the Sasakawa Peace Foundation, indicates that "Researches on the ocean science tends to focus on such issues as seabed resources development and geophysics. Researches of marine physics, chemistry and biological environment, as well as technological innovation are equally important for marine security, not only for environmental protection." All of these are why the application of science and technology to ocean policy is a very urgent issue [6–8].

4.2 Possibility of Ocean Policy Based on Science and Technology Policy

With regard to the applicability of science and technology to ocean policy, Sect. 3 in 5th Science and Technology Basic Plan indicates clearly that "As a "oceanic state" that ranks as sixth in the world in terms of the size of the country's exclusive economic zone (EEZ), it is important that Japan strive steadily to improve its STI to a level befitting this status. Some examples of marine-related science and technology efforts include technologies for ocean surveys and observation—including areas of sea ice, deep seas, and below the seabed—and technologies for contributing to sustainable development and utilization of the seas. This includes marine resources (including biological resources), transportation, tourism, and environmental conservation, as well as technologies to help ensure the safety of the seas, and the scientific knowledge and fundamental technologies necessary to support all these efforts. While engaged in ongoing collaboration with the Headquarters for Ocean Policy and the Strategic Headquarters for Space Development in order to ensure coordination between the Basic Plan on Ocean Policy and the Basic Plan on Space Policy, CSTI is pursuing initiatives aimed at developing solutions to R&D challenges relating to the oceans and space."

And the 2nd Basic Plan on Ocean Policy states that "With regard to research and development of marine science and technology, in consideration of the Science and Technology Basic Plan and deliberations of the Subdivision on Ocean Development of the Council for Science and Technology, the government should intensively promote research and development for the five policy needs: (1) projection of and adaptation to global warming and climate change, (2) development of marine energy and mineral resources, (3) conservation of marine ecosystems and sustainable use of living resources, (4) development of marine renewable energy and (5) response to natural disasters."

Based on these plans, coordination between the science and technology policy and the ocean policy seems likely to be promoted effectively. However, based on the above-mentioned findings, at least from the ocean policy point of view, we conclude that there remain some issues to be addressed with respect to the coordination between the science and technology and the ocean policy. Therefore, we suggest that construction of the framework for mutual advantages is needed for the future coordination between the two (Table 1).

Table 1. Targets and indicators of SDG 14 (Source: United Nations Official Website)

Targets		Indicators	
1.4.1	By 2025, prevent and significantly reduce marine pollution of all kinds, in particular from land-based activities, including marine debris and nutrient pollution	14.1.1	Index of coastal eutrophication and floating plastic debris density
1.4.2	By 2020, sustainably manage and protect marine and coastal ecosystems to avoid significant adverse impacts, including by strengthening their resilience, and take action for their restoration in order to achieve healthy and productive oceans	14.2.1	Proportion of national exclusive economic zones managed using ecosystem-based approaches
1.4.3	Minimize and address the impacts of ocean acidification, including through enhanced scientific cooperation at all levels	14.3.1	Average marine acidity (pH) measured at agreed suite of representative sampling stations
1.4.4	By 2020, effectively regulate harvesting and end overfishing, illegal unreported and unregulated fishing and destructive fishing practices and implement science-based management plans, in order to restore fish stocks in the shortest time feasible, at least to levels that can produce maximum sustainable yield as determined by their biological characteristics	14.4.1	Proportion of fish stocks with in biologically sustainable levels
1 4.5	By 2020, conserve at least 10% of coastal and marine areas, consistent with national and international law and based on the best available scientific information	14.5.1	Coverage of protected areas in relation to marine areas

(continued)

Table 1. (*continued*)

Targets		Indicators	
1.4.6	By 2020, prohibit certain forms of fisheries subsidies which contribute to over capacity and overfishing, eliminate subsidies that contribute to illegal, unreported and unregulated fishing and refrain from introducing new such subsidies, recognizing that appropriate and effective special and differential treatment for developing and east developed countries should be an integral part of the World Trade Organization fisheries subsidies negotiation	14.6.1	Progress by countries in the degree of implementation of international instruments aiming to combat illegal, unreported and unregulated fishing
1.4.7	By 2030, increase the economic benefits to Small Island developing States and east developed countries from the sustainable use of marine resources, including through sustainable management of fisheries, aquaculture and tourism	14.7.1	Sustainable fisheries as a percentage of GDP in small Island developing States, least developed countries and all countries
1.4.a	increase scientific know edge, develop research capacity and transfer marine technology, taking into account the intergovernmental Oceanographic Commission Criteria and Guidelines on the Transfer of Marine Technology, in order to improve ocean heath and to enhance the contribution of marine biodiversity to the development of developing countries, in particular small island developing States and east developed countries	14.a.1	Proportion of total research budget allocated to research in the field of marine technology
1 4.b	Provide access for small-scale artisanal fishers to marine resources and markets	14.b.1	Progress by countries in the degree of application of a legal/regulatory/policy/institutional framework which recognizes and protects access rights for small-scale fisheries
1.4.c	Enhance the conservation and sustainable use of oceans and their resources by implementing international law as reflected in UNCLOS, which provides the legal framework for the conservation and sustainable use of oceans and their resources, as recalled in paragraph 158 of The Future We Want	14.c.1	Number of countries making progress in ratifying, accepting and implementing through legal, policy and institutional frameworks, ocean-related instruments that implement international law , as reflected in the United Nation Convention on the Law of the Sea, for the conservation and sustainable use of the oceans and their resources

5 Conclusion

We have focused on the inclusion and development of science and technology in developed and industrialized countries based on modern Japan's efforts in order to present some observations on its prospects. We now observe difficulty of inclusion and development of science and technology within societies only by prescribing it in a book.

In this presentation, we have focused on Japan's ocean policy and considered inclusion and development of science and technology. The ocean policy supported by science and technology will contribute to the achievement of SDGs. SDG 14, titled "Life Below Water", obliges us to "Conserve and sustainably use the oceans, seas and marine resources for sustainable development". As is generally known, how to include and develop science and technology is important in order to balance economic development with environmental conservation in a sustainable manner. And the economic development compatible with environmental conservation contributes to the realization of "blue economy" [9–11].

In addition, we cannot overlook the importance of human capacity building. However, education in Japan, particularly the higher education suffers from the so-called "reform fatigue" by the efforts led the government (Ministry of Education, Culture, Sports, Science and Technology), and is unable to demonstrate its potential for human capacity building. Therefore, to change the environment in order to facilitate human capacity building for inclusion and development of science and technology is also important.

Acknowledgement. This work was supported by JSPS Grants-in-Aid for Scientific Research (KAKENHI) Grant Number JP18K12714 (managed by Meiji University).

References

1. Komori, Y.: Civil-military relations in Japan from 1904 to 1937: from new institutional perspective. Doctoral thesis (Meiji University) (2012)
2. Komori, Y.: An analysis of civil-military relations: focusing on excessive involvement in the tactical and operational areas by civilians. Stud. Polit. Sci. Econ. **49**(4), 579–605 (2013)
3. Komori, Y.: A study of politico-military relations: focusing on the relationship between civilian control and national security. Stud. Polit. Sci. Econ. **50**(3), 863–889 (2014)
4. The Ocean Policy Research Institute. The Sasakawa Peace Foundation Website. (https://www.spf.org/opri-j/publication/projects/ocean-policy/. Accessed 14 May 2018
5. Komori, Y., Matsuura, Y., Gojo, R.: A basic study on legislation by house members: focusing on the issues and prospects. JSN J. Special Edition, 275–288 (2017)
6. Terashima, H., et al.: Report on Japan's Ocean Policy 2016. OPRI-SPF, Tokyo (2017)
7. Furukawa, K., Komori, Y.: Future challenges in promoting the comprehensive management of coastal zones as seen in the evaluation of the second basic plan on ocean policy. In: Japanese Association for Coastal Zone Studies 29th National Conference Proceedings (2017)

8. Komori, Y.: Maritime Security Initiatives in Japan and Future Challenges: An opportunity to evaluate the second Basic Plan on Ocean Policy. FROM THE OCEANS: Intelligence Analysis (Special Edition) (2018)
9. Sunami, A., et al.: Report on the Development of Integrated Coastal Management Model Site Projects 2017. OPRI-SPF, Tokyo (2018)
10. Sunami, A., et al.: Guidebook for Community Development Incorporating the Ocean ~ Towards Realization of the Blue Economy ~ Ways of Thinking on Integrated Coastal Management and Its Implementation. OPRI-SPF, Tokyo (2018)
11. Murakami, Y., Komori, Y.: Realizing blue economy at coastal communities and the roles of fishers' associations". In: Japanese Association for Coastal Zone Studies 30th National Conference Proceedings (2018)

Dhaka University Telemedicine Programme, Targeting Healthcare-Deprived Rural Population of Bangladesh and Other Low Resource Countries

K. Siddique-e Rabbani[1]([✉]), Abdullah Al Amin[1], Zihad Tarafdar[1],
Md. Abu Yousuf[1], A. K. M. Bodiuzzaman[1],
Ahmad Imtiaz Khan[1], Papia Chowdhury[1], Kamrul Hussain[1],
Shahed Md. Abu Sufian[1], Maruf Ahmad[1], Md. Moniruzzaman[1],
and Ashir Ahmed[2]

[1] Department of Biomedical Physics and Technology,
University of Dhaka, Dhaka, Bangladesh
rabbani@du.ac.bd
[2] Faculty of Information Science and Electrical Engineering,
Kyushu University, Fukuoka, Japan

Abstract. Most current telemedicine efforts focus on tertiary care, general doctors being available at the patient end. In low resource countries (LRC), qualified doctors do not want to live in villages where the majority population lives. Therefore, telemedicine is the only solution. Besides, the technology should be indigenously developed to be effective and sustained. We developed necessary technology indigenously including web based software and online diagnostic devices like stethoscope and ECG. More devices are under development. Targeting primary or secondary care we deployed the system through an entrepreneurial model, giving video conferencing and online prescription by the consulting doctor. All data are archived for future reference and analysis. We also developed a mobile phone version using which roving operators can provide a doctor's consultation to rural patients right at their homes, which has proved very useful for women, children, elderly and the infirm. The software also provides monitoring with provision for analyses for feedback. Starting in 2013 we have so far given consultation to more than 18,500 rural patients, paying a small fee, and the acceptance is increasing. At present more than 40 rural centres are active which can choose from a panel of 15 doctors who are providing consultation from places of their own. We are also planning to organize body tissue collection for pathological investigation at the telemedicine centres through arrangements with pathological centres in the neighbourhood. We feel this system can be spread throughout the LRCs benefitting the majority of the global population who are deprived at present.

Keywords: Telemedicine · Low resource countries ·
Indigenous telemedicine technology ·
Dhaka University Telemedicine Programme

© Springer Nature Switzerland AG 2019
C. Stephanidis (Ed.): HCII 2019, LNCS 11786, pp. 580–598, 2019.
https://doi.org/10.1007/978-3-030-30033-3_45

1 Introduction

In Bangladesh 64% of the total population of about 165 million lives in villages [1] and one doctor is available for every 1847 people on average, equivalent to about 5.4 doctors per 10,000 [2]. However, due to socio-economic conditions, all doctors live in cities or towns. Therefore, in real terms, to about 105 million of this population, the number of doctors available is virtually 'zero'. This 105 million population lives in about 87,000 villages [3] for whom the Government established 421 semi-rural hospitals (Upazilla Health Complex - UHC) each having 30 to 50 beds and to serve about 250,000 people [4]. However, most of these people reside many miles away from these hospitals; the dilapidated condition of the connecting roads and lack of proper transports make the travel a big hassle. Furthermore, due to prevailing socio-economic conditions, the Government finds it very difficult to retain all the designated doctors in these UHCs. While the number of doctors designated for each UHC is 10 to 15, hardly a fraction of them, mostly general practitioners, may actually be present and available for consultation [5]. Specialist posts mostly remain vacant. Naturally, there are long queues and the quality of consultation suffers due to the large number of patients served by a few overworked doctors. In some villages, a doctor, who has a root in that area, comes for a scheduled day in a week to give consultation to as many patients as possible. However, such doctors are not available for day to day consultation.

Due to all the above-mentioned factors, unless there is an emergency, the rural people, particularly women, children, the infirm and the elderly mostly go without treatment or they get medicines prescribed by village quacks or drug sellers who are not qualified to do so. This often leads to maltreatment, disabilities, and life-threatening complications. The time, cost and hardship that the patient and the family have to go through can easily be guessed; the whole family is ruined in some cases. Medicine shops selling simple to sophisticated drugs abound in the rural areas and consultation of unqualified people leads to large scale misuse of steroids, NSAIDS, and antibiotics. The last has become a global scare now, contributing to antibiotic resistance against which the world may appear helpless soon. A similar situation exists in most low resource countries (LRC) of the world.

Therefore, a telemedicine system appropriate to the local conditions could be the best solution to the above problem. Very simply stated, Telemedicine is basically 'medicine at a distance', through a connectivity medium. Some perfectionists argue that a doctor has to see the patient face to face, touch and palpate the patient, so telemedicine should not be promoted. Realistically, the people we are talking about will not have the opportunity to see a doctor at all, as mentioned above. So, 'something is better nothing' is the main argument in favour of telemedicine. One has to make compromises in view of the realistic problems in the present day world. One cannot have ideal conditions always.

To give a very brief history, the telemedicine system in its rudimentary form started very early, with the advent of telephones in the early part of the twentieth century. Electro Cardio-graphic (ECG) data were sent to remote doctors over telephone networks by Willem Einthoven, father of ECG [6]. Subsequently, voice consultations of remote doctors were performed using radio technology. In the early 1950s, radiographic images were transmitted using television technology, mainly for military personnel working in remote areas. However, telemedicine took a back seat for a considerable length of time until the 1990s when an expanding internet technology rejuvenated activities in telemedicine with fresh vigour. With the proliferation of mobile networks in most low resource countries providing widespread internet access, telemedicine through the internet has become a viable option again. Video consultation of city dwelling doctors can be brought to the rural people, even right to their homes using PCs or mobile smartphones. Even a doctor employed somewhere may provide consultation during leisure periods, increasing the capacity of a doctor to serve more patients and thus virtually increasing the doctor-patient ratio.

The present work gives an account of a successful telemedicine programme in Bangladesh which covers most aspects of the activity through fully indigenous development. The system design, technology including software and hardware for some online diagnostic devices, deployment modality, and implementation – everything has been done through the efforts of various appropriate groups or individuals under a single leadership at the Department of Biomedical Physics & Technology of the University of Dhaka [7]. Branded 'Dhaka University Telemedicine Programme (DUTP)', it has taken the outcome of R&D at the university to the general masses, targeting self-sustainability, a unique effort in a low resource country like Bangladesh. Where many other efforts in telemedicine investing large amounts of funds have dwindled away within a few years of initiation in the country, DUTP, having a very meagre amount of funds at its disposal, has sustained since 2013 and is progressing at a slow and steady pace, learning through the activity and modifying the system design, technology and mode of deployment accordingly and appropriately. For this success, DUTP has already received national and international awards in e-health/telemedicine category, namely, (i) Brac-Manthan Award 2016 - Winner, national level, at Dhaka, Bangladesh (ii) Manthan South Asia Award 2016 - Finalist, regional level, at Gurgaon, India (iii) World Summit on the Information Societies (WSIS) Forum Award-2017 – Championship, at Geneva, Switzerland and (iv) 3rd Commonwealth Digital Health Award 2018 – Winner, at Colombo, Sri Lanka. Designed and developed through practical experience in a low resource country like Bangladesh, the technology and modality of implementation make it very appropriate and scalable.

2 Methods

The first thing needed in designing a telemedicine system for the rural areas of a low resource country is to understand and assess the need properly, to understand the rural people, their economy, culture and practices, and of existing infrastructure and facilities related to health and to telemedicine, which differs widely from that available in the cities. Side by side, challenges, and obstacles also need to be assessed and considered. Secondly, one needs to understand the practical level of entry for telemedicine in these situations. Is it needed for primary, secondary or tertiary care? Also one needs to consider the level of expertise that will be available in a sustained way in a rural area of the target region, as is exemplified by the absence of qualified doctors there, even after a huge effort by the Government over many decades.

2.1   System Design

The first design was for telemedicine centres at the rural areas where an operator will register a patient, carry out minimum physical and clinical measurements and enter the data manually into the computer, all of which will be saved in the cloud. Then the operator will link up the patient to a city-based doctor through video consultation as shown in Fig. 1. Necessary online diagnostic devices will be used to provide additional diagnostic information to the doctors, if required. The doctor will generate a prescription with software support to make it error free taking a minimum time of the doctor.

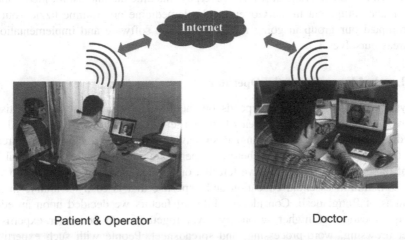

Patient & Operator   Doctor

Fig. 1. Basic telemedicine operation through the internet with patient and operator at a rural centre and doctor at the cities or towns.

2.2   Level of Healthcare

It is well understood that if an ailment is treated early this can save many patients from later complications, even death or disabilities. This could also reduce the demand for tertiary care to a great extent, saving national resources as well as that of the affected person and the family. Therefore, our focus was primary and secondary care, not tertiary care. Besides, it is obvious that telemedicine cannot handle emergencies and interventions requiring invasive procedures.

For tertiary care in telemedicine, one would need a minimum of modern diagnostic devices and the presence of a qualified doctor at the patient end, which is not the realistic scenario for Bangladesh and many LRCs. Incidentally, our entry into tele-medicine was led by a requirement for tertiary care by the UHCs of the Bangladesh Government. The leader of our group was invited to a seminar organized by the Health Ministry of the Bangladesh Government in 2010 where it was first announced that many of the UHCs have been equipped with modern video conferencing facility, procured from an international supplier, which will help in providing consultation of expert doctors from the cities. The motivation was the difficulty in retaining expert doctors at the UHCs, as mentioned before. However, there was no plan to add diagnostic equipment, as the ones available from advanced countries are very expensive and unaffordable. This prompted our group in developing a few online diagnostic devices for telemedicine that could send data over the internet. The personnel at the Government had suggested the requirement for four items initially, (i) Stethoscope, (ii) ECG, (iii) Microscope and (iv) X-ray View-box. The idea was that medical technologists were available to provide the interface to the patients for the above tests, to prepare microscope slides and to take X-ray images using film-based machines that were available at the UHCs.

Our group developed all the four items at low cost within a year and delivered a sample each to the Government [8]. However, by this time the interest for incorporating locally made equipment in the Government telemedicine programme fizzled out and this prompted our group in going into telemedicine software and implementation in rural areas ourselves.

2.3   Level of Expertise of the Operator

The system design very much depends on the level of education and expertise of manpower available in a rural area of the target region who may be trained as a telemedicine operator easily. In Bangladesh, having a qualified doctor in rural areas is out of the question, as mentioned before. Expert paramedics are also not available in most of these regions. Therefore, we felt that our system should be designed to work with the minimum essential education and expertise that is easily available in most rural areas of Bangladesh. Considering different factors we decided upon an educational qualification of higher secondary level together with computer expertise in internet browsing, word-processing, and spreadsheet. People with such expertise is available in most rural areas of Bangladesh. So it would only be necessary to train them in using our software for telemedicine and the software for the essential online diagnostic devices. Besides, they will need to perform a minimum of physical and clinical measurements, i.e., height, weight, temperature, blood pressure (using either automatic or manual equipment), blood glucose and haemoglobin (using strip based finger prick devices), that do not need any type of medical license. We felt that we can train such people in less than a week to start the service. Anyone having weaknesses in certain issues may be improved upon later, through video conferencing. Of course, we will take tests before giving a 'pass' certificate that a person can successfully provide the service needed in our telemedicine programme. We also obtained permission from the Government authorities regarding the qualifications and training of the telemedicine operators.

2.4   Level of Telemedicine

Technology for telemedicine may have several levels as mentioned below.

i. Audio only, where consultation is given through telephone or mobile phone only. Information conveyed through body language remains missing. Again, it depends on how much a patient can convey his or her conditions to a doctor through audio only. Besides, the doctor cannot give a written prescription, so it is limited to advices and a few common over the counter (OTC) drugs or medications. However, in reproducing the names of medicines or the doses, there is a chance that the patient will make mistakes. If the patient has a mobile smartphone, the doctor may send a written prescription which will eliminate the above error. If the patient has a feature phone, the names of medicines may be sent through messaging facilities.

ii. Addition of Video to the above through video conferencing facility of internet, either using a PC or a mobile smartphone. A video consultation allows the patient to see a doctor and vice versa where the body language can be seen allowing a better communication. Besides the doctor can have a visual assessment of the patient's appearance. On the other hand, seeing a doctor on the screen gives a feeling of assurance to the patient which is very important in medicine. Here again, possible errors in reproducing the names of medicines by the patient remain and the treatment remains limited to advice and OTC drugs. However, if the service integrates written prescription generation by the doctor and printing facility at the patient end, the error can be eliminated. Most of the telemedicine operational these days use this modality.

iii. Addition of online diagnostic devices to the above may provide the maximum benefit of the internet in telemedicine. If the doctor can get such diagnostic information immediately, the quality of consultation would improve significantly. Possibilities in an LRC setting are, listening to heart or lung sounds using a digital stethoscope, seeing the insides of the ear or throat using appropriate endoscopic camera, seeing skin images for dermatological problems, observing ECG traces, observing ultrasound images, and so on. In some cases, if medical technologists are available in the rural areas, telepathology may also be practiced, through digital microscopic images. Telemedicine is still in its infancy. Once it gets popular more and more online digital diagnostic devices may be expected to appear on the market through continuing R&D.

2.5 Diagnostic Devices for Our System

From the very beginning, we targeted the highest form of telemedicine, i.e., the one with integrated diagnostic devices. With the leader having a background of a few decades of developing medical and research equipment indigenously including computerized equipment, and with the expertise in modern computer and internet technology of the youths in the team, we have attained a capability of developing many of such essential devices indigenously. We designed and developed the telemedicine system with indigenously acquired expertise and skill, albeit boosted with short periods of working in foreign laboratories with experts. We design equipment in a manner so that these can be repaired and manufactured in most LRCs with the limited infrastructure available thus allowing the use of the devices over prolonged periods, almost through the whole of the expected lifetime of equipment.

Besides, we have a philosophy of not taking patents on our innovation. Rather, we have plans to teach qualified scientific and engineering personnel in the LRCs after the technology of a product gets matured through some years of field trial and dissemination. This thought stems out from the observation that the huge technology disparity existing in the world has pushed almost 80% of the population into a life of disgrace and humility, a scenario which is unacceptable to any sensible human being. We feel that unless the devices can be manufactured locally, the expected life of a device cannot be attained, which is clear from the decades of experience throughout the world. Besides, growing local capability for R&D and production will allow innovations appropriate to the particular region besides delivering the products to the people at the lowest possible cost.

As mentioned before, we had developed four items for telemedicine for the Government. Out of this the ECG device was designed and developed fully indigenously, from scratch, while the others were essentially improvisations of standard commercial devices. The digital stethoscope was made using a good quality chest piece of a commercial acoustic stethoscope and inserting a microphone into a cut segment of the attached rubber tube, with adequate acoustic insulation. The electrical output of the microphone goes to the audio input of a PC or a mobile smartphone. It may also be taken to the USB input through a commercial USB soundcard dongle. The microscope image was digitized using a high-quality webcam with a glass lens mounted appropriately over the eyepiece of the microscope. This gives an essentially digital microscope with a cost that is much less than a commercially available one with the same quality. The digital X-ray View-box was similarly developed placing a high-quality webcam in front of the screen of a locally made View-box.

The ECG device was essentially developed out of a single channel circuitry with software switching to any one of the desired 12 leads at a time, thus acquiring all the 12 lead ECG sequentially. The ECG trace is acquired through a USB interface and the raw signal is displayed in real time. Every 4-s data is stored and transferred to another window while sending the data to a remote computer over the internet at the same time. In the end, through a mouse click, all the 12 lead traces are combined into a single page display, suitable for viewing by a cardiologist for diagnosis, as an XML or a pdf file. This single page image file can be sent to the doctor as a downloadable file through email. Thus a doctor located anywhere with an internet connection and the requisite software can observe the traces every 4 s, almost in real time, or can receive the combined 12 lead data through email, without the need of any specialized software.

The sequential single channel option has several advantages. Firstly, the circuit is simplified and the cost is low. Secondly, this simplification helps minimize disorders, which increases with complexity. Thirdly, all the 12 lead signals go through a single amplifier keeping the relative outputs the same even if the amplifier gain changes a little over time. With 12 lead parallel ECG machines, individual amplifiers are used for each of the channels. Thus if the amplification of a single channel changes a little, the relative sizes of the ECGs will be different, which will mislead the cardiologist into giving a wrong diagnosis. Fourthly, 4-s traces each of the 12 leads give a total observation over 48 s. Thus if a patient has an intermittent beat loss, chances of detecting such disorders are more in 48 s than in only 4 s as acquired in a 12 lead parallel machine.

The real-time transmission of ECG has a big advantage. If an operator makes a mistake in getting any of the individual ECG traces, the doctor can immediately notice it from the remote end and ask for repeat measurement of that individual lead only. This makes life easy for everyone involved, particularly for the patient. Had it not been real time, and if some of the measurements are wrong, then the patient will have to take the trouble of coming to the centre again later for a repeat measurement. Pictures of all the four items developed and the ECG display screen are given in Figs. 2, 3, 4 and 5. Some of our devices are working through two decades in our country.

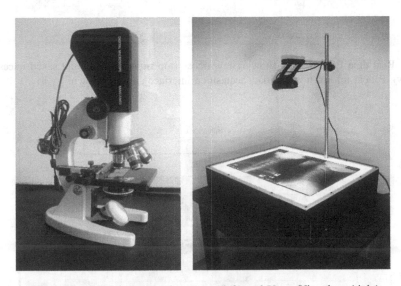

Fig. 2. Improvised digital microscope (left) and X-ray View-box (right)

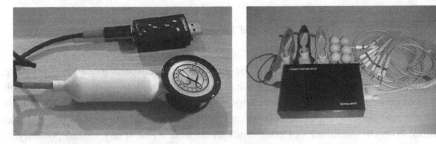

Fig. 3. Improvised digital stethoscope (left) and indigenously designed and developed 12 lead diagnostic ECG device, which connects to a PC through USB port.

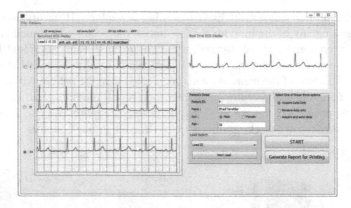

Fig. 4. Real time ECG display showing raw traces (top right window) and saved traces (left window). Patient information and data acquisition interface are also shown.

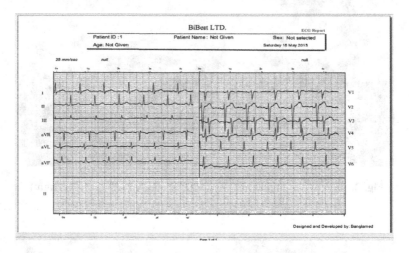

Fig. 5. Combined 12 lead ECG display

Standard basic measurements like height, weight, temperature, blood pressure, blood glucose, blood hemoglobin, etc., are carried out using low-cost devices available in the local market. The idea is that such equipment can easily be replaced at a low cost.

We are also developing other online devices like localized lung ventilation and tele-palpation, both of which are our own innovations and when ready would possibly be the world's first in telemedicine. We are also taking up programmes to incorporate ultrasound scanners, otoscope, retinoscope, etc., using low-cost commercial devices.

2.6 Our Software

2.6.1 Basic Requirements

The initial work involved the development of a basic telemedicine software with Electronic Health Record (EHR) and a few integrated online diagnostic devices like a stethoscope and ECG with individual software. A field trial taken up during 2013–2015 indicated the initial success of the envisaged basic model. However, the software was basic and would not be able to cater to the requirements envisaged for its further expansion based on the experience. Therefore, based on this experience the whole software was redesigned and developed afresh with the following requirements [9]:

i. It should be web-based, with cloud storage of all medical records (Electronic Health Records-EHR) including written texts, images and acquired data from integrated medical devices. Thus it would be platform independent.

ii. It has to be robust.

iii. It has to be user-friendly to its users, namely, the rural operators, consulting doctors and administrators, with a graphical user interface (GUI) and the maximum use of local language.

iv. It has to give each patient an identity for future reference.

v. All data have to be secure and available only to appropriate persons.

vi. It should integrate a video conferencing facility within the same platform.

vii. It should have a computer-aided prescription generation tool linking databases of drugs (medicines), and other medical or clinical advice. The latter will need to be created in this software.

viii. It should have a web-based monitoring facility for the administrators which should have some analytical features with a graphical presentation of necessary data, which can be expanded as the need arises.

ix. It should be optimized for slow internet connectivity, as is encountered in Bangladesh.

Each of these areas was individually addressed by developing corresponding tools and finally put together to make it an integrated, user-friendly telemedicine platform capable to work efficiently in Bangladesh. An Action Research (AR) approach applied in the socio-technical context dictated the most part of the research and development process. Participations of relevant stakeholders of the system were ensured in all the stages of the "design to deployment" cycle of this project. In contrast to many typical workflows followed in such developments, the software development concentrated on evolutionary improvements adopting existing technology and tools, rather than focusing on radical innovation by introducing new forms of technologies. First, a working prototype was developed which was put to use by our deployment team. Subsequently, the software was expanded, modified and refined over the years to add newer features and to incorporate critical feedbacks coming from the users – the rural operators, consulting doctors and administrators.

Thus developed, our software appears to be very appropriate and robust, suited to our specific needs.

2.6.2 Operation of the Software

At the rural centre, an operator registers a patient, if new, giving a unique ID. For a returning patient, only the ID is used to retrieve all previous data. The mobile phone number, if any, will work as an alternative ID. The operator then measures and records basic physical data like age, gender, height, weight, temperature, blood pressure, and the chief complain of the patient, as described by the patient, in local language or dialect, which are all saved in the cloud storage. If there are X-ray images, previous handwritten prescriptions or reports, these are also uploaded into the record. A screenshot of an operator interface with initial patient data is given in Fig. 6.

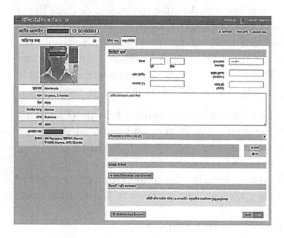

Fig. 6. A typical user interface for the operator to register a new patient, entering basic physical data, chief complain, adding previous clinical information and choosing a doctor from the panel.

The operator then connects the patient to an available doctor, who downloads the patient data page and goes through it before initiating a video conference. At present popular video conference software, 'Skype' is being used. However, we already have developed our own video conferencing software as a part of the main software, waiting to be implemented soon. The doctor finds out the details of the illness by questioning the patient directly and rewrites the chief complain in medical terms. If needed, the doctor may ask the operator to place the stethoscope on specified places on the body to listen to body sounds. Here again, the

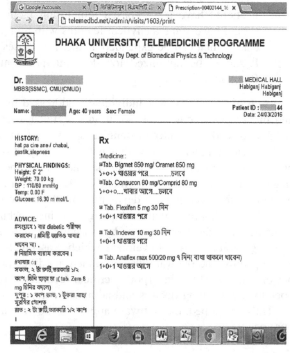

Fig. 7. A typical prescription page showing a mix of local language, Bangla, and English.

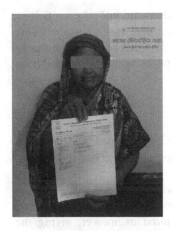

Fig. 8. A rural patient with a printed prescription.

doctor initially listens to the sound through Skype, but this is not good enough for heart sounds as Skype cuts off low-frequency sounds. Skype is mainly used to check if the placement of the chest piece is correct or not. Then the operator records a few seconds of sounds using a free sound software named 'Audacity', and then sends the saved file through Skype. The doctor also listens to the audio file using Audacity, which gives a good rendition of the heart sounds. Thus this uses 'store and forward' technique rather than a live transmission. Here again, we have recently developed our own audio recording software, integrated to the main telemedicine software. Here we can adjust the frequency filters ourselves for live transmission of heart sounds. This will be deployed soon.

Then the doctor generates a prescription which is aided by databases of medicines, symptoms, and advice. After a confirmation check, the doctor uploads the prescription to the cloud storage when the operator downloads it and gives a printout to the patient. A screenshot of a prescription page is given in Fig. 7 and a rural patient with a copy of a prescription is shown in Fig. 8.

2.6.3 Overall Project Monitoring and Analysis Needs

Evaluating the performance of a telemedicine project in a systematic way is crucial to the success and sustainability of a telemedicine project. All telemedicine projects irrespective of its clinical and application context requires some means to monitor and analyse the delivered service quantitatively. Useful tools to visualize the project performance and generate a customised report based on a set of varying parameters help project managers to take decisions related to financial and operational management. The clinical data accumulated and stored

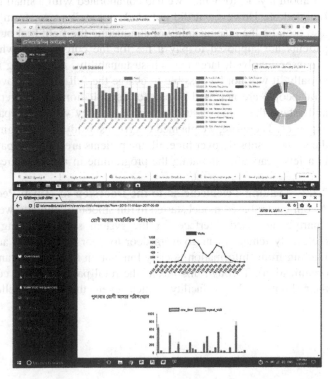

Fig. 9. Screenshots of typical analytical pages showing different statistical parameters

in the database, as telemedicine project keeps running and operational, is essentially a big data and can be immensely useful to the researchers for data analysis in the future too, which may also help a Government in its health care planning and in situations of emergency. Figure 9 shows typical screenshots of two pages giving information on some statistical parameters.

2.7   Implementation

We not only developed the necessary technology, we also implemented the solution in the field. So we had to innovate modes of deployment appropriate to our rural areas.

2.7.1   Mode of Deployment: Through Entrepreneurs

Typical social interventions by different groups, particularly NGOs with large funding, implement programmes in villages through their own hired manpower, giving the services mostly 'free'; at no cost to the recipients. It shows some quick success in the beginning, but as the funding exhausts, the whole programme stops. Again, initiatives taken up by the Government for services of similar nature at huge subsidies suffer due to lack of commitment and dedication, bureaucratic obstacles and self-interests of the people having political influence. Considering all these factors, we decided to choose an entrepreneurial model where a local person would establish a telemedicine centre where patients will come to consult remote doctors, appointed by us, using our telemedicine system. After developing an early version of the software we ran a field trial, for about a year, for which we had collaborated with a small NGO in a small region in Bangladesh. However, it did not work out well so we from the University of Dhaka also took up the responsibility of conducting the field trial ourselves. In our model the patients are supposed to pay a fee for the consultation which would cover all the expenses involved, targeting self-sustainability, in the long run. We understood that initially, it will not be possible to charge the full fee to recover the expenses since the rural people are not used to pay for consultations. However, with time, as they will understand the value of such consultation, they will be prepared to pay the necessary expenses. Therefore, we planned to give a subsidy in the beginning, gradually reducing the share of subsidy over time, till the patients are ready to pay the full amount, maybe in a few years after initiating the programme in a certain area.

2.7.2   Taking Telemedicine to the Doorstep of Rural People

As our centre based model started to run smoothly enough, we also developed a mobile smartphone based interface for the system so that roving telemedicine operators, preferably females, can go from door to door in the rural areas. This received some funding from 'Information Society Innovation Fund-Asia' (an Australia based funding organization). Through this means the rural patients could consult doctors right from their homesteads, a facility which even the city dwellers cannot get always.

Fig. 10. Some screenshots of the mobile phone interface

This was very useful for women, children, the elderly and the infirm. Some screenshots of the interface are shown in Fig. 10. Through a small funding from the Edward M Kennedy Centre in Bangladesh, we put the mobile phone system on field trial for 4 months in four rural areas through teams of two female roving operators each. They went from door to door in the villages. However, since most of the houses in the villages have tin walls and tin roofs, the mobile signals were poor indoors. Therefore, most of the consultations were carried out outside the house as shown in Fig. 11.

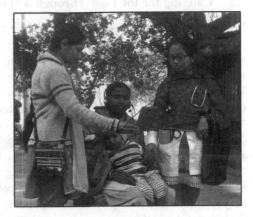

Fig. 11. Roving telemedicine operators providing consultation of city doctors to a village woman at her doorstep.

We also embarked upon developing a portable online diagnostic device with multiple sensors and measurement devices. All the data will be acquired by an onboard microcontroller and the digital data will be sent to a mobile smartphone through a Wi-fi link, for further data transfer over the internet. The work is yet to be completed. Figure 12 shows the initial prototype of the motherboard with 8 slots for 8 measuring devices including temperature, ECG, lungs ventilation monitor, etc. The box shown on the left will hold the whole device, to be carried by the roving telemedicine operators.

Fig. 12. Initial prototype of the motherboard for a multi sensor and measurement unit for a portable telemedicine device, to be fitted inside the box shown on the left.

2.8 Catering for the Poor Through a 'Trust' Based System

We also realized that there are people in the villages who do not have enough cash to pay for medicines even if they get a 'free' consultation, because of which they do not seek treatment at all, leaving themselves at the mercy of nature. We wanted that nobody should be left out of the services, so we organised a poor fund, both centrally and locally, so that people with true need may be given support to cover consultation and medicine costs up to a certain ceiling. To minimize misuse of such funds we tried a 'trust-based system' through invoking the self-esteem and self-responsibility among all people involved in the whole programme, patients, operators, entrepreneurs, doctors, and administrators. However, this trust-based system needs to be integrated with a campaign based on a philosophy of 'serving others' as a purpose of life rather than serving self-interests only. Through such a policy and effort, the management became very simple, not requiring continuous policing that we find in all activities around us in the present day. Of course, we believed that such a policy will only succeed if there were honesty and sincerity in the leadership, which we tried to maintain. However, for the rare cases of misuse of the trust, one needs to be vigilant, to identify and to take necessary steps sensibly and logically if something of this nature happens. In fact, through the five years of deployment of this scheme, such undesirable situations never occurred.

2.9 Connectivity and Power

We took advantage of the available mobile phone internet connectivity. For video consultation with doctors, a 3G mobile network is needed. Most regions of Bangladesh has good coverage of the 3G network although there are some places with 2G network still now. Again, in some places with 3G, the speed fluctuates, video consultation gets interrupted. Our solution was initially limited to areas with 3G connectivity hoping that within a few years, when our telemedicine system proliferates, 3G will be available in most places. Already 4G mobile phone connectivity is available in some cities and towns. In developing the system, we had to keep the drop in speed in mind.

In some areas where the mobile phone signal flickers, one may use a locally made booster fixed on top of a bamboo pole to get a better signal. Again, where mobile phone network is not available, radiolink may be used, although requiring much higher cost. However, so far in the 40 or more rural areas where we are providing service, such extra infrastructure was not needed.

One also needs electrical power for a laptop and a printer. Again initially in all the centres where we are providing service, electrical power is available. During power interruptions, which is frequent in many places, a Laptop usually provides backup for a few hours. Printing of prescriptions may be done later when power resumes. Fortunately, mobile phone networks have power backups, so the network is available even when the grid electricity fails. Alternatively, the centres may use battery powered ac sources (called UPS or IPS) for continued service. However, we kept the option open for centres to use alternative sources of power like diesel generators or solar PV if these can be afforded.

2.10   How Would the Doctors Operate?

In many telemedicine systems around the world, the organisers have call centres where salaried doctors work in shifts full time. We realized that in Bangladesh situation, work in a telemedicine facility will not give doctors much credit for their careers. So it will not be possible to retain full-time doctors initially. Besides, we would not have so many patients to engage full-time doctors in the beginning. Therefore, we designed a system where a doctor can provide consultation from his or her own place, in between his or her other work engagements, using a PC or a mobile smartphone. The idea was that if we have a large pool of doctors in this way, the patients will not have to wait for long. Eventually, the software will be developed to manage this model efficiently, but we are managing this scheme through a semi-manual system at present, and it has not caused much of a problem so far.

2.11   Feedback Study

Some small scale studies were carried out to assess the ease of use and satisfaction of our telemedicine system by the doctors and operators. Studies were also carried out on patients to assess their satisfaction and comparative advantages in terms of time, cost and visit, against existing facilities they have.

3   Results

We started a field trial of our PC based telemedicine system in a district of Bangladesh in collaboration with a small NGO, using our joint resources, in 2013 at 5 rural centres. Here we used our early version of the software. The operators were provided with the online stethoscope and ECG, both developed by us as mentioned before, and the doctors with good quality headphones. At that time we had only one full-time doctor giving consultation. Towards the end of this period, we were fortunate to get a reasonable funding from 'Access to Information (a2i)' project of the Bangladesh Government, which was a programme supported by USAID and UNDP. This trial proved a success, giving more than 1,500 consultations during this period.

However, with the experience obtained we revised the software fully and obtained permission from the Government to deploy the service throughout Bangladesh from our department of Biomedical Physics & Technology. We also obtained permission from the University authority to use the name, 'Dhaka University Telemedicine Programme (DUTP)' and to use the University logo. With fresh vigour we started deploying the system throughout Bangladesh in November 2015. We advertised in national newspapers to seek for entrepreneurs to set up telemedicine centres at their own locality, particularly in the rural areas. We trained their operators at the University for three days only, which appeared to be adequate. At present, more than 40 rural centres are providing this service and 16 doctors are on the roll, mostly general practitioners (GP), who provide consultation following their own time schedule. One programme co-ordinator works under the team leader to organize and manage all the entrepreneurs, operators and doctors, and to oversee the quality of service.

From November 2015 till 31 January 2019, the number of consultations provided is more than 17,000, making the total number of consultation given from the beginning in 2013 to more than 18,500. The monthly number of patients taking consultation through our system is increasing steadily. The percentage of patients coming back for treatment is about 10% which shows that the people are satisfied with the service. More than 75% of the patients served are women, children and elderly, many of whom would not have consulted a doctor had our service not been available. This proves that our telemedicine technology and implementation modality has achieved its expected function.

As mentioned before, we had a field trial of a mobile phone-based telemedicine in the field, to provide doctors' consultations right at the doorsteps of the rural population. The above figure for women, children and elderly rose to 95% and shows the need and efficacy of this version [10].

People in the rural areas are not used to get treatment for early stages of illness and are not ready to pay for doctor's consultation. We are trying to change this mindset through the local version of the idiom, 'A stitch in time saves nine'.

4   Discussion

Most telemedicine solutions available from the advanced countries target tertiary care; specialised online diagnostic equipment and doctors or highly trained paramedics being available at patient-end. On the other hand, in a low resource country, such qualified manpower is not available at the patient end in the rural areas as mentioned above. Besides, the imported specialised online diagnostic equipment are very expensive, and cannot be afforded by low resource countries, where such equipment are needed in large numbers. Furthermore, due to warm and humid weather and erratic electrical power supplies with abnormal high and low voltages occurring, such equipment become out of order very quickly, even within months of installation. It is a common experience that if an imported equipment becomes out of order it cannot be repaired economically in a low resource country. Lack of technical expertise and spares are two major causes. Combined with this is the technology 'secrecy' maintained by most manufacturers, which has become aggravated through the introduction of microcontroller based equipment in the recent times, where nothing can be done if one does not have access to the software programme, irrespective of the level of technical expertise available. Therefore, the out-of-order equipment has to be simply thrown away, stopping the service altogether for prolonged periods of time till adequate budget becomes available for a replacement. Sometimes, it never happens and the service remains suspended for indefinite periods.

Therefore, our attempts at indigenous development of an internet-based telemedicine system are very timely and appropriate, particularly for primary and secondary healthcare. As mentioned before, if the people get good primary and secondary care, the requirement for tertiary care will be much reduced, saving resources of both the nation and the individual families besides saving many people from lifelong sufferings or disabilities, even untimely death.

In addition to standard video consultation, we have developed some integrated online diagnostic devices through which the condition of a patient is better assessed by a doctor instantly. Being indigenously developed, these devices are affordable, repairable locally at low cost and have long usable life. We not only developed necessary technology, but we also implemented the solution in the field as well using innovative ideas and are continually improving the system, both in software and hardware and in deployment modality, using the feedback received. Thus the system has become very appropriate and robust for a country like Bangladesh and has received satisfactory appreciation of all stakeholders – patients, operators, doctors, and administrators.

We took advantage of the available mobile phone internet connectivity and our mode of deployment is through rural entrepreneurs who establish local telemedicine centres where patients come and consult a doctor paying fees, targeting self-sustainability.

The operator would choose from a pool of doctors who are available at any given time. The doctors can be at home, office or on travel. Operators need not be paramedics, nor need extensive training. Chosen to have computer expertise, a few days training in using both the software and the diagnostic devices was adequate. All data are archived in cloud storage for subsequent referencing. Innovation was everywhere.

The system is being continuously enhanced through practical feedback from users, which has made it very satisfactory. This was also the outcome of a random survey of the doctors and rural telemedicine operators and patients.

Already BRAC, one of the largest global NGOs originating from Bangladesh joined our Telemedicine programme on an experimental basis. We will soon discuss with them how we can expand the service to cover more people in the rural areas of Bangladesh and other low resource countries. We are also planning to organize body tissue collection for pathological investigation at the telemedicine centres through arrangements with pathological centres in the neighbourhood. Again, to provide investigation by remote specialists, digital microscopic images will be sent through the internet. For this, we have already converted microscopes using webcams. We also plan to add low-cost commercial ultrasound scanners to the system.

If an ailment is treated early through a qualified doctor in a better way through an improved telemedicine system with integral diagnostic devices, this can save many patients from later complications, even death or disabilities. 'A stitch in time saves nine' is the slogan of our indigenous telemedicine technology, targeting primary and secondary healthcare in rural areas of low resource countries where there are no doctors. Besides, this will also reduce the misuse of steroids and antibiotics, the latter causing a global scare. We are not patenting our innovations and would disseminate technology to qualified people in all low resource countries of the world so that they can provide such affordable and sustainable healthcare at low cost.

Acknowledgments. (i) International Science Programme (ISP), Uppsala University, Sweden for overall funding of the research of the Department of Biomedical Physics & Technology, (ii) Access to Information (a2i) of Bangladesh Government (supported by UNDP and USAID) for funding support during field trial and later promotion, (iii) Information Society Innovation Fund (ISIF) -Asia, a funding window of Asia Pacific Network Information Centre (APNIC), Australia, for development of the mobile smartphone version including the portable diagnostic unit, (iv) Edward M Kennedy (EMK) Centre, Dhaka, for field trial of the mobile phone version of the telemedicine system, (v) Farm Fresh Dairy for part funding of the development of the online diagnostic devices, (vi) Beximco Pharma and (vii) several individual donors for funding towards implementation of the telemedicine programme, and (viii) Relevant Science & Technology Society (RSTS), Bangladesh for organizing the poor fund.

References

1. https://data.worldbank.org/indicator/SP.RUR.TOTL.ZS?locations=BD
2. https://thefinancialexpress.com.bd/health/bangladesh-has-one-doctor-for-every-1847-people-1519053209
3. http://www.kabirhat.com/village/
4. http://app.dghs.gov.bd/inst_info/other/uhc.php
5. http://www.theindependentbd.com/printversion/details/169590
6. Rashid, B., Shannon, G.A.: History of Telemedicine: Evolution, Context, and Transformation. Mary Ann Liebert Inc., New Rochelle (2009)
7. Rabbani, K.S., Amin, A.A., Abir, A.R., Bodiuzzaman, A.K.M., Khan, A.I., Tarafdar, M.Z.: A rural health monitor with telemedicine. In: Galigeke, R.R., et al. (eds.) Biomedical Engineering, pp. 77–82. Narosa Publishing House, New Delhi (2011)
8. Rabbani, K.S., Raihan Abir, A., Bodiuzzaman, A.K.M.: Design and development of a low cost personal computer based ECG monitor. Bangladesh J Med Phys **4**, 115–125 (2011)
9. Tarafdar, Z.: Software development for a secure telemedicine system for slow internet connectivity, Ph.D. thesis, Department of Biomedical Physics & Technology, University of Dhaka, Dhaka (2018)
10. Md. Abu Sufian, S.: System analysis of center based & doorstep based telemedicine systems including design & implementation of the latter, MS thesis, Department of Biomedical Physics & Technology, University of Dhaka, Dhaka (2017)

Differences in Relationships and Risk Factors Associated with Hypertension, Diabetes, and Proteinuria Among Urban and Rural Adults in Bangladesh

-Findings from Portable Health Clinic Research Project 2013–2018-

Fumihiko Yokota[1]([⊠]) and Ashir Ahmed[2]

[1] Institute of Decision Science for Sustainable Society, Kyushu University,
Fukuoka, Japan
fumihiko.yokota.2011@gmail.com
[2] Graduate School of Information Science and Electrical Engineering,
Kyushu University, Fukuoka, Japan

Abstract. Objective: The aim of this study was to compare the relationships and risk factors with hypertension, diabetes, and proteinuria between urban office workers at Dhaka city and rural community residents at Bheramara sub-district who participated in a mobile health check-up service called portable health clinic (PHC).

Methods: Data were collected from 271 urban office workers at Dhaka city in 2018 and 2,890 rural community residents at Bheramara sub-district between 2013 and 2016, who agreed to participate in the PHC. Data included basic socio-demographic and health check-up information. Descriptive statistics were conducted to compare the relationships with three main outcome variables (hypertension, diabetes, and proteinuria) and independent variables (ex, age, sex, pulse rates, and body mass index (BMI)).

Results: The percentage of participants who were overweight or obese was higher among urban participants (51%) than rural participants (35%), whereas in rural participants, the percentage of being underweight was higher (11%) than in urban participants (0.4%). Among participants who had proteinuria, 60% in urban and 34% in rural participants had hypertension and 10% in urban and 14% in rural and had diabetes. Among those who had diabetes, 26% in urban and 45% in rural participants had hypertension and 3% in urban and 55% in rural participants had proteinuria. Among participants who had hypertension, 9% in urban and 37% in rural participants had proteinuria 12% in both urban and rural participants had diabetes.

Conclusions: Hypertension, diabetes, and proteinuria were highly co-existed particularly among rural participants. Obesity is more prevalent among urban participants. PHC services is important for screening a large number of unaware and undiagnosed diabetic, hypertensive, and proteinuria patients both in rural and urban Bangladesh.

© Springer Nature Switzerland AG 2019
C. Stephanidis (Ed.): HCII 2019, LNCS 11786, pp. 599–610, 2019.
https://doi.org/10.1007/978-3-030-30033-3_46

Keywords: Diabetes · Hypertension · Proteinuria · Complications · Comorbidities · Portable health clinic

1 Introduction

Hypertension, diabetes, and proteinuria have enormous public health significance in both developed and developing countries because these conditions are associated with increased risks of developing complications, such as cardiovascular disease (CVD) and chronic kidney disease [1–5]. In Bangladesh, such non-communicable diseases (NCD) account for nearly 60% of all deaths [6, 7]. According to a recent report from the World Health Organization (WHO), Bangladesh has a high burden of hypertension among the adult population, with an estimated prevalence of 24% [8]. A meta-analysis of diabetic studies conducted in Bangladesh estimated that the prevalence of diabetes among adults had more than doubled, from 4% in 1995–2000 to 9% in 2006–2010 [1], and projected to 13% by 2030 [9]. Under such conditions, both diabetes and hypertension are known to be risk factors for proteinuria [10], which is an early marker of kidney damage and a manifestation of chronic kidney disease [11, 12]. In addition, proteinuria is known to be a common complication of both hypertension and diabetes [4, 8, 10, 13]. Despite a need for the prevention of hypertension, diabetes, and proteinuria in Bangladesh, few studies have compared the levels of the co-existence of these diseases both at urban and rural areas in Bangladesh. The relationships among hypertension, diabetes, and proteinuria and their risk factors have previously been well documented worldwide and also prevalence of diabetes, hypertension and proteinuria in Bangladesh was previously reported [10]. However few studies has investigated the relationships for these three diseases jointly in a combined approach both in urban and rural Bangladesh. In addition, several previous studies found geographical differences in the relationships and factors associated with proteinuria, diabetes, and hypertension [12, 14, 15]. It will be meaningful to compare the differences in relationship among these diseases between urban and rural areas in Bangladesh in order to find any potential differences of factors associated with these three diseases comparing with other different areas of Bangladesh or other countries.

In Bangladesh, a mobile health check-up system called "portable health clinic" (PHC) was introduced in Bangladesh. PHC is an e-health service delivery system that includes a set of medical sensor devices in a briefcase to allow mobile health check-up and tele-medicine services using Skype in remote rural areas [16–19] (Fig. 1). This PHC service, as a role of early detection of NCD, has been implemented by Grameen Communications in Bangladesh since 2010, and it had reached nearly 35,000 people at 32 locations at the beginning of 2017 [20]. Both in rural and urban areas of Bangladesh, the PHC service has been implemented by healthcare entrepreneurs as a social business for the sustainable provision NCD prevention services.

The aim of this study was to compare the relationships among hypertension, diabetes, and proteinuria and their risk factors who participated in PHC services in urban Dhaka and rural sub-district in Bangladesh.

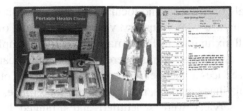

Fig. 1. Portable health clinic box, healthcare entrepreneur, and health check-up result

2   Methods

2.1   Urban Data Source and Data Collection Procedures in Dhaka City

Urban data were collected from all office workers who agreed to participate in PHC health check-up services in August 2018 in Grameen Compound, Dhaka, Bangladesh. In Grameen Compound, there are several different offices such as Grameen Banks, Grameen Communications, other non-government organizations and private companies with more than 500 workers. Participants were office workers from these organizations aged 35 years or older who voluntary visited at PHC service point which were set at the Grameen Communication building within the compound. Prior to the implementation of PHC services, awareness events and prior notification to each office were made to inform about availabilities of PHC services. These PHC services were scheduled and arranged by project staff from Grameen Communications. Healthcare workers and other staff from Grameen Communications provided PHC services and survey interviews in Bangla. Participant basic socio-demographic, behavioral and health related information were collected using a standardized questionnaires. During the PHC health check-up, the following anthropometric and clinical data were measured or tested; (1) height, (2) weight, (3) hip circumference, (4) waist circumference, (5) body temperature, (6) systolic blood pressure, (7) diastolic blood pressure, (8) blood glucose, (9) blood hemoglobin, (10) urinary glucose, (11) urinary protein, (12) urinary urobilinogen, (13) urinary pH, (14) pulse rate, and (15) blood cholesterol. The result of each health check-up test was ranked into one of four different color-coded risk levels as follows: green (healthy), yellow (caution), orange (affected), and red (emergent). Detailed methodologies including privacy and security of collecting patient's personal health data have been described elsewhere [16, 17, 19].

2.2   Rural Data Source and Data Collection Procedures at Bheramara Sub-district

Rural data were collected from all community residents who agreed to participate in PHC health check-up services between September 2013 and April 2016 in Bheramara sub-district. According to the 2011 Bangladesh census, the Bheramara sub-district has a population of 208,000 in six unions [21]. Bheramara was chosen because of higher prevalence of proteinuria than other regions of Bangladesh [16], scares of previous studies at Western rural areas of Bangladesh, and established collaborative research partnerships with local governments and local communities of Bheramara. Participants were individuals of any age who voluntary visited at least one of eight PHC service points that covered all six unions in Bheramara. Prior to the implementation of PHC services, community awareness events were held in Bheramara to inform about availabilities of PHC services at these eight services points. Each of eight service points were located near rural village markets, near the counselor's office, and near elementary schools. These PHC services were scheduled and arranged by project staff from Grameen Communications. Healthcare entrepreneurs were locally recruited and trained as social entrepreneurs by Grameen Communications to provide PHC services in Bangla once every two weeks. Each health check-up service had a nominal fee. For example, a blood pressure test was 10 Taka and a blood glucose test was 30 Taka. Most participants did not undergo all health check-up tests but selected the tests according to their requirements. Participant basic demographic information, such as age, sex, and location, was collected using a standardized registration sheet. Procedures of PHC health check-up were the same as those conducted for urban participants.

2.3 Dependent and Independent Variables and Measurements

The main outcome variables were hypertension, diabetes, and proteinuria. Hypertension was defined as a systolic blood pressure more than 140 mmHg or a diastolic blood pressure more than 90 mmHg. Based on the definition, the hypertension variable was dichotomously coded as "yes" or "no." Blood pressure was measured using an A&D UA-772PBT. This device can measure not only blood pressure but also pulse rate and arrhythmia. Diabetes was defined as a blood glucose level more than 200 mg/dL at the time of the PHC health check-up. This definition was based on WHO criteria, and diabetes was classified dichotomously as "yes" or "no." A casual blood glucose level was measured, as the time from the participant's last meal was not asked. Diabetes was measured using the Medisafe Fit (Terumo, Tokyo, Japan). A drop of blood was taken from each participant's middle fingertip. Proteinuria was defined as a protein level of more than or equal to 30 mg/dL in urine. It was measured using the dipstick method with Urine Test Stripes Uric 3 V, which provides a color scale that indicates five levels of protein as follows: absent (<10 mg/dL), trace (10–20 mg/dL), 1 + (≥ 30 mg/dL), 2 + (>100 mg/dL), and 3 + (>500 mg/dL). Based on the definition, proteinuria was binary classified as "yes" or "no." The independent variables were overweight or obesity and other socio-behavioral variables. The WHO criteria were used to define all variables. Overweight and obesity were defined as body mass index (BMI) values of more than 25 and 30 kg/m^2, respectively.

2.4 Data Analysis

Bivariate analysis was performed to describe the inter-relationships among hypertension, diabetes, and proteinuria. Pearson's chi-square test (bivariate analysis) was performed to describe the unadjusted association between dependent and independent/control categorical variables. All statistical analyses were performed using SPSS version 21 (IBM Corp., Armonk, NY). A P-value < 0.05 was considered significant.

3 Results

A total of 271 office workers from urban Dhaka Grameen Compound participated in PHC health check-up services and survey questionnaire during the study period. In contrast, a total of 2890 rural individuals from Bheramara sub-district participated in PHC health check-up services during the study period. Among these individuals, those younger than 15 years (19 cases) and those who had missing or inconsistent data (4 cases) were excluded from the analysis. Thus, the total sample size for analysis was 2867 (Supplement Figure). The most popular health check-up item selected by the participants was blood glucose test for diabetes (n = 2539), followed by blood pressure for hypertension (n = 2411) and pulse rate (n = 2396) (Supplement Figure). Only 18.8% (n = 539) and 15.3% (n = 440) of the participants underwent measurement for height/weight and urinary protein, respectively.

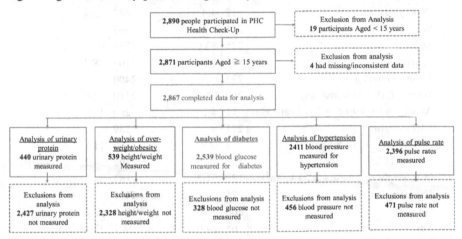

Supplemental Figure: Flow diagram showing rural participant exclusion and the final sample size from Bheramara sub-district

The mean age of urban participants was 50 years with the range between 34 and 77 years old, whereas the mean age of rural participants was 44 years with the wider rage between 15 and 95 years old. In urban participant, over 80% were male compared to 61% male among rural participants. An abnormal pulse rate was noted in 4% of the urban and 12% of rural participants. More than half of the urban participants (51%) were overweight or obese, compared to only 35% in the rural participants. In addition, 11% of the rural participants were underweight while only 0.4% of the urban participants were underweight. The percentages of urban participants who had hypertension, diabetes, and proteinuria were 24%, 11%, and 4%, respectively, whereas the percentages of rural participants who had hypertension, diabetes, and proteinuria were 37%, 18%, and 32%, respectively (Table 1).

Table 1. Socio-demographic characteristics and health status among individuals who partici-pated in the portable health check-up at Urban (Grameen Complex Dhaka city) and Rural (Bheramara sub-district), Bangladesh

Items	Urban (Dhaka city)		Rural (Bheramara sub-district)	
	N	%	N	%
Age (years)	271	Mean = 49.6 Range = 34–77	2867	Mean = 44.1 Range = 15–95
Age groups 1	271		2867	
15–29 years	0	0	424	14.8
30–39 years	35	12.9	739	25.8
40–49 years	78	28.8	671	23.4
50–59 years	146	53.9	591	20.6
≥ 60 years	12	4.4	442	15.4
Sex	271		2867	
Male	225	83.0	1758	61.3
Female	46	17.0	1109	38.7
Pulse rate category	271		2400	
Normal (50–100 beats/min)	260	95.9	2110	87.9
Abnormal (≤ 49 or ≥ 101 beats/min)	11	4.1	290	12.1
BMI category	271		539	
Underweight (<18.5 kg/m^2)	1	0.4	60	11.1
Normal (18.5–25 kg/m^2)	131	48.3	292	54.2
Overweight or Obese (≥ 25 kg/m^2)	139	51.3	187	34.7
Hypertension	271		2411	
No	206	76.0	1510	62.6
Yes	65	24.0	901	37.4
Type II Diabetes	271		2539	
No	240	88.6	2091	82.4
Yes (Blood Glucose => 200 mg/dl)	31	11.4	448	17.6
Urinary Protein test	270		440	
Negative (−) < 14 mg/dL	247	91.5	200	45.5
Trace (−/+) 15–29 mg/dL	13	4.8	101	23.0
Positive (+1) 30–99 mg/dL	9	3.3	121	27.5
Positive (+2 or +3) ≥ 100 gm/dL	1	0.4	18	4.1

Table 2a presents the unadjusted associations of independent variables with hypertension, diabetes, and proteinuria among urban participants. Urban participants with obese (BMI => 25) had significantly higher percentage of having diabetes (15%) than those without obese (8%) (P < 0.039). In addition, urban participants with obese

(BMI => 25) had significantly higher percentage of having proteinuria (7%) than those without obese (1%) (P < 0.012). The percentage of urban participants who had hypertension was significantly higher among those who had proteinuria (60%) than those who did not have proteinuria (23%) (P < 0.015).

Table 2a. Unadjusted association of independent variables with hypertension, diabetes, and proteinuria among office workers at urban Dhaka city, Bangladesh

Item	Hypertension (N=271)			Diabetes (N=271)			Proteinuria (N=271)		
	n/N	%	P for Diff.	n/N	%	P for Diff.	n/N	%	P for Diff.
Age groups 2	N		0.228			0.210			0.660
30–39 years	6/35	17.1		1/35	2.9		2/35	5.7	
40–59 years	58/224	25.9		28/224	12.5		8/224	3.6	
≥60 years	1/12	8.3		2/12	16.7		0/11	0	
Age groups 3	N=271		0.214			0.065			0.380
30–39 years	6/35	17.1		1/35	2.9		2/35	5.7	
≥40 years	59/236	25.0		30/236	12.7		8/235	3.4	
Sex			0.169			0.364			0.519
Female	8/46	17.4		4/46	8.7		2/45	4.4	
Male	57/225	25.3		27/225	12.0		8/225	3.6	
Pulse rate category			0.095			0.635			0.057
Normal	60/260	23.1		30/260	11.5		8/259	3.1	
Abnormal	5/11	45.5		1/11	9.1		2/11	18.2	
Obese			0.270			0.039			0.012
25<	29/132	22.0		10/132	7.6		1/131	0.8	
25=>	36/139	25.9		21/139	15.1		9/139	6.5	
Hypertension						0.476			0.015
No				23/206	11.2		4/205	2.0	
Yes				8/65	12.3		6/65	9.2	
Type II Diabetes			0.476						0.678
No	57/240	23.8					9/239	3.8	
Yes =>200mg/dl	8/31	25.8					1/31	3.2	
Urinary Protein			0.015			0.678			
No (- & -+)	59/260	22.7		30/260	11.5				
Not include -+	6/10	60.0		1/11	10.0				

Table 2b presents the unadjusted associations of independent variables with hypertension, diabetes, and proteinuria among rural participants. Both hypertension and diabetes were significantly associated with age group (P < 0.001). The percentage of participants with hypertension was significantly higher among those with overweight or obesity (47%) than among those without overweight or obesity (24%) (P < 0.001), among those with diabetes (49%) than among those without diabetes (35%) (P < 0.001), and among those with proteinuria (35%) than among those without proteinuria (25%) (P = 0.026). The percentage of participants with diabetes was significantly higher among those with hypertension (23%) than among those without hypertension (14%) (P < 0.001) and among those with proteinuria (13%) than among those without proteinuria (5%) (P < 0.004). The percentage of participants with proteinuria was significantly higher among those with diabetes (55%) than among those without diabetes (29%) (P < 0.004) and among those with hypertension (38%) than among those without hypertension (27%) (P < 0.026).

Table 2b. Unadjusted association of independent variables with hypertension, diabetes, and proteinuria among voluntary community participants at Bheramara sub-district in rural Bangladesh

Items	Hypertension (N = 2,411)			Diabetes (N = 2,539)			Proteinuria (N = 440)		
	n/N	%	P for Diff.	n/N	%	P for Diff.	n/N	%	P for Diff.
Sex	N = 2411		0.34	N = 2539		0.015	N = 440		0.081
Male	541/1462	37.0		257/1574	16.3		73/254	28.7	
Female	360/949	37.9		191/965	19.8		66/186	35.5	
Age groups	N = 2411		<0.001	N = 2539		<0.001	N = 440		0.86
15–39 years	264/993	26.6		103/1013	10.2		61/190	32.1	
40–49 years	231/568	40.7		116/602	19.3		30/106	28.3	
50–59 years	241/505	47.7		130/531	24.5		24/72	33.3	
≥60 years	165/345	47.8		99/393	25.2		24/72	33.3	
Pulse rate	N = 2388		<0.001	N = 2139		0.12	N = 408		0.033
Normal	756/2099	36.0		322/1892	17.0		101/351	28.8	
Abnormal	140/289	48.4		50/247	20.2		24/57	42.1	
Overweight/obesity	N = 536		<0.001	N = 490		0.48	N = 385		0.50
No	83/350	23.7		34/320	10.6		78/264	29.5	
Yes	87/186	46.8		19/170	11.2		35/121	28.9	
Hypertension	-	-	-	N = 2154		<0.001	N = 412		0.026
No	-	-	-	191/1344	14.2		81/298	27.2	
Yes	-	-	-	182/810	22.5		43/114	37.7	
Diabetes	N = 2154		<0.001	-	-	-	N = 407		0.004
No	628/1781	35.3		-	-	-	108/378	28.6	
Yes	182/373	48.8		-	-	-	16/29	55.2	
Proteinuria	N = 412		0.026	N = 407		0.004	-	-	-
No	71/288	24.7		13/283	4.6		-	-	-
Yes	43/124	34.7		16/124	12.9		-	-	-

Among participants who had proteinuria, 60% in urban and 34% in rural participants had hypertension and 10% in urban and 14% in rural and had diabetes. Among those who had diabetes, 26% in urban and 45% in rural participants had hypertension and 3% in urban and 55% in rural participants had proteinuria. Among participants who had hypertension, 9% in urban and 37% in rural participants had proteinuria and 12% in both urban and rural participants had diabetes (Fig. 2).

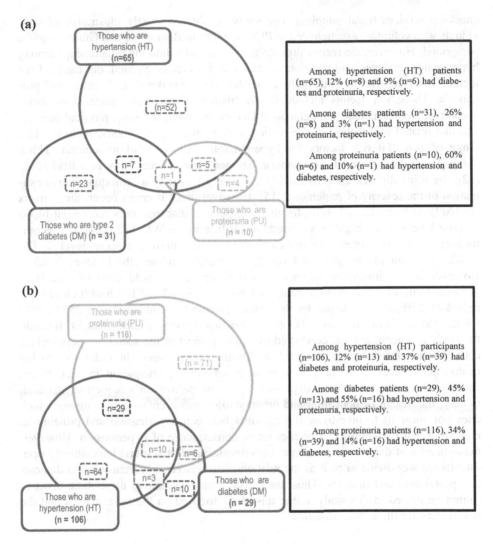

Fig. 2 (a) Numbers of participants who had complications of proteinuria, hypertension, and diabetes among urban participants at Dhaka city, Bangladesh (n = 271). (b) Numbers of participants who had complications of proteinuria, hypertension, and diabetes among rural participants at Bheramara sub-district, Bangladesh (n = 389: those who received urine test, blood pressure test, and blood glucose test)

4 Limitations of the Study

This study has some limitations. First, the study's urban and rural samples from PHC health check-ups are unlikely to be representative of all adults in Bheramara sub-district (Rural) and Dhaka (Urban) office workers. Our participants are likely to be unhealthy individuals who were willing to participate in (urban samples) or paid for PHC health check-up services (rural samples). The study results are strictly illustrative of individuals who voluntarily participated in PHC services in Bheramara and Grameen office compound. However, the results provide general insights into the relationships among hypertension, diabetes, and proteinuria and their risk factors. Second, our data did not include other key factors potentially associated with hypertension, diabetes, and proteinuria. These key factors include family history of diabetes/hypertension, socioeconomic, environmental, and behavioral factors including smoking, physical activity, and diet-related information of the participants. Further studies should include wider range of potential risk factors for hypertension, diabetes, and proteinuria. Third, although the dipstick test for proteinuria has been used successfully in a field study [22], the urine dipstick analysis used in this study was only a semi-quantitative estimation of the severity of proteinuria [15]. However, even if errors occur, these errors are likely to be random. Fourth, for the diagnosis of diabetes, only the casual blood glucose level (≥ 200 mg/dL) was used. According to the WHO [23, 24], the recommended diagnostic criteria for diabetes are a fasting plasma glucose level ≥ 126 mg/dL, a 2-hour plasma glucose level ≥ 200 mg/dL, and an HbA1c level $\geq 6.5\%$. However, it was difficult to implement these criteria in our field study of rural Bangladesh. Fifth, of the 2890 rural samples who participated in PHC health check-ups, only 440 (15%) decided to pay for the urinary protein test compared with 2539 (88%) for the blood glucose test and 2411 (83%) for blood pressure measurement. Because the study in Bheramara was conducted as a pilot project of the social business service delivery model for locally recruited healthcare entrepreneurs in order to provide healthcare services sustainably in a rural community, participation in each health check-up item was completely dependent upon the participant's request or demand. Finally, the design of both rural and urban studies was a cross-section survey which does not allow us to investigate the causality between hypertension and proteinuria, indicating that proteinuria can be a cause or consequence of hypertension. However, the dynamics of diabetes in relation to hypertension and proteinuria have already been established worldwide as well as the relationships between hypertension and diabetes and proteinuria and diabetes. Thus, the causal pathways among these three diseases cannot be misled in this study, rather this study focused on the relationships and the risk factors for these three diseases.

5   Conclusions

Despite these limitations, this study provided insight into diabetic complications with proteinuria and/or hypertension. Hypertension, diabetes, and proteinuria were highly co-existed particularly among rural participants. Obesity is more prevalent among urban participants. PHC health check-up services in rural and urban Bangladesh was found to be effective to screen a large number of unaware and undiagnosed diabetic, hypertensive, and proteinuria patients at the early disease stage before the development of complications/comorbidities. The study also found other key risk factors for hypertension, such as older age (≥ 40 years), overweight/obesity, and abnormal pulse rate. For the prevention of complications/comorbidities in NCD, a combined set of health check-up services using PHC should be promoted, particularly for those older than 40 years of age and those having hypertension, diabetes, or proteinuria particularly in rural Bangladesh. Future studies on the risk factors of proteinuria, diabetes, and hypertension in Bangladesh should consider other potential factors including socio-economic factors, health-related behavioral factors, and environmental factors in other geographic areas of Bangladesh.

Acknowledgement. This research project was supported by Toyota Motors, Grameen Communications, Bangladesh, and Kyushu University, Japan. I would like to thank all who supported and participated in the project. Particular thanks are owed to Dr. Naoki Nakashima, Dr. Rafiqul Islam, Dr. Mriko Nishikitani, Dr. Kimiyo Kikuchi, Dr. Yasunobu Nohara, Dr. Rieko Izukura, Ms. Nazneen Sultana, Mr. Md. Rajib Chowdhury, Mr. Kazi Mozaher Hossein, Mr. Mehdi Hasan, and Ms. Masuda Begum Sampa who provided valuable comments and assistance. This study is also supported by the Future Earth Research Fund, grant number 18-161009264; and the Kyushu University QR Program, grant number 30105.

Conflict of Interest. The authors report no conflicts of interest.

Ethics and Consent. Data collection from each participant was performed in accordance with the Declaration of Helsinki. The study was approved by the ethics committee at the Kyushu University Institutional Review Board (#24-048). Verbal informed consent was obtained from all participants who received detailed explanation about the study purposes by the field research assistants.

References

1. Saquib, N., Saquib, J., Ahmed, T., Khanam, M.A., Cullen, M.R.: Cardiovascular diseases and type 2 diabetes in Bangladesh: a systematic review and meta-analysis of studies between 1995-2010. BMC Publ. Health **12**, 434 (2012)
2. Pesola, G.R., et al.: Dipstick Proteinuria as a predictor of all-cause and cardiovascular disease mortality in Bangladesh: a prospective cohort study. Prev. Med. **78**, 72–77 (2015)
3. Modesti, P.A., et al.: Relationship between hypertension, diabetes, and proteinuria in rural and urban households in Yemen. J. Hum. Hypertension. **27**, 572–579 (2013)
4. Anupama, Y.J., Hegde, S.N., Uma, G., Patil, M.: Hypertension is an important risk determinant for chronic kidney disease: results from a cross-sectional, observational study from a rural population in South India. J. Hum. Hypertension **31**(5), 369–370 (2017)
5. Farag, Y.M.K., et al.: Burden and predictors of hypertension in India: results of SEEK (Screening and Early Evaluation of Kidney Disease) study. BMC Nephrol. **15**, 42 (2014)
6. WHO. Diabetes Country Profiles, Bangladesh (2016). http://www.who.int/diabetes/country-profiles/bgd_en.pdf?ua=1. Accessed 17 Aug 2019
7. WHO. Bangladesh Country Profile: Noncommunicable Disease (NCD) (2018). http://www.who.int/nmh/countries/bgd_en.pdf. Accessed 17 Aug 2019
8. Moniruzzaman, M., Taleb, A., Rahman, S., Acharyya, A., Islam, F.A., Ahmed, S.M.A.M., Zaman, M.M.: Prevalence of hypertension among the Bangladeshi adult population: a meta-analysis. Reg. Health Forum World Health Organ. Bangladesh **17**(1) (2013)
9. International Diabetes Federation. IDF Diabetes Atlas. 6th edition (2013). ISBN: 2-930229-85-3
10. Hasan, M.J., et al.: Prevalence of diabetes mellitus, hypertension and proteinuria in a rural area of Bangladesh. Commun. Based Med. J. **1**(2), 8–13 (2012)

11. Iseki, K., Ikemiya, Y., Iseki, C., Takishita, S.: Proteinuria and the risk of developing end-stage renal disease. Kidney Int. **63**(4), 1468–1474 (2003)
12. Jafar, T.H., Chaturvedi, N., Gul, A., Khan, A.Q., Schmid, C.H., Levey, A.S.: Ethnic differences and determinants of proteinuria among South Asian subgroups in Pakistan. Kidney Int. **64**, 1437–1444 (2003)
13. Gallieni, M., Ene-Iordache, B., Aiello, A., Tucci, B., et al.: Hypertension and kidney function in an adult population of West Bengal, India: role of body weight, waist circumference, proteinuria and rural are living. Nephrology **18**(12), 798–807 (2013)
14. Spanakis, E.K., Golden, S.H.: Race/ethnic difference in diabetes and diabetic complications. Curr. Diab. Rep. **13**(6), 814–823 (2013)
15. Ramirez, S.P., Mcclellan, W., Port, F.K., Hsu, S.I.: Risk factors for proteinuria in a large, multiracial, Southeast Asian population. J. Am. Soc. Nephrol. **13**(7), 1907–1917 (2002)
16. Nohara, Y., et al.: Health checkup and telemedical intervention program for preventive medicine in developing countries: verification study. J. Med. Internet Res. **17**(1), e2 (2015)
17. Ahmed, A., Rebeiro-Hargrave, A., Nohara, Y., Kai, E., Hossein Ripon, Z., Nakashima, N.: Targeting morbidity in unreached communities using portable health clinic system. IEICE Trans. Commun. **E97-B(3)**, 540–545 (2014)
18. Nakashima, N., et al.: An affordable, usable and sustainable preventive healthcare system for unreached people in Bangladesh. Stud. Health Technol. Inform. **192**, 1051 (2013)
19. Nakashima, N., Hiramatsu, T., Ghosh, P.P., Islam, R., Kobayashi, K., Inoguchi, T.: Evaluation of "Portable Health Clinic" with BAN standard for 10K subjects in Bangladesh. In: Conference Proceedings of the IEEE Engineering in Medicine and Biology Society, pp. 1672–1675 (2013)
20. Grameen Communications Website. Global Communication Center. Portable Health Clinic. http://ghealth.gramweb.net/. Accessed 27 June 2017
21. Bangladesh Bureau of Statistics (BBS). District Statistics 2011, Kushtia. Bangladesh Bureau of Statistics. Statistics and Information Division, Ministry of Planning, December 2013
22. Fatema, K., et al.: Screening for chronic kidney diseases among an adult population. Saudi J. Kidney Dis. Transplant. **24**(3), 534–541 (2013)
23. WHO. Definition and diagnosis of diabetes mellitus and intermediate hyperglycemia, report of a WHO/IDF Consultation (2006). http://www.who.int/diabetes/publications/diagnosis_diabetes2006/en/. Accessed 17 August 2019
24. WHO. Use of Glycated Haemoglobin (HbA1c) in the Diagnosis of Diabetes Mellitus, Abbreviated report of a WHO Consultation (2011). http://www.who.int/cardiovascular_diseases/report-hba1c_2011_edited.pdf. Accessed 17 August 2019

Author Index

Printed in the United States
By Bookmasters